William Edward Story, Louis N. Wilson, Mass.) Clark University (Worcester

Clark University, 1889-1899, decennial celebration

William Edward Story, Louis N. Wilson, Mass.) Clark University (Worcester

Clark University, 1889-1899, decennial celebration

ISBN/EAN: 9783741151439

Manufactured in Europe, USA, Canada, Australia, Japa

Cover: Foto ©Thomas Meinert / pixelio.de

Manufactured and distributed by brebook publishing software
(www.brebook.com)

William Edward Story, Louis N. Wilson, Mass.) Clark University (Worcester

Clark University, 1889-1899, decennial celebration

PREFACE.

This volume is intended not only to commemorate the Decennial Anniversary of Clark University, but also to make the Public acquainted with its aims and ideals, and with the character, scope, and amount of the work it has already done. Ever since it opened its doors to students it has confined itself to truly post-graduate work in a few departments, and has admitted such students only as gave promise of the ability not only to pursue the courses here offered with advantage to themselves, but to benefit the world by advancing science along the lines here represented. It has thus taken a distinct position as a training school for college professors and scientific investigators. Such a policy is conducive neither to large numbers of students nor to popular appreciation. But, small as the university is and few as are its departments, it takes great satisfaction in pointing to this volume as, in some sense, a record of its work and its methods. The list of titles of the publications of its past and present members is a witness of the quality and quantity of what it has accomplished. We believe that Clark University, opening, as it did, at the beginning of a new university epoch in this country, has had some special influence in suggesting new lines of scientific research.

The five foreign professors who took part in the Decennial Celebration were selected as the most eminent available scientific men in their respective lines in Europe; this was the first visit of each to America, and four of them came here solely for this anniversary. Their lectures are here reproduced *in extenso* and have not been published elsewhere. The lectures of Professors Picard and Boltzmann are given in the languages in which they were delivered, and those of Professors Ramón y Cajal, Mosso, and Forel in translations made by members of the Faculty and revised by representatives of the departments to which they severally belong. For these laborious services the editors desire to extend their very particular thanks to the individuals who have rendered them.

The reports of departments were prepared especially for this occasion, and include not only an account of the work actually done during the decade, but also a statement by the officer in charge of each department of its aims and ideals and the lines along which it hopes to advance. The responsibility for the content and form of each report rests with the individual in whose name it is published; all modifications by the editors having been made in the form of suggestions to the writers and adopted only with their consent. It is perhaps unnecessary to say that no attempt has been made to secure uniformity in the various articles, excepting in the titles and in minor details of arrangement.

The editors extend their hearty thanks to the authors of the several portions of the volume for their cordial coöperation and for the friendly spirit in which suggestions have been received, and to all members of the Faculty for assistance in reading the proof-sheets.

WILLIAM E. STORY,
LOUIS N. WILSON,
Editors.

TABLE OF CONTENTS

REPORTS OF DEPARTMENTS

SCIENTIFIC LECTURES

DELIVERED IN CONNECTION WITH THE DECENNIAL CELEBRATION

HISTORICAL SKETCH.

HISTORICAL SKETCH.

Clark University was founded by the munificence of Jonas G. Clark, a native of Worcester County, whose plans, conceived more than twenty years before, had gradually grown with his fortune. His affairs had been so arranged as to allow long intervals for travel and study. During eight years thus spent, the leading foreign institutions of learning, old and new, were visited, and their records gathered and read. These studies centred about the means by which the highest culture of one generation is best transmitted to the ablest youths of the next, and especially about the external conditions most favorable for increasing the sum of human knowledge. To the improvement of these means and the enlargement of these conditions, the new University was devoted.

It was the strong and express desire of the founder that the highest possible academic standards be here forever maintained; that special opportunities and inducements be offered to research; that to this end the instructors be not overburdened with teaching and examinations; that all available experience, both of older countries and our own, be freely utilized; and that new measures, and even innovations, if really helpful to the highest needs of modern science and culture, be no less freely adopted; in fine, that the great opportunities of a new foundation in this land and age be diligently explored and improved.

He chose Worcester as the seat of the new foundation after mature deliberation, — first,

Because its location is central among the best colleges of the East, and by supplementing rather than duplicating their work, he hoped to advance all their interests and to secure their good will and active support, that together they might take further steps in the development of superior education in New England; and secondly,

Because he believed the culture of this city would insure that enlightened public opinion indispensable in maintaining these educational standards at their highest, and that its wealth would insure the perpetual increase of revenue required by the rapid progress of science.

As the first positive step toward the realization of these long-formed plans, Mr. Clark invited the following gentlemen to constitute with himself a Board of Trustees: —

STEPHEN SALISBURY, A.B., Harvard, 1856; Universities of Paris and Berlin, 1856–58; LL.B., Harvard, 1861; President Antiquarian Society since 1887; State Senator, 1892–95.

CHARLES DEVENS, A.B., Harvard, 1838; LL.B., Harvard, 1840; Major-General, 1863; Associate Justice of the Massachusetts Superior Court, 1867–73; Associate Justice of the Massachusetts Supreme Judicial Court, 1873–77, and again, 1881–91; Attorney-General of the United States, 1877–81; LL.D., Columbia and Harvard, 1877; Died January 7, 1891.

GEORGE F. HOAR, A.B., Harvard, 1846; LL.B., Harvard, 1849; United States House of Representatives, 1869–77; Member Electoral Commission, 1876; United States Senate since 1877; Chairman of Judiciary Committee, 1891—; LL.D., William and Mary, Amherst, Harvard, and Yale.

WILLIAM W. RICE, A.B., Bowdoin, 1846; admitted to Bar, 1854; United States House of Representatives, 1876–86; LL.D., Bowdoin, 1886. Died March 1, 1896.

JOSEPH SARGENT, A.B., Harvard, 1834; M.D., Harvard, 1837; London and Paris Hospitals, 1838–40. Died October 13, 1888.

JOHN D. WASHBURN, A.B., Harvard, 1853; LL.B., Harvard, 1856; Representative, 1876–79; State Senate, 1884; United States Minister to Switzerland, 1889–92.

FRANK P. GOULDING, A.B., Dartmouth, 1863; Harvard Law School, 1866; City Solicitor, 1881–93.

GEORGE SWAN, A.B., Amherst, 1847; admitted to Bar, 1848; Member of Worcester School Board, 1879–90; Chairman of High School Committee, 1887–90.

The following gentlemen have been added to the Board since to fill vacancies caused by death. In place of Dr. Sargent: —

EDWARD COWLES, A.B., Dartmouth, 1859; M.D., Dartmouth, 1862, and College of Physicians and Surgeons, N. Y., 1863; Assistant Surgeon, U. S. A., 1863–72; Resident Physician and Superintendent Boston City Hospital, 1872–79; Medical Superintendent McLean Asylum since 1879; Professor of Mental Diseases, Dartmouth Medical School, since 1885; Clinical Instructor in Mental Diseases, Harvard Medical School, since 1888.

In place of General Devens:

THOMAS H. GAGE, M.D., Harvard, 1852; President Massachusetts Medical Society, 1886–88.

On petition of this Board, the Legislature passed the following

ACT OF INCORPORATION. CHAPTER 133.

COMMONWEALTH OF MASSACHUSETTS, IN THE YEAR ONE THOUSAND EIGHT HUNDRED AND EIGHTY-SEVEN. AN ACT TO INCORPORATE THE TRUSTEES OF CLARK UNIVERSITY IN WORCESTER.

Be it enacted by the Senate and House of Representatives in General Court assembled, and by authority of the same, as follows:—

SECTION 1. Jonas G. Clark, Stephen Salisbury, Charles Devens, George F. Hoar, William W. Rice, Joseph Sargent, John D. Washburn, Frank P. Goulding and George Swan, all of the city of Worcester, in the Commonwealth of Massachusetts, and their successors, are hereby made a corporation by the name of the Trustees of Clark University, to be located in said Worcester, for the purpose of establishing and maintaining in said city of Worcester an institution for the promotion of education and investigation in science, literature and art, to be called Clark University.

SECTION 2. Said corporation may receive and hold real or personal estate by gift, grant, devise, bequest or otherwise, for the purpose aforesaid, and shall have all the rights, privileges, immunities, and powers, including the conferring of degrees, which similar incorporated institutions have in this Commonwealth.

SECTION 3. Said corporation shall have the power to organize said University in all its departments, to manage and control the same, to appoint its officers, who shall not be members of said corporation, and to fix their compensation and their tenure of office; and said corporation may provide for the appointment of an advisory board and for the election by the Alumni of said University to fill any vacancies in said board.

SECTION 4. The number of members of said corporation shall not be less than seven nor more than nine, and any vacancy therein may be filled by the remaining members at a meeting duly called and notified therefor; and when any member thereof shall, by reason of infirmity or otherwise, become incapable, in the judgment of the remaining members, of discharging the duties of his office, or shall neglect or refuse to perform the same, he may be removed and another be elected to fill his place, by the remaining members, at a meeting duly called and notified for that purpose.

SECTION 5. This Act shall take effect upon its passage.

House of Representatives, March 30, 1887, Passed to be Enacted.

CHARLES J. NOYES, *Speaker.*

Senate, March 31, 1887, Passed to be Enacted.

HALSEY J. BOARDMAN, *President.*

During the previous five years, Mr. Clark had gradually acquired a tract of land, comprising over eight acres, located on Main Street, about a mile from the heart of the city, with additional tracts near by. This land has considerable elevation above that part of the city, is a watershed sloping to the southeast, insuring sanitary excellence and a wide and picturesque view. A park reservation of about 25 acres, directly opposite, has been set apart by the city, and named University Park.

Plans for a main building were submitted to the Board by Mr. Clark, which were approved, and its erection was at once begun. The corner-stone was laid with impressive ceremonies, October 22, 1887. This building is plain, substantial, and well appointed, 204 x 114 feet, four stories high and five in the centre, with superior facilities for heating, lighting, and ventilation, and has been constructed of brick and granite, and finished throughout in oak. On the whole it is a model of stability and solid workmanship. It contains a total of 90 rooms, and in its tower is a clock with three six-foot illuminated dials, which was presented by the citizens of Worcester. The elevations and ground plan are published, and the heating, lighting, ventilation, walls, floors, etc., etc., are described in detail in the *Third Official Announcement.*

On April 3, 1888, G. Stanley Hall, then a professor at Johns Hopkins University, was invited to the presidency. The official letter conveying the invitation to the president contained the following well-considered and significant expression of the spirit animating the trustees: —

"They desire to impose on you no trammels; they have no friends for whom they wish to provide at the expense of the interests of the Institution; no pet theories to press upon you in derogation of your judgment; no sectarian tests to apply; no guarantees to require, save such as are implied by your acceptance of this trust. Their single desire is to fit men for the highest duties of life, and to that end, that this Institution, in whatever branches of sound learning it may find itself engaged, may be a leader and a light."

This invitation was accepted May 1, and the president was at once granted one year's leave of absence, with full salary, to visit universities in Europe. This year was diligently improved in gathering educational literature and collecting information and advice from leading authorities. Many reports based upon this work have already been made in the *Pedagogical Seminary* and more are in course of preparation.

During the absence of the president a Chemical Laboratory was begun. This building in its main body has three stories, in its eastern wing four, in its southwestern two. It contains 68 rooms. The outer walls are 2 feet in thickness and the partition walls from 12 to 16 inches. All partitions are of brick, so that the building is nearly fireproof. The two large laboratories are 24 x 58 feet and 22 feet high. This building is also described with plans in the *Third Official Announcement.*

The opening exercises were held in a hall of the University, seating 1500 people, on Wednesday, October 2, 1889. The late General Charles Devens presided, and made an opening address. Addresses were made by Senator George F. Hoar and the president. The founder of the University stated his purpose as follows: —

"When we first entered upon our work it was with a well-defined plan and purpose, in which plan and purpose we have steadily persevered, turning neither to the right nor to the left. We have wrought upon no vague conceptions nor suffered ourselves to be borne upon the fluctuating and unstable current of public opinion or public suggestions. We started upon our career with the determinate view of giving to the public all the benefits and advantages of a university, comprehending full well what that implies, and feeling the full force of the general understanding, that a university must, to a large degree, be a creation of time and experience. We have, however, boldly assumed as the foundation of our institution the principles, the tests, and the responsibilities of universities as they are everywhere recognized — but without making any claim for the prestige or favor which age imparts to all things. It has therefore been our purpose to lay our foundation broad and strong and deep. In this we must necessarily lack the simple element of years. We have what we believe to be more valuable — the vast storehouse of the knowledge and learning which has been accumulating for the centuries that have gone before us, availing ourselves of the privilege of drawing from this source, open to all alike. We propose to go on to further and higher achievements. We propose to put into the hands of those who are members of the University, engaged in its several departments, every facility which money can command — to the extent of our ability — in the way of apparatus and appliances that can in any way promote our object in this direction. To our present departments we propose to add others from time to time, as our means shall warrant and the exigencies of the University shall seem to demand, always taking those first whose domain lies nearest to those already established, until the full scope and purpose of the University shall have been accomplished.

"These benefits and advantages thus briefly outlined, we propose placing at the service of those who from time to time seek, in good faith and honesty of purpose, to pursue the study of science in its purity, and to engage in scientific research and investigation — to such they are offered as far as possible free from all trammels and hindrances, without any religious, political, or social tests. All that will be required of any applicant will be evidence, disclosed by examinations or otherwise, that his attainments are such as to qualify him for the position that he seeks."

After careful consideration it was decided to begin with graduate work only and in the following five departments:

I. Mathematics.
II. Physics, Experimental and Theoretical.
III. Chemistry, Organic, Inorganic, Physical, and Crystallography.
IV. Biology, including Anatomy, Physiology, and Paleontology.
V. Psychology, including Neurology, Anthropology, and Education.

Mathematics is sometimes called the queen of all the sciences. As the latter become exact, they approximate it, and are fructified by its spirit and its methods. Its antiquity, its disciplinary value, its rapid and recent development, make it obviously indispensable. Physics is the field of the most immediate application of mathematics, and deals with the fundamental forces of the material universe, — heat, sound, light, electricity, — and the underlying problems of form and motion generally, with their vast field of application in such sciences as astronomy and dynamic geology. Chemistry, with its great and sudden development, revealing marvellous order and harmony in the constitution of matter, is rapidly extending its dominion over industrial processes. Biology, which seeks to fathom the laws of life, death, reproduction, and disease, that underlies all the medical sciences, in its broader aspects has taught man in recent decades far more concerning his origin and nature than all that was known before. Psychology, or the study of man's faculties and their education, is a new field into which all the sciences are bringing so many of their richest and best ideas, which is now so full of promise for the life of man.

A sub-department of Education was established in 1892, and the department of Chemistry was temporarily discontinued in 1894.

To express more explicitly the character and policy of the institution, the Trustees voted to approve and publish the following statement: —

"As the work of the University increases, its settled policy shall be always to first strengthen departments already established, until they are as thorough, as advanced, as special, and as efficient as possible, before proceeding to the establishment of new ones.

"When this is done and new departments are established, those shall always be chosen first which are scientifically most closely related to departments already established; that the body of sciences here represented may be kept vigorous and compact, and that the strength of the University may always rest, not upon the number of subjects, nor the breadth or length of its curriculum, but upon its thoroughness and its unity.

"This shall in no wise hinder the establishment, by other donors than the founder, of other and more independent departments if approved by the Trustees.

"While ability in teaching shall be held of great importance, the leading consideration in all engagements, reappointments, and promotions shall be the quality and quantity of successful investigation."

By thus limiting the work of the University in the beginning to five departments, it appeals only to advanced men who desire to specialize in one or more of these fundamental sciences, leaving college students who require a larger range of studies, as well as those who desire to devote themselves to language and literature, historical, technical, or professional studies, to go elsewhere. Hence our work must be post-graduate. This requires the best professors and apparatus, more books and journals, and necessitates a system of fellowships, scholarships, and provisions for original research. It thus becomes a training-school for professors. This is the most expensive of all educational work, seeks the fewest but the best men from the widest area, and to succeed must be helpful in elevating the academic standards of the country to a higher plane. It requires the highest degree of wisdom and foresight on the part of the Founder and the Trustees, and possibly some sacrifices of local sympathy and support at first, till the nature of the work is well understood. It requires the greatest effort and devotion to work on the part of the Faculty and students. But the cause is itself an inspiration. It appeals to the future, the country, and to the world, and seeks quality more than numbers. It is in the current of all the best tendencies in the best lands, and is now the ideal of perhaps every eminent man of science everywhere. The inauguration and steady maintenance of this clear and simple policy gives the University a reason for being, and a distinct individuality it could not otherwise have, and also a real leadership in this epoch of awakening and transition, which is the golden time of opportunity for new institutions, and brings them to the front. Such a period as the present gives the latter even greater relative influence and prominence than would be possible in periods of less public interest in education. New institutions can and should lead, set new fashions, and be the first upon the higher planes. Older institutions are retarded by conservatism and must advance more slowly, but when they move they carry great momentum. This condition makes the present a moment of perhaps unprecedented opportunity, which has been long looked for and long delayed, and which renders both funds and labor in this field more precious than they have been, or will be when it is past. We may all be content if our University can transmit to future generations by means of its organization, plan, and methods the best and highest educational tendencies and movements now stirring the souls of the best men of the world, and uniting men of all lands, races, creeds, and stations in a larger if not also a deeper consensus of belief than history has ever known before.

Our University does not draw its chief earnings from, or do most of its teaching for, undergraduates, and our so-called graduate students do not take undergraduate courses. This makes the proportion of expenditure to income very high here, and indeed we can admit and do justice to but comparatively few students. Most of those who come here have spent one or more years after graduation in teaching, or in study in Europe or elsewhere. Most of those who have been members here have already obtained professorships or other academic positions elsewhere. The proportion of such is hardly excelled by the *Ecole Normale* of Paris, the special function of which is to train professors from other collegiate institutions. Every student who obtains original results is expected to present them in the form of lectures to his department, and thus to acquire experience in teaching under criticism. The work of the educational department deals with problems and history of higher educational institutions, and is adapted to all the body of fellows and scholars, and seeks to increase the efficiency of every man both as a teacher of his own specialty and in general helpfulness to the institution with which he is to be connected.

Since the opening of the University not less than five hundred books, memoirs, theses, or articles[1] have been published by members of the University, which attempt to make additions to the sum of human knowledge. These contributions are of very different orders of value, but together they constitute a body of knowledge in which the institution takes special pride. Every member of the University is expected to make at least one long and serious effort of this kind. Indeed, had its publications no value as contributions to knowledge, its educational value is the highest for mature men. Such effort gets minds into independent action, gives a sense of authority and of true mental freedom, which no amount of acquisition can bring. It brings out new powers of mind and of will, and, while one of the chief

[1] A list of these publications will be found at the end of this volume.

marks by which true University work is distinguished from that of lower grades, is in the line of all present tendencies to place doing above knowing from the kindergarten up. Work that is published enlarges the sphere of interests of the author, subjects him to the higher test of being judged by his peers elsewhere, and brings in the potent and salutary stimulus of wider competition. This baptism of ink has often marked a new birth of ideals and ability in young men. Modern as distinct from earlier culture culminates in the man-making training of will and judgment thus given. Such work, too, gives teaching a new power and zest. Instruction to a fit few by an investigator who stands on the frontier and has once felt the light and heat in which discovery is wrought out is inspiring, and is very different from information imparted at lower levels by teachers further removed from the work of discovery and creation.

Clark University is exclusively what is called in Europe a Philosophical Faculty, or a part of one so far as yet developed, devoted to a group of the *pure sciences* which underlie technology and medicine, but does not yet apply its work to these professional fields. These or a college course could be added with relatively less expense. Our method has brought us face to face with many new problems. Our efforts at solving some of these are described in the department reports which follow. Like all new institutions, we have not entirely escaped trials, but we trust we have learned their lesson, and shall be the better and stronger for them. Instead of dispersing our energies in university extensions, we have followed the opposite course of university concentration, like the *Ecole Pratique* of France. Accepting the plain lesson of history that the best educational influences work from above downward, that universities create the material of culture, while lower institutions are the canals for its distribution, we have sought aid for the latter work by an educational sub-department and summer school. We are not like the Smithsonian Institute, the Naples school, the *Reichsanstalt*, academies of science, etc., devoted solely to research, but have to make our lectures more condensed and fewer than usual, because addressed to advanced men, and to devise ways of making *seminary* and *laboratory*, two of the noblest words in the vocabulary of higher education, more effective. We have tried to effect systematic exchanges with foreign institutions, — and our library has profited largely from this source, — and have sought by all the above means to aid in giving to universities and to professors the position due them in a time when sciences have come to underlie all the arts of peace and war, and when the world, in all its activities, industry and trade, professions, legislation, is coming to be more and more controlled by experts, thus trained to the frontier of their specialties.

The degree of Doctor of Philosophy has been conferred upon candidates, whose names, together with the dates of their final examinations and the subjects of their dissertations, are given later in this volume.

Other historical facts are given in the President's Address at the Decennial Celebration.

REQUIREMENTS FOR THE DEGREE OF DOCTOR OF PHILOSOPHY.

At least two years, and in most cases three years, of graduate work will be necessary for this degree. Examinations for it, however, may be taken at any time during the academic year when, in the judgment of the University authorities, the candidate is prepared. A prearranged period of serious work at the University itself is indispensable.

For this degree the first requirement is a dissertation upon an approved subject, to which it must be an original contribution of value. To this capital importance is attached. It must be reported on in writing by the chief instructor before the examination, printed at the expense of the candidate, and at least one hundred copies given to the University. In case, however, of dissertations of very unusual length, or containing very expensive plates, the Faculty shall have power, at the request of the candidate, to reduce this number of presentation copies to fifty.

Such formal or informal tests as the Faculty shall determine, shall mark the acceptance of each student or fellow as a candidate for this degree. One object of this preliminary test shall be to insure a good reading knowledge of French and German. Such formal candidature shall precede by at least one academic year the examination itself. (See special rules below.)

The fee for the doctor's degree is $25, and in every case it must be paid and the presentation copies of the dissertation must be in the hands of the Librarian before the diploma is given. In exceptional cases, however, and by special action of the Faculty, the ceremony of promotion may precede the presentation of the printed copies of the dissertation. The latter, however, must always precede the actual presentation of the diploma.

An oral but not a written examination is required upon at least one minor subject in addition to the major, before an examination jury composed of at least four members, including the head of the department and the President of the University, who is authorized to invite any person from within or without the University to be present and to ask questions. The jury shall report the results of the examination to the Faculty, which, if it is also satisfied, may recommend the candidate for the degree.

For the bestowal of this degree, the approbation of the Board of Trustees must in each case be obtained. They desire that the standard of requirements for it be kept the highest practicable, that it be reserved for men of superior ability and attainment only, and that its value here be never suffered to depreciate.

It is to the needs of these students that the lectures, seminaries, laboratories, collections of books, apparatus, etc., are specially shaped, and no pains will be spared to afford them every needed stimulus and opportunity. It is for them that the Fellowships and Scholarships are primarily intended, although any of these honors may be awarded to others.

SPECIAL RULES.

I. *Residence.* — No candidate shall receive the degree of Doctor of Philosophy without at least one year's previous residence.

II. *Candidature for the Doctor's Degree.* — Every applicant for the doctor's degree shall fill out before October 15th the regular application blank provided at the office. This schedule shall be submitted to the head of the department and the instructor in the major subject. Before affixing their signatures they shall satisfy themselves, in such manner as they may desire, as to the fitness of the applicant.

III. When countersigned, this schedule shall be filed with the President, who will appoint an examiner to serve with a representative of the major subject as a committee to determine the proficiency of the applicant in French and German.

IV. In case of a favorable report by this committee the applicant shall be a regular candidate for the degree.

V. Candidates complying with all preliminary conditions, including the examinations in French and German, before November 1st, will be allowed to proceed to the doctor's examination at any time between May 15th following and the end of the academic year.

VI. *Dissertation.* — The dissertation must be presented to the instructor under whose direction it was before written, and reported upon by him before the final examination. In every case the dissertation shall be laid before the jury of examination, at the time of examination, in form suitable for publication. This provision shall not, however, preclude the making of such minor changes later as the chief instructor may approve.

VII. The dissertation shall be printed at the expense of the candidate, and the required copies deposited with the Librarian within one calendar year from the 1st of October following the examination. The candidate alone will be held responsible for the fulfilment of these conditions.

VIII. The favorable report of the chief instructor, filed in writing with the Clerk of the University, shall be a sufficient imprimatur or authorization for printing as a dissertation. The printed copies shall bear upon the cover the statement of approval in the following words, over the name of the chief instructor: —

A Dissertation submitted to the Faculty of Clark University, Worcester, Mass., in partial fulfilment of the requirements for the degree of Doctor of Philosophy, and accepted on the recommendation of (name of the chief instructor).

IX. *Examinations for the Doctor's Degree.* — The examinations for the doctor's degree may be held at any time during the academic year, provided that at least one academic year has elapsed since the completion of the preliminaries of candidature, except in the case of fulfilment of these conditions between the beginning of any academic year and November 1st of that year, to which case Rule V. applies. The examinations shall be held at such hours and places as the President may appoint.

X. Examinations may also be held during the regular vacations of the University, but for these an additional fee of five dollars to each examiner, and the reasonable travelling expenses of any examiners who are out of town, all payable in advance, will be required.

XI. All these special rules shall go into force immediately as far as practicable, and shall govern all applicants for degrees in the academic year 1899–1900.

THE DECENNIAL CELEBRATION.

The work of Clark University is so technical and special that it is necessarily more or less withdrawn from popular interest. It has no commencements, and comes in very little contact with the public or the press in Worcester, or indeed with collegiate institutions in other parts of the country. This is a disadvantage so far as local or general public interest in its work is concerned, but the fact that it does not exercise many of the usual functions of a college is also a distinct advantage to its scientific work. The close of the tenth year of its existence presented an opportunity to bring before the public, in a simple way, befitting at once its size and its quality, a presentation of the work it has accomplished in the past and of its hopes and needs for the future. Early last winter the President began to consider plans of marking this anniversary, and, with the efficient aid of the Faculty, they gradually took definite shape. A personal appeal was then made to a number of public-spirited and wealthy citizens of Worcester, and the scheme was rendered feasible by the generosity of the following gentlemen, who donated the sums affixed to their names: —

Mr. Stephen Salisbury,	$1000	Mr. C. Henry Hutchins,	$500
Mr. Philip W. Moen,	500	Mr. William E. Rice,	500
Mr. Thomas H. Dodge,	200	Mr. Orlando W. Norcross,	200
Mr. Edward D. Thayer, Jr.,	200	Mr. Matthew J. Whittall,	150
Mr. Charles S. Barton,	100	Mr. A. Swan Brown,	100
Mr. John H. Coes,	100	Mr. Loring Coes,	100
Mr. Andrew H. Green,	100	Mr. James Logan,	100
Mr. Arthur M. Stone,	100	Mr. Joseph H. Walker,	100
John O. Marble, M.D.,	50	Mr. Frederick L. Coes,	25

Charles L. Nichols, M.D., $25.

It was decided that the close of the tenth academic year should be celebrated (1) by courses of lectures delivered by distinguished foreign scientific men, (2) by public exercises, and (3) by an evening reception.

A conference was then held concerning the most prominent leaders in Europe in branches especially cultivated at the University, and after some correspondence the following persons were invited to give from two to four lectures each: —

Emile Picard, Professor of Mathematics at the University of Paris.

Ludwig Boltzmann, Professor of Theoretical Physics at the University of Vienna.

Angelo Mosso, Professor of Physiology and Rector of the University of Turin.

Santiago Ramón y Cajal, Professor of Histology and Rector of the University of Madrid.

August Forel, late Professor of Psychiatry at the University of Zürich and Director of the Burghölzli Asylum.

Under the direction of a committee consisting of Assistant Professor A. G. Webster and Professor W. E. Story, the following forms of invitation to the various parts of the programme were prepared: —

The President, Trustees, and Faculty of

Clark University

in Worcester, Massachusetts,

request the honor of your presence

at a series of Scientific Lectures to be delivered

in connection with the Celebration of the

completion of the Tenth Academic Year

of the University,

July fifth, sixth, seventh, and eighth,

eighteen hundred and ninety-nine.

Please reply.

The President, Trustees, and Faculty of

Clark University

request the honor of your presence

at the Celebration of the completion of the

Tenth Academic Year of the University

on Monday morning, July the tenth,

eighteen hundred and ninety-nine,

at half past ten o'clock.

Worcester, Massachusetts.

Please reply.

The President, Trustees, and Faculty
request the pleasure of your company
at Clark University
Monday evening, July the tenth,
from eight to eleven o'clock.

Please reply.

The invitations to the lectures were sent to such persons as were considered to be particularly interested in the subjects in question, of whom over one hundred accepted. Many declinations were inevitable and expected, owing to the unfavorable season of the year and, perhaps in part, to the somewhat too short notice given. The lecturers all arrived in due season, and were entertained as follows: —

Professor Emile Picard,	by Professor W. E. Story.
Professor Ludwig Boltzmann,	by Assistant Professor A. G. Webster.
Professor Angelo Mosso,	by President G. Stanley Hall.
Professor S. Ramón y Cajal,	by Hon. Stephen Salisbury.
Professor August Forel,	by Dr. Adolf Meyer.

The lectures were held in the large lecture-room on the first floor, and were well attended. Professors Picard and Cajal lectured in French, and Professors Boltzmann, Mosso, and Forel in German. Their lectures are printed in full elsewhere in this volume.

Many social functions occurred during the week ending July 8. On Wednesday evening, Professor Story received informally the attendants on the lectures of Professors Picard and Boltzmann; on Thursday evening President Hall gave a reception to all the visitors; and on Friday afternoon and evening the whole company was entertained by Hon. Stephen Salisbury at the Quinsigamond Boat Club house.

The second part of the celebration occurred on Monday morning, July 10, beginning at 10.30, in the University. The professors had adopted academic costume, and many distinguished guests were seated upon the platform. The exercises opened with prayer by the Rev. Alexander H. Vinton, Rector of All Saints' Church.

A few extracts from congratulatory letters were read by Professor Story, which are printed elsewhere in this volume. Brief congratulatory addresses were made by President Faunce, of Brown University, representing the New England college presidents; and Professor Bowditch of the Harvard Medical School, representing the higher scientific institutions of the state.

President Faunce said: —

"I count it a very happy fact that the first occasion on which I am to officially speak, representing Brown University, is at this anniversary at Clark University. I bring you to-day greetings from an institution of the higher learning founded in 1764 to a university founded in 1887. It is safe to say that Clark University has done more to widen the confines of human knowledge than any other American college in one hundred and fifty years.

"When Professor J. P. Cooke, of Harvard, applied to the Faculty for chemicals and apparatus for experiment, he was told he must secure the materials at his own expense, and that he must be responsible for any explosions or damage in consequence of his experiments. From that day to this is a long step. Our method of applying nature has been transformed within a very few years. The distance between Achilles' coach and the English stage-coach is not the same as that between the stage-coach and the Empire State express. The difference between the Phenician galleys and the *Bon Homme Richard* is not the difference between the *Bon Homme Richard* and the modern battleship. The little world of Shakespeare has become one vast universe of learning, and the field has broadened almost infinitely in all directions, and the goal is the far-off divine event toward which the whole creation moves.

"In this movement of scholarship the enrichment of one institution is the enrichment of all, the enfeeblement of one is the enfeeblement of all. You have received at this celebration, almost Spartan-like in its simplicity, the congratulations not alone of America, but of Berlin and Munich and Vienna, because your advance and success is the advance of all. Only geographically and superficially are the leaders of modern scholarship divided, and so we congratulate you, not because you have duplicated existing plants, but that you have filled a place hitherto unfilled and have broken new ground.

"Here among all the institutions of learning you have not detracted from the success of other institutions, you have placed fresh laurels on the heads of each. All of us feel a warm interest and admiration for this University because of the simple, quiet, and noble work done within these walls."

Dr. Bowditch said that he was quite unprepared to say much, and he thought it just as well, for he belonged, in the words of Dr. Holmes, to the "silent profession." He paid a tribute to the felicitous speech of Dr. Faunce, which left him little to say. Dr. Bowditch spoke of the great work in scientific research being conducted by the institution, and, after some wishes for its prosperity, congratulated the youngest college in the name of the oldest college in Massachusetts.

Then followed the address by President Hall, printed elsewhere in this volume.

The honorary degree of DOCTOR OF LAWS, *honoris causâ*, was then conferred, for the first time, upon the five foreign professors in the following terms: —

"By virtue of the authority vested by the Commonwealth of Massachusetts in the Board of Trustees of Clark University, and by them delegated to me, I now create you Doctor of Laws, *honoris causâ*, and by this token [presenting diploma] invest you with all the dignities thereunto appertaining." Brief responses were made, of which translations follow.

LUDWIG BOLTZMANN.

THE problem of science is a twofold one: first, to advance our knowledge of nature independently of any practical application; and second, to make practical applications of the knowledge gained. Although to a superficial observer it may seem that the latter is of greater importance, the development of humanity has shown in the most convincing way that the first kind of activity is not only of paramount importance, but that the leading rôle belongs to it. In fact, it is only thanks to the pioneers of science who, laying aside all practical applications, penetrate deeper and deeper into the essence and arrangement of the forces of nature, that humanity has obtained that sway over the laws of nature which makes possible the present practical achievements.

The German universities have devoted themselves at all times to the nurture of pure science apart from its practical applications, although but one of the four university faculties is consecrated to it, and that one not entirely. It must be considered as a good omen, therefore, that here in America, which is usually taken to be the land of practical men, the ideal of a place entirely consecrated to the service of pure science, unattainable in Germany, has found its realization, so that I, who am body and soul a German professor, deem it a great honor to have conferred on me in this place, the greatest distinction which the University can grant. While desiring Clark University to flourish and thrive in the intimate conviction that the whole scientific world is interested in her prosperity, I express my thanks to the President and all its members for the high honor bestowed upon me to-day.

SANTIAGO RAMÓN Y CAJAL.

I OFFER my most cordial thanks to Clark University for the honorable distinction she has bestowed upon me in spite of my small deserts by granting to me the degree of doctor of laws by this learned body, the remembrance of which will never fade from my memory. This honor I deem to be the prize of the greatest value which my modest researches have procured for me, and the one which will encourage me most in my worship of the laboratory tasks and of the study of nature. This honorary distinction, as well as the invitation which Clark University condescended to make me to take part in the conferences for solemnizing the tenth anniversary of its foundation, shows once more that the men of science know of no frontiers, and that they form a universal family, whose solidarity and fellow-feeling place them high above the wrangle of material interests and selfish struggles of nationalities.

It was truly a happy idea to create in America a university of higher studies, devoted not only to the labor of teaching, but also very especially to giving impulse to pure science. It has been said many times, but never enough, that there is no lasting industrial progress if it is not connected, as a brook with its source, with the creation of original science.

No matter how great the practical genius of a nation, it is impossible for it to preserve its political, commercial, and industrial hegemony, unless it comes out intellectually superior to other nations, unless it attends with equal care to the laboratory and to the mill, to the ideas as well as to the inventions, to the philosophy and to the science which guide as well as to the art which carries out.

This happy alliance between theory and practice is what places Germany to-day at the head of civilization. It would be easy to adduce numberless examples of the supremacy which industry, founded on science, holds over empirical industry created at haphazard according to the inventive character of each nation. I will quote only two — the chemical industry of the aniline dyes created chiefly in Germany, which assures to that nation an immense wealth; and the optical industry representing all kinds of apparatus (microscopes, photographical and astronomical object-glasses) which sprung up under the inspiration of the great mathematicians, Abbe, Rudolph, Goertz, and others, and which by its manifest superiority over that of other nations procures to Prussia a monopoly which makes the whole world her tributary.

That is the right way, the only one which leads to glory, wealth, and power. I trust that the creation of Clark University may give the signal for founding in America other similar institutions embracing a still larger number of branches of science, and having as their primary object the wresting of secrets from nature, supplying industry and arts with principles and facts capable of fruitful applications, forming the research spirit of the new generation, freeing it from the clogs of routine and imitation, and finally forming the foundation of a splendid civilization superior in groundwork, as well as in form, to that of the European nations.

August Forel.

I thank you heartily for the great honor you have bestowed upon me by conferring upon me the degree of doctor of laws, *honoris causâ*, of Clark University. But I accept this honor less in my own person than as a representative of Switzerland at your celebration — in the name of my little fatherland. Although nowadays the Swiss Federation disappears beside the powerful republic of the United States, yet she prides herself still on being the little old mother of democracy, which has fought for her free rights for centuries, and has maintained them up to the present day. I offer my heartiest congratulations for the brilliant success which Clark University has achieved during the short time of its existence in the high domains of philosophy, pedagogy, and of many a scientific foundation of social questions. But we must also offer our heartiest thanks and congratulations for the generous and magnificent gifts of American citizens for the furtherance of scientific and social progress. Allow me to add a wish. Let Clark University continue to pursue — under the successful guidance of her excellent President, Professor G. Stanley Hall — her researches in the regions of psychology and pedagogy together with those on the brain and its life, and thus to further the investigation and the building up of truth in the teeth of all prejudices. Let her help to bury the old roads of barren metaphysical dogmas and speculations, and thus develop in its entirety the only fruitful ethically built-up progressive method of scientific investigation in these domains, as a blessing to our posterity and for the good of a better and happier humanity.

ANGELO MOSSO.

I OFFER my thanks to Clark University for the honor bestowed upon me. I shall carry with me to Italy a happy remembrance of the many proofs of sympathy and friendship which I have received in the University and the city of Worcester. It is not only the expression of my gratitude that I offer you, but also my great admiration for all that I saw in your University, and especially the development in experimental psychology under the happy impulse which the President has given to this branch of science. It is not only on my own account that I offer you my thanks, it is also because, on my return to Italy, I hope to found in the University of Turin a school of experimental psychology.

EMILE PICARD.

I OFFER my heartiest thanks to the President and Professors of Clark University for the degree just conferred upon me. I have been also greatly touched by the honor you bestowed upon me by inviting me to give a few lectures during this academic celebration. Your desire was thus to bear witness to your sympathy with men of science in France. We follow on our side, in France, with great interest the American scientific movement, and we rejoice in seeing closer relations established between our universities and those of this country. Science treads its ascending march on different roads, and research work requires to-day the most varied aptitudes. The initiative and the energy which are prevalent in this country will not be wanting in occasions for displaying themselves, and, in all branches of studies, the American scientists will be able to erect something equivalent to those large telescopes by means of which your astronomers have made such beautiful discoveries. It is in the universities which, like this one, are devoted to research, that the scientific movement is bound to have its origin. From everything I have seen and heard for the last few days, I am certain that the eminent professors of this University devote themselves with success to this noble task, and I beg to offer my most sincere wishes for the continuance of the brilliant development of Clark University.

The exercises concluded with prayer by Dr. Vinton.

The closing exercise of the decennial was a reception which was attended by between five hundred and six hundred ladies and gentlemen of Worcester. The arrangements had been made under the direction of Assistant Professor Henry Taber and Professor William E. Story. The large lecture-room and corridors were decorated with festoons of green and white, the flags of the United States and of the native countries of the foreign guests, and with potted plants. A collation was served in the library, and many pieces of apparatus were exhibited in operation in the physical and psychological laboratories.

The following persons received: President G. Stanley Hall, Miss Florence E. Smith of Newton Centre, Mass., Mrs. A. W. Beals of Stamford, Conn., Hon. Stephen Salisbury, Dr. Edward Cowles, Miss Gage, Professor and Mrs. William E. Story, Assistant Professor and Mrs. Arthur G. Webster, Assistant Professor and Mrs. Clifton F. Hodge, Assistant Professor Edmund C. Sanford, Miss Sanford, Assistant Professor Henry Taber, Dr. and Mrs. A. F. Chamberlain, the foreign lecturers, Señora Ramón y Cajal, and Frau Boltzmann.

The press of Worcester gave very full and detailed accounts of all that transpired during the week except the scientific lectures, all of which were in foreign languages and upon very technical subjects.

The following original documents have been bound and filed in the University library: —

(1) The congratulatory letters, telegrams, etc.

(2) The correspondence with the foreign lecturers, and the letters of acceptance and declination from American professors.

(3) The letters of acceptance and declination to the reception in the evening.

The weather was somewhat warm during the first few days, but was clear and cool on Saturday, Sunday, and Monday. The hospitality of Worcester people was all that could be desired.

CONGRATULATIONS.

The following extracts are taken from many hundred congratulatory letters, personal, official, and from institutions and educators of all grades and many lands.

Congratulations on the conclusion of the University's first decade, and best wishes for the successful continuance of the work it has undertaken.

William McKinley, Washington, D.C.,
President of the United States.

The attraction will be strong to all who are interested in the great subjects which these distinguished men will discuss, or in intellectual eminence for its own sake. Your occasion will be the most distinguished gathering that will occur in all New England this summer. . . .

The high plane of the work done at Clark University, the only institution in our country exclusively devoted to original research and the instruction of advanced investigators, so far as I am aware, is well known to all who have followed the course of the University. Modestly, and without ostentation, it has pursued its noble ideals. If, under your able direction, its means were more extensive, the University would, doubtless, become the centre of a still larger circle of influence in the training of men for the prosecution of original research and the conduct of similar work in other institutions. I trust that your own large plans and those of the founder of the University may enjoy a complete realization, and that its future may be crowned with the high success which so great an enterprise rightly deserves.

Felicitating the honored founder, yourself, the trustees, and your colleagues in the faculty upon the great occasion you are soon to celebrate,

David J. Hill, Washington, D.C.,
Assistant Secretary of State.

It is one of the chief regrets of my life that I cannot attend the celebration of Clark University. Be assured that no reason personal to myself has prevented my attendance. I have seriously considered the question of crossing the Atlantic for the purpose, and coming back here immediately afterward. But that seems impracticable.

We have to congratulate the University upon ten years of success. It was not to be expected that an institution whose aim is to lift the university education, not only of this country, but of the world, to a higher plane, and to break out a new and untrodden path, should command popularity in the beginning, or that its success should at once be recognized by the general public. But we have no cause for regret or for discouragement. Teachers whom we have educated are found in institutions of the first class in all parts of the country, and all parts of the world have sent representatives to receive our instruction. This is largely due to the wise and far-sighted intelligence of the founder, and, next, to your own constant and self-sacrificing labors.

There have been times during these ten years when we have been tempted to think that the people of Worcester have been cold, and have been lacking in the liberality which we had hoped from them when we started. But in looking at the history of other institutions which are now useful and flourishing, it will be seen that they had in the beginning a like experience. I remember well a time when it almost seemed impossible to get the people of Worcester to endow a public library. But the hour came and the man came, and our public library is now munificently endowed and is a model of library administration. The Polytechnic Institute had its day of small things. But the liberality of two citizens of Worcester of the same name and race, whose two lives seem almost like the prolonged life of one individual, came to its aid, and it is now doing its work with large endowments, and its scheme has been copied by other institutions all over the country. I do not for a moment doubt that the time will come when our endowments will enable us to maintain in the entire circle of university education the position which we have taken and hold with regard to a few subjects. Already an eloquent orator, formerly head of the National Catholic University at Washington, has referred to Clark as "that little institution in Worcester which has added a new story to university education, and

'Which allures to brighter worlds and leads the way.'"

An eminent professor of science from the English Cambridge declared at a meeting in the British Association, in the presence of famous scholars from all parts of the world, that there is one thing that England envies America, and that is Clark University.

There is nothing except the country itself which ought to inspire a deeper devotion in its children than a university. As time goes on this feeling, made up of love and gratitude, will be found in fullest measure among the alumni of Clark. As they go out to reap the harvests of success in life, they will repay to their alma mater, in their own way, the great debt they owe her. When that time comes I have no fear that her endowments will not be ample to accomplish the work she has undertaken. In the meantime those of us to whom the confidence of the founder has committed a share in her administration must renew our own vows of fidelity to her service.

Among the many public honors which the undeserved kindness of my fellow-citizens has bestowed upon me, I count none higher than my selection as one of the first board of trustees of this institution. I trust that your celebration will be full of delight for those who gather there, that they will look forward with bright hopes to the future, and that an immortality of fame and usefulness may await the institution which now celebrates its tenth birthday.

GEORGE F. HOAR,
United States Senator.

I learn from your formal letters of invitation that you are to celebrate the close of the first decade of Clark University. It is one of the most wonderful careers to be chronicled in the history of American education. I congratulate you on your eminent success in conducting your University in so efficient a manner toward the improvement and elevation of pedagogy in the United States. Your movement is all the more valuable because it challenges the aims and purposes of the present existing education. It is an elementary force in making the American teachers circumspect and reflective, and causing them to seek deeper principles on which to ground their practice and on which to improve it. Hoping that there will be a long series of equally useful decades in the history of Clark University and in your own successful directorship of that institution,

W. T. HARRIS, Washington, D.C.,
Commissioner of Education.

I cannot refrain from offering my congratulations to the President, Trustees, and Faculty for securing the services of such distinguished lecturers, as well as for the marked success that has attended Clark University during the first decade of its existence.

WILLIS L. MOORE, Washington, D.C.,
Chief of Weather Bureau.

I must add my profound appreciation of the great work for the highest science that is being accomplished by you. The solid knowledge that constitutes "Science" is a rather slow growth — it can only advance in proportion as man frees himself from ancient errors and evolves higher powers of observation and reason. The fine work done at Clark, the excellent memoirs published by its professors, and now these attractive lectures, give us all the assurance that your labors for the highest attainments in the study and teaching of science will be abundantly rewarded.

CLEVELAND ABBE, Washington, D.C.,
Weather Bureau.

Congratulating you on the successful rounding out of the first decade of the University, and with best wishes for the success of the institution in the future,

W. J. MCGEE, Washington, D.C.,
Smithsonian Institution.

I send you most cordial greetings on the interesting occasion, and hope the future of Clark will be as successful as the past, and that your plans for scientific research may be realized in the fullest degree.

CARROLL D. WRIGHT, Washington, D.C.,
Commissioner of Labor.

One may well be envious of the gratification that the generous founder of Clark University must feel at the world-wide recognition of its achievements during the very first decade of its existence.

To have established a just claim upon the regard of foremost men associated with educational establishments in this country and in Europe is of great significance.

The work that the University has done and is doing will continue to attract to its halls those rare geniuses who, impressed with the transcendent importance of the science of Pedagogy, of Physiology and Psychology, seek with unfailing diligence to penetrate their inmost depth. This work can scarcely fail to exercise a beneficial influence upon the schools of the country, and become a distinguished attraction to the city which is fortunately the home of the University, whose citizens will give it welcome and encouragement and markedly recognize the munificence of its founder, as well as the labors of those who have in so brief a time established it among the foremost seats of learning.

ANDREW H. GREEN,
214 Broadway, New York City.

As I shall not be able to be present during the exercises on Monday, July 10, celebrating the completion of the tenth academic year of Clark University, I desire to express in writing my feelings of sympathy and my strong desire for the success of the University, and also to extend to you and your co-workers my sincere congratulations on this auspicious occasion.

It is probably true that the initiative step of the institution was not fully understood or appreciated by the public, but during the past ten years it has, under your able and judicious direction, steadily pursued a course well calculated to win its way to public confidence and to an abiding position among the most eminent and distinguished institutions of learning in the civilized world.

The entire exercises attending the celebration are calculated to draw aside the mystic veil, and when the occasion shall have been numbered among past events, the general public will be led to see and know Clark University in the future as it has been seen and known in the past by distinguished foreign scientists and educators.

Yes, rest assured, President Hall, that before the last hour of the present century has been struck by the unerring and mighty hand of time, Clark University, the far-seeing, noble, and generous founder, together with the University's learned and distinguished first president, will have been crowned by truth and justice with the laurel wreath of victory, exalted merit, and universal appreciation.

THOMAS H. DODGE, Esq.,
Worcester.

JAMES BRYCE begs to be permitted to offer his congratulations upon that occasion.

Will you please convey to them my best wishes for the continued prosperity of Clark University. It has a high mission; for gathering in new knowledge is a much nobler task than distributing that which is known, useful as the latter may be.

I feel confident that when your present age is lengthened tenfold and your successors celebrate the centenary, they will hold up a great record of influence for good in the States and in the world.

PROFESSOR MICHAEL FOSTER,
University of Cambridge, England.

Though thus tardily, it is none the less heartily, that I congratulate you and your colleagues and fellow-citizens in this celebration — and this not simply on reaching your first natural period of retrospect, but on the worthy manner of the celebration also. You are certainly setting forth a feast of rare and varied intellectual fare, and thereby also giving a great lesson to us in the Old World of that return to the international unity of universities, which it is fitting that you in America should lead. Again accept these my best wishes for the celebration, with hearty congratulations upon your vigorous and productive youth — with confident hope also of your yet more productive maturity.

PROFESSOR T. W. GEDDES,
University of Edinburgh, Scotland.

ARTHUR BIENAYMÉ (Toulon, France) addresses to the President his most sincere prayers for the prosperity of the University.

I address my wishes for the brilliant future of your University.

PROFESSOR ALFRED BINET,
Paris, France.

I find it unfortunately impossible to avail myself of your invitation, for I certainly would have desired to enter into personal relations with men who join to their high science a largeness of view seldom to be met with.

PROFESSOR JULES TANNERY,
Paris, France.

My congratulations on the completion of the tenth academic year of the University, with my best wishes for its increase and prosperity.

PROFESSOR ADOLF BAGINSKY,
University of Berlin, Germany.

I avail myself of this occasion to express my heartiest wishes for the further prosperity of your University. I rejoice at the admirable way in which you are to celebrate the foundation of your institution, thereby showing that it is to remain what it has hitherto been: the home of scientific investigation and culture.

PROFESSOR MAX DESSOIR,
Berlin, Germany.

I express my heartiest wishes for the prosperity of your University, whose scientific activity has so soon won for it a high place among the universities of your country.

PROFESSOR BENNO ERDMANN,
Bonn, Germany.

In your effort to unite the nations under the banner of unselfish science, accept my most cordial congratulations and wishes for prosperity.

PROFESSOR PAUL FLECHSIG,
University of Leipzig, Germany.

I request you to receive my sincerest congratulations to this academical solemnity, and the expression of my hope, that your institution, highly advanced through many difficulties and sacrifices, may enjoy the most splendid prosperity for many secula.

PROFESSOR ERNST HAECKEL,
University of Jena, Germany.

I send to you and Clark University best wishes for success.

PROFESSOR FELIX KLEIN,
University of Göttingen, Germany.

Permit me to express my warmest wishes for the future prosperity of your University, which, called to life ten years ago, has already won such deserved success.

PROFESSOR KÜHNE,
University of Heidelberg, Germany.

Accept my heartiest congratulations on your approaching celebration, and may it be the dawn of a still more momentous era than the preceding one has already been.

PROFESSOR OSWALD KÜLPE,
University of Würzburg, Germany.

May the following decennium of Clark University be prosperous in its development and rich in scientific results.

PROFESSOR LINDEMANN,
University of München, Germany.

I express my good wishes on the occasion of the celebration.

PROFESSOR MAX NOETHER,
University of Erlangen, Germany.

I do not want to let slip the opportunity of expressing my best wishes for the University which has done so much for science, and is spoken of, particularly in Germany, with the highest respect and esteem.

PROFESSOR BAUER,
University of München, Germany.

With the best wishes for the growth and success of your University,

PROFESSOR W. REIN,
University of Jena, Germany.

I offer my best wishes for the welfare and progress of the University.

PROFESSOR C. RUNGE,
Hannover, Germany.

Permit me to send my heartiest congratulations on this celebration. Under your guidance Clark University has, in the ten years of its existance, already won for itself a high reputation in the whole scientific world. May the second decennium continue like the first to advance and increase science, and may it be granted to you, Mr. President, for many years to come to be the standard-bearer of the scientific labors of Clark University.

PROFESSOR HERMANN SCHILLER,
University of Giessen, Germany.

Wishing the University further prosperity and progress,

PROFESSOR F. SCHUR,
Karlsruhe, Germany.

I remember my sojourn in America and the kind reception which I met with in Worcester. I should rejoice to have the opportunity to renew the hospitality shown me by yourself and by your colleagues.

PROFESSOR E. STUDY,
University of Greifswald, Germany.

May the young University, which has already developed so auspiciously, continue according to the old saying: *Vivat, floreat, crescat!*

PROFESSOR WALDEYER,
University of Berlin, Germany.

I should have also been especially desirous of bringing to you my own recognition of what has hitherto been accomplished and my cordial wishes for the future. I follow with great interest particularly the psychological works which proceed from your University and are published in the *American Journal of Psychology*. I have always received from them the impression that the psychological and pedagogical departments of your University belonged to the most important institutions of their kind.

May Clark University complete the second decennium of its existence with like, and where possible, increasing glory!

PROFESSOR W. WUNDT,
University of Leipsic, Germany.

Accept my warmest wishes for the development of the University.

PROFESSOR ED. WEYR,
University of Prague, Austria.

I feel a great pleasure in congratulating your Clark University on the celebration of the festival; and allow me to express the hope that your University may extend its activity with every year to the honor of its President, its Trustees, and all its Members.

PROFESSOR S. E. HENSCHEN,
University of Upsala, Sweden.

I beg you to receive my cordial congratulations on the occasion of the beautiful decennium which your University has completed. I hope that this seat of learning shall have a future correspondingly to the excellent manner in which it has begun its life.

PROFESSOR H. HÖFFDING,
University of Copenhagen, Denmark.

I beg to present my sincere congratulations upon the erection of a scientific centre, the decennium of which you are to celebrate in so fitting a manner.

PROFESSOR ZEUTHEN,
University of Copenhagen, Denmark.

I send you the best wishes for the success of your celebrated University,

PROFESSOR VITO VOLTERRA,
University of Turin, Italy.

Eternal prosperity to the vigorous propagator of light.

PROFESSOR STEPHANOS,
University of Athens, Greece.

DR. WESLEY MILLS (McGill University, Montreal, Canada) wishes the University every success in the future.

With best wishes for the continued prosperity of Clark University,

PROFESSOR J. SQUAIR,
University of Toronto, Canada.

PRESIDENT ANGELL (University of Michigan) congratulates them on the useful work which the University has already accomplished.

With hearty congratulations for what you have already achieved as President of Clark University, and in full assurance of a great future before you,

HENRY BARNARD, Hartford, Conn.,
Ex-U. S. Commissioner of Education.

WILLIAM W. BIRDSALL (President Swarthmore College) desires to extend congratulations upon the completion of the tenth year of Clark University.

I congratulate you most heartily on the splendid work which Clark University has accomplished during the ten years of its existence. Nothing in our educational work has reflected greater honor upon the American system than the high ideals so successfully maintained at Clark University.

PRESIDENT JOHN E. BRADLEY,
Illinois College.

Good wishes to the University in all its undertakings, and congratulations to President, Trustees, and Faculty upon the completion of ten years of distinguished usefulness.

PROFESSOR C. L. BRISTOL,
New York University.

My deepest wish is that Clark may do as much more for the advancement of science and the deepening of the true university spirit in the next decennium as it has in the one now closing.

PROFESSOR EDWARD F. BUCHNER,
Teachers' College, New York City.

I beg leave to extend to you my most sincere congratulations on the work that Clark University has accomplished under your guidance, since the time of its founding, ten years ago.

As a Fellow of the University, I enjoyed opportunities for work that other institutions could not afford, and I found your efforts to provide books, instruments, and material as effectual as they were untiring.

As a Graduate I have found inspiration in your zeal for the furtherance of all that can advance education and science.

I have followed the development of the University with pride. The first high ideals have not been lowered, and Clark remains, as it was at its foundation, a University for Universities.

PROFESSOR H. C. BUMPUS,
Brown University.

No undertaking nor movement has made so clear and definite impress upon the educational thought of America nor established guiding lines of control so distinctly in pedagogical and psychological progress as the suggestions and tendencies which have emanated from Clark University. Though the institution is yet in its infancy, though the students in point of numbers have been limited, yet its influence has penetrated every state in the Union, has entered practically every educational institution of the land, from university to kindergarten, and has quickened the spirit of educational conferences, from those of national repute to those of the little teachers' meetings of the village school.

Granting the truth of the educational view for which Clark University stands, and allowing for the singularly forceful methods of instruction by the President and Faculty within the institution, and the energy with which its mission has been prosecuted, it is nevertheless still a marvel that its influence should have become, in this brief space, so widespread and vigorous. The facts which stand prove the wisdom of the plan of an institution which should be exclusively graduate, selecting as its students a limited number of mature thinkers who should be inspired by the power which ever comes from the contact with original investigation and a faculty of original investigators.

FREDERICK BURK, *President State Normal School, San Francisco, and*
President Clark University Alumni Association of California.

I send my best wishes for the success of the anniversary exercises and for the continued and enlarged prosperity of the University.

PRESIDENT NATHANIEL BUTLER,
Colby University.

Kindly accept my congratulations upon the completion of your tenth academic year.

PROFESSOR R. H. CHITTENDEN,
Director Sheffield Scientific School.

I desire to congratulate the Faculty of the University on the great work accomplished within a comparatively short period.

BROTHER CHRYSOSTOM,
Manhattan College.

We rejoice with your many friends in the successful rounding out of Clark University's first decade. It is a consolation to the generous benefactor that the world recognizes the merit of the Institution, which his munificence established and maintains. Coming into existence the same year, holding similar views as to the place of graduate work, having the highest ideals of university endeavor, striving earnestly to realize them in spite of all difficulty, our two Universities have always felt strong attachments for one another, and a more than ordinary interest in one another's success. The Catholic University tenders you its most cordial greeting on this the day of your rejoicing. It bids me extend to you and through you to the University its most sincere wishes for still higher and greater success in its chosen fields.

THOS. J. CONATY, Washington, D. C.,
Rector Catholic University.

With many congratulations on the past ten years' work of the University,

PROFESSOR CHARLES R. CROSS,
Massachusetts Institute of Technology.

PROFESSOR C. B. DAVENPORT (Harvard University) desires to express his appreciation of the brilliant example of research as a primary university function which Clark University has for a decade set.

The University and all connected with it are to be congratulated.

PROFESSOR ELLERY W. DAVIS,
University of Nebraska.

I desire to express my appreciation of the splendid work done by Clark University during these ten years.

PROFESSOR NATHANIEL F. DAVIS,
Brown University.

I must content myself with rejoicing over the unique intellectual enterprise you are carrying out. I may not be informed regarding such matters, but it seems to me you have accomplished a sort of scientific *coup d'état* in getting such a group of scholars to come to America upon the occasion of your anniversary. As a disciple of Clark University, and an admirer of everything it stands for, I take pride in the impression that must necessarily be made upon American scholarship by the visit of such men. I congratulate all of you, and hope that everything you desire in connection with the series of lectures may be realized.

PROFESSOR GEORGE E. DAWSON,
Bible Normal College, Springfield, Mass.

PRESIDENT DROWN of Lehigh University begs for his colleagues and for himself, to offer his hearty congratulations to the President, Trustees, and Faculty of Clark University on the completion of a decade of usefulness in the higher education, marked by distinguished services in many lines of original research.

Permit me to express my admiration of the work you have done and are doing.

PROFESSOR WILLIAM P. DURFEE,
Hobart College.

Let me assure you that we are all grateful for what Clark University is doing for sound education in this country, and I can only hope that you may have many successful years in the development of the work which you are doing.

S. T. Dutton, Brookline, Mass.,
Superintendent of Schools.

In the opinion of many who have studied there, the peculiar advantage of Clark University is mainly attributable to the close and personal relations between professors and students under which the work is conducted. The formal lecture delivered to a body of men in the class-room has but little of the stimulative force imparted by a conversational discussion with the man alone in the lecturer's private study, and too great praise can hardly be given to the members of the faculty of Clark for their constant and generous sacrifice of time to this most helpful method of instruction. The frequent assignment throughout the course of problems involving research leads to the best of training for the later performance of original work, and the presentation in the lecture-room of the results thus obtained gives experience in the work of the lecturer. In perhaps no other institution are these methods of the personal conference and the "colloquium" so constantly applied; no doubt such methods are impossible in most larger universities at present; and one can hardly imagine such a course followed with more kindness and devotion at any time than is now the case at Clark.

Professor Frederick C. Ferry,
Williams College.

I take this means of expressing my interest in the noble success of the University, and of wishing it continuance and increase.

Rabbi Charles Fleischer,
Boston, Mass.

Congratulating you and the University upon these years of achievement,

Alice C. Fletcher,
Washington, D.C.

I rejoice in the prosperity of your institution because it is one which sends forth its light, not only for the few, but for the many.

President Wm. Goodell Frost,
Berea College.

Though my stay with you was short, yet it meant the inspiration that took me abroad and pushed me on to undertake important work.

Professor John P. Fruit,
William Jewell College.

The Johns Hopkins University sends its cordial greetings to the President, the Trustees, and the Faculty of Clark University, on the completion of its first decennium, with congratulations upon its successful maintenance of high ideals, and with best wishes for its continued prosperity and power.

PRESIDENT DANIEL C. GILMAN.

I must add my congratulations on the success of your work, and my good wishes for its continuance on even a larger scale.

PROFESSOR GEORGE L. GOODALE,
Harvard University.

Every educator especially owes a debt of gratitude to Clark for the fearless work it has done in breaking down blind prejudice and advancing the truth.

PROFESSOR JOHN Y. GRAHAM,
University of Alabama.

You have certainly arranged a most dignified and impressive series of lectures — wholly congruous with the work which you have been doing during the decade.

PROFESSOR EDWARD H. GRIFFIN,
Johns Hopkins University.

You will please accept the assurance that I am very glad indeed that your institution, which has already done so much for the cause of progressive education, has thus shown its vitality and power of endurance. No doubt these ten years have meant much struggle and anxiety on the part of those whose heart was in the work. Others may be able to express their appreciation of this work with greater eloquence, but none can be more sincere and thankful than I am. Truly, if there is such a thing as a science of education in this country now, Clark University . . . (has) contributed the largest share toward this accomplishment. To me (its) work has meant an awakening and uplifting hardly equalled by any other influences that have worked upon my soul. May your anniversary week be a thorough success.

PROFESSOR M. P. E. GROSZMANN,
Milwaukee, Wis.

Allow me to extend cordial congratulations on the auspicious event.

PROFESSOR CHARLES W. HARGITT,
Syracuse University.

I extend for the University of Maine hearty congratulations, and wish continued prosperity for the future.

PRESIDENT A. W. HARRIS,
University of Maine.

I send you my hearty congratulations on your decennial celebration.

PRESIDENT WALTER L. HERVEY,
Teachers' College, New York City.

I congratulate you and the Trustees and Faculty upon these successful years of your University work, and upon this most appropriate mode of celebrating the anniversary. It is a mode worthy of universal following, and will, without doubt, be more and more adopted by our institutions of higher learning.

PROFESSOR G. H. HOWISON,
University of California.

Allow me to offer my congratulations to you especially, and to your associates, for the marked success which has attended the career of Clark University. We have felt that it not only increases the resources of high education for youth, but it stands for progress and enlightenment in the commonwealth and the country at large. There is a justifiable pride on the part of those who love earnestness and progress in educational matters, as they review the past of this institution, into whose good name and wide scope of influence you have thrown so much of your personal enthusiasm as well as your scholarly ability.

REV. EDWARD A. HORTON,
Boston, Mass.

I have many pleasant memories of a year's profitable work at Clark, and rejoice in the continued success of Clark University.

PROFESSOR L. S. HULBURT,
Johns Hopkins University.

The programme presented is most attractive and inspiring. I congratulate you upon the successful work of the past ten years.

DR. HENRY M. HURD, Baltimore, Md.,
Superintendent Johns Hopkins Hospital.

I can't help expressing to you my feeling of satisfaction, and repeating the satisfaction I heard such men as Cattell, Royce, Van Gieson, Munsterberg, and Putnam express, with the excellent good taste and refinement of your little celebration. All the refinements of the world seem now to take refuge in the smaller things; the bigger ones are getting too big for any virtue to remain with them. You have done something original and succeeded perfectly, from the point of view of the passive "assistant."

PROFESSOR WILLIAM JAMES,
Harvard University.

I beg you to accept my heartiest congratulations. Each year, I sincerely believe, finds me more grateful and appreciative of the privileges I enjoyed at

Clark, and especially do I realize more and more what you yourself did for me. I trust you may be spared health and vigor many years to come in your labor, for you are doing a great work.

GEORGE E. JOHNSON, Andover, Mass.,
Superintendent of Schools.

I have been very deeply interested in the work of Clark University, and in the way it has held to its high purposes regardless of pressure of all sorts in other directions. . . . Stanford congratulates Clark on ten years' noble work for high thought and accurate investigation.

PRESIDENT DAVID S. JORDAN,
Leland Stanford Jr. University.

For myself and all the staff of the University of California, I send you hearty congratulations and good wishes. You have not attempted to do as many things as some other universities, but what you have attempted you have done exceedingly well. If excellent work is the standard of true success, you have been successful among the foremost.

May your achievements and your reputation gain still greater lustre, and your educational work confer still larger benefits on succeeding generations.

PRESIDENT MARTIN KELLOGG,
University of California.

May I say that I think you have taken a most admirable course in the character of this celebration, and that I wish you every success, not only on this occasion, but in all the future years of the University.

PROFESSOR J. S. KINGSLEY,
Tufts College.

I regret more than I can express my inability to be present at the decennial celebration of your noble institution, and to hear the splendid series of lectures which you have provided.

PROFESSOR JOSEPH LECONTE,
University of California.

It is a pleasure to me to join in the celebration of the first decade of Clark University. The method of celebrating the event is, I think, exceedingly fitting. I enjoyed several of the most interesting years of my life in the lecture-rooms and laboratories of Clark, and always recall them with great satisfaction.

PROFESSOR J. S. LEMON, Washington, D.C.,
Columbian University.

Clark University stands unique among the universities of this country in the work which it is attempting to do. No other institution has done more in the line of original investigation, nor given during the same period greater inspiration to the educators of the country.

PROFESSOR G. W. A. LUCKEY,
University of Nebraska.

Permit me to congratulate heartily the President, Trustees, and the Faculty of Clark University upon the completion of the tenth academic year of the University.

PRESIDENT GEORGE E. MACLEAN,
University of Nebraska.

We appreciate the great work done by Clark University, and send every best wish for the future.

PRESIDENT JAMES G. K. MCCLURE,
Lake Forest University.

I have the highest feelings of regard for Clark University, for I feel that I owe much to it. Its conception is the broadest and best of all our institutions, and I hope the time will come when it can broaden out, and, all obstacles being removed, go on to its full completeness.

PROFESSOR WILLIAM S. MILLER,
University of Wisconsin.

When one thinks of the amount of light that has spread from Clark University and of the place that it fills in American education to-day, it is hard to realize that no such institution was in existence ten years ago. Please accept my most sincere congratulations to this auspicious event, with the hope that a long series of years of vigorous activity may be granted to you, so that you may lead the University to ever new achievements, and continue to benefit the cause of education in the future, as you have so splendidly done in the past. *Vivat, floreat, crescat.*

PROFESSOR F. MONTESER,
New York University.

It is with very great regret that I find it impossible to attend the rich celebration you have prepared for the friends of Clark University and of all the forward movements in science for which you have made Clark University stand, and wish the University long-continued and increasing prosperity.

PROFESSOR E. H. MOORE,
University of Chicago.

My participation in the treasures you offered was thus limited to one day — but this one day, with the three lectures I listened to, and the very interesting men I met, was so agreeable and valuable that I feel the desire to thank you warmly for the distinguished and exquisite pleasure. I take special pleasure in combining with my personal thanks my congratulations to the high success of the celebration and my very best wishes for the next ten years in the life of Clark University.

PROFESSOR HUGO MÜNSTERBERG,
Harvard University.

Permit me to express here my sincere admiration and respect for the aims, ideals, and plans of Clark University; these are of such an ideal character that they are bound to interest profoundly every man who loves science for its own sake.

PROFESSOR J. U. NEF,
University of Chicago.

Permit me to offer my hearty congratulations on the work done and the progress made in the ten years of Clark's existence, to express the hope that the future may be marked by even greater achievements.

PRESIDENT CYRUS NORTHROP,
University of Minnesota.

Clark University does well to celebrate in such a becoming manner the noble service which she has rendered to higher education in this country. May the next ten years be no less fruitful and helpful to those who have become accustomed to look to Clark University for inspiration and guidance.

PROFESSOR F. W. OSBORN,
Adelphi College, Brooklyn, N. Y.

I write to congratulate you most cordially upon your celebration of the completion of the tenth academic year of Clark University.

PROFESSOR HENRY F. OSBORN,
Columbia University.

Allow me to congratulate you upon these lectures, and also upon the remarkable results which you have been able to accomplish in ten years in connection with Clark University.

PROFESSOR G. T. W. PATRICK,
University of Iowa.

The Provost, Trustees, and Faculty of the University of Pennsylvania present their cordial congratulations to the President, Trustees, and Faculty of Clark University on the happy completion of the tenth academic year of the University.

The President, Trustees, and Faculty of Clark University certainly deserve the thanks of all those interested in the cause of education.

PROFESSOR GEORGE H. PRICE,
Vanderbilt University.

Pray accept congratulations on the completion of a decade of grand work, and on the prospects of even better work for the future.

JOHN T. PRINCE, West Newton, Mass.,
Agent State Board of Education.

I send my heartiest congratulations on the great achievements of Clark University during its first decade, and express my sincerest desire that its usefulness may continue and expand for many centuries to come.

PROFESSOR ERNST RICHARD,
New York City.

PRESIDENT H. W. ROGERS (Northwestern University) desires to extend the congratulations of Northwestern University, as well as his own, upon the great success of Clark University and the distinction it has attained in the academic world.

JAMES E. RUSSELL (Dean, Teachers' College, New York) wishes to convey to the President of the University his best wishes for the continued success and prosperity of the institution.

PRESIDENT L. CLARK SEELYE (Smith College) offers his hearty congratulations on the important educational work it has already accomplished.

With sincere thanks and hearty congratulations on the auspicious occasion,

PROFESSOR JAMES SETH,
Columbia University.

Meanwhile I wish to join in the many congratulations I am sure you will receive upon the quiet and dignified, but none the less eminent, manner in which Clark University has carried on the work of the past decade, and upon the manner in which it has reflected honor upon American scholarship in science and philosophy.

ALBERT SHAW, New York, N. Y.,
Editor Review of Reviews.

We shall always be grateful for the work that has already been accomplished by the University, and especially for the ideals which it has brought to the colleges and universities of the West. With high personal regard and warmest congratulations from our faculty,

PRESIDENT WILLIAM F. SLOCUM,
Colorado College.

With best wishes for the success of the celebration and for the continued prosperity of your institution,

PRESIDENT F. H. SNOW,
University of Kansas.

Allow me to congratulate the University upon its happy completion of ten years' life and work, and to wish it a long and prosperous future.

PROFESSOR FREDERICH STARR,
University of Chicago.

I wish to send my cordial congratulations and my wish that the next ten years may witness the coming to the University of such ample endowments as will enable it to accomplish its high ideals.

PRESIDENT JAMES M. TAYLOR,
Vassar College.

Please accept my best wishes for continued prosperity.

PRESIDENT W. O. THOMPSON,
Ohio State University.

I do not like to let the present occasion pass without intimating to you my appreciation and admiration of the methods and aims of university work for which Clark University has stood in the past, and will, I hope, stand in a long and prosperous future. My recent visit to Worcester merely confirmed a belief which I have long held, — that the type of man that Clark University calls to its professorial chairs, and the type of man that it sends into active life at the close of its three or four years of graduate study, are types that represent the highest ideal of scholarship, and are the very salt of American society. I hope, most sincerely, that the coming celebration will prove to be the door through which you and the University pass to greatly extended activity upon your own high level.

PROFESSOR E. B. TITCHENER,
Cornell University.

I wish to express my sincere appreciation of the service to education and investigation which Clark University is thus undertaking, a service which is eminently in harmony with the work of Clark University from the beginning.

PROFESSOR JAMES H. TUFTS,
University of Chicago.

I wish to extend my hearty congratulations on the successful work of the University during the last ten years, and my best and most hearty good wishes.

PROFESSOR JOHN M. TYLER,
Amherst College.

PROFESSOR HENRY B. WARD (University of Nebraska) extends to the President, Trustees, and Faculty his congratulations upon the occasion, and best wishes for the continued success of the institution.

I express my sincere congratulations.

PROFESSOR SHO WATASE,
University of Chicago.

With best wishes for the success of the University,

PROFESSOR J. B. WEEMS,
Iowa State College.

Please accept congratulations upon the honorable record of these ten completed years. The distinguished service of yourself and the University have made the whole world your debtor.

PRESIDENT B. L. WHITMAN, Washington, D. C.,
Columbian University.

The Clark University ideal as I understood it, when connected with its early work, is the ideal which I place above any others thus far proposed, and I hope that it may find strong friends to help it forward.

PROFESSOR CHARLES O. WHITMAN,
University of Chicago.

PROFESSOR A. W. WRIGHT (Yale University) sends congratulations and best wishes for the prosperity of the University.

DECENNIAL ADDRESS.

By G. Stanley Hall, President of the University.

It has been said that decades are the best periods for studying historic tendencies because they are long enough to contain a rich array of facts and events, and short enough to be grasped by a single mind in the stage of its prime. The ten years since Clark University was opened, the close of which, by the coöperation of a few beneficent public-spirited citizens of Worcester, we have sought to mark in a very quiet but dignified way that should befit at once its size and its quality, constitute distinctly the most important decade in the educational history of this country. The mere index of a few of the well-known and accomplished facts of these years has an eloquence beyond all words. They have witnessed the establishment of the Catholic University at Washington, with its strong faculty and its handful of picked graduates from the seventy Catholic colleges of the country, the only university in the land besides Clark devoted solely to graduate work, an institution related to us, not only by a strong tie of sympathy in the struggle and sacrifice for ideals and high standards, but by my own long and personal friendship with the first rector, and by the fact that its present head was our Worcester neighbor and kindly friend. The Leland Stanford University, now one of the richest in the world, was planned and endowed by a long-time friend of our Founder, and the wife of that founder lately told me that she still counts ours among her wisest and most trusted advisers. The University of Chicago, with possibilities of increase brighter and larger than any other, from the very first the most rapid academic growth in history, has leaped into existence with a Minerva-like completeness, owing in no small part its first impulse to higher creative work in science to the sagacity of the chief trustee of its Ogden Fund, our fellow-townsman, Andrew H. Green, and which is still more closely affiliated to us by the fact that so many of the leading members of its faculty honored us by doing three years of their best work here, and for which we still cherish a little of the feeling of a poor but proud and noble mother for her great son. The new Methodist University at Washington has begun the unfoldment of large and well-matured plans, for the fulfilment of which the vitality of the strong religious body behind it is perhaps the best of guarantees. The millions already provided and about to be expended at the State University of California which will involve transformation and enlargement perhaps greater than all that has hitherto been done there, very comprehensive and valuable as that is; the magnificent new architectural installation at Columbia and the federation of so many other affiliated institutions about it, with all the possibilities of our greatest metropolis open before it; the steady development, whether for good or for ill, of the plan of a great national university, to which at least all state, if not private, colleges and universities may be tributary as feeders, and which shall command all the vast resources of science in Washington, unify them, and add the new vitalizing function of research and perhaps teaching, a scheme that has enlisted most of the educational leaders of the land and is sure of eventual fulfilment,—such are some of the events which have seemed to many to threaten the academic preëminence of New England, and even of the East, in the future; that have stirred to their very foundations the older and more conservative institutions, and caused transformations not all apparent from the outside, but which involve hardly less than an ultimate revolution of academic sentiments, methods, and ideals. Fellowships, not for the indigent who need support while preparing for the professions, but to give leisure, opportunity, and incentive for full development to talent, the choicest of all national products; research, with books, apparatus, above all, leaders competent to guide and inspire; new post-graduate departments for non-professional specialization, with their own laboratories and libraries; seminaries where experts discuss the latest literature, best methods, instruments, and results of investigation; new journals devoted to the speedy publication of such studies; new chairs and topics; a growing and ever widening distinction between receptive learning and active creation,—these and the gradual completion of a system that is truly national, and has not its apex in Europe, where hundreds of our graduates still go yearly to get what it should be a matter of simple patriotism to supply at home, must suffice to mark the direction and progress of these years in which institutions and work alike are becoming more and more plastic to the changing and ever more imperative needs of learning and science which have themselves celebrated triumphs during the decade which could not even be enumerated within the hour. It is no wonder that many old academic problems have become obsolete and new ones have arisen, and that present demands in men, methods, and instruments have changed from those of ten years ago.

Again, within this time a wave of doubt and opposition to the public support of intermediate education passed over the country, but the reaction against that tendency has made the last few years preëminently the age of high schools. More and statelier buildings than ever before, longer courses and more of them, many modifications suggested by committees and others, great increase in the number of students, rich and well-planned departures like the Tome Institute, Mrs. Emmons Blaine's new normal foundation, and several others contemplated or assured but not yet established, the new associations of high schools and colleges covering now all sections of the country, the ever increasing collegiate character of the work done in such institutions, and the consequent development of a distinct, and in some places urgent, small college problem, — all this shows that even secondary education, the last stage to be reached by reforms, has here been stirred and quickened as never before.

If we extend our view to lower grades, we find all plastic and changing. This stronghold of conservatism is invaded by the spirit of reform, often revolution, and sometimes even of rather wild experimentation. New journals, pedagogical chairs, new methods, the new school hygiene, broader views that relate teaching to all the great problems of science, statecraft, and religion, have arisen, which have brought the university and kindergarten and all between them into an organic unity, yet fitting all features of the system to the vast variety of individual differences of character, temperament, and ability. In this field, I think, the closing decade has witnessed a change greater than the preceding quarter of a century. New and better minds are enlisted, educational topics are of increasingly central interest in the press and more dominant in the church and pulpit, education is becoming more professional and scientific, recognizing the necessity of expert leadership and mastery, and is at last assuming its rightful and larger power, and its normal basal all-conditioning place as at bottom a biological science, revealing to us how state, church, home, literature, science, art, and all else have their ultimate justification only in so far as they are effective in bringing human beings to the ever fuller maturity of mind and body on which civilization depends, and which it is the work of education to accomplish in the world. This is increasingly necessary as our country grows in population and in territorial expansion, and educational progress is coming to be recognized by history as the chief standard by which to test all other advancement. Europe has progressed during this decade, although with less rapidity, along nearly all these lines, and the next decennial promises not less, but more advance. In such a time it is, indeed, glorious to be alive, and to be young is heaven, for hope is even brighter than memory.

No time in the history of the country could have been more favorable than the beginning of this period for a great and new university foundation. The epoch-making work of the Johns Hopkins University, which for the preceding decade had made Baltimore the brightest spot on the educational map of the country, and was the pioneer in the upward movement, had leavened the colleges and roused them from the life of monotony and routine which then prevailed, and kindled a strong and widespread desire for better things. The significance of the work of that institution can hardly be overestimated. But financial clouds had already begun to threaten this great Southern luminary, and there were indications that, if the great work it had begun was to be carried on, parts of it, at least, must be transplanted to new fields.

It was at this crisis that our munificent Founder entered the field with the largest single gift ever made to education in New England, and one of the largest in the world, and with the offer of more to come, if sufficient coöperation was forthcoming. He selected Worcester as the site of his great enterprise with a piety to the region of his nativity worthy of the greatest respect and emulation, and in addition to the fulfilment of his pledges gave it the benefit of his own previous wide studies of education in Europe, and contributed wisely matured plans and constant personal oversight and labor for years. It is as strenuously engaged in this highest of all human endeavors that the world knows him, and that we shall remember him, and I am sure that we all unite to-day first of all in sending him in the retirement his health demands (although it cannot assuage his interest to see the work of his hands prosper) our most cordial greetings and our most hearty congratulations.

With a dozen colleges within a radius of one hundred miles doing graduate work, the plainest logic of events suggested at once a policy of transplanting to this new field part of the spirit of the Johns Hopkins

University, and taking here the obvious and almost inevitable next step by eliminating college work, although the chief source of income by fees was thereby also sacrificed, and thus avoiding the hot and sometimes bitter competition for students, waiving the test of numbers, and being the first upon the higher plane of purely graduate work, selecting rigorously the best students, seeking to train leaders only, educating professors, and advancing science by new discoveries. It was indeed a new field wide open and inviting, the cultivation of which was needed to complete our national life; the preliminary stages of its occupancy all finished, yes, necessary almost as a work of rescue for the few élite graduates who wished to go beyond college but not into any of the three professions, and who had had hitherto a pathetically hard time. The call to the President gave assurance of the highest aims and of perfect academic freedom, a pledge that has been absolutely kept. He was sent to Europe a year on full pay to learn the best its institutions could teach, and the Faculty that first fore-gathered here has never been excelled in strength, if indeed it has ever been equalled anywhere for its size. Story, an instructor at Harvard, colleague and friend of Sylvester, formerly acting editor of the chief mathematical journal of the country and co-head of his department at Baltimore, founder of another journal here, who has enriched his department by contributions, the list of which printed elsewhere in this volume tells its own story; Michelson, who while here accepted an invitation of the French Government to demonstrate in Paris his epoch-making discoveries in the field of light, which he did while on our pay-roll — lately especially honored by learned societies at home and abroad, now head of one of the best-equipped and largest laboratories in the world, and still continuing his brilliant contributions to the sum of human knowledge; Whitman, now head of another great university laboratory, trainer of many young professors, founder and editor of the best and most expensive biological journal, head of Woods Holl marine laboratory and summer school, one of the best of its kind in the world, himself a contributor to his science; Michael, than whom America had not produced a more promising or talented chemist, the list of whose published works would be far too long to read here; Nef, perhaps our most brilliant young chemist, and now head of one of the largest and best-equipped laboratories in the world, and with a power of sustained original work rarely excelled; Mall, now full professor at the Johns Hopkins University, and head of the great new anatomical laboratory and museum there, whose published contributions are admirable illustrations of both the great caution and boldness needed by a student in his field; Boas, the leading American in physical anthropology, now a professor at Columbia; Loeb, almost the first expert that this country could boast in the new physical chemistry in the sense of Ostwald, now head of his department in the University of the city of New York; Bolza, an almost ideal teacher, suggesting the great Kirchoff in the perfection of his demonstrations; the brilliant and lamented Baur, leader of the expedition to the Galapagos Islands made possible by the gift of Worcester's patron saint of so many good enterprises, Mr. Salisbury; Donaldson, now dean of the graduate school of the University of Chicago, author of the best handbook in English on the brain, with a caution, poise, and diligence befitting the successful investigator in that dangerous but fascinating field; Mulliken, suddenly placed in a position of great difficulty, discharged its duties with rare ability and discretion for one so young; Lombard, now professor in Michigan, genial, assiduous, a gifted teacher and enthusiastic student; White, scholarly, able, a born teacher and student; McMurrich, an untiring investigator and a lucid inquirer after knowledge; those now here, who have since become so well-known, Burnham, Chamberlain, Hodge, Perott, Sanford, Taber, and Webster; these, not to mention many others, then only fellows, but who have achieved so much in their work and positions since, — these are the men and others whose presence on this spot, whose high intercourse and whose stimulating personal contact with each other, whose ardor and devotion in the pursuit of knowledge, whose healthful emulation in achievement, made this almost classic ground and the cynosure of the eyes of all those in this country who love science for its own sake. With the wealth, wisdom, and interest of our Founder, with the high character and culture of our Board of Trustees, with the intelligence of such a community of old New England, with an atmosphere of intellectual freedom, with unique and precious exemption from the drudgery of excessive teaching and examinations, with the youth of the Faculty, none of whom had reached the zenith of their maturity, with substantial and ample buildings, abundant and forthcoming funds for equipment, few rules and almost no discipline or routine of faculty meetings, the motto on our seal, *fiat lux*, our university color white, — is it any wonder if some of our young men saw visions and dreamed dreams, or perhaps in some cases fell in love with the highest ideals, or that the very memory of the first stage of our history is to-day, as it has been in darker hours, a most precious memory and a basis of an all-sustaining hope?

To these days of our prime to which our former students and professors recur with joy, and in whose breasts the processes of idealization of them have already begun, days which were pervaded by sentiments of joy and hope very like those which animated the best years of the Johns Hopkins University, we have often reverted since in soberer hours with longing thoughts of what might have been had the University continued in all its pristine strength. Not one weak, dull, or bad man in our Faculty, all given not only leisure, but every possible incentive to do the very best work of which they were capable, with a Founder and a board of control who realized that a new endowment should do new things, and that the best use of money is to help the best men, we entered a field very largely new and with as bright prospects as we could wish.

But life has its contrasts and competitions. The reductions of our force, which occurred at the end of the third year, and to us almost beyond precedent, although helpful elsewhere, may be ascribed to fate, disease, or to the very envy of the gods. Some incidents should remain unwritten, but it should be known that our Trustees foresaw from the beginning of the year one of the gravest of crises, and met it with an unanimity, a wisdom, and a firmness which even in the light of all that has transpired since, I think, could not be improved on. The pain of it all has faded, the glad hand has been extended and accepted by nearly if not quite all who left us; the lessons of adversity have been learned and laid well to heart, and we hope and believe that these and all their attendant incidents may be considered closed.

Although nearly half our Faculty and students left us in the hegira, and our income had dropped in almost the same proportion, and only the departments of psychology and mathematics remained nearly intact, we fortunately had left in every department young men as promising as any in the land. They needed simply to grow, and never has there been such an environment for a faculty to develop as in this "paradise of young professors," as a leading college president has called this University. To Darwin the greatest joy of life was to see growth; and to see the unfoldment of these youthful, intellectual élite, and to feel the sense of growth with them as all near them must, is a satisfaction almost akin to the rapture of discovery itself. Now the years have done their work, and our Faculty, although smaller, was never stronger, never more prolific.

stimulating, and attractive to students, in proportion to its size, than it is to-day. There has never been such loyalty to the institution and its ideals, such readiness to endure the petty and the great economies now necessary, such prompt and frequent refusals of larger salaries elsewhere, and so strong a sentiment that, so long as a man has growth in him, our incentive, opportunity, and plan of work are of more value than a large increase of salary.

These changes involved, however, but little reduction of the number of instructors or of students, but materially decreased for a time the efficiency of the University. Since the end of the third year the President, who was not required to teach, has done full professorial duty in addition to that of administration, has established a seminary at his house three hours each week through the entire academic year, and founded and conducted at his own expense a new educational journal. The income-bearing summer school has been organized and conducted during the past seven years with the active and efficient coöperation of a large local advisory board under the direction of Colonel E. B. Stoddard and Charles M. Thayer, Esq., by which its social character, that has contributed much to its success, has been established on a high plane. The summer school represents only the departments of biology, psychology, and pedagogy, is open to every one of either sex on the payment of a small fee, is popular rather than technical in its scientific character, has been numerously attended, and in all ways is directly in contrast with the work of the year. Hardly a ripple has marred the harmony within the University during these last seven years, and every man, student and instructor alike, has been hard at work and enthusiastic for our own unique and individual method and plan.

This institution must be judged from within and by educational and scientific experts, and the commendations which we have lately received from leading specialists, some of which are printed elsewhere in this volume, have been so numerous, spontaneous, and hearty in response to our invitation to be present, as almost to rival in cordiality and loyalty to the now so definitely developed Clark idea and Clark spirit that of our three alumni associations of the Pacific Coast, Illinois, and Indiana organized during the present year.

Scientific work must be weighed and not measured, so that numbers tell but little. Clark University has been instrumental in training well-nigh three hundred professors or special academic instructors, has numbered over twelve hundred different persons enrolled in its summer school, not counting the hundreds who have attended more than one session. These, especially the former, are in a sense our epistles known and read of all men. The other output of a university like ours is its scientific work, and here we have five hundred publications based upon work done here, of which twenty-five are books. The University now publishes three journals, with hope of a fourth as a more permanent way of marking the beginning of its second decade.

Small as we are, if our departments and students are measured by the significant criterion of the number of the doctorates annually conferred here, we rank among the best and largest institutions of the land. Although our fellowship funds have declined, and that, too, in the midst of a competition, which never existed or was hitherto dreamed of, our numbers of late years have slightly but steadily increased, although at the same time we could go on forever and do invaluable work of research and publication like the French Ecole des Hautes Etudes, or a few other Old World institutions, even if we had no students; and, indeed, America may need in the future, if, indeed, she does not already, at least, one such academic endowment for research only. One thing, at least, is true so far, hardship has no whit lowered our aims or diluted our quality, but if anything has had the reverse influence; and I fervently trust (and think I can speak on this point with confidence for the entire Faculty) that this may be the case throughout all the infinite future that endowments like this in a country like ours have a right to expect. Although influences are too subtly psychological to be traced, I am writing our history, and find it a most inspiring theme, and I believe it adds already a very bright and hopeful page to the records of higher education in the country, and one which history will brighten to epochal significance. It has, on the whole, in it one clear note, not of discouragement, but of hope and confidence.

Have we duly considered, even the best of us, what a real university is and means, how widely it differs from a college, and what a wealth of vast, new, and in themselves most educative problems it opens? A college is for general, the university for special, culture. The former develops a wide basis of training and information, while the latter brings to a definite apex. One makes broad men, the other sharpens them to a point. The college digests and impresses second-hand knowledge as highly vitalized as good pedagogy can make it, while the university, as one of its choicest functions, creates new knowledge by research and discovery. The well-furnished bachelor of arts, on turning from the receptivity of knowing to creative research, is at first helpless as a new-born babe, and needs abundant and personal direction and encouragement before he can walk alone; but when the new powers are once acquired they are veritable regeneration. He scorns the mere luxury of knowing, and wishes to achieve, to become an authority and not an echo. His ambition is to know how it looks near and beyond the frontier of knowledge, and to wrest if possible a new inch of territory from the nescient realm of chaos and old night, and this becomes a new and consuming passion which makes him feel a certain kinship with the great creative minds of all ages, and having contributed ever so little, he realizes for the first time what true intellectual freedom is, and attains intellectual manhood and maturity. This thrill of discovery, once felt, is the royal accolade of science, which says to the novice, stand erect, look about you, that henceforth you may light your own way with independent knowledge.

This higher educational realm is full of new "phenomena of altitude." Faculties, instead of discussing and elaborating plans for commencement ceremonies, hearing recitations, preparing and then reading the results of examination papers, and carefully marking each individual exercise, grinding in the old mills of parietal regulations, discipline, and the rules of conduct needful to civilize the adolescent *homo sapiens ferus*, revising requirements for admission, tacking and shaping the policy to gather in more students and keep ahead of others in the struggle to get the best connections with high and fitting schools, are occupied with far different problems wherever the university spirit has a true and real embodiment. Here first of all men must be discriminated, and great issues hang upon the success in differentiating superior from indifferent young men. To detect the early manifestations of talent and genius in the different fields of intellectual endeavor, which some presidents and professors can, and others so eminently lack the power to do, is the crucial doorkeeping problem, where great privileges are to be awarded to great promise. This is almost a life and career saving function for not only the young professors and students, but for the university. Men are not equal, and there must be a touchstone of mental aristocracy to discriminate $500 from $10,000 men.

Second, having selected these, the university should bestow freely its needed aid and equipment, and the professor his choicest time and knowledge, to perfect the precious environment by which the later stages of growth, so liable to be lost, but on the full development of which civilization itself hangs, and perfected. How to select the best, ripest, and most *fruitful* topics for investigation requires an almost prophetic ken in which differences in individual professors are immense. To study individuals enough to adapt each theme to each personality is another problem as new as it is delicate and difficult. The right solution of both these is the large half *of* the work. The professor should give his best suggestion, with no reservation for himself, and the able student should not be an apprentice to serve his master, but should be distinctly educated toward leadership himself from the first.

Having thus sown fit seed in fit soil, it must be watched and watered with constant suggestion. The best and newest literature; the most effective and original apparatus that can be devised and if possible made on the spot; how to insure in the best form and place the speedy publication of work and to bring it under the eye of all experts; how to avoid conflict and duplication; how general or how special thesis subjects and work should be to best combine the two sometimes more or less divergent ends of discovery and education; the requirements for perhaps the choicest of all degrees, the doctorate of philosophy; the best modes of individual examination for it; the number and relation of subjects required; the migration of students so as to insure not only the best environment for each, but to give to professors not only in the same department, but in different institutions, the same stimulus that was felt when the elective system aroused the dry-as-dust professors to unwonted effort lest their class-rooms be left vacant; the kindred question of the relative value of graduate work at home and abroad for each student and for each department; the fit federation of graduate clubs and their thirty-five hundred members in the twenty-three American institutions now recognized in the yearbook; the great problem of printing and special journals together with interchange of monographs; the vast new library problems of purveying for highly specialized, but very voracious, appetites which make the true university librarian a man of far different order from others, and gives him a wealth of new problems of exchange, foraging, etc.; to maintain the true relations between lecture work and individual guidance while duly emancipating the professors from the drudgery of elementary teaching and mass treatment of great bodies of students; the many and wide-reaching differences between pure and applied science, and the practical methods by which this distinction is maintained; the danger of great aggregations of students and the advantages of few; the wide differences between the new kind of professor needed in the university and those in the college, where no provision is made for the advancement of learning, and the tests are mainly pedagogic; the even greater contrasts between scholarship funds for the aid of poverty to professional careers, which are a doubtful advantage even in colleges where they belong, and the true university fellowship as above described; the growing dominance and need of expertness in all fields for which graduate departments must prepare as well as for professorship alone, — these and many great questions like them, destined more and more to eclipse all others which are just looming up, and for the irrigation and ventilation of which we hope to establish here soon a new educational journal — such questions constitute this opening field of what may be called the higher educational statesmanship.

The hastiest glance at the situation on an anniversary like this would be incomplete unless we turned toward the future. Our own needs here are many and our wants urgent, but our faith is firm that in a community like this the time will soon come when no wills will be drawn by wealthy people without carefully considering the conclusion of the largest parliamentary report ever made, which fills near a score of volumes, was many years in the making, and describes all the public bequests ever made in England. The substance of the conclusion of that most competent tribunal that has ever spoken upon this subject is that *the best of all uses of public benefactions is, not for charity to the poor or even the sick and defective, noble and Christlike as those charities are, not for lower education or religion, beneficient as these are, but rather for affording the very best opportunities for the highest possible training of the very best minds in universities, because in training these the whole work of church, state, school, and charity is not only made more efficient, but raised to a higher level, and in this service all other causes are at the same time best advanced.* I beg respectfully, but with all my heart and mind, to urge this conclusion by the highest human authority upon all those contemplating the bestowment of funds where they will accomplish most for the good of man.

Our very best department is the library, which is so well endowed that we do not at present need to expend the income of the fund. In this respect the sagacity and benevolence of our Founder has been more than sufficient for our needs up to the present time, and our most efficient and courteous librarian has found many means and devices, new to the most advanced library science, of bringing out its utmost efficiency for our work, and of making it in all the pregnant sense of that word attractive to all who once come within the sphere of its influence. His work amply merits all the growing recognition that it and his rare personnel are so steadily gaining. His special report contains new suggestions and experiences.

The large and new demands upon the Public Library caused by the presence of an university for research which involved a material addition to its work, which is likely to increase in proportion to our growth, should be distinctly recognized. The special privileges needed by investigators have often been a strain upon the capacity of both its officers, its methods of administration and service, and the resources of its alcoves. The Public Library has on the whole well met the test, and I desire here to express, not only for myself personally, but for the other members of the University our gratitude to the city, the Trustees, and particularly to the accomplished head of the library itself, whose coöperation, with his able corps of assistants, has been a factor in an important part of our work.

Our two strongest departments are mathematics and psychology. These two, as has been often said, are the root and heart of all other branches. Mathematics is the grammar of all the sciences that deal with inanimate nature, and the study of the human mind and soul opens the field where all animate nature celebrates her highest triumph and which underlies all the humanities. While we could expend with profit much more than at present, perhaps the entire resources of the University, upon these departments, or perhaps, even upon each of them, they are best equipped and least in immediate need. We have books, journals, professors, means of speedy publication, and well-developed traditions, and can claim, we think with modesty, to be doing creditable work.

Our greatest and most pressing need, according to the policy first formulated of strengthening the departments already established before founding new ones, is to enlarge the biology to an independent position, with due provision for botany and the related subject of paleontology. The foundations of a building for this group of studies is already laid on the grounds, and its completion, with an endowment of $150,000 or $200,000 with what we now have, would give us a strong department able to compete successfully with the best; perhaps we may sometime dedicate such a building and department to the name of some honored public-spirited citizen of Worcester.

Physics, like biology, now represented by a single able and promising man, needs enlargement to the same degree, with an annex department of astronomy and astrophysics, and for the same sum could, in addition to what we now have, be put upon a creditable footing.

The chemical building, admirably planned after careful studies of all the best in Europe, and well equipped, especially for organic work, has no endowment, and needs for its full development the income of at least a quarter of a million of dollars.

Anthropology, so greatly needed in this land, but so lacking in academic installation and tradition here, is already a precious germ with one worthy representative, has been cherished from the first with us, and it, too, needs enlargement and independence.

If we pass over into the humanities, there are, of course, the two great groups of philology and literature, ancient and modern, and a historical group culminating in political economy, sociology, and a grand department of international law, nowhere adequately represented in this country, and for the establishment of which somewhere Senator Hoar, acting president of the Board of Trustees, the first citizen of Massachusetts, competent to-day to fill any one of four professional chairs in any university, in learning, experience, character, and position more nearly the American Gladstone than any other, has been so distinguished an advocate.

Education, now coming to be the largest philosophy of life and the natural field of applied psychology, needs a more adequate representation, and with a quarter of a million of dollars for an ideal university school for children, we would almost guarantee in five years to make this place an educational Mecca, by short circuit methods now well demonstrated but nowhere embodied, which would greatly increase the efficacy and reduce the expense and ease the labor of the lower grades of education in this country.

Our summer school has become one of the largest and highest grade institutions of its kind in the country, and appeals especially to heads of fitting schools, with whom it would be important for us to be *en rapport* if we had a college; to normal schools, whose faculties are a growing field for the employment of our pedagogical graduates; to young instructors in colleges, superintendents, parents, etc. If our two weeks could become a summer quarter counting toward a degree, and if the summer school could be adequately endowed and furnished, with the interest which one department of our work has already enlisted among the teachers of our country, the best of whom could spend their summer here in work, this, too, could be made an institution of which any city or university might well be proud.

We urgently need without delay the means for establishing a university printing office, where we can publish our journals at less expense and do our own printing; and if this should grow to larger dimensions and develop a life of its own, that, too, might be welcomed.

These needs are all on the university plane, where the beginnings already made are precious beyond words, wrought out as they have been with so much pain and labor, and the highest effort of so many choice spirits. May the day never dawn when this in our country most sorely needed and prayerfully cherished academic tradition shall fade or be broken. The investments of wealth and effort already made are too great, and achievements already attained and future promise too bright, to permit this ever to be an open question here.

Satisfied, yes proud, as we are to-day to submit to Worcester, to sister institutions, and the country, the records of our work when compared with our means, we have lived, and even now live and walk, let us confess it, to a great extent in faith and hope, looking confidently to a future larger than our past has been, with steadfast and immovable conviction that our cause is the very highest of all the causes of humanity, but ready even ourselves, if need be, to labor on yet longer in the captivity of straitened resources, being fully persuaded that our redeemer liveth and that in due time he shall appear.

THE DEPARTMENT OF MATHEMATICS.

BY WILLIAM EDWARD STORY.

PAST AND PRESENT STAFF.

WILLIAM EDWARD STORY, Ph.D., Professor of Mathematics since 1889.

OSKAR BOLZA, Ph.D., Associate in Mathematics, 1889–92.

HENRY TABER, Ph.D., Docent in Mathematics, 1889–92; Assistant Professor of Mathematics since 1892.

JOSEPH DE PEROTT, Docent in Mathematics since 1890.

HENRY S. WHITE, Ph.D., Assistant in Mathematics, 1890–92.

FELLOWS AND SCHOLARS.

HENRY BENNER, Fellow in Mathematics, 1889–90.

L. P. CRAVENS, Scholar in Mathematics, 1889–90.

ROLLIN A. HARRIS, Ph.D., Fellow in Mathematics, 1889–90.

J. F. MCCULLOCH, Fellow in Mathematics, 1889–90.

WILLIAM H. METZLER, Fellow in Mathematics, 1889–92.

J. W. A. YOUNG, Fellow in Mathematics, 1889–92.

LEVI L. CONANT, Scholar in Mathematics, 1890–91.

ALFRED T. DE LURY, Fellow in Mathematics, 1890–91.

JAMES N. HART, Scholar in Mathematics, 1890–91.

THOMAS F. HOLGATE, Fellow in Mathematics, 1890–93.

JOHN I. HUTCHINSON, Scholar in Mathematics, 1890–91; Fellow in Mathematics, 1891–92.

FRANK H. LOUD, Scholar in Mathematics, 1890–91.

N. B. HELLER, Scholar in Mathematics, 1891–92.

LORRAIN S. HULBURT, Fellow in Mathematics, 1891–92.

JOHN MCGOWAN, Scholar in Mathematics, 1891–92.

ERNEST B. SKINNER, Scholar in Mathematics, 1891–92.

L. WAYLAND DOWLING, Scholar in Mathematics, 1892–93; Fellow in Mathematics, 1893–95.

JOHN E. HILL, Fellow in Mathematics, 1892–95.

HERBERT G. KEPPEL, Scholar in Mathematics, 1892–93; Fellow in Mathematics, 1893–95.

THOMAS F. NICHOLS, Scholar in Mathematics, 1892–93; Fellow in Mathematics, 1893–95.

F. E. STINSON, Scholar in Mathematics, 1892–93; Fellow in Mathematics, 1893–95.

W. J. WAGGENER, Scholar in Mathematics and Physics, 1892–93.

WARREN G. BULLARD, Scholar in Mathematics, 1893–96.

SCHUYLER C. DAVISSON, Fellow in Mathematics, 1895–96.

FREDERICK C. FERRY, Fellow in Mathematics, 1895–98.

JOHN S. FRENCH, Scholar in Mathematics, 1895–96; Fellow in Mathematics, 1896–98.

E. W. HETTNER, Fellow in Mathematics, 1895–98.

†S. EDWARD RYERSON, Fellow in Mathematics, 1895–96. Died March 25, 1896.

HUGH A. SNEPP, Scholar in Mathematics, 1895–96.

JAMES W. BOYCE, Fellow in Mathematics, 1896–99.

HERBERT O. CLOUGH, Scholar in Mathematics, 1896–97.

A. HARRY WHEELER, Scholar in Mathematics, 1896–99.

LINDSAY DUNCAN, Scholar in Mathematics, 1897–99.

FREDERICK H. HODGE, Scholar in Mathematics, 1897–98; Fellow in Mathematics, 1898–99.

HALCOTT C. MORENO, Scholar in Mathematics, 1897–98; Fellow in Mathematics, 1898–.

STEPHEN E. SLOCUM, Scholar in Mathematics, 1897–98; Fellow in Mathematics, 1898–.

JOHN N. VAN DER VRIES, Scholar in Mathematics, 1897–98; Fellow in Mathematics, 1898–.

FRANK B. WILLIAMS, Scholar in Mathematics, 1897–98; Fellow in Mathematics, 1898–.

ELWIN N. LOVEWELL, Scholar in Mathematics, 1898–99.

LOUIS SIFF, Scholar in Mathematics, 1898–99.

ORLANDO S. STETSON, Scholar in Mathematics, 1898–99.

SPECIAL STUDENTS.

GEORGE F. METZLER, Ph.D., Honorary Fellow in Psychology, 1891–92.

CALVIN H. ANDREWS, Mathematics and Pedagogy, 1894–95.

WALTER E. ANDREWS, Mathematics and Pedagogy, 1894–95.

Whole number of students in mathematics in 10 years	44
Aggregate attendance (including 4 who remain in 1899–1900) . . .	83 years.
Average number of students per year	8
Average attendance per student	2 years.

Mathematics occupies a peculiar position relatively to the arts and sciences. It is, par excellence, an art, inasmuch as its chief function is to solve problems, — not such examples as are given in the text-books, and which serve only as exercises in the application of methods, but any problems that may arise in human experience and for whose correct solution sufficient data are at hand. When any line of investigation, to whatever subject it may refer, has been carried so far that exact reasoning may be applied to it, mathematics is the authority to which the results of observation are submitted for the final determination of their consistency and the conclusions that may be drawn from them, and furnishes the means of applying these conclusions to the prediction of phenomena not yet observed. No science and no branch of technology is exact, that is, capable of predicting with certainty what will happen under given conditions, unless it rests upon a mathematical foundation. Astronomy, physics, and applied mechanics already have this foundation to a considerable extent, while the other sciences are still in the inductive stage, in which material is being collected with which, it is to be hoped, such foundation will ultimately be laid. Mathematics is also a science, inasmuch as it has accumulated a large body of systematic knowledge involving and leading to the methods that it employs in its solutions. These methods are of such a peculiar nature, differing so widely from other methods, that a special course of training is requisite if any one would learn to use them, and their number and variety have become so great that a lifetime would not suffice to acquire familiarity with them all. But new problems are continually arising and demanding new methods, and we need, therefore, a body of men who shall devote themselves especially to the task of supplying this demand. While the colleges are engaged in general liberal education, teaching a variety of subjects that develop the mental faculties (and no subject is more efficient than mathematics for this purpose) and make the student acquainted with his own tastes and powers, thus enabling him to determine the life-work for which he is best fitted, it is the special function of the university to extend the limits of human knowledge, and to train those who have unusual intellectual talents to employ them to the best advantage. We believe this object is best accomplished by an institution devoted solely to it, and whose teachers' energies are not diverted by the lower, though no less important, aims of the college.

When the policy that should characterize this University was under discussion, the first point decided was that its work should be strictly post-graduate, and that it should not compete with other institutions in the work that is generally recognized as undergraduate. In accordance with this principle, the mathematical department fixed its standard of admission so as to require such a knowledge of mathematics as can be obtained in the average American college, and laid out upon this foundation a curriculum of its own, as extensive and as thorough as circumstances allowed. In elaborating the details of this curriculum, we have kept in mind the fact that those who pursue post-graduate studies in pure mathematics almost always look forward to careers as professors in colleges or other higher institutions of learning; and we have taken the view that, other things being equal, the ideal teacher is a master of his subject, not only conversant with the general principles of all its more important branches, the problems that have arisen in each, the methods that have been devised for the solution of these problems, and the results that have been obtained, but also unbiassed, ready and sound in judgment, and actively engaged in scientific research. We believe that the training that is best adapted to produce efficient specialists is also the training that is best adapted to produce efficient teachers of specialties.

While desirous of supplying all possible facilities to those who wish to pursue studies in special branches, and to those who, already occupying permanent positions, have but a limited leave of absence, we have made it our chief object to provide a thorough training for those who, having just completed a college course, have not yet entered upon their life-work. This provision consists of such courses of lectures, seminaries, and individual assistance as should enable a faithful student endowed with the proper natural ability to satisfy the requirements for the degree of Doctor of Philosophy at the end of his third year with us. The requirements for this degree have been determined by our conception of the ideal teacher, as already stated. To acquire the necessary breadth of knowledge of mathematics as a whole, the candidate is expected to attend, during his first two years, specified courses of lectures on the general principles, methods, and results of all the more important branches of pure mathematics, to supplement these lectures by private reading, and to take an active part in the seminary. In the seminary, a special topic, more or less directly connected with the subject of some lecture, is assigned, from time to time, to each student, who is required to read it up and make an oral report upon it before the class. Advanced courses of lectures on special subjects that vary from year to year are also given, and each candidate for the degree is expected to attend a number of such courses. The student spends the greater part of his third year in the original investigation, under the constant personal guidance of one of the instructors, of a topic of his own selection. In preparing for this investigation, he is required to make a practically complete bibliography of the subject, and to read all the more important available articles that have been written on it. The results of the investigation, embodied in a dissertation suitable for printing, must be submitted to the instructor under whose direction the work was done, and must receive his approval before the candidate will be admitted to the final examination for the degree. This approval will not be given unless the dissertation is satisfactory in form and completeness and the results are sufficiently novel and important to constitute a real contribution to science. The dissertation is, in fact, the main criterion by which the candidate is judged, and no amount of other work will compensate for its defects. The ability of our graduates to carry on research and the excellence of the work actually done is assured by the regulation that each dissertation accepted by us as worthy of the degree shall be printed with the explicit approval of a member of our Faculty. It is evident that, whereas any one that has the necessary preparation and taste for mathematics may profit by the advantages here afforded, only those who have a certain amount of mathematical genius can secure the degree.

In making appointments to fellowships and scholarships we have endeavored to maintain the same high standard. We are on the lookout for mathematical geniuses; but it is difficult to determine from the evidence of others whether candidates come up to our standard or not; so that we have adopted the general policy of giving the best appointments to those only that have been with us for at least one year, and about whom we are in position to judge for ourselves. Of course, this policy could not be carried out during the earlier years of the University, and its effect is apparent in the fact that, whereas seventy-five per cent of the students that entered the mathematical department during the first three years remained with us but one year, only twenty per cent of those that have been admitted during the last seven years left at the end of their first year. I do not mean to imply that those who left before completing our course were inferior in ability to those who remained three years, but we desire particularly to encourage men who can and will go forward to the degree.

Nearly all of those who have studied mathematics with us have adopted teaching as a profession, two-thirds are now members of college faculties, and one-third are engaged in higher school work. Those who have received the doctor's degree have generally secured at once desirable positions in which to begin their life-work, and most of them have already acquired for themselves, by distinguished ability, very decided influence in the institutions with which they are connected. Of those who have left without the degree fully one-half ought to have continued, and would have done so but for want of pecuniary means; and we have been obliged to turn away many men of very great promise on account of our inability to assist them in providing the means of subsistence during the unproductive period of student life. We could employ for fellowships, with decided advantage, ten times the amount now at our disposal.

Although, as I believe, students will find here a broader post-graduate curriculum in mathematics and greater personal attention from the instructors than at any other university in the country, we need greater facilities to make our course what it ought to be. Four-fifths of the instruction in the department is now given by two men, and we are compelled to give in alternate years lectures on fundamental subjects that ought to be given every year. As I have said, we lay great stress upon the ability of our students to investigate; but this faculty can be fully developed only under the personal guidance of one who is himself in the habit of investigating and who has the facilities and opportunities necessary for such work. A teacher's usefulness is greatly increased by the inspiration that comes from a personal identification with his subject, from the fact that he has ideas of his own about it, and that he has extended it by his individual exertions; and the investigator can have no greater incentive to search for new results than the opportunity to present his thoughts and discoveries to an intelligent and appreciative class in the lecture-room. But the necessity of teaching many subjects simultaneously distracts the mind and is fatal to research. The ideal conditions for an instructor in an institution like this would be those under which he could teach one subject at a time, and that a subject that he was himself developing, and follow this subject with his class to such a point as to bring into evidence the scope and importance of his own work. To apply this method to the courses that are actually given here would require the services of three additional instructors in mathematics. We are actually laboring under the disadvantage that some of the important branches now taught by us are not of such paramount interest to any one of our instructors as to be the subject of his personal investigation. We are compelled to restrict ourselves to elementary courses in many branches that ought to be carried to a much higher point, and to omit altogether from our consideration applications of mathematics to statistics, to the arts, and to other sciences. Applications to physics receive the attention of the physical department, to be sure, but the mathematical department ought to do much more than it is at present able to do in preparing students for higher work in physics. The number of instructors necessary for such advanced work as we do is not to be determined by the number of our students, but by the number of subjects taught.

Again, every expert investigator finds himself continually obliged to spend much time in details that could just as well be worked out by a younger man, to whom such work would be of immense advantage, not only as an exercise in the practical application of methods, but also as furnishing the opportunity for a prolonged study of the workings of an investigator's mind; and example is worth more than precept in the development of the faculty of investigation. We ought to have the means of retaining our best graduates for a year or two as personal assistants to the instructors, during which period they might also be gaining experience in the class-room by teaching a few hours a week under the supervision of one of the regular instructors. Such work is not drudgery, and would be, I think, sufficiently attractive to an ambitious young man to induce him to remain with us on a moderate stipend while he is waiting for such appointment as may seem to him desirable.

It is almost universally assumed that a mathematician needs no material equipment other than brains, with, possibly, a few books. However true this assumption may have been some decades ago, — and I fancy that its truth then rested solely upon the difficulty of procuring such equipment, — it is not true now, as must be apparent to any one who studied carefully the German educational exhibit at the World's Fair in Chicago. Ten years ago our department started out with a fair nucleus for a mathematical library and a moderate collection of models, to which we have not been able to make many additions. We have very few of the older mathematical works that illustrate the history of the subject, and we need particularly complete sets of many important mathematical journals and the transactions of learned societies. In these journals and transactions have appeared most of the original investigations to which, as investigators ourselves, we have continual occasion to refer, both for suggestions and to avoid apparent plagiarism and the unnecessary duplication of research. We should also be greatly assisted in our class-work by a more complete collection of models.

In short, what I have in mind as a model mathematical department for post-graduate work would have, say, four professors and assistant professors, each having his personal assistant, and at least two instructors of lower grade for the more elementary work, and would be provided with a complete mathematical library and with all the apparatus that it is now possible to procure, with suitable provision for the purchase of new books and apparatus as they appear in the market.

These schemes are not incapable of realization, although, perhaps, opposed to the traditions of education in this country. This University has never had any traditions excepting such as were based upon high ideals. Its mathematical department was not modelled after that of any other institution, but was determined by the conception of what would constitute perfection in such a department. We have always lived up to our ideals, in so far as we have done anything, without regard to considerations of material interest. We are not here to do what is done elsewhere, and we do not acknowledge that it would be best for us to do what other institutions, in their experience, have thought wisest. We propose to adopt no temporary policy that we shall sometime want to abandon, confident that the ideal university of the future will be ideal from the very root and not a graft upon inferior stock.

When the doors of the University were first opened to students, in the fall of 1889, the mathematical staff consisted of William E. Story, Professor, Oskar Bolza, Associate, and Henry Taber, Docent; a year later it was increased by the appointment of Joseph de Perott, Docent, and Henry S. White, Assistant; and in 1892 Drs. Bolza and White resigned their positions to accept Associate Professorships in the University of Chicago and Northwestern University, respectively, and Dr. Taber was promoted to an Assistant Professorship, thus leaving the department with practically the same teaching force as it had during the first year.

The instruction has been given by lectures, seminaries, and individual conferences. The number of lectures (of fifty minutes each) was sixteen a week the first year, nineteen and twenty a week in the second and third years, respectively, and about fourteen a week, on the average, each year since. In some years courses of lectures on certain mathematical subjects having important physical applications have been given by Assistant Professor Webster of the Department of Physics.

The subjects of the lecture courses given during the ten years include the following: —

1. The History of Arithmetic and Algebra among various peoples from the earliest times to 1650 A.D.
2. Theory of Numbers (introductory).
3. Theory of Numbers (advanced).
4. Numerical Computations.
5. Theory of Quadratic Forms.
6. Finite Differences.
7. Probabilities.
8. Theory of Errors and the Method of Least Squares.
9. Theory of Functions of a Real Variable.
10. Linear Transformations and Algebraic Invariants (introductory).
11. Theory of Substitutions, with applications to algebraic equations (introductory).
12. Theory of Transformation Groups.
13. The Application of Transformation Groups to Differential Equations.
14. Finite Continuous Groups.
15. Klein's Icosahedron Theory.
16. Simultaneous Equations, including Restricted Systems.
17. Theory of Functions of a Complex Variable, according to Cauchy, Riemann, and Weierstrass (introductory).
18. Definite Integrals and Fourier's Series (introductory).
19. Ordinary Differential Equations (introductory).
20. Ordinary Differential Equations (advanced).
21. Partial Differential Equations (introductory).
22. Elliptic Functions, according to Legendre and Jacobi (introductory).
23. Weierstrass's Theory of Elliptic Functions.
24. Elliptic Modular Functions.
25. Abelian Functions and Integrals.
26. Theta-Functions of Three and Four Variables.
27. Riemann's Theory of Hyperelliptic Integrals.
28. Riemann's Surfaces and Abelian Integrals.
29. Conic Sections by modern analytic methods (introductory).
30. Quadric Surfaces by modern analytic methods (introductory).
31. General Theory of Higher Plane Curves (introductory).
32. Plane Curves of the Third and Fourth Orders.

33. General Theory of Surfaces and Twisted Curves (introductory).
34. Surfaces of the Third and Fourth Orders.
35. Twisted Curves and Developable Surfaces (advanced).
36. Applications of the Infinitesimal Calculus to the Theory of Surfaces.
37. Rational and Uniform Transformations of Curves and Surfaces.
38. Enumerative Geometry.
39. Analysis Situs.
40. Hyperspace and Non-Euclidean Geometry.
41. Modern Synthetic Geometry (introductory).
42. Quaternions, with applications to geometry and mechanics.
43. Multiple Algebra, including matrices, quaternions, "Ausdehnungslehre," and extensive algebra in general.
44. Symbolic Logic.

Courses designated as "introductory" are given at least as often as every other year, and attendance on them is required of all candidates for the degree of Doctor of Philosophy that take mathematics as their principal subject. The other courses, intended primarily for the more advanced students, have been given less frequently and with particular reference to the suggestion of topics for original investigation.

In connection with his lectures, Assistant Professor Taber has conducted a weekly seminary for students in their first or second year, for the purpose of cultivating in them an active attitude toward the subjects treated, instead of the passive attitude usually resulting from hearing lectures. Topics related to those of the lectures have been discussed by the students, and their work has been criticised both with reference to rigor of demonstration and manner of presentation. In this way some of the advantages of the laboratory and the practice school are brought into the field of mathematics. Professor Story, with the assistance of the other instructors, has directed the more advanced students individually in the systematic investigation of special topics that promised to afford opportunity for the discovery of new results and methods, — a task that has sometimes required the professor to hold weekly three-hour conferences with each of four students during nearly the entire academic year; but we believe the results have justified this unusual expenditure of energy.

The average annual number of students taking mathematics as their chief study has been about eight, the average duration of their residence was about two years, and more than one-third of them have received (or will undoubtedly receive) the Doctor's degree, which is a decided improvement in every respect over the record of the first three years. The published investigations of these students are enumerated in the Bibliography at the end of this volume.

The researches of an instructor in an institution of this kind are not to be judged solely by the number and magnitude of his printed papers, as many of them are naturally turned over, in a more or less incomplete form, to his pupils for further investigation and more adequate presentation; at least it seems most natural and desirable that an instructor should suggest to his pupils subjects for investigation on which he has himself worked, and for whose treatment he has found adequate methods.

My chief subjects of investigation have been: —

1. Hyperspace and Non-Euclidean Geometry.
2. Algebraic Invariants.
3. Curves on Ruled Surfaces, and Restricted Equations.
4. The History of Mathematics prior to the invention of the infinitesimal calculus, and
5. A Mathematical Curriculum for Primary and Secondary Schools.

I have developed systematically the general theory of space of any number of dimensions from assumptions that are precisely analogous to those on which the scientific treatment of threefold space is usually based, and which we recognize as the results of experience. In accordance with this general theory, I have thoroughly investigated the properties of loci of the first and second orders and some special loci of higher orders. The introduction of the most general kind of measurement has then led me to an equally thorough study of parallel and perpendicular loci, the curvature of loci, areas, and volumes in the most extended sense. The first part of these results has already appeared in the *Mathematical Review*, and I hope to publish the remainder within a short time.

Ever since the appearance of Clebsch's "Theorie der binaeren algebraischen Formen," toward the end of the year 1871, when I was studying in Berlin, I have taken a lively interest in the theory of algebraic invariants, — an interest that was greatly augmented by my association with Sylvester at the Johns Hopkins University in 1876. I had thought all along that there ought to be a direct process by which all such invariants could be obtained, but my efforts to find it had failed. A course of lectures on invariants that I have given every year or two since the opening of Clark University caused me to renew my attempts, and the classic paper of Hilbert in the 36th volume of the *Mathematische Annalen*, in which a process devised by Mertens (and which I regarded as indirect, inasmuch as it involved quantities extraneous to the matter in question) suggested a new line of research, which happily led at length to the long-sought direct process. I then applied this process, as Hilbert had applied Mertens's process, to the proof of Gordon's theorem that all the invariants of any finite system of quantics of finite orders can be expressed rationally in terms of a finite number of such invariants. These results were published in the *Mathematische Annalen* and in the *Proceedings of the London Mathematical Society*. I have spent much time in trying to find, by means of the process, an extension of Cayley's formula for the number of linearly independent ground-forms of a single binary quantic (extended by Sylvester to any system of binary quantics) to the case of quantics involving three or more variables, but so far without success.

In my lectures on surfaces of higher orders and twisted curves I have paid particular attention to the algebraic curves that lie upon a given algebraic surface. If the given surface is ruled, the curves on it can be classified in such a way that certain problems relating to a curve can be solved when the class of the curve is known. My investigations in this direction have been communicated to my students, some of whom have already solved such problems. In connection with my investigations on twisted curves, I have also made a systematic study of restricted equations, and have carried the determination of the orders of such systems much farther than had been done before.

I have lectured at various times on the early history of mathematics, with special reference to the development of arithmetical and algebraic symbolism, and have collected a large number of systems of such symbols, which I hope sometime to utilise for a monograph on the subject.

In connection with a course of lectures delivered for two years at the Summer School, I arranged a mathematical curriculum for primary and secondary schools, which will be published when I can find the leisure necessary to prepare the explanatory text.

At my request, Assistant Professor Taber has furnished the material for an account of his personal researches, which involves such a complete and excellent history of the theory of matrices that it seems to me inadvisable to abbreviate it; I therefore append it to this report at length, for the benefit of those readers who may be interested in the subject.

Dr. Taber's researches have been devoted to the development of the theory of matrices, and its application to bilinear forms, multiple algebra, and theory of finite continuous groups. The calculus or theory of matrices was invented by Professor Cayley (see his "Memoir on the Theory of Matrices," *Phil. Trans.*, 1858), and has proved an instrument of great power in the theory of linear transformation, bilinear forms, and for the investigation, generally, of the projective group.[1] In order to explain the work done by Dr. Taber in this direction, a few words of explanation will be necessary to describe the work done by Cayley and others.

Associated with any linear substitution

$$x_i' = \sum_{j}^{n} a_{ij}x_j \quad (i = 1, 2, \cdots n)$$

is the bilinear form $A = \sum_i^n \sum_j^n a_{ij}x_iy_j$, which may be regarded as representing this substitution, or *vice versa*; and, in the theory of matrices, we do not need to distinguish between this linear substitution and the associated bilinear form, or between either and the matrix $\begin{pmatrix} a_{ij} \\ i, j = 1, 2, \cdots n \end{pmatrix}$ common to both. If now B denotes the bilinear form $\sum_i^n \sum_j^n b_{ij}x_iy_j$, or its associated linear substitution, $A \pm B$ will denote the bilinear form $\sum_i^n \sum_j^n (a_{ij} \pm b_{ij})x_iy_j$, or its associated linear transformation; and AB will denote the bilinear form $\sum_i^n \sum_j^n \left(\sum_s^n a_{is}b_{sj}\right)x_iy_j$, or its associated linear substitution (obtained by the composition of the linear substitutions A and B). Equivalence between two bilinear forms or linear substitu-

[1] By means of this calculus very important results have been obtained by Cayley himself, by Sylvester, Frobenius, Fom, Weyr, Study, and others; and, by methods essentially similar, Kronecker obtained important theorems on the orthogonal group to which reference is made below.

tions, A and B, is denoted by writing $A = B$. Further, in what follows, I will denote the identical transformation, represented by $\dot{\sum}_i x_i y_i$, and A^{-1} the form, or substitution, satisfying the symbolic equation $AA^{-1} = A^{-1}A = I$; $\acute{A}$ will denote the bilinear form $\dot{\sum}_i \dot{\sum}_j a_{ji} x_i y_j$ transverse or conjugate to $A = \dot{\sum}_i \dot{\sum}_j a_{ij} x_i y_j$, and $|A|$ will denote the determinant of the matrix A. A is said to be symmetric if $\acute{A} = A$, and alternate, or skew symmetric, if $\acute{A} = -A$.[1]

Cayley was, perhaps, led to the invention of this calculus by his researches upon orthogonal substitution, *Crelle* (1846), Vol. 32. For in *Crelle*, Vol. 50, three years before the publication of his memoir on matrices, he expressed the results of these researches in the notation of matrices. Thus Cayley showed that the general expression for the proper orthogonal substitution in n variables is $(I - B)(I + B)^{-1}$, where B denotes an arbitrary alternate, or skew symmetric, linear substitution; and this expression gives Cayley's determination of the coefficients of a proper orthogonal substitution in n variables as rational functions of the essential parameters, $\frac{1}{2}n(n-1)$ in number.

Again, in his "Memoir on the Automorphic Linear Transformation of a Bipartite Quadrate Function" (*Phil. Trans.*, 1858), Cayley showed that the general automorphic linear transformation (linear transformation into itself) of a symmetric (alternate) bilinear form $A = \dot{\sum}_i \dot{\sum}_j a_{ij} x_i y_j$ with cogredient variables and of non-zero determinant, may be represented by $(A + X)^{-1}(A - X)$, where X is an arbitrary alternate (symmetric) bilinear form. This expression gives in the first case (when A is symmetric) Hermite's determination of the general proper automorphic linear transformation of a symmetric bilinear form, and, in the second case (when A is alternate), Cayley's determination of the transformation into itself of an alternate bilinear form. Further, in this same memoir Cayley showed how to reduce, to the solution of a system of n^2 linear equations, the rational determination of the n^2 coefficients of the automorphic linear transformation of a general bilinear form A (neither symmetric nor alternate) with cogredient variables and of non-zero determinant. Namely, he showed that the general formula for such a substitution is

[1] In the first case $a_{ji} = a_{ij}$, in the second $a_{ji} = -a_{ij}$ $(i, j = 1, 2, \cdots n)$.

$(A + X)^{-1}(A - X)$, where X satisfies the condition $(\breve{A})^{-1}\breve{X} + A^{-1}X = 0$. This result includes the determination of the general automorphic transformation of A, when A is symmetric and when A is alternate. It also includes Cayley's determination of the coefficients of an orthogonal substitution to which it reduces when $A = I$.

In what follows G will denote the group of proper automorphic linear transformations of A (the x's and y's being cogredient), and G' the proper orthogonal group. A transformation T of G (or of G') is termed *singular* if -1 is a root of its characteristic equation (namely, $|T - \rho I| = 0$); otherwise, *non-singular*. Every non-singular transformation of group G (or G') is given by Cayley's formula, and may be termed a *Cayleyan* transformation of the group.[1] No singular transformation of group G is given by Cayley's expression or determination. But for A alternate, also when A is neither symmetric nor alternate provided $|\breve{A} \pm A| \neq 0$, Dr. Taber showed in 1894 (*Proc. Am. Acad. Arts and Sciences*, Vol. 29) that group G is generated by the Cayleyan transformations of the group,— each transformation T of this group being obtained by the composition of a finite number of Cayleyan transformations. In the same paper Dr. Taber also showed that the sub-group of orthogonal transformations of G is, similarly, generated by the non-singular orthogonal transformations of this sub-group, when A is alternate, and when $\breve{A} \neq \pm A$ provided $|\breve{A} \pm A| \neq 0$.

This theorem is similar to a theorem relating to the orthogonal group (group G') established by Kronecker in 1890 ("Ueber orthogonale Systeme," *Sitzungsberich. d. Preuss. Akad.*), who showed that this group is generated by the Cayleyan transformations of the group, each transformation T of this group being obtained by the composition of two Cayleyan transformations,— the coefficients of each of the Cayleyan transformations being rational functions of the coefficients of T.

In 1895 (*Math. Ann.*, Vol. 46) Dr. Taber showed that, if A is real and alternate, every real transformation T of G can be obtained by the composition of two real Cayleyan transformations of this group. This theorem was obtained independently and extended widely by Dr. Loewy, who in 1896 (*Math. Ann.*, Vol. 48) showed that, if A is irreducible

[1] For the case in which A is symmetric, the determination of the coefficients of T, given by Cayley's formula, is properly Hermite's; but it is not convenient to distinguish here between this case and the other two cases, namely, when A is alternate, or is neither symmetric nor alternate, when the determination is Cayley's.

(which case includes that in which A is alternate), every transformation of G, real or imaginary, can be obtained by the composition of two Cayleyan transformations of the group, and that, therefore, when A is irreducible, there is no transformation of the kind termed by Foss *essentially singular*,[1] that is to say, which cannot be obtained by the composition of two non-singular, or Cayleyan, transformations.

For a reducible form A not every singular transformation of G can be obtained by the composition of two Cayleyan transformations of this group. Nevertheless, Dr. Taber showed in 1897 (*Math. Review*, Vol. 1) that in every case the Cayleyan transformations of G form a group by themselves; that the composition of any number of Cayleyan transformations of G results in a transformation that can be obtained by the composition of two Cayleyan transformations of this group; and that thus the composition of Cayleyan transformations never gives rise to an essentially singular transformation.

It is to be noted that from Cayley's formula for a transformation T of G, namely,

$$T=(A+X)^{-1}(A-X)=(I-A^{-1}X)(I+A^{-1}X)^{-1},$$

we derive

$$X=A(1-T)(1+T)^{-1};$$

and, therefore, the parameters, namely, the coefficients of X, which enter into the determination of T, can be expressed rationally in the coefficients of T and of A.[2] Similarly, in the memoir by Kronecker mentioned above, he has shown that the coefficients of the two Cayleyan transformations, whose composition gives the general transformation T of group G', can be expressed rationally in the coefficients of T. For A real, alternate, and orthogonal, Dr. Taber gave, in the paper in the *Mathematische Annalen* mentioned above, the determination of the coefficients of the two Cayleyan transformations C_1 and C_2, whose composition gives any real transformation T of G, as rational functions of the coefficients of T and of A. This determination of C_1 and C_2 he has since extended to the case in which T is imaginary, and A any alternate bilinear form.[3]

Dr. Taber has pointed out that the transformations of G, both when A is irreducible and when A is reducible, are in general of two essentially

[1] *Abhand. d. k. Bayer. Akad. d. Wiss.*, II. Cl., XVII. Bd., II. Abth. 1890, p. 77.

[2] Between these parameters when A is neither symmetric nor alternate n^2 equations persist.

[3] See papers to appear in *Proc. Am. Acad. of Arts and Sciences*, Vol. 36.

different kinds. The difference between the two kinds of transformations of G is given by the following theorem:—

(I.) *If we designate a transformation of group* G *as of the first or second kind according as it is or is not the second power of a transformation of the group, then every transformation of the first kind is the* m*th power of a transformation of the group, for any positive integer* m, *and can be generated by the repetition of an infinitesimal transformation of the group. A transformation of the second kind, by definition not an even power of any transformation of the group, is always the* $(2m+1)^{th}$ *power of a transformation of the group for any odd exponent* $2m+1$. *But no transformation of the second kind can be generated by an infinitesimal transformation of the group.*

(II.) *Every Cayleyan transformation of group* G *is a transformation of the first kind; whereas, a non-Cayleyan transformation is, in general, of the second kind.*[1]

Dr. Taber has also given the conditions necessary and sufficient that a transformation T of group G may be of the first kind for the case in which A is symmetric (which includes the case when $A = I$, in which case G becomes G'), and for the case when A is alternate.[2]

Dr. Taber has shown that, if A is neither symmetric nor alternate and

[1] This was proved for the orthogonal group in 1896, *Bull. Am. Math. Soc.*, Vol. 3. At the conclusion of this paper it was stated that a precisely similar theorem held for what is here designated as group G. In the *Math. Ann.*, 1896, Vol. 46, the theorem was proved for group G when A is alternate; for the case in which A is symmetric, in the *Proc. Lond. Math. Soc.*, 1896, Vol. 26; and for the general case, in the *Math. Review*, 1897, Vol. 1.

[2] For the orthogonal group, to which G reduces when $A = I$, the conditions necessary and sufficient that a transformation shall be of the first kind were given by Dr. Taber in a communication to the American Academy of Arts and Sciences, March, 1895. (See *Proceedings*, Vol. 30, p. 361.) The necessity and sufficiency of these conditions was afterwards shown in *Proc. Lond. Math. Soc.*, 1896, Vol. 26, and the theory for the orthogonal group extended to group G for A symmetric. It was not explicitly stated in this paper that the conditions given for the orthogonal group hold for G when A is symmetric, being so obvious a consequence of the considerations adduced. This does not seem to have been recognized by Dr. Loewy, who refers to this paper but gives the necessary and sufficient conditions, *Math. Ann.*, Vol. 48, when A is symmetric as an extension of Dr. Taber's theorem for group G'.

For A alternate the necessary and sufficient conditions were given by Dr. Taber in a communication to the American Academy of Arts and Sciences, January, 1896. (See *Proceedings*, Vol. 31, p. 342.) The necessity of these conditions has previously been shown by Dr. Taber in the *Math. Ann.*, Vol. 46. In Vol. 49 (1897), Dr. Loewy gave the conditions as sufficient, undoubtedly without knowledge of Dr. Taber's priority in the statement of this theorem.

$|\check{A} \pm A| \neq 0$, group G contains no transformation of the second kind. This theorem leads, for the case mentioned, to the following rational representation of any transformation of this group, namely,

$$[(A+X)^{-1}(A-X)]^2,$$

where $(\check{A})^{-1}\check{X} + A^{-1}X = 0$. Moreover, Dr. Taber has shown that the sub-group of orthogonal transformations of G contains no transformation of the second kind when A is alternate.[1]

The determination of the congruent transformations between two bilinear forms is the natural generalization of the problem to determine the automorphic linear transformations of A. A determination of the transformations between A and B depending on the solution of a single equation of degree n has been given by Dr. Taber (*Mathematical Review*, Vol. 1, 1897), which holds for any case whatever in which A and B are both symmetric or both alternate.

The theory of matrices, or bilinear forms, is closely related to the theory of Hamilton's linear vector functions. In the *American Journal of Mathematics*, Vol. 12, Dr. Taber has given a development of the theory of matrices, proving many of the fundamental theorems, from the point of view of Hamilton's theory.

One of Sylvester's most important contributions to the theory of matrices was a general formula, given in the *Comptes Rendus*, Vol. 94, 1882, expressing any power, integral or fractional, of the bilinear form or matrix A as a polynomial in A of degree $n-1$. Thus, if $B = A^\mu$, where μ is any fraction, and if $\rho_1, \rho_2, \ldots \rho_n$ are the roots of the characteristic equation of A, we have

$$B = \Sigma \rho_1^\mu \frac{(A-\rho_2 I)(A-\rho_3 I)\cdots(A-\rho_n I)}{(\rho_1-\rho_2)(\rho_1-\rho_3)\cdots(\rho_1-\rho_n)}.$$

By means of this theorem the determination of a matrix or linear substitution whose μth power is equivalent to A is reduced to the solution of a single algebraic equation of degree n. This formula was afterwards extended by Sylvester to any function of the matrix A.[2] Thus we have

$$f(A) = \Sigma f(\rho_1) \frac{(A-\rho_2 I)(A-\rho_3 I)\cdots(A-\rho_n I)}{(\rho_1-\rho_2)(\rho_1-\rho_3)\cdots(\rho_1-\rho_n)}.$$

[1] See *Bull. Am. Math. Soc.*, Series 2, Vol. 2, pp. 6 and 161.

[2] *Johns Hopkins Univ. Circulars*, No. 28, Vol. 3, p. 34.

Neither of these formulæ applies unless the roots of the characteristic equation of A are all distinct. For the general case, in which the roots of the characteristic equation have any given multiplicities, a formula for $f(A)$ has been given by Dr. Taber.[1] Thus, if the distinct roots of the characteristic equation are $\rho_1, \rho_2, \cdots \rho_r$, respectively of multiplicity $m_1, m_2, \cdots m_r$, and if $A^{(i)} = A_1^{(i)} \cdots A_{i-1}^{(i)} A_{i+1}^{(i)} \cdots A_r^{(i)}$, where $A_j^{(i)}$ denotes

$$[(A-\rho_j I)^{m_j} - (\rho_j-\rho_i)^{m_j} I]^{m_i} : [(-1)^{m_i}(\rho_j-\rho_i)^{m_i m_j}],$$

then

$$f(A) = \sum_{i=1}^{r}\left[f(\rho)I + (A-\rho_i I)\frac{\partial f(\rho)}{\partial \rho} + \cdots + \frac{(A-\rho_i I)^{m_i-1}}{(m_i-1)!}\frac{\partial^{m_i-1} f(\rho)}{\partial \rho^{m_i-1}}\right]_{\rho=\rho_i} A^{(i)}.$$

For $m_1 = m_2 = \cdots m_r = 1$, this reduces to Sylvester's formula.

The theory of matrices stands in a very special and important relation to the theory of higher complex quantity (multiple algebra). Namely, a class of systems of complex numbers with n^2 units arises from the theory of lineal transformation, — that is to say, a matrix of n^2 elements gives rise to a system of n^2 units e_{ij} with the special multiplication table $e_{ij}\, e_{jk} = e_{ik}$, $e_{ij}\, e_{kl} = 0$ for $j \neq k$. Multiple algebras (systems of complex numbers) of this class have been termed by Mr. Charles S. Peirce quadrate algebras, or quadrates; and Peirce has shown that the p units of any system of complex numbers (the p units of any multiple algebra) can be expressed linearly in terms of the n^2 units of a quadrate.[2] Whence it follows that the theory of any system of complex numbers is identical with the theory of the combination by multiplication, addition, and subtraction, of a certain system of p matrices.

The first quadrate algebra, namely, that with four units, is identical with the quaternions with the imaginary (Hamilton's bi-quaternions), as was first explicitly pointed out by Professor Benjamin Peirce. That is to say, by substituting for the original units e_{ij} a certain system of four linearly independent linear functions of the four units we obtain a system of complex numbers, $1, i, j, k$, which can be substituted for the original units, and whose multiplication table is $i^2 = j^2 = k^2 = -1$, $1i = i1$, etc., $ij = -ji = k$, etc. Let now i', j', k' be a new system of quaternion unit vectors having the multiplication table $i'^2 = j'^2 = k'^2 = -1$, $i'j' = -j'i' = k'$, etc. And let a third system of units be formed by the combination of these two sys-

[1] *Math. Ann.*, Vol. 46, p. 561. See also *Proc. Am. Acad. of Arts and Sciences*, 1892, Vol. 27, p. 46 *et seq.*

[2] See *Am. Jour. Math.*, Vol. 4, pp. 123 and 125.

tems, it being assumed that each of the one system of quaternion unit vectors is commutative with each unit vector of the other system. That is to say, that $ii' = i'i$, $jj' = j'j$, etc. We get thus sixteen units, 1, i, j, k, i', j', k', and the nine binary products ii', jj', etc. Dr. Taber has shown that the system of units thus obtained is identical with the quadrate of sixteen units. The same is true if we had combined the four original units of the quadrate with four units, namely, e_{rs} $(r, s = 1, 2)$ with a similar system of another quadrate, viz., e'_{rs} $(r, s = 1, 2)$, — assuming that $e_{rs}e'_{rs} = e'_{rs}e_{rs}$. The resultant system has sixteen units, and is the quadrate with sixteen units.[1] Dr. Taber has established a general theorem including the one just given. Namely, he has shown that, if $n = mp$, the quadrate of n^2 units is a compound of two quadrates severally with m units and p units, the units of one quadrate system being commutative with each unit of the other quadrate.[2] Whence it follows that if the prime factors of n are δ_1, $\delta_2, \cdots \delta_\omega$ and $n = \delta_1^{\mu_1}\delta_2^{\mu_2}\cdots\delta_\omega^{\mu_\omega}$, the quadrate of n^2 units is a compound of μ_1 quadrates each with δ_1^2 units, μ_2 quadrates each with δ_2^2 units, etc.

The general projective group holds a position of special importance in Lie's theory of finite continuous groups. For the adjoined group Γ of any finite continuous group G, by means of which the sub-groups of G are determined, will, if the equations of transformation of this group are properly chosen, appear as a sub-group of the general projective group. Thus the theory of matrices is of importance in the investigation of certain problems of Lie's theory, since this calculus furnishes a convenient instrument for the treatment of the general projective group.

The chief theorem of Lie's theory states that if a system of infinitesimal transformations satisfies certain conditions, they generate a group with continuous parameters, each of whose finite transformations can be generated by an infinitesimal transformation of the group.[3] In 1892 Professor Study made the extremely important discovery that this theorem is subject to certain limitations, — showing that an exception to this theorem existed in the case of the special linear homogeneous group in

[1] *Am. Jour. Math.*, Vol. 12, p. 391.

[2] *Ibid.* This theorem was obtained independently, but subsequently, by Professor Study. See "Math. Papers of Internat. Math. Congress of 1893," p. 376.

[3] *Transformationsgruppen*, Vol. 1, pp. 73, 158; *Continuierliche Gruppen*, p. 390. Lie originally defined a finite continuous group, substantially (*Trans. Grp.*, p. 3), as a group with continuous parameters. Ultimately, he assumed that in a continuous group as thus defined each transformation can be generated by an infinitesimal transformation of the group (*Contin. Grp.*, p. 679).

two variables, namely, that not every transformation of this group can be generated by an infinitesimal transformation of the group.[1] Subsequently, in 1893 (*Am. Jour. Math.*, Vol. 16), Dr. Taber showed that the orthogonal group in n variables (for $n \leq 4$) also presents an exception to Lie's theorem; and in 1895 gave, in a communication to the American Academy of Arts and Sciences, the conditions necessary and sufficient that a proper orthogonal substitution may be generated by an infinitesimal orthogonal substitution.[2]

For $n > 2$ also, the special linear homogeneous group in n variables is continuous only in the neighborhood of the identical transformations. For two variables, Study gave the conditions necessary and sufficient that a transformation of this group may be generated by an infinitesimal transformation of this group. Dr. Taber gave, in 1896 (*Bull. Am. Math. Soc.*, Series 2, Vol. 2, p. 231), these conditions for n variables; also the conditions necessary and sufficient that a transformation of the special linear homogeneous group may be the mth power of a transformation of this group. From these conditions it appears that the nth power of any transformation of this group can be generated by an infinitesimal transformation of this group; and that the transformations of this group can be divided into as many genera as there are prime factors of n. Thus, if δ is a prime factor of n, there are transformations of this group whose n/δth power, but no lower power, can be generated thus.[3]

Dr. Taber has shown that the following groups are not continuous, except in the neighborhood of the identical transformations, namely, the group G, mentioned above, for A symmetric or alternate, and in general when A is neither symmetric nor alternate, provided either $|\bar{A} + A|$ or $|\bar{A} - A|$ is equal to zero.[4] For all these groups the infinitesimal transformations satisfy Lie's criterion.

Dr. Taber has also shown that the following groups are continuous, namely, group G when $|\bar{A} \pm A| \neq 0$, the sub-group of orthogonal transformations of G, for A alternate, and the group of automorphic linear transformations of a bilinear form $A = \sum_{1}^{n}{}_{i}\sum_{1}^{n}{}_{j} a_{ij}x_i y_j$, of non-zero determinant, the x's and y's being contra-gredient.[5]

[1] *Leipziger Berichte*, 1892.
[2] See *Proc.*, Vol. 30, p. 551. This result is referred to above on p. 77.
[3] See *Bull. Am. Math. Soc.*, Series 2, Vol. 3, p. 9.
[4] See p. 77, note 1.
[5] See p. 77 above, also *Proc. Am. Acad. Arts and Sciences*, Vol. 31, p. 181.

Investigations upon the continuity of the groups in two and three variables have been carried on under Dr. Taber's supervision by certain of the students in the mathematical department. Dr. E. G. Rettger has investigated the continuity of all the two and three fold groups, fifty-nine in number, enumerated by Lie, *Continuierliche Gruppen*, pp. 288 and 519; and shown that twenty-one of these groups are discontinuous.[1] Mr. F. P. Williams has investigated the continuity of certain groups of the plane, not treated by Mr. Rettger; and Mr. S. E. Slocum has pointed out the nature of Lie's error in his demonstration of the fundamental theorem referred to above.[2]

If a system of real infinitesimal transformations satisfy a modification of the Lieschen criterion, Lie states that they generate a real continuous group, that is, a group with continuous parameters, each transformation of which can be generated by an infinitesimal transformation of the group. But this theorem is subject to certain modifications.

Dr. Taber has shown that the group of real proper orthogonal transformations is continuous;[3] also that in the groups of real transformations enumerated below not every transformation can be generated by an infinitesimal transformation of the group, namely, —

- the real projective group,[4]
- the general and special real linear groups,
- the general and the special real linear homogeneous groups,
- the sub-group of real transformations of G, for A real and either alternate or symmetric.

Further, that if G denotes either of the groups just enumerated, the first part (I) of the theorem of p. 77 holds. And he has given the conditions necessary and sufficient, for each of the first three of the groups just enumerated, that a transformation of this group may be generated by an infinitesimal transformation of this group.[5]

Let G denote a group generated by the composition of r one-fold

[1] *Proc. Am. Acad. of Arts and Sciences*, Vol. 33.

[2] See papers to appear in Vol. 35 of the *Proc. Am. Acad. of Arts and Sciences*.

[3] *Bull. Am. Math. Soc.* for July, 1894. See also *Proc. Am. Acad. of Arts and Sciences*, Vol. 27, p. 163.

[4] For the real projective group this was first pointed out by Professor H. B. Newson, *Kansas Univ. Quart.*, 1895.

[5] *Bull. Am. Math. Soc.*, Series 2, Vol. 3, p. [illegible] et seq. Also *Proc. Am. Acad. of Arts and Sciences*, Vol. 31, p. 336, and Vol. 32, p. 77.

groups (each containing the identical transformation), namely, $G_1^{(1)}$, $G_1^{(2)}$, $\cdots G_1^{(r)}$, whose infinitesimal transformations satisfy Lie's criterion. It may happen that a transformation T of one (or more) of these one-fold groups, as $G_1^{(u)}$, combined with any transformation of another of the one-fold sub-groups, as $G_1^{(v)}$ (in particular with the infinitesimal transformation of $G_1^{(v)}$), results in a transformation that cannot be generated by an infinitesimal transformation of G. Any such transformation T, together with any transformation T of G that cannot be generated by an infinitesimal transformation of this group, may be termed *singular;* all other transformations of G will then be *non-singular.* In a paper, of which an abstract was read at the February meeting of the American Mathematical Society, 1899, Dr. Taber showed that, if G is a sub-group of the projective group, any singular transformation of G can always be obtained by the composition of two non-singular transformations of G; and moreover that, if T is any singular transformation of G not generated by an infinitesimal transformation of G, a transformation T_ρ generated by an infinitesimal transformation of G, can always be found which can be made to approach as nearly as we please to T by taking ρ sufficiently small, so that $\lim_{\rho=0} T_\rho = T$.

DEPARTMENT OF PHYSICS.

By Arthur Gordon Webster.

STAFF.

Albert Abraham Michelson, Ph.D., Professor of Physics, 1889–92.
Arthur Gordon Webster, Ph.D., Docent in Mathematical Physics, 1890–92; Assistant Professor of Physics, 1892–.

FELLOWS AND SCHOLARS.

Louis W. Austin, Scholar in Physics, 1890–91; Fellow, 1891–92.
Frank K. Bailey, Scholar in Physics, 1898–99.
William P. Boynton, Scholar in Physics, 1894–95; Fellow, 1895–97.
Arthur L. Clark, Scholar in Physics, 1896–97; Fellow, 1897–98.
D. Ellis Douty, Scholar in Physics, 1898–99.
William F. Durand, Scholar in Physics, Nov.–Dec., 1889.
Thomas W. Edmondson, Fellow in Physics, 1894–96.
Benjamin F. Ellis, Scholar in Physics, 1892–93.
T. Proctor Hall, Scholar in Physics, 1890–91; Fellow, 1891–93.
†Benjamin C. Hinde, Fellow and Assistant in Physics, 1892–93. Died Feb. 6, 1894.
Richard J. Holland, Ph.D., Honorary Fellow in Physics, 1893–94.
James Edmund Ives, Scholar in Physics, 1897–98; Fellow, 1898–.
Sidney J. Lochner, Scholar in Physics, 1892–93.
Alexander McAdie, Fellow in Physics, 1889–90.
Alfred G. Mayer, Assistant in Physics, 1889–90.
Rolla R. Ramsey, Scholar in Physics, 1898–99.
Stanley H. Rood, Scholar in Physics, 1893–94.
†Clarence A. Saunders, Fellow in Physics, 1892–95. Died Dec. 19, 1896.
Benjamin F. Sharpe, Fellow in Physics, 1894–96; 1897–98.
Robert R. Tatnall, Ph.D., Honorary Fellow in Physics, 1897–98.
Samuel N. Taylor, Fellow in Physics, 1893–96.
Frank L. O. Wadsworth, Fellow in Physics, 1889–90; Assistant, 1890–92.
Arthur J. Warner, Scholar in Physics, 1889–90.
Albert P. Wills, Scholar in Physics, 1894–95; Fellow, 1895–97.

SPECIAL STUDENTS.

Ervin W. Howard, 1892-93.
Albert B. Kimball, 1893-94.
William Nelson, 1892-93.
Joseph O. Phelon, 1892-93.
Arthur L. Rice, 1892-93.
Stanley H. Rood, 1892-93.
Clayton O. Smith, 1892-93.
Hugh M. Southgate, 1892-93.

The work of a Department of Physics in a university at the present time may be best understood after a brief survey of some of the chief achievements of the science during the present century. As we in this country have our attention called more frequently to the achievements of applied than to those of pure science, it is worth while to dwell somewhat upon the influence of pure science upon applied, and upon its contribution to the progress of civilization. At the beginning of the century, the various subjects that together make up the science of Physics were in a very imperfect state. Of heat, light, sound, electricity, and magnetism, little that we now accept was known, while of that little still less had been applied to practical matters. The science of mechanics, upon which the whole superstructure of physics must inevitably rest, had indeed been set upon a firm basis by the immortal Newton, while its principles had recently been formulated by the distinguished mathematician Lagrange, in a way so broad and powerful that it has not since been improved upon. The science of pure mathematics had of course arrived at a high degree of perfection, and many of the leading mathematicians had devoted their best efforts to the subject of mechanics. But while a large number of investigators had laid the foundations of our present knowledge by the method of experiment, the habit of questioning nature, instruments in hand, had as yet by no means become general. This habit of direct experimental research is certainly in large degree to be credited to the present century. Without stopping to enumerate the leading achievements of physics during the century, let us take as illustrations a few leading cases. Nothing has, perhaps, done more to change the face of the earth, from the point of view of man, than the invention of the steam-engine and of the railway thereby made possible, of the telegraph and telephone, while the transmission of energy by electricity bids fair to rival them in importance. Let us then briefly consider what led to these inventions. At the beginning of the century it was universally held that heat was a substance, which could be put into, or removed from, ordinary matter. It is to the experiments of one of our own countrymen, the celebrated Count Rumford, that was due the original assault on this notion, the last blow at which was delivered by the Englishman, James Prescott Joule, in his great discovery of the mutual convertibility of heat and mechanical work, and of the doctrine of the Conservation of Energy. This discovery, so simple that it may be understood by every one, namely, that for whatever we do we get an exact equivalent, neither more nor less, is the fundamental truth of physical science. It is in physics the supreme achievement of the century. Until it was discovered, a true understanding of the principles of the steam-engine could not be arrived at, although the way had been prepared by the theoretical work of a French engineer, the illustrious Sadi Carnot. To Carnot and Joule, then, we owe the two laws of the new science of Thermodynamics, or the relations between heat and work, which lie at the basis of all steam, gas, oil, or other heat engines, as well as of all freezing machines, and of transmission or storage of energy by means of compressed gases. It would be well, therefore, for all intending investors in new and promising compressed or liquid air companies, no matter how attractively advertised, to find out what thermodynamics has to say of the propositions advanced.

The foundations having been laid by the experimental work of Joule and the theoretical work of Carnot, the required knowledge of the properties of steam and other vapors used in engines and cooling machines was furnished by a masterly series of experimental researches of the distinguished French physicist, Henri Regnault, who was set at work by the French government, and whose work has ever since been classical. No engineer could to-day design an engine without making use of the data thus furnished.

Let us pass on to the telegraph. Here again it was the patient work of our countryman Henry, working quietly with purely scientific aims in his little laboratory in Albany, — it was Henry's investigations on the electromagnet that made feasible the invention by Morse of the recording telegraph, which is still in use more than any other system all over the world. It is, however, when we come to the great question of submarine telegraphy that we see most emphatically the practical contribution of pure science. The problem of telegraphing through an insulated wire immersed in water is totally different from the corresponding one for a land line, and for years seemed hopeless of solution. The construction of a cable reaching from Europe to America was such a costly undertaking as to deter the most venturesome capitalists, unless they could be previously furnished with a reasonable guarantee of success. It was here that the work of William Thomson, to-day known as Lord Kelvin, our greatest living physicist, furnished the necessary assurance. Taking up the purely mathematical problem of the propagation of an electrical impulse in a submarine cable, he for the first time set its mode of working in a clear light, and by means of his solution predicted that the American cable, if constructed in accordance with his specifications, was bound to work. Led by faith in this statement, Cyrus W. Field collected the money, the cable was laid, and the cable worked. That the first cable of 1858 lasted but little more than a month was due to the unfortunate mode of working adopted by the chief electrician, a so-called practical man, who would however have been much better off if he had possessed the theoretical knowledge of Professor Thomson. To-day twelve working cables span the Atlantic, representing an investment of eighty-five million dollars. Is this too large a sum to credit to theoretical physics? The problem of telegraphy that is to-day most interesting is that of telephoning across the Atlantic, and I feel no hesitation in saying that before this can be accomplished a large amount of theoretical research will be necessary, together with such experimental work as may be carried on in laboratories like ours, and is now being carried on by Professor Pupin of Columbia University, before a single dollar is sunk under the sea.

The question of electric power transmission is one whose genesis is easy for all to remember. All do not remember, however, that far from electrical science being, as the newspapers maintain, in its infancy, the laws governing our dynamos and motors were discovered in the first quarter of the century, mainly by two princes among workers in physics, the Frenchman Ampère and the Englishman Faraday. The achievement of Ampère in discovering the laws of the action of electrical currents in producing magnetic forces upon each other was, in its combination of mathematical and experimental brilliancy, one of the most remarkable achievements in the annals of science. Still more important practically were the discoveries of Faraday, who deduced unaided all the laws upon which the working of dynamo-machines depends.

Another illustration of our point is the wireless telegraphy of Marconi, of which we hear so much in the newspapers to-day. What the newspapers do not tell us is that the electrical waves made use of in telegraphing across the English Channel were predicted in a paper published in 1864 by the great English physicist, Clerk-Maxwell, who completely remodelled the theory of electricity as it then existed. Twenty-three years afterward his predictions were experimentally verified by Heinrich Hertz, who thus rendered the practical results of Marconi possible.

These researches, far-reaching as were their practical results, were carried on by purely scientific workers, solely for the interest that they presented by increasing our knowledge. This should always be the position of the scientist, for, if he turns aside, attracted by the seductive paths of moneymaking, he is almost sure to lose the prize of the great discovery.

Let us now turn to the present means of advancing our scientific knowledge. It is not to be overlooked that many of the great discoveries above mentioned were made with very simple apparatus and with very modest facilities. When we see the very primitive instruments of Ampère, Henry, and Faraday, we are led to wonder that they could produce such accurate results. The days of such work are however over. It is now possible to add to the knowledge already so richly harvested only by experiments of the most careful nature and by measurements of great refinement, involving often complicated and expensive apparatus. It is for this reason that the great laboratories have sprung up, which we find in such large numbers both in this country and in Europe. Until about a quarter of a century ago there were none. It had, however, come to be recognized that, in order to make an investigator of a student, it was necessary not only that he should hear lectures, but that he should himself have practice in experimentation and in the making of exact measurements. For these purposes, courses of instruction in physical measurements were planned, and laboratories where they might be practically carried on were erected. One of the earliest of these teaching laboratories was that of the Massachusetts Institute of Technology, presided over by Professor Pickering, now director of the Harvard College Observatory. Later came the laboratories at Yale, Harvard, Cornell, Johns Hopkins, Chicago, and Columbia, costing between one and two hundred thousand dollars each. In each case is to be added the sum of from twenty to fifty thousand dollars for equipment with apparatus. During the same time a large number of physical laboratories have been built in Europe, some of them involving a still larger expenditure of money, notably the one at Zürich, in which the Swiss government invested about a quarter of a million of dollars. At all these laboratories both teaching and the performance of research were contemplated, and an idea of the results achieved may be obtained from the statement that from the Johns Hopkins laboratory have issued upwards of five hundred papers, and from those of Harvard and Cornell in the neighborhood of one hundred each.

Besides these institutions so immediately connected with teaching, another type of laboratory has made its appearance within the last ten years. Of this the most conspicuous example is the German Imperial Physico-technical Institute, which is separated from teaching, and is intended solely for the performance of research, especially for the performance of such measurements as would require resources exceeding those possessed by private or university laboratories. The work performed in this great institution has been of the highest class, and has drawn the attention of other governments to the desirability of establishing such national laboratories, with the result that England has now followed the example of Germany, though upon a smaller scale. A further example is presented in the Faraday-Davy research laboratory in London, the gift of a private individual, Mr. Ludwig Mond, a successful technical chemist, who in this most appropriate manner recognized the debt of applied to pure science by the foundation of a laboratory devoted especially to the furtherance of research in physical chemistry.

What, then, has been the position occupied by Clark University in the ranks of this march of progress? Naturally it has been a modest one. Without a separate laboratory building, with a small equipment, and a staff reduced to the minimum, it has of course not been able to rival in quantity the work of its greater predecessors. It may, however, be remarked that limitations of size are not necessarily limitations of quality. The relatively small number of students coming here have received greater individual attention than would have been possible at more crowded institutions. In spite of our limited space and equipment, it has always been found possible to put in possession of each student apparatus suitable for the performance of original research, and to give him what is more important, minute personal direction and encouragement. In this manner students coming to us from the colleges, often ill prepared for the severe mathematical work so necessary to the physicist, but to which they have been little accustomed, are rapidly pushed on, and recover their places in line.

The Department of Physics was, during the first three years of the history of the University, under the direction of the distinguished physicist, Professor Albert A. Michelson, who was then called from it to take the conduct of the larger department at the University of Chicago. During his stay at Clark Professor Michelson was engaged in research in the field of optics, inventing a method for the study of radiations from both celestial and terrestrial bodies, by means of an instrument devised by him, and depending on the interference of light. By means of this ingenious and elegant method, valuable results in connection with spectroscopy and the measurement of small astronomical objects were obtained, upon which a number of papers were published. Before the termination of his labors here, Professor Michelson was invited by the International Bureau of Weights and Measures to make, by means of his new apparatus, a comparison between the international standard of length and the length of a certain wave of light, thus establishing a natural unit of length. A new apparatus having been designed and constructed under the direction of Mr. F. L. O. Wadsworth, preliminary observations were made at the University, and, obtaining leave of absence, Professor Michelson and Mr. Wadsworth proceeded to Paris, where the experiment was carried out with marked success, constituting a performance in metrology that will undoubtedly become classical.

During his conduct of the department, Professor Michelson delivered usually one lecture a week, on various subjects concerning the Theory of Light, especially connected with his own researches. Upon the beginning of the incumbency of the writer, a consecutive course in theoretical or mathematical physics was planned, and has been regularly delivered, the course covering five lectures a week for a term of two years. Perhaps the principal claim that can be made for the department is the stress that has been laid upon the subject of mathematical physics, undoubtedly the most difficult branch for the student, and one which has not yet become popular in this country, yet which is of prime importance, and without which none can hope to reach the highest position in the science. A gratifying testimonial to the truth of this contention is furnished by the recent arrival at the University of two students, both doctors of philosophy from German universities, who have come here impressed with their need for more study of mathematical physics.

In this course the several parts of the subject are treated in regular order, as parts of a logically connected whole, starting from the fundamental basis of dynamics. The course is attended by every student in the department, and he is held responsible for a knowledge of its subject-matter in his examination for the doctor's degree. It is safe to say that in this respect the requirement for the degree is not exceeded at any institution in the country. The regular courses of the cycle are as follows: —

1. Dynamics. — General Methods, Canonical Equations, Methods of Hamilton and Jacobi, Systems of Particles, Rigid Bodies.
2. Newtonian and Logarithmic Potential Functions, Attraction of Ellipsoids.
3. Elasticity, Hydrodynamics, Wave and Vortex Motion, Dynamical Basis of Sound and Light.
4. Electricity and Magnetism.
5. Optics, Physical and Geometrical. — Elastic and Electromagnetic Wave-theories.
6. Thermodynamics, Thermo- and Electro-Chemistry, Kinetic Theory of Gases.
7. The Partial Differential Equations of Mathematical Physics.
   Laplace's Equation, Equation of Thermal and Electrical Conduction, Equation of Wave-motion, Telegrapher's Equation, Developments in Series, Legendre's, Laplace's, Bessel's, and Lamé's Functions.

Besides these, it has been the practice to deliver each year at least one new course, so that certain courses are delivered occasionally. A number of courses in pure mathematics have also been delivered at various times, supplementing those of the mathematical department. These extra courses have been as follows: —

Dynamics of Cyclic and Oscillatory Systems, with applications to the Theory of Electricity, Sound, and Light.

Comparison of the Theories of the Ether.

Theory of Functions of Real and Complex Variables.

Definite Integrals, Fourier's Series.

Ordinary Differential Equations.

Linear Differential Equations, particularly of the second order.

Elliptic Functions (notation of Weierstrass), with certain physical applications, including the theory of the Top.

Orthogonal Surfaces and Curvilinear Coördinates, and their applications.

Of the lectures in the above course one volume, on the theory of electricity and magnetism, has been published, and has apparently been of use to teachers in other institutions. Other volumes are in course of preparation.

In addition to the lectures, a weekly colloquium or meeting for the discussion of questions in experimental physics has been held. Here reports upon current articles in the leading physical journals are delivered by the students, and the most important classical determinations are also taken up, in order that familiarity may be gained with the methods of the masters of research. These meetings have been of great help to students, and have given them practice in presenting their ideas before an auditory. Beside the work of instruction, research has been carried on in the laboratory by every student and the professor. When a student arrives at the University he is at first put at work upon a subject designed to test his powers, and to give him familiarity with the principles of exact measurement. When he has shown his ability, he is encouraged to undertake a research for himself, under the continual guidance of the professor. In this way the undertaking of research before the necessary experience has been gained is prevented, and the publication of trifling or ill-considered articles is discouraged. As a rule a student devotes at least two years to the preparation of a doctor's dissertation. Thus the number of published researches is limited. Six doctor's dissertations have been published, and another is ready for publication. Beside these a number of other researches, both theoretical and experimental, have been published, one of which latter was honored by a substantial money prize in an international competition. These researches have not been confined to any one branch of physics, but have dealt with molecular physics, electricity, magnetism, and sound. Most of them have been of such a nature that the student was forced, not to work in a single narrow specialized line, but to gain a large amount of experience in various parts of the subject. A research of this nature is of far more value to the student than one performed simply for the purpose of gaining him a degree, and dealing only with a narrow range of ideas.

The subjects of the dissertations have been as follows: Mr. T. P. Hall worked out a new method for the determination of the surface tension of liquids, suggested by Professor Michelson, in which the pull upon a film of liquid was directly weighed by a balance. Mr. C. A. Saunders made a determination of the velocity of electric waves in parallel wires, by a direct method, in which the wave-length and period of the waves were measured, the latter by photographing the periodic spark giving rise to the wave by means of a revolving Foucault mirror, the wave-length by measuring the length of the wires, which was made to be a quarter wave-length by means of electrical resonance. This research demanded a large amount of time, and elaborate apparatus. In connection with the revolving mirror a convenient method devised by the writer for maintaining a constant angular velocity was made use of. Mr. T. W. Edmondson determined the distances necessary for the formation of a spark at varying potentials between spheres of different sizes in air and in various insulating liquids, the potentials being measured by means of an absolute attracted disk electrometer. Mr. S. N. Taylor made a comparison between the important cadmium element devised by Weston with the well-known Latimer Clark standard cell, in which he compared their electromotive forces by means of an electro-dynamometer, obtaining results agreeing remarkably well with those obtained by a quite different method at the German Reichsanstalt. Mr. W. P. Boynton carried out an experimental verification of the theory of the action of the peculiar high-frequency induction coil invented by Elihu Thomson and Tesla, which had never been mathematically treated in detail, not to say experimented upon. This work involved a large number of difficult measurements, including the currents, potentials, and frequencies of oscillation involved in the working of the apparatus. The results were in excellent agreement with the theory, considering the difficulty of the experiments. Mr. A. P. Wills undertook the development of a new and ingenious method, suggested by the writer, but materially improved by him, for measuring the magnetic permeability of substances, whether magnetic or diamagnetic, differing so little in this respect from air as to be not amenable to the usual methods. By means of a simple arrangement involving the use of a slab of the substance suspended in the field of a powerful electromagnet with peculiarly shaped pole-pieces, the effect was measured by the pull on a sensitive balance, so that accurate results were easily obtained. This work of Mr. Wills resulted in his being received into the laboratory of Professor du Bois, one of the leading authorities in magnetism, in Berlin, where he performed a number of other interesting pieces of research in the same subject. Mr. B. F. Sharpe spent the greater part of three years in developing a method devised by the writer for the measurement of the intensity of sound, a measurement of more than ordinary difficulty. The instrument depends upon the application of Michelson's interference methods to the measurement of the very small distances involved in the vibration of plates set in motion by sound. The interference bands observed in an interferometer, of which one movable mirror is fixed upon a plate of thin glass forming the back of a resonator, are observed through a moving telescope, or have their motion photographically registered. In this manner a very sensitive means of measurement is obtained, and it is possible to measure sound in absolute measure, even when it is rapidly varying in intensity, a result not before attainable. The applications of this method which have been already suggested are very numerous and important.

Mention should not be omitted of the labors of Mr. F. L. O. Wadsworth, who, as assistant to Professor Michelson, by his untiring energy and especial skill in the design and construction of apparatus, contributed in large measure to the success of the researches of the latter.

The most important experimental paper published by the writer was a determination of the period of electrical oscillations in a circuit containing a condenser and a coil, the purpose of the investigation being to verify the formula of Lord Kelvin, all the constants of the apparatus being measured in absolute measure. For the research a new instrument was devised capable of breaking two electrical contacts at instants separated by a very small measured interval of time. The instrument was very sensitive, permitting the appreciation of less than a millionth of a second. This research, already begun in the attempt to improve a method for the determination of the ratio of the two units of electricity, was found to correspond to a question proposed by a committee in Paris having in charge the prize established by Elihu Thomson, and being submitted for the competition, was awarded the prize of five thousand francs.

During the first year of the history of the University a considerable sum was spent upon a set of meteorological instruments, especially for the study of atmospheric electricity, and research was begun in this subject by Mr. Alexander McAdie, of the Weather Bureau, who has now become a recognized authority upon the subject of lightning discharges. This work came to an end upon the departure of Mr. McAdie from the University, but it might with advantage be resumed, with the addition of observations of phenomena of terrestrial magnetism.

In concluding this report, it will not be out of place to speak of the needs and ideals of the department for the future. It is extremely desirable that the courses in mathematical physics be repeated every year, instead of once in two years as at present, this being as often as the time and strength of a single lecturer will allow him to cover the subject. If this were done, students could then begin each year at the most appropriate part of the course, without waiting for the natural beginning in their second year, as is now necessary for those students coming in alternate years. Even more desirable than aid in instruction is assistance in experimental work. Research in the laboratory can be carried out much more economically if a number of assistants are available to carry out details, leaving the professor free for the more important work of planning and personally attending to the more difficult parts of the work.

One of the most important adjuncts of the department, the workshop, in which a skilled mechanic is constantly employed in the construction of apparatus for research, is capable of great extension of facilities. The absolute necessity of this work cannot be too strongly emphasized, and the department could even at the present moment profitably employ two or three men instead of one. Research in physics demands instruments of great exactness, complication, and cost, so that the maintenance of such a department in which research is done entails more expense than that of any other scientific department, except engineering. Each particular research requires much of the apparatus used in it to be particularly designed, so that in view of the frequent changes necessitated before it exactly fits its purpose, and of the fact that it is impossible as a rule to find it kept in stock by dealers, it is more economical to have apparatus constructed in the workshop of the department under the eye of the professor than to have it made elsewhere.

In designing an ideal laboratory, one of the first things to be considered would accordingly be a workshop well equipped with modern machine tools, with an ample and convenient source of power for driving them, and with a large electric storage plant, both as a source of supply for investigations in electricity and magnetism, and for the purpose of furnishing power in smaller quantities than would require the main supply. An optical shop would greatly increase the capability of a laboratory for work in light. That such a suggestion is not extravagant is shown by the fact that Professor Michelson's new and ingenious echelon spectroscope was constructed by methods devised by him in the workshop of his laboratory, and could not have been so well constructed anywhere else. The famous diffraction gratings of Professor Rowland have for years furnished a further striking example, forcing European physicists to send to this country for their supply.

A laboratory should be provided with the means for the determination of the important physical constants of nature, such as the velocity of light and of electric waves, of the Newtonian constant of gravitation, of the mechanical equivalent of heat, and of the fundamental relation between electricity and magnetism, the so-called "v" of Maxwell. Thus it would be possible not only to initiate students into the most precise methods, but even to hope to improve upon classical determinations. Ample facilities should be always at hand for the comparison and calibration of the important physical standards of measurement, such as those of length, time, mass, of electrical and magnetic quantities. The small facilities in this line possessed even by our national government are in painful contrast to what is seen in Europe, particularly in the German Imperial Physico-technical Institute, in which a million or more of dollars is invested.

Beside the matter of accurate measurements of well-known phenomena lies the wider field of research in fields which are sure to prove fertile in new discoveries. The great domain of electrical waves, a creation of the last decade, although already exploited by scores of observers, is still full of interesting problems, that are sure to yield a rich reward to those who shall devise more perfect methods of investigation. The field of spectroscopy, whether in its terrestrial or celestial applications, is an enormous one. To this is to be added the study of radiations in general, of whatever character. The recent discovery of Röntgen was followed quickly by hundreds of researches bearing on the rays discovered by him, resulting in the discovery of several closely allied forms of radiation, and in a greatly increased interest in the phenomena of electrical discharges in vacuum tubes. Here remain a multitude of questions to be decided. The nature of cathode and of Röntgen rays remains to be settled, and will probably be one of the achievements of the early years of the next century. Research on the liquefaction of gases, and on the properties of bodies at temperatures not far removed from the absolute zero, until recently limited to a few observers possessing far more than ordinary facilities, will soon furnish a field for the labors of many, who will undoubtedly be well repaid. The many relations predicted by the recent applications of thermodynamics, especially in the domain of physical chemistry, remain in large measure to be verified. The science of meteorology, hitherto largely an empirical one, remains to be put upon a satisfactory theoretical basis, and presents many problems for the physicist to attack in his laboratory. The same may be said of geology, which is, for example, vitally concerned with the thermal properties of rocks and other materials of the substance of the earth, and with many problems concerning the physics of the earth's crust.

The foregoing is but a brief sketch of the field of physical investigation. The enthusiasm of one devoted to the performance of research, and considering it the most attractive form of human endeavor, would enable him to enlarge the subject over many more pages than are here available. The field is enormous, and each new discovery leads to new paths of inquiry. It is obvious that, in order to enter upon these attractive fields of work, one must be provided with large resources. Is it unreasonable to look forward eagerly to the day when Clark University shall possess a well-equipped physical laboratory building, fitted out with the utmost that our knowledge can suggest, in which we may hope to contribute our just share toward the enlargement of the boundaries of science, and thus to the welfare of humanity?

DEPARTMENT OF BIOLOGY.

By Clifton F. Hodge.

PAST AND PRESENT STAFF.

Charles O. Whitman, Ph.D., Professor of Animal Morphology, 1889–92.
Franklin P. Mall, M.D., Adjunct Professor of Anatomy, 1889–92.
Henry H. Donaldson, Ph.D., Assistant Professor of Neurology, 1889–92.
Warren P. Lombard, M.D., Assistant Professor of Physiology, 1889–92.
Clifton F. Hodge, Ph.D., Assistant and Fellow in Neurology, 1889–91; Assistant Professor of Physiology and Neurology, 1892–.
J. P. McMurrich, Ph.D., Docent in Morphology, 1889–91; Assistant Professor of Morphology, 1891–92.
Adolf Meyer, M.D., Docent in Psychiatry, 1895–.
†George Baur, Ph.D., Docent in Comparative Osteology and Paleontology, 1890–92. Died June 25, 1898.
John C. Cardwell, M.D., Assistant in Physiology, 1889–91.
Sho Watase, Ph.D., Lecturer and Assistant in Morphology, 1890–92.

FELLOWS AND SCHOLARS.

Franklin W. Barrows, M.D., Fellow in Physiology, 1893–94.
Charles L. Bristol, Fellow in Morphology, 1891–92.
Hermon C. Bumpus, Fellow in Biology, 1889–90.
Albert C. Eycleshymer, Fellow in Morphology, 1891–92.
Charles L. Edwards, Ph.D., Fellow in Morphology, 1890–92.
R. R. Gurley, M.D., Fellow in Biology, 1895–96.
Homer Gage, M.D., Honorary Scholar in Anatomy, 1889–90.
Edwin O. Jordan, Fellow in Morphology, 1890–92.
Herbert P. Johnson, Fellow in Morphology, 1891–92.
F. C. Kenyon, Ph.D., Fellow in Biology, 1895–96.
†W. E. Lockwood, M.D., Fellow in Physiology, 1891–92. Died June 23, 1897.
Frank R. Lillie, Fellow in Morphology, 1891–92.
A. D. Mead, Fellow in Morphology, 1891–92.
William S. Miller, M.D., Honorary Scholar, 1889–90; Scholar in Anatomy, 1890–91; Fellow in Anatomy, 1891–92.
James R. Slonaker, Fellow in Biology, 1893–96.

Colin C. Stewart, Scholar in Physiology, 1894–95; Fellow in Physiology, 1895–97.
Frederick Tuckerman, M.D., Ph.D., Fellow in Anatomy, 1889–90.
William M. Wheeler, Fellow in Morphology, 1890–91; Assistant, 1891–92.

SPECIAL STUDENTS.

James Jenkins, Special Student in Biology, 1894–95.
Preston Smith, Special Student in Physiology, 1899.
W. G. Watts, Laboratory Steward and Special Student, 1889–91.

HISTORICAL REVIEW.

It will be seen from the above list of appointments that the department was organized to cover animal biology. Animal morphology, vertebrate anatomy, physiology, comparative osteology and paleontology, and neurology, which forms the natural transition to psychology, and has been classed in that department, formed a compact and well-selected group with which to begin work. This organization was still further strengthened by a strong force of organic chemists in this fundamental department.

A good share of the equipment necessary for different lines of research work already in progress or planned by the different appointees had been ordered during the previous summer, so that the work of the whole department began practically with the opening of the University. Zeiss microscopes of the most approved patterns and with full complements of apochromatic eye-pieces and objectives, Thoma microtomes, together with those of Minot, the Minot-Zimmerman, Schanze, and others, complete assortments of chemical reagents, stains and laboratory tools, apparatus and glassware, all were supplied with liberality. Abundant and suitable rooms were also placed at the department's disposal in the main university building. Two large rooms and a convenient dark room for photographic purposes on the fourth floor were assigned to physiology and were devoted to laboratory and lecture-room with workshop equipped with lathe and tools for working both wood and metals. Four large rooms on the third floor were arranged to accommodate anatomy and morphology for laboratories, lecture-room and drafting room; and, in addition, four small rooms adjoining supplied office and library for the head of the department, and private laboratories for three of the docents and assistants. Two rooms on the second floor, adjoining the psychological department, were assigned to neurology, the one for private laboratory and office of Assistant Professor Donaldson, the other for his general laboratory. All of these rooms were equipped with water and gas, and some with hoods to render them the most convenient and ideal laboratories possible, and the morphological laboratories were furnished with five large aquaria, the largest being eight feet in length, all supplied with running water, and a large number of smaller glass aquaria which made it possible to keep all sorts of aquatic animals both summer and winter.

While the chief emphasis both as to equipment and disposition of the instructor's time was given to research, the side of instruction toward breadth and depth of view, so necessary to the highest type of investigation, was not neglected. Models of the brain (Auzoux, Aeby, Ziegler), as well as Ziegler's models of classic embryological types, and a complete set of Leuckart & Nitche's zoölogical charts, and an extensive library of wall charts copied from various monographs and text-books, all these, supplemented by anatomical and zoölogical specimens, gathered as rapidly as possible to form the nucleus of a museum, imparted the best possible quality to the work of instruction. In fact, instruction and research began together and went hand in hand, the one aiding the other.

Professor Whitman immediately began courses of lectures fundamental to the doctrine of evolution. The first of these treated, entirely from original sources, the historical development of Comparative Anatomy, beginning with its renaissance in the works of Marco Aurelio Severino ("Zootomia Democritæa, id est Anatome generalis totius animalium opificii libris quinque distincta," 1645), and bringing the subject down to the discussions, just preceding the Darwinian epoch, between Etienne Geoffroy Saint Hilaire and Georges Cuvier (1830). As Professor Whitman himself announced with reference to this early course: "Attention will be directed particularly to the origin and development of historic ideas, tendencies, methods, and schools, as presented in the early iatric and physiological stages of Zoötomy; in the works of Haller, Geoffroy, and Cuvier; in the 'Anatomie Philosophique' of the French, and the 'Naturphilosophie' of the Germans; in the doctrines of the 'Scale of Nature,' 'Unity of Composition,' and of 'Types'; in the hypotheses of Evolution and Epigenesis, in Homology and Teleology, etc. The biographical side of the subject will also receive due consideration, especially in the cases of such representative men as Malpighi, Swammerdam, and Leeuwenhoek of the seventeenth century, and Haller, Buffon, Daubenton, Linné, John Hunter, Camper, Vicq-d'Azyr, Kielmeyer, Geoffroy, and Cuvier of the later period."

A second and third historical course was devoted respectively to the subjects of Generation and Comparative Embryology. These courses, compactly coördinated, and following logically on the development of comparative anatomy, were likewise worked up from original sources in Aristotle, Harvey, John Hunter, Wolff, Von Baer, and others, and led naturally up to the modern doctrines of heredity as developed by Lamarck, Darwin, Weismann, and their followers. Especially in the course in Comparative Embryology, the present phase of biological work, cytological technique and terminology, were fully treated, together with matters of interest in recent discussions as to origin and maturation of ova and spermatozoa, phenomena of fecundation, cleavage of the ovum, with comparison of different types of cleavage and experimental researches in cleavage, gastrular and pre-gastrular stages, their different types and derivations, germ layers, the trochosphere, budding and fission, formation of the embryo in invertebrates and vertebrates, together with that of double and multiple monsters, and, finally, the course culminated in a discussion of the origin and significance of metameric segmentation.

Simultaneously with these courses Dr. McMurrich lectured on the cœlenterates and platyhelminths, sifting all discoverable evidences for cœlenterate ancestry of the worms, the origin of segmentation, and the significance of cœlenterate structure in gastrular stages of vertebrate embryos. Dr. Baur on the side of paleontology discussed the osteology of reptiles and mammals, living and extinct. Dr. Bumpus also lectured on the affinities of the crustacea.

For two years, as a means of uniting still further instruction and research, and of keeping all members of the department in touch with one another, an active biological club was maintained. Monthly meetings were held, and at each a carefully prepared lecture was read and discussed. The subjects of these lectures indicate to such an extent the lines of interest developed in the department, that a list for 1890–92 is given in full.

1. Scope and Aims of the Club. — C. O. Whitman.
2. Ideas on the Origin of the Galapagos Islands and the Origin of Species. — Geo. Baur.
3. Insect Metamorphosis. — W. M. Wheeler.
4. The Origin and Significance of the Blastopore. — J. P. McMurrich.
5. Nitrification and Nitrifying Organisms. — E. O. Jordan.
6. The Animal Ovum. — Sho Watase.

1. The Salisbury Expedition to the Galapagos Islands. — Geo. Baur.
2. The Third Eye of Vertebrates. — A. C. Eycleshymer.
3. Some Points in the History of Bacteriology. — E. O. Jordan.
4. Amphimixis in the Protozoa. — H. P. Johnson.
5. Nervous System of Mollusca. — F. R. Lillie.
6. Germ Cells. — Sho Watase.
7. Mammalian Spermatogenesis. — Sho Watase.
8. Metamerism in Arthropoda. — W. M. Wheeler.

The scope of work of the morphological section will be seen more fully in the list of investigations which follows, under the heading of Research Work, which has been grouped together for all divisions of the biological department.

In Vertebrate Anatomy, Dr. Mall lectured for three successive years on the histology of tissues arising from the mesoderm, on the development of serous and blood spaces in vertebrates, and on the development, histology, and comparative anatomy of the organs arising from the endoderm. Dr. Tuckerman lectured in connection with his research work, on the gustatory organs of mammals, and Dr. Miller likewise on the lobule of the lung with its blood-vessels.

In Physiology Dr. Lombard devoted a series of lectures of a year each, supplemented by numerous demonstrations, to the following subjects: —

1. Physiology of Muscle and Nerve.
2. Physiology of Circulation and Respiration and the Nervous Mechanisms by which they are regulated.
3. Physiology of Muscle, Nerve, and Spinal Cord.

Dr. Cardwell gave a number of lectures upon Animal Locomotion and Coördination. And Drs. Hodge and Jordan lectured respectively on the Physiology of Spinal and Peripheral Ganglia, and the Physiology of Leucocytes.

A convenient laboratory was fitted up with microscopes, microtomes, and all needed instruments, materials, and reagents for neurology. A number of brain and other neurological specimens were prepared for purposes of instruction and demonstration, and the best neurological models were purchased with this end in view.

Dr. Donaldson lectured during 1889–90 on the anatomy of the central nervous system in man; and in 1890–91 completed the course by treating the peripheral nervous system and discussing at length the various physical measures, so-called, of intelligence as found in the brain, its size, weight, convolution, thickness of cortex, and relative development of lobes, as these have been presented in the history of neurology. The course was repeated in 1891–92, together with a practice course in the laboratory on the histology of the nervous system.

A seminary which met once a week was devoted to the reading of papers on neurological topics, both of historical and current interest, and to reports on work in progress in the laboratory.

The primary aim of the department, as Professor Whitman expressed it, is to make "research men," men imbued with the spirit and desire for original investigation. This purpose is seen in all the courses of instruction and becomes even more patent in the number of investigations actually in progress in the different laboratories of the department. In fact, the serious work of every member was research, for which lecture and seminary combined to form an appropriate historical and philosophical background.

During this period, Professor Whitman being in charge of Woods Holl Marine Laboratory, practically all the men in morphology continued their studies there through the summer seasons, taking microscopes, apparatus, and reagents from the University. Lectures were also given at Woods Holl by Professors Donaldson, Lombard, and McMurrich, and Drs. Watase, Wheeler, and Jordan assisted Professor Whitman with the laboratory instruction.

The following résumé is given to present a general picture of the spirit and scope of the department's work during this three-year period.

RESEARCH WORK.

Professor Whitman, in addition to editing the *Journal of Morphology*, equipping and directing a new and complicated laboratory, and giving regular lectures, spent most of his time investigating the Hirudinea, publishing a series of papers on their classification, with descriptions of new species, on their metamerism, and on their hypodermic impregnation by means of spermatophores. "Specialization and Organization," "The Naturalist's Occupation," and other papers show that he was following lines of more general interest both in scientific work and in public education.

Dr. Baur was delving in problems of fundamental importance in comparative osteology of vertebrates, morphology of the vertebrate skull, carpus, ribs, etc., and working out the descriptions of a number of forms discovered during his successful paleontological expeditions. A good share of his work grouped itself about the plan of his great expedition to the Galapagos Islands, which was finally made possible by the munificence of the Hon. Stephen Salisbury, together with contributions from Professor H. F. Osbourn and from the Elizabeth Thompson Science Fund. This trip Dr. Baur made (in company with Mr. C. F. Adams) between May and October of 1890, visiting all the islands, excepting Narborough, Wenman, and Culypepper. Extensive collections of both flora and fauna were obtained, which were worked up by Dr. Baur himself and by specialists both in this country and in Europe. The main general result of the expedition was a demonstration of the fact that the life on these islands is harmonious, and hence that the islands themselves must be explained on the subsidence theory, rather than on that of emergence as held by Darwin, Wallace, and others.

Dr. McMurrich devoted his time chiefly to investigating the morphology and embryology of the Actinozoa, and from these researches derived his conclusions as to the phylogeny of the group. Dr. Watase was at work on various fundamental problems on the cell, caryokinesis, cleavage of the ovum, spermatogenesis, and sex differentiation.

The research work of other members of the department was distributed as follows: Mr. Johnson investigated the morphology and biology of the Stentor. Mr. Lillie studied the embryology of Unio. Dr. Wheeler worked upon the embryology of the Insecta, and in that connection investigated the neuroblasts in the Arthropod embryo. Dr. Bumpus completed his study, already under way, upon the embryology of the American lobster. Dr. Edwards studied the embryology of the Holothurians. Dr. Jordan studied the life history and embryology of the common newt; and Mr. Eycleshymer made a special investigation of the development of the optic vesicle in the amphibian embryo.

In the closely allied field of vertebrate anatomy, Dr. Mall was making a minute study of a human embryo, investigating the formation of the lesser peritoneal cavity in birds and mammals, the motor nerves of the portal vein, and also completed his important work on a new connective tissue element, the reticulated connective tissue, with its distribution in the body. Dr. Tuckerman carried on an extended research on the gustatory organs of a series of animals, and their development in man. Dr. Miller also worked out the minute anatomy of the lung, and by a most exhaustive and varied method succeeded in demonstrating for the first time the manner of ending of the terminal bronchi, together with their relations to the arteries, veins, and capillary system. On the side of practical surgery Dr. Homer Gage conducted a series of experiments on intestinal suture.

In physiology Dr. Lombard continued his investigations on effect of fatigue on voluntary muscular contractions and alterations in strength which occur in severe muscular work, and on the conditions, barometric pressure, temperature, sleep, food, alcohol, and tobacco, which effect voluntary effort. Dr. Cardwell investigated the physiology of the cerebellum with relation to animal locomotion and coördination.

For neurology Dr. Donaldson was pursuing a similar plan with that followed by Dr. Whitman in morphology, viz., gathering the history of the science from original sources, and reducing to uniform statements, tables, and curves all the data as to size and weight, both relative and absolute, of the brain. In this connection he made an exhaustive study, both gross and microscopical, of the brain of Laura Bridgman. An extended series of observations was also being carried on in the laboratory upon the influence of hardening reagents upon brain weight and specific gravity. Dr. Hodge worked for two years (1889–91) on the physiology of nerve cells, their diurnal fatigue and recovery in sleep, and their recovery from effects of electrical stimulation. Dr. Donaldson, with Dr. Bolton, completed a study of the size of the cranial nerves in man, and Dr. Bolton studied microscopically the spinal cord of a horse affected with spring halt.

The above gives, in the main, a picture of the work in progress during the first three years of the department's existence. All but one or two of the researches mentioned have been published, together with others not cited. For place of publication and the complete record the reader is referred to list of publications by members of the University for the corresponding years.

If one science is entitled to claim the special interest of the founder more than another, biology is that science; and in the organization of this department, the aim above all else was to make it the most ideal possible place for biological research. Foundations were laid at this time for a special building more adequately to house this flourishing department. How well the ideal was realized may be seen from the estimate of Professor Whitman, whose experience in the laboratories of three continents entitles him to an opinion. Writing in 1899, he says, "The Clark University Ideal, as I understood it when connected with its early work, is the ideal which I place above any other thus far proposed, and I hope it may find strong friends to help it forward." Unencumbered by the burden of undergraduate courses, untrammelled by red tape and traditions, the laboratory formed for three brief years a veritable garden spot in the field of biological history in this country. It was a place where each man was free to devote all his best energies to just that which he wanted most to discover; where the best thing a man could possibly do for himself constituted the highest service he could render to the University.

A "Flying Squadron," has been suggested as the most fitting definition for a university. Scarcely had this splendid organization been attained than it was carried off bodily, almost, to lay foundations for the biological department in a new university. While no higher tribute could have been paid to Clark University, it has left the department sadly crippled both for men and means for work.

Since 1892 biology has been represented by but a single instructor, Dr. Hodge, who was recalled from the University of Wisconsin, with the title of Assistant Professor of Physiology and Neurology. For the first year Dr. Hodge offered only courses on the physiology, anatomy, and embryology of the nervous system. During the succeeding years, owing to the great need of having the subject presented, a course in general biology has been given, the aim of which is to present the fundamental principles of the science. A sense of the importance of this course has grown from year to year, with the conviction that the subject finds too little representation in most of our educational institutions; and it is hoped, as soon as practicable, to develop it into a solid course, historical, philosophical, and practical, to extend through all of two and possibly three years of university study. The main courses offered by Dr. Hodge have related to anatomy and physiology of the nervous system, both comparative and human, including the sense organs as well, and to the entire field of physiology and to that of embryology, especially of the nervous system and sense organs. These have been supplemented, wherever possible, by laboratory courses. A seminary meeting, usually one evening weekly, has been maintained, the plan of which has been, in the main, to spend a year upon each of the three following topics: 1, history of medicine, with special reference to physiology, epochs, schools, and men; 2, history of, and present discussion centring about, the doctrine of evolution; 3, development of neurology. A journal club, meeting weekly, has aided to bring all members of the department together for discussion of articles in current literature. In general, all seminaries and courses of instruction have been given with reference to furnishing aid and stimulus to students in their research work.

In addition to the above, on the teaching side, Dr. Hodge has become interested in lines, especially of biological education in elementary schools. A definite standpoint for elementary nature study has been developed, which is a distinct reaction against the tendency toward technicality, classification, and minutiæ which have come to constitute so large a part of our elementary science courses. It is planned to include this in the general biology course by way of discussing the question, What aspects of biological science shall be taught in the elementary school? The kind of physiology which should form a part of elementary education has also been given considerable attention. Both subjects have formed the basis for courses in the summer school.

In passing to consider the research work of the department since Dr. Hodge took charge of it, a word as to its general purpose and plan will simplify the discussion.

Science, in this country especially, has become unnecessarily arrogant. We hear on all sides such expressions as "pure science," a term which Huxley wished had never been invented, "truth for truth's sake" or "science for the sake of science," and the "uselessness" of science is made a boast. An important truth is stated in these expressions; for science is of such paramount use and importance to mankind that to discuss this point with one who says it is not, is clearly "casting pearls before swine." Possibly another reason for resorting to these expressions is that the human values attaching to knowledge are so enormous that we have no measures or terms with which to adequately express them. However this may be, if science have a faith worthy of respect, it should result in mutual benefit to share it so far as possible with a reasonable and intelligent public.

A research laboratory is an institution the business of which is to investigate those problems which have either never been attempted or have hitherto baffled all efforts of the human mind to solve. These problems are not far to seek, but crowd upon our lives at every point. The values attaching to their solutions can be expressed only in terms of human life and happiness, compared with which the output of Klondikes and Cripple Creeks is but the small change of the hour. It is clearly recognized that we may not be able to estimate the value of truth until it be discovered, and that the investigator himself, who is willing to devote his time and energies to the work, should be the one to estimate its values, and that he should have the greatest freedom to select the task for which he knows himself to be best fitted. Still, one must be a man before he can be a scientist, and fundamental human values must be in the main the same for all. And it would seem to be the first duty of a research laboratory to devote its resources to the work of solving those problems which concern human life most closely, and possess the greatest human importance. A laboratory owes no less than this to a community; or, better stated, a laboratory is that part or organ of a community differentiated to perform the special function of discovering and making available whatever truth is of greatest value to its common life.

In deciding the directions, therefore, which research work shall take, the above general policy has been followed, and it is a satisfaction to note that the same sentiment was prominently expressed at the founding of the University. On that occasion Mr. Hoar spoke as follows: —

"Speaking now for myself alone, I have little sympathy with that arrogant and disdainful spirit with which some men who undertake, with little title, to represent science in this country, sneer at any attempt to make use of the forces she reveals to us for the service of mankind. Some one said the other day that science was becoming a 'hod-carrier.' I do not see why the term 'hod-carrier' should express the relation rather than the term 'benefactress.' I do not see, either, that there is anything degrading in the thought that the knowledge of the learned man enables him to lift the burden beneath which humanity is bowed and bent. I do not know that science is exempt from the divine law, 'He that is greatest among you, let him be the servant of all.' If the great forces of the universe perform all useful offices for man, if the sunshine warm and light our dwellings, if gravitation move the world and keep it true to its hour, nay, if it keep the temple or cathedral in its place when the hod-carrier has builded it, I do not see why it should not lend its beneficent aid to him also. Our illustrious philosopher advised his countryman to "hitch his wagon to a star." The star will move no less serenely on its sublime pathway when the wagon is hitched to it. I do not know that any archangel or goddess, however resplendent the wings, has ever yet been constructed or imagined without feet. I do not know that any archangel, however glorious, has ever been created or imagined without sympathy for suffering humanity.

"I look for great advantage to the country, both in wealth and power and in the comfort and moral improvement of the people, by the application of science to the useful arts."

The manner in which this fundamental purpose has been carried out thus far may now be seen in part in the lines of work which have been carried out, and, more fully, in plans for the future.

In this country of, so-called, nervous tension, nervousness and nervous prostration, nothing could be of greater value to the common life than knowledge of the fundamental laws of the working of nerve protoplasm. It is only in discovery and obedience to these laws that we may hope for escape from present evils and possession of sane and permanent national health. Consequently lines of investigation upon the physiology of the nerve cell have been kept open from the beginning. Continuing the studies mentioned in speaking of an earlier period in the history of the laboratory, the nerve cell has been studied *during* its electrical stimulation and also in connection with changes which occur in the process of aging and in death from old age. Dr. Barrows has investigated its appearance under various kinds of diet and when the body has been deprived of food, Dr. Stewart has studied the effect of alcohol on the cells of the cerebrum, cerebellum, and spinal cord. Drs. Starbuck and Lancaster respectively studied effects on the nerve cell of artificial (by means of electrical stimulation) and natural fatigue carried to an extreme degree. Dr. Kenyon devoted a year to a most successful study of the brain of the honey-bee. Dr. Burk devoted considerable time in working out the medullation of the brain in puppies. Dr. Goddard tested by especially rapid methods of preparation theories as to the possible amœboid movements of nerve cells in conditions of activity and sleep. Further experiments are now in progress on the influence of alcohol, and work has been begun on the effect of other chemical substances, notably strychnine, morphine, and nicotine on nerve cells. For the purpose of making possible a more practical study of the human brain, a brain microtome has been devised in the laboratory by Dr. Goddard, with suggestions from Dr. Hodge. This instrument is constructed on principles new to such microtomes thus far made, and has rendered it possible to cut sections of the entire human brain in any desired plane with the ease and uniformity with which smaller sections are cut by the ordinary microtomes. The blade of this microtome was made, and presented to the University, by the firm of Loring, Coes, & Co. of Worcester.

A research less closely connected with the general plan, but still essentially upon the nervous system, was carried out by Dr. Slonaker upon the eyes of vertebrates.

This line of work in the physiology of the nervous system is one which the department proposes to continue, as opportunities and properly prepared men present themselves, until, it is hoped, the American public may be able to live on more amicable terms with its "nerves."

In order to attack, in a more fundamental manner, problems centring about the nerve cell and its normal activities, it has been necessary to make a wide detour of investigation in two directions. The first of these has consisted in a study of the microscopical appearances of lymph as compared with different special protoplasms under various methods of hardening and staining. This has proved to be a matter of fundamental importance to histology in general, and has demonstrated that, until we are able to gain some definite notion as to the substances in question, it is useless to go on figuring and describing "granulations," and "fibrillæ," "alveoli," and the like.

The other line of research to which study of the rhythms of the nerve cell has led logically is that of the physiological conditions in general which underlie and determine phases of animal activity. In other words, if we wish to learn the condition of nerve cells in states of rest and fatigue, we must study first the normal rhythms of activity and rest of our animal. Knowing this, we may be able to examine the nerve tissues at any desired point in the curve of functional activity. And in order to gain the fundamental laws of nervous activity, we need to study these rhythms of sleep and waking, rest and activity, which make up the normal flow of an animal's life, in a *series* of animals. This fundamental work has not been done for more than one or two forms as yet, and for those only in a preliminary way. Dr. Aikin's study of vorticella, which showed that a one-celled animal is capable of continuous activity so long as food and environment remain suitable, was the first on the subject. Stewart's experiments on the influence of barometric pressure and diet, including alcohol, on the diurnal activity of rats and mice, together with Dr. Hodge's similar work on dogs and squirrels, serve further to indicate the possibilities in this field. These studies have pointed to the fact that the activity of each animal conforms to a type as to periods and rhythms which is characteristic of the species, and that the total amount of work developed is profoundly influenced by physiological conditions thus far investigated. These researches have been suspended for the present, but it is hoped to push the work in the near future along two main lines. The first of these aims to discover the typical rhythms of physiological activity for a series of animals, both invertebrate and vertebrate. It would seem that these physiological types are of even greater ultimate interest and philosophical importance than the purely structural and morphological types from which the comparative anatomists have worked out the evolutionary series. When this has been done, we shall be in position for the first time in the history of biological science to study human rhythms of activity and repose in the light of similar rhythms of the animal series, and to gain, possibly, some notion as to a norm for human work. The second line of study in this field essays to analyze the physiological conditions under which any particular animal is able to develop the greatest possible amount of normal activity. This is no less a problem at bottom than the study of the physiological conditions which underlie the highest possible types of human life and activity.

The question naturally arises at this point as to what position the biological department of Clark University assumes upon some of the wider aspects of the science.

Since the times when Aristotle employed the armies of Alexander the Great to collect specimens for his museums from all the then known world, the greater portion of biological effort has been directed toward classification and naming of animal and plant species. The uttermost corners of the earth have been searched to the tops of the mountains and dredged to the deepest ocean depths, all to discover some new species of animal or plant, while the common plants and animals of our dooryards are known scarcely more than in name. This classification work, extending from Aristotle in Greece through Linné and Cuvier, Buffon and Brehm, to Agassiz in America, has been in part necessary and important. But, when it is possible to find single species which have been christened ten or even twenty times, it is safe to insist that the passion for naming things has been carried too far. This passion for names is characteristic of a certain period in infancy in the individual, and, we may hope, in the growth of a science as well; and while it gives the best promise for the future, is it not time to hope that this phase of biology may wane, and the maturer work of learning the really important facts concerning animals and plants be seriously undertaken? These facts of paramount importance have to do with the functions of species, the work species do in the world. As a matter of fact, to work in classification by methods of external characters the monumental work of Darwin and Wallace has long since put a final period. Species are not fixed immutably, but are plastic and normally variable. Embryological studies, even by Louis Agassiz himself, proved that animals repeat simpler stages of organization each in its own life history. With the doctrine of evolution the whole method of the science has been changed. Deeper characters than those on the surface must be discovered, and only such as reveal blood relationships and indicate the true position of the species in the line of evolutionary descent can be of permanent importance in the new classification. Thus the past two decades have been devoted in biological laboratories largely to tracing most minutely the embryology of different species, and in exhaustive studies into comparative anatomy and embryology combined. There has been a constant gravitation, naturally enough, to again consider the findings of the microscope, arrangements of cells, and all the infinite variety of granule and rod and fibril as fixed entities, rather than again as plastic and possibly changing with every phase of functional activity. There has thus been no limit to the careful drawing and figuring and coloring of what are supposed to be important structures in living protoplasm. This may all be well enough as pastime. But where the idea of functional changes has been left out of account, the work is builded on the sand. It is like studying and mapping the positions, forms, and colors of the clouds by means of the nice adjustments of the telescope. Many of the books of the past decade will be museum junk before 1910, if they are not already. We need to realize in our modern laboratories that turning the crank of a microtome in and of itself has no more educational value, possibly not so much, as turning the crank of a grindstone. In fact, our theories of *laboratory research* and even of *laboratory instruction* in the brief period in which these have come into prominence have gone far astray. In drifting away from all considerations of human good and even common sense, our modern laboratory work is in the same danger of becoming an end in itself that sunk the old classification into a worse than imbecile waste of time.

Furthermore, *progress* is the word which has characterized every expression of the purpose of the biological department. The advancement of science has been its fundamental *raison d'être* from the beginning. There is little danger that the world will have too many institutions devoted to the serious work of advancing science. The great difficulty has been, and, we may add, still is, that, after a period of great achievement, the inevitable tendency asserts itself to spin round and round about it as though there were nothing else ahead worth working for. The endless discussions of the past two decades reminds one of the hollow disputations of the scholastics. The coursing over and over again of the ground covered so well by Darwin and Wallace, and even by Aristotle, in great part, has been enough to raise the shades of some of these good men to urge us to cease hairsplitting and trifling, and go forward into the great field which their works have opened up.

Their great contributions have consisted in demonstrating the plasticity of living forms, and the field which this presents is that of infinite possibilities of perfection and utilization in the future. It has opened up before us, instead of the dead finality, the idiotic circle with its endless round of "vanity of vanities," of the old philosophy, an infinite future of progress. In this progress Science must worthily lead, but may well hold Art by the hand, lest the doing of science, which is its consummation in virtue, fall behind, and Science, herself, languish for very lack of sustenance.

We expect great help for the present status of biological science from Brooks's "Foundations of Zoölogy." To the question which he imagines Aristotle to ask: "Is not the biological laboratory which leaves out the ocean and the mountains and meadows a monstrous absurdity?" this department would answer — Yes. And it would add that it is not enough to bring our laboratories to the ocean and make fine trips to the mountains and the ends of the earth, unless these great factors become a real part of the scientific quest.

In a word, with the so-called *discovery* and naming of a species of animal or plant, and even with its embryonic and adult anatomization, biological science has scarcely touched the great problem which the species presents. With the half million species of animals and plants of which Science has told us scarcely more than the names, Art has stumbled haltingly along, with all too little help from Science, toward the perfection and utilization of a very few, our domesticated species. Even with these few the scientific biology of no single one has been adequately worked out, and we are practically in the beginnings of scientific studies as to the influence of environment in cultural conditions, and as to the possibilities for improvement in cross fertilization. Biological science owes to the world not only knowledge of the name, form, and structure of a species; it owes as well a clear statement of what the species does, considered as a force in nature; and further, the method by which this force can best be utilized. And this is no whit less pure science because incalculable human values attach to the knowledge. Biologically we are now at a stage comparable from the standpoint of physical science with that of the sail-boat and the stage-coach, before science had discovered, and discovered a way to utilize, the forces of steam and electricity. And we find, when we study carefully what one animal or a plant can *do*, and multiply this by the number of individuals in the species, values and magnitudes, which we scarcely possess terms to express. Add to the total amounts of forces which different species represent, the nicety of adjustment, the adaptation of means to ends, the intelligent direction of the forces, which make comparative psychology a part of biology, and we begin to realize the importance of biology as a science. No seed is too small to contain the power, under proper conditions, of covering the world with plants of its kind; and, not only that, but generation after generation it may be capable of indefinite improvement. The most minute organisms, the bacteria, possess very few interesting features of form or structure that we are able to discover, but they have the power to determine the ultimate food supply of all animal life, on the one hand; and, on the other, to cause the disease, suffering, and death of untold numbers of animals, and even human beings. Insects, on the one hand, have created flowers and fruits by their work of cross fertilization, and, on the other, have laid a tax on human industries heavier than that of bad government and even of war.

Since the side of function, of the actual work which a species can do, presents the greatest ultimate value connected with knowledge of living things, if modern biology does not go forward into this great field, its whole past history from Aristotle down will be an arrested development.

The laboratory that undertakes this work must be a unique affair as biological laboratories go now. It should have greenhouses, terraria and aquaria, aviaries and insectories, in order to provide the essential elements of normal environment where the life and work of species may be conveniently studied in both their daily rhythms and in their larger life cycles. It should especially have easily accessible the actual normal environment of the species under investigation, the pond, ocean, stream, grove, forest, hill, mountain, field, and garden, where results obtained in the laboratory can be readily tested and confirmed in the actual environment of nature. In fact, during favorable seasons much of this line of laboratory work might well be done out of doors. A laboratory of this kind need not be expensive, but should consist largely of rooms adapted for individual investigators, so that researches upon the life and work of a number of different forms may be carried on with the least possible mutual disturbance and interference. This is an absolute essential to investigations of this class. It should also be provided with sunny and sanitarily perfect quarters for not only keeping, but rearing and breeding, a considerable variety of animals.

These and many other considerations render it imperative, if work of the best quality is to be turned out, that a biological laboratory have a building of its own. At present this lack has been one of the chief obstacles to prosecution of the important lines of work indicated. They cannot be successfully studied in rooms used for other purposes, or in a building shaken by the running of powerful dynamos and other heavy machinery. Natural rhythms and periods of rest and activity may be profoundly influenced by these disturbing conditions, and results thus largely vitiated. As already stated, the foundations for a biological laboratory have been laid, and an inexpensive building would greatly facilitate the work of the department. It ought to be erected under the idea, now gaining ground, that a laboratory should be a somewhat temporary building, which could be altered and reconstructed from time to time as new problems arise.

The matter of biological nature study has already been referred to, and it is the opinion that such a research laboratory should be in organic relationship with elementary education and the public school. It is believed that this side of nature, the side of movement and activity, is the natural side of approach for the child. It is peculiarly akin to that animism of childhood which projects life and action even into inanimate things. It is this side of living nature, which, from its intrinsic fascinations and varied affinities with the passionate activity of child life, is calculated to create enduring love of nature; and the vast human values and interests connected with it constitute the most natural wellspring for love of science.

In line with this idea, two nature-study leaflets have already been printed, upon, respectively, the "Biology of the Common Toad" and the "Biology of Our Common Birds." Both of these were written by Dr. Hodge, and he has thus far assumed all financial responsibility for their publication. He also has in course of preparation similar studies on a series of biological subjects, insects, fishes, and reptiles, flowers, fruit, and forest trees, bacteria and moulds, and a few others, which will provide ample materials for nature study from the standpoint above indicated for the entire school course. On the one hand, such connection between the biological laboratory and the schools will furnish channels for the distribution of information to the public, and, on the other, may be made to supply, not only stimulus, but assistance to its work as well.

Bacteriology is a recently created department of biology which has claimed recognition as an independent science by reason of its wonderful development since about 1880, when the discoveries of Koch, Pasteur, and Lister revealed the causal relations which exist between these minute organisms and disease. We can express the enormous values of scientific knowledge of these germs only in terms of human life itself. And it is a worthy refutation of the charge sometimes brought against science that it disregards the welfare of humanity that, as Professor Ludwig said, laboratories devoted to other lines of biological work have been depopulated, because their students have flocked into this new and important field. The bacteria are coming to be recognized as one of the most, if not the most, important element in the environment of animal and even plant species; hence their consideration is essential in such studies as have been outlined above, which aim to determine the influence of environmental conditions upon the activity, health, and vigor of species. Still the pathological side will not be able long to dominate the science of biology; and even with relation to diseased conditions, the side of normal function, physiology proper, must remain preëminent. In fact, it may even now be stated as the highest contribution of bacteriology, that it has revealed the fact that the highest possible health level is the best practical safeguard against inroads of microbic disease. Still the great importance of the subject has made it cause for regret that the resources of the department have not permitted the establishment of a well-equipped bacteriological laboratory. The next step in the development of the department should be in this direction.

The library of the biological department has been selected with a view to making it the best possible working library for those engaged in biological research.

THE DEPARTMENT OF PSYCHOLOGY.

BY EDMUND CLARK SANFORD.

PAST AND PRESENT STAFF.[1]

G. STANLEY HALL, Ph.D., LL.D., President of the University and Professor of Psychology and Education since 1889.

HENRY H. DONALDSON, Ph.D., Assistant Professor of Neurology, 1889–92.

CLIFTON F. HODGE, Ph.D., Assistant in Psychology, 1890–91; Assistant Professor of Physiology and Neurology since 1892.

EDMUND C. SANFORD, Ph.D., Instructor in Psychology, 1889–92; Assistant Professor of Psychology since 1892.

WILLIAM H. BURNHAM, Ph.D., Docent in Pedagogy, 1890–92; Instructor in Pedagogy since 1892.

BENJAMIN IVES GILMAN, Instructor in Psychology, 1892–93.

ALEXANDER F. CHAMBERLAIN, Ph.D., Lecturer in Anthropology since 1892.

FRANZ BOAS, Ph.D., Docent in Anthropology, 1889–92.

B. C. BURT, A.M., Docent in Philosophy, 1889–90.

ALFRED COOK, Ph.D., Docent in Philosophy, 1889–90.

HERMAN T. LUKENS, Ph.D., Docent in Pedagogy since 1895.

ARTHUR MACDONALD, A.M., Docent in Ethics, 1889–91.

ADOLF MEYER, M.D., Docent in Psychiatry since 1896.

CHARLES A. STRONG, Docent in Philosophy, 1890–91.

FELLOWS AND SCHOLARS.

H. AUSTIN AIKINS, Ph.D., Fellow in Psychology, 1892–93; Honorary Fellow, 1893–94.

ERNEST ALBEE, Scholar in Psychology, 1889–90; Fellow, 1890–91.

ARTHUR ALLIN, Ph.D., Honorary Fellow in Philosophy, 1895–96.

N. P. AVERY, Scholar in Psychology, 1895–96.

THOMAS P. BAILEY, JR., Ph.D., Fellow in Psychology, 1892–93.

[1] As this list shows, the Department of Psychology has included, Anthropology, Criminology, Neurology, Psychiatry, Education, and Philosophy. The report of work in Neurology has been incorporated by Dr. Hodge with that in Physiology and Biology.

Henry R. Baker, Student in Psychology, 1894–95; Fellow, 1895–96; Honorary Fellow, 1896–97, and 1898–99.

John A. Bergström, Fellow in Psychology, 1891–94.

Eugene W. Bohannon, Scholar in Pedagogy, 1895–96; Fellow in Psychology, 1896–98.

Frederick E. Bolton, Honorary Fellow in Psychology, 1897–98.

Thaddeus L. Bolton, Scholar in Psychology, 1890–91; Fellow, 1891–93.

Ernest N. Brown, Scholar in Psychology, 1891–92.

Elmer B. Bryan, Scholar in Philosophy, 1898–99.

William L. Bryan, Fellow in Psychology, 1891–93.

Frederic Burk, Scholar in Psychology, 1896–97; Honorary Fellow, 1897–98.

Will G. Chambers, Scholar in Psychology, 1897–98.

Walter Channing, Honorary Scholar in Psychology, 1889–90; Honorary Fellow, 1890–92.

Oscar Chrisman, Fellow in Pedagogy, 1892–94.

Robert Clark, Scholar in Pedagogy, Jan., 1898–June, 1899.

Charles W. Clinton, Fellow in Psychology, 1897–98.

Frederick W. Colegrove, Honorary Fellow in Psychology, 1898–99.

Thomas R. Croswell, Scholar in Pedagogy, 1895–97.

Henry S. Curtis, Fellow in Psychology, 1895–97.

Arthur H. Daniels, Fellow in Psychology, 1892–93.

George E. Dawson, Fellow in Psychology, 1895–97.

Fletcher B. Dresslar, Scholar in Psychology, 1891–93; Fellow, 1893–94.

Frank Drew, Scholar in Psychology, 1892–93; Fellow, 1893–95.

Frederick Eby, Scholar in Pedagogy, 1898–99.

Stafford C. Edwards, Scholar in Pedagogy, 1897–98.

A. Caswell Ellis, Scholar in Pedagogy, 1894–95; Fellow in Psychology, 1895–97.

H. L. Everett, Scholar in Psychology, 1896–97; Honorary Fellow, 1897–98.

Daniel Folkmar, Fellow in Psychology, 1889–90.

Clemens J. France, Scholar in Psychology, 1898–99.

J. Irwin France, Scholar in Psychology, 1896–97.

Alexander Fraser, Fellow in Psychology, 1891–92.

John P. Fruit, Scholar in Psychology, 1891–92.

Henry H. Goddard, Scholar in Psychology, 1896–97; Fellow, 1897–99.

Cephas Guillet, Scholar in Psychology, 1895–96; Fellow, 1896–98.

John A. Hancock, Fellow in Pedagogy, 1893–94.

S. B. Haslett, Scholar in Psychology, 1898–99.

Clark W. Hetherington, Fellow in Psychology, 1898–99.

†R. C. Hollenbaugh, Ph.D., Scholar in Psychology, 1892–93. Died July 6, 1893.

William A. Hoyt, Scholar in Pedagogy, 1893–94.

Edmund B. Huey, Scholar in Psychology, 1897–98; Fellow, 1898–99.

D. D. Hugh, Fellow in Psychology, 1895–96.

John P. Hylan, Fellow in Psychology, 1895–97.

Tilmon Jenkins, Scholar in Pedagogy, 1897–98.
George E. Johnson, Scholar in Pedagogy, 1893–94; Fellow, 1894–95.
E. A. Kirkpatrick, Scholar in Psychology, 1889–90; Fellow, 1890–91.
Milton S. Kistler, Scholar in Pedagogy, 1897–98.
Linus W. Kline, Scholar in Psychology, 1896–97; Fellow, 1897–98; Honorary Fellow, 1898–99.
William O. Krohn, Ph.D., Fellow in Psychology, March–June, 1892.
E. G. Lancaster, Scholar in Psychology, 1895–96; Fellow, 1896–97.
James S. Lemon, Scholar in Psychology, 1891–93; Student, 1893–94.
James E. Le Rossignol, Ph.D., Fellow in Psychology, May–July, 1892.
James H. Leuba, Scholar in Psychology, 1892–93; Fellow, 1893–95; Honorary Fellow, 1895–96.
Ernest H. Lindley, Fellow in Psychology, 1895–97.
George W. A. Luckey, Fellow in Psychology, 1894–95.
Frank H. McAnney, Scholar in Psychology, 1898–99.
George F. Metzler, Ph.D., Fellow in Psychology, 1891–92.
Dickinson S. Miller, Fellow in Psychology, 1889–90.
Herbert Nichols, Fellow in Psychology, 1889–91.
C. A. Orr, Scholar in Psychology, 1889–90.
George E. Partridge, Special Student in Philosophy, 1895–96; Scholar in Psychology, 1896–98; Fellow, 1898–99.
T. Richard Prede, Special Student in Philosophy and Pedagogy, 1895–96; Honorary Scholar in Philosophy, 1896–97.
Daniel E. Phillips, Scholar in Psychology, 1894–March, 95; Honorary Scholar, Jan.–June, 97; Fellow, 1897–98.
Jefferson R. Potter, Scholar in Pedagogy, 1890–91.
J. O. Quantz, Ph.D., Honorary Fellow in Psychology, 1897–98.
J. F. Reigart, Scholar in Psychology, 1890–91.
Robert J. Richardson, Fellow in Psychology, 1898–99.
Edwin W. Runkle, Ph.D., Honorary Fellow in Psychology, Jan.–June, 1899.
Albert Schinz, Ph.D., Honorary Fellow in Psychology, 1897–98.
Alva R. Scott, Honorary Scholar in Psychology, 1894–95; 1896–97.
Colin A. Scott, Fellow in Psychology, 1894–96.
E. W. Scripture, Ph.D., Fellow in Psychology, Jan.–June, 1891; 1891–92.
Charles H. Sears, Ph.D., Honorary Fellow in Pedagogy, 1897–99.
Albert E. Segsworth, Honorary Fellow in Psychology, 1893–94.
John C. Shaw, Scholar in Pedagogy, 1895–96; Fellow in Psychology, 1896–97.
Henry D. Sheldon, Fellow in Pedagogy, 1897–99.
Frederic D. Sherman, Ph.D., Honorary Fellow in Psychology, 1898–99.
Toshihide Shinoda, Honorary Scholar in Pedagogy, 1889–90.
Maurice H. Small, Scholar in Psychology and Pedagogy, 1895–96; Fellow in Psychology, 1896–98.
Willard S. Small, Scholar in Psychology, 1897–98; Fellow, 1898–99.
Frank E. Spaulding, Ph.D., Honorary Fellow in Psychology, 1894–95.

Edwin D. Starbuck, Fellow in Psychology, 1895-97.

J. Richard Street, Scholar in Pedagogy, 1895-96; Fellow in Psychology, 1896-98.

Charles H. Thurber, Honorary Fellow in Pedagogy, Jan.-April, 1899.

Frederick Tracy, Fellow in Psychology, 1892-93.

Norman Triplett, Fellow in Psychology, 1898-99.

Gerald M. West, Ph.D., Fellow in Anthropology, 1890-91; Assistant, 1891-92.

Guy M. Whipple, Scholar in Psychology, 1897-98.

Minosuke Yamaguchi, Scholar in Psychology, 1897-98.

Albert H. Yoder, Scholar in Pedagogy, 1893-94.

Lewis E. York, Scholar in Pedagogy, 1897-98.

HISTORICAL SKETCH OF THE WORK IN GENERAL PSYCHOLOGY.

The ten years covered by the history of the Psychological Department in this University have been eventful in the history of Psychological Science in the country at large.

Before 1880 the science was taught as a stepping-stone to metaphysics and ethics; its method was chiefly introspective; laboratories were unheard of; and genetic and comparative psychology were a *terra incognita*. During the early part of the eighties, however, the idea that psychology was an independent science, to be advanced by experiment and systematic observation, was gradually taking root, and in 1888 and 1889 began a vigorous growth. New interest was taken in the subject, laboratories began to be opened, and a special journal was started for the publication of psychological investigations (*The American Journal of Psychology*). Since that time the interest has continued; the laboratories have increased at the rate of three or four a year till they now number between thirty and forty, are found in almost all the leading universities of the country, are often liberally supported, and in some cases surpass the best European laboratories in equipment; and many workers trained at home and abroad have entered the field. In 1892 the American Psychological Association was started, and now numbers over one hundred members, nearly all actively interested in psychological teaching or investigation. A little later genetic and comparative psychology appeared in an awakened interest in the study of childhood; and more recently still have been extended into a new and fruitful study of the mind and habits of animals. Since 1894 a second psychological journal, *The Psychological Review*, has been published; and many articles of psychological interest appear in the *Pedagogical Seminary* (especially on Child Study) and in the other educational magazines. It is with such a period of vigorous interest in psychology and of rapid growth in facilities that our own ten years' history coincides.

In turning now to this more particularly, I shall speak first of the work in experimental psychology, which, though by no means the whole of the new movement, has been so far rather its centre and characteristic mark, and afterward of that of a more general character.

The distinctive feature of American laboratories generally is the extent to which they are used for psychological teaching as distinct from psychological investigation. Both foreign and home laboratories have the double purpose of instruction and research, but in the American laboratories a little greater emphasis seems to be laid on their pedagogical usefulness. This emphasis is doubtless due in part to more deep-seated differences between American and foreign universities, but it has been favored also by the feeling that a general acquaintance with laboratory problems and methods should precede the undertaking of original investigation. In the case of the Clark laboratory, it has been further enforced by the number of students of pedagogy for whom a psychological groundwork must be provided.

The advantage of laboratory teaching of psychology is that of all proper laboratory teaching, namely, that the student is brought face to face with that about which he is studying, and knows the thing itself at first hand rather than what some text-book or lecturer may say about it. For those who intend to take up experimental investigation later, it is of course the natural apprenticeship.

Such elementary laboratory teaching demands some sort of manual or guide that can be put into the hands of the students, a fact that became painfully evident in the first years of the department; and as at the time none whatever existed, it was necessary to make one. A beginning was made with manuscript sheets struck off on the mimeograph. Later these were worked over in part in a series of articles in the *Journal of Psychology*, and, finally, again revised and enlarged, this part was regularly published, six chapters in 1894, and the remainder last year, making altogether a volume of about 450 pages covering the topics of sensation and perception. This work seems to have supplied a genuine need — at least, has met with a wide acceptance in American laboratories.

Up to the year just passed the laboratory course has not extended beyond the usual laboratory topics of sensation and perception, reaction-times, Weber's law, and the like. But, beginning with the year 1898–99, an important enlargement was made by the addition of laboratory practice in comparative psychology. Under the special guidance of Dr. Kline, opportunities have been given for the study of the habits and mental life of a number of more or less typical animals. Starting with the microscopical amœba, paramecium, and vorticella, the list has been extended upward to include earthworms, slugs, fish, chickens, white rats, and kittens. Though lectures have been regularly delivered, demonstrations made, and seminaries held in connection with the laboratory work, the development of this practice course in both experimental and comparative psychology, together with the manual mentioned and the similar though briefer work of Dr. Kline, is regarded as the most important product of the Clark laboratory on its teaching side.

The scientific work of the laboratory has resulted in ten or twelve extended researches and in a considerable number of briefer studies. It is not easy in short space to give an intelligible account of studies upon a variety of topics so considerable as these have covered, but it has seemed to the writer that a list of the titles of papers published, with a few lines of explanation where necessary, might serve the purpose.

STUDIES FROM THE PSYCHOLOGICAL LABORATORY.

Time and Rhythm.

NICHOLS: The Psychology of Time. *Am. Jour. of Psy.*, Vol. 3, pp. 453–529, and Vol. 4, pp. 60–112 (1891). (Dissertation.) Republished in book form by Henry Holt, New York, 1891.

A general discussion of the time problem. The experimental portion shows that a period of practice in keeping time at a slow rate tends to slow a quicker rate tried immediately afterward, and *vice versa*, thus demonstrating a dependence of time judgments upon artificially acquired rhythms.

BOLTON, T. L.: On the Discrimination of Groups of Rapid Clicks. *Ibid.*, Vol. 5, pp. 294–310 (1893).

An indirect determination of the fineness of discrimination for very short periods of filled time.

BOLTON, T. L.: Rhythm. *Ibid.*, Vol. 6, pp. 145–238 (1894). (Dissertation.)

A general account of the subject. The experimental portion deals with the subjective rhythms observed in uniform series of sounds, and with the structure of the rhythmic feet which result when sounds of different length or intensity are regularly introduced in an otherwise uniform series.

HAMLIN, ALICE J.: On the Least Observable Interval between Stimuli addressed to Disparate Senses and to Different Organs of the Same Sense. *Ibid.*, Vol. 6, pp. 564–575 (1895).

Experimental determination of the interval that must separate nearly simultaneous sensations in order that their order may be recognized. Experiments with clicks and flashes, flashes and shocks, separate clicks heard by the two ears, etc., and with indifferent and with specially directed attention.

WHIPPLE: On Nearly Simultaneous Clicks and Flashes. *Ibid.*, Vol. 10, pp. 280–286 (1899).

A study of the reason for the difference between the results of Dr. Hamlin and of earlier European observers in the matter of which order of stimuli (click-flash or flash-click) could be more readily recognized. Dr. Hamlin's results are confirmed and the difference proved not to lie in the fact that the European observers had made use of series of pairs of clicks, which had been supposed a possible cause.

Memory.

BOLTON, T. L.: The Growth of Memory in School Children. *Ibid.*, Vol. 4, pp. 362–380 (1892).

A study by the memory-span method on upwards of fifteen hundred children, made in connection with the anthropometric studies of Dr. Boas, together with a theoretical treatment of the statistical curves obtained.

BERGSTRÖM: Experiments upon Physiological Memory by Means of the Interference of Associations. *Ibid.*, Vol. 5, pp. 356–369 (1893).

The Relation of the Interference to the Practice Effect of an Association. *Ibid.*, Vol. 6, pp. 433–442 (1894).

An Experimental Study of Some of the Conditions of Mental

Activity. *Ibid.*, Vol. 6, pp. 247–274 (1894). (These three papers were united to form a Dissertation.)

A pack of eighty cards (eight cards each of ten different kinds) is sorted according to the kinds, and after an interval re-sorted, but with such an arrangement that each kind occupies a different place on the table. The second sorting takes longer because of interference between the new associations and those formed in the first sorting, and the excess of time required measures indirectly the persistence of the first set of associations. The first paper gives curves showing the rate of falling away of the first associations (curves of forgetting) determined by this method. The second paper, by an ingenious application of the same method, shows that the interference power of any association is practically equal to the fixity given it by practice,—in other words, "that the work of breaking up a habit is roughly proportional to the work of forming it." The third paper gives determinations of the variations in mental ability during the work hours of the day made upon several different subjects and with different sorts of tests.

DANIELS: The Memory After-image and Attention. *Ibid.*, Vol. 6, pp. 558–564 (1895).

The aim was to measure the native persistence of bare impressions as distinguished from that which they show when received with attention and held by association. The time was found to be very short, not more than five or ten seconds.

SMITH, THEODATE L.: On Muscular Memory. *Ibid.*, Vol. 7, pp. 453–490 (1896).

A painstaking comparative study of the memory of nonsense syllables learned with and (as far as possible) without the coöperation of the vocal mechanism. The memory assisted by even incipient movements was, in all cases, distinctly better,—a result further confirmed by a similar study on various combinations of the manual signs of the deaf-mute alphabet learned with and without execution of the hand postures involved.

COLEGROVE: The Time required for Recognition. *Ibid.*, Vol. 10, pp. 286–292 (1899).

A chronoscopic study of the time required for deciding whether a picture suddenly presented had been seen before or not.

Psychology of Movement.

BRYAN, W. L.: On the Development of Voluntary Motor Ability. *Ibid.*, Vol. 5, pp. 125–204 (1892). (Dissertation.)

A study of the rate, precision, and strength of voluntary movements in the case of adults, and of a large number of school children from six to sixteen years old. Differences due to fatigue, to increasing age, to sex, to bilateral asymmetry, and the like, are carefully worked out; the mathematical treatment of the statistics (thanks in part to suggestions from Dr. Boas) is unusually full and rigid.

REIGART AND SANFORD: On Reaction-times when the Stimulus is Applied to the Reacting Hand. *Ibid.*, Vol. 5, pp. 351–355 (1893).

The experiments bring into question the statement of Exner that reactions are slower when the stimulus is applied to the reacting hand.

HANCOCK: A Preliminary Study of Motor Ability. *Pedagogical Seminary*, Vol. 3, pp. 9–29 (1894).

The Relation of Strength to Flexibility in the Hands of Men and Children. *Ibid.*, Vol. 3, pp. 308–313 (1895).

The first is a study of the spontaneous movements of school children from five to seven years old, — of the swayings and tremors displayed in efforts to stand still with eyes open or closed, or to hold the hand or forefinger still, — movements analogous to those of nervous disease. The second paper shows for the persons tested (20 men, 22 boys, and 11 girls), greater flexibility in the hands of the men as measured by the extent to which the joints could be flexed voluntarily. Both papers are of avowedly pedagogical interest.

LANCASTER: Warming Up. *Colorado College Studies*, Vol. 7, pp. 16–20 (1898).

Based upon ergographic experiments.

Sensation and Perception.

SCRIPTURE: Einige Beobachtungen über Schwebungen und Differenztöne. *Philos. Studien*, Vol. 7, pp. 630–632 (1892).

A brief experimental study of beats and difference tones produced by forks sounding separately on either side of the head.

DRESSLAR: On the Pressure Sense of the Drum of the Ear and "Facial Vision." *Am. Jour. of Psy.*, Vol. 5, pp. 344–350 (1893).

The study shows that the faculty of the blind of recognizing the presence or absence of neighboring objects, which has been credited to some sort of obscure visual sensation in the skin of the face, or to sensations of pressure mediated by the drum of the ear, is probably a matter of hearing.

KROHN: An Experimental Study of Simultaneous Stimulation of the Sense of Touch. *Journal of Nervous and Mental Disease*, N. S., Vol. 18, pp. 169–184 (1893).

Based chiefly on experiments made in the Clark laboratory.

LEUBA: A New Instrument for Weber's Law, with Indications of a Law of Sense Memory. *Am. Jour. of Psy.*, Vol. 5, pp. 370–384 (1893).

Weber's law demonstrated in the classification of artificial stars. The law of sense memory suggested is that memories of intensities of sensation tend to shift toward the middle of the usual scale of intensities.

DRESSLAR: A New Illusion for Touch and an Explanation for the Illusion of Certain Cross Lines in Vision. *Ibid.*, Vol. 6, pp. 275–276 (1894).

This illusion is similar to that of the Poggendorff illusion in vision, and the obvious explanation in the case of the touch illusion is extended to the visual one.

SANFORD: A New Visual Illusion. *Science*, Feb. 17, 1893.

A visual illusion involving false judgments.

DRESSLAR: Studies in the Psychology of Touch. *Am. Jour. of Psy.*, Vol. 6, pp. 313–368 (1894). (Dissertation.)

The study is in three sections: 1. On the Education of the Skin with the Æsthesiometer, particularly of its bilateral effects; 2. Experiments on Filled and Open Space for Touch, showing that filled space seems larger when the finger moves over it, or when the extents compared are moved under the resting finger; 3. On Apparent Weight as affected by Apparent Size and Shape — tests upon school children and adults.

Circulation and Respiration.

DAWSON: Effects of Mental States upon Circulation. (Records in the instructor's hands but not worked up as yet.) Preliminary note in the Proc. of the Am. Psychological Ass'n, *Psychological Review*, Vol. 4, pp. 119–121 (1897).

An extended study made with the plethysmograph applied simultaneously to the hand and eye.

WHIPPLE: The Influence of Forced Respiration on Psychical and Physical Activity. *Am. Jour. of Psy.*, Vol. 9, pp. 560–571 (1898).

The effect of very rapid breathing on eight simple tasks involving sensory or motor activities, or both. Effects slight in most cases; physical strength and endurance seem to be increased, while discriminative powers seem to be depressed.

Comparative Psychology.

KLINE: Methods in Animal Psychology. *Ibid.*, Vol. 10, pp. 256–279 (1899).

Discussion of methods, and presentation of the results of experiments upon vorticellæ, wasps, chicks, and white rats.

SMALL, W. S.: Notes on the Psychic Development of the Young White Rat. *Ibid.*, Vol. 11, pp. 80–100 (1899).

The study consists of a careful record of the bodily and mental development of the white rat from birth onward for a number of weeks.

Studies on Miscellaneous Topics.

CALKINS, MARY WHITON: Statistics of Dreams. *Ibid.*, Vol. 5, pp. 311–343 (1893).

A careful analytical and statistical study of dreams, recorded immediately after waking by two subjects during a period of six or eight weeks. An effort to get as full a picture as possible of normal dream-life.

LUCKEY: Some Recent Studies of Pain. *Ibid.*, Vol. 7, pp. 108–123 (1895).

A review of recent literature on the physiology and psychology of pain.

MILES, CAROLINE: A Study of Individual Psychology. *Ibid.*, Vol. 6, pp. 534–558 (1895).

A *questionnaire* study of a number of special points, made on one hundred students in Wellesley College. Such topics are considered as: How do you know your right hand from your left? How do you concentrate attention? Fears as children? Things causing anger? Favorite color? Earliest memories? Early ideals? etc. (This study and the preceding, though not experimental, were made in connection with the work of the laboratory.)

DREW: Attention: Experimental and Critical. *Ibid.*, Vol. 7, pp. 533–576 (1896). (Dissertation.)

The experimental portion of this paper consists of three sections: 1. Reaction and Association Times with Differing Degrees of Distraction; 2. A Qualitative Study of Associations with Full and with Distracted Attention; 3. A Study of the Apparent Order of nearly Simultaneous Stimuli with variously Directed Attention.

HYLAN: The Fluctuation of Attention. *Psychological Review*, Monograph Supplement, No. 6, pp. 1–78 (1898).

An experimental and expository paper, the experiments approaching the question in several different ways.

HUEY: Preliminary Experiments in the Physiology and Psychology of Reading. *Am. Jour. of Psy.*, Vol. 9, pp. 575–586 (1898).

Tests of rate of reading in vertical and horizontal directions, of the importance for recognition of the first and last parts of words, and of the actual movements of the eye in reading, determined by apparatus attached to the eye. This study was continued during the year 1898–99, with results that are nearly ready for publication.

Technical Matters.

The following papers have been chiefly concerned with technical matters and apparatus.

SCRIPTURE: Psychological Notes. *Ibid.*, Vol. 4, pp. 577–584 (1892).

On the method of regular variation; The least perceptible variation in pitch; The faintest perceptible sound; Notation for intensity; A constant blast for acoustical purposes; Some psychological terms.

SCRIPTURE: An Instrument for Mapping Hot and Cold Spots on the Skin. *Science*, Vol. 19, p. 258 (1892).

DRESSLAR: A New and Simple Method for comparing the Perception of Rate of Movement in the Direct and Indirect Fields of Vision. *Am. Jour. of Psy.*, Vol. 6, p. 312 (1894).

SANFORD: A Simple and Inexpensive Chronoscope. *Ibid.*, Vol. 3, pp. 174–181 (1890).

A New Pendulum Chronograph. *Ibid.*, Vol. 5, pp. 384–389 (1893).

Some Practical Suggestions on the Equipment of a Psychological Laboratory. *Ibid.*, Vol. 5, pp. 429–438 (1893).

Notes on New Apparatus. *Ibid.*, Vol. 6, pp. 575–584 (1895).

The Vernier Chronoscope. *Ibid.*, Vol. 9, pp. 191–197 (1898).

While these studies have been going on in the laboratory, the work in philosophy and education, and in the non-laboratory sections of psychology, has been carried forward with perhaps even greater vigor. President Hall, Dr. Burnham, Dr. Boas, Dr. Chamberlain, Dr. Meyer, Messrs. MacDonald, Strong, Gilman, and others, have lectured on various aspects of the history of philosophy, pedagogy, psychiatry, æsthetics, criminology, and anthropology. Some account of the work in education, anthropology, and psychiatry will be found below in the special reports of Drs. Burnham, Chamberlain, and Meyer; the rest will be spoken of here.

The work of instruction has been carried on by means of seminaries as well as lectures, and to a great extent also in the more informal but most effective way of personal conference with individual students.

It is not possible from data now at hand to give a complete list of the courses given by President Hall, but at different times he has lectured upon the History of Philosophy, Ancient, Mediæval, and Modern (taking philosophy in a sense wide enough to include psychology, education, and medicine); on Cosmology, on General Psychology, on Morbid Psychology (with clinics at the Worcester Lunatic Hospital), on Genetic Psychology (both in the animal series and in the child), Educational Philosophy and Practice, Child Study, Adolescence, Curricula, Teaching of Special Subjects, and upon other pedagogical topics. In addition to these lectures,

President Hall has, almost from the first, conducted a weekly seminary, meeting in the evening at his own house. Here members of the department have reported on the progress of their investigations and received the benefit of mutual criticism, or have united in the study of some special author or topic. Notes of the discussions of the seminary during a period when chief attention was given to Plato have been published by Dr. H. Austin Aikins in the *Atlantic Monthly* (September and October, 1894), under the title, "From the Reports of the Plato Club." President Hall has also directed the research of the greater part of the men in the department, recommending topics, methods, literature, and lines of thought, and in some cases has gone so far as to enter into joint authorship with the students, taking their incomplete results and putting them into shape for publication.

In the first years after the opening of the University, President Hall was assisted in the philosophical teaching by Dr. Alfred Cook, Dr. B. C. Burt, and Mr. C. A. Strong as Docents. During the year 1889–90, Drs. Burt and Cook gave courses on Greek philosophy and on modern philosophy from Locke to Kant; and in 1890–91, Mr. Strong gave a brief course on the history of psychology among the Greeks from Thales to Aristotle, — an abstract of the lectures being later published in the *American Journal of Psychology*, Vol. 4, pp. 177–197 (1891). During 1892–93, Mr. Benjamin Ives Gilman, as Instructor in Psychology, lectured on Pleasure and Pain, and pursued independent investigations on the theory of musical consonance. Abstracts of his lectures are to be found in the *American Journal of Psychology*, Vol. 6, pp. 1–60 (1893). Mr. Arthur MacDonald, as Docent in Ethics, devoted himself to theoretical and practical studies in criminology, lecturing on that topic during the first year of the University and conducting a seminary, with occasional lectures, during the second. Since 1891 all the philosophical teaching of the department has been done by President Hall himself.

The research of this section of the psychological department has been devoted for the most part to questions that are too large and too unmanageable for successful treatment in the laboratory, — questions of the origin and development of mental life in the race and in the child, of adolescence and sex, of emotion, of religion, and the like. Its scope and nature will be apparent from the following list of studies: —

Child Study and Psychogenesis.

TRACY: The Language of Childhood. *Am. Jour. of Psy.*, Vol. 6, pp. 107–138 (1893).

The Psychology of Childhood. Boston, 1893. 94 pp. (Includes a reprint of the preceding.) (Dissertation.)

The first paper is a careful study of extant data on the physiology, phonetics, and psychology of infant language, together with new material gathered by the author. The second is a similar treatment of sensation, emotion, intellection, and volition as they appear in very young children.

SHAW: A Test of Memory in School Children. *Pedagogical Seminary*, Vol. 4, pp. 61–78 (1896).

An account of tests made with a carefully prepared story, which was read to the children to test memory and lines of greatest interest. Statistics of about seven hundred papers from children ranging from the third year of school life to those in the higher classes of the high school.

HALL AND ELLIS: A Study of Dolls. *Ibid.*, Vol. 4, pp. 129–175 (1896).

A study of the various aspects of the interest in dolls and of ways in which they are used in play, based upon numerous replies to two *questionnaires*.

SMALL, M. H.: The Suggestibility of Children. *Ibid.*, Vol. 4, pp. 176–220 (1896).

A record of experiments both on groups of children and on separate individuals, together with a large number of returns from a *questionnaire*, with pedagogical inferences and applications.

CURTIS: Inhibition. *Ibid.*, Vol. 6, pp. 65–113 (1898). (Dissertation.)

The four sections of the paper present: 1. A Summary of Facts and Theories, Psychological, Biological, and Neurological; 2. An Account of the Influence of Different forms of Activity on one Another; 3. A Study of Restlessness in Children; and 4. Pedagogical Inferences from the Foregoing. The third section gives results of experiments and observations by the author together with *questionnaire* returns. The term "inhibition" is taken in a very wide sense.

PARTRIDGE: Reverie. *Ibid.*, Vol. 5, pp. 445–474 (1898).

A study of 337 *questionnaire* returns on day dreams and related phenomena. The physical signs, the subjective state, the causes and conditions, the content, and the awakening are considered. An appendix contains records of the efforts of 330 children to describe an imaginary animal, and of an attempt to gather statistics as to hypnagogic images from upward of 800 children.

DAWSON: A Study of Youthful Degeneracy. *Ibid.*, Vol. 4, pp. 221–258 (1896).

A careful study of about 60 degenerate youths (including 26 boys and 26 girls from the state reform schools of Massachusetts) as to Vitality, Head and face configuration, Anomalies of physical structure, Keenness of senses, Intellectual ability, Parentage, and Environment.

HALL: Some Aspects of the Early Sense of Self. *Am. Jour. of Psy.*, Vol. 9, pp. 351–395 (1898).

A study of the growth and development of self-consciousness based on *questionnaire* returns. Making acquaintance with hands, feet, and other parts of the body, external and internal; influence of dress and adornment; experiences with mirrors; various pet names; childish conceptions of the soul; questionings of children about their own identity, present reality, etc.; the effect of social environment, beginning especially with the mother.

Psychology of Religion.

DANIELS: The New Life: a Study of Regeneration. *Ibid.*, Vol. 6, pp. 61–106 (1893). (Dissertation.)

A study of adolescence in its anthropological and psychological aspects, with special reference to conversion and other religious experiences occurring at that period, the whole being an effort to show the means by which the fundamental truths of religion and theology may be restated in accord with science and life.

LEUBA: A Study of the Psychology of Religious Phenomena. *Ibid.*, Vol. 7, pp. 309–385 (1896). (Dissertation.)

Based upon noted cases of conversion found in religious literature, on material gathered by *questionnaire* and in personal interviews. The headings of the first part are: The religious motive, Analysis of conversion, Sense of sin, Self-surrender, Faith, Justification, Joy, Appearance of newness. The second part treats of the current doctrines of justification, faith, will, determinism, and the doctrine of the grace of God as related to the experiences described. An appendix contains a number of the cases in full.

STARBUCK: A Study of Conversion. *Ibid.*, Vol. 8, pp. 268-308 (1897).

Contributions to the Psychology of Religion: Some Aspects of Religious Growth. *Ibid.*, Vol. 9, pp. 70-124 (1897). (Dissertation.)

The first paper is a study of sudden conversions; the second of more gradual changes of a similar character. Both are based almost exclusively on *questionnaire* returns; the first on 137 cases, the second on 196. The topics in the first paper are: Age of conversion, Motives and forces leading to conversions, Experiences preceding conversion, The change itself, Post-conversion phenomena, Other experiences similar to conversion, General view of conversion. Those of the second paper are: Statistics of material, Adolescent phenomena, The period of reconstruction, External influences, Cases without marked stages of growth, Adult religious consciousness, Ideals, Significance of the facts.

LEUBA: The Psycho-physiology of the Moral Imperative. *Ibid.*, Vol. 8, pp. 528-559 (1897).

An analysis of the phenomena of conscience, together with argument to show that the "moral imperative" is the psychical correlate of certain activities of the cerebro-spinal system (taken as the neural basis of the life of relation) as opposed to activities of the sympathetic system (taken as the neural basis of the vegetative and emotional life).

Philosophy and Criticism.

KIRKPATRICK: Observations on College Seniors and Electives in Psychological Subjects. *Ibid.*, Vol. 3, pp. 168-173 (1890).

A study of *questionnaire* returns from college seniors as to their reasons for studying philosophical and psychological subjects, benefit gained, authors most impressive, and special topics found most interesting.

HALL: Contemporary Psychologists. I., Prof. Eduard Zeller. *Ibid.*, Vol. 4, pp. 156-175 (1891).

An account of the life and writings of Zeller.

FRASER: Visualization as a Chief Source of the Psychology of Hobbes, Locke, Berkeley, and Hume. *Ibid.*, Vol. 4, pp. 230-247 (1891).

The Psychological Foundation of Natural Realism. *Ibid.*, Vol. 4, pp. 429-450 (1892).

The Psychological Basis of Hegelism. *Ibid.*, Vol. 5, pp. 472–495 (1893).

These papers are the result of an effort toward a "psychology of philosophy." The first two trace the influence of concepts derived from vision and from touch on the philosophic schools in question, and the third the influence of those derived from galvanism.

BAILEY: Ejective Philosophy. *Ibid.*, Vol. 5, pp. 465–471 (1893).

An attempt to describe briefly the philosophical "signs of the times."

LEUBA: National Destruction and Construction in France as seen in Modern Literature and in the Neo-Christian Movement. *Ibid.*, Vol. 5, pp. 496–539 (1893).

A review of these topics under the following heads: Artist sensualists, The quest for new sensations, Nihilism and pessimism, School of the decadents, Literary critics, Chronicles, The tormented, The Neo-Christian movement.

ALLIN: The "Recognition-theory" of Perception. *Ibid.*, Vol. 7, pp. 237–248 (1896).

Recognition. *Ibid.*, Vol. 7, pp. 249–273 (1896).

The first paper is a critique of a theory of perception widely held in the past and present; the second is an analytical, critical, and expository account of the mental experience of recognition.

Mental and Physical Peculiarities.

SCRIPTURE: Arithmetical Prodigies. *Ibid.*, Vol. 4, pp. 1–59 (1891).

Accounts of a large number of phenomenal calculators collected from widely scattered sources; analysis and discussion of their mental peculiarities, and pedagogical inferences.

KROHN: Pseudo-chromesthesia, or the Association of Colors with Words, Letters, and Sounds. *Ibid.*, Vol. 5, pp. 20–41 (1892).

A summary of literature with presentation of several new cases, and a discussion of the theory of the phenomenon, followed by a bibliography.

LINDLEY: A Preliminary Study of some of the Motor Phenomena of Mental Effort. *Ibid.*, Vol. 7, pp. 491–517 (1896).

A study, on the basis of a *questionnaire* and special tests, of the tricks and peculiarities of movement and posture that accompany mental effort.

LINDLEY AND PARTRIDGE: Some Mental Automatisms. *Pedagogical Seminary*, Vol. 5, pp. 41–60 (1897).

A *questionnaire* study of 495 cases of such mental automatisms as the avoidance of stepping on cracks, counting objects unnecessarily, grouping objects like small patterns in wall paper into regular figures, and the picking out the middle one of rows of objects.

PHILLIPS: Genesis of Number Forms. *Am. Jour. of Psy.*, Vol. 8, pp. 506–527 (1897).

A study, based on over 2000 cases (974 school children, and nearly 700 normal school pupils and adults personally questioned), showing the almost universal presence of number forms, though often in very rudimentary condition.

COLEGROVE: Individual Memories. *Ibid.*, Vol. 10, pp. 228–255 (1899). (Dissertation.)

The paper is a study of some sixteen hundred replies to a *questionnaire* on earliest memories, period of life best remembered, forgetfulness and false memories, aids to memory, etc. This paper is an extract from a more extended work on memory in general.

Emotion.

HALL: A Study of Fears. *Ibid.*, Vol. 8, pp. 147–249 (1897).

Discussion of the chief fears of seventeen hundred people mostly under twenty-three years of age, together with description of methods used in reducing the original reports for general treatment. Fears of high places and falling, of losing orientation, of being shut in, of water, of wind, of celestial objects, of fire, of darkness; dream fears; shock; fears of thunder, of animals, of eyes, of teeth, of fur, of feathers; special fears of persons, of solitude, of death, of diseases; moral and religious fears; fear of the end of the world, of ghosts; morbid fears; school fears; and the repression of fears, — are all treated in separate sections.

HALL AND ALLIN: The Psychology of Tickling, Laughing, and the Comic. *Ibid.*, Vol. 9, pp. 1–41 (1897).

A study based upon about seven hundred *questionnaire* returns. The following rubrics are treated: The Physical act of laughing, Tickling, Animals and their acts, Recovery from slight fear, Laughter at calamity, Practical jokes, Caricature, Wit, Laughter at what is forbidden or secret, at the naïve and unconscious, Animal laughter, Miscellaneous items, and Notes on literature.

HALL: A Study of Anger. *Ibid.*, Vol. 10, pp. 516–591 (1899).

A general summary of very widely gathered literary material, followed by a discussion of over two thousand *questionnaire* returns; General descriptions of the state, Causes (with many sub-heads), Subjective variations, Physical manifestations (with many sub-heads), Anger at inanimate and insentient objects, Venting anger, Reaction, Control, Treatment, Miscellaneous aspects.

Miscellaneous Topics.

MACDONALD: Ethics as Applied to Criminology. *Journal of Mental Science*, Vol. 37, pp. 10–16 (1891).

Criminal Aristocracy, or the Maffia. *Medico-Legal Journal*, Vol. 9, pp. 21–26 (1891).

LE ROSSIGNOL: The Training of Animals. *Am. Jour. of Psy.*, Vol. 5, pp. 205–213 (1892).

A review of literature on the subject.

KROHN: Facilities in Experimental Psychology at Various German Universities. *Ibid.*, Vol. 4, pp. 585–594 (1892); Vol. 5, pp. 282–284 (1892).

Notes on Heidelberg, Strasburg, Zurich, Freiburg, Munich, Prag, Berlin, Leipzig, Halle, Jena, Bonn, and Göttingen.

LEMON: Psychic Effects of the Weather. *Ibid.*, Vol. 6, pp. 277–279 (1894).

A preliminary note on the general question.

SCOTT: Sex and Art. *Ibid.*, Vol. 7, pp. 153–226 (1896).

The study traces the higher enthusiasms of art and religion, as well as the passions of sex, to the "fundamental quality of erethism found in every animal cell." Beginning with erethism, the following topics are discussed: Specialization among cells, Separation of the sexes, Radiation, Selection, Combat, Courting, Fear and anger, Sex and care for young, The æsthetic capacity, Courting instinct in the lower races, Tattooing, Clothing, Shame, Jealousy and fear, Symbolism and fetichism, Phallicism, Modern phallicism, General features and laws of courting, Degeneration, Perversion, Ecstasy, Æsthetics, Conclusion.

SCOTT: Old Age and Death. *Ibid.*, Vol. 8, pp. 67–122 (1896). (Dissertation.)

Old age and death treated from biological and physiological standpoints, together with discussion of 226 returns to a *questionnaire* designed to bring out the ideas of young people and others with regard to the aged, to death, and to a future life.

PARTRIDGE: Blushing. *Pedagogical Seminary*, Vol. 4, pp. 387–394 (1897).

A *questionnaire* study (120 cases, all normal school pupils): Objective and subjective aspects, After-effects, Physiology, Psychology, Blushing and sex.

PARTRIDGE: Second Breath. *Ibid.*, Vol. 4, pp. 372–381 (1897).

A study based upon about two hundred *questionnaire* returns. The following are the headings: Physical second breath, Mental second breath, Over-play and *abandon* in children, Reaction, Physiology of second breath.

LINDLEY: A Study of Puzzles with Special Reference to the Psychology of Mental Adaptation. *Am. Jour. of Psy.*, Vol. 8, pp. 431–493 (1897). (Dissertation.)

The subject is introduced by a consideration of the biology and psychology of play in general, followed by the classification of puzzles. The time and conditions of greatest interest in puzzles are treated on the basis of *questionnaire* returns. This is followed by a report of extended experiments made upon school children to discover their growth in ability to deal with the difficulties presented by puzzles.

KLINE: The Migratory Impulse *vs.* Love of Home. *Ibid.*, Vol. 10, pp. 1–81 (1898). (Dissertation.)

A biological and psychological study combining the results of experiments upon animals with those of a *questionnaire*. Such topics as the Influence of temperature, Spring fever, Migrations of wild and domestic animals and of man, Wandering tendency in men, women, and children, Love of home, and homesickness, are treated.

QUANTZ: Dendro-psychoses. *Ibid.*, Vol. 9, pp. 449–506 (1898).

A study on material gathered from biology, anthropology, and *questionnaire* returns of the psychic influence of experiences with trees, Biological evidence of man's descent from arboreal ancestors, Psychical reverberations from ancestral experience, Tree worship, The life tree, The tree in folk-medicine, The tree in child life, The tree in poetry.

BOLTON, F. E.: Hydro-psychoses. *Ibid.*, Vol. 10, pp. 171–227 (1899). (Dissertation.)

A study, similar to the last, on the psychic effects of experiences with water: Evidences of man's pelagic ancestry, Origin of animal life, Animal retrogression to aquatic life, Water in primitive conceptions of life, in philosophical speculation, Sacred waters, Water deities, Lustrations and ceremonial purifications by water, Water in literature, Feelings of people at present toward water.

GODDARD: The Effects of Mind on Body as evidenced by Faith Cures. *Ibid.*, Vol. 10, pp. 431–502 (1899). (Dissertation.)

"Christian Science," "Divine Healing," hypnotism and other forms of mental treatment of disease are briefly considered; and "Mental Science," taken as a type, is treated fully from data gathered by extended correspondence and from hospital records. In the remainder of the paper the following topics appear: Positive testimony of the influence of mind on disease, Failures in the practice of mental therapeutics, Hypnotism as a therapeutic agent, Theory of mental therapeutics, Psychological problems suggested, Résumé and conclusions.

STREET: A Genetic Study of Immortality. *Pedagogical Seminary*, Vol. 6, pp. 267–318 (1899). (Dissertation.)

A study of the origin and characteristics of ideas of the soul, immortality, heaven, and a future life, made on the basis of the reports of the thoughts of deaf mutes before training, on about five hundred replies to a *questionnaire*, and on other material. Biological, psychological, and moral aspects of the belief in immortality are also considered.

Besides the studies of these lists, which have been printed, a number more have been made and are in the hands of the instructors practically ready for publication. Others still have been made and the data submitted without complete writing out; a good part of these will ultimately be made use of either in themselves or as the basis for further research along the same lines.

After this outline of work done in the past, a few words may be permitted with reference to the future of the department. This, like its past, must be closely connected with the general progress of psychological science, and the question naturally becomes that of the directions in which progress may be most reasonably expected. Let me begin, as before, with the laboratory.

It seems to me that the two lines of greatest promise, conceding readily the importance of continuing research along lines already undertaken, are those of comparative and of individual psychology. Work has already been begun in both fields. Especially in comparative psychology much has already been done by the biologists, but much remains yet to be done. There is surprisingly little accurate knowledge of the mental life of even the commonest animals; there are many anecdotes, but not many reliable observations, and very few experiments. In this field lie the questions of instinct and heredity, belonging alike to psychology and biology, to which run back so many of the most fundamental and practical of even strictly psychological questions. Much may also be expected from the full introduction into psychology of the comparative method which has so broadened and enriched other sciences in which it has been applied. The conception of mind, as of something not narrowly human or confined to a few higher animals, but as in some sort present in all animals, even the lowest, with a history as long as evolution, opens up vistas to which psychologists have been too little accustomed. Much surely is to be expected from this closer alliance of psychology with biology.

While the theoretical interest of comparative psychology is thus hardly to be overestimated, the practical interest of the efforts toward an individual psychology is hardly less important. We know something about the mental differences of our fellow-men, but we know very little about them in a scientific way. What underlies temperament? What are the laws of the growth of character? Why do some pupils do well with some teachers and not with others? What is the best treatment for reform school boys? How shall one deal with exceptional and peculiar children in the family? Individual psychology ought to answer such questions as these, and many others. It is clear, of course, that many of these questions extend far beyond the possibilities of the laboratory, but the methods and standpoint and training of the laboratory will play no small part in their final solution, and justify attacking them from that side.

Closely connected with individual psychology, but lying a little further from the laboratory, is another field which might be called the "psychology of the permanent apperceptive groups" — the study of the mental attitudes, that is, that result from the fundamental experiences of life, a study of apperception which does not stop at demonstrating the fact of mental habit, but goes on to investigate the effect of one sort of mental habit upon the rest; how, for example, the fact of fatherhood or a severe sickness may alter character distinctly and permanently. These topics have not been neglected, but many questions remain that would well repay the worker of proper equipment and insight. Coördinate with these are the study of the more complex emotions, of religion and of æsthetics, all of which promise much and should have an important place in a psychological department as a counterweight to the laboratory. It is on the data obtained from the study of these topics and those of the last group, with others like them, that true mental and moral hygiene must rest. Fortunately, here also we have beginnings.

Beyond these again, there are topics of great popular interest, like those of Christian science and psychical research, upon which the layman has a right to ask an expert opinion from science, and on which psychology, after careful investigation, can and ought to speak.

What any particular department of psychology can do in realizing these promises of the future, must depend upon the resources in men and materials that it can command. Work in comparative psychology can be begun at once wherever suitable accommodations can be provided for the animals,—proper housing, cages, aquaria, and such attendance as shall insure the health and happiness of the animals, which are essential factors in any reliable study of their behavior,—and a properly qualified observer can be secured. The first of these requirements is easier to fill at present than the second, for as yet too few persons have equipped themselves both as psychologists and naturalists, but this lack will not long exist if the subject is taken up in earnest. For the portion of individual psychology that comes within the scope of the laboratory, there is need of new instruments of at least a relative precision, many of which must yet be devised or slowly perfected by trial and failure, which involves a liberal subsidy. For any of the more general problems mentioned, the first requisite is men of proper natural equipment and training. Not every man of learning is fitted to handle them, and those devoted to them must not be so much taken up with the routine and responsibility of elementary teaching, that they lack the time and spirit for ardent research. And these men, once secured, must be liberally supplied with such help in the way of books and other materials as they need. Of these three things,—quarters for comparative psychology, apparatus for individual psychology, and an enlargement of the staff,—the last is, in all ways, by far the most important. Competent and enthusiastic investigators can work with inadequate facilities, but no facilities can take the place of the men or of the freedom from routine teaching. The Clark department has already made such efforts in all these lines as its opportunities have permitted. Its ten years' history justifies the prophecy that, with enlarged opportunities, it would make more than commensurate return in an increase of the advanced teaching and research for which it was originally organized.

PSYCHO-PATHOLOGY.

By Adolf Meyer.

It is hardly necessary to insist to-day on the remarkably suggestive influence which pathology has had on the biology of man, and especially on psychology. Many of the most fundamental changes in psychology are directly traceable to problems furnished by the study of abnormal life, clinical and post-mortem pathology, and experimental reproduction of diseases and of symptom-complexes. Under these conditions it is evident that the curriculum of a psychologist, and of biologists generally, is quite incomplete without, at least, some touch with results and problems of general pathology, and more especially of neuro- and psycho-pathology.

Starting from the experience that certain types of psycho-pathology lead very promptly into paths which have nothing to do with biology, and put themselves directly on pre-biological traditions, it was considered best to develop a course which would begin with the principles of general pathology, the abnormalities of the most general biological factors, *i.e.* with a chapter properly belonging to any general biology. In this field, the experience in the domain of neurology and of psychiatry would have to be worked up more carefully, as far as possible in constant touch with the broader biological concepts.

Medicine, barely deserving the attribute of an applied science, is not rich in literature breathing the biological spirit. To a great extent it stands on a pre-biological, materialistic standpoint, and the orthodox practitioner of medicine is usually anxious to keep to materialism and to profess ignorance of the psychological aspect; and, again, many of those who look upon the psychological manifestations in their patients very rapidly acquire one of the traditional exclusive standpoints, dangerously near certain mystical concepts. The psychology of hypnotism, of hysteria, even that of aphasia, give good instances of such tendencies. It is consequently desirable to build up a course from the elementary to the more difficult, and starting from the least contested foundations to proceed to the less comprehensible points.

The plan outlined in the lectures and clinics of the spring of 1897 gives an idea of the work.

The course during the year covered the following ground: —

1. Introductory remarks on general biological conceptions. The general biological principles applied to the study of abnormal life. Relation between neurology and psychology, neuro-pathology and psychiatry, neurological and psychical phenomena from the biological standpoint. Application of the point of view to alcoholic intoxication and to several forms of mental disease. Demonstration: Cases of Febrile Delirium, General Paralysis, Catatonia, and Idiocy.

2. Review of the general pathology on the ground of the aspect-hypothesis. The terms "disease," "residual," "defective formation," and "defective *Anlage*." Clinical and post-mortem pathology and their share in general pathology. Only clinical pathology furnishes data on the psychological and physiological side. Plan of clinical study. Anatomical study. Our knowledge of the macroscopic and microscopic lesions of the nervous system and the underlying pathological processes, defective growth and nutrition, intoxication, abnormal function. Local disorders: Abnormal circulation, local intoxications, traumatic disorders, over activity, perverted function. Demonstration of abnormal brains and histological changes.

3. The general plan of the nervous system and illustrations of diseases of the various parts (levels). The neural tube; the segmentary arrangement and the elements of the segments within the lowest level. The middle level apparatus — cerebellum, midbrain, and forebrain, and their afferent and efferent connections. Demonstrations: (1) Traumatic paralysis of the nervus peroneus. (2) Infantile paralysis. (3) Cases of hemiplegia. (4) Lead paralysis (Remak type). (5) Alcoholneuritis. (6) Locomotor ataxia.

4. The principles of localization. The meaning of the connections of neurones by numerous collaterals, of the "interruptions of the tracts by gray matter," of the term "centre." Description of the most important "centres," the lesions of the apparatus of mimic movements, the sensorimotor areas, the principal "sensory" projection fields. An outline of the principles of aphasia and its forms, of hemianopsia. Highest level symptoms. Demonstration: Hemiplegia with hemianopsia; two cases of hemiplegia with motor aphasia; one case of sensory aphasia. Reference to a case of Brown-Sequard paralysis.

5. General outline of mental diseases. Explanation of Kraepelin's classification. Illustration of a paradigm of mental disease: General Paralysis, its etiology, symptomatology, and principal types. Demonstration of six cases.

6. Toxic psychoses and psychoses of disturbed metabolism. Summary of the data of psycho-physiological study of fatigue and intoxication furnished by the school of Kraepelin. Review of the methods and the results. Application to the clinical problems. Demonstration: Delirium Tremens, Subacute Alcoholic Insanity. Cretinism. Dementia Præcox and Catatonia.

7. Periodic Insanity compared with the types of Verbloedungsprocesse. Demonstration of further types of Catatonia and of Periodic Insanity; "Acute Mania," "Acute Melancholia."

8. Short sketch of Senile Dementia and demonstration of a case. Constitutional psychoses. Résumé of the methods and aims of individual psychology (Cattell, Münsterberg, Jastrow, Kraepelin, Gilbert, Binet et Henri, Guicciardi and Ferrari). Value of "types" of character or constitution. Their formation. Dominant ideas. Mysophobia as a type of Neurosis of Fear. Development of Paranoia; cases of Paranoia.

In the spring of 1896 a similar course of demonstrations had been given (see the outline, *American Journal of Psychology*, April, 1896, Vol. 7, pp. 449–450). In the spring of 1898 only one lecture was possible (on the methods of individual psychology, especially Kraepelin's work) and a short course of four clinics in the spring of 1899. The desire to extend the studies into research work has remained unfulfilled. Several attempts failed because the possibilities for such work were not mature, neither on the side of the hospital nor on the part of the University.

The general principles of the work at Clark University tend toward the education of workers. So far the sub-department of psycho-pathology has been purely didactic, covered by the lectures of President Hall, on the topics which have specially attracted psychology, *e.g.*, border-line phenomena, as seen in neurotic people, prodigies, and geniuses; defectives, such as the blind, deaf, criminal, idiotic; mental and nervous diseases, epilepsy, phobias, neurasthenia, hysteria; morbid modifications of will, personality, emotion, etc., and by the above attempt at giving a course with clinics based on general pathology.

The research work along these lines depends on two important conditions. For systematic work the organization of a clinic is necessary, and on the part of the worker a fair knowledge of general and special pathology (in its broadest sense — the knowledge of abnormal life, not merely pathological anatomy and bacteriology) is an absolute pre-requisite.

A training in general and special pathology on the ground of a complete course of biology must be regarded as an absolutely necessary pre-requisite for research in psycho-pathology. Whether most courses of medicine offer what is needed, and whether a medical education should be required, is a matter of some doubt; since much of the ordinary medical course is business training rather than work in pathology in the true sense of the word, leaving out almost intentionally the broader aspects which we have to require more especially for research in our lines; and most of the medical courses are so overburdened that the training in the history of human thought and philosophical criticism is completely crowded out, and this important safety-valve and balancing apparatus is almost missing in the medical curriculum.

The other point, the creation of clinical possibilities, is not less difficult. Our attempt at the Worcester Insane Hospital has hardly matured sufficiently to allow of much research work. The work which forms the foundation of research must be done first, and the reorganization begun in 1896 is only just beginning to furnish the material for some studies suggested by Dr. Sanford, and some investigations on more closely psychiatric questions.

The study of the most protracted disorders of human life requires such a patient spirit of work and an atmosphere of such tenacious adherence to solid working principles, that the predilection for fads and the haste for results are nowhere more lamentable. Should it be the good fortune of this department to get strengthened by the State, as well as by the University, a psychiatric clinic and research-station might grow up. Efforts of this character are being made in New York by an institute independent of the hospitals. Our plan is rather to develop the research-station on the basis of the clinical work. The constant contact with a field of experience such as a clinic offers furnishes the safest working basis and prevents one from running away with hasty speculation derived from too limited a number of facts. The best field for getting problems for work is that of actual observation, such as a clinic only can afford. To pick out curiosities merely will never lead to a psycho-pathology worth its name.

ANTHROPOLOGY.

BY ALEXANDER FRANCIS CHAMBERLAIN.

THE history of the Department of Anthropology at Clark University forms an important chapter in the history of the study of anthropology in America, since it was the first educational institution to distinctly recognize anthropology as a subject of graduate study leading to the degree of Doctor of Philosophy.

The first official announcement of the University, published in May, 1889, included, under the work to be undertaken in the Department of Psychology, the following subjects: "The Psychology of Language; Myth, Custom, and Belief anthropologically considered." With the opening of the academic year, anthropology was established as Section C of the Department of Psychology, and a laboratory and departmental library provided, with proper facilities for original investigation and research. The laboratory contained crania for practical study, necessary craniographic and craniometric instruments, together with the usual tools of the anthropologist working in the field.

The library of the University, besides a special anthropological collection, contains a very complete selection of the literature on applied ethics (criminology), embracing the chief works of the English, Italian, French, and German writers. In the psychological library will be found also many works relating to the subjects which anthropology and psychology treat of in common.

In 1889 Dr. Franz Boas (now Professor of Anthropology at Columbia University, New York), a graduate of the University of Kiel, who was already well known through his researches among the Eskimo of Baffin Land and the Indians of Alaska and British Columbia, was appointed Docent in Anthropology, which position he held until the close of the academic year, 1891–92, when he assumed the duties of director of the sub-department of physical anthropology at the World's Columbian Exposition, taking with him his fine collection of crania. At the University Dr. Boas continued his studies of the anthropology of the Northwest Coast, paying especial attention to a monograph on "The Mythologies of the North Pacific Coast," which he prepared for publication, and to osteological studies of the material collected during his several journeys.

In the summer of 1890 Dr. Boas was engaged in investigating the anthropology, ethnology, and linguistics of the Indian tribes of the coast of British Columbia, under the auspices of the British Association for the Advancement of Science. His report, presented to the Leeds meeting in 1891, treated of the customs and beliefs of the Bella Coola, who were shown to be of Salishan stock, besides containing a general review of the physical characteristics of the Indians of the North Pacific coast, with a discussion of the problem of mixed races. Studies of the Chemakum and Chinook languages were also continued and articles prepared for publication. Early in 1890, the approval of the school authorities having been obtained, an extensive series of anthropological measurements was begun in the schools of the city of Worcester, and carried to successful completion. Preparations were also made for the inauguration of similar investigations in other parts of the Union and in Canada. These measurements were undertaken with the object of studying the growth of children as influenced by varying conditions. The investigations in Worcester were carried on by Dr. Boas, with the assistance of the following members of the University: Dr. G. M. West, Mr. A. F. Chamberlain, Mr. T. L. Bolton, Mr. J. F. Reigart. In the spring of 1891 preparations were made for extensive anthropological measurements of the American Indians, under the auspices of the World's Columbian Exposition, Dr. Boas being placed in charge of the sub-department of physical anthropology. In prosecution of these investigations, the following students of the University, trained in the anthropological laboratory, were engaged during the summer: Dr. G. M. West, in Quebec and the maritime provinces of Canada; Mr. T. F. Holgate, in eastern Ontario; Dr. T. Proctor Hall, in western Ontario; Mr. T. L. Bolton, in Idaho and Utah. Other observers were similarly employed in Alaska, British Columbia, the northwest territories of Canada, Labrador, Dakota, Wisconsin, Washington, Oregon, New Mexico, Yucatan, etc. The chief object of the extensive investigation thus begun is to show the distribution of types over the American continent, and to settle, if possible, disputed points regarding the physical anthropology of the Indians. In the summer of 1891 Dr. Boas resumed his investigations of the Indians of British Columbia for the British Association, and also visited the last survivor of the Chinook tribe, from whom he obtained very valuable ethnologic and linguistic data.

During the academic years, 1889–92, Dr. Walter Channing, of Brookline, Mass., Honorary Fellow of the University, carried on original investigations in the laboratory of the department.

In November, 1890, Dr. G. M. West (afterward Instructor in Anthropology in the University of Chicago), a graduate of Columbia College, was appointed Fellow (and afterward Assistant) in Anthropology, and devoted himself to the consideration of its physical side, taking a large part in the anthropometric investigations begun in the Worcester schools. During the summer of 1891 Dr. West was engaged in anthropological measurements of the Indian tribes of Quebec and the maritime provinces of Canada. Appointed Assistant in Anthropology in 1891, he continued in that position until the close of the academic year 1891–92, when he became associated with Dr. Boas in the sub-department of anthropology in the World's Columbian Exposition, having charge of the anthropological investigations during Dr. Boas's absence in Europe.

During the Docentship of Dr. Boas the lectures of the department were as follows:—

1. A course of lectures on: Physical Anthropology, Osteology, and particularly Craniology. The Physical Character of the living subject: Anatomy of Races. In connection with these lectures practical work was carried on in the laboratory.

2. A course of lectures on: The Anthropology of Africa, embracing the consideration of the geographical distribution, physical characters, languages, and culture of the native tribes.

3. A course of lectures on: The Application of Statistics to Anthropology.

In the spring of 1892 Dr. West delivered a course of lectures on The Growth of School Children, based upon the results obtained in the Worcester schools. These lectures have been published in *Science* and the *Archiv für Anthropologie*.

In the spring of 1890 Mr. A. F. Chamberlain, a graduate of the University of Toronto, then Fellow in Modern Languages in University College, Toronto, who had been a student in ethnology under the late Sir

Daniel Wilson, was appointed to the first fellowship created in anthropology in the University. Previous to entering upon the course of study for the doctorate, Mr. Chamberlain had made special investigations of the Algonkian Indian languages, and these he continued, offering as his thesis an original monograph, "The Language of the Mississagas of Skūgog," which was published in 1892. Other briefer essays in the same field have appeared in the *Proceedings of the Canadian Institute* (Toronto), *Canadian Indian*, *American Anthropologist*, *Journal of American Folk-Lore*, *Proceedings of the American Association for the Advancement of Science*, etc., during the years 1888–99.

Time snatched from busy hours from 1891 to 1893 was devoted to original investigations in the language and folk-lore of the Canadian French, some results of which have been published in *Modern Language Notes* (Baltimore), Vols. 6–8. In 1892 was published the result of an extensive investigation of the use of "Diminutives in *-ing*," in the Platt-Deutsch (Low German) dialects, another study from which field, "Color Comparisons in the Low German Dialects," subsequently appeared.

In the spring of 1891 Dr. Chamberlain delivered a brief course of lectures on "The Relationship of Linguistics to Psychology and Anthropology." In the fall of the same year he assisted in the anthropometric investigations carried on in the schools of the city of Worcester under the direction of Dr. Boas, and in April–May, 1892, superintended the measurements of some 15,000 school children in Toronto, Canada, the results of which work are being from time to time published (see *Report of Commissioner of Education*, 1896–97, Vol. 2) by Dr. Boas, under whose auspices it was carried out.

From June to October, 1891, he was absent among the Kootenay Indians of southeastern British Columbia and Northern Idaho, having been selected by the committee of the British Association for the Advancement of Science to carry on anthropological investigations among the Indian tribes of northwestern Canada. His report (discussing in detail the ethnography, physical anthropology, mythology, and language of this comparatively unknown aboriginal people) was presented at the Edinburgh (1892) meeting of the Association and printed, with an introduction by Horatio Hale, as the "Eighth Report on the Northwestern Tribes of Canada" (London, 1892, 71 pp.). Other briefer studies, botanical, linguistic, mythological, psychological, based upon the material gathered during this expedition, have been published in the *American*

Anthropologist, American Antiquarian, Journal of American Folk-Lore, Verhandlungen der Berliner anthropologischen Gesellschaft, Archivio per l'Antropologia, Am Ur-Quell, Science, etc. The great mass of material, however, is still in process of preparation for publication, and will, when complete, make some four good-sized treatises or volumes as follows: —

1. Kootenay Indian Art. An Interpretative and Comparative Study of some Three Hundred Drawings of Natural Objects, Human Beings, Animals, etc., made by various Indians of the Upper and Lower Kootenay.
2. Mythology of the Kootenay Indians. A Comparative and Interpretative Study of some Fifty Animal Tales and Legends of the Kootenay Indians. With original Indian Text, Translation, Explanatory Notes, etc.

3–4. Dictionary of the Kootenay Language, with Introduction on Grammar and Morphology. Part I., Kootenay-English; Part II., English-Kootenay.

As much time as could reasonably be spared from other duties has been devoted to the long and difficult task of compilation and revision of these original studies.

During his tenure of the Lectureship in Anthropology, Dr. Chamberlain has lectured twice a week throughout the academic year, the following courses having been delivered: —

1892–93. Mythology of the North American Indians.

The syllabus and bibliography of this detailed interpretative study have been published in the "Third Annual Report of the President to the Trustees of Clark University," 1893, pp. 123–125, 141–161. Several of the lectures have appeared in full, or in abstract, in the *Journal of American Folk-Lore*.

1893–94. General Course: The Science of Anthropology in its Relations to Psychology and Pedagogy. Special Courses: (*a*) Comparative Mythology of Ancient Greece and Italy; (*b*) Child Life among Primitive Races, the American Indians especially.

The introductory lecture of this course, under the title "Anthropology in Universities and Colleges," with brief historical bibliography, has been published in part in the *Pedagogical Seminary*, Vol. 3, pp. 48–60. An abstract of one of the lectures in course (*b*) has appeared as "Notes on Indian Child Language," in the *American Anthropologist*, Vol. 3, pp. 237–241; Vol. 6, pp. 321–322.

1894–95. Besides the course in General Anthropology, the following brief special courses were delivered: Anthropology and Ethnology of Sex; The Child amongst Primitive Peoples; Comparative Mythology of America and the Old World; Psychology of Primitive Languages; The Beginnings of Art and Language; The Æsthetical Ideas of Primitive Peoples.

The lectures on the "Psychology of Primitive Languages" were based upon original investigations among the Algonkian Indians of Canada, and the Kootenay Indians of British Columbia, and abstracts of several of them have been published in the *American Anthropologist*, Vol. 7 (1894), pp. 68–69, 186–192; *Verhandlungen der Berliner anthropologischen Gesellschaft*, 1893, pp. 421–425, 1895, pp. 551–556; *Archivio per l' Antropologia e la Etnologia* (Firenze), Vol. 23 (1893), pp. 393–399.

The lectures on "The Child among Primitive Peoples," delivered also in popular form at the Summer School in July, 1894, have been elaborated and published as a book, with the title "The Child and Childhood in Folk-Thought" (New York, Macmillan, 1896).

1895–96. Besides the course in General Anthropology, the following special and briefer courses were delivered: Anthropometry of Children and Youth; The Emotions and their Expression among Primitive Races; The Idea of the Soul among Primitive Peoples; Crime and Degeneracy among the Lower Races of Man; Origin and Development of the Family; Sociological History of Woman.

Two of the lectures on "The Emotions and their Expression among Primitive Peoples" have appeared in part in the *American Journal of Psychology*, Vol. 10, pp. 301–305, "Fear," and Vol. 6, pp. 585-592, "Anger."

1896–97. Besides the course in General Anthropology, the following briefer special courses were delivered: The Philosophy of Primitive Mythologies; Origin and Development of Social Institutions; Race-Psychology; The Anthropology of Childhood; Civilization and Evolution.

One of the lectures in the course on "The Philosophy of Primitive Mythology" appears, under the title "Folk-Lore and Mythology of Invention," in the *Journal of American Folk-Lore*, Vol. 10 (1897), pp. 89–100.

1897–98. Besides the course in General Anthropology, the following briefer special courses were delivered: The Anthropology of Sex; Primitive Children and Children of Civilized Races; Social Evolution; Origin and Development of Primitive Religions; Anthropometry.

1898–99. Besides the course in General Anthropology, the following special briefer courses have been delivered: Child Study in Italy, Variation and Degeneration, Heredity and Environment.

Outside of the academic and summer school courses the following lectures and addresses on topics of general interest have been delivered from time to time in Worcester and elsewhere: —

1892. Aims and Methods of Anthropometry. Principals and Teachers of Grammar Schools, Toronto.
1892. Optimism. Canadian Club, Clark University, Worcester.
1893. Savage Views of Nature. Natural History Society, Worcester.
1893. The American Indian. Men's Association, Pilgrim Church, Worcester, Mass.
1894. Woman's Rôle in the Development of Religion and Civilization. Fortnightly Club, Woonsocket, R.I.
1895. The World's Debt to the Red Man. Natural History Society, Sterling, Mass.
1895. The Mother and the Child in the Story of Religion and Civilization. South Unitarian Church, Worcester, Mass.
1896. Childhood. Conference of Lend-a-Hand Clubs, Lowell, Mass.
1896. The American Indian. Universalist Church, New Britain, Conn.
1896. The Making of Abraham Lincoln. South Unitarian Church, Worcester, Mass.
1897. Johanna Ambrosius. Lend-a-Hand Clubs, South Unitarian Church, Worcester, Mass.
1897. Youth. Lend-a-Hand Conference, Boston, Mass.
1897. Lincoln and Darwin. South Unitarian Church, Worcester, Mass.
1897. In Memoriam: Henry George. South Unitarian Church, Worcester, Mass.
1897. The Unitarian Church and Alcoholism. Conference of Unitarian Churches, Barre, Mass.
1898. Primitive Nature Study. Jacob Tome Institute, Port Deposit, Md.
1899. The Child and the Criminal. Monday Morning Club (Universalist Ministers), Boston, Mass.

At the meetings of various scientific societies, 1890–99, the following papers have been presented, those marked * having been published since their delivery: —

1. American Folk-Lore Society: —

   1890. *Nanibozhu among the Otchipwe, etc.
   1892. *Physiognomy and Physical Characteristics in Folk-Lore and Folk-Speech.
   1892. Christ in Folk-Lore.
   1893. Mythology of the Columbian Discovery of America.
   1895. *Poetical Aspects of American Aboriginal Speech.
   1896. *Folk-Lore and Mythology of Invention.
   1898. *American Indian Names of White Men and Women.

2. Modern Language Association of America: —

   1891. *The Use of Diminutives in *-ing* by some writers in Low German Dialects.

3. American Association for the Advancement of Science: —

1893. Primitive Woman as Poet.
1894. *Translation into Primitive Languages. (Abstract.)
1894. *Incorporation in the Kootenay Language.
1894. *Primitive Anthropometry and its Folk-Lore. (Abstract.)
1895. *Kootenay Indian Personal Names.
*Word Formation in the Kootenay Language.

4. British Association for the Advancement of Science: —

1892. *Kootenay Indians.
1897. *Kootenay Indian Drawings. (Abstract.)
1897. *The Kootenays and their Salishan Neighbors. (Abstract.)

5. Berliner Anthropologische Gesellschaft: —

1893. *Wurzeln aus der Sprache der Kitonaqa-Indianer.
1895. *Beitrag zur Pflanzenkunde der Naturvölker America's.

6. International Congress of Anthropology (Chicago): —

1893. *The Coyote and the Owl. (Tales of the Kootenay Indians.)

Dr. Chamberlain has been a Councillor of the American Folk-Lore Society (1894), Secretary of the Anthropological Section of the American Association for the Advancement of Science (1894), and one of the secretaries of the Anthropological Section of the British Association for the Advancement of Science (1897).

Since 1894 anthropology has been represented on the programme of the Summer School of the University, and each year Dr. Chamberlain has delivered a course of twelve daily lectures upon anthropological questions and topics of more or less interest to the teacher and to the general public. These courses have been as follows: —

1894. Anthropology of Childhood. (The Child Among Primitive Peoples.)
1895. Pedagogical and Psychological Aspects of Anthropology.
1896. Anthropology of Childhood. (New Series.)
1897. Anthropological Aspects of Childhood.
1898. The Beginnings of Education and Educational Institutions. — Primitive Pedagogy.
1899. Educational Aspects of Human Evolution.

At the various summer schools the following topics have also been popularly treated in evening lectures: —

1898. (a) The Philosophy of Childhood with the Poets.
(b) The Genius of Childhood.

1897. (*a*) The Divinity of Childhood.
(*b*) The Attitude of Primitive Peoples toward Nature.
1898. The Childhood of Genius.
1899. (*a*) The Prophecy of Childhood.
(*b*) The Making of a Genius. (Abraham Lincoln.)

Anthropology, while comparatively a new, is by no means an uncommon, subject of academic instruction, and the time has distinctly passed when it should be called upon to plead for its existence, or to make an *oratio pro domo.*

Very many of the great European universities have specifically recognized anthropology as worthy of the highest positions in their gift, and, in this country, institutions like Harvard, Columbia, Chicago, and the University of Pennsylvania have endued this department with the full dignity of a professorship. Moreover, nearly twenty other colleges and universities in America now offer instruction in anthropology, as such, while Sociology, one of the most important branches of the science, is to be found on the curriculum of all such institutions as are making any efforts whatsoever to keep abreast of the times. Other branches of anthropology, such as Comparative Philology, Comparative Religion, Race Psychology, Anthropometry, Archæology, Culture-History, etc., are finding more and more acceptance with the higher institutions of learning.

Both with respect to original research and to academic lectures, the representatives of anthropology in American universities have no reason to fear comparison with the professors and instructors in any other branch of science, and their influence in broadening and humanizing some of the more belated and conservative of the kindred branches of human knowledge can hardly be overestimated.

It is a significant fact that the latest and most complete academic recognition of anthropology, the promotion of Dr. Franz Boas to a professorship in Columbia University, does just honor to one who began his academic career as a Docent in Clark University in 1890. How much of the interest in anthropology in other institutions of learning can be legitimately traced to this University, which, in 1892, conferred the first Ph.D. ever granted in America for research and investigation in anthropological science, cannot readily be ascertained, but its influence, both direct and indirect, has been, no doubt, as it still is, very great. Proofs of this are not wanting in the curricula of more than one of the higher institutions of learning, while the course in anthropology in the University of Illinois, offered by Dr. Arthur H. Daniels, a graduate of Clark University, is directly due to the initiative and encouragement of the department of anthropology.

Through the lectures delivered at the University and during the Summer School, the anthropological department has exercised an ever increasing influence, which has been added to by the appearance of one series of these lectures in book form. Another point of contact with the teaching profession throughout the country lies in the use of the department as a sort of bureau of information upon many and varied topics of educational science. During the last year, especially, very many requests for such information have been received and responded to, often in detail and as the result of personal research. To the students of the University the department of anthropology has always emphasized the great value of a bibliographical knowledge of the subject under investigation, and its services have always been at their disposal.

In this University anthropology ranks as a branch of psychology, and to promote and advance it as such has been the constant aim and endeavor of its representative on the Faculty. The lectures have been such as to correlate with the instruction given in philosophy, psychology, and pedagogy, and their object has been to furnish the students in those departments with the most recent results of anthropological investigations, and to imbue them with that wider and deeper thought that comes from the contemplation of the history of individual and of racial man, and to lay firm foundations upon which in years to come may rise a complete and perfectly equipped department of anthropology. A glance at the theses and essays in the departments of philosophy and psychology will demonstrate the way in which the department has advantaged those who have proceeded to their degrees in this University, such subjects as "Regeneration," "Dolls," "Migration," "Hydro-Psychoses," "Dendro-Psychoses," "Immortality," "Teaching Instinct," "Philosophy of Education," "Adolescence," "Degeneracy," etc., naturally calling upon anthropology for its quota of fact and information, which has often been quite large and significant. Especially has this been the case since "Child-study" has loomed up so largely in the field of education, for questions of heredity and environment, recapitulation, atavism and reversion, degeneration, variation, genius, and the like, must receive from anthropology, more or less, their true orientation and interpretation, — the science of the child would be helpless without the science of man, the story of the individual not half understood without the story of the race. The greater prominence now being given to individual psychology, brings psychology also into closer and better touch with anthropology. That the first woman to hold a fellowship in any department in Harvard University was an anthropologist is a fact, which, taken in connection with the great amount of excellent original work done in anthropology by women, both in Europe and in America, augurs well for the future advancement of the science, when all institutions offering post-graduate instruction in anthropology and facilities for original investigation shall have been opened to women upon the same terms as to men. The composite character of the population of the United States, the existence within its borders of several entirely distinct races, and the addition to these resulting from the recent acquisition of outlying and distant possessions, must inevitably tend to make anthropology more and more a real academic necessity, no less than a constant factor in the determination of national welfare and progress. Unless every sign fails, the history of anthropology in the next quarter century of American university life will compare in brilliancy with that of any other science similiarly stimulated and environed.

At this University, anthropology has accomplished, as the record of the publications of the department shows, results out of proportion to its financial resources and the facilities for investigation and research made possible thereby. With other departments in the University it has striven to overcome these serious handicaps as much as might be, and what has already been done must serve to indicate what can be done in the future, if the department is generously and satisfactorily endowed. Nowhere else, perhaps, can the "sinews of science," rightly employed, give ampler or juster returns, if the past foreshadows the years to come.

Clark University, the first institution in America to recognize anthropology as a fit and proper subject for post-graduate researches and investigation leading to the degree of Ph.D., and the first university to confer such a degree, can justly hope for that recognition which comes to the pioneers in all great educational movements.

But before the department can labor at its best, it must have the best means of research and investigation, be equipped as well, at least, as any similar department in any other institution in the country. Given these, it can do as good work, or even better.

The professorships at Harvard, Columbia, Chicago, and Pennsylvania, the Thaw Fellowship at Harvard, the library of 20,000 books and pamphlets in a single branch of anthropology at the University of Pennsylvania, and the laboratory and museum facilities of all these institutions which have come into such rich fruition during the last ten years, point the way for us, if the good work of the past is to increase and multiply. For comparison with the present state of affairs at this University, the following data from the most recent official publications of the universities concerned, institutions which offer post-graduate courses in anthropology and confer the degree of Ph.D. in that department, will suffice (sociology, etc., not included): —

Harvard: Professor; Instructor; Thaw Fellow ($1050); Hemenway Fellow ($500); Winthrop Scholar ($200).
Chicago: Associate Professor; one Fellow.
Columbia: Professor; two Instructors; President's University Scholar ($150); one Fellow; two Scholars.

One cannot escape seeing the necessity of enlargement and further endowment at this University, if anthropology is to prosper fully.

Before the great things of which it is capable can, in all their rounded completeness, be accomplished here, changes and improvements must take place, and the following are among those most needed or most desirable: —

(1) The department must ultimately be dignified by the existence of a professorship, if it is to continue to hold its own among the similar departments in other great educational institutions. Anthropology can wait, as it has waited, but it scarcely deserves that refusal of academical advancement, which is, of necessity, bound up with straitened financial conditions.

(2) A complete departmental library, which shall include all current periodicals and journals of anthropological interest and afford immediate access to the very latest American and foreign publications in all branches of anthropological science, is an absolute necessity. The advantage of having all these under one roof and procurable immediately after their issuance is inestimable.

(3) A thoroughly equipped laboratory, for special researches and investigations, is also among the things first to be desired, and what investigators now, or formerly connected with the University, have done in this field is a full guarantee that such an addition to the facilities of the University would be well utilized and appreciated.

(4) A museum, which shall contain materials and specimens illustrating the parallel development of the individual and the race, is also a *desideratum*, for this truly anthropological theory, so fecund for education and psychology, has yet to undergo that stern test which zoölogy, paleontology, and geology have so successfully sustained.

(5) Generous endowment of fellowships and scholarships (intra-mural and extra-mural) and other aids in investigation and field work is absolutely necessitated by any adequate instalment of anthropology.

(6) More, perhaps, than is the case with most other departments, liberal allowances for clerical work and for travelling expenses, the lack of which so often delays good studies and inconveniences good men, are necessary, and the department must be congratulated on what has been achieved in the absence of all these. Often to be able means to accomplish.

Judged both by the work accomplished here and the status of anthropology in other universities, the department has every reason to ask and every right to expect such increased endowment as will enable it to make the next ten years of its existence as notable as the same period in the history of anthropology in any of the higher institutions of learning, European or American.

PEDAGOGY.

By William Henry Burnham.

Soon after the opening of the University, President G. Stanley Hall entered upon the duties of Professor of Psychology and Education. During the first academic year no pedagogical courses were given, but toward the close of the year Dr. William H. Burnham, the writer of this report, was appointed Docent in Pedagogy and sent to Europe by the University to study educational institutions, methods, etc. During the year 1890–91, courses of lectures on pedagogy were given in the psychological department by Drs. Hall and Burnham, and a seminary met weekly for the study and discussion of educational subjects. In 1893 the educational courses were designated as a sub-department of psychology offering a minor for the doctor's degree. But the work has remained most intimately connected with that in psychology and anthropology.

In any natural development of these three subjects, the subject-matter overlaps and is interrelated. In this University no attempt has been made to mark a line of division between them. Specially close has been the connection between psychology and pedagogy, most of the students in one subject taking courses in the other. Such vital connection of the two subjects has mutual advantages. Pedagogy is based upon psychology and owes to it the inspiration and stimulus to scientific work, and psychology owes to pedagogy the suggestion of some of its most fruitful fields of investigation.

With a limited staff no attempt has been made to cover the whole field of pedagogy; but by choosing specially important parts of the field, and by extending the courses over two or three years, an effort has been made to show how the subject should be studied. By this method lectures have been given on the history of the modern reform movement in education, begun on the one hand by the early Italian Humanists, and on the other by Comenius, the present organization of schools in England, France, and Germany, the Evolution of the Teaching Profession, the Historical and Critical Study of Educational Principles, Mental and Physical Development, Educational Psychology, and School Hygiene, including the Hygiene of Instruction. Other courses have been given by Drs. Hall, Burnham, and Lukens on the following among other topics: History of Methods in Reading, Physical Education, Child-study, Adolescence, Ideal School, Herbartian Pedagogy, History of Curricula, and leading present topics in education.

A great variety of subjects have been studied in connection with the seminaries, and the results of many of these studies have appeared in the *Pedagogical Seminary*, an educational journal edited by G. Stanley Hall and published at the University, beginning in 1891. The work of the department is best seen, however, by noting its aims, methods, and concrete results.

The aim of the department is twofold: first, to give instruction and training to those who are preparing to be professors of pedagogy, superintendents, or teachers in higher institutions; second, to make scientific contributions to education. These two ends are so closely related that the pursuit of one involves much of the work required for the other also. Suitable preparation for the course involves so much of general education as is usually indicated by the B.A. degree. A good reading knowledge of French and German is of vital importance, and an acquaintance with elementary psychology is desirable, it being taken for granted, of course, that those who intend to teach have adequate knowledge in their own special departments.

Assuming that a student has adequate preparation, three things are essential for higher pedagogical training: first, a general knowledge of the organization of education in different countries and of literature in the field of education, including the history of education, psychology in its relation to education, and school hygiene; second, actual experience in teaching, together with observation of good teaching, and some direct study of educational institutions of different character and grade; third, some experience in independent research, involving not only the thorough study of all authorities upon a subject, and of all work that has been done in the same field in different countries, but also original investigation leading to a scientific contribution.

These three kinds of work may be done simultaneously or successively.

In some of the best higher pedagogical seminaries in Germany they are done simultaneously. Students study and report upon educational and psychological literature. They visit classes of different grades, observing the work of regular teachers, and also teach in a practice school. At the same time they endeavor to investigate some special problem. In this University the study of educational literature, by lectures and independent reading, and the investigation of some problem, are usually carried on simultaneously; but practical experience in teaching must be gained before or after the University course. There are some advantages in doing actual teaching simultaneously with the study and investigation of educational problems. Direct experience in the school makes investigation more vital and practical, and is an important control in scientific research. But, while at present the University has no practice school, as a matter of fact, most of those who have been members of the educational department have had experience in teaching before coming to the University; and the lack of direct connection with the schools is in part supplied by visits to educational institutions. Moreover, there is no rigid line between instructors and students in the department. Both are teachers and learners in turn. Special emphasis is placed upon the importance of research; and much of the time of the instructors is spent in consultation with individual students in regard to their investigations. President Hall especially has given a large amount of attention to directing this work. The research undertaken has been largely in the field of genetic psychology and related subjects; and the students have been assisted by the instructors in psychology, anthropology, and neurology. A great variety of topics, however, have been studied; and a large part of the investigations have yielded results for publication. The papers[1] that have already appeared may be roughly classified as follows: —

Contributions to the Physiology and Psychology of Development.

BOHANNON, E. W.: A Study of Peculiar and Exceptional Children. *Pedagogical Seminary*, Oct., 1896, Vol. 4, pp. 3–60.

Based upon answers to a *questionnaire* reporting over a thousand cases.

[1] Many of the papers mentioned in this list are quite as much products of the department of psychology as of that of pedagogy; and, on the other hand, the pedagogical department has contributed to many of the psychological studies mentioned above.

BOHANNON, E. W.: The Only Child in a Family. *Pedagogical Seminary*, April, 1898, Vol. 5, pp. 475–496.

From a study of reports of 381 only children, it appears that only children are below the average in vitality and unusually subject to mental and physical defects of a grave character, and that, lacking the important education from the constant companionship of other children, they need special pedagogical care and training.

BURK, FREDERICK: Growth of Children in Height and Weight. *Am. Jour. of Psy.*, April, 1898, Vol. 9, pp. 253–326.

A comprehensive résumé of the numerous studies in this field, with a discussion of their pedagogical significance.

BURK, FREDERICK: From Fundamental to Accessory in the Development of the Nervous System and of Movements. *Pedagogical Seminary*, Oct., 1898, Vol. 6, pp. 5–64.

A contribution to the physiology of development, especially a study of the evolution of hand movements in the development of the normal child. From a comprehensive review of the various neurological and psychological studies upon this subject, the author makes among others the following conclusion: that there is an early period in the development of each part or process when the purpose of education must be to follow the fixed innate heredity line of tendency (fundamental education); that there follows a later period in an activity's development when it passes partially out of the control of racial habit and becomes more plastic to present environment (accessory education). Presented as a dissertation.

BURNHAM, WM. H.: The Study of Adolescence. *Ibid.*, June, 1891, Vol. 1, pp. 174–195.

A brief introduction to the study of the adolescent problem.

BURNHAM, WM. H.: Individual Differences in the Imaginations of Children. *Ibid.*, March, 1893, Vol. 2, pp. 204–225.

Based upon literature and reports by students at the Worcester Normal School.

CHRISMAN, OSCAR: The Secret Language of Children. *Science*, Dec. 1, 1893, Vol. 22, p. 303.

CROSWELL, T. R.: Amusements of Worcester School Children. *Pedagogical Seminary*, Sept., 1899, Vol. 6, pp. 267–371.

A study of the amusements of two thousand children based upon reports by the children. A contribution to the problem of variation in play as conditioned by age, sex, nationality, locality, and season. The results indicate as characteristic of the games of adolescence the coöperation of a number of individuals to secure a definite end, and the delight in contest in contrast with the individualistic amusements of earlier years.

HALL, G. STANLEY: Initiations into Adolescence. *Proc. Am. Antiq. Soc.*, Worcester, Mass., Oct. 21, 1898, Vol. 12, pp. 367–400.

Includes a detailed account of certain rites of primitive peoples, and discusses the relation of adolescent instincts in religion.

LANCASTER, E. G.: The Psychology and Pedagogy of Adolescence. *Pedagogical Seminary*, July, 1897, Vol. 5, pp. 61–128.

A comprehensive study by the *questionnaire* method. With a résumé of the work of others and practical suggestions. Presented as a dissertation.

YODER, A. H.: The Study of the Boyhood of Great Men. *Ibid.*, Oct., 1894, Vol. 3, pp. 134–156.

Based upon the study of a large number of biographies.

Studies of Special Branches of Education from the Genetic Point of View.

ELLIS, A. CASWELL: Sunday-school work and Bible Study in the Light of Modern Pedagogy. *Ibid.*, June, 1896, Vol. 3, pp. 363–412.

An attempt to suggest the psychological method of religious instruction, together with an historical sketch of the Sunday-school idea.

JOHNSON, G. E.: Education by Plays and Games. *Ibid.*, Oct., 1894, Vol. 3, pp. 97–133.

Presents a classified list of about five hundred plays and games with a study of their educational value.

HOYT, WM. A.: The Love of Nature as the Root of teaching and learning the Sciences. *Ibid.*, Oct., 1894, Vol. 3, pp. 61–86.

Based chiefly upon literature, with pedagogical suggestions.

LUKENS, HERMAN T.: Preliminary Report on the Learning of Language. *Ibid.*, June, 1896, Vol. 3, pp. 424–460.

Traces the stages in a child's learning to talk, and presents much data in regard to pronunciation and the development of the sentence.

LUKENS, HERMAN T.: A Study of Children's Drawings. *Ibid.*, Oct., 1896, Vol. 4, pp. 79–110.

A genetic study based upon original reports and observations.

PHILLIPS, D. E.: Number and its Application psychologically considered. *Ibid.*, Oct., 1897, Vol. 5, pp. 221–281.

Includes a study of over two thousand arithmetic papers prepared by children in the schools, the results of a *questionnaire* research, a critical estimate of many text-books, and a discussion of the general subject from the genetic standpoint.

STREET, J. R.: A Study in Moral Education. *Ibid.*, July, 1897, Vol. 5, pp. 5–40.

Based upon the reminiscent answers of adolescents to a *questionnaire*. The results suggest the great rôle of imitation, instruction, the sentiments, and heredity in moral action, and emphasize the significance of habit.

STREET, J. R.: A Study in Language Teaching. *Ibid.*, April, 1897, Vol. 4, pp. 269–293.

Studies in School Hygiene.

BURNHAM, WM. H.: Outlines of School Hygiene. *Ibid.*, June, 1892, Vol. 2, pp. 9–71.

Includes, besides a general survey of school sanitation, brief studies of such topics as fatigue, the period of study, school furniture, the hygiene of writing, etc.

BURNHAM, WM. H.: Bibliography of School Hygiene. *Proc. N. E. A.*, 1898, pp. 505–523.

A selected list of 436 titles.

CHRISMAN, OSCAR: The Hearing of Children. *Pedagogical Seminary*, Dec., 1893, Vol. 2, pp. 397–441.

A résumé of the investigations of the hearing of school children in different countries. Practically complete to the date of publication, with practical suggestions collected from different authorities.

DRESSLAR, F. B.: Fatigue. *Ibid.*, June, 1892, Vol. 2, pp. 102–106.

An introduction to the general subject of mental fatigue.

DRESSLAR, F. B.: A Sketch of Old Schoolhouses. *Ibid.*, June, 1892, Vol. 2, pp. 115–125.

A brief historical contribution to school hygiene.

Principles, Methods, and Organization of Education.

CROSWELL, T. R.: Courses of Study in the Elementary Schools of the United States. *Ibid.*, April, 1897, Vol. 4, pp. 294–335.

Devoted especially to state and city courses and legal requirements.

ELLIS, A. CASWELL: Suggestions for a Philosophy of Education. *Ibid.*, Oct., 1897, Vol. 5, pp. 159–201.

The closing chapter of an extended historical study of the philosophy of education presented as a dissertation.

HALL, G. STANLEY: Child Study the Basis of Exact Education. *Forum*, Dec., 1893, Vol. 16, pp. 429–441.

LUKENS, HERMAN T.: The Correlation of Studies. *Educational Review*, Nov., 1895, Vol. 10, pp. 364–383.

POTTER, J. R.: History of Methods of Instruction in Geography. *Pedagogical Seminary*, Dec., 1891, Vol. 1, pp. 415–424.

Specially an account of German methods, based upon literature.

SCRIPTURE, E. W.: Education as a Science. *Ibid.*, June, 1892, Vol. 2, pp. 111–114.

A plea for experimental education with report of illustrative experiments.

SEARS, CHARLES H.: Home and School Punishments. *Ibid.*, March, 1899, Vol. 6, pp. 159–187.

Based upon literature and the answers to a *questionnaire*.

The Training of Teachers.

BURK, FREDERICK L.: The Training of Teachers. *Atlantic Monthly*, Oct., 1897, Vol. 80, pp. 547–561, and June, 1898, Vol. 81, pp. 769–779.

BURNHAM, WM. H.: Higher Pedagogical Seminaries in Germany. *Pedagogical Seminary*, Dec., 1891, Vol. 1, pp. 390–408.

A sketch of the history and present character of the different kinds of pedagogical seminaries for training teachers for the higher schools in Germany, based on literature and personal observation.

BURNHAM, WM. H.: Some Aspects of the Teaching Profession. *Forum*, June, 1898, Vol. 25, pp. 481–495.

HALL, G. STANLEY: American Universities and the Training of Teachers. *Ibid.*, April and May, 1894, Vol. 17, pp. 148–159, 297–309.

HALL, G. STANLEY: The Training of Teachers. *Ibid.*, Sept., 1890, Vol. 10, pp. 11–22.

HALL, G. STANLEY: Research the Vital Spirit of Teaching. *Ibid.*, July, 1894, Vol. 17, pp. 558–570.

PHILLIPS, D. E.: The Teaching Instinct. *Pedagogical Seminary*, March, 1899, Vol. 6, pp. 188–245.

A study of the phenomena of leadership and teaching among animals and children, of the lives and motives of the great teachers, and of training in relation to the teaching instinct, including a contribution by the *questionnaire* method. Presented as a dissertation.

REIGART, J. F.: The Training of Teachers in England. *Ibid.*, Dec., 1891, Vol. 1, pp. 409–416.

A brief sketch based upon literature.

Miscellaneous.

BURK, FREDERICK L.: Teasing and Bullying. *Pedagogical Seminary*, April, 1897, Vol. 4, pp. 336–371.

Based on returns to a *questionnaire*.

HALL, G. STANLEY: Boy Life in a Massachusetts Country Town Thirty Years Ago. *Proc. Am. Antiq. Soc.*, Worcester, Mass., Oct. 21, 1890, N. S., Vol. 7, pp. 107–128.

An historical contribution showing the many-sidedness of the home education of the New England country boy.

HALL, G. STANLEY: The Case of the Public Schools. *Atlantic Monthly*, March, 1896, Vol. 77, pp. 402–413.

HALL, G. STANLEY: The Love and Study of Nature: a Part of Education. *Agriculture of Massachusetts*, 1898, pp. 134–154. Lectures delivered before the Massachusetts State Board of Agriculture at Amherst, Dec. 6, 1898.

Treats of the child's attitude toward nature.

HANCOCK, JOHN A.: An Early Phase of the Manual Training Movement. *Ibid.*, Oct., 1897, Vol. 5, pp. 287-292.

A brief historical sketch of the old manual labor school.

JOHNSON, G. E.: Contribution to the Psychology and Pedagogy of Feeble-minded Children. *Ibid.*, Oct., 1895, Vol. 3, pp. 246–291.

Reports result of tests of memory span, motor ability, and association, in feeble-minded children at the Massachusetts School for the Feeble-minded at Waltham, together with an historical introduction and practical suggestions for their education.

KISTLER, MILTON S.: John Knox's Services to Education. *Education*, Oct., 1898, Vol. 19, pp. 105–116.

KLINE, LINUS W.: Truancy as Related to the Migratory Instinct. *Pedagogical Seminary*, Jan., 1898, Vol. 5, pp. 381–420.

Includes a comparison of the physical condition of truants as shown by anthropometric tests with that of public school children.

SHELDON, HENRY D.: The Institutional Activities of American Children. *Am. Jour. of Psy.*, July, 1898, Vol. 9, pp. 425–448.

Based largely on returns to a *questionnaire*.

SMALL, M. H.: Methods of manifesting the Instinct for Certainty. *Pedagogical Seminary*, Jan., 1898, Vol. 5, pp. 313–380.

A comprehensive study of oaths based upon 2,263 answers to a *questionnaire* and a vast amount of literature.

Such have been the methods of the department, and such in part the work done. The aim has been to treat a few subjects in a broad way, rather than to exhaust the field of conventional pedagogy. The necessity and the advantages of this method are obvious from a brief consideration of the subject of education, both theoretical and practical.

Jean Paul Richter quotes the French artist who required from a good director of the ballet, besides the art of dancing, only geometry, music, poetry, painting, and anatomy. "But," he adds, "to write upon education means to write upon almost everything at once; for it has to care for and watch over the development of an entire . . . world in little,—a microcosm of the macrocosm. . . . If we carried the subject still further, every century, every nation, and even every boy and every girl, would require a distinct system of education, a different primer and domestic French governess, etc."[1] The subject of pedagogy is still more encyclopædic to-day than when Jean Paul Richter wrote these words. Its foundation involves the whole physiology and psychology of development in the individual, and the history of culture in the race, and its superstructure includes, not only all the various forms and systems and methods of education, but the study of the influence of environment in the widest sense.

The conventional views minimize both the difficulties and the importance of the subject. It is said that pedagogy is applied psychology or applied child study, and again that pedagogy must get its norms from the history of education and from child study. This statement will do if one knows what it involves. The history of education means the history of civilization from its earliest traceable genesis among primitive peoples. It means a study of types of culture and the conditions of their development. In a word, it is a study of the evolution of education. Child study means, too, the study of the physiology and psychology of development in man. The science of development aims to give a complete description of all the stages of physical development from infancy to maturity, to show their sequence and their relation to the acquisition of organic, sensory, motor, and psychic processes. As far as psychology goes, it is genetic psychology, which means more than is frequently connoted by child study. Adult psychology is one thing, relatively fixed, except for variations incident to environment or the individual. Child psychology, even for a single individual and a given environment, varies continually because the individual is in the process of growth and rapid development of function. It is one thing for the infant, a very different

[1] Richter, "Levana, or the Doctrine of Education," Author's Preface.

thing for the child who can walk and talk, still another at that plateau in the curve of development that seems to come somewhere between nine and twelve for girls and ten and fourteen for boys, still another for the adolescent. The variation is seen in the period of a single year, almost with the changing moons. This is true, not only on account of the grosser acquisitions, but is seen in the sequence of interests and activities. Child psychology is protean. It varies not only with the individual and the environment, but especially with the stage of development. Further, the science of development includes comparative psychology. Not only must the child mind be compared with the adult mind, but the stages of development in the child should be compared with the stages of development in animals, the faculties of the child with those in animals, the motor ability and activities of the child with those in animals. And again, the stages of development in the child must be compared with those in the race; ontogenesis in relation to phylogenesis must be studied.

All this is scientific study, not directly practical. Before deriving the norms for practical pedagogy, a propædeutic study must be made. As Professor James has said: "Psychology is a science, and teaching is an art; and sciences never generate arts directly out of themselves. An intermediary inventive mind must make the application by using its originality." This mediating function is represented by two somewhat vaguely defined branches of pedagogy — educational psychology, and the general principles and methods of education.

Again, after the general principles of education have been derived from psychology and history, and the theoretical norms established, they must be verified by practical educational experiments. This brings us to the practical side of pedagogy represented by such subjects as the organization of schools, the art of teaching, and special didactics. And parallel with the art of teaching in its derivation from the science of development is school hygiene, which studies especially the conditions that favor the healthy development of the school child. Thus pedagogy is both theoretical and practical, at once a science (at least potentially) and an art.

Such is the subject which, as the Italian proverb runs, is always poor and naked, and, in the words of a German writer, has long sat as a drudge at the academic hearth, and whose highest recognition in the great universities has usually been as the handmaid of philosophy. Everybody believes in education, yet few believe in pedagogy. The reasons for this are obvious. Apart from a few fundamentals that are almost commonplace, pedagogy has lacked a solid body of scientific knowledge and universally accepted principles. Worse than this, it has lacked a definite method and a definite ignorance.

Most of the works on the history of education are padded with accounts of second-rate writers and second-rate books that happen to be labelled educational; while the really great educators have often been neglected, and educational movements have been described as isolated currents in the progress of civilization, without regard to their vital connection with political, social, and industrial movements. The method has been the elementary method of studying and describing isolated facts without regard to historical perspective and causal relations; and even the works of the classic writers have been chiefly the repetition and recasting of a few old truths which had been forgotten or were ignored at the time in which the reformers lived. For example, Comenius two hundred and fifty years ago taught that we must study nature by the inductive method and adapt education to the sequence of the stages of natural development; but his writings were forgotten, and again and again the reformers have had to teach again to a new generation the simplest principles of the Comenian didactic. Most of the books on the educational systems of to-day, in like manner, consist of the barren details of organization and method, and the description often of inferior teachers and schools. The forces that have produced these teachers and schools, the significance of the educational movements, have not been seen; and the philosophical, social, and religious thought that has determined educational ideals has not been studied. These isolated facts are barren. Their real significance is in their relation to other facts. We cannot, for example, understand the educational events in England to-day unless we know something of the wider relations of the school movement. The wrangling over the question whether the parish of Eastbourne shall have a school board, or whether the school education of the parish shall continue to be supplied by voluntary schools, means a great deal more than a difference in taxes of a few pence in the pound. This petty struggle is a part of the great movement for the disestablishment of the Church of England. The commissioning of a new fellow for university extension work marks another step in the progress of the democratic ideal, which, no longer satisfied with provision for elementary education for every child, now demands also for each individual, according to his ability, a share in higher education. A new endowment for a technical school by the Worshipful Society of Goldsmiths, or the like, may indicate a new dread of democracy on the part of certain monopolists quite as much as any special interest in industrial education. Oxford itself, with all its marvellous beauty and idealism, the stronghold of conservatism, cannot keep aloof from the great social, industrial, and educational movements outside. No better illustration could be chosen to show the progress of the democratic ideal in education. At the beginning of Queen Victoria's reign one could not even study at Oxford without subscribing to the Thirty-nine Articles. A few years ago Jowett advocated opening the university honors and emoluments to the world, admitting anybody to any university examination without restriction of sect, class, race, age, or residence. As was remarked at the time, if fifty or perhaps twenty years ago a radical undergraduate were to have made such suggestions, he would have stood a chance of being expelled from the university, as Shelley was, for blasphemy; now they are the last words of Jowett, quoted with approval before the vice-chancellor.

To miss these larger aspects is to miss everything of permanent value. Historical literature in education has relatively little importance for its direct practical teachings; but the importance of the history of education as a culture subject can hardly be put too high. Education represents one of the deepest human interests, more vital than politics, and well-nigh as universal as religion. The history of education is the history of the development of civilization. It aims at nothing less than the study of the school as a factor in the development of culture in relation to the other factors in education, — the home, the church, the farm, the workshop, the playground, and the rest. And it aims at the study of educational movements in their genesis, and in relation to political, social, industrial, scientific, and literary movements. This involves not merely the study of educational writers so-called and school systems, but the study of types of culture and the causes that condition them.

Likewise in the other parts of the field the failure to recognize the wider significance of the subjects studied, and the attempt to build systems before the foundations were laid, have brought pedagogy into disrepute. But in recent years the conviction has grown that educational problems must be studied inductively; and, better still, important contributions by the inductive method have actually been made. This has put life into the subject and given hope for the future. Take child study as an illustration. The significance of the modern study of children is not merely the renewed emphasis on the old truth of adapting education to the stages of development, but the insight that the only way to make this principle vital is concrete inductive study to find out just what are the stages of natural development. Thus every fact in regard to general development or individual variation is deemed significant, and the student is willing to wait for a new science of development before attempting a permanent pedagogical system.

During the past ten years the opportunities for truly scientific work in education have been shown as never before, methods of investigation have been demonstrated, and in part the foundations of a science have been laid. The things now needed are trained men and facilities. With them a solid content of scientific knowledge can be acquired that will place historical and social pedagogy on as firm a basis as general history and sociology, and genetic pedagogy on a scientific footing comparable to that of psychology. School hygiene has already its methods and a solid body of knowledge, but it needs special laboratories for instruction and research, either independent or in connection with psychology, physiology, and anthropology.

The work in pedagogy in this University, although the practical aspects of the subjects studied have not been neglected, has been chiefly in the more scientific and theoretical parts of the field. It is not less important on this account. Pedagogical study, like research in any other field of history or science, is valuable for its own sake without regard primarily to practical results. It is its own justification and its own reward. With the nucleus of solid scientific contributions that now exists, no university can long afford to omit courses in education from its curriculum, whether they have any practical value or not. Such scientific studies, however, cannot be divorced from the practical art of education. The studies of children have emphasized the doctrine that the aim of childhood is its own development, and the best guarantee of normal maturity is normal childhood and immaturity; in a word, they have emphasized the principles of normal development. But these principles are no longer pedagogical abstractions; they are greatly modifying the practical work of education, causing greater regard for individual children rather than uniform classes, for health rather than scholastic products, for a psychological order of instruction adapted to the capacity and interests of children rather than logical sequence and articulation of grades. In a word, they are causing courses of study and methods to be reconstructed with regard to the one fundamental principle of fostering normal growth and development. To mention a few details, ten years ago school baths, adjustable seats and desks, and vertical script, were vagaries of university theorists; to-day they are deemed essentials in the best schools. Ten years ago suggestions of periodic disinfection of school apparatus and school text-books, of investigating pupils' individual capacity and power to resist fatigue, and of adapting education to individual capacity and interest, in elementary and secondary schools, were likely to be ridiculed; now their soundness has been demonstrated by practical experiments.

What part this University has had in this movement, it is not easy to say; but it has always advocated such reforms in the regular courses of lectures; many addresses on topics in school hygiene and pedagogy have been given outside the University before schools and teachers' meetings; students from this University have become school superintendents, teachers in secondary schools, professors of pedagogy or psychology in normal schools, professors of pedagogy in colleges and universities; and teachers and educators from all parts of the country have attended lectures on pedagogy during the sessions of the Summer School.

To make a department of pedagogy what it should be, it is necessary that the whole field of education be covered by lectures as far as possible, that the more elementary courses be given every year, that research should be extended to the multitude of topics that offer opportunity for study. Nowhere in the world is a complete course in pedagogy covering all the important parts of the field given. Here and there throughout this country and Europe are offered a few truly scientific courses, but the subject will hardly attain its due academic dignity until somewhere in one university are given courses which approximate an adequate treatment of the whole field. That this University might approximate a complete course in the subject are needed an addition to the staff, especially for the study of historical and social pedagogy, the establishment of special fellowships for educational research, a laboratory for school anthropometry and school hygiene, a great enlargement of the educational museum, a pedagogical library like that of the *Musée pédagogique* in Paris, where educational literature of every kind, both good and bad, may be collected; and, finally, a model school for the objectification of ideals, under the direction of competent teachers who should safeguard the interests of the pupils, but offer to university students opportunities for observation, and in some cases for practice in school work.

The aim of such a course in pedagogy, like that of the more limited course already given in this University, would be twofold: first, to contribute something to the body of knowledge in regard to education, the content of pedagogy; and, second, to give practical training to students preparing to become teachers. These two aims are quite in harmony, for an essential in the training of a teacher is the development of those permanent professional interests and that professional apperception and prevision acquired by the study of the more scientific parts of pedagogy.

PHILOSOPHY.

By G. Stanley Hall.

In addition to my own work in psychology and education, reported in the preceding articles by my colleagues, Drs. Sanford and Burnham, and in editing the *American Journal of Psychology* and the *Pedagogical Seminary*, I have lectured during the last eight years on the History of Philosophy. This course is felt to be of cardinal importance for those studying either psychology or education, to give them breadth of view, to teach what great problems have interested the race, and to give a repertory of general ideas that will obviate some of the dangers of specialization.

The course begins with a very brief survey of Oriental speculation, treats the pre-Socratic Greek thinkers with considerable detail and with constant reference to their fragmentary texts. Great stress is laid upon Plato, and from a quarter to half of all his works are read aloud by the students in turn from Jowett's translation, and on these dialogues the examination for the doctorate is in some part based. Even for those who read some Greek, the use of the English translation is preferred, because more can be gained from Plato by men of this grade by extensive reading than by intensive and critical study of text. Discussions often arise in this work. Aristotle is treated in the same manner, and selections and sometimes large portions of some of his works are read in English. From twelve to twenty lectures are given on the later schools, ending with Plotenus and Proclus. This usually concludes the work of the first year.

Until two years ago the second year began with the rise of scholasticism and the third ended with Schopenhauer, Lotze, Hartmann, and contemporary writers. Special effort has always been made to go considerably outside the stock text-book field and to deal to some extent with the history of science, with some reference to medicine and with very slight reference to literature, art, etc. The texts of Spinoza, Locke, Berkeley,

Hume, Kant, Fichte, Schelling, Hegel, Schopenhauer, and Lotze have been used at different times and with very different results. Ethics, logic, metaphysics, and aesthetics are included in this course, and no special courses in any of these subjects have been given, although logical and ethical questions are treated in my psychological course. Considerable time is always given to epistemology.

Two years ago, after considerable previous preparation, a course in Christology and Patristics was inserted between the ancient and the modern course as above described. The life of Jesus was treated concisely and reverently from the standpoint of psychology, which is felt to be very different from that of the current lives of Jesus. This course, although at present being repeated with amplification, is still too incomplete to warrant any final report upon its utility. On the whole this historic course, which occupies three years, is earnestly recommended to all students of psychology, religion, education, or any of the humanities, and has generally been taken by all.

During the past eight years I have opened my house one evening every week of the academic year to all students in the department of psychology and related themes from seven to ten o'clock. We began by discussing philosophical topics assigned beforehand to leaders in turn. One year most of the time of this seminary was devoted to reading and discussing Jowett's Plato.[1] Schopenhauer, Kant, and Hegel were tried for briefer periods, but gradually, as the numbers have increased and as the rule that each man should devote a portion of his time to some original investigation has prevailed, the evening has been occupied by each student in turn, who presents his thesis or subject, or a part of it, which is then freely discussed by the other members. The debates are often animated, as nearly every standpoint is represented. There are clergymen, young professors from other institutions, Hegelian idealists, Kantian epistemologists, and men of empirical science, and from these various directions nearly every subject is really illuminated. Attendance is never enforced, and the light refreshments served in the middle of the evening have never been an attraction, but only a welcome break from continued tension. The attendance for the last few years has rarely been

[1] See a somewhat disguised account of the first semester's work in two articles by H. Austin Aikins, entitled "From the Reports of the Plato Club." *Atlantic Monthly*, Sept. and Oct., 1894, Vol. 74, pp. 359–366, 470–480.

under fifteen and rarely over forty, so that the entire freedom and informality of conversation has been the rule. The themes assigned in a way described later have been presented here in so compact and forcible a way, that the seminary has been one of the most effective agents in my own education, and I think all its members share my sentiments in this respect. Here the new work on which each individual is spending so much of his year's time is pooled for the common benefit, the reader has the healthful stimulus of emulation in interesting his audience, acquires valuable practice in the methods of effective presentation, and always receives help in the way of new literature, references, the pointing out of defects in argument or method; and conflicts are thus most surely avoided. Often other professors from the University attend, and the list of distinguished guests from abroad who have either participated in the discussions or introduced matter of their own is a long and dignified one. There is rarely any lack of interest or reluctance to discuss, and very infrequently is the animation too great for healthful mental circulation. Here nearly everything that has been done by the student members of this department of the University has been carefully wrought over, some of it more than once.

Such stimulus I believe to be unsurpassed in educational value. The dialectic give and take of the conversational method, the mental alertness of debate, the charm of friendly intercourse upon high themes, which Lotze, like some of the ancients, thought the highest joy of life and the consummate fruition of friendship, are here combined in judicious proportions most favorable to growth. Some European seminaries are devoted to discussions of minute points; in others the student is simply a literary forager for the professors; quite frequently some author is read; but for our American needs, at least for Clark University, I think the method now settled upon is more educative than any other that I have seen.

A word should be said concerning student lectures. At various periods during the decade each member of the department has been requested to take his turn in presenting some subject in due form before the class, taking my place at the lecturer's desk, and developing his theme with the aid of charts, blackboard, and specimens if need be; and at the close of the lecture I have a personal interview, stating very frankly any faults of manner, automatism, voice, method of presentation, etc., liable to interfere with his usefulness as instructor or lecturer. More often, in place of an original lecture, each man takes his turn in digesting with extracts some book or chapter of a standard work in the history of philosophy, with the same criticisms. This personal relation together with the many hours spent each week with individuals, elsewhere spoken of, has been, I believe, of great value.

At the beginning of the year (or, for those who have already spent a year at the University, near the close of the spring term) careful lists of subjects which seem to the instructors in the department ripe for investigation are prepared. Each jots down all suggestions in this direction during the year, and all now meet to compare themes, consider whether they have already been treated, what new books and apparatus each will necessitate, by what paths each can best be approached and which are likely to yield the best and (what for thesis work is of great importance) the most certain results of value. Conferences with each individual are then held and each is urged to select some theme, either because it is congenial or because it represents a field he desires to enter, and to devote some considerable portion of the year to the effort to master it and to add something new, however small, to the sum of the world's knowledge.

A really good subject has aspects or divisions that bring the student into contact with each professor in the department, and each gives everything in the way of information, stimulus, and references that he possibly can. Our plan has always been to allow the student to print such work over his own name and to have full credit, although he usually makes acknowledgements at the close of his paper to his helpers. This plan we have found very congenial and stimulating to students, and it has avoided all questions of ownership rights in intellectual property. Again, a good subject must be midway between a very large and general and a very minutely special standpoint. The student must not waste his energy in vague generalities on the one hand, nor must he be shut up to some petty problem, perhaps fitting into and aiding the professor's special work, being thus unduly subordinated and apprenticed to him, as is so common in Germany. Fitting the problem to the man so that it will enlist all his interest and focus his knowledge and effort is half the work.

In beginning more or less independent research like this, our best college graduates are often in a sense suddenly reduced back to infancy and need constant individual help to go alone. For the last ten years most of several afternoons a week of my own time has been given in the laboratory, library, and conference room in trying to assist and direct young men to launch out in some modest yet effective way, as becomes them, on the great life of discovery. Some, often the best scholars, are so tied to authority that it is hard for them to be brought to realize that the best things have neither been done nor said in the world, and that mastery of the text-book is not final. Others are strongly inclined to repeat experiments, multiply observations, and accumulate numbers, and find it hard to make a serious study of the real significance of their data. Some approach subjects with preconceived ideas and speculate in a deductive way, abhorring details which others get lost in. Every type of philosophical opinion and every shade of temperament, every degree of intellectual enterprise at almost every rate of progress, is represented. Some are strong in the literary, historical, and antiquarian side of their topic; others in its experimental technique or in statistical presentation and tabulation or in literary form; some at once tend to lose themselves in aspects of the subject that are so large that, instead of coming to a conclusion in an academic year, they begin to anxiously plan a life work and anticipate remote difficulties; while others can see absolutely nothing in topics of great range and significance except some over elaborately fortified or proven fact.

This form of modern university work is a new kind of high Socratic midwifery, but in my opinion it is the most beneficial of all the points of contact between professor and student. Some must be encouraged; others must be roundly scolded. Some would devote all their time to an interesting work of this kind, while others dawdle with it as a mere side issue of doubtful educational value. A few do not want it, but are contented with receptivity of what others have done. Restless ones often seek change of theme, so that great discretion and great patience are needed in this work.

Its rewards, however, are incomparably great. Having once discovered a fact or made ever so small an original contribution and had the baptism of printer's ink, the novitiate is henceforth a changed man. His ideals of culture, standards of attainment and excellence, and his methods of work are slowly revolutionized from this centre. Instead of being a passive recipient, his mind has tasted a free and creative activity which puts him on his mettle like the first taste of blood to a young tiger. He has learned that achievement and not possession is the end and aim; his mind has been brought to a *focus* in such a way that he now knows what real concentration means as never before. He realizes that almost every subject in the universe, if broadly seen, is connected with every other, and that the cosmos, like his own mind, is knit together into a unity of a higher order. In all his works and ways he is more independent and more inclined to seek, do, know, and experience for himself. By such personal conference with individuals at all stages of their preparation in such a work, which need not be a doctor's dissertation and often is not, I am convinced, after a decade of experience here and some years of the same work at the Johns Hopkins, that this is the highest criterion of an academic teacher's real efficiency in his vocation, and that it is as much above the mass teaching of the lecture-room as talent is above mere learning. The necessity of this work is one of the chief reasons why truly university work must always be done, if not at small institutions, at least in squads so small that they can be thus individualized.

Having brought this work to some degree of completion, as should be done at the close of each academic year, even at some sacrifice of scientific quality (because educational values should take precedence even over this, where the two conflict), an indispensable requisite is publicity and that without delay. Any institution or department that confers a doctorate upon the ground of a dissertation that is unpublished conceals that upon which the chief value of the degree rests. The older the student the more stress should be laid upon this part of the work as compared with acquisition. In most departments, science is progressing so rapidly and work is so often duplicated that the necessity of announcing beforehand the theme of each research has often been urged, and any considerable interval between the completion of a work and its publication involves danger of anticipation by others, as well as general loss of value from the progress of science, which is always slowly leaving everything behind. Chiefly to avoid this danger the journals of this University were established, in which, without the cost to the students generally insisted upon elsewhere and with the advantage of a more or less extended international circulation among experts, everything can be speedily brought to the knowledge of those most interested and competent. To know that results will thus appear without delay is itself a real stimulus, and it is fortunate that evaluation of such work is coming to be a more and more prominent factor in determining appointments to university positions. The quality of mind which makes success here is infinitely more inspiring to students, even of lower grades, than the rehearsal of second-hand knowledge perhaps many removes from its source. Very much might be said upon the effect of research as a stimulant to the teacher, while, from still another point of view, the fact that the instructor has entered the great arena and submitted his productions to the critical estimate of experts, gives his pupils confidence in him as an authority and not a mere echo. The provision of a sufficient number of reprints for circulation among special journals that will notice each work, and for exchange with other productive workers or departments, is another one of the new university problems unknown to the college, to the fuller exploitation of which the new journal here contemplated and elsewhere spoken of will be devoted.

Great importance has always been attached here to the methods of bringing students into immediate and personal contact with the latest literature, especially upon the topics of their theses or those related to the original researches upon which they may be engaged. The exchanges of the journals constitute a carefully selected list of nearly three score periodicals, all of which, besides those regularly subscribed for by the library, are immediately available. Besides these the journals receive a large number of the most important books and pamphlets within their field, especially from American, English, French, and German houses. These works together with the smaller resources of my own library, which mainly supplements that of the University, are at the disposal of students, who are often encouraged to write brief book notices for publication. The frequent personal conferences with each student in the department keeps the instructor's mind alert to find out and bring to the immediate notice of each anything bearing upon his theme. Meetings are occasionally held in my library, where I spend the evening going through my shelves, taking out the books that I deem most important and that have helped me most, briefly characterizing each, and passing it around for actual inspection. If I had at my disposal an hour's time of a dozen of the most eminent men to utilize in such a way as would be of greatest benefit to me, I think I should ask them to do precisely this, for they would thus be giving me to some extent a key to their own intellectual activity and direction. Where this method is extended to monographs and pamphlet publications, the collection of which our system of exchanging theses promises to greatly enrich, its value is still greater for special students.

Genetic psychology, which one sub-department of this University so conspicuously represents, is far larger than the child-study of mothers' clubs or teachers' associations. It is simply the entrance of Darwinism into the field of mind. Underneath it lies the great transforming conception that the soul is as complex, as old, and as gradually unfolded as the body, and like it must be studied comparatively in view of all that the psychic life of the lower or even the lowest organisms can teach us. The new methods cross-section the old classification methods which make memory, will, perception, imagination, etc., so many faculties, and seek to trace the origins of the higher mental powers to their faintest beginnings near the dawn of animal life. The most fundamental activities are those whose roots extend lowest down in the scale of existence, and these are also they that send their tops highest. The conception that mind, as we know it in consciousness, has been developed out of something very different that, like organic forms, tends to vary and change indefinitely is a new conception and is sure eventually to reconstruct out of new and old elements a far larger and more adequate city of Man-soul with reformed administrative, educational, religious, and other functions. This movement appears in biology in the tendency to study psychic phenomena in the most rudimentary and microcosmic organisms. It appears again in the new and careful studies of instinct in the higher animals, where conditions can be varied and educational experiments conducted with great precaution and detail. Another root of the genetic movement is in the anthropology of myth, custom and belief among primitive and savage peoples; another in the studies of degenerative types among the defective classes, where decay has inverted the evolutionary order.

It is on this foundation that the child-study movement rests, and its amazing development cannot be adequately explained without a due appreciation of this wider field. The minute observation and annotation, the measuring and weighing of a single child, or the collective study of one topic upon the basis of returns from very large numbers of children with the help of questionnaires, anthropometric work with its carefully wrought out averages, — all this appeals to the instinctive love of children; out of it has grown the new conception of childhood as the most generic period of life, wherein the limitations of individuality are not yet so painfully apparent as in adults, and it has given us new conceptions concerning the nature of genius, the laws of growth, the origin of fear, anger, love, the conditions of health, the nascent periods of maximal interest in special lines and topics, until at last education seems likely to have under it a far more solid and scientific foundation than it has ever yet attained. While this subject has as yet occupied but a slight and recent portion of our curriculum, so much has already been accomplished as to warrant the very fairest hopes for the future. Among the first results likely to be witnessed are the gradual transformation of the methods of teaching and of investigating the problems of the special philosophical disciplines somewhat analogous to the transformation of anatomy and morphology under the influence of embryology. How far this movement will extend among the other university studies, and whether with or without any new coördination of the successive stages of individual growth with the historic development of different philosophical systems as first presented by Hegel, it is impossible to foretell.

THE LIBRARY.

By Louis N. Wilson, Librarian.

From the foundation of the University the library has been considered an important factor and has received a great deal of attention from the Founder, President, and Faculty. Immediately upon his appointment, the President requested each member of the University to draw up a list of books in his special field, laying particular stress upon important serials and special monographs. These lists were carefully collated, duplicates weeded out, and arranged in order for purchase. The total number of items amounted in June, 1889, to upward of fifteen thousand, a very large proportion being books and journals in foreign languages. In order to secure for the University the best possible rates, lists of standard works, both in sets and single volumes, were submitted for competition to a number of well-known booksellers both in this country and in Europe. This necessitated some delay, but it was fully warranted by the resultant saving in cost.

To illustrate this point, the figures submitted by five firms for an identical list of 742 items are given here, viz.: $1806.30, $1810.90, $1971.86, $2055.89, $2166.41, showing a maximum difference of $360.11.

After carefully comparing all the lists sent in, and taking into consideration the condition of the books offered, orders were placed with firms in New York, Boston, London, Paris, Berlin, Leipzig, and Vienna.

During the past few years, owing to our very peculiar and constantly changing customs and postal regulations, it has become more and more desirable to import from Europe through some responsible bookseller in this country, in order to avoid the frequent and often vexatious annoyances consequent upon individual importations. Having decided upon a particular bookseller, orders were freely placed with the understanding that the library should receive the lowest possible rates consistent with good service, and from time to time lists were sent to other firms in order to be assured that the agreement was faithfully carried out. A recent test of this kind showed the following quotations for thirty-five volumes, $105.26, $107.57, $120.00. In general, the plan has worked exceedingly well.

During the summer of 1889, while these orders were being executed, Mr. Clark placed the first books in the library by donating about thirty-two hundred volumes. A large proportion of these, on history, biography and travel, were given with the original bookcases as they had stood in his own private library. Another part of the collection consisted of the following sets of bound periodicals, almost all complete down to the end of 1883: *Atlantic Monthly, Blackwood's Magazine, Century Magazine, Cornhill Magazine, Edinburgh Review, Fortnightly Review, Gentleman's Magazine, Harper's Magazine, Littell's Living Age, Macmillan's Magazine, North American Review, North British Review, Notes and Queries, Popular Science Monthly, Putnam's Magazine, Quarterly Review,* and *Scribner's Monthly,* also a set of the Report on the Scientific Results of the Voyage of H. M. S. *Challenger*, during the years 1872–76. Yet a third part consisted of a large number of rare old books, some of which are fine examples of early printing when there was no title-page, no pagination, date, or printer's name, and where the initial letters were omitted to be inserted later by hand. Of these fine old volumes, the following are mentioned as examples:—

Paulus de Sancta Maria Scrutinium scripturarum. Probably the oldest book in our library, with no title-page, colophon, pagination, or signatures. Rubricated throughout.

Rationale divinorum officiorum. Supposed to have been printed at Basle in 1474–75.

Astexanis Suma. Libri VIII., de preceptis, de virtutibus et viciis; de sacramentis de sacro penitentie, de sacramento ordinis, de excommunicatione; de matrimonio. Venetiis, 1478.

Roberti Caraczoli de Licio de timore divinorum judiciorum ac de morte. Nuremberge, 1479.

Alberti de Padua expositio Evangeliorum dominicalium totius anni et concordancia quatuor evangelistarum in passionem dominicam a Nicolao Vinckelspickel. Ulm, 1480.

Sancti Thome de Aquino ordinis predicatorum super quarto libro sententiarum preclarum opus. Venetiis, 1481.

Liber moralitatum elegantissimus magnarum rerum naturalium lumen anime dictus. 1482.

Sancti Hieronimi Vite Patrum Sanctorum Egiptiorum. Nurnberg (Koburger) 1483.

Blondi Flavii historiarum ab inclinatione Romanorum Imperii, libri XI. Venetiis per Octavianum Scotum. 1483.

Johannis de Turrecremata questionum dignissimarum cum solutionibus earumdem, etc. Daventriæ, 1484. A work of the celebrated Spanish Dominican Juan de Torquemada.

Legende de sancti composte per Jacobo de Voragine. Venetia, 1484.

An old German almanac beautifully printed in red and black and pasted on one of the covers of *Hieronimi Vitæ Patrum.* It runs from 1486 to 1579, and was probably printed at the earlier date.

Summa Rainerij de Pisis. Venetiis, 1486.

Liber Cronicarum cum figuris et imaginibus ab initio mundi usque nunc temporis Impressum ac finitum in vigilia purificationis Marie in imperiali urbe Augusta a Johanne Schensperger. Anno ab incarnatione domini 1497. The so-called *Nuremberg Chronicle,* with numerous woodcuts by Wolgemuth, the master of Albrecht Durer.

Sermones Pomerii de Tempore Hyemales et Estivales et sermones quadragesimales per Helbartum de Themeswar. Hagenaw, 1502. With rubricated initials.

Pauli Jovii elogia virorum bellica virtute illustrium veris imaginibus supposita, quae apud Musæum spectantur. Florentiæ, 1551.

Ramusio, Primo volume, & Terza edizione delle navigationi et viaggi. Venetia, Giunti, 1563. The first volume of Ramusio's well-known collection of voyages and travels, containing among other things Pigafetta's log during the first voyage around the world under Magalhães.

Missale Romanum, ex Decreto Sacrosancti Concilii Tridentini restitutum, Pii V. Pont. Max. jussu editum. Venetiis, apud Juntas, 1602.

The Bible: that is the Holy Scriptures contained in the Old and New Testament. London, 1610. A copy of the so-called Breeches Bible.

Missale Romanum, ex Decreto Sacrosancti concilii Tridentini restitutum, Pii V. Pont. Max. jussu editum et Clementis VIII. auctoritate recognitum. Ingolstadii, 1610.

Montanus (Arnoldus) De Nieuwe en Onbekende Weereld of Beschryving van America. Amsterdam, 1671. An old description of America in Dutch.

Esquemeling (John) and Ringrose (Basil), History of the Bucaniers of America. London, 1695. Esquemeling, who spent many years at Tortuga, gives here a very graphic account of the buccaneers.

Armenian Bible. Venice, 1805. Fleeing from the persecution of their orthodox brethren, the Catholic Armenians of the mechitaristic order established themselves at the island of San Lazzaro, granted them by the Republic of Venice. Many a learned volume issued from their press, of which this is a specimen.

New Testament in Lettish language. Mitau, 1816.

Select Fables; with cuts, designed and engraved by Thomas and John Bewick, previous to the year 1784; together with a Memoir and a descriptive catalogue of the works of Messrs. Bewick. Newcastle, 1820. Thomas Bewick is considered the restorer of wood engraving in England.

Cookson (Mrs. James). Flowers drawn and painted after nature in India. 1834.

In addition to a number of books presented to the library by President Hall, we are indebted for gifts to the following citizens of Worcester: Hon. George F. Hoar, Mr. Henry J. Howland, Hon. Henry L. Parker, Mr. Samuel H. Putnam,[1] the late Hon. W. W. Rice, Hon. Stephen Salisbury, Hon. John D. Washburn, and Hon. John E. Russell of Leicester.

To receive the books temporary wooden stacks were erected in the main library room, and so substantially were they constructed that they are still serviceable. Solid oak shelving was put up on both sides of the reading-room, adjoining the main library room, with a three-foot projecting shelf three and a half feet from the floor, upon which the current numbers of periodicals are displayed.

To the problem of cataloguing and classification, always a difficult one, both the President and the members of the Faculty gave a good deal of time and attention. It was felt that the scheme of classification must not be too rigid, and that nothing should be allowed to interfere with the free use of the books by all members of the University. The books were first carefully classified upon the shelves by departments, and marked as follows: —

A. Works of General Reference.
B. Journals.
C. Mathematics.
D. Physics.
E. Chemistry.
F. Zoölogy.
G. Physiology.
H. Pathology.
I. Psychology.
J. Philosophy.
K. Ethics.
L. Criminology.
M. Anthropology.
N. Education.
O. Botany.

The various subdivisions in each department may be inferred from that of the mathematical department.

[1] A copy of "*Justini historici clarissimi in Trogi Pompeii historias Libri XLIIII.*" *Venice, Jenson. 1470.* Duke de Noailles' copy of the *editio princeps*. "*Virorum illustrium vitae ex Plutarcho Graeco in Latinum versae Solerterque, cura emendate feliciter expliciunt:*" *per Nicolaum Jenson Gallicum Venetiis impressae. 1478, die. II Januarii.* 2 vols. "The Scientific Papers of James Clerk Maxwell." Edited by W. D. Niven, F. R. S. The University Press, Cambridge, 1890. 2 vols.

C.—MATHEMATICS.

In Mathematics, C, the books are grouped in ten divisions, designated by the numerals 1, 2, 3, 4, 5, 6, 7, 8, 9, 0, immediately following the letter C; every division is subdivided into sections of which each is designated by a second numeral following that indicating the division. The cipher, 0, always denotes a miscellaneous division or section. The mathematical works are arranged on the shelves in accordance with the following classification, the subdivisions of which, however, are not all used at present. The italicized part of each title is that printed on the sliding shelf label.

C 1. HISTORY AND PHILOSOPHY.
- C 1. 1. *Bibliography.*
- C 1. 2. *History.*
- C 1. 3. *Biography.*
- C 1. 4. *Philosophy.*

C 2. COLLECTIONS.
- C 2. 1. *Works,* complete and select.
- C 2. 2. *Compendia,* Dictionaries.
- C 2. 3. *Tables. Formulæ.*

C 3. SYMBOLISM AND OPERATION.
- C 3. 1. *Symbolic Methods.*
- C 3. 2. *Operations.*
- C 3. 3. *Multiple Algebra* (ref. C 5).
- C 3. 4. *Symbolic Logic.*
- C 3. 0. *Miscellaneous Symbols.*

C 4. ARITHMETIC.
- C 4. 1. *Elementary Arithmetic.*
- C 4. 2. *Continued Fractions.*
- C 4. 3. *Numerical Series.*
- C 4. 4. *Finite Differences* and Summation.
- C 4. 5. Permutations and *Combinations.*
- C 4. 6. *Probabilities.*
- C 4. 7. *Theory of Numbers.*

C 5. ALGEBRA. (For Multiple Algebra see C 3. 3.)
- C 5. 1. *Elementary Algebra.*
- C 5. 2. *Determinants.*
- C 5. 3. *Theory of Equations.*
- C 5. 4. *Simultaneous Equations.*
- C 5. 5. *Transformation.*
- C 5. 6. *Invariants.*

C 6. INFINITESIMAL CALCULUS.
- C 6. 1. Limits and *Infinite Series.*
- C 6. 2. Functions of a *Real Variable.*
- C 6. 3. *Differential Calculus.*
- C 6. 4. *Integral Calculus.*
- C 6. 5. *Total Differential Equations.*
- C 6. 6. *Partial Differential Equations.*
- C 6. 7. Functions Derived from Differential Equations. *Spherical Harmonics.*
- C 6. 8. *Calculus of Variations.*

C 7. THEORY OF FUNCTIONS.
- C 7. 1. *General Theory.*
- C 7. 2. *Algebraic Functions.*
- C 7. 3. *Exponential* and Trigonometric *Functions.*
- C 7. 4. *Elliptic Functions* and Integrals.
- C 7. 5. *Hyperelliptic* and Abelian *Functions* and Integrals.
- C 7. 6. *Various Functions* (fuchsiennes, etc.).
- C 7. 7. Functions of *Several Variables.*

C 8. Geometry.
- C 8. 1. *Elementary Geometry* and Trigonometry.
- C 8. 2. *Analysis Situs.*
- C 8. 3. *Analytic Geometry* in General.
- C 8. 4. *Projective Geometry.* Modern Synthetic Geometry.
- C 8. 5. Special Systems of *Geometric Analysis.*
- C 8. 6. *Plane Loci* in particular.
- C 8. 7. *Loci in 3 Dimensions* in particular.
- C 8. 8. Hyperspace and *Non-Euclidean Geometry.*
- C 8. 9. *Applications of Geometry.*

C 9. Extensive Algebra (ref. C 3. 3).
- C 9. 1. Geometric *Representation of the Imaginary.*
- C 9. 2. *Quaternions.*
- C 9. 3. *Geometric Algebras* (Clifford).
- C 9. 4. *Ausdehnungslehre* (Grassmann).
- C 9. 5. *Equipollences* (Bellavitis).

C 0. Miscellaneous.
- C 0. 1. *Apparatus.*
- C 0. 2. *Recreations,* Games, Puzzles, etc.
- C 0. 9. *Paradoxes* and Paradoxers. Circle-squaring, etc.

As B is the general designation of periodicals, each periodical exclusively devoted to one department is designated by B, followed by the letter of the department to which it belongs, thus:

B C. Mathematical Periodicals.

B A. Miscellaneous Periodicals. Transactions of learned societies, etc.

So long as the number of books in any section is very small, they are grouped under the division to which that section belongs, and are designated only by the number of that division. All books which refer to several divisions are placed in the division C 2 (collections), and all books referring to several sections of any one division are grouped under that division, unless they refer but slightly to more than one division or section. Volumes of a set are not separated, but the whole set is classed as if it were a single volume. Otherwise, every book is placed in the narrowest division or section to which it belongs.

The library has two card catalogues:—

I. An author's catalogue arranged alphabetically with miscellaneous and anonymous sections, so that nearly all books in the library are represented in it.

II. A subject catalogue which is at the same time a shelf and an inventory catalogue. This is arranged as follows: Every volume and every pamphlet has its card, so that each card represents a volume. All the books are classified and arranged upon the shelves according to the departments, divisions, and subdivisions, but under each subdivision books are placed alphabetically by authors. While each case, tier, and shelf is permanently labelled, the demarcation between the subdivisions is made by sliding shelf label holders bearing the subject, division, and subdivision. These label holders being movable, the subdivisions can easily be enlarged as new books are added.

In mathematics, for instance, C 1, history and philosophy, comes first, with the first subdivision, C1, 1, bibliography. First on the top shelf, and therefore first in the catalogue drawer set apart for these tiers, comes bibliography, beginning with authors in A, and so on through the alphabet to the end of the subject. Then come history, biography, etc., on through mathematics and the other departments, the order of cards being identical with the order of the books upon the shelves, reading down the tiers as down a printed page.

In the drawers the book cards are separated by red cards projecting on the right above the others, and on these projections the tier and shelf divisions are marked; they are also separated by blue cards projecting above the others on the left-hand side, on which the subjects are marked. Whenever the position of any book is changed, it is only necessary to make a corresponding change in the position of its card. The shelf position of each book is marked in pencil, not upon these cards, but upon each card in the author's catalogue, and in the book itself, in order that it may be readily found and replaced.

New books, after being entered in the author's catalogue, are kept in a case reserved for them for a few weeks before being permanently placed on the shelves and entered in the inventory catalogue.

A full list of all serial publications taken by the library is kept in a special drawer of the catalogue case, so that a person unfamiliar with the library may ascertain, with very little trouble, what periodical publications are to be found here.

Worcester is fortunate in possessing an excellent Public Library of more than 120,000 volumes, and well supplied with serial publications. In the early years of the University, it was the hope of the Founder that we might confine our purchases to such books and journals as were not to be found in the Public Library, and that the two might supplement each other; this plan was largely carried out in the earlier years, but later the needs of our students demonstrated the necessity of the duplication of the more important scientific publications, though we still depend upon the Public Library for works of a less special character, and our students have availed themselves of the library privileges thus extended to them to the fullest extent.

Besides its indebtedness to the Worcester Public Library the University is under great obligations to the following for frequent loans: Library of the Surgeon-General's Office, Washington, D.C.; Library of Harvard University; The City Library Association of Springfield, Mass.; Boston Public Library; Public Library, Cleveland, Ohio; Trinity College Library and Case Memorial Library, of Hartford, Conn.; Library of Yale University; Forbes Library, Northampton, Mass.; Library of Vassar College; and many others. Several of these libraries have freely lent us books and volumes of serial publications, often of the greatest importance to those engaged in research work. No library, however large, can hope or expect to be prepared to meet all the calls upon it, and a glance at the diverse and advanced character of the publications issued from this University[1] shows how varied and numerous are the demands upon this department.

To the Library of the American Antiquarian Society we are especially indebted for the kindly spirit of coöperation invariably shown. While strictly a reference library, its officers have ever been ready and willing to make reasonable exceptions in aid of the cause of historical and scientific research.

The library is a veritable laboratory, and is looked upon as a work-room, and not as a museum with contents too sacred to be profaned by use. It is a favorite meeting-place for professors and students, where the heads of departments meet their men to direct their reading and demonstrate to them how to make the best use of a well-selected collection of scientific books. The books are readily accessible to every member of the University, and there is no limit to the number that may be taken out. Each one enters the volumes he takes out upon a printed form provided for that purpose; if not returned at the end of ten days, they are renewed by the librarian for another period of ten days, at which time they must be returned, but may be taken out again upon the following day.

The library is open to all persons outside the University who are interested in any of its lines, and its books are freely lent to such persons, who are thus placed for the time being upon the same footing as members of the University; and, while we borrow during term time an average of fifty volumes a month, we lend as freely. The library is rich in

[1] See Bibliography at the end of this volume.

certain special lines, and is often used by experts from other universities, state and national institutions.

President Hall has an exceptionally fine private library, especially rich in pamphlets and special monographs in the various fields of philosophy, psychology, and education. During these ten years all students have been permitted to draw upon it as freely as upon the University library, and the efficiency of this department has been largely due to Dr. Hall's broad-minded and liberal conception of the function of the printed volume. In his various courses he frequently gives demonstrations of books, pointing out the best books in each subject, the best to buy, the best to read, emphasizing and explaining the strong points in each, etc.

In spite of the absolute freedom of the library, the loss of books has been surprisingly small. Once a year the books are carefully checked by means of the shelf cards, and in very few years have the losses amounted to more than two or three volumes. The missing volumes one year frequently turn up later, so that a careful estimate recently made shows the actual money value of the books lost in ten years to be less than fifty dollars.

Almost all who are interested in libraries have ideals as to the future development of their special fields, and the librarian has attempted, in the course of the past ten years, to formulate an ideal of an university library. He alone is responsible for his views, and is encouraged to state them here by the fact that the President and Faculty have given him the greatest freedom and their warmest support in all matters pertaining to his department.

The ideal library should be housed in its own building, and not relegated to rooms in a building constructed for other purposes. In constructing such a building, the chief end in view should be to provide every facility for the use of books, and this end should never be sacrificed for architectural features or artistic purposes. Each department in the University should have a working library in its own rooms, but whatever books are placed in these department libraries should be duplicated in the main library. The building should be large enough to allow the book shelves to be arranged around the rooms, leaving the greatest amount of open space in the centre. Movable working desks, liberally supplied with conveniences for writing, and containing ample drawer space for note-books and papers, are much to be preferred to the large fixed tables usually found in library buildings. The shelving should be of the most approved modern type, insuring economy of space and the proper care of the books, and the highest shelf within easy reach from the floor. The rooms should be provided with every possible convenience, including a sufficient number of comfortable chairs, with cozy nooks and corners inviting to a quiet half-hour with a book, when one would otherwise be disinclined to read. That the light should be good, the ventilation absolutely perfect, and the attendants have but one purpose — the service of the readers — are obvious essentials.

In these days of rapid multiplication of new libraries and enlargement of many older ones, there is a great demand for complete sets of serial publications, and many of the important journals are growing rapidly scarce and difficult to obtain. It is, therefore, particularly desirable in an institution of this character to procure, as soon as possible, full sets of all the serial publications in its various departments and on all allied subjects, and every effort should be made, and no expense spared, to procure all the scientific contributions by specialists in the work represented here, or in departments likely to be of service in research work.

The current numbers of all these publications should be placed before the members of the University promptly, as it is imperative that those engaged in original investigation be advised of the latest literature on the subject, or of the work others are doing along similar lines.

A most important part of a good library is its catalogue. The day has gone by when men can afford to spend hours in hunting among a mass of books to ascertain what the library possesses upon a given subject, or to rely upon the memory of the librarian and attendants, be they ever so erudite. While, therefore, the aim should be to keep in printed and card form a list of all the books and articles that have been written upon a given subject, nothing should be allowed to interfere with the prompt cataloguing under subject headings of everything that the library possesses. Two questions always arise here, first, "Where can I find a list of all printed matter upon my subject?" and secondly, "How much of that printed matter is to be found in this library?" A complete card catalogue can be so arranged as to answer perfectly these two questions.

In this, as in every well-regulated library, printed forms should be provided to encourage readers to make suggestions and complaints to the library committee; the latter, in no case, to pass through the hands of the librarian.

The subject of binding is always an important one, and we feel very keenly the need of united action on the part of all the libraries of the city in this respect. A careful inquiry has developed the fact that between $4000 and $5000 is expended yearly by the various institutions in this city for this purpose. There are unmistakable signs that the art of bookbinding, which has for ages commanded the services of eminent craftsmen, as well as of men and women eminent in art, is receiving increased attention from book lovers here, and the time may not be far distant when this question will be taken up by a committee representing the different libraries.

There would seem to be no reason also why the various institutions should not, in the near future, devise a system of coöperation, as is already proposed in Toronto, by means of which the resources of all the libraries in the city could be drawn upon by each.

REPORT OF THE TREASURER.

At the first meeting of the Trustees of Clark University, May 4, 1887, Mr. Clark proposed to give: —

(1) "The sum of $300,000 (payable as the same shall be needed) to the General Working or Construction Fund to be applied in the erection of buildings and equipping them with such appliances and facilities as may be deemed necessary for putting the University in good working order."

(2) "The sum of $100,000, the income of which shall be devoted to the support and maintenance of a University Library."

(3) "The sum of $600,000, the income of which is to be devoted to the general uses of the University in its support and management, and which for the sake of convenience may be called the University Endowment Fund."

"The Library and the Endowment Funds are never to be diminished, and no part of the principal is in any event ever to be applied to the objects to which the income of each is to be devoted. If by any accident or loss, either of said funds shall at any time become impaired, then the income of each of said funds shall be added to the principal until such impairment is made good and the funds restored to their original amounts."

In addition to the foregoing gifts, Mr. Clark then and subsequently conveyed to the Trustees of the University, real estate, the valuation of which on the books of the assessors of the city of Worcester is $135,600.

In the Treasurer's Annual Statement for the year ending August 31, 1899, which follows, is an account of the Library and University Endowment Funds.

The amounts expended for construction and equipment of buildings under the terms of Mr. Clark's first proposal have been as follows: —

Construction of the Main University Building . . .	$159,780.60
Construction of the Chemical Laboratory	56,131.94
Equipment of the Main Building	18,480.28
Equipment of the Chemical Laboratory	14,801.47
Apparatus and Supplies	29,082.73
	$278,277.02

Additional land was purchased by Mr. Clark for the University at an expense of	$12,233.04
The balance to make up the proposed $300,000 . . was subsequently expended in the additional equipment of the different departments.	9,489.94

A statement of the expenses of the several departments for the years 1890–98, inclusive, including the amounts expended in the original equipment above mentioned, is appended.

	1890.	1891.	1892.	1893.	1894.
Mathematics . . .	$ 6,664.49	$ 7,235.00	$ 7,856.30	$ 6,926.40	$ 5,906.64
Physics	17,214.20	7,820.96	6,768.46	3,567.78	2,530.60
Chemistry	26,834.24	7,491.00	6,298.46	2,693.26	1,537.64
Biology	26,083.29	15,429.70	12,782.58	8,676.47	2,066.20
Psychology . . .	13,604.17	11,400.00	7,059.16	7,696.05	6,564.00
Education	730.00	1,650.00	1,151.26	1,686.13	1,576.67
Library	15,368.04	6,733.11	1,279.64	1,334.45	2,566.83
Administration . .	5,829.00	2,900.00	3,000.00	3,600.00	2,600.00
Expenses	9,067.43	6,162.92	4,183.77	6,963.01	6,773.51
Fellowships . . .	3,660.00	4,360.00	7,240.00	5,280.00	4,980.00
	$125,974.86	$68,782.01	$57,070.02	$48,518.58	$34,000.40

	1895.	1896.	1897.	1898.
Mathematics	$ 5,900.00	$ 5,900.00	$ 5,900.00	$ 5,900.00
Physics	2,529.07	2,393.05	2,918.78	2,173.00
Biology	2,072.71	2,200.00	2,300.00	2,054.24
Psychology	6,015.16	7,010.00	7,010.00	6,676.38
Education	1,512.29	1,250.00	1,250.00	1,250.00
Library	1,628.72	1,740.16	2,456.00	3,608.16
Administration	2,600.00	2,600.00	2,600.00	2,600.00
Expenses	3,434.13	4,319.80	4,237.82	3,100.98
Fellowships	4,740.00	4,620.00	3,420.00	1,500.00
	$30,032.41	$32,032.99	$32,122.55	$28,862.96

In addition to the endowment and gifts, which have already been referred to, Mr. Clark has given to the University for its general purposes: —

1889–90	$12,000
1890–91	50,000
1891–92	26,000
1892–93	18,000
	$106,000

The University has received from Mrs. Eliza W. Field "a fund of $500 to be called the John White Field Fund, the income of which is to provide for the minor needs of a Scholar or Fellow."

There was also presented to the Trustees of the University by Hon. George S. Barton of Worcester $5000, the income of which is to be devoted to the aid of "some one or more worthy native born citizens of the city of Worcester, who may desire to avail themselves of the advantages of the institution."

Hon. Henry L. Parker, in the summer of 1892, in behalf of many citizens of Worcester, presented the University with a tower clock and the sum of $781.80 to provide for its maintenance, which fund is known as the Clock Fund.

REPORT OF THE TREASURER TO THE TRUSTEES FOR THE YEAR ENDING AUGUST 31, 1899.

To the Trustees of Clark University,

Gentlemen, — I have the honor to submit herewith my annual report for the year ending August 31, 1899.

The total receipts of the University from Sept. 1, 1898 to Aug. 31, 1899, inclusive, were	$48,595.53
The total disbursements during the same period were	37,130.27
Leaving a balance on hand Sept. 1, 1899, of	$11,465.26

(A.)

The items of income are as follows: —

Gross Income of the University Endowment Fund	$28,407.33
Gross Income of the Library Fund	5,258.46
Gross Income of the University	1,586.00
Gross Income of the Summer School, 1899	1,388.50
Subscriptions to the Fund for the Decennial Celebration	4,150.00
From the Field Fund	20.00
Balance from previous year	7,785.24
Total	$48,595.53

(B.)

The expenditures have been as follows: —

For the Department of Mathematics	$ 6,300.00
For the Department of Physics	2,641.11
For the Department of Biology	2,012.25
For the Department of Psychology	7,966.82
For the Department of Education	1,250.00
Administration	2,700.00
Expense	4,720.87
Field Scholarship	20.00
Expenses of Summer School	889.85
Expenses of the Decennial Celebration	3,156.85
Library Expenses	3,474.08
Sinking Fund	700.00
Jonas G. Clark on account of premiums	900.00
Accrued interest repaid	389.44
	$37,130.27

(C.)

The incidental earnings of the University from fees, etc., were . $ 1,586.00

(D.)

Account of the Summer School for 1899: —

Receipts	$ 1,388.50
Expenses	889.85
Balance carried to University Account	$ 498.65

(E.)

Subscriptions to the Decennial Celebration: —

Receipts	$ 4,150.00
Expenses	3,156.85
Balance on hand appropriated to the publication of this volume	$ 993.15

(F.)

The University Endowment Fund is invested as follows: —

		Book value.	Market value. Sept. 1, 1899.
Oregon Railway and Navigation Co., 4s		$110,000.00	$112,750.00
West Shore R. R. Co., 1st Mtg., 4s, 2361		75,000.00	84,750.00
City of Cambridge, Sewer Loan, 6s, 1905		20,000.00	22,600.00
Norwich and Worcester R. R. Co., 4s, 1927		75,000.00	84,000.00
Rutland R. R., 1st Mtg., 6s, 1902		25,000.00	26,500.00
Wilkesbarre and Eastern R. R., 1st Mtg., 5s, 1942		9,600.00	10,600.00
Hereford Ry. Co., 4s, 1930		8,350.00	10,000.00
Chicago and Eastern Illinois R. R., 1st Consol. Mtg., 6s, 1934		10,000.00	13,700.00
1st Mtg. Sink. F., 6s, 1907		1,000.00	1,145.00
Wayne Co., Michigan, 4s		30,000.00	31,200.00
Northern Ohio Ry. Co., 1st Mtg., 5s		3,000.00	3,180.00
Lowell, Lawrence, and Haverhill St. Ry., 1st Mtg., 5s		15,000.00	15,750.00
Worcester and Suburban St. Ry., 1st Mtg., 5s		6,000.00	6,240.00
Worcester and Marlboro St. Ry., 1st Mtg., 5s		10,000.00	10,400.00
Atchison, Topeka and Santa Fé Ry. Co.		28,000.00	
Gen. Mtg., 4s	$18,500.00		18,500.00
Adj., 4s	10,000.00		8,800.00
Certif. Gen. Mtg., 4s	250.00		250.00
Second Ave. R. R. Co., New York, 1st Consol. Mtg., 5s, 1948		25,000.00	30,000.00
15 shares Worcester National Bank		2,250.00	2,700.00
71 shares Norwich and Worcester R. R.		14,603.50	15,620.00
Deposit in Worcester Co. Inst. for Savings		5,000.00	5,000.00
Deposit in Five Cents Savings Bank		10,000.00	10,000.00
100 shares Fitchburg (preferred)		10,300.00	11,800.00
35 shares New York, New Haven, and Hartford R. R.		6,982.50	7,630.00
100 shares Worcester Traction Co. (preferred)		10,700.00	10,450.00
New England Yarn Co., 5s		11,000.00	11,495.00
Lake Shore Collaterals, 3½s		50,000.00	50,000.00
Invested in premiums		15,230.00	
Cash in Worcester National Bank		28,920.25	28,920.25
		$614,136.25	$634,480.25

The gross income of the University Endowment Fund was		$28,407.33
There was paid from this: —		
To Sinking Fund to provide for premiums	$700.00	
To Jonas G. Clark on account of premiums . . .	900.00	
Accrued interest repaid	389.44	$1,989.44
Leaving net income carried to University Account . .		$26,417.89

(G.)

The Library Fund is invested as follows: —

	Book value.	Market value. Sept. 1, 1899.
50 shares Washington National Bank, Boston .	$ 5,527.00	$ 6,000.00
25 shares Tremont National Bank, Boston . .	1,766.00	(In liquidation)
50 shares Merchants' National Bank, Boston .	7,934.60	8,600.00
50 shares National Bank of Republic, Boston .	7,994.88	8,750.00
50 shares Union National Bank, Boston . .	6,829.50	7,150.00
50 shares Second National Bank, Boston . .	9,162.50	8,850.00
50 shares New England National Bank, Boston .	8,237.50	7,825.00
50 shares Atlas National Bank, Boston . .	6,293.50	5,750.00
61 shares State National Bank, Boston . .	6,938.01	7,167.50
15 shares Suffolk National Bank, Boston . .	1,527.21	1,650.00
50 shares Eliot National Bank, Boston . .	6,598.00	7,150.00
50 shares National Bank of Commerce, Boston .	5,552.62	5,625.00
50 shares Boylston National Bank, Boston .	6,530.75	5,850.00
43 shares Old Boston National Bank, Boston .	4,527.63	5,074.00
10 shares City National Bank, Worcester . .	1,500.00	1,500.00
15 shares Norwich and Worcester R. R. stock .	3,000.00	3,300.00
Northern Ohio R. R. Bonds, 5s	4,000.00	4,240.00
15 shares New York, New Haven, and Hartford R. R.	2,992.50	3,270.00
Invested in premiums	150.00	
Deposit in Worcester National Bank . . .	2,273.05	2,273.05
	$99,335.25	$100,024.55

The gross income of the Library Fund was: —

From dividends and interest	$4,085.77
Rebate on bank tax, ...	1,172.67
Balance carried to Library Expense Account .	$5,258.44

(H.)

The Library Expense Account: —

Unexpended balance from previous years	$3,091.18	
Credits for books sold	412.38	
Income of the Library Fund for 1899	5,258.46	$8,762.02
The expenses, including $900 for administration, heat and light, were		3,886.46
Leaving a balance Sept. 1, 1899, of		$4,875.56

(I.)

The George S. Barton Fund, deposited in the Worcester Co. Inst. for Savings, amounts to . .	$7,239.24
Income during the year	278.43

(J.)

The John White Field Fund, deposited in the Worcester Co. Inst. for Savings, amounts to	$653.22
Income during the year	25.74

(K.)

The Clock Fund, deposited in the Five Cents Savings Bank, amounts to	$878.40
Income during the year	33.93

(L.)

The Sinking Fund, to provide for premiums, is deposited in the Worcester Five Cents Savings Bank, and amounts to	$2,670.42

(M.)

The salaries of the University Faculty were . .	$19,990.00

(N.)

Fellowships and Scholarships	$1,310.00

(O.)

Salaries of employees	$2,135.00

(P.)

Apparatus and supplies	$870.18

Respectfully submitted,

THOMAS H. GAGE, *Treasurer.*

We have examined the books and accounts and securities of Clark University, and find them to be correct and as stated in the foregoing treasurer's report for the year ending August 31, 1899.

JAMES P. HAMILTON,
T. H. GAGE, JR.,
Auditors.

Em Picard

LECTURES ON MATHEMATICS.

By Professor Émile Picard.

Première Conférence.

Sur l'Extension de quelques Notions Mathématiques, et en particulier de l'Idée de Fonction depuis un siècle.

Mes premiers mots seront pour adresser ... de cette Université qui m'a fait l'honneur de ... charger de prendre la parole devant quelques ... C'est un honneur auquel je suis très sensible ... que les études mathématiques se développent ... et nous suivons ce mouvement avec une très vive ... *American Journal of Mathematics* compte parmi les ... les plus importants ... de remarquables ... toujours pour ... grand profit et intérêt ... de la Société mathématique ... excellente revue historique et critique qui tient ses lecteurs au courant des travaux les plus récents. J'ai appris aussi que cette Société allait fonder un nouveau recueil ... à des mémoires plus étendus; je ne doute pas ... brillant avenir. Dans les trois causeries que ... je ne puis songer à aborder un sujet spécial ... paration particulière. Nous allons rester dans ... rapide coup d'œil sur l'extension de quelques ... en particulier, de l'idée de fonction depuis un siècle.

I.

Toute la science mathématique repose sur ... être dépendantes ... deux ou plusieurs ... sidère le premier ... l'analyse. Il a ... se rendit compte ... extraordinaire ... d'à beaucoup une ... a été très heu... Newton ... Si Newton ... avaient pensé ... n'ont pas ... ou qui est ... le calcul

LECTURES ON MATHEMATICS.

By Professor Emile Picard.

Première Conférence.

Sur l'Extension de quelques Notions Mathématiques, et en particulier de l'Idée de Fonction depuis un Siècle.

Mes premiers mots seront pour adresser mes remerciments au Conseil de cette Université qui m'a fait l'honneur de m'inviter à ces fêtes et m'a chargé de prendre la parole devant quelques mathématiciens américains. C'est un honneur auquel je suis très sensible, car nous savons en France que les études mathématiques se développent rapidement en Amérique et nous suivons ce mouvement avec une très vive sympathie. Votre *American Journal of Mathematics* compte parmi les journaux périodiques les plus importants et renferme de remarquables mémoires, et je lis toujours pour ma part avec grand profit et intérêt le Bulletin de la Société mathématique américaine, excellente revue historique et critique qui tient ses lecteurs au courant des travaux les plus récents. J'ai appris aussi que cette Société allait fonder un nouveau recueil destiné à des mémoires plus étendus; je ne doute pas qu'il ne soit appelé à un brillant avenir. Dans les trois causeries que nous allons avoir ensemble, je ne puis songer à aborder un sujet spécial qui demanderait une préparation particulière. Nous allons rester dans les généralités et jeter un rapide coup d'œil sur l'extension de quelques notions mathématiques et en particulier, de l'idée de fonction depuis un siècle.

I.

Toute la science mathématique repose sur l'idée de fonction c'est à dire de dépendance entre deux ou plusieurs grandeurs, dont l'étude constitue le principal objet de l'analyse. Il a fallu longtemps avant qu'on se rendît compte de l'étendue extraordinaire de cette notion; c'est là d'ailleurs une circonstance qui a été très heureuse pour les progrès de la Science. Si Newton et Leibnitz avaient pensé que les fonctions continues n'ont pas nécessairement une dérivée, ce qui est le cas général, le calcul différentiel n'aurait pas pris naissance; de même les idées inexactes de Lagrange sur la possibilité des développements en séries de Taylor ont rendu d'immenses services. Sans vouloir trop généraliser, on peut dire que l'erreur est quelquefois utile, et que, dans les époques vraiment créatrices, une vérité incomplète ou approchée peut être plus féconde que la même vérité accompagnée des restrictions nécessaires; l'histoire de la science confirme plus d'une fois cette remarque et, pour rappeler encore Newton, il est heureux qu'il ait eu au début de ses recherches pleine confiance dans les lois de Kepler. Les géomètres du siècle dernier, sans remonter plus haut, ne raffinaient pas sur l'idée de fonction; pour eux, une fonction d'une variable est une fonction qu'on peut représenter par une courbe formant un trait continu; ce sont ces fonctions qu'Euler appelait *functiones continuae*. La question de la représentation d'une fonction arbitraire sous une forme analytique dans laquelle interviennent seulement les opérations fondamentales de l'arithmétique effectuées un nombre fini ou infini de fois, se posa, semble-t-il pour la première fois à propos du problème des cordes vibrantes. D'Alembert avait donné l'intégrale de l'équation

$$\frac{\partial^2 y}{\partial t^2} = a^2 \frac{\partial^2 y}{\partial x^2}$$

sous la forme $f(x + at) + \phi(x - at)$. Daniel Bernoulli montra qu'on pouvait satisfaire à l'équation différentielle et aux conditions aux limites par une série trigonométrique, et il affirma que cette série donnait la solution la plus générale. Ce fut l'occasion d'une longue discussion entre Bernoulli, Euler et Lagrange. Pour ces grands géomètres, une fonction arbitraire était toujours la fonction arbitraire susceptible d'être représentée par un trait continu. En 1807, dans un mémoire célèbre, et, plus tard, dans sa théorie analytique de la chaleur, Fourier montra l'extrême importance des séries trigonométriques; il a, le premier, osé affirmer que toute fonction pouvait être représentée entre 0 et 2π par un développement de cette nature, et, ce qui est le point capital, qu'un même développement pouvait entre ces limites représenter des fonctions qu'on considérait comme distinctes, c'est à dire correspondant graphiquement à des arcs de courbes différentes. Il est très instructif d'étudier dans la théorie de la chaleur de Fourier les voies diverses que le célèbre géomètre a suivies pour avoir les coefficients du développement. La détermination de ces coefficients à l'aide des intégrales classiques ne vient qu'en second lieu ; cette détermination avait d'ailleurs été indiquée auparavant, quoique d'une manière incidente, par Euler. Dans une première méthode, Fourier obtient les coefficients en envisageant une infinité d'équations du premier degré à une infinité d'inconnues ; c'était une recherche audacieuse pour l'époque, et nous ne devons pas nous attendre à trouver dans cette étude toute la rigueur que nous exigeons aujourd'hui. Il n'en faut pas moins se souvenir que Fourier eut le premier la hardiesse de résoudre des systèmes d'une infinité d'équations linéaires à une infinité d'inconnues. Il y a d'ailleurs en analyse plus d'une question où se présentent de tels systèmes. C'est le cas quand on veut chercher le développement du quotient de deux séries trigonométriques, et aussi, quand ayant à intégrer une équation différentielle linéaire à coefficients périodiques, on veut y satisfaire par une fonction périodique ou au moyen du produit d'une telle fonction par une exponentielle ; ce dernier cas se présente dans plusieurs problèmes de mécanique céleste et en particulier dans les beaux travaux de M. Hill sur le mouvement du périgée de la lune. M. Poincaré a posé les principes d'une étude rigoureuse des systèmes d'équations en nombre infini, spécialement dans le cas des systèmes homogènes. Il introduit dans cette théorie les déterminants d'ordre infini, et un fait inattendu ressort de ses recherches, à savoir que des égalités en nombre infini peuvent dans certains cas être remplacées par une infinité d'inégalités. Il y a d'ailleurs en analyse bien d'autres questions où on se trouve en présence d'une infinité d'équations et il y aura un jour un chapitre intéressant à écrire sur l'intégration d'un nombre infini d'équations différentielles avec une infinité de fonctions inconnues. Mais revenons aux séries trigonométriques. En poursuivant rapidement leur histoire, nous arrivons à la période où Cauchy, Abel, et Dirichlet soumettent à une révision sévère les principes fondamentaux de l'analyse mathématique. Le mémoire de Dirichlet sur les séries de Fourier est resté un modèle de rigueur ; l'illustre auteur précise les conditions pour que l'on puisse affirmer qu'un développement trigonométrique avec les coefficients de Fourier représente une fonction donnée dans l'intervalle de 0 à 2π, et ces conditions sont restées dans la science sous le nom de conditions de Dirichlet. Elles sont seulement suffisantes, mais on ne peut espérer dans cette théorie trouver, sous une forme pratique, des conditions à la fois nécessaires et suffisantes. Il est certain aujourd'hui, grâce surtout aux travaux de Du Bois-Reymond, qu'une fonction continue n'est pas nécessairement toujours développable en série trigonométrique ; la condition suffisante de M. Lipschitz formulée par l'inégalité $[f(x+h)-f(x)] < kh^a$ $(a > 0)$, en désignant par k une constante fixe, a un grand caractère de généralité, et il en est de même du théorème de M. Camille Jordan sur la légitimité du développement pour les fonctions à variation bornée.

Le mémoire de Riemann sur les séries trigonométriques est célèbre dans l'histoire de ces séries; on peut dire en deux mots, pour le caractériser, qu'il abandonne le point de vue de Dirichlet, et qu'au lieu de chercher des conditions suffisantes, sa principale préoccupation est de trouver des conditions nécessaires. A un autre point de vue encore, le mémoire de Riemann marque une date parce qu'il continue cette révision des principes du calcul infinitésimal commencée par Abel et Cauchy; la distinction entre les fonctions intégrables et les fonctions non intégrables y apparaît pour la première fois, et on peut dire qu'il résulte des travaux de Riemann qu'il y a des fonctions continues n'ayant pas de dérivées.

On doit à M. G. Cantor la réponse à une question importante: une fonction peut-elle être représentée entre 0 et 2π de plusieurs manières par une série trigonométrique? En d'autres termes, *zéro* peut-il être représenté par un développement trigonométrique où les coefficients ne soient pas tous nuls? Indépendamment du résultat lui-même, le mémoire de M. Cantor est digne d'intérêt parce que, dans une question depuis longtemps posée, des notions concernant les ensembles de points viennent jouer un rôle utile. Etant donné un ensemble de points entre 0 et 2π, M. Cantor appelle ensemble dérivé l'ensemble de ses points limites, et on peut définir ainsi de proche en proche les dérivées successives d'un ensemble. Si la dérivée $n^{ème}$ d'un ensemble se réduit à un nombre limité de points, l'ensemble sera dit de la $n^{ème}$ espèce. M. Cantor établit que si dans l'intervalle $(0, 2\pi)$ une série trigonométrique est nulle pour toutes les valeurs de x à l'exception de celles qui correspondent aux points d'un ensemble d'espèce n, pour lequel on ne sait rien de la série tous les coefficients seront nuls.

II.

J'ai insisté, peut-être un peu longuement, sur les séries trigono métriques. Indépendamment de leur importance dans les applications et particulièrement en physique mathématique, elles ont joué un rôle considérable dans l'évolution de la notion de fonction; c'est leur étude qui a appelé l'attention sur des circonstances, qui ne nous étonnent plus aujourd'hui, mais qui paraissaient jadis invraisemblables, comme, par exemple, ce fait que la limite vers laquelle tend une série de fonctions continues peut n'être pas égale à la valeur de la série en ce point. Les précautions à prendre dans la dérivation des séries ont été aussi suggérées par les séries trigonométriques; on peut faire remonter à cet exemple les nombreuses recherches effectuées depuis Cauchy sur la dérivation et l'intégration des séries, auxquelles M. Osgood ajoutait il y a quelques années un important complément dans son mémoire sur la convergence non-uniforme.

Le développement d'une fonction en série trigonométrique est aussi le type le plus simple de développements très généraux qui se présentent dans les applications; Fourier, ici encore, a été un précurseur. L'étude du refroidissement d'une sphère, en supposant que la température ne dépende que du temps et de la distance au centre, l'a conduit à un développement où, au lieu des lignes trigonométriques des multiples x, $2x$, ..., nx de la variable, figurent les lignes trigonométriques de a_1x, a_2x, ..., a_nx, les a désignant les racines en nombre infini d'une certaine équation transcendante, et il a esquissé une théorie de ces sortes de développements. Cette étude a été reprise par Cauchy dans plusieurs mémoires qui forment une des applications les plus remarquables de ce que le grand analyste appelait le calcul des résidus. Sous des conditions très générales relatives à l'équation transcendante, Cauchy a démontré en toute rigueur la légitimité des développements pour une fonction satisfaisant d'ailleurs aux conditions de Dirichlet, et ainsi se sont trouvés considérablement généralisés les résultats du mémoire classique de l'illustre géomètre allemand.

D'autres développements d'un caractère encore plus général se rencontrent en physique mathématique, et ont fait l'objet des travaux de Poisson, de Sturm et de Liouville et de bien d'autres, mais ici se présentent, au point de vue de la rigueur complète, des difficultés que l'on a réussi à surmonter que dans un petit nombre de cas. Je citerai seulement l'exemple très simple du refroidissement d'un mur indéfini dont les faces extrêmes sont maintenues à la température zéro; on suppose d'ailleurs que la chaleur spécifique soit une fonction de l'abscisse x correspondant à chaque tranche, de telle sorte que l'on a pour la température V l'équation aux dérivées partielles

$$\frac{\partial^2 V}{\partial x^2} = A(x)\frac{\partial V}{\partial t},$$

où $A(x)$ est une fonction continue et positive de x dans l'intervalle (a, b) de l'épaisseur du mur. Envisageons l'équation linéaire ordinaire

$$\frac{d^2y}{dx^2} + k \cdot A(x)y = 0$$

et les valeurs positives de k en nombre infini, $k_1, k_2, \cdots, k_n \cdots$, pour lesquelles il existe une intégrale de l'équation précédente s'annulant en a et b. A chaque valeur de k_i correspond une intégrale $y_i(x)$ de cette équation (déterminée à une constante près), et le problème qui se présente est de développer une fonction $f(x)$ s'annulant en a et b sous la forme

$$f(x) = \Sigma B_i y_i(x).$$

La démonstration rigoureuse de ce développement résulte des dernières recherches de M. Stekloff, s'aidant des travaux antérieurs de M. Poincaré sur les équations de la physique mathématique. Il semble bien qu'il soit indispensable pour l'entière rigueur de supposer que $f(x)$ a des dérivées des deux premiers ordres; nous sommes loin d'atteindre ici à la généralité des conditions de Dirichlet pour le développement en série trigonométrique qui rentre d'ailleurs comme cas particulier (celui où $A(x)$ est une constante) dans le cas précédent.

III.

L'histoire des développements en séries que je viens de retracer rapidement nous donne un remarquable exemple de l'intime solidarité qui unit à certains moments l'analyse pure et les mathématiques appliquées. En plus d'une occasion, ce sont celles-ci qui ont donné l'impulsion en posant les problèmes, et c'est un fait assurément remarquable que des questions concernant les cordes vibrantes ou la propagation de la chaleur aient conduit les géomètres à approfondir la notion si complexe de fonction. L'histoire de la science mathématique offrirait d'ailleurs dès le debut des exemples analogues; nos facultés d'abstraction ne trouvent primitivement à s'exercer qu'en partant de certains faits concrets, et c'est sans doute en réfléchissant aux procédés empiriques des praticiens égyptiens leurs prédécesseurs que les premiers géomètres grecs créèrent la science géométrique. Mais ces vues risqueraient de m'entraîner trop loin. Je tiens seulement à ajouter qu'il ne faudrait pas professer une opinion trop systématique sur cette marche parallèle de la théorie pure et des applications, comme le faisait avec Laplace, Fourier, Poisson la brillante école française de physique mathématique du commencement de ce siècle. Pour eux, l'analyse pure n'était que l'instrument, et Fourier, en annonçant à l'Académie des sciences, les travaux de Jacobi, disait que les questions de la philosophie naturelle doivent être le principal objet des méditations des géomètres. "On doit désirer, ajoutait-il, que les personnes les plus propres à perfectionner la science du calcul dirigent leurs travaux vers ces hautes applications si nécessaires au progrès de l'intelligence humaine." Ce désir très légitime ne doit pas être exclusif; ce serait méconnaître d'abord la valeur philosophique et artistique des mathématiques; de plus des spéculations théoriques sont restées pendant longtemps éloignées de toute application, quand un moment est venu où elles ont pu être utilisées. On n'en peut pas citer d'exemple plus mémorable que le concept des sections coniques élaboré par les géomètres grecs, qui resta inutilisé pendant deux mille ans, jusqu'au jour où Kepler s'en servit dans l'étude de la planète Mars. Les questions s'épuisent pour un temps, et il n'est pas bon que tous les chercheurs marchent dans la même voie. Peu d'années après que Fourier écrivait les lignes que je viens de rappeler, apparaissait Évariste Galois qui aurait, s'il avait vécu davantage, rétabli l'équilibre en ramenant les recherches vers les régions les plus élevées de la théorie pure, et ce fut un malheur irréparable pour la science française que la mort de Galois, dont le génie allait exercer une action si profonde sur les parties les plus variées des mathématiques.

Avec cette digression, nous semblons être bien loin, messieurs, de notre promenade à travers l'idée de fonction depuis le commencement de ce siècle. Elle n'était cependant pas inutile, pour montrer qu'un moment devait arriver où les spéculations sur la théorie des fonctions de variables réelles se poursuivraient sans souci immédiat des applications et prendraient de plus en plus un caractère philosophique. Nous avons déjà dit qu'il résultait indirectement des travaux de Riemann qu'une fonction continue n'a pas nécessairement une dérivée. Weierstrass donna le premier exemple d'une fonction continue n'ayant de dérivée pour aucune valeur de la variable, et il fit connaître au sujet des fonctions continues une proposition qui nous ramène aux développements en séries, mais ici les termes sont des polynomes. D'après Weierstrass, toute fonction continue dans un intervalle peut être développée en une série de polynomes qui est absolument et uniformément convergente dans cet intervalle. La démonstration de l'illustre géomètre est très compliquée; elle prend comme point de départ une intégrale considérée par Fourier dans la théorie de la chaleur, qui permet d'obtenir la fonction considérée comme la limite d'une fonction transcendante entière dépendant d'un paramètre, quand celui-ci tend vers zéro. C'est de là que Weierstrass déduit la possibilité de représenter d'une manière approchée par un polynome toute fonction continue dans un intervalle fini, d'où se tire alors de suite le résultat énoncé. On peut arriver beaucoup plus rapidement au théorème de Weierstrass en partant de l'intégrale classique de Poisson dans la théorie des séries trigonométriques; elle montre facilement que la fonction, supposée définie dans un intervalle moindre que 2π, peut-être représentée avec telle approximation que l'on voudra par une série limitée de Fourier, et on passe de suite à une représentation approchée par un polynome; cette démonstration s'étend à des fonctions continues d'un nombre quelconque de variables. M. Volterra est arrivé aussi très simplement au théorème qui nous occupe en remarquant qu'une fonction continue est représentable avec telle approximation qu'on voudra par une ligne polygonale convenable; celle-ci conduit à une série de Fourier uniformément convergente, et en la réduisant à un nombre suffisamment grand mais limité de termes on retombe sur le résultat indiqué plus haut. Le théorème de Weierstrass présente un réel intérêt philosophique, en même temps qu'il peut avoir quelque utilité au point de vue du calcul pratique; on en a aussi quelquefois fait usage pour la démonstration de certaines propositions.

Les développements en séries de polynomes spéciaux sont d'un grand intérêt, mais ils ne peuvent s'appliquer qu'à des fonctions satisfaisant à des conditions particulières. Ainsi, dans son mémoire sur l'approximation des fonctions de très grands nombres, M. Darboux a étudié les développements d'une fonction suivant les polynomes de Jacobi provenant de la série hypergéométrique. Les conditions sont encore celles de Dirichlet; pareillement aussi dans le cas où la fonction devient infinie, elle doit rester intégrable. Il y a cependant une différence quand la fonction devient infinie pour les points extrêmes. Dans le cas des polynomes de Legendre, une fonction qui deviendrait infinie d'un ordre égal ou supérieur à $\frac{1}{2}$ pour $x = \pm 1$ ne serait pas développable, quoique les coefficients aient un sens.

IV.

Si nous revenons aux fonctions prises dans toute leur généralité, on reconnait vite la nécessité d'établir avec un soin extrême certaines propositions que l'on accorde aisément pour les fonctions usuelles. C'est ce qu'avait déjà reconnu Cauchy dans son Analyse algébrique; les travaux de Hankel, le mémoire de M. Darboux sur les fonctions discontinues, le beau livre de M. Dini et les études plus récentes des géomètres italiens montrent bien les précautions nécessaires dans ce genre de recherches. Ainsi, une fonction de deux variables réelles peut être continue par rapport à x et par rapport à y sans être continue par rapport à l'ensemble des deux variables, comme M. Dini en a indiqué des exemples. Parmi les travaux les plus récents sur ces questions délicates, je m'arrêterai un instant sur un mémoire de M. Baire qui renferme de curieux résultats. L'auteur a réussi à trouver la condition nécessaire et suffisante pour qu'une fonction $f(x)$ d'une variable réelle puisse être représentée par une série simple de polynomes; l'énoncé suppose certaines notions sur la discontinuité d'une fonction par rapport à un ensemble de points: une fonction peut être ponctuellement ou totalement discontinue par rapport à cet ensemble. La condition obtenue est que la fonction soit ponctuellement discontinue par rapport à tout ensemble parfait. M. Baire se pose aussi une question singulière sur les équations linéaires aux dérivées partielles. Envisageons l'équation

$$\frac{\partial f}{\partial x}+\frac{\partial f}{\partial y}=0. \tag{1}$$

Si je vous demandais quelles sont les fonctions satisfaisant à cette équation, vous me répondriez sans doute que les fonctions de $x-y$ répondent seules à la question. M. Baire n'en est pas absolument sûr; il remarque que la théorie du changement de variables suppose la continuité des dérivées qu'on emploie; si on suppose seulement l'existence des dérivées $\frac{\partial f}{\partial x}$ et $\frac{\partial f}{\partial y}$ de la fonction cherchée f, on ne peut pas faire le changement de variables classique. Il faut une analyse délicate pour établir que la fonction f, supposée continue par rapport à l'ensemble des variables x et y, et satisfaisant à (1) est une fonction de $x-y$; la conclusion reste douteuse si f est seulement continue par rapport à x et par rapport à y.

Au point de vue géométrique les recherches générales sur les fonctions ne sont pas non plus sans intérêt; elles nous apprennent à nous défier de nos conceptions les plus simples. Quoi de plus simple semble-t-il qu'une courbe dont les coordonnées x et y sont des fonctions continues d'un paramètre t variant entre a et b. M. Peano a cependant montré qu'on peut choisir ces deux fonctions de telle sorte que, quand t varie entre a et b, le point (x, y) puisse prendre une position quelconque dans un rectangle. À certains points (x, y) pourront correspondre d'ailleurs, dans l'exemple de M. Peano, deux ou quatre valeurs de t. Ce résultat est au premier abord déconcertant; il dérange nos idées sur les surfaces et sur les courbes. Voici encore un résultat singulier obtenu tout récemment par M. Lebègue; il y a d'autres surfaces que les surfaces développables qui sont applicables sur un plan. On peut à l'aide de fonctions continues obtenir des surfaces correspondant à un plan de telle sorte que toute ligne rectifiable du plan ait pour correspondante une ligne rectifiable de la surface, et la surface n'est cependant pas réglée.

De tels exemples montrent la subtilité des recherches auxquelles doivent se livrer aujourd'hui ceux qui veulent approfondir la notion de fonction prise dans son extrême généralité. Ces études sont en bien des points intimement liées aux spéculations sur la notion même de nombre. Nous rejoignons ici une école de philosophie mathématique qui s'est brillamment développée depuis quelque trente ans, école qui se livre à une minutieuse analyse sur la nature du nombre. On ne peut s'empêcher d'être frappé du nombre considérable de publications parues dans ces dernières années et se rapportant à cette mathématique philosophique; elles sont bien en accord avec les tendances générales de l'époque où nous vivons, et où l'esprit humain applique dans des directions variées une critique de plus en plus pénétrante. Ces spéculations raffinées ont même pénétré dans l'enseignement élémentaire, ce qui est à mon avis très regrettable. Mais il ne s'agit pas ici d'enseignement; je ne recherche pas non plus l'intérêt que ces études présentent pour le philosophe; il me parait très réel, et on doit souhaiter que de jeunes philosophes s'engagent dans cette direction après s'être initiés sérieusement aux mathématiques. Je ne veux me placer qu'au point de vue de la mathématique. De bons esprits contestent que les spéculations dont je parle aient quelque importance pour les mathématiques positives et ils craignent de voir beaucoup de talent dépensé dans des recherches stériles. Je comprends très bien leurs craintes mais je ne partage pas entièrement leur avis. Il y a lieu sans doute de faire des distinctions. Certaines questions sont d'un intérêt purement philosophique et n'auront jamais vraisemblablement la moindre utilité pour les mathématiques, comme, par exemple, de savoir si la priorité appartient au nombre cardinal ou au nombre ordinal, c'est à dire si l'idée de nombre proprement dit est antérieur à celle de rang ou si c'est l'inverse. Mais dans d'autres cas, il n'en est plus de même ; ainsi il est vraisemblable que la théorie des ensembles de M. Cantor, que nous avons déjà rencontrée deux *fois* sur notre chemin, est à la veille de jouer un rôle utile dans des problèmes qui n'ont pas été posés exprès pour être une application de la théorie. Ne regrettons donc pas cet effort hardi sur l'idée de nombre et sur celle de fonction, car la théorie des fonctions de variables réelles est la véritable base de l'analyse mathématique.

V.

Il faut bien, il est vrai, reconnaître que la notion générale de fonction est très vague, et nous ne pouvons obtenir des résultats de quelque étendue qu'en faisant des hypothèses particulières. Qu'est ce qui a guidé plus ou moins consciemment dans le choix de ces hypothèses ? Il résulte de ce que nous avons dit sur les rapports entre l'analyse et les applications aux phénomènes naturels, que celles-ci ont plus d'une fois guidé le mathématicien dans son choix. Une hypothèse essentielle a été celle de la continuité. Suivant le vieil adage "natura non facit saltus" nous avons le sentiment, on pourrait dire la croyance, que dans la nature il n'y a pas de place pour la discontinuité. Il est utile quelquefois de conserver le discontinu dans nos calculs, par exemple quand nous regardons comme nulle la durée du choc en mécanique rationnelle, ou quand nous réduisons à une surface les couches de passage dans plusieurs questions de physique; mais nous savons que, pour si petite qu'elle soit, les chocs ont une certaine durée et les physiciens nous ont appris à mesurer l'épaisseur des couches où se produisent dans plusieurs phénomènes des variations très rapides. L'idée de dérivée s'impose déjà moins ; elle répond cependant au sentiment confus de la rapidité plus ou moins grande avec laquelle s'accomplit tel ou tel phénomène. L'hypothèse relative à la possibilité de la dérivation d'une fonction a donc une origine analogue à celle de la continuité. Je ne veux pas dire qu'au point de vue du nombre l'idée de continuité soit aussi claire au fond qu'elle en a l'air, mais il ne s'agit ici que de la notion du continu physique tirée des données brutes des sens.

Dans d'autres cas, on ne voit pas de cause du même ordre dans la particularité imposée à la fonction ; il en est ainsi, ce me semble, pour la propriété des fonctions dites analytiques c'est à dire des fonctions qui dans le voisinage d'une valeur arbitraire de la variable peuvent être développées en séries de Taylor. Les fonctions étudiées les premières, comme les fonctions rationnelles, l'exponentielle, les lignes trigonométriques, jouissant de cette propriété, l'attention se sera sans doute trouvée appelée sur elle; et ensuite la facilité avec laquelle cette hypothèse a permis d'aborder certaines questions a fait acquérir aux fonctions analytiques une importance considérable. C'est donc à leur commodité dans nos calculs qu'elles doivent le grand rôle qu'elles jouent.

On ne sait pas d'ailleurs, pour une fonction définie seulement pour les valeurs réelles de la variable, quelles sont les conditions de légitimité du développement en série de Taylor. Une fonction de x peut avoir des dérivées de tout ordre pour toute valeur de la variable, et n'être cependant pas développable. On doit à M. Borel un résultat remarquable concernant les fonctions d'une variable réelle définie dans un certain intervalle et ayant dans cet intervalle des dérivées de tout ordre. Si l'intervalle est $(-\pi, +\pi)$, la fonction peut être représentée par un développement de la forme

$$\sum_{0}^{\infty} (A_n x^n + B_n \cos nx + C_n \sin nx).$$

Ces diverses remarques m'amènent à dire un mot d'une école de géomètres qui ne veulent rien voir en dehors des fonctions analytiques, et d'une manière plus générale de l'importance, peut-être exagérée, qu'a prise dans les travaux modernes la théorie des fonctions analytiques. C'est mutiler singulièrement l'analyse que de vouloir se borner à des développements aussi particuliers que les séries entières, alors que l'on peut former tant de développements d'une autre nature qui ne peuvent jamais être représentées par de telles séries. Sans doute, les fonctions les plus usuelles sont analytiques, et on pourrait nous demander de citer des exemples dans la solution desquels interviennent des fonctions non analytiques, tandis que les données sont analytiques. Ils ne sont pas courants; ce sont les équations aux dérivées partielles qui probablement les fourniront le plus facilement. Le suivant, dû à M. Borel, me paraît digne d'être signalé. Envisageons l'équation

$$\frac{\partial^2 u}{\partial x^2} - a^2 \frac{\partial^2 u}{\partial y^2} = f(x, y),$$

où a est une irrationnelle convenablement choisie, et $f(x, y)$ une certaine fonction analytique de x et y de période 2π pour x et y. Pour l'équation de cette forme citée par M. Borel, il y a une seule solution périodique et cette solution n'est pas analytique. Soit a un nombre incommensurable tel que $\frac{m_i}{n_i}$ étant l'une quelconque des réduites du développement de α en fraction continue, on ait

$$|m_i - n_i\alpha| < e^{-n_i^4 - m_i^4}$$

on forme

$$\phi(x, y) = \Sigma a^{m_i} b^{n_i} \cos(m_i^2 x) \cos(n_i^2 y) \quad (a < 1, b < 1).$$

C'est une fonction non analytique. Posons d'autre part

$$\frac{\partial^2\phi}{\partial x^2} - \alpha^4 \frac{\partial^2\phi}{\partial y^2} = \psi(x, y), \tag{1}$$

la fonction ψ sera analytique. Donc si on prend l'équation (1) à priori et qu'on cherche une solution périodique, en x et y, il n'y en a qu'une; c'est ϕ qui n'est pas analytique.

C'est encore, en se plaçant à un autre point de vue, qu'il paraît mauvais de réduire la théorie des fonctions à la théorie des fonctions analytiques. Il y a de nombreuses questions, où le fait pour les données d'être analytiques ne donne aucune facilité pour la solution, et où on risque, en portant trop son attention sur cette nature des données, de chercher la solution dans des voies sans issues. Pour le problème du refroidissement de la barre dont je parlais plus haut, qu'importe que les fonctions données $A(x)$ et $f(x)$ soient ou non analytiques? Ce n'est pas tout; il y a un dernier point sur lequel je tiens à insister. Il peut arriver que la circonstance d'avoir à faire à des fonctions analytiques conduise à une solution, mais il se peut que celle-ci ne se présente pas sous la forme la plus favorable, forme à laquelle on arrive au contraire en faisant abstraction de la nature analytique des données. La théorie des équations différentielles fournirait des exemples à l'appui de cette assertion; bornons nous à citer le théorème fondamental du Calcul Intégral relatif à l'existence de l'intégrale de l'équation différentielle $\frac{dy}{dx} = f(x, y)$. Ce sont les démonstrations ne supposant pas que la fonction f soit analytique, qui donnent le plus grand intervalle comme région où l'intégrale est certainement déterminée; l'analyste, qui suppose analytique la fonction réelle $f(x, y)$ et veut n'envisager que des séries entières, est conduit par son mode de démonstration à un domaine plus restreint.

J'ai simplement eu pour but dans ce qui précède de montrer qu'il ne faut pas restreindre systématiquement la notion de fonction. D'une manière générale, admirons des systèmes très bien ordonnés, mais méfions nous un peu de leur apparence scolastique, qui risque d'étouffer l'esprit d'invention. Il ne s'agit pas, bien entendu, de nier la grande importance actuelle de la théorie des fonctions analytiques, mais il ne faut pas oublier qu'elles ne forment qu'une classe très particulière de fonctions, et on doit souhaiter qu'un jour vienne où les mathématiciens élaborent des théories de plus en plus compréhensives; c'est ce qui arrivera peut-être au siècle prochain, si l'idée de fonction, dont je vous ai bien incomplètement esquissé l'histoire, continue son évolution. Mais, pour le moment nous sommes encore au dix-neuvième siècle; j'aurai l'occasion demain et après demain de faire amende honorable aux fonctions analytiques, qui depuis trente ans ont fait, comme vous savez, l'objet de travaux considérables.

VI.

Nous venons de voir les vastes perspectives qu'ouvre l'extension de plus en plus grande de la notion de fonction. Il faudra certainement montrer dans cette voie beaucoup de prudence, et ne pas entreprendre avant l'heure des recherches qui resteraient stériles; mais il n'est pas douteux qu'un jour viendra où l'analyste sentira le besoin d'étendre le domaine de ses recherches. L'extension de l'idée de fonction n'est pas la seule qu'aient poursuivie en ce siècle les mathématiciens qui s'intéressent aux principes de la science; la question des quantités complexes a vivement excité l'intérêt, d'autant plus qu'une certaine obscurité planait sur elle, qu'entraînait le mot un peu mystérieux de quantités imaginaires. Le sujet ne présente plus rien aujourd'hui de mystérieux. Dans un mémoire publié en 1884 Weierstrass a développé une théorie des nombres complexes. Il suppose que l'on considère des nombres de la forme

$$x_1 e_1 + x_2 e_2 + \cdots + x_n e_n,$$

où les x sont des nombres réels ou imaginaires ordinaires. Les e sont de purs symboles. On fait l'hypothèse que la somme, la différence, le produit et le quotient de deux nombres de l'ensemble font eux-mêmes partie de cet ensemble. Les produits $e_p e_q$ $(p, q = 1, 2, \cdots, n)$ sont donc des expressions $E_{p,q}$ linéaires et homogènes en $e_1, e_2, \cdots, e_n$ qui jouent le rôle essentiel dans la théorie. Weierstrass suppose de plus que les théorèmes dits *commutatif* et *associatif* subsistent tant pour l'addition que pour la multiplication. Pour l'addition, ils sont vérifiés d'eux-mêmes; pour la multiplication, ils s'expriment par les égalités

$$ab = ba, \quad (ab) \cdot c = a \cdot (bc).$$

a, b, c étant trois nombres quelconques de l'ensemble. Ces conditions conduisent à certaines relations entre les coefficients des formes linéaires $E_{p,q}$. A tout système de formes $E_{p,q}$ vérifiant ces conditions correspondra un ensemble de nombres complexes. Les nombres complexes que nous venons de définir diffèrent seulement en un point des nombres complexes ordinaires. Quand n est supérieur à deux, il peut exister des nombres différents de zéro dont le produit par certains autres nombres est nul. Weierstrass appelle ces nombres des diviseurs de zéro. M. Dedekind a montré qu'en général les calculs avec ces nombres complexes se ramenaient aux calculs de l'algèbre ordinaire; d'une manière plus précise, si le carré d'un nombre ne peut être nul sans que ce nombre soit nul, on peut aux n unités complexes primitives substituer n autres unités (le déterminant de la substitution n'étant pas nul) de telle sorte que pour ces nouvelles unités $e'_1, e'_2, \ldots, e'_n$ on ait

$$e'^2_i = e'_i, \quad e'_i e'_k = 0 \ (i \neq k),$$

d'où l'on conclut que les calculs relatifs aux nombres complexes précédents se ramènent à des calculs relatifs aux nombres réels ou complexes ordinaires.

Nous avons admis que les lois commutative et associative subsistaient dans l'algèbre précédente. On s'est placé à un point de vue plus général en supposant que, seule, la loi associative subsistait [c'est à dire $(ab)c = a(bc)$]. On a alors une algèbre beaucoup plus générale; celle-ci est complètement déterminée par le système des expressions linéaires $E_{p,q}$. Un exemple célèbre d'un système à quatre unités e_1, e_2, e_3, e_4 est fourni par les quaternions d'Hamilton

$$e_1 = 1, \quad e_2 = i, \quad e_3 = j, \quad e_4 = k,$$

avec les relations

$$\begin{aligned} i^2 = j^2 = k^2 &= -1 \\ ij = -ji &= k \\ jk = -kj &= i \\ ki = -ik &= j. \end{aligned}$$

Une remarque très intéressante de M. Poincaré ramène toute la théorie des quantités complexes à une question concernant la théorie des groupes. Elle consiste en ce qu'à chaque système d'unités complexes correspond un groupe continu (au sens de Lie) de substitutions linéaires à n variables, dont les coefficients sont des fonctions linéaires de n paramètres arbitraires, et inversement. Cette idée a été approfondie par M. Scheffers qui a été ainsi conduit à partager les nombres complexes en deux classes, suivant que le groupe qui leur correspond est intégrable ou non intégrable. A cette dernière classe appartient le groupe correspondant aux quaternions, et ceux-ci sont les représentants les plus simples de cette catégorie de nombres complexes. Le rapprochement entre la théorie des groupes de Lie et les nombres complexes fait disparaître le mystère qui semblait planer sur ceux-ci, et la véritable origine des symboles est ainsi bien mise en évidence. On peut se demander si ce symbolisme est susceptible d'accroître la puissance de l'Analyse. En France, les géomètres qui s'intéressent à ces calculs sont très peu nombreux; je sais qu'au contraire en Angleterre et, je crois aussi, dans ce pays les quaternions sont très appréciés. Je ne les ai pas assez maniés moi-même, pour me rendre compte si leur emploi en mécanique ou en physique mathématique simplifie les calculs d'une manière très appréciable; il y a probablement là surtout une affaire d'habitude. Le point vraiment intéressant serait de savoir si ces quantités complexes présenteront un jour quelque intérêt pour l'analyse générale, comme il arrive pour les imaginaires ordinaires. Les essais tentés jusqu'ici dans cette voie ne paraissent pas avoir été heureux; mais, maintenant que le lien avec la théorie des groupes est complètement mis en évidence, il n'est pas impossible que de nouvelles tentatives n'aboutissent à quelque résultat intéressant.

Les idées de nombres réel ou complexe, la notion de fonction sont à la base même de l'analyse; il y a encore une autre notion que le travail mathématique de ce siècle a conduit à élargir considérablement. L'idée d'espace forme la matière même de la géométrie; elle aussi a été soumise à une critique pénétrante qui a renouvelé les bases de la géométrie. Je n'en referai pas l'histoire depuis Gauss, Bolyai et Lobatschevski, histoire très souvent racontée, ni ne prendrai parti dans les querelles que se font encore à ce sujet les philosophes. Je veux dire seulement un mot de l'intérêt qu'ont eu pour les mathématiques les spéculations sur la nature de l'espace. Dans le mémoire célèbre de Riemann, apparaissent pour la première fois les notions relatives à la courbure de l'espace dans les différentes directions, c'est-à-dire les $\frac{n(n-1)}{2}$ fonctions invariantes caractéristiques d'une multiplicité à n dimensions; une vive impulsion a été ainsi donnée à la théorie des formes quadratiques de différentielles. Pour ne citer qu'un exemple, j'indiquerai seulement la forme

$$\frac{dx^2 + dy^2}{y^2}$$

qui donne le carré de l'élément d'arc dans la géométrie de Lobatchevski ; et il est intéressant de rappeler le rôle qu'elle a joué dans les recherches de M. Poincaré sur la formation des groupes fuchsiens. Après Riemann, Helmholtz posa la question sur un autre terrain: son idée fondamentale consiste à porter l'attention sur l'ensemble des mouvements possibles dans l'espace dont on fait l'étude. Le grand physicien traitait ainsi par avance de problèmes se rattachant à la théorie des groupes. Celle-ci n'était pas encore créée à l'époque où Helmholtz écrivait son mémoire ; il a commis quelques erreurs après tout secondaires, mais il n'en a pas moins la gloire d'avoir le premier regardé une géométrie comme l'étude d'un groupe. Les recherches d'Helmholtz furent reprises complètement par Lie ; elles lui offraient une magnifique occasion d'appliquer son admirable théorie des groupes de transformations. Dans ces études, l'espace est à priori regardé comme une multiplicité, et, en prenant le cas de trois dimensions, un point est défini par trois quantités (x, y, z). Un mouvement dans l'espace n'est autre chose qu'une transformation

$$x' = f(x, y, z), \; y' = \phi(x, y, z), \; z' = \psi(x, y, z)$$

valable pour une portion de l'espace. On suppose que tous les mouvements possibles forment un groupe à six paramètres, qu'ils laissent invariable une fonction des coordonnés de deux points quelconques, qu'enfin le mouvement libre soit possible, comme disait Helmholtz. Lie démontre alors que l'espace euclidien et les espaces non euclidiens sont les seuls qui satisfassent à ces conditions. Au point de vue où s'est placé Lie, l'étude des principes de la géométrie peut être regardée comme épuisée, mais il se borne à considérer une petite portion de l'espace. Clifford et Klein ont appelé l'attention sur la question de la connexité de l'espace qui est extrêmement intéressante ; nous ne savons rien sur la connexité de l'espace où nous vivons. On peut aussi chercher à approfondir le postulat de l'espace regardé comme une multiplicité, et subordonner la conception métrique de l'espace à la conception projective avec von Staudt, Cayley et Klein ; mais je dois me contenter de rappeler ces directions diverses.

J'ai seulement, messieurs, voulu montrer dans cette conférence quelles perspectives ouvre aux chercheurs l'extension de nos idées sur les fonctions, sur le nombre et sur l'espace. Si l'élaboration mathématique est aussi féconde au siècle prochain qu'elle l'a été en ce siècle, l'analyse différera beaucoup dans cent ans de ce qu'elle est aujourd'hui; on maniera peut-être couramment les fonctions les plus extraordinaires, et on verra très clair dans des espaces ayant beaucoup de dimensions et des connexités élevées. Pour se représenter l'état de la mathématique en l'an 2000, il faudrait l'imagination de l'auteur de "Looking Backward"; il est malheureux que M. Bellamy dans son roman ne nous ait pas parlé des mathématiques à cette époque. Comme l'humanité, s'il faut l'en croire, aura alors beaucoup de loisirs, les mathématiques seront sans doute extrêmement florissantes et les problèmes qui nous arrêtent aujourd'hui ne seront plus que des jeux d'enfants pour nos successeurs.

Seconde Conférence.

Quelques Vues Générales sur la Théorie des Équations Différentielles.

Je voudrais aujourd'hui jeter un coup d'œil sur la théorie des équations différentielles, qui joue en analyse un rôle considérable et dont les progrès importent vivement à ses applications; c'est un domaine très vaste et j'éprouve quelque embarras à faire un choix entre les directions si diverses où s'est développée cette théorie. Les géomètres du siècle dernier ne paraissent pas s'être préoccupés d'établir rigoureusement l'existence des intégrales des équations différentielles; ils intégraient, quand ils le pouvaient, les équations qui se présentaient dans leurs recherches, sans se soucier de ces théorèmes d'existence, comme on dit aujourd'hui, auxquels nous attachons beaucoup d'importance. C'est à Cauchy que l'on doit les premières recherches précises sur ces questions; le champ en est très vaste, et il ne l'a pas parcouru en entier, mais, au moins dans le cas où les fonctions et les données sont analytiques, il a indiqué les principes qu'ont suivis tous ses continuateurs. Dans les théorèmes relatifs à l'existence des intégrales, on emploie des méthodes différentes suivant que les équations et les données sont supposées ou non analytiques.

I.

Plaçons nous d'abord dans le premier cas, de beaucoup le mieux élaboré. L'idée essentielle de Cauchy consiste dans la considération des fonctions majorantes. On sait que les difficultés résident surtout dans la démonstration de la convergence de certaines séries entières que les équations différentielles permettent de former. Cauchy y parvient par des comparaisons avec d'autres équations facilement intégrables. Pour les équations différentielles ordinaires, il n'y avait à faire après Cauchy que des simplifications de forme, et, pour le cas d'une seule équation aux dérivées partielles, quel que soit le nombre des variables, le grand géomètre avait indiqué aussi les points essentiels de la démonstration, que Mme. Kovalevski, dans un mémoire resté classique, a présentée sous une forme très simple. Le théorème fondamental est alors le suivant : Si on a une équation aux dérivées partielles d'ordre n relative à une fonction z de $p+1$ variables indépendantes $x, x_1, \cdots, x_p$ et que l'équation contienne la dérivée d'ordre n, $\frac{\partial^n z}{\partial x^n}$, une intégrale sera en général déterminée si on se donne pour $x = a$ les valeurs de z et de ses dérivées par rapport à x jusqu'à l'ordre $n-1$; ces données sont des fonctions holomorphes de $x_1, x_2, \cdots, x_p$ dans le voisinage de $a_1, a_2, \cdots, a_p$. On peut donc dire, en s'appuyant sur cet énoncé que l'intégrale générale de l'équation considérée dépend de n fonctions de p variables indépendantes. C'était un point auquel on tenait beaucoup autrefois de savoir de combien de fonctions arbitraires dépendait l'intégrale générale d'une équation aux dérivées partielles ; certains résultats paradoxaux avaient cependant déjà appelé l'attention comme les formes diverses de l'intégrale générale de l'équation de la chaleur $\frac{\partial^2 z}{\partial x^2} = \frac{\partial z}{\partial y}$, qui se présentait tantôt avec une, tantôt avec deux fonctions arbitraires. De tels résultats ne nous étonnent plus aujourd'hui, quand il s'agit comme ici de fonctions analytiques. Nous n'avons qu'à nous rappeler qu'un nombre fini quelconque de fonctions à un nombre quelconque de variables indépendantes ne présente pas, au point de vue arithmétique, une plus grande généralité qu'une seule fonction d'une seule variable, puisque dans l'un et l'autre cas l'ensemble des coefficients des développements forme simplement une suite énumérable. Aussi s'explique-t-on que M. Borel ait pu établir que toute intégrale analytique d'une équation aux dérivées partielles à coefficients analytiques peut être exprimée à l'aide d'une formule ne renfermant qu'une seule fonction arbitraire d'une variable réelle.

Nous venons de considérer une seule équation aux dérivées partielles. L'étude des systèmes d'équations différentielles présentait de plus grandes difficultés. Une première question est tout d'abord restée longtemps sans réponse; il était possible de se demander s'il pouvait exister des systèmes qui comprennent un nombre illimité d'équations distinctes c'est à dire ne pouvant pas se déduire par différentiation d'un certain nombre d'entre elles. M. Tresse a établi qu'un système d'équations aux dérivées partielles étant défini d'une manière quelconque, ce système est nécessairement limité, c'est à dire qu'il existe un nombre fini s, tel que toutes les équations d'ordre supérieur à s, que contient le système, se déduisent par de simples différentiations des équations d'ordre égal ou inférieur à s. Il importait ensuite de se rendre compte de la nature des éléments arbitraires figurant dans l'intégrale générale. Mme. Kovalevski n'avait examiné que certains systèmes composés d'équations en nombre égal à celui des fonctions inconnues et résolubles par rapport aux dérivées d'ordre le plus élevé de chacune des fonctions, ces dérivées étant relatives à une même variable x. M. Riquier d'abord, puis M. Delassus ont donné sous des formes différentes la solution du problème dans le cas général; M. Delassus arrive par des changements de variables à obtenir une forme canonique complètement intégrable, et montre que l'intégration d'un tel système à m variables se ramène à l'intégration successive de m systèmes de Mme. Kovalevski contenant successivement 1, 2, ⋯, m variables; c'est en partant de cette propriété qu'on peut démontrer facilement l'existence des intégrales analytiques, et déterminer les fonctions et constantes initiales en nombre fini dont dépendent ces intégrales.

Il semble y avoir eu longtemps chez les mathématiciens quelques hésitations sur ce qu'on devait entendre par intégrale générale d'une équation aux dérivées partielles. Si l'on se borne aux cas où il ne figure dans les équations que des éléments analytiques, et si l'on n'envisage que les intégrales analytiques, on considère aujourd'hui, conformément à l'opinion de M. Darboux, qu'une intégrale est générale, si on peut disposer des arbitraires qui y figurent, fonctions et constantes, de manière à retrouver les solutions dont les théorèmes de Cauchy et de ses successeurs nous ont démontré l'existence. Antérieurement, Ampère s'était placé à un autre point de vue; dans son grand mémoire sur les équations aux différences partielles, il s'exprime ainsi: "Pour qu'une intégrale soit générale, il faut qu'il n'en résulte entre les variables que l'on considère et leurs dérivées à l'infini que les relations exprimées par l'équation donnée et par les équations que l'on en déduit en la différentiant." Il est bien clair qu'il s'agit de relations ne renfermant aucune des quantités arbitraires qui figurent dans l'intégrale considérée. Les avis étaient partagés entre les géomètres, et on se demandait s'il y a identité entre la définition d'Ampère et celle de Cauchy. M. Goursat a montré bien nettement, sur différents exemples, qu'une intégrale peut être générale au sens d'Ampère sans être générale au sens de Cauchy.

Il ne faudrait pas conclure des divers travaux qui précèdent, que, tout en envisageant seulement des intégrales et des équations analytiques, l'étude des conditions déterminant les intégrales d'un système d'équations aux dérivées partielles soit actuellement achevée. Les théorèmes généraux indiqués font connaître certaines données qui déterminent une intégrale, mais celle-ci peut être déterminée par une infinité d'autres conditions. Il n'est pas douteux que les types à trouver de ces théorèmes d'existence sont en nombre infini. Prenons l'exemple très simple de l'équation

$$\frac{\partial^2 z}{\partial x\,\partial y} + a\frac{\partial z}{\partial x} + b\frac{\partial z}{\partial y} + cz = 0.$$

Une intégrale est déterminée par la condition de se réduire pour $x = 0$ à une fonction donnée de y, et pour $y = 0$ à une fonction donnée de x: voilà un genre de déterminations d'une intégrale qui ne rentre pas dans les conditions du théorème général de Cauchy. Les conditions très variées, qui peuvent déterminer les intégrales des équations aux différences partielles appellent encore de nombreuses recherches.

II.

Nous venons de nous placer au point de vue de la théorie des fonctions analytiques. Comme je le disais hier, il y a souvent grand intérêt, non seulement à un point de vue philosophique, mais même en quelque sorte au point de vue pratique, à adopter des hypothèses plus générales. C'est encore à Cauchy que l'on doit pour les équations différentielles ordinaires la démonstration de l'existence des intégrales sans supposer les équations analytiques. Sa méthode, bien naturelle et bien simple, consiste à regarder les équations différentielles comme limites d'équations aux différences. On peut faire sur cette méthode de Cauchy une remarque très intéressante; elle est susceptible de fournir des développements en séries des intégrales qui *convergent tant que les intégrales restent continues, et laissent continues les coefficients différentiels.* En ce sens, elle est supérieure aux autres méthodes qui ont été proposées. Ainsi, pour prendre un exemple, soit le système d'équations

$$\frac{dx_i}{dt} = X_i(x_1, x_2, \cdots, x_n) \qquad (i = 1, 2, \cdots n)$$

où les X sont des polynomes. On peut représenter les intégrales de ce système prenant pour $t = 0$ les valeurs $x_1^0, x_2^0, \cdots, x_n^0$ par des développements de la forme

$$P_1(x_1^0, x_2^0, \cdots, x_n^0, t) + \cdots + P_n(x_1^0, x_2^0, \cdots, x_n^0, t) + \cdots$$

les P étant des polynomes en $x_1^0, x_2^0, \cdots, x_n^0$ et t, et ces développements sont convergents tant que les intégrales restent des fonctions continues de t.

D'autres méthodes ont été proposées pour démontrer l'existence des intégrales, comme la méthode des approximations successives qui donne pour les séries une convergence très rapide, mais ces séries ne convergent pas nécessairement dans tout le champ où les intégrales sont continues.

Pour une équation différentielle ordinaire d'ordre n, on suppose généralement, quand on veut établir l'existence des intégrales, qu'on se donne pour une valeur de x les valeurs de la fonction et de ses dérivées jusqu'à l'ordre $n - 1$, mais on pourrait prendre beaucoup d'autres données; et c'est ce qui arrive notamment dans les applications du calcul des variations. Ainsi pour une équation du second ordre, il arrive qu'une intégrale soit déterminée par les conditions de prendre pour x_0 la valeur y_0 et pour x_1 la valeur y_1. On a peu travaillé jusqu'ici dans cet ordre d'idées, et cependant maintes conditions initiales sont aussi intéressantes que celles adoptées dans le théorème général classique. Les recherches entreprises dans cette voie ont conduit à quelques résultats par l'emploi de méthodes d'approximations successives, et on a pu ainsi reconnaître des cas singuliers de divergence dans l'emploi de ces méthodes d'approximation.

Si nous passons maintenant aux équations aux différences partielles, les équations et les données n'étant pas nécessairement analytiques, nous nous trouvons dans un domaine très étendu où on n'a fait que les premiers pas. Il faut déjà quelque soin pour établir l'existence des intégrales de l'équation linéaire

$$\frac{\partial f}{\partial x} + X(x, y)\frac{\partial f}{\partial y} = 0$$

sans supposer que $X(x, y)$ soit analytique. Pour les équations d'ordre supérieur, il n'y a qu'un petit nombre de types pour lesquels on puisse définir avec précision ce que l'on entend par intégrale générale. Ils ont généralement pour origine des problèmes de géométrie infinitésimale ou de physique mathématique; les variables et les fonctions restent ici réelles. Prenons, comme exemple, l'équation

$$\frac{\partial^2 z}{\partial x \partial y} + a\frac{\partial z}{\partial x} + b\frac{\partial z}{\partial y} + cz = 0$$

où a, b, c sont des fonctions continues de x et y, sur laquelle Riemann a écrit quelques pages extrêmement remarquables. Soit un arc de courbe MP tel que toute parallèle à Ox et à Oy le rencontre au plus en un point; nous nous donnons les valeurs de z et $\frac{\partial z}{\partial x}$ sur cette courbe. Il y aura une intégrale et une seule, continue ainsi que ses dérivées partielles du premier ordre, satisfaisant aux conditions données, et elle sera définie dans le rectangle de côtés parallèles aux axes et ayant M et P pour sommets opposés. On voit combien cet énoncé est d'une nature plus précise que ceux qui ont été donnés antérieurement en nous plaçant au point de vue de la théorie des fonctions analytiques, où pour une équation comme celle-ci on établit seulement l'existence d'une solution dans le voisinage d'une courbe, voisinage déterminé avec très peu de précision. L'exemple si simple que nous avons choisi montre encore qu'il n'existe pas toujours d'intégrale continue ainsi que ses dérivées premières satisfaisant aux conditions données sur un arc de courbe; il en sera ainsi quand sur cet arc il y aura une tangente parallèle à l'un des axes. Voici un second exemple dans le même ordre d'idées; on peut relativement à l'équation

$$\frac{\partial^2 u}{\partial x^2} + \frac{\partial^2 u}{\partial y^2} - \frac{\partial^2 u}{\partial z^2} = 0$$

se donner les valeurs de u et de $\frac{\partial u}{\partial z}$ pour les points d'un cercle C situé dans le plan $z = z_0$; l'intégrale ainsi définie est déterminée à l'intérieur des deux cônes de révolution passant par la circonférence C et de génératrices parallèles à celles du cône $x^2 + y^2 - z^2 = 0$.

Les conditions déterminant une intégrale peuvent prendre des formes très diverses. Ainsi des conditions de continuité sont susceptibles de remplacer certaines données: c'est un fait auquel nous sommes très habituée, mais qui n'en est pas moins très remarquable. L'équation du potentiel a provoqué dans cette voie de nombreuses recherches, et le théorème fondamental auquel Riemann a donné le nom de Dirichlet, après avoir été approfondi par Schwarz et Neumann, a encore fait récemment l'objet des recherches de M. Poincaré. Des problèmes analogues ont été posés et résolus pour un grand nombre d'équations, par exemple pour l'équation

$$\frac{\partial^2 u}{\partial x^2} + \frac{\partial^2 u}{\partial y^2} + a\frac{\partial u}{\partial x} + b\frac{\partial u}{\partial y} + cu = 0$$

pour laquelle une intégrale continue est déterminée par ses valeurs sur un contour fermé dans toute région où le coefficient c est négatif; de telles questions ne sont d'ailleurs pas limitées aux équations linéaires.

Ces divers exemples caractérisent bien la nature des théorèmes d'existence des intégrales, quand on ne se place pas au point de vue de la théorie des fonctions analytiques. Il y a là un ordre immense de recherches également intéressantes pour la théorie pure et pour les applications de l'analyse. Sans même aborder de questions entièrement nouvelles, que de points seraient à reprendre dans les travaux célèbres des physiciens géomètres de la première moitié du siècle, de Fourier, de Poisson, de Cauchy même, si on voulait y apporter la rigueur que l'on exige aujourd'hui en mathématiques.

Je dois ajouter d'ailleurs, comme transition entre les deux directions relatives aux généralités sur les équations aux dérivées partielles, qu'il existe des classes très étendues d'équations dont *toutes* les intégrales sont analytiques. Citons les équations linéaires d'ordre n à deux variables indépendantes: dans une région du plan où toutes les caractéristiques sont imaginaires, toute intégrale bien déterminée et continue ainsi que ses dérivées partielles jusqu'à l'ordre n est nécessairement analytique. Il y a aussi de nombreuses équations non linéaires ayant toutes leurs intégrales analytiques.

Je viens de parler des caractéristiques d'une équation; c'est là un sujet en connexion étroite avec les théorèmes généraux d'existence qui viennent de nous occuper. Les caractéristiques sont certaines multiplicités jouissant de propriétés particulières relativement à une équation donnée, multiplicités singulières en ce qu'elles ne définissent pas une intégrale contrairement à ce qui arrive en général pour les multiplicités contenant les mêmes éléments. Tandis que la notion de caractéristiques est aujourd'hui très nette pour les équations ou systèmes d'équations à deux variables indépendantes, elle a encore besoin d'être approfondie dans le cas de plus de deux variables.

III.

Si, quittant les généralités relatives à l'existence des intégrales, nous voulons parler de la recherche effective des intégrales et de l'étude d'équations particulières, l'embarras est grand de tenter des classifications dans un ensemble considérable de travaux, et nous sentons combien ces classements sont toujours défectueux par quelque endroit. Peut-être pourrait-on tout d'abord distinguer l'ancienne école mathématique, et le mot "*ancienne*" ne veut pas dire qu'elle ne continue pas à prospérer. C'est l'École d'Euler, de Lagrange, de Monge dans son immortel ouvrage sur les applications de l'analyse à la géométrie, d'Ampère dans son célèbre mémoire de 1817 sur les équations aux différences partielles. En France, cette école des analystes géomètres pour qui les problèmes de géométrie infinitésimale sont l'occasion de belles recherches analytiques, a pour chef M. Darboux. Ses Leçons sur la Théorie des surfaces sont aujourd'hui un livre classique qui a rappelé l'attention sur des questions quelque temps négligées. Relativement à l'intégration effective des équations du second ordre, pendant de longues années après la publication du mémoire d'Ampère, il n'avait été rien ajouté d'essentiel à la théorie développée par le grand géomètre. En 1870, M. Darboux publia un mémoire renfermant des vues profondes et originales qui est fondamental dans l'histoire de cette théorie. Depuis cette époque, divers géomètres ont développé des méthodes plus ou moins analogues. M. Goursat vient de rassembler dans un ouvrage considérable les méthodes proposées, en y ajoutant ses découvertes personnelles sur ces questions difficiles. On peut caractériser toutes ces recherches, en disant qu'on s'y propose de trouver explicitement des intégrales avec le plus grand degré possible d'indétermination. Quelquefois, les méthodes sont des indications de marche à suivre quand telle circonstance heureuse se présente, et on cherche des classes d'équations pour lesquelles il en soit ainsi; dans d'autres cas, on renonce au moins temporairement à l'intégration complète, et on recherche des solutions de plus en plus étendues au moyen de transformations convenables comme, par exemple, celles de M. Bianchi pour l'équation des surfaces à courbure constante.

Les idées du grand géomètre norvégien, Sophus Lie, dont la science déplore la perte récente, ont exercé aussi depuis vingt ans une grande influence dans l'étude des équations différentielles sous le point de vue qui nous occupe en ce moment. La théorie des groupes de transformations, une des plus belles créations mathématiques de ce siècle, est venue apporter un élément incomparable de classification ; elle a permis de faire une vaste synthèse en donnant une origine commune à des notions éparses qui paraissaient sans liens.

Je disais tout à l'heure que nos classifications se plient difficilement à la complexité des choses. Certains problèmes se trouvent à un confluent, où se rencontrent l'ancienne École de Monge et d'Ampère et l'École plus récente qui se rattache à la théorie moderne des fonctions. Monge avait intégré l'équation des surfaces minima, et c'est là un de ses titres de gloire. Ses formules ont été transformées par Weierstrass, et alors a apparu le lien entre la théorie des fonctions d'une variable complexe et la théorie des surfaces minima. Un problème appelle vivement l'attention dans cette théorie : c'est le problème de Plateau relatif aux surfaces minima passant par un contour donné. Il a été résolu seulement dans des cas très spéciaux ; je crois qu'en exerçant la sagacité des analystes il sera quelque jour l'occasion de progrès importants dans l'analyse générale.

IV.

J'ai surtout parlé jusqu'ici des équations aux dérivées partielles. La théorie des équations différentielles ordinaires est plus spéciale, d'autant que quelques uns ont une tendance à la regarder comme un chapitre de la théorie des fonctions analytiques. Après les remarques que j'ai faites hier, je n'ai pas besoin d'ajouter que ce n'est pas là mon opinion ; je vous ai indiqué plusieurs problèmes qui ne relèvent en rien de la théorie des fonctions analytiques, et il me suffira de citer encore l'extension des idées de Galois aux équations différentielles. Ceci dit, il n'est pas douteux que les progrès de la théorie des fonctions analytiques ont exercé la plus heureuse influence sur certains points de la théorie des équations différentielles ordinaires. Je ne ferai que rappeler le mémoire célèbre de Puiseux sur les fonctions algébriques, dans lequel étudiant à un point de nouveau les plus simples des équations différentielles à savoir les quadratures, il révèle l'origine de la périodicité des intégrales de différentielles algébriques. Les recherches de Briot et Bouquet ne sont pas moins classiques ; les auteurs y étudient les circonstances singulières qui peuvent se présenter dans une équation du premier ordre quand le coefficient différentiel devient infini ou indéterminé. Il faut se reporter à près de cinquante ans en arrière pour bien juger ce mémoire, où pour la première fois est mis en évidence le rôle des points singuliers dans l'étude des fonctions; ces notions nous sont bien familières aujourd'hui, mais nous ne devons pas oublier que ce sont les mémoires de Puiseux et de Briot et Bouquet qui en ont montré la haute importance. Il semble que le mémoire de Briot et Bouquet aurait dû être immédiatement l'origine de travaux dans la même voie, mais bien des années se passèrent avant qu'il ne fût repris et complété. C'est en Allemagne, sous l'influence de l'enseignement de Weierstrass que nous voyons d'abord reparaître l'étude des singularités des équations différentielles, et cela pour les équations différentielles linéaires. Il est vraiment curieux que Briot et Bouquet, après avoir traité le cas plus difficile des singularités d'une équation non linéaire, fût-elle du premier ordre, n'aient pas songé à s'occuper des équations linéaires, laissant à M. Fuchs l'honneur de fonder une théorie, dont l'illustre géomètre allemand a fait lui-même des applications du plus haut intérêt, et qui a provoqué un nombre immense de recherches. On remplirait des bibliothèques avec les mémoires composés depuis trente ans sur la théorie des équations linéaires. Je ne puis songer à vous parler des nombreuses classes d'équations dont l'étude a été faite. En restant dans les généralités, je rappelle seulement que l'étude des points singuliers présente une grande différence suivant que ce point singulier est régulier, comme dit M. Fuchs, ou présente les caractères d'un point singulier essentiel. Ce dernier cas est de beaucoup plus difficile; M. Thomé a formé des séries satisfaisant formellement à l'équation, mais qui en général ne sont pas convergentes. Remarquons à ce propos que Briot et Bouquet ont les premiers montré qu'une équation différentielle pouvait conduire à une série en général divergente; leur exemple bien simple est l'équation

$$x^2\frac{dy}{dx} = ax + by$$

vérifiée par une série entière dont le rayon de convergence est nul. Cette petite constatation a appelé l'attention sur un fait d'une importance capitale, et qui ne se rencontre que trop fréquemment dans les applications; les développements purement formels sont nombreux en mécanique analytique et mécanique céleste, où ils font le désespoir des géomètres. Pour les équations linéaires, ces développement ont un certain intérêt, comme l'a montré M. Poincaré, au point de vue de la représentation asymptotique des intégrales. On peut d'ailleurs obtenir et de bien des manières, une représentation analytique des intégrales autour du point singulier. Je dois enfin mentionner, relativement aux points singuliers irréguliers, les recherches de M. H. von Koch qui a tiré très heureusement parti dans cette question des résultats obtenus sur les déterminants d'ordre infini.

Revenons aux équations du premier ordre. Briot et Bouquet ont surtout étudié les singularités en faisant les réductions au type

$$x\frac{dy}{dx} = f(x, y)$$

où f est holomorphe et s'annule pour $x = 0$, $y = 0$, et leurs recherches ont été depuis complétées par la connaissance de la forme analytique des intégrales au voisinage du point singulier. Le cas plus compliqué de l'équation

$$x^m\frac{dy}{dx} = f(x, y) \qquad (m \geqq 2) \tag{1}$$

n'avait fait jusqu'à ces derniers temps l'objet d'aucune recherche depuis les quelques lignes que lui avaient consacrées Briot et Bouquet. Cette étude vient d'être reprise simultanément par M. Horn et par M. Bendixson. Ces auteurs se servent d'une méthode convenable d'approximations successives dont j'indiquerai le principe. Nous supposons expressément que x reste réel et se rapproche de zéro par valeurs positives, et posons

$$f(x, y) = by + F(x, y)$$

F ne contenant pas de terme du premier degré en y indépendant de x. Si la partie réelle de b est positive, l'équation précédente a une infinité d'intégrales tendant vers zéro en même temps que x, et elle n'en a qu'une quand la partie réelle de b est négative. Les deux cas peuvent être traités en faisant les approximation successives

$$x^m\frac{dy_1}{dx} = by_1$$

$$x^m\frac{dy_2}{dx} = by_2 + F(x, y_1)$$

$$\cdots\cdots\cdots\cdots$$

$$x^m\frac{dy_n}{dx} = by_n + F(x, y_{n-1})$$

et on obtient ainsi une représentation analytique des intégrales (ou de l'intégrale). Il existe un développement

$$a_1 x + a_2 x^2 + \cdots + a_n x^n + \cdots$$

satisfaisant *formellement* à l'équation (1), mais dont le rayon de convergence est nul en général; c'est la généralisation de la remarque de Briot et Bouquet, et on peut ajouter que la dérivée d'ordre n de toutes les intégrales considérées tend vers $1 \cdot 2 \cdots n \cdot a_n$, quand x tend vers zéro. De plus, quand il y a une infinité d'intégrales tendant vers zéro en même temps, elles sont *toutes* représentées asymptotiquement par le même développement, ce qui est évidemment défavorable pour l'intérêt que peut présenter une telle représentation asymptotique. Les méthodes précédentes sont d'ailleurs susceptibles de s'étendre à un système d'équations différentielles. Je ferai encore une remarque importante sur l'équation (1); le cas où la partie réelle de b est nulle échappe complètement à la méthode. L'équation a en général des intégrales qui ne tendent vers aucune limite pour $x = 0$. On se trouve alors, sur un exemple très simple, en présence des difficultés considérables que l'on rencontre dans plusieurs questions de mécanique analytique; c'est en vain que l'on a tenté jusqu'ici de procéder par approximations successives convergentes et les développements essayés sont en général divergents.

Quoi qu'il en soit des difficultés restant encore à surmonter, des progrès sérieux ont été réalisés ces dernières années dans l'étude des intégrales des équations non linéaires au voisinage des points singuliers mis en évidence par la forme même de l'équation différentielle. De tels points singuliers sont les seuls que puissent avoir les intégrales quand il s'agit d'une équation linéaire, mais il en est autrement pour les équations non linéaires. En dehors des points singuliers, qui sont *apparents* sur l'équation, il peut y en avoir d'autres variables d'une intégrale à l'autre. Les équations du premier ordre ne présentaient pas à cet égard de bien grandes difficultés. En se bornant aux équations différentielles algébriques, tous les points singuliers qui ne sont pas apparents ne peuvent être que des points critiques algébriques. Des exemples simples montraient que pour les équations d'ordre supérieur au premier, il n'en était plus de même et qu'il pouvait y avoir des points essentiels mobiles; l'attention avait été appelée sur ce point quand on avait voulu étendre aux équations du second ordre à points critiques fixes les méthodes qui avaient réussi pour les équations du premier ordre possédant la même propriété. La difficulté signalée restait entière, quand M. Painlevé est venu faire une importante distinction et signaler un fait inattendu. Les points singuliers mobiles peuvent se partager en deux classes, les points singuliers algébriques ou transcendants pour lesquels l'intégrale et ses dérivées acquièrent une valeur déterminée finie ou infinie, et les points singuliers essentiels. M. Painlevé a établi que, dans les équations différentielles algébriques, le cas où les points singuliers essentiels sont mobiles est un cas exceptionnel. Ces équations se trouvent ainsi partagées en deux classes, une classe générale pour laquelle l'intégrale générale n'a pas de singularités essentielles mobiles, et une classe singulière. L'intérêt de cette distinction est très grand dans l'étude de quelques classes particulières d'équations différentielles.

V.

Arrêtons nous spécialement sur le cas où la variable et les fonctions restent réelles; c'est le cas intéressant pour les applications. Nous désignerons par t la variable indépendante qui sera, si l'on veut, le temps. Pour étudier quantitativement les fonctions définies par les équations différentielles, c'est à dire pour pouvoir évaluer numériquement les valeurs de ces fonctions, on doit désirer d'avoir des représentations de celles-ci permettant de les calculer pour un intervalle de temps aussi grand que possible. Il y a des classes assez étendues d'équations différentielles, d'après la forme desquelles on est assuré d'obtenir des développements valables pour toute valeur de t. Un cas très simple est celui des équations

$$\frac{dy_i}{dt} = f_i(t, y_1, y_2, \cdots, y_n) \qquad (i = 1, 2, \cdots, n).$$

On suppose que les fonctions f restent continues pour toutes les valeurs réelles et finies de t et des y, et que de plus les dérivées $\frac{df_i}{dy_k}$ restent en valeurs absolues moindres qu'un nombre fixe. La méthode de Cauchy ou la méthode des approximations successives donne pour les y des développements valables pour toute valeur du temps.

En supposant que les fonctions f soient analytiques et régulières pour toute valeur réelle finie ou infinie de t et des y, on peut procéder autrement dans la recherche d'un développement valable pour toute valeur du temps. Il suffit de faire, avec M. Poincaré, une représentation conforme, sur un cercle situé dans le plan d'une variable z, d'une bande très petite dans le plan de la variable t (supposée un instant complexe), bande parallèle à l'axe réel, ce qui revient à poser

$$s = \frac{e^{t} - 1}{e^{t} + 1}.$$

On peut ici procéder encore d'une autre manière en se rappelant que M. Painlevé a établi que toute fonction holomorphe d'une variable réelle dans un intervalle peut être développée en une série de polynomes dont les coefficients dépendent linéairement des valeurs de la fonction et de ses dérivées pour une valeur particulière $t = t_0$.

Il y a des cas où l'équation ne rentre pas dans les types précédents, et où l'on sera cependant, au moins pour certaines intégrales, assuré de la possibilité d'un développement toujours valable. Je citerai comme premier exemple les équations

$$\frac{dx}{dt} = -ax + f\left(\frac{1}{t}, x, y\right), \quad \frac{dy}{dt} = -by + F\left(\frac{1}{t}, x, y\right)$$

où a et b sont deux constantes positives ; f et F désigne des séries holomorphes en $\frac{1}{t}$, x et y, et ne renfermant pas de termes constants et de termes du premier degré en x et y. Il est aisé d'établir que, pour $t = t_0$ suffisamment grand, les valeurs initiales étant suffisamment petites, les intégrales correspondantes tendront vers zéro pour $t = \infty$. De tels exemples sont malheureusement très rares ; on peut encore citer les problèmes de mécanique où il y a une fonction des forces. Chacun sait que l'équilibre est stable, dans le voisinage d'une position où la fonction des forces est maxima, mais ce résultat classique provient de l'étude *indirecte* des équations différentielles ; le même problème nous montre vite combien une étude *directe* serait désirable, et combien de difficultés restent à vaincre. Ainsi, supposons qu'il n'y ait pas de fonction de forces et bornons nous à un point matériel. Ecrivons les équations

$$\frac{d^2x}{dt^2} = ax + by + \cdots \qquad \frac{d^2y}{dt^2} = a'x + b'y + \cdots \tag{2}$$

où les seconds membres sont des développements suivant les puissances de x et y, et convergents pour x et y assez petits. Le point $x = 0$, $y = 0$ correspond-il à une position d'équilibre stable ? Il est impossible actuellement de répondre à cette question. Il y a peut-être quelques mécaniciens qui croient que la nature de l'équilibre dépend seulement des termes du premier degré dans le second membre. Nous nous garderons bien de leur en vouloir, car c'était au fond l'erreur de Lagrange, mais il est clair qu'en réduisant les équations à la partie linéaire, on peut avoir une solution stable qui cesse de l'être quand on rétablit les termes d'ordre supérieur. Les équations (2) présentent une particularité curieuse qui mérite d'être signalée. On peut se proposer de trouver une intégrale première

$$F(x, y, x', y') = C \qquad \left(x' = \frac{dx}{dt}, y' = \frac{dy}{dt}\right)$$

F étant en holomorphe en x, y, x', y', et commençant par des termes du second degré. Or on trouve une telle fonction F au point de vue formel, mais la série ainsi obtenue ne converge pas en général. J'ajoute que, si la force dépendait non seulement de la position du point mais de la vitesse, c'est-à-dire si dans (2) les seconds membres dépendaient aussi de x' et y', la recherche de la fonction F ne pourrait plus généralement être effectuée, mais il serait plus facile de répondre à la question relative à la stabilité.

Quand on a aucune notion de la grandeur de l'intervalle pour lequel les fonctions définies par les équations différentielles sont continues, on peut cependant trouver des développements valables pour tout le temps pendant lequel les fonctions resteront continues. J'ai dit tout à l'heure que l'on pouvait déduire de tels développements de la méthode classique de Cauchy; c'est là un résultat intéressant, mais malheureusement il n'a guère qu'un intérêt théorique, car il semble bien difficile de déduire de ces développements quelques renseignements sur le champ où les intégrales restent continues.

Il y aura cependant des cas où certaines propriétés auxiliaires des équations permettent d'avoir des renseignements sur le champ où les intégrales restent continues. Que l'on prenne, par exemple, les six équations classiques en $p, q, r, \gamma, \gamma', \gamma''$ relatives au mouvement d'un solide pesant suspendu par un point; l'intégrale des forces vives et l'intégrale $\gamma^2, \gamma'^2, \gamma''^2 =$ const. permettent de reconnaître que les six fonctions précédentes resteront finies pour toute valeur du temps, et nous sommes alors assuré que pour ce problème la méthode de Cauchy donne des développements valables pour toute valeur du temps.

VI.

A l'ordre d'idées qui nous occupe, se rattachent les travaux de M. Poincaré sur les solutions périodiques, et sur les solutions asymptotiques. L'étude des solutions périodiques d'une équation différentielle présente un intérêt particulier. Je connais peu d'exemples où on puisse trouver directement une solution périodique. Dans ses travaux sur ce sujet, M. Poincaré procède par voie indirecte; il profite de la présence d'une constante très petite dans les équations, et il raisonne par continuité en partant d'une solution périodique pour la valeur zéro de cette constante. Il serait à désirer que l'on pût pénétrer par une autre voie dans l'étude des solutions périodiques. Quant aux solutions asymptotiques à une seule solution, leur étude résulte de développements analytiques simples; mais l'existence dans certains cas particuliers de solutions doublement asymptotiques, c'est à dire de solutions asymptotiques pour $t = -\infty$ à une solution périodique et de nouveau asymptotiques pour $t = +\infty$ à cette même solution était extrêmement cachée, et leur découverte a demandé un effort considérable.

L'étude des courbes définies par les équations différentielles est surtout une étude qualitative. Si l'on considère d'abord une équation du premier ordre et du premier degré

$$\frac{dx}{X} = \frac{dy}{Y} \quad (X \text{ et } Y \text{ polynomes en } x \text{ et } y) \tag{2}$$

l'étude des points singuliers généraux se déduit des résultats de Briot et Bouquet. Ces points se partagent en trois types, que M. Poincaré appelle des cols, des nœuds et des foyers. Un point singulier d'une nature déjà plus compliquée est fourni par ce que M. Poincaré appelle un centre, qui en général présente de l'analogie avec les foyers mais autour duquel dans certains cas l'intégrale constitue une courbe fermée. On a alors un exemple de solutions périodiques dont la période dépend des conditions initiales. Les travaux les plus récents sur les points singuliers de courbes intégrales de l'équation (2) sont dus à M. Bendixson; le savant géomètre suédois a établi en particulier que s'il existe pour l'équation (2) une courbe intégrale allant à l'origine avec une tangente déterminée, toutes les courbes intégrales allant à l'origine y parviendront avec des tangentes déterminées.

L'étude des courbes intégrales ne doit pas être bornée au voisinage des points singuliers; on doit chercher à se rendre compte de leur forme sur le plan tout entier ou sur la sphère en faisant une perspective. Si l'on chemine, pour l'équation (2), sur une courbe intégrale, qu'arrivera-t-il? Cette courbe peut être fermée de telle sorte qu'on reviendra au point de départ; elle peut aussi avoir un des foyers comme point asymptote. Elle peut avoir encore pour courbe asymptote une courbe fermée satisfaisant d'ailleurs à l'équation différentielle. Ces courbes fermées, que M. Poincaré appelle *cycles limites* jouent un rôle capital, et c'est dans les cas où il est possible de se rendre compte de leur position que la discussion de l'équation peut être faite d'une manière complète.

Pour les équations du premier ordre mais de degré supérieur les difficultés sont beaucoup plus grandes. L'étude des points singuliers généraux a été faite; elle trouve en particulier son application dans des problèmes comme celui des lignes de courbure d'une surface passant par un ombilic. L'étude des courbes dans tout le plan est singulièrement compliquée par un fait qui ne pouvait se rencontrer pour les équations du premier degré. Il peut arriver qu'une courbe intégrale couvre une aire, c'est à dire puisse se rapprocher autant qu'on voudra d'un point arbitraire dans une aire.

D'après les difficultés que présentent encore les équations du premier ordre, il est clair que pour les équations d'ordre supérieur au premier l'étude qualitative des intégrales sollicitera longtemps encore l'effort des chercheurs. Au point de vue analytique, une circonstance importante est à noter. Tandis que pour le premier ordre, on peut tirer parti dans quelques cas comme celui des centres de certains développements en série, il arrive au contraire ici dans les cas correspondants que les développements analogues sont purement formels; nous en avons vu un exemple en parlant tout à l'heure de la stabilité de l'équilibre. Remarquons à ce propos que les questions d'instabilité sont beaucoup plus faciles à traiter que les questions de stabilité comme il résulte des intéressantes recherches de M. Liapounoff. Quand il y a une fonction des forces l'équilibre est stable si, pour cette position, la fonction des forces est maxima. Quant aux positions d'équilibre pour lesquelles cette dernière condition n'est pas remplie, on les a toujours regardées comme instables, mais leur instabilité n'avait pas été démontrée. M. Liapounoff l'a établie en particulier pour le cas que l'on peut appeler général où la non existence du maximum de la fonction des forces se reconnait par les termes du second ordre.

Je citerai seulement un exemple relatif aux courbes intégrales d'une équation d'ordre supérieur au premier. Dans un mémoire récent, M.

Hadamard vient d'étudier les lignes géodésiques des surfaces à courbures opposées et à connexion multiple ayant un nombre limité de nappes infinies. Il établit que les tangentes aux lignes géodésiques passant par un point de la surface, et restant à distance finie, forment un ensemble parfait non continu. Ce résultat est intéressant au point de vue de la disposition des lignes géodésiques de la surface; il montre qu'il existe des lignes géodésiques se rapprochant d'une géodésique fermée déterminée, puis abandonnant celle-ci pour se rapprocher d'une autre, puis passant à une troisième, et ainsi de suite indéfiniment. Il montre de plus que l'allure des courbes intégrales peut dépendre dans certains cas, des propriétés discontinues je veux dire *arithmétiques* des constantes d'intégration. C'est sur cette idée que je veux m'arrêter; dans la théorie des équations différentielles comme en maintes parties des mathématiques, les recherches sont obligées de prendre un caractère arithmétique. C'est *l'arithmétisation* des mathématiques dont parlait M. Klein dans un article récent.

J'ai essayé, messieurs, en restant dans les généralités et sans prendre aucune classe particulière d'équations, de faire une sorte de carte géographique sommaire de la théorie des équations différentielles. Beaucoup de voies sont ouvertes et dans des directions très variées; sur plus d'un point, les questions sont seulement posées, mais elles paraissent bien posées; et nous nous rendons compte, ce qui a son prix, de la nature des difficultés qu'il faudra vaincre. C'est une étroite alliance entre les disciplines les plus diverses qui amènera maintenant de nouveaux progrès. Il n'est plus permis aujourd'hui au géomètre inventeur d'être l'homme d'un seul point de vue, et il faut nous résigner à de grandes complications. C'est un privilège que les sciences mathématiques partageront probablement dans l'avenir avec d'autres sciences. Espérons seulement que des hommes de génie viendront, de loin en loin, donner au moins pour un temps l'illusion de la simplicité.

Troisième Conférence.

Sur la Théorie des Fonctions Analitiques et sur quelques Fonctions Spéciales.

La théorie des fonctions de variables complexes est devenue aujourd'hui une branche considérable de l'analyse mathématique. Elle doit son brillant essor à la découverte de quelques propositions générales parmi lesquelles se trouvent au premier rang les théorèmes de Cauchy sur les intégrales prises le long d'un contour. Ces lois générales des fonctions analytiques appliquées à des fonctions spéciales donnent souvent avec facilité leurs principales propriétés. L'application de ces lois constitue une méthode synthétique, et des résultats auxquels avaient conduit une longue série de transformations de calculs apparaissent quelquefois avec une évidence intuitive. La théorie des fonctions elliptiques en offre un mémorable exemple, et n'y a-t-il pas quelque chose de merveilleux à intégrer avec M. Hermite le long d'un parallélogramme de périodes et à obtenir ainsi d'un trait de plume les principales propriétés des fonctions doublement périodiques? La façon dont Riemann pose et résout dans sa dissertation inaugurale le problème des intégrales abéliennes n'est pas moins digne d'être méditée comme exemple d'une méthode synthétique dans la théorie des fonctions.

I.

Il n'est plus douteux aujourd'hui que les principes essentiels qui sont à la base de la théorie n'aient été connus de Gauss. On sait que celui-ci ne publia pas ses recherches sur ce sujet. On ne peut guère admettre qu'il n'en ait pas saisi la haute importance; fidèle à sa devise "pauca sed matura" il attendait sans doute de s'être livré à une plus longue élaboration, quand Cauchy fit connaître ses découvertes. On doit donc regarder Cauchy comme le véritable fondateur de la théorie appelée à un si grand avenir; non pas certes qu'il l'ait présentée sous une forme didactique. Ouvrant des voies nouvelles, son esprit toujours en travail se souciait peu de donner à ses conceptions une forme parfaite. On suit le travail d'invention dans maintes publications de Cauchy, notamment quand on parcourt dans ses Œuvres Complètes les notes innombrables extraites des Comptes-Rendus. Dans la théorie qui nous occupe, une place à part doit être faite à l'idée fondamentale d'étendre la notion de l'intégrale définie en faisant passer la variable par une succession de valeurs imaginaires; cette conception a été la source des plus belles découvertes, et la représentation d'une fonction par une intégrale le long d'un contour fermé gardera à jamais le nom d'intégrale de Cauchy.

Le point de départ de Riemann se rapproche beaucoup de celui de Cauchy; il est très philosophique de prendre comme base les deux équations simultanées

$$\frac{\partial u}{\partial x} = \frac{\partial v}{\partial y}, \quad \frac{\partial u}{\partial y} = -\frac{\partial v}{\partial x}$$

et de réduire ainsi la théorie des fonctions d'une variable complexe à l'étude de ces deux équations simultanées aux dérivées partielles. En même temps apparaissent les liens entre cette étude et plusieurs questions de physique mathématique comme le mouvement permanent des fluides sur un plan et celui de l'électricité sur une plaque conductrice; et tous ces problèmes sont susceptibles d'être généralisés si au plan simple dans lequel se ment la variable (x, y) on substitue le plan multiple de Riemann. Les deux relations écrites plus haut amènent à considérer l'équation $\Delta u = 0$, équation qui contient toute la théorie des fonctions d'une variable complexe, et parmi les problèmes qu'on peut se poser sur cette équation le plus célèbre est celui de la détermination d'une intégrale par ses valeurs sur un contour fermé. Une application d'une autre nature concerne la géométrie; je veux parler du problème des cartes géographiques qui amène à la question de la représentation conforme d'une aire sur une autre.

Weierstrass a édifié la théorie des fonctions de variables complexes sur une autre base que Cauchy et Riemann, en partant des développements en séries entières; en France, ces développements avaient été aussi envisagés par M. Méray qui n'avait pas connaissance des leçons de Weierstrass. Le mémoire publié en 1876 par l'illustre analyste de Berlin, qui a fait connaître à un public plus étendu les résultats développés depuis longtemps dans l'enseignement du maître, a été le point de départ d'un grand nombre de travaux sur la théorie des fonctions. Cauchy avait déjà obtenu d'importants résultats sur le développement en sommes ou en produits infinis de certaines catégories de fonctions. Il était réservé à Weierstrass et à ses disciples de traiter ces questions dans toute leur généralité. La décomposition des fonctions entières, c'est à dire des fonctions uniformes et continues dans tout le plan, en facteurs primaires est un des plus admirables théorèmes de l'analyse moderne; chacun de facteurs primaires est le produit d'un facteur linéaire par une exponentielle. Les développements des fonctions uniformes en sommes et en produits infinis ont fait ensuite l'objet d'un grand nombre de travaux parmi les quels il faut citer tout particulièrement le mémoire de Mittag-Leffler qui a abordé ces problèmes avec la plus grande généralité possible. Je rappellerai aussi un mémoire de M. Runge auquel des recherches toutes récentes viennent de redonner de l'actualité, où se trouve en particulier établi que toute fonction holomorphe dans un domaine connexe peut dans ce domaine être développée en une série de polynomes.

Cauchy et ses disciples français, en étudiant la théorie des *fonctions* uniformes, n'avaient pas pénétré dans l'étude de ces points singuliers appelés aujourd'hui points singuliers essentiels, dont le point $z = 0$ pour la fonction $e^{\frac{1}{z}}$ donne l'exemple le plus simple. La considération des facteurs primaires permit à Weierstrass de montrer que dans le voisinage d'un point essentiel isolé une fonction uniforme peut se mettre sous la forme d'un quotient de deux fonctions uniformes n'ayant pas de pôles dans le voisinage de a; Weierstrass montra aussi que dans le voisinage d'un tel point la fonction s'approche autant que l'on veut de toute valeur donnée. On a plus tard complété ce résultat, en établissant que dans le voisinage d'un point singulier essentiel isolé la fonction prend rigoureusement une infinité de fois toute valeur donnée, une exception seulement étant possible pour deux valeurs particulières au plus. La démonstration de ce théorème se déduit de la considération d'une fonction présentant précisément la propriété qu'on veut démontrer être impossible; cette fonction est la fonction modulaire de la théorie des fonctions elliptiques, mais ses points singuliers ne sont pas isolés. Un corollaire du théorème indiqué conduit à la proposition suivante relative aux fonctions entières: si, pour une fonction entière $G(z)$ il existe deux valeurs a et b telles que les deux équations $G(z) = a$ et $G(z) = b$ aient seulement un nombre limité de racines, la fonction $G(z)$ est un polynome.

De nombreuses tentatives ont été faites pour démontrer directement les théorèmes précédents sans recourir à la théorie des fonctions elliptiques. Pour le théorème sur les fonctions entières, M. Hadamard avait réussi à l'établir quand, la fonction entière étant représentée par $\sum a_m x^m$, on a $(a_m) < \frac{1}{[1 \cdot 2 \cdots m]^{\alpha}}$, α étant positif. Plus récemment M. Borel est arrivé à le démontrer pour toutes les fonctions entières et même à le généraliser considérablement.

Les travaux de M. Hadamard et de M. Borel publiés dans ces dernières années sont extrêmement remarquables. Dans ces recherches, une notion importante introduite par Laguerre, celle du genre d'une fonction entière, joue un rôle capital; ce qui fait l'intérêt de cette notion, c'est qu'elle est intimement liée à la distribution des racines de la fonction. M. Poincaré avait fait le premier la remarque que le genre d'une fonction entière est en relation étroite avec l'ordre de grandeur de la fonction pour les grandes valeurs de la variable. M. Hadamard a cherché une limite du genre à l'aide des coefficients du développement, et il a établi que si le coefficient de z^m est moindre que $\frac{1}{(1 \cdot 2 \cdots m)^{\frac{1}{\lambda}}}$, la fonction est de genre E en désignant par $E+1$ l'entier immédiatement supérieur à λ. Il a réussi aussi à démontrer que, en désignant par $\phi(m)$ une fonction croissant indéfiniment avec m, si le coefficient a_m décroit plus vite que $\frac{1}{[\phi(m)]^m}$ la $p^{ième}$ racine a un module supérieur à $(1-\epsilon)\phi(p)$ où ϵ est infiniment petit pour $p=\infty$. De ses résultats, M. Hadamard a fait une belle application à l'étude de la distribution des racines d'une fonction célèbre considérée par Riemann dans son mémoire sur les nombres premiers.

Dans son travail sur les zéros des fonctions entières, M. Borel a eu surtout pour objet la démonstration de l'impossibilité de certaines identités. Soit $\mu(r)$ une fonction positive croissant indéfiniment avec r. Désignons par $G_i(z)$ une fonction entière dont le module maximum pour $(z)=r$ est inférieur à $e^{\mu(r)}$, et $H_i(z)$ une fonction entière dont le module maximum est supérieur à $[\mu(r)]^{1+\alpha}$, α étant positif; l'identité

$$G_0(z)+G_1(z)e^{H_1(z)}+\cdots+G_n(z)e^{H_n(z)}=0$$

ne peut avoir lieu que si tous les G sont identiquement nuls. En particulier pour $n=2$, une pareille identité ne peut exister, G_0 étant une constante, G_1 et G_2 des polynomes : c'est le théorème énoncé plus haut sur les fonctions entières.

Après ces résultats sur les fonctions holomorphes dans tout le plan, revenons aux séries entières dont le rayon de convergence est fini. Une telle série donne, pour employer le langage de Weierstrass, un élément de fonction, en supposant bien entendu que le rayon de convergence n'est pas nul. L'extension analytique d'un tel élément joue un rôle capital dans la théorie de Weierstrass; il est dans cette étude du plus haut intérêt d'avoir des renseignements sur les singularités de la fonction sur le cercle de convergence. Le mémoire de M. Darboux sur l'approximation des fonctions de très grand nombres, les recherches plus récentes de M. Hadamard, de M. Borel et de M. Fabry ont conduit à des résultats d'un haut intérêt. Je ne veux signaler qu'une conséquence curieuse, entrevue déjà par M. Pringsheim : c'est qu'une série entière a en général son cercle de convergence comme coupure. On sait que Weierstrass a le premier indiqué un exemple d'un série entière ne pouvant être prolongée analytiquement au delà de son cercle de convergence, et cet exemple détourné provenait de la théorie des fonctions elliptiques. Il est vraiment singulier que l'on ait eu autrefois quelques difficultés pour trouver des exemples de ce que l'on doit considérer maintenant comme la circonstance la plus fréquente.

Parmi les méthodes proposées pour l'étude de la série prolongée au delà de son cercle de convergence, il en est deux qui sont particulièrement simples. La première, employée par M. E. Lindelöff repose sur la théorie de la représentation conforme; la seconde utilise la notion de série divergente sommable résultant des travaux de M. Borel. Cette notion semble devoir jouer dans plusieurs questions d'analyse un rôle important. J'en indiquerai en deux mots le principe. Soit une série, $u_0 + u_1 + \cdots u_n + \cdots$; on lui associe la fonction de a:

$$u(a) = u_0 + u_1 a + \frac{u_2 a^2}{1 \cdot 2} + \cdots + \frac{u_n a^n}{1 \cdot 2 \cdots n} + \cdots$$

L'expression

$$s = \int_0^\infty u(a) e^{-a} da$$

peut avoir un sens quand la série initiale est divergente; on la regarde alors comme la limite de la série. En appliquant cette notion à la progression géométrique qui représente $\frac{1}{1-z}$, et en se servant de l'intégrale de Cauchy, on est alors conduit à une expression analytique qui dans bien des cas représente la fonction dans une aire extérieure au cercle de convergence.

Je ne puis songer à rappeler, ne fût-ce que d'un mot, les études les plus importantes faites tout récemment sur le prolongement analytique. Arrêtons nous seulement sur un résultat que vient de publier M. Mittag-Leffler. Considérons, avec l'éminent géomètre suédois, un élément de fonction dans son cercle de convergence, et sur chaque rayon suivons la fonction jusqu'à ce que nous rencontrions un point singulier, celui-ci pouvant d'ailleurs être à l'infini. On ne garde sur chaque rayon que la portion comprise entre le centre et le premier point singulier, et on obtient ainsi une aire que M. Mittag-Leffler appelle *l'étoile* correspondant à l'élément de fonction. Il montre qu'on peut obtenir une représentation de la fonction dans toute l'étoile, sous la forme d'une série ayant pour termes des polynomes en x dont les coefficients sont linéaires par rapport aux coefficients du développement initial; de cette façon, quand on a en un point la valeur d'une fonction analytique et de toutes ses dérivées, on peut obtenir à l'aide de ces seules données une représentation de la *fonction* valable dans toute une étoile. Ce résultat pourra peut-être avoir un certain intérêt pour la théorie des équations différentielles; il faut toutefois observer que dans ce cas la méthode de Cauchy, comme nous l'avons dit hier, conduit au même résultat. Ainsi les séries considérées hier (page 18), constituent des développements valables dans une étoile.

Nous avons, dans ce qui précède, considéré un élément de fonction, c'est à dire que la série

$$a_0 + a_1 x + \cdots + a_m x^m + \cdots \tag{1}$$

avait un rayon de convergence différent de zéro. Si la série précédente ne converge que pour $x = 0$, elle ne représente rien et il semble qu'il n'y ait aucun problème à se poser à son sujet. Cependant nous avons donné hier des exemples d'équations différentielles conduisant à de tels développements; la dérivée d'un ordre quelconque m de certaines intégrales dans un certain angle ayant l'origine pour sommet tend vers $1 \cdot 2 \cdots m \cdot a_m$ quand x tend vers zéro à l'intérieur de l'angle convenable A. Ces conditions relatives aux valeurs des dérivées ne peuvent manifestement déterminer une seule fonction dans l'angle A près de l'origine, car on peut à une première fonction ajouter une exponentielle de la forme $e^{-\frac{1}{x^a}}$ (a étant convenablement choisie) dont toutes les dérivées sont nulles à l'origine; mais, en appliquant sa méthode de sommation des séries divergentes, M. Borel est conduit à imposer une condition supplémentaire et à obtenir alors, dans des cas étendus, une fonction unique déterminée par la série divergente (1).

II.

Les divers travaux que je viens de rappeler montrent avec quelle activité les analystes se sont occupés dans ces derniers temps des généralités concernant les *fonctions* analytiques d'une variable. La théorie générale des fonctions de plusieurs variables avance beaucoup moins rapidement; les questions qui se posent ici sont beaucoup plus difficiles, tant en elles-mêmes que par le défaut d'une représentation qui *fasse* image. Nous suivons une variable complexe sur son plan, mais avec deux variables complexes nous nous trouvons dans un espace à quatre dimensions, où de plus les diverses coordonnées ne se présentent pas symétriquement. Au lieu de *deux* équations, nous avons *quatre* équations aux dérivées partielles auxquelles doivent satisfaire deux fonctions de quatre variables. L'élimination d'une des fonctions conduit pour l'autre à un système de quatre équations aux dérivées partielles qui remplace l'équation de Laplace, mais qui n'a pas été étudié directement comme cette dernière équation. Il semble qu'on ne puisse pour ce système se poser aucun problème analogue à celui de Dirichlet et de Riemann; nous ne trouvons ici aucune analogie entre le cas d'une variable et celui de deux variables.

A un autre point de vue, le développement de Taylor à deux variables peut bien servir à définir un élément de fonction, mais nous n'avons rien d'analogue au cercle de convergence. Que sont les régions de convergence pour un tel développement? Il faudrait considérer des surfaces dans l'hyperespace à quatre dimensions; aucune règle n'étant connue à cet égard, on se borne à considérer deux cercles assez petits dans les plans respectifs des deux variables, cercles à l'intérieur desquels la série est convergente.

Les théorèmes généraux sur les fonctions analytiques de deux variables complexes sont peu nombreux. Une remarque souvent utile a été faite il y a longtemps par Weierstrass; elle a en quelque sorte pour objet de mettre en évidence, dans une fonction de n variables holomorphes autour de $x_1 = 0, \cdots, x_n = 0$, et s'annulant pour ces valeurs des variables, la partie de la fonction qui s'annule. Weierstrass montre que autour de $x_1 = \cdots = x_n = 0$ la fonction peut se mettre sous la forme d'un produit de deux facteurs holomorphes, dont l'un ne s'annule pas à l'origine et dont l'autre est un polynome par rapport à l'une des variables. Une autre proposition d'une démonstration délicate est due à M. Poincaré et a pour objet de généraliser le théorème de Weierstrass relatif aux fonctions uniformes d'une variable n'ayant à distance finie que des pôles, fonctions qui peuvent se mettre sous la forme d'un quotient de deux fonctions entières. Pareillement une fonction de deux variables qui, pour toutes les valeurs finies des variables présente le caractère d'une fonction rationnelle peut être mise sous la forme d'un quotient de deux fonctions entières. Ce beau théorème a été étendu par M. Cousin, qui a suivi une toute autre voie, aux fonctions d'un nombre quelconque de variables.

On doit encore à M. Poincaré un résultat bien saillant: je veux parler de l'extension aux intégrales doubles du théorème fondamental de Cauchy relatif aux intégrales simples prises le long d'un contour. Il n'y a pas de difficulté à définir une intégrale double d'une fonction $F(x, y)$ de deux variables complexes x et y

$$\iint F(x, y)\,dx\,dy$$

sur un continuum à deux dimensions situé dans l'hyperespace à quatre dimensions qui correspond aux deux variables complexes. Si le continuum est fermé, et qu'on puisse le réduire à une ligne où à un point sans que F cesse d'être continue, l'intégrale sera nulle. Ce résultat conduit à poser un grand nombre de questions. Si F est une fonction rationelle, il y a lieu de considérer les *résidus* de l'intégrale double; ces résidus s'expriment par des périodes d'intégrales abéliennes ordinaires. Si F est une fonction algébrique de x et y, on aura à envisager les *périodes* de l'intégrale double, et on voit s'ouvrir un vaste champ de recherches. On s'aperçoit d'ailleurs bien vite que si certaines analogies subsistent avec le cas d'une variable, il en est beaucoup d'autres qui disparaissent entièrement. Des intégrales le long d'un contour ont donné à Cauchy le nombre des racines d'une équation contenues dans ce contour, mais dans la question correspondante du nombre des racines communes à deux équations simultanées, les intégrales doubles n'ont aucun rôle à jouer; ce sont des intégrales triples étendues à un certain continuum à trois dimensions qui interviennent dans cette recherche.

Je parlais tout à l'heure de la dissymétrie qui se présente au point de vue réel dans la théorie des fonctions de deux variables complexes. Il était intéressant de rechercher si il n'est pas possible de généraliser les deux équations aux dérivées partielles de la théorie d'une fonction d'une variable. Le problème est évidemment indéterminé; tout dépend de la propriété de ces équations sur laquelle on porte spécialement son attention. On peut se placer au point de vue suivant: rechercher tous les systèmes d'équations aux dérivées partielles relatifs à n fonctions de n variables indépendantes et telles que, si $u_1, u_2, \cdots u_n$ et $v_1, v_2, \cdots v_n$ désignent deux solutions quelconques, les v considérées comme fonctions des u satisfassent au même système. Cette propriété appartient évidemment aux deux équations $\frac{\partial u}{\partial x} = \frac{\partial v}{\partial y}, \frac{\partial u}{\partial y} = -\frac{\partial v}{\partial x}$. La recherche de ces systèmes peut se faire d'une manière régulière, et peut se déduire de la connaissance des certains groupes d'ordre fini; ainsi tous les systèmes du type précédent d'équations aux dérivées partielles du premier ordre pourront être obtenus à l'aide des groupes linéaires et homogènes à n variables. Il est possible que, parmi tous ces systèmes, il en est qui présentent quelque intérêt particulier, et avec lesquels on puisse édifier une théorie plus ou moins analogue à la théorie d'une fonction d'une variable complexe. Le cas de $n = 3$ ne donne rien d'intéressant; pour

$n = 4$, on pourrait prendre d'abord le groupe linéaire qui donne naissance aux quaternions, il lui correspond un système d'équations différentielles qui présente peut-être quelque intérêt.

Cette extension de la théorie des fonctions d'une variable complexe n'est pas la seule qui ait été proposée. M. Volterra a cherché dans une autre voie en considérant des fonctions de ligne, ce qui l'a conduit à d'intéressantes relations différentielles et à quelques problèmes analogues à ceux de Dirichlet. L'avenir dira si ces extensions sont simplement des curiosités ou si elles présentent quelque intérêt général.

III.

Quittons maintenant les généralités et jetons un coup d'œil sur quelques fonctions spéciales. Il n'en est pas qui aient été plus étudiées que les fonctions algébriques d'une variable; c'est en faisant leur étude que Puiseux, dans un mémoire resté célèbre, a appelé l'attention sur l'intérêt que présentait la considération de la variable complexe. On a quelque peine à se représenter qu'il a paru merveilleux que $\sqrt{z}$ et $-\sqrt{z}$ puissent être considérées comme deux déterminations d'une même fonction; c'est dans ce mémoire aussi qu'apparait pour la première fois l'origine de la périodicité.

La théorie des fonctions algébriques est devenue un confluent où se rencontrent les notions les plus diverses; chacun, suivant ses goûts, peut y trouver les points de vue qu'il préfère. Avec les méthodes de Weierstrass, nous trouvons la précision extrême qui caractérise son école, et le souci constant de n'introduire aucune considération étrangère à la théorie des fonctions fût ce au prix de détours longs et pénibles. Celui qui aime le langage et les formes de raisonnement de la géométrie analytique suivra Brill et Noether dans leur théorie si féconde des groupes de points. Ceux enfin qui recherchent les grands horizons auront plaisir à lire Riemann qui, avec la merveilleuse conception de la surface qui porte son nom, rend, pour ainsi dire, intuitifs les points les plus délicats de la théorie. Ce serait d'ailleurs une vue étroite que de regarder seulement la belle conception de Riemann comme une méthode simplicative. Pour Riemann, le point essentiel est dans la conception *à priori* de la surface connexe, formée d'un nombre limité de feuillets, et dans le fait qu'à une telle surface conçue dans toute sa généralité correspond une classe de courbes algébriques. De plus, on peut envisager des surfaces de Riemann à un nombre infini de feuillets, et les travaux de Poincaré ont montré le rôle utile qu'elles peuvent jouer dans l'étude des fonctions non uniformes. On sait aussi l'importance qu'avait pour Riemann le problème de la représentation conforme; le cas de la représentation conforme des aires à connexions multiples a *été* traité par M. Schottky dans un très beau mémoire où l'auteur se montre disciple de Weierstrass, mais qui se rattache naturellement à l'ordre d'idées de Riemann. A une aire plane percée de p trous, envisagée comme ayant une face supérieure et une face inférieure correspond une courbe algébrique de genre p; la question de la représentation conforme de deux aires revient alors à la correspondance entre les points de deux courbes algébriques.

Aux courbes algébriques se rattachent des fonctions extrêmement remarquables d'une variable; ce sont les fonctions que M. Poincaré appelle *fuchsiennes* et que M. Klein désigne sous le nom de fonctions automorphes. Pour les courbes des genres *zéro* et *un*, on peut exprimer les coordonnées par des fonctions uniformes d'un paramètre, méromorphes dans tout le plan (fonctions rationnelles et fonctions doublement périodiques). Il était naturel de chercher, pour les courbes de genre supérieur à *un*, une représentation paramétrique par des fonctions uniformes. Des tentatives variées ont probablement été faites pour résoudre cette question, en cherchant à réaliser cette expression par des transcendantes n'ayant que des pôles à distance finie. De telles tentatives, on le sait aujourd'hui, ne pouvaient réussir, car on peut établir que, entre deux fonctions uniformes dans le voisinage d'un point qui est pour chacune d'elles un point singulier essentiel isolé, ne peut exister une relation algébrique de genre supérieur à l'unité. Les transcendantes à employer sont d'une nature beaucoup plus compliquée; les unes ont un cercle comme coupure au delà duquel elles ne peuvent être prolongées analytiquement, les autres sont définies dans tout le plan, mais elles ont sur un cercle une infinité de points singuliers essentiels formant, d'après la dénomination de M. Cantor, un ensemble parfait qui n'est pas continu. Les célèbres mémoires de M. Poincaré sur les fonctions fuchsiennes et les belles recherches de M. Klein sur le même sujet forment un des plus beaux chapitres écrits dans ces vingt dernières années sur la théorie des fonctions. Les fonctions automorphes forment une généralisation extrêmement étendue et remarquable des fonctions modulaires étudiées par M. Hermite dans la théorie des fonctions elliptiques, et des fonctions considérées par M. Schwarz en faisant dans certains cas l'inversion du rapport de deux solutions de l'équation hypergéométrique. Toute cette théorie est d'ailleurs étroitement liée à la théorie des équations linéaires, et c'est un des résultats les plus saillants obtenus par M. Poincaré qu'avec des transcendantes analogues aux fonctions fuchsiennes on puisse intégrer les équations différentielles linéaires à coefficients algébriques n'ayant que des points singuliers réguliers (au sens de M. Fuchs).

Parmi les transcendantes se rattachant aux fonctions algébriques citons encore les intégrales de fonctions à multiplicateurs étudiées tout particulièrement par M. Appell. Ce sont des fonctions n'ayant sur la surface de Riemann que des pôles ou des points singuliers logarithmiques, et dont toutes les déterminations se déduisent de l'une d'entre elles par des substitutions de la forme $(u, au+b)$; elles généralisent par suite les intégrales abéliennes pour lesquelles les a sont égaux à l'unité. Un beau résultat obtenu par M. Appell est que ces fonctions se présentent dans la recherche des coefficients des fonctions abéliennes de deux variables quand on les développe en séries trigonométriques. On a aussi recherché les cas où l'inversion d'une intégrale de fonction à multiplicateurs conduit à une fonction uniforme, mais la conclusion a été négative, c'est à dire que dans ce cas la courbe algébrique est nécessairement du genre zéro ou du genre un, et la fonction uniforme obtenue se ramène où des transcendantes connues.

IV.

Les équations différentielles forment une mine inépuisable pour obtenir des fonctions spéciales. Les équations linéaires ont ainsi conduit à des fonctions jouissant de propriétés bien définies. Pour les équations non linéaires, M. Fuchs appela le premier l'attention sur les équations algébriques du premier ordre à points critiques fixes et montra comment on peut reconnaître qu'on se trouve dans ce cas. M. Poincaré fit voir ensuite qu'on pouvait ramener ce cas à des quadratures ou aux équations de Riccati. M. Painlevé a étendu ces résultats en considérant les équations du premier ordre dont les intégrales n'ont qu'un nombre limité de valeurs autour de l'ensemble des points critiques mobiles. Une des conclusions de ses recherches est que l'intégrale, supposée transcendante, de toute équation algébrique du premier ordre qui satisfait à la condition précédente, est une fonction algébrique de l'intégrale d'une équation de Riccati dont les coefficients dépendent algébriquement de ceux de l'équation donnée. On peut se proposer des problèmes analogues pour les équations différentielles algébriques d'ordre supérieur au premier. Il se présente ici des difficultés considérables; l'une d'elles tient au fait suivant:

tandis que toute transformation biuniforme d'une courbe algébrique en elle-même (avec singularités isolées) est nécessairement birationnelle, il peut arriver au contraire qu'une transformation biuniforme d'une surface algébrique en elle-même ne soit pas birationnelle. Une seconde difficulté, non moins grave, consiste dans l'existence possible de singularités essentielles mobiles. J'ai indiqué hier la distinction faite à cet égard par M. Painlevé entre la classe générale d'équations ne possédant pas de tels points et la classe singulière.

En cherchant à étendre aux équations du second ordre à points critiques fixes la méthode qui avait réussi à M. Poincaré pour les équations du premier ordre jouissant de la même propriété, on est arrêté immédiatement par la première difficulté signalée plus haut, et c'est seulement dans le cas où l'intégrale générale de l'équation est supposée dépendre algébriquement des deux constantes d'intégration que l'on peut poursuivre l'étude sans de sérieuses difficultés; on retombe d'ailleurs sur des transcendantes déjà connues. M. Painlevé a fait une étude complète des autres cas qui peuvent se présenter; l'intégrale générale peut encore être une fonction algébrique d'une seule des constantes, ou enfin dépendre d'une manière transcendante des deux constantes (de quelque façon qu'on les choisisse). Ce dernier cas seul est irréductible aux transcendantes classiques, c'est à dire ne peut être ramené aux quadratures et aux équations linéaires. Ce cas se présente d'ailleurs effectivement, et M. Painlevé a formé explicitement toutes les équations du second ordre de la forme

$$y'' = R(y, y', x)$$

où R est rationnel en y', algébrique en y et analytique en x; elles se laissent ramener à *douze* types canoniques très simples. J'indiquerai seulement deux de ces équations pour lesquelles l'intégrale générale est uniforme,

$$y'' = 6y^2 + x$$
$$y'' = 2y^3 + xy + a \quad (a = \text{constante numérique})$$

L'intégrale générale de l'une et l'autre équation est une *fonction* uniforme et méromorphe de x dans tout le plan, et cette intégrale est une transcendante vraiment nouvelle. Ces exemples précis montrent combien M. Painlevé a poussé jusqu'au bout ses profondes recherches.

Je me bornerai à dire, relativement aux équations du troisième ordre, que l'intégrale générale peut avoir des lignes de points singuliers essentiels. On en a facilement des exemples en considérant l'équation différentielle algébrique du troisième ordre à laquelle satisfait une fonction automorphe d'une variable.

V.

Le champ des fonctions spéciales de plusieurs variables complexes, dont l'étude a été quelque peu approfondie, est assez limité. La théorie des *fonctions abéliennes* a fait l'objet d'un nombre considérable de travaux qui sont trop classiques pour que je m'y arrête ici; les mémoires de Riemann et de Weierstrass, les études de M. Hermite sur la transformation des fonctions abéliennes sont dans toutes les mémoires. Après les études *faites* sur les fonctions fuchsiennes d'une variable, il était naturel de chercher des transcendantes analogues pour le cas de deux variables; on devait d'abord se demander s'il existe des groupes *discontinus* contenus dans le groupe linéaire à deux variables

$$\left(u, v; \frac{a'u+b'v+c'}{au+bv+c}, \frac{a''u+b''v+c''}{au+bv+c}\right). \qquad (1)$$

Un seul exemple d'un tel groupe, mais bien peu utile, s'offrait à l'esprit, celui du groupe à quatre périodes. Aucun exemple analogue au groupe modulaire ne se présentait, et il n'y avait rien à demander sur ce point à la théorie des fonctions abéliennes, au moins sous sa forme classique. Par quoi d'ailleurs se trouverait remplacée ici la condition imposée aux substitutions d'un groupe fuchsien, de conserver un certain cercle? L'étude des formes quadratiques ternaires à indéterminées conjuguées vint permettre de former en grand nombre les exemples cherchés. M. Hermite avait, il y a longtemps, montré l'intérêt au point de vue arithmétique des formes quadratiques binaires à indéterminées conjuguées; les formes ternaires indéfinies conduisirent à de nombreux groupes du type (1), discontinus à l'intérieur d'une certaine hypersurface de l'espace à quatre dimensions. Cette surface remplace la circonférence de la théorie des groupes fuchsiens. Les groupes du type précédent furent appelées *groupes hyperfuchsiens;* on se rend aisément compte que leur recherche générale constitue, comme pour les groupes fuchsiens, un problème uniquement d'ordre algébrique; mais, toute représentation géométrique faisant défaut, cette recherche directe serait tellement pénible qu'elle est réellement impraticable. Aussi les exemples fournis par des considérations arithmétiques sont-ils extrêmement précieux.

Aux groupes hyperfuchsiens correspondent des fonctions uniformes restant invariables par les substitutions du groupe.

Des exemples de fonctions hyperfuchsiennes d'une nature différente peuvent être fournis par les séries hypergéométriques de deux variables. Une telle série, fonction de x et y dépendant de quatre paramètres arbitraires λ, μ, δ_1, et δ_2 satisfait à un système de trois équations linéaires aux dérivées partielles du second ordre, ayant trois solutions communes linéairement indépendantes. Désignant celles-ci par ω_1, ω_2, ω_3, on peut chercher dans quels cas les quotients

$$\frac{\omega_2}{\omega_1} = u, \quad \frac{\omega_3}{\omega_1} = v$$

donnent pour x et y des fonctions uniformes de u et v. Les conditions sont très simples ; si on prend deux quelconques des quatre quantités λ, μ, δ_1 et δ_2, soit, par exemple λ et δ_1, la différence $\lambda + \delta_1 - 1$ doit être l'inverse d'un nombre entier positif, et pareillement si on prend trois quelconques de ces quantités, soit λ, μ et δ_1, la différence $2 - \lambda - \mu - \delta_1$ est encore égal à l'inverse d'un entier positif. Je citerai l'exemple $\lambda = \mu = \delta_1 = \delta_2 = \frac{3}{5}$ pour lequel le polyèdre fondamental du groupe est tout entier à *l'intérieur* de l'hypersurface limité.

On peut généraliser les fonctions fuchsiennes en considérant d'autres groupes discontinus que les groupes hyperfuchsiens. Une substitution birationnelle entre deux variables u et v n'est pas nécessairement linéaire, et ce serait un problème intéressant mais difficile de former tous les groupes discontinus au moins dans une certaine région de l'hyperespace (u, v) de substitutions birationnelles. En dehors des groupes linéaires (hyperfuchsiens) on a seulement considéré jusqu'ici les groupes formés de substitutions de la forme

$$\left(u, \frac{au + b}{cu + d}\right), \quad \left(v, \frac{a'v + b'}{c'v + d'}\right)$$

et des substitutions où u est remplacé par une fonction linéaire de v et inversement. Ce sont les groupes *hyperabéliens* qui rentrent évidemment dans les types des substitutions quadratiques ; il y a dans ce cas deux domaines frontières. Il y aura sans doute des découvertes intéressantes à faire un jour dans le champ très vaste des groupes discontinus de substitutions birationnelles, et des fonctions correspondantes (dans le cas où il en existera, comme il arrive pour les fonctions hyperfuchsiennes et hyperabéliennes).

VI.

Nous avons rappelé tout à l'heure le brillant développement de la théorie des fonctions algébriques d'une variable; les progrès ont été beaucoup plus lents dans le champ de deux variables. C'est un sujet en pleine élaboration, et que l'on attaque de plusieurs côtés. Clebsch, se plaçant au point de vue de la géométrie analytique, signala le premier que, pour une surface algébrique de degré m, certaines surfaces d'ordre $m-4$ devaient jouer le rôle que jouaient les adjointes d'ordre $m-3$ par rapport à une courbe de degré m. L'étude de ces surfaces d'ordre $m-4$ a été reprise par M. Noether dans un mémoire de grande importance. En se plaçant au point de vue de la théorie des fonctions, voici l'origine de ces surfaces. Si on cherche les intégrales doubles

$$\int\int R(x, y, z)dx\,dy \qquad (f(x, y, z) = 0)$$

restant toujours finies, intégrales qu'on appelle les intégrales doubles de première espèce, on trouve qu'elles sont de la forme

$$\int\int \frac{Q(x, y, z)dx\,dy}{f'_z}$$

Q étant un polynome d'ordre $m-4$. Le nombre p_g de ces polynomes linéairement indépendants est ce que l'on appelle le genre *géométrique* de la surface; un pareil nombre est manifestement un invariant. Jusqu'ici les analogies sont complètes avec les courbes; il y a des intégrales doubles de première espèce, comme il y a des intégrales abéliennes de première espèce. Mais une première différence va de suite se manifester. Il faut calculer le nombre des arbitraires qui figurent dans les polynomes Q d'ordre $m-4$ se comportant aux points multiples de la surface de telle manière que l'intégrale reste finie. Or on peut trouver par une formule précise le nombre des conditions ainsi entraînées, mais seulement pour un polynome d'un ordre suffisamment grand N; si donc on fait dans cette formule $N = m-4$, il est possible que l'on trouve un nombre différent de p_g; on désigne le nombre que donne la formule à laquelle je fais allusion par p_n, et on l'appelle le genre numérique de la surface. Le cas le plus général est celui où $p_n = p_g$; quand il n'y a pas égalité, on a $p_n < p_g$ et la surface est dite irrégulière, tandis qu'elle est régulière si $p_n = p_g$. Cayley a le premier appelé l'attention sur la curieuse circonstance qui précède; Zeuthen et Noether établirent ensuite l'invariance du nombre p_a, quand il n'est pas égal à p_g. Les surfaces réglées offrent un exemple de surface irrégulière; en désignant par π le genre d'une section plane arbitraire de la surface, on a

$$p_a = -\pi, \quad p_g = 0.$$

Il y a pour une surface des polynomes adjoints d'ordre quelconque. On peut les définir facilement au point de vue transcendant. Si la surface a une position arbitraire par rapport aux axes, le polynome $P(x, y, z)$ sera un polynome adjoint si l'intégrale double

$$\iint \frac{P(x, y, z)\,dx\,dy}{f'_z}$$

reste finie à distance finie; la surface $P = 0$ est une surface adjointe. M. Enriques a donné une très remarquable interprétation géométrique de la différence $p_g - p_a$. Les adjointes d'ordre $m - 4 + r$ découpent sur une section plane déterminée d'ailleurs arbitraire une série linéaire de groupes de points qui peut n'être pas complète si r est assez petit. Désignons par ω_r le *défaut* de cette série linéaire par rapport à la série complète; on a

$$p_g - p_a = \sum_{r=1} \omega_r$$

la somme dans le second membre ne comprend qu'un nombre limité de termes, les ω étant certainement nuls à partir d'une valeur assez grande de r. La formule précédente est fondamentale dans l'étude du genre numérique.

Nous avons parlé plus haut des intégrales doubles de première espèce relatives à une surface. On peut aussi développer une théorie des intégrales doubles de *seconde espèce* dont la définition est la suivante: ce sont les intégrales qui deviennent infinies comme

$$\iint \left(\frac{\partial U}{\partial x} + \frac{\partial V}{\partial y}\right) dx\,dy \qquad (\alpha)$$

U et V étant des fonctions rationnelles de x, y et z [$f(x, y, z) = 0$]. Le nombre des intégrales distinctes de seconde espèce, c'est à dire des intégrales dont aucune combinaison linéaire n'est de la forme (α) est fini; c'est un invariant de la surface. Mais il n'en est plus ici, comme dans le cas des courbes pour lesquelles le nombre des intégrales abéliennes distinctes de seconde espèce était égale à $2p$; le nouvel invariant d'une classe de surfaces algébriques n'est pas lié au genre, soit géométrique soit numérique.

La considération des intégrales doubles ne se présente pas seule. On peut aussi envisager des intégrales de différentielles totales de la forme

$$\int P(x, y, z)\,dx + Q(x, y, z)\,dy$$

où P et Q sont rationnelles en x, y et z, et il y a encore lieu de parler des intégrales de première et de seconde espèce. Mais ici de telles intégrales n'existent pas en général, c'est à dire pour une surface prise arbitrairement, et c'est une question assez délicate que de reconnaître si une surface possède des intégrales de seconde espèce en dehors des fonctions rationnelles.

Les questions de connexité présentent aussi un grand intérêt dans la théorie des fonctions algébriques de deux variables indépendantes, mais quelques précautions sont ici nécessaires. Pour une surface déterminée, et en procédant d'une manière bien précisée, on peut obtenir deux nombres correspondant à la connexion linéaire et à la connexion à deux dimensions; le premier p_1 est véritablement un invariant pour toute transformation birationnelle, tandis que le second p_2 peut être influencé par la présence de points fondamentaux dans la correspondance birationnelle. C'est un résultat remarquable que le nombre $p_1 - 1$ représente le nombre des intégrales de différentielles totales distinctes de seconde espèce relatives à la surface. Pour une surface arbitrairement choisie, il n'y a pas d'intégrale de seconde espèce et on a $p_1 = 1$.

On voit que les points de vue de la géométrie analytique, de la théorie des fonctions et de la géométrie de situation se retrouvent aussi dans l'étude des surfaces algébriques, mais il faut se méfier des analogies avec la théorie des courbes. Tout, dans ce nouveau domaine, se présente d'une manière plus compliquée.

Voici encore un exemple de cette complexité. Les courbes dont le genre est nul forment la classe très restreinte des courbes unicursales. Au contraire les surfaces pour les quelles $p_g = 0$ sont extrêmement variées, et on peut dans ce cas considérer un nouvel invariant que M. Enriques a découvert et qu'il appelle le *bigenre*. On peut le definir aisément dans le cas où la surface f de degré m n'a qu'une ligne double. On envisagera à cet effet le système des surfaces d'ordre $2m - 8$ (ne se composant pas de f et d'une surface d'ordre $m - 6$) ayant comme ligne double la courbe double de f; le bigenre P est la dimension augmentée d'une unité de ce système. Cette notion a permis à M. Castelnuovo d'établir un théorème réellement merveilleux; il s'agit des conditions nécessaires et suffisantes pour qu'une surface soit unicursale. On pouvait penser que ces conditions seraient très compliquées et non susceptibles d'une forme simple; il n'en est rien, elles se réduisent à $p_a = 0$, $P = 0$. Mais je dois m'arrêter, me bornant à citer seulement le mémoire si élégant de M. Humbert sur les surfaces hyperelliptiques qui donnent un très intéressant exemple de surfaces irrégulières pour les quelles $p_a = -1$, tandis que $p_g = 1$.

Nous avons, messieurs, jeté un rapide coup d'œil sur quelques unes des branches de la science mathématique. Vous avez pu vous apercevoir plus d'une fois de l'embarras dans lequel je me suis trouvé, quand j'ai voulu, pour les nécessités de mon exposition, faire une classification dans certaines théories. La pénétration réciproque des diverses disciplines est aujourd'hui en effet un fait capital et sera de plus en plus la source d'importantes découvertes. A cet égard, il y a une grande différence entre notre époque et des temps un peu antérieurs. Nous avons peine aujourd'hui à comprendre certaines histoires où on voit des géomètres mépriser des analystes et inversement; nous sentons que l'ère des écoles fermées et étroitement attachées à un seul point de vue est pour toujours terminée. Il est bien vraisemblable que l'érudition jouera à l'avenir un plus grand rôle qu'autrefois en mathématiques. Les mathématiciens perdront peut-être ce privilège de la précocité qui étonne tant de personnes; ils se rapprocheront des physiciens et des naturalistes qui doivent en général commencer plus tard leurs travaux personnels. En terminant, je me permettrai de donner un conseil aux étudiants mathématiciens qui m'ont fait l'honneur de m'écouter; je leur recommanderai de ne pas se cantonner trop tôt dans des recherches spéciales. Il leur faut acquérir d'abord des vues générales sur les diverses parties de notre science, sans lesquelles leurs efforts risqueraient de rester stériles, et qui leur coûteraient plus tard un bien plus grand effort.

Ludwig Boltzmann.

[redacted] [redacted]

[illegible] GRUND[illegible] [illegible]
[illegible]LEICHUNGEN [illegible]

Von Professor [illegible]

Erste Vor[illegible]

[illegible] Mechanik ist eine [illegible]
[illegible] mit solchen [illegible]
[illegible] in dem [illegible]
[illegible] besteht. Die [illegible]
von [illegible]
[illegible] dass die vollendete[illegible]
[illegible] als die Grundl[illegible]
[illegible] von Legrange, [illegible]
[illegible]
[illegible] Es scheint
[illegible]
[illegible] man die [illegible]
[illegible] mit dem gleichen [illegible]
[illegible] diese [illegible]
[illegible]
[illegible] ist [illegible]
[illegible]hafte [illegible]
[illegible] Mechanik [illegible]
[illegible] der [illegible]
[illegible]

ÜBER DIE GRUNDPRINCIPIEN UND GRUNDGLEICHUNGEN DER MECHANIK.

Von Professor Ludwig Boltzmann.

Erste Vorlesung.

Die analytische Mechanik ist eine Wissenschaft, welche schon von ihrem Begründer Newton mit solchem Scharfsinne und solcher Vollendung ausgearbeitet wurde wie es in dem gesammten Gebiete menschlichen Wissens fast ohne Beispiel dasteht. Die grossen Meister, welche auf Newton folgten, haben das von ihm errichtete Gebäude noch weiter gefestigt, und es hatte den Anschein, dass eine vollendetere und einheitlichere Schöpfung des Menschengeistes als die Grundlehren der Mechanik, wie sie uns in den Werken von Lagrange, Laplace, Poisson, Hamilton etc. entgegentreten überhaupt nicht denkbar wäre. Gerade die Begründung der ersten Principien schien von diesen Forschern mit einem Scharfsinne und einer logischen Consequenz durchgeführt, die allezeit das Vorbild lieferten, welchem man die Begründung der übrigen Wissenszweige, wenn auch nicht immer mit dem gleichen Erfolge, nachzubilden suchte. Es schien lange ganz unmöglich dieser Begründung überhaupt noch etwas hinzu zu fügen oder daran etwas zu ändern.

Um so auffallender und unerwarteter ist es, dass gegenwärtig hauptsächlich in Deutschland ziemlich lebhafte Controversen gerade über die Grundprincipien der analytischen Mechanik entstanden sind. Es ist dies gewiss nicht so zu verstehen, als ob die Ehrfurcht und Bewunderung, die wir dem Genius eines Newton, Lagrange oder Laplace zollen, dadurch irgend wie geschmälert werden sollte. Diese haben aus den kleinen Anfängen, welche sie vorfanden, eine für alle Zeiten mustergültige Herrin geschaffen. Sie hatten so viel des thatsächlich Neuen heraus zu arbeiten, dass sie sich nur aufgehalten und dem einheitlichen Eindruck geschadet hätten, wenn sie bei gewissen Schwierigkeiten und Dunkelheiten zu lange verweilt hätten. Aber seitdem ist unsere Kenntnis von Thatsachen bedeutend gewachsen, unser Verstand ist geschult, so dass viele Vorstellungen, welche zu Zeiten Newtons noch den Gelehrten Schwierigkeiten machten, nun zum Gemeingut aller geworden sind. Dadurch erhielt man Musse die Construktion des Newton'schen Gebäudes gewissermassen mit der Lupe zu betrachten, und siehe es ergaben sich manche Schwierigkeiten, wie sie sich ja dem Menschengeiste immer gerade da am meisten entgegen stellen, wo er die einfachsten Grundlagen der Erkenntnis zu analysiren strebt.

Diese Schwierigkeiten sind freilich mehr philosophischer oder wie man heutzutage sagt, erkenntnistheoretischer Natur. Wir Deutsche sind schon oft und viel verlacht worden wegen unserer Neigung zur philosophischen Speculation und in früherer Zeit sicher oft mit Recht. Eine von den Thatsachen abgekehrte Philosophie hat nie etwas Brauchbares hervorgebracht und kann es nicht hervorbringen. Von unmittelbar greifbarem Nutzen ist es vor allem, unsere Kenntnis der Thatsachen durch Experimente zu erweitern und auch unsere wissenschaftliche Naturkenntnis wird zunächst und am ausgiebigsten in dieser Weise gefördert. Aber trotz alledem scheint die Neigung die einfachsten Begriffe zu analysiren und sich über die Grundoperationen unseres Denkens Rechenschaft zu geben im Menschengeiste unbezwinglich.

Viel hat sich auch die Methode dieser Analyse im Verlaufe der Zeit vervollkommnet, so dass dieselbe heutzutage wenn auch noch keineswegs sofort praktisch fruchtbringend, doch lange nicht mehr so wesenlos ist, wie die alte Philosophie. Im Verlaufe der Geschichte erfährt ja das ganze Culturbild der Menschheit stete und bedeutende Schwankungen. Die Deutschen sind nicht mehr die unpraktischen Träumer von ehemals. Sie haben es auf allen Gebieten der Experimentalwissenschaft, der Technik, Industrie, und Politik bewiesen. Die Bestrebungen der Amerikaner waren naturgemäss anfangs behufs Unterjochung des Grundes und Bodens der rein praktischen Thätigkeit der Industrie und Technik zugewandt. Aber sie sind es längst nicht mehr ausschliesslich und schon weist Amerika auf allen Gebieten der abstrakten Wissenschaft Forscher auf, die den hervorragensten Europas vollkommen ebenbürtig zur Seite stehen. Da sie daher, meine Herren, einen Deutschen zu Vorträgen in ihrem Lande geladen haben, so will ich es wagen ein Gebiet der Erkenntnistheorie mit ihnen zu betreten.

Ich will zunächst wieder zurück kommen auf die Bedenken, welche gegen die Fundamente der Newton'schen Mechanik erhoben worden sind oder (besser gesagt) zu den Stellen, wo diese noch einer näheren Beleuchtung, einer Analyse der Schlussweise und Sichtung der Begriffe zu bedürfen scheinen. Bei Aufstellung der Bewegungsgesetze betrachtet Newton die Bewegung der Körper als eine absolute im Raume. Der absolute Raum ist aber nirgends unserer Erfahrung zugänglich. Erfahrungsmässig gegeben sind immer nur die relativen Lagenänderungen der Körper. Es wird also da gleich zu Anfang vollständig über die Erfahrung hinausgegangen, was gewiss bedenklich ist in einer Wissenschaft, welche sich nur die Aufgabe stellt Erfahrungsthatsachen darzustellen. Diese Schwierigkeit ist natürlich dem Genius Newtons keineswegs entgangen. Allein dieser glaubte ohne den Begriff eines absoluten Raumes zu keiner einfachen Formulirung des Trägheitsgesetzes gelangen zu können, um die es ihm an erster Stelle zu thun war und ich glaube, dass er hierin auch Recht behalten hat; denn so viel diese Schwierigkeit auch beleuchtet oder durchdacht wurde, so ist doch kaum ein wesentlicher Fortschritt erzielt worden. Neumann führt statt des Newton'schen absoluten Raumes einen räthselhaften idealen Bezugskörper ein, womit er offenbar ganz ebenso wie Newton über die Erfahrung hinausgeht. Streintz stellt sich die Aufgabe derartige Begriffe oder Körper zu vermeiden, indem er lehrt wie man mittelst der Bewegung eines Gyroskops, auf welches keine oder bekannte Kräfte wirken relativ gegen ein gewähltes Coordinatensystem entscheiden kann, ob für dieses Coordinatensystem die Newton'schen Bewegungsgesetze gelten, ob es ein brauchbares Bezugsystem ist. Allein diese Streintz'schen Betrachtungen scheinen für die Fundamentirung der Mechanik wenig brauchbar, da sie ja bereits die Bewegungsgesetze eines rotirenden Kreisels und die Beurtheilung, ob auf denselben Kräfte wirken oder nicht, voraussetzen, wozu schon die Kenntnis der Newton'schen Bewegungsgesetze erforderlich ist. Lange versucht allerdings die Formulirung des Trägheitsgesetzes ohne irgend ein Bezugsystem bloss durch Betrachtung der relativen Bewegung. Sie gelingt ihm auch, fällt aber so complicirt und weitschweifig aus, dass man sich nur schwer entschliessen wird ein so wenig übersichtliches Gesetz an Stelle der einfachen Newton'schen Formel zu setzen. Selbstverständlich geht auch der Vorschlag Mach's Gerade, welche durch die Gesammtheit aller Massen der Welt bestimmt sind oder der Vorschlag den Lichtäther an Stelle des absoluten Raums zu setzen, beide freilich in ganz anderer Weise über die Erfahrung hinaus. Ersterer Vorschlag knüpft nämlich wieder an rein ideale transcendente Begriffe an, wogegen letzterer eine Aussage macht, welche zwar erfahrungsmässig möglicherweise bewiesen werden könnte, aber es gewiss noch nicht ist. Es müsste denn für den Äther eine ganz andere Mechanik gelten, dieser müsste etwa selbst die Ursache des Trägheitsgesetzes nicht aber demselben unterworfen sein. Eine gleiche Schwierigkeit begegnet man bei Einführung des Begriffs der Zeit. Auch diese wird von Newton als eine absolute eingeführt, während uns eine solche niemals gegeben ist, sondern immer bloss die Gleichzeitigkeit des Verlaufs mehrerer Vorgänge. Jedoch ist hier die Abhilfe leichter, indem man von einem Vorgange ausgeht, der sich immer periodisch unter ganz gleichen Umständen wiederholt. Freilich ist es nicht möglich absolute Gleichheit der Umstände herzustellen, doch kann man im höchsten Grade wahrscheinlich machen, dass alle Umstände, die überhaupt wesentlichen Einfluss haben, die gleichen sind. Man kann dies noch dadurch erhärten, dass man verschiedenartige Vorgänge von dieser Eigenschaft (die Erddrehung, die Schwingungen eines Pendels, einer Chronometerfeder) untereinander vergleicht. Die Übereinstimmung aller dieser Vorgänge in der Anzeige gleicher Zeiten schliesst dann jeden Zweifel an der Brauchbarkeit der Methode aus.

Eine dritte Schwierigkeit betrifft die Begriffe der Masse und Kraft. Dass die Newton'sche Definition der Masse als Quantität der Materie eine nichts sagende ist, wurde längst erkannt. Aber auch bezüglich des Verhältnisses der Kraft zur Masse ergeben sich Zweifel. Ist die Masse das allein Existirende und die Kraft nur eine Eigenschaft derselben oder ist umgekehrt die Kraft das wahrhaft Existirende oder ist ein Dualismus zweier getrennter Existenzen (Masse und Kraft) anzunehmen, so dass die Kraft eine von der Materie getrennt existirende Ursache der Bewegung der ersteren ist. Hinzu kam in neuerer Zeit noch die Frage, ob auch der Energie Existenz zuzuschreiben ist oder ob gar letztere das allein Existirende ist.

Es war vor allen Kirchhoff, welcher in diesem Punkte schon der Art der Fragestellung entgegentrat. Oft ist ein Problem schon halb gelöst, wenn die richtige Methode der Fragestellung gefunden ist. Kirchhoff wies es nun zurück, dass es Aufgabe der Naturwissenschaft sei, das wahre Wesen der Erscheinungen zu enträthseln und ihre ersten metaphysischen Grundursachen anzugeben. Er reducirte die Aufgabe der Naturwissenschaft vielmehr darauf, die Erscheinungen zu beschreiben. Kirchhoff nannte dies noch eine Beschränkung der Aufgabe der Naturwissenschaft. Wenn man aber so recht in die Art und Weise, ich möchte sagen in den

Mechanismus unseres Denkens eindringt, so möchte man fast auch das leugnen.

Alle unsere Vorstellungen und Begriffe sind ja nur innere Gedankenbilder, wenn ausgesprochen Lautcombinationen. Die Aufgabe unseres Denkens ist es nun, dieselben so zu gebrauchen und zu verbinden, dass wir mit ihrer Hilfe allezeit mit grösster Leichtigkeit die richtigen Handlungen treffen und auch andere zu richtigen Handlungen anleiten. Die Metaphysik hat sich da dem nüchternsten praktischsten Standpunkte angeschlossen, die Extreme berühren sich. Die begrifflichen Zeichen, welche wir bilden, haben also nur eine Existenz in uns, die äussern Erscheinungen können wir nicht mit dem Masse unserer Vorstellungen messen. Wir können also formell derartige Fragen aufwerfen, ob bloss die Materie existirt und die Kraft eine Eigenschaft derselben ist oder ob letztere von der Materie unabhängig existirt oder ob umgekehrt die Materie ein Erzeugnis der Kraft ist; aber es haben alle diese Fragen gar keine Bedeutung, da alle diese Begriffe nur Gedankenbilder sind, welche den Zweck haben die Erscheinungen richtig darzustellen. Besonders klar hat dies Hertz in seinem berühmten Buche über die Principien der Mechanik ausgesprochen, nur stellt Hertz daselbst als erste Forderung die auf, dass die Bilder, welche wir uns construiren, den Denkgesetzen entsprechen müssen. Gegen diese Forderung möchte ich gewisse Bedenken erheben oder wenigstens sie etwas näher erläutern. Gewiss müssen wir einen reichen Schatz von Denkgesetzen mitbringen. Ohne sie wäre die Erfahrung vollkommen nutzlos; wir könnten sie gar nicht durch innere Bilder fixiren. Diese Denkgesetze sind uns fast ausnahmslos angeboren, aber sie erleiden doch durch Erziehung, Belehrung, und eigene Erfahrung Modifikationen. Sie sind nicht vollkommen gleich beim Kinde, beim einfachen ungebildeten Manne, oder beim Gelehrten. Wir werden dies auch einsehen, wenn wir die Denkrichtung eines naiven Volkes wie der Griechen mit der der Scholastiker des Mittelalters, und diese wieder mit der heutigen vergleichen. Gewiss gibt es Denkgesetze, welche sich so ausnahmslos bewährt haben, dass wir ihnen unbedingt vertrauen, sie für aprioristische unabänderliche Denkprincipien halten. Aber ich glaube doch, dass sie sich erst langsam entwickelten. Ihre erste Quelle waren primitive Erfahrungen der Menschheit im Urzustand, allmälig erstarkten sie und verdeutlichten sich durch complicirtirte Erfahrungen bis sie endlich ihre jetzige scharfe Formulirung annahmen; aber als unbedingt oberste Richter möchte ich die Denkgesetze nicht anerkennen.

Wir können nicht wissen ob sie nicht doch noch die eine oder andere Modification erfahren werden. Man erinnere sich doch mit welcher Sicherheit Kinder oder Ungebildete überzeugt sind, dass man durch das blosse Gefühl die Richtung nach oben von der nach unten an allen Orten des Weltraums müsse unterscheiden können und wie sie daraus die Unmöglichkeit der Antipoden deduciren zu können glauben. Würden solche Leute Logik schreiben, so würden sie das sicher für ein a priori evidentes Denkgesetz halten. Ebenso wurden anfangs gegen die Copernicanische Theorie vielfach aprioristische Bedenken erhoben und die Geschichte der Wissenschaft weist zahlreiche Fälle auf, wo man Sätze bald begründete, bald widerlegte mittels Beweisgründen, die man damals für evidente Denkgesetze hielt, während wir jetzt von ihrer Nichtigkeit überzeugt sind. Ich möchte daher die Hertz'sche Forderung dahin modificiren, dass in so weit wir Denkgesetze besitzen, welche wir durch stete Bewahrheitung in der Erfahrung als zweifellos richtig erkannt haben, wir die Richtigkeit unserer Bilder zunächst an diesen erproben können, dass aber die letzte und alleinige Entscheidung über die Zweckmässigkeit der Bilder in dem Umstande liegt, dass sie die Erfahrung möglichst einfach und durchaus treffend darstellen und dass gerade hierin wieder die Probe für die Richtigkeit der Denkgesetze liegt. Haben wir die Aufgabe des Denkens überhaupt und der Wissenschaft insbesondere in dieser Weise erfasst, so ergeben sich uns Consequenzen welche im ersten Augenblick etwas Frappirendes an sich haben. Eine Vorstellung von der Natur werden wir falsch nennen, wenn sie uns gewisse Thatsachen unrichtig darstellt oder wenn es offenbar einfachere gibt, welche die Thatsachen klarer darstellen, besonders wenn sie allgemein bewährten Denkgesetzen widerspricht, doch sind immerhin Theorien möglich, welche eine grosse Zahl von Thatsachen richtig darstellen in andern Punkten aber unrichtig sind, denen also eine gewisse relative Wahrheit zukommt. Ja es ist sogar möglich, dass wir in verschiedener Weise ein System von Bildern der Erscheinungen construiren können. Jedes dieser Systeme ist nicht gleich einfach, stellt die Erscheinungen nicht gleich gut dar. Aber es kann zweifelhaft, gewissermassen Geschmacksache sein, welches wir für das Einfachere halten, durch welche Darstellung der Erscheinungen wir uns mehr befriedigt fühlen. Die Wissenschaft verliert hiedurch ihr einheitliches Gepräge. Man hielt doch ehedem daran fest, dass es nur *Eine* Wahrheit geben könne, dass die Irrthümer mannigfaltig seien, die Wahrheit aber nur eine einzige ist. Dieser Ansicht muss von unserem jetzigen Standpunkte entgegen getreten werden, freilich ist der Unterschied der neuen Ansicht gegenüber der alten ein mehr formeller. Es war nie zweifelhaft, dass der Mensch niemals den vollen Inbegriff aller Wahrheit zu erkennen vermöge. Diese Erkenntniss ist nur ein Ideal. Ein ähnliches Ideal besitzen wir aber auch gemäss unserer jetzigen Vorstellung. Es ist das vollkommenste Bild, das alle Erscheinungen in der einfachsten und zweckmässigsten Weise darstellt. Wir wenden daher nach der einen Anschauungsweise den Blick mehr auf das unerreichbare Ideal, welches nur ein einheitliches ist, nach der andern auf die Mannigfaltigkeit des Erreichbaren.

Wenn wir nun die Überzeugung haben, dass die Wissenschaft bloss ein inneres Bild, eine gedankliche Construction ist, welche sich mit der Mannigfaltigkeit der Erscheinungen niemals decken, sondern nur gewisse Theile derselben übersichtlich darstellen kann, wie werden wir zu einem solchen Bilde gelangen? wie es möglichst systematisch und übersichtlich darstellen können? Es war früher eine Methode beliebt, welche der von Euclid in der Geometrie angewandten nachgebildet ist und daher die Euclidische heissen soll. Dieselbe geht von möglichst wenigen, möglichst evidenten Sätzen aus. In den ältesten Zeiten wurden diese als a priori evident, als direkt dem Geiste gegeben betrachtet, weshalb man sie als Axiome bezeichnet. Später dagegen schrieb man ihnen lediglich den Charakter von hinlänglich verbürgten Erfahrungssätzen zu. Aus diesen Axiomen wurden dann bloss mit Hilfe der Denkgesetze gewisse Bilder als nothwendig deducirt und man glaubte so einen Beweis gefunden zu haben, dass diese die einzig möglichen seien und nicht durch andere ersetzt werden könnten. Als Beispiel führe ich die Schlüsse an, welche zur Ableitung des Kräfteparallelogramms oder des Ampère'schen Gesetzes oder des Beweises dienten, dass die zwischen zwei materiellen Punkten wirkende Kraft in die Richtung ihrer Entfernung fallen und eine Function dieser Entfernung sein müsse.

Aber die Beweiskraft dieser Schlussweise geriet allmälig in Miscredit, der erste Schritt hiezu war der, dass man wie schon früher geschildert von einer a priori evidenten Grundlage zu einer bloss erfahrungsmässig bewährten überging. Man sah ferner ein, dass auch die Deduktionen aus jener Grundlage nicht ohne zahlreiche neue Hypothesen gemacht werden konnten, und so wies endlich Hertz darauf hin, dass namentlich im Gebiete der Physik unsere Überzeugung von der Richtigkeit einer allgemeinen Theorie im Wesen noch nicht auf der Ableitung derselben nach der Euclidischen Methode, sondern vielmehr darauf beruhe, dass diese Theorie in allen bisher bekannten Fällen uns zu richtigen Schlüssen in Bezug auf die Erscheinungen leite. Er machte von dieser Ansicht zuerst in seiner Darstellung der Maxwell'schen Grundgleichungen der Lehre von der Elektricität und dem Magnetismus Gebrauch, indem er vorschlug sich um deren Ableitung aus gewissen Grundprincipien gar nicht zu bekümmern, sondern sie einfach an die Spitze zu stellen und die Rechtfertigung hievon darin zu suchen, dass man nachweisen könne dass sie hinterher überall mit der Erfahrung übereinstimme; denn diese bleibt doch schliesslich die einzige Richterin über die Brauchbarkeit einer Theorie, deren Urtheil inapellabel und unerschütterlich ist. In der That wenn wir auf die Gegenstände näher eingehen, welche mit dem Gegenstande am meisten zusammenhängen, das Trägheitsgesetz, das Kräfteparallelogramm und die übrigen Fundamentalsätze der Mechanik, so werden wir die verschiedenen Beweise, welche in allen Lehrbüchern der Mechanik für jeden einzelnen dieser Sätze geliefert werden, bei weitem nicht so überzeugend finden, als die Thatsache, dass sich alle aus dem Inbegriffe aller dieser Sätze gezogenen Consequenzen so ausgezeichnet in der Erfahrung bestätigt haben. Die Wege, auf denen wir zu den Bildern gelangten, sind nicht selten die verschiedensten und von den mannigfaltigsten Zufällen abhängig.

Manche Bilder wurden im Verlauf von Jahrhunderten durch das Zusammenwirken vieler Forscher erst allmälig construirt, wie die der mechanischen Wärmetheorie. Manche wurden von einem einzigen, genialen Forscher, aber oft wieder auf sehr verschlungenen Umwegen, gefunden und erst dann von andern in die verschiedenartigste Beleuchtung gerückt, wie die besprochene Maxwell'sche Theorie der Elektricität und des Magnetismus. Es wird nun eine Darstellungsweise geben, welche ganz besondere Vorzüge aber auch wieder ihre Mängel besitzt. Diese Darstellungsweise besteht darin, dass wir eingedenk unserer Aufgabe, bloss innere Vorstellungsbilder zu construiren, anfangs lediglich mit gedanklichen Abstractionen operiren. Hiebei nehmen wir noch gar keine Rücksicht auf etwaige Erfahrungsthatsachen. Wir bemühen uns lediglich mit möglichster Klarheit unsere Gedankenbilder zu entwickeln, und aus denselben alle möglichen Consequenzen zu ziehen. Erst hinterher, nachdem die ganze Exposition des Bildes vollendet ist, prüfen wir dessen Übereinstimmung mit den Erfahrungsthatsachen, motiviren also in dieser Weise erst hinterher, warum das Bild gerade so und nicht anders gewählt werden musste, worüber wir vorher nicht die leiseste Andeutung geben. Wir wollen dies als die deduktive Darstellung bezeichnen. Die Vorzüge dieser

Darstellung liegen auf der Hand. Sie lässt zunächst gar keinen Zweifel darüber aufkommen, dass sie nicht die Dinge an sich selbst bieten will, sondern bloss ein inneres geistiges Bild und dass ihr Bestreben bloss darin besteht dieses geistige Bild zu einer geschickten Bezeichnung der Erscheinungen zu formen. Da die deduktive Methode nicht fortwährend äussere uns aufgezwungene Erfahrungen mit inneren von uns willkürlich gewählten Bildern vermengt, so ist es ihr weitaus am leichtesten diese letzteren klar und widerspruchsfrei zu entwickeln. Es ist nämlich eines der wichtigsten Erfordernisse dieser Bilder, dass sie vollkommen klar sind, dass wir niemals in Verlegenheit sind, wie wir sie in jedem bestimmten Falle formen sollen und dass wir jedes Mal das Resultat eindeutig und unzweifelhaft aus denselben ableiten können. Gerade diese Klarheit leidet durch zu frühe Vermischung mit der Erfahrung und wird bei der deduktiven Darstellungsweise am sichersten gewahrt. Dagegen tritt bei dieser Darstellungsweise besonders die Willkürlichkeit der Bilder scharf hervor, indem man mit ganz willkürlichen Gedankenconstructionen beginnt und deren Notwendigkeit nicht anfangs motivirt sondern erst hinterher rechtfertigt. Davon, dass nicht auch andere Bilder erdacht werden könnten, die ebenso mit der Erfahrung stimmen würden, wird kein Schatten eines Beweises geliefert. Es scheint dies ein Fehler zu sein, ist aber vielleicht gerade ein Vorzug, wenigstens für denjenigen, der die früher auseinandergesetzte Ansicht von dem Wesen jeder Theorie hat. Ein wirklicher Fehler der deduktiven Methode besteht dagegen darin, dass der Weg nicht sichtbar wird, auf welchem man zur Auffindung des betreffenden Bildes gelangte. Aber es ist ja im Gebiete der Wissenschaftslehre die Regel, dass der Zusammenhang der Schlüsse dann am deutlichsten hervortritt, wenn man diese möglichst in ihrer natürlichen Reihenfolge und ohne Rücksicht auf den oft krummen Weg auseinandersetzt, auf welchem dieselben gefunden wurden. Hertz hat auch im Gebiete der Mechanik in seinem bereits citirten Buche ein Muster einer solchen rein deduktiven Darstellung gegeben. Ich glaube den Inhalt des Hertz'schen Buches hier als bekannt voraussetzen zu können und mich daher auf eine ganz kurze Charakteristik desselben beschränken zu dürfen. Hertz geht von materiellen Punkten aus, welche er als reine Gedankenbilder betrachtet. Auch die Masse definirt er ganz unabhängig von aller Erfahrung durch eine Zahl, die wir uns jedem materiellen Punkte beigelegt denken müssen, nämlich die Anzahl der einfachen Massenpunkte, welche er enthält. Aus diesen abstrakten Begriffen construirt er eine zunächst natürlich bloss wie die Punkte selbst in Gedanken vorhandene Bewegung. Der Begriff der Kraft fehlt dabei vollständig. An ihre Stelle treten gewisse Bedingungen, welche sich in der Form von Gleichungen zwischen den Differenzialen der Coordinaten der materiellen Punkte schreiben. Diese letzteren sind nun mit gegebenen Anfangsgeschwindigkeiten ausgestattet und bewegen sich in jeder folgenden Zeit nach einem sehr einfachen Gesetze, welches sobald die Bedingungsgleichungen gegeben sind, die Bewegung für alle Zeiten eindeutig bestimmt. Hertz spricht es dahin aus, dass die Summe der mit den Massen multiplicirten Quadrate der Abweichungen der materiellen Punkte von der geradlinigen, gleichförmigen Bewegung für jeden Zeitmoment ein Minimum sein muss oder noch kürzer, dass die Bewegung in den geradesten Bahnen geschieht. Es hat dieses Gesetz die grösste Ähnlichkeit mit dem Gauss'schen Principe des kleinsten Zwanges, ja es ist gewissermassen derjenige spezielle Fall, der eintritt, wenn man das Gauss'sche Princip auf ein System von Punkten anwendet, welche zwar einem Zwange, aber keinerlei sonstigen äussern Kräften unterworfen sind.

Ich habe in meinem Buche welches den Titel hat "Vorlesungen über die Principe der Mechanik" ebenfalls eine rein deduktive Darstellung der Grundprincipe derselben versucht, aber in ganz anderer Weise, weit mehr an die gewönliche Behandlung der Mechanik anknüpfend. Ich gehe wie Hertz von reinen Gedankendingen, exakten materiellen Punkten aus; ich beziehe deren Lage auf ein ebenfalls gedachtes rechtwinkliges Coordinatensystem und denke mir ein geistiges Bild von der Bewegung derselben zunächst in folgender Weise construirt. Jedesmal, wenn sich zwei derselben in irgend einer Entfernung r befinden, soll jeder derselben eine Beschleunigung in der Richtung von r erfahren, welche eine Function $f(r)$ dieser Entfernung ist, über die später nach Belieben verfügt werden kann. Es sollen ferner die Beschleunigungen beider Punkte in einem zu allen Zeiten unveränderlichen Zahlenverhältnisse stehen, welches das Massenverhältnis der beiden materiellen Punkte definirt. Wie wir uns die Bewegung aller materiellen Punkte zu denken haben, das ist dann eindeutig durch die Angabe bestimmt, dass die wirkliche Beschleunigung jedes Punktes die Vectorsumme aller für ihn nach der früheren Regel gefundenen Beschleunigungen ist und sich zur schon vorhandenen Geschwindigkeit des Punktes ebenfalls so addirt wie Vectorgrössen addirt werden. Woher diese Beschleunigungen kommen und warum ich gerade die Vorschrift gebe sich das Bild in dieser Weise zu construiren wird nicht weiter discutirt. Es genügt dass das Bild ein vollkommen klares ist, welches in genügend vielen Fällen durch Rechnungen im Detail ausgearbeitet werden kann. Dasselbe findet seine Rechtfertigung erst darin, dass sich die Function $f(r)$ in allen Fällen so bestimmen lässt, dass die gedachte Bewegung der eingebildeten materiellen Punkte in ein naturgetreues Abbild der wirklichen Erscheinungen übergeht.

Wir haben durch diese Behandlungsweise, welche wir die rein deductive genannt haben, die Frage nach dem Wesen der Materie, der Masse, der Kraft, freilich nicht gelöst, aber wir haben diese Fragen umgangen, indem wir ihre Voranstellung vollständig überflüssig gemacht haben. In unserem Gedankenschema sind diese Begriffe ganz bestimmte Zahlen und Anweisungen zu geometrischen Constructionen, von denen wir wissen, wie wir sie denken und ausführen sollen, damit wir ein brauchbares Bild der Erscheinungswelt erhalten. Was die eigentliche Ursache sei, dass die Erscheinungswelt sich gerade so abspielt, was gewissermassen hinter der Erscheinungswelt verborgen ist und sie treibe, das zu erforschen, betrachten wir nicht als Aufgabe der Naturwissenschaft. Ob es Aufgabe einer andern Wissenschaft sei und sein könne, oder ob wir da nicht vielleicht bloss nach Analogie mit anderen vernünftigen Wortzusammenstellungen hier Worte aneinandergefügt haben, welche in diesen Verbindungen keinen klaren Gedanken ausdrücken, das kann hier vollständig dahingestellt bleiben. Wir haben durch diese deductive Methode ebenso wenig die Frage nach dem absoluten Raume und der absoluten Bewegung gelöst; allein auch diese Frage hat keine pädagogischen Schwierigkeiten mehr; wir brauchen sie nicht mehr beim Beginne der Entwickelung der mechanischen Gesetze vorzubringen, sondern können sie erst besprechen, wenn wir alle mechanischen Gesetze abgeleitet haben. Denn da wir ja anfangs ohnehin nur gedankliche Constructionen vorführen, so nimmt sich ein gedachtes Coordinatensystem keineswegs fremdartig unter denselben aus. Es ist eben eins der verschiedenen uns verständlichen und geläufigen Constructionsmittel aus denen wir unser Gedankenbild zusammensetzen, nicht mehr und nicht weniger abstract, als die materiellen Punkte, deren Bewegung relativ gegen das Coordinatensystem wir uns vorstellen und für welche allein wir zunächst die Gesetze aussprechen und mathematisch formuliren. Beim Vergleiche mit der Erfahrung finden wir dann, dass ein unveränderlich mit dem Fixsternhimmel verbundenes Coordinatensystem praktisch vollkommen ausreicht um die Übereinstimmung mit der Erfahrung zu sichern. Was für ein Coordinatensystem wir einstens werden zu Grunde legen müssen, wenn wir einmal die Bewegung der Fixsterne durch mechanische Formeln ausdrücken könnten, diese Frage steht auf unserm Repertoire an allerletzter Stelle und wir können jetzt alle die Hypothesen von Streintz, Mach, Lange etc. welche eingangs erwähnt wurden mit Leichtigkeit discutiren, da uns alle Gesetze der Mechanik bereits zur Verfügung stehen. Wir kommen nicht in dieselbe Verlegenheit wie früher, wo wir diese complicirten Betrachtungen der Entwickelung des Trägheitsgesetzes hätten voranstellen müssen. Freilich haben wir dafür bei der deductiven Methode wieder einen Beweis zu liefern, der bei den alten Methoden überflüssig war. Da wir bei den letzteren direct von den Erscheinungen ausgingen, so verstand es sich von selbst, dass die Gesetze der Erscheinungen nicht von der Wahl des lediglich hinzugedachten Coordinatensystems abhängen können, und es musste eben frappiren, dass sich diese Gesetze anders und viel complicirter ausnehmen, wenn wir ein sich drehendes Coordinatensystem einführen. Bei der deductiven Methode aber haben wir von vorne herein dem Coordinatensystem im Bilde die gleiche Rolle angewiesen wie den materiellen Punkten. Es ist ein integrirender Bestandtheil des Bildes und es kann uns nicht Wunder nehmen, dass dieses verschieden ausfällt, wenn wir das Coordinatensystem anders wählen. Wir müssen hier im Gegentheil aus dem Bilde selbst den Beweis liefern, dass dieses sich nicht ändert, wenn wir beliebige andere Coordinatensysteme einführen, so lange sich diese nicht relativ gegen einander drehen oder nicht mit Beschleunigung relativ gegen einander bewegen.

Wir wollen nun die zuletzt besprochene Darstellungsweise meines Buches mit der Hertz'schen vergleichen. Herr Classen hat meine Darstellung als eine Polemik gegen Hertz aufgefasst und die Sache so dargestellt, als ob ich mir einbildete etwas unbedingt Besseres als Hertz vorgebracht zu haben. Nichts weniger als dies. Ich erkenne die Vorzüge des Hertz'schen Bildes unbedingt an, aber nach dem Principe, dass es möglich und wünschenswert ist, für ein und dieselbe Erscheinungsgruppe mehrere Bilder aufzustellen, glaube ich, dass mein Bild neben dem Hertz'schen noch seine Bedeutung hat, indem es gewisse Vorzüge aufweist, welche dem Hertz'schen fehlen. Die Principe der Mechanik, welche Hertz aufstellt, sind von ausserordentlicher Einfachheit und Schönheit. Sie sind natürlich nicht vollständig frei von Willkürlichkeit, aber ich möchte sagen die Willkürlichkeit ist auf ein Minimum beschränkt. Das von Hertz unabhängig von der Erfahrung construirte Bild hat eine gewisse innere Vollendung und Evidenz. Es enthält an sich nur wenig willkürliche Elemente. Hingegen steht offenbar mein Bild weit zurück. Letzteres enthält weit mehr Züge, welche den Stempel davon an sich tragen, dass sie nicht durch eine innere Notwendigkeit bestimmt sind, sondern bloss eingefügt wurden, um hinterher dann eben die Übereinstimmung mit den Erfahrung zu ermöglichen. Es enthält auch eine ganz willkürliche Function und von den vielen Bildern, welche entstehen, wenn dieser Function alle möglichen Formen ertheilt werden, entsprechen nur ganz wenige wirklichen Vorgängen, während man beim Hertz'schen Bilde sofort sieht, dass wenn überhaupt einige, so doch jedenfalls nur wenige andere Bilder möglich sein können, welche sich einer gleichen Einfachheit und inneren Vollendung erfreuen, so weckt mein Bild sofort die Idee, dass es wohl noch so manche andere geben mag, welche die Erscheinungen mit gleicher Vollkommenheit darstellen. Trotzdem giebt es aber wieder Punkte, in denen mein Bild dem Hertz'schen überlegen ist. Hertz kann zwar einige Erscheinungen in directer Weise, aus seinem Bilde erklären, oder wie wir lieber sagen wollen, mittelst desselben darstellen, so die Bewegung eines materiellen Punktes auf einer vorgeschriebenen Fläche oder Kurve oder die Drehung eines starren Körpers um einen fixen Punkt, beides wolgemerkt, so lange keine fremdartigen äussern Kräfte vorhanden sind. Man stösst aber sofort auf Schwierigkeiten, sobald man die gewöhnlichsten in der täglichen Erfahrung vorkommenden Vorgänge darstellen will, bei denen Kräfte wirken. Betrachten wir zunächst eine der allgemeinsten und wichtigsten Naturkräfte, die Gravitation. Als Fernkraft dürfen wir dieselbe vom Hertz'schen Standpunkte natürlich nicht auffassen. Es sind nun zwar zahlreiche Versuche gemacht worden, sie durch Wirkung eines Mediums mechanich zu erklären. Allein es ist bekannt, dass keiner derselben zu einem recht bestimmten, entscheidenden Resultate geführt hat. Einer der bekanntesten ist die schon von Lesage aufgestellte, später von Lord Kelvin, Isenkrahe und andern wieder aufgenommene Theorie der Molekularstösse. Dieselbe ist abgesehen davon, dass ihre exacte Durchführbarkeit, noch immer zweifelhaft, ist für die Hertz'sche Theorie unbrauchbar, weil schon die Erklärung eines einzigen elastischen Stosses aus derselben Schwierigkeiten bereitet, wie wir sogleich sehen werden. Man müsste also erst eine ganz neue Theorie schaffen, die Gravitations-wirkung etwa durch Wirbel, Pulsationen oder Ähnliches erklären, wobei die Theilchen des betreffenden Mediums ebenfalls nicht durch Kräfte im alten Sinne, sondern bloss durch Bedingungsgleichungen von der Form, wie sie Hertz aufstellt verknüpft sein dürften. Selbst, wenn dies gelingen sollte, so hiesse dies doch zu einem ganz willkürlichen Bilde greifen, welches höchst wahrscheinlich im Verlaufe der Zeit durch ein ganz anderes ersetzt werden müsste. Der Vorwurf, welchen Hertz gegen die alte Mechanik erhebt, dass sie ein viel zu weites Bild gibt, indem von allen möglichen die Kraft darstellenden Functionen $f(r)$ nur ganz wenige eine praktische Verwendung haben lässt sich in verstärktem Masse gegen sein eigenes Bild kehren, sobald man dasselbe auf bestimmte Fälle anwenden will. Schon bei der Anwendung auf die Gravitation muss man aus allen möglichen Medien, welche Fernwirkung vermitteln könnten irgend ein bestimmtes auswählen, worin wohl noch mehr Unbestimmtheit und Willkürlichkeit liegt als in der Wahl gewisser Functionen $f(r)$.

Die elektrischen und magnetischen Kräfte hat bekanntlich Maxwell in seinen ersten Arbeiten mit Erfolg durch die Wirkung eines Mediums erklärt. Allein abgesehen davon, dass dieses Medium einen höchst complicirten Bau hatte und von Eigenschaften strotzte, die den Stempel der Willkürlichkeit und eines rein provisorischen Charakters an sich trugen, so wäre es für Hertz wieder nicht einmal brauchbar, indem seine Theile ebenfalls von Kräften im alten Sinne der Mechanik zusammengehalten werden. Ja auch die Eigenschaften der elastischen, tropfbarflüssigen und gasförmigen Körper müssten durch neue Bilder ersetzt werden, da die bisherigen alle auf die Annahme von zwischen den Theilchen wirkenden Kräften gegründet sind. Man hat also nur folgende Wahl, entweder man lässt die Natur des Mechanismus, welcher die Gravitation, die elektrischen und magnetischen Erscheinungen erzeugen soll, unbestimmt und willkürlich. Dadurch entsteht eine unerträgliche Unanschaulichkeit, indem man genöthigt ist immer mit Gleichungen zu operiren, von denen man nur einige ganz allgemeine Eigenschaften kennt, deren spezielle Form aber vollständig unbekannt ist, oder man bemüht sich einen bestimmten Mechanismus zu wählen, wodurch man dann wieder in eben so viele Willkürlichkeiten als Schwierigkeiten verwickelt wird.

Doch ich will noch an einem viel einfacheren Beispiele die Schwierigkeiten zeigen, auf welche die Anwendung des Hertz'schen Fundamentalgesetzes schon in den trivialsten Fällen stösst.

Es seien drei Massen m_1, u und m_2 mit der Bedingung gegeben, dass sowohl die Entfernung $m_1 u$ als auch die $u m_2$ stets gleich derselben Grösse a sein soll. Lassen wir dann die Masse u immer kleiner werden, so erhalten wir einen vollkommen dem Geiste der Hertz'schen Mechanik entsprechenden Fall, der uns ein getreues Bild des folgenden Naturvorgangs gibt. In einer elastischen Hohlkugel von der Masse m_1 bewege sich eine kleine elastische Vollkugel; die Differenz der Radien sei $2a$. Wir haben also hier ein Beispiel eines und desselben Naturvorganges, welcher auf zwei ganz verschiedenen Wegen erklärt werden kann, einestheils aus der Molekulartheorie, anderstheils nach der von Hertz angegebenen Methode. Aber so verhalten sich nicht alle Vorgänge. Schon der ganz triviale Fall des Stosses zweier elastischen Vollkugeln ist aus dem Hertz'schen Schema nur durch zeimlich willkürlich gewählte Mechanismen oder complicirte Annahmen über ein Zwischenmedium ableitbar, da ja die Hertz'sche Methode Ungleichungen ausschliesst. Es führt also die Hertz'sche Methode schon in den einfachsten Fällen zu den grössten Complicationen.

Ich betone hier nochmals, dass diese Ausführungen keineswegs den Zweck haben sollen, den hohen Wert des Hertz'schen Bildes zu leugnen, welcher in der logischen Einfachheit seiner Grundprincipien besteht. Es wäre ja möglich, dass man in ferner Zukunft einmal alle Wirkungen durch Medien erklären kann, deren Eigenschaften nicht phantastisch gewählt, sondern durch die Natur der Sache in nahe liegender und unzweideutiger Weise geboten werden. Es wäre möglich, dass die Theilchen dieser Medien nicht Kräfte im alten mechanischen Sinne aufeinander ausüben, sondern dass man mit Bedingungsgleichungen im Hertz'schen Sinne zwischen den Coordinaten der Elementartheilchen ausreichen würde. Von diesem Augenblicke an hätte die Hertz'sche Mechanik in unzweifelhafter Weise den Sieg davongetragen und alle andern Darstellungen hätten nur mehr historisches Interesse. Ob man das einstige Eintreffen eines solchen Zeitmomentes für wahrscheinlich hält oder nicht ist natürlich eine reine Geschmackssache. Bewiesen ist nicht einmal die Möglichkeit einer derartigen Entwicklung unserer Erkenntnis. Wir werden daher auf unserem gegenwärtigem Standpunkte zu jenem Ideale mit Bewunderung aufblicken, auch das Unserige zur Beförderung der Annäherung an dasselbe beitragen. Aber einstweilen werden wir solche einfache und unmittelbar brauchbare Bilder, welche sich jetzt schon ins Detail durchführen lassen neben den Hertz'schen nicht entbehren können.

Zweite Vorlesung.

Ich habe in der vorigen Vorlesung zwei Bilder der mechanischen Erscheinungen besprochen, welche beide rein deductiv sind, das Hertz'sche und das in meinem Buche über Mechanik dargestellte. Das letztere unterscheidet sich dem Wesen nach nicht von den älteren Theorien der Mechanik. Ich bemühte mich nur diese durch eine möglichst consequente Darstellung gegen etwaige Einwürfe besonders gegen die Bedenken zu sichern, welche Hertz in der Vorrede seines Buches gegen die ältere Mechanik erhebt. Gerade zu diesem Zwecke schien sich die rein deductive Darstellung am besten zu eignen, weil sie das Bild ganz unabhängig von den Thatsachen in möglichster Klarheit zu entwickeln erlaubt. Man könnte jedoch das Bild auch nach der entgegengesetzten Methode entwickeln, indem man unmittelbar von den Thatsachen ausginge, wie sie sich der unbefangenen Beobachtung bieten, aus diesen Thatsachen die Bilder erst allmälig entstehen liesse und jede Abstraction erst dann einführte, wenn sie auf keine Weise mehr abgewiesen werden kann. Diese letztere Darstellung wollen wir die inductive nennen. Dieselbe hat der deductiven gegenüber den Nachtheil, dass die Bilder von Anfang an nicht so rein hervortreten, daher ihre innere Consequenz nicht so klar zu übersehen ist. Allein sie hat auch wieder den Vortheil, dass sie an Stelle der lange Zeit hindurch rein abstracten von der Wirklichkeit abgekehrten Darstellungsweise der deduktiven Methode rein an das unmittelbar Gegebene und Geläufige anknüpfende setzt und möglichst klar erkennen lässt, wie die abstracten Bilder entstanden sind und warum wir gerade zu diesen Bildern unsere Zuflucht nehmen. Um die Vorzüge und Nachtheile der deductiven Methode mit der inductiven zu vergleichen, wäre es nicht ganz zweckmässig die im vorigen Vortrage geschilderte Methode mit den älteren in der Mechanik üblichen Darstellungsweisen zu vergleichen, da die letzteren beide Methoden vermischen und dadurch wie mir scheint die Klarheit beeinträchtigen. So werden in der Regel sehr bald abstracte Begriffe, wie der des materiellen Punktes, der Masse etc., eingeführt, diese aber nicht, wie von uns in der vorigen Vorlesung als rein gedankliche Werkzeuge aufgefasst. Es werden vielmehr davon mehr oder minder unbestimmte und nichts sagende Definitionen gegeben. So wird der materielle Punkt als ein Körper definirt, welcher so klein ist, dass seine Ausdehnung vernachlässigt werden kann. Man meint damit etwa, dass seine Trägheitsmomente bezüglich einer durch seinen Schwerpunkt gehenden Axe gegenüber denen bezüglich einer andern Axe verschwinden, die sich davon in einer Entfernung befindet, die von der Grössenordnung der Entfernungen ist, welche bei unsern Experimenten für gewöhnlich vorkommen oder Ähnliches. Da aber der Begriff des Trägheitsmomentes, Schwerpunkts etc. noch nicht entwickelt worden ist, so wüsste ich nicht was man sich unter einem Körper, an dem eine der wichtigsten Eigenschaften, nämlich die Ausdehnung vernachlässigt werden kann, denken soll. Die Masse wird oft definirt durch die Wirkung einer und derselben Kraft auf verschiedene Körper, aber wie soll man constatiren, dass die Kraft dieselbe ist, wenn sie einmal auf diesen einmal auf jenen Körper wirkt? Es wird daher das Beste sein, wenn wir versuchen noch eine neue rein inductive Darstellung der Grundprincipien der Mechanik wenigstens mit einigen Strichen zu skizziren. Wir bleiben dabei unserm Princip treu, dass wir vorläufig keineswegs eine einzige beste Darstellung der Wissenschaft erstreben, sondern dass wir es für nützlich halten möglichst viele verschiedene Darstellungen zu versuchen, von denen jede ihre besondern Vorzüge, freilich auch wieder jede ihre Mängel hat. Das Hauptaugenmerk wird dabei wieder darauf zu richten sein alle Inconsequenzen und logischen Fehler zu vermeiden, keinen Begriff oder keine Annahme stillschweigend einzuschmuggeln, sondern uns aller gemachten Hypothesen mit möglichster Klarheit bewusst zu werden. Es versteht sich von selbst, dass ich hier bei der Kürze der mir zur Verfügung stehenden Zeit nicht die ganze Mechanik erschöpfend darstellen kann. Ich werde nur versuchen einige Andeutungen zu geben. Es wäre wol auch kaum möglich eine so schwierige Aufgabe auf einmal ganz der Lösung zuzuführen. Viel wird an dem ersten Versuche noch mangelhaft sein und erst allmälig werden sich die Begriffe sichten und die Darstellungsweisen vervollkommnen. Wir werden da gerade denjenigen Weg einschlagen müssen, der dem in der vorigen Vorlesung geschilderten und in meinem Buche über Mechanik verfolgten, direct entgegengesetzt ist. Die abstracten Begriffe des materiellen Punktes, der Masse, Kraft etc., von denen wir dort ausgingen, werden wir nun zwar auch nicht ganz vermeiden können; denn sie sind einmal die Grundpfeiler, auf welche die Mechanik aufgebaut ist. Aber wir werden sie jetzt so spät als möglich einführen und während wir sie früher postulirten, werden wir jetzt möglichst an die Erfahrung anknüpfen und unsere Resultate daraus zu deduciren suchen. Daher sind jetzt auch diejenigen Gesetze, welche früher die einfachsten schienen, nicht voranzustellen, wie z. B. das Trägheitsgesetz. Dieses wird gewöhnlich dahin ausgesprochen, dass ein materieller Punkt, welcher jedem äusseren Einflusse entzogen ist, sich geradlinig und gleichförmig bewegt. Abgesehen von der Schwierigkeit, die im Begriffe des materiellen Punktes liegt, können wir nun aber keinen Körper so weit von allen übrigen entfernen, dass er jedem Einflusse entzogen ist und wäre dies möglich, so könnten wir seine Bewegung nicht mehr beobachten, geschweige denn deren Geradlinigkeit und Gleichförmigkeit constatiren. Wenn man aber das Trägheitsgesetz an Körpern verificiren will, an denen sich alle darauf wirkenden Kräfte das Gleichgewicht halten, so müsste man die gesammte Lehre vom Gleichgewichte schon vorausschicken. Man pflegt also in der gewöhnlichen Darstellung Abstractionen und Thatsachen vielfach zu vermischen, was zu vermeiden eben im folgenden unsere Hauptaufgabe sein soll, da wir uns vornehmen streng von reinen Erfahrungsthatsachen auszugehen.

Die erste Unbequemlichkeit, die uns hiebei entgegentritt ist folgende: Früher hatten wir es bei Aufstellung der ersten Grundprincipien mit rein Gedachtem zu thun, das wir in unserer Idee formen können, wie wir wollen, und wovon wir verlangen können, dass es immer exact unseren Anforderungen entspricht, jetzt dagegen wollen wir von den direct beobachteten Erscheinungen ausgehen, welche immer sehr zusammengesetzt und complicirt sind. Wollen wir daraus Grundgesetze gewinnen, so müssen wir die Erscheinungen immer generalisiren und idealisiren, so dass wir schon nicht mehr ganz exacte Thatsachen vor uns haben sondern Vorgänge, welche in der Natur immer nur mit grösserer oder geringerer Annäherung realisirt sind. Wir können es daher auch nicht ganz vermeiden Vorstellungen und Thatsachen zu vermengen aber wir suchen dies wenigstens auf das kleinste Mass zurück zu führen und bestreben uns es nicht versteckt zu thun, sondern wo wir dazu gezwungen sind uns dessen klar bewusst zu bleiben.

Die Erscheinungen, welche uns gegeben sind, haben eine ausserordentlich verschiedene Natur. Die einfachsten bestehen in Ortsveränderungen eines Körpers, welcher dabei weder seine Gestalt noch seine sonstigen Eigenschaften irgendwie zu verändern scheint. Schon diese einfache Erscheinung ist in gewisser Beziehung eine idealisirte. In den wenigsten Fällen ändert der Körper seine Gestalt absolut gar nicht; ja alle, selbst die unveränderlichsten Körper können durch sehr starke Kräfte zerbrechen, durch Hitze, chemische Wirkungen, zu völliger Veränderung ihrer

Eigenschaften veranlasst werden. Aber es gibt sehr viele Körper, die doch ihre Gestalt während der mannigfaltigsten Bewegungen durch lange Zeit nicht bemerkbar ändern. Wir nennen sie feste Körper und bilden uns das Ideal eines absolut unveränderlichen Körpers, welchen wir einen starren nennen. Andere Körper, die Flüssigkeiten ändern während ihrer Bewegung ihre Gestalt in der mannigfaltigsten Weise, entweder bei (natürlich wieder nur angenähert) gleich bleibendem Volumen, (die tropfbaren Flüssigkeiten) oder unter steter sehr merkbarer Änderung des Volumens, (die Gase). Man kann die letzteren Erscheinungen auf die erstern zurückführen, indem man annimmt, dass die Flüssigkeiten aus sehr vielen sehr kleinen Theilchen bestehen, deren Bewegung unabhängig von einander, die Gestaltänderung hervorruft. Ändert sich dabei die durchschnittliche Entfernung je zweier Nachbartheilchen, so ist dieselbe auch mit Volumänderung verknüpft. Es ist nun die Frage, soll man sich die Anzahl dieser Theilchen mathematisch unendlich oder bloss sehr gross aber endlich denken. Viele Erfahrungsthatsachen deuten darauf hin, dass die letztere Annahme gemacht werden muss, welche auch philosophisch die befriedigendere ist. Aber da eine unzweifelhafte experimentelle Entscheidung bisher nicht erfolgt ist, so wollen wir getreu den Principien, nach denen wir jetzt vorzugehn beabsichtigen, diese Frage vollständig in suspenso lassen.

Alle Ortsveränderung heissen Bewegungen. Die Lehre von den Bewegungserscheinungen ist die Mechanik, welche sich in die Geo-, Hydro- und Aero-mechanik abtheilt, je nachdem man es mit der Bewegung fester, tropfbarer oder gasförmiger Körper zu thun hat. Die Mechanik umfasst ihrer Definition gemäss auch die Bedingungen, unter denen sich ein Körper garnicht bewegt.

Es gibt noch vielerlei Erscheinungen der Schall, die Wärme, das Licht, die elektrischen und magnetischen Erscheinungen, die gänzliche Änderung der Eigenschaften von Körpern bei chemischen Prozessen, die Geruchs-, Geschmackerscheinungen etc. Letztere sind wahrscheinlich nur spezielle Fälle von Verdampfungs- oder chemischen Erscheinungen, und daher für die Physik von geringerer Wichtigkeit, welche ja die Action auf die Nerven und die Fortleitung durch dieselben bis zum Bewusstwerden der Physiologie und Psychologie überlässt. Aber sie müssen hier doch ebenfalls erwähnt werden.

Es ist unzweifelhaft nachgewiesen, dass den Schallerscheinungen Bewegungen der Körper zu Grunde liegen. Naturgemäss suchte man auch Licht, Elektricität und Magnetismus, so wie die chemischen Erscheinungen durch Bewegungserscheinungen gewisser hypothetischer Medien oder hypothetischer kleinster Theile zu erklären und bis vor Kurzem war wohl jeder Physiker überzeugt, dass hiemit dem Wesen nach die eigentliche Aufgabe der Physik ausgesprochen sei. Erst vor wenigen Decennien wurde unwiderleglich nachgewiesen, dass die besonders in Deutschland früher allgemein verbreitete Theorie der elektrischen und magnetischen Fluide mit den Thatsachen nicht in Übereinstimmung gebracht werden kann. Man wurde nun vorsichtiger, man suchte zwar die elektrischen und magnetischen Erscheinungen zunächst wieder durch mechanische Wirkung eines Mediums zu erklären, allein da man hiebei nicht zu einem bestimmten eindeutigen Erfolge gelangte, so neigen in neuester Zeit manche Physiker zur Ansicht, dass es wol ein übereilter Schluss sei, dass sich alle Erscheinungen durch Bewegungsphänomene müssten erklären lassen oder in unsere Ausdrucksweise übertragen, dass es vielleicht gar nicht möglich sei durch die Bilder von Ortsveränderungen von Punkten und Körpertheilen allein sich ein ausreichendes Bild der Erscheinungen zu verschaffen; dass man dazu noch qualitativ verschiedene Bilder wie dielektrische und magnetische Polarisationen, chemische Zustände oder anderes dazunehmen müsse. Es würde dadurch die Einheit der Naturwissenschaft ausserordentlich leiden, da man auf keinen Fall die alten einfachen Bilder vermeiden könnte und uns noch eine Menge fremdartiger dazu einführen müsste. Es würde dann auch die Bedeutung der Mechanik als Grundlage der gesammten Naturwissenschaft, auf welcher alle übrigen Theorien derselben beruhen, in Frage gestellt. Aber immer hätte noch die Mechanik als die Lehre der einfachsten Erscheinungen, ohne die irgend welche andere nicht denkbar sind, allen andern physikalischen Theorien voranzugehn. Wenn man daher auch einerseits nicht leugnen kann, dass der Beweis der mechanischen Erklärbarkeit aller Naturerscheinungen noch nicht geliefert ist, so ist doch sicher ebenso wenig ein Beweis geliefert, dass gewisse Naturerscheinungen nicht durch mechanische Bilder erklärbar sein könnten, und man kann höchstens die Ansicht aussprechen, dass bei gewissen Naturerscheinungen der Versuch einer mechanischen Erklärung heute noch zu früh kommt. Die allgemeine Frage an sich kann erst nach Jahrhunderten entschieden oder wenigstens in ein wesentlich neues Licht gerückt und geklärt werden. Wir wollen uns daher mit der Discussion des "Für" oder "Wider" hier nicht aufhalten, sondern kehren zur Bewegung eines festen Körpers K zurück, den wir sogleich idealisiren, indem wir ihn als absolut starr denken. Wir fassen denselben nicht etwa als einen materiellen Punkt, sondern als einen erfahrungsmässig gegebenen, wenigstens dem Scheine nach continuirlich ausgedehnten Körper auf. Wir müssen freilich wieder sogleich mit einer Abstraction einsetzen; wir können die Bewegung des Körpers nicht auf einmal als Ganzes erfassen, da er ja (wenigstens für uns scheinbar) aus unendlich vielen Theilen besteht. Wir können bloss die Bewegung einzelner Punkte desselben klar mit dem Auge und Gedanken verfolgen. Wir wollen daher sehr kleine Stellen desselben A, B, C, . . . mit feinen selbstverständlich ebenfalls starr mit dem Körper verbundenen Marken bezeichnen etwa mit feinen Farbepunkten, Mehlstäubchen oder durch die Kreuzung zweier feiner Linien etc. Wenn wir eine ausserordentlich enge Höhlung in den Körper bohren, so können wir auch Punkte im Innern desselben wirklich bezeichnen und wir können es auch ohne die Höhlung in Gedanken, wenn wir uns etwa einen geometrisch ähnlichen hohlen oder durchsichtigen oder sonst an dieser Stelle zugänglichen Körper vorstellen. Es ist freilich schon wieder eine Idealisirung, wenn wir uns diese bezeichneten Stellen als mathematische Punkte denken; allein wir bleiben doch dem thatsächlich Realen viel näher, wenn wir die Bewegung des ausgedehnten Körpers durch solche Punkte beschreiben und an erster Stelle einfache Gesetze für die Mechanik ausgedehnter Körper zu gewinnen suchen, als wenn wir direkt mit den Gesetzen für die Bewegung einzelner materieller Punkte beginnen. Wir können jetzt genauer beschreiben, was es heisst, wenn wir sagen die Gestalt eines Körpers ändert sich während seiner Bewegung nicht. Wir können durch Anlegen eines Massstabes oder zweier Zirkelspitzen, die wir dann auf einen Massstab übertragen die Entfernung je zweier beliebiger Punkte des Körpers K d. h. zweier beliebiger hervorgehobener Marken auf demselben messen. Wenn dieselbe für alle Punktepaare zu allen Zeiten unverändert bleibt, so sagen wir die Gestalt des Körpers ist unveränderlich. Für die Unveränderlichkeit des Massstabes oder Zirkels haben wir freilich keine objective Garantie, sondern nur die empirische, dass uns dieselben an allen Körpern, welche schon dem Augenscheine nach ihre Gestalt nicht ändern, die richtige Anzeige liefern. Wenn alle festen Körper in gleicher Weise ihre Dimensionen mit der Zeit ändern würden, so könnten wir dies natürlich nicht bemerken. Wir haben auch durchaus nicht die Absicht zu erklären, wieso es feste Körper gibt, wieso wir die Entfernungen der damit fest verbundnen

Marken messen können. Wir nehmen dies als Erfahrungsthatsachen hin, nur die Gesetze der Veränderung der Entfernungen der Marken verschiedener Körper oder auch desselben Körpers falls dieser nicht starr ist, wollen wir durch unsere Vorstellungsbilder darstellen.

Vorbedingung jeder wissenschaftlichen Erkenntniss ist das Princip der eindeutigen Bestimmtheit der Naturvorgänge, auf die Mechanik angewandt der eindeutigen Bestimmtheit aller Bewegungen. Dasselbe sagt aus, dass die Bewegungen der Körper nicht rein zufällig bald so, bald anders vor sich gehn, sondern dass sie durch die Umstände, unter denen sich der Körper befindet, eindeutig bestimmt sind. Wenn jeder Körper sich wie er wollte bewegte, wenn unter gleichen Umständen bald diese, bald jene Bewegung je nach Zufall erfolgte, so könnten wir dem Verlaufe der Erscheinungen nur neugierig zusehen nicht ihn erforschen. Auch hierin liegt wieder eine Unbestimmtheit, die Umstände, unter denen die Bewegung irgend eines Körpers vor sich geht, umfassen streng genommen das ganze Universum. Dasselbe ist nie zweimal im selben Zustande. Wir müssen also unsere Bedingungen dahin reduziren, dass immer dieselbe Bewegung erfolgt, wenn die unmittelbare Umgebung sich in demselben Zustande befindet. Wir sind hier bei der inductiven Methode wieder in einer weit ungünstigeren Lage als bei der Deductiven. Denn da wir bei der letztern mit der Aufzählung der Wirkungsgesetze ohne Rücksicht auf jede Erfahrung beginnen, so liegt es ganz in unserer Hand gleich anfangs willkürlich festzustellen, von welchen Umständen die Bewegung eines Körpers abhängt und welche darauf ohne Einfluss sind. Bei der inductiven Methode hingegen müssen wir den Begriff der unmittelbaren Umgebung eines Körpers, deren Zustand auf seine Bewegung von Einfluss ist, nach der Erfahrung bestimmen. Nach der Nahewirkungstheorie sind es nur die unmittelbar anliegenden Volumelemente, welche die Bewegung irgend eines Volumelementes bestimmen. Nach dieser Theorie wirkt die Erde nicht direct anziehend auf den schweren Körper sondern sie wirkt nur auf die Volumelemente eines Mediums, durch welche sich die Wirkung bis zum schweren Körper fortpflanzt. Aber wenn wir den Principien unserer jetzigen Darstellungsweise treu bleiben wollen, so dürfen wir nicht die Nahewirkungstheorie zur Basis des gesammten Gebäudes der Mechanik machen, wir dürfen vielmehr hiezu nur Gesetze verwenden, welche nichts Willkürliches enthalten, sondern uns durch die Erfahrung eindeutig und notwendig aufgedrängt werden. Die Nahewirkungstheorie aber, so wahrscheinlich sie vielleicht manchem a priori erscheint, geht doch vollständig über das rein Thatsächliche hinaus und kann heutzutage noch keineswegs ins Detail ausgearbeitet werden. Wir würden da in denselben Fehler verfallen, den wir der Hertz'schen Darstellungsweise vorgeworfen haben. Wir müssten entweder ganz willkürliche spezielle Hypothesen für die Art und Weise der Nahewirkung erfinden oder uns mit allgemeinen unbestimmten Vorstellungen über dieselbe begnügen.

Wir müssen daher die ganze Erde zur Umgebung des schweren Körpers rechnen aber Mond und Sterne dabei ausser Acht lassen, da letztere keinen bemerkbaren Einfluss ausüben. Es ist also wieder eine reine Annahme, welche wir erst nachträglich durch die Erfahrung rechtfertigen müssen, dass wir die unmittelbare Umgebung immer so abzugrenzen vermögen, dass wir alles Wesentliche einschliessen und dass wir so factisch zu einer Aufstellung von Bewegungsgesetzen gelangen können.

Wie werden wir uns nun bei unserer jetziger Darstellungsweise dem absoluten Raume und der absoluten Zeit gegenüber verhalten? An einem Theile des absoluten Raumes können wir keine Zirkelspitze einsetzen sondern nur an materiellen Körpern. Wir können daher nur die Bewegung von materiellen Körpern relativ gegen einander bestimmen. Wir dürfen jetzt nicht wie bei der deductiven Methode das Gedankenbild eines fingirten Coordinatensystems unter die von uns gegenwärtig allein betrachteten realen Körper mengen. Dem Geiste unserer Methode entsprechend müssen wir vielmehr unsere Betrachtungen möglichst dem historischen Entwickelungsgange der Mechanik anschliessen. Galilei hat die einfachen Bewegungsgesetze gefunden, indem er die Bewegung relativ gegen die Erde studirte. Seinem Beispiele folgend werden wir daher ausser dem Körper K, dessen Bewegung wir beschreiben wollen, noch ein System von anderen Körpern in die Betrachtungen mit einbeziehen, welche die Bedingung erfüllen, dass alle ihre Punkte ihre Entfernungen von einander nicht ändern, dass sie also alle relativ ruhen. Dieses System nennen wir das Bezugssystem. Wenn wir daher die Bewegung eines festen Körpers gegen ein Bezugssystem studiren und wenn A, B, C . . . markirte Punkte des ersteren, E, F, G . . . solche des letztern sind, so ändern sich weder die Entfernungen AB, AC . . . noch EF, EG . . . und unsere Aufgabe besteht bloss darin, die Gesetze der Veränderungen, der Entfernungen AE, AF, BF . . . aufzustellen. Natürlich sind hiebei auch wieder vielerlei Idealisirungen notwendig. Wir werden kein System von Körpern als Bezugssystem auffinden können, welche so beschaffen sind, dass sie zu allen Zeiten relativ gegeneinander ihre Lage absolut beibehalten. Es genügt, wenn diese Bedingung angenähert durch genügend lange Zeit erfüllt ist.

Ferner können wir nicht wissen, ob wir dieselben Gesetze erhalten, wenn wir das eine oder andere Bezugssystem wählen. Wir werden daher jedenfalls ein solches Bezugssystem zu wählen haben, dass wir einfache Gesetze für die Bewegung erhalten. Es zeigt sich in der That, dass die Gesetze, welche wir bei zu Grundelegung des Fixsternhimmels als Bezugssystem erhalten nicht ohne kleine Correctionen auf die Bewegung relativ gegen die Erde angewandt werden können und es muss als ein für die Entwickelung der Mechanik ausserordentlich günstiger Zufall bezeichnet werden, dass der Einfluss der Erddrehung auf die verschiedenen Bewegungen, welche wir auf ihrer Oberfläche beobachten ein so ausserordentlich geringer ist. Sonst wäre es weit schwieriger gewesen die Grundgesetze der Mechanik herzuleiten. Diesem Umstande ist es zu verdanken, dass wir für die Bewegungen auf der Erde den Erdkörper als Bezugssystem wählen können. Wir erhalten hiedurch einfache Gesetze, denen die wirklichen Bewegungen freilich nicht mit absoluter Genauigkeit folgen, aber die Abweichungen sind so gering, dass sie sich fast der Beobachtung entziehen. Dies könnten wir freilich nicht a priori wissen; aber es ist kein logischer Fehler, wenn wir zunächst die Gesetze der Relativbewegung gegen die Erde studiren. Finden wir einfache Gesetze, so ist es wieder kein logischer Fehler, deren Anwendung auf die Bewegung der Planeten relativ gegen das Fixsternsystem zu versuchen. Bei dieser Erweiterung zeigt sich dann erst einestheils, dass sie auch für den ersten Fall angenähert richtig sein müssen, andererseits aber, dass derselbe doch kleiner Correctionen bedarf. Diese Correctionen sind so klein dass sie uns bei Auffindung der Gesetze aus den irdischen Bewegungen nicht störten, dass sie aber jetzt nachdem wir ihre Grössenordnung kennen gelernt haben doch mit feinen Hilfsmitteln beobachtet werden können. Dass die wirklichen Bewegungen dann gerade die durch diese Correctionen bedingten Eigenthümlichkeiten zeigen, rechtfertigt nachher in glänzender Weise unsere Methode. Hiemit ist wieder die pädagogische Schwierigkeit beseitigt, welche durch die Relativität aller Bewegungen bedingt wird. Die Frage, auf welches Bezugssystem wir die Fixsternbewegungen zu beziehen haben, ist hiemit freilich nicht gelöst, aber es liegt in keiner Weise eine Notwendigkeit vor, diese Frage vor Aufstellung der sämmtlichen Gesetze der Mechanik zu behandeln.

Wir haben bisher über die Gestalt und Anordnung der Körper des zu Grunde gelegten Bezugssystems keine besondere Annahme gemacht. Es hat nun keine Schwierigkeit mit denselben drei fixe auf einander rechtwinklige Gerade verbunden zu denken, welche man als Coordinatenaxen wählen kann. Die Lage jedes an dem betreffenden Körper markirten Punktes ist dann zu jeder Zeit durch dessen rechtwinklige Coordinaten bezüglich dieses Coordinatensystems bestimmt. Wenn sich diese mit der Zeit nicht ändern, so befindet sich der Körper in relativer Ruhe gegen das Bezugssystem. Wenn sie sich ändern, so ist er in Bewegung. Um den letztern Fall beschreiben zu können, ist noch die genaue Fixirung des Zeitmasses erforderlich. Gerade so wie wir schon mit Hülfe des Augenmasses oder des Tastgefühles grössere räumliche Ausdehnungen von kleineren unterscheiden, einen genauen zahlenmässigen Ausdruck der Raumgrösse aber nur durch Vergleich mit einem rationell construirten Massstabe gewinnen können, so können wir auch schon durch das Gefühl (den Zeitsinn) längere Zeiträume von kürzern unterscheiden, müssen uns aber ein genaues quantitatives Zeitmass durch die Hilfsmittel verschaffen, welche schon in der ersten Vorlesung angedeutet wurden. Wir müssen uns da vor allem eine Reihe von Vorgängen verschaffen, bei denen wir vollkommen oder besser gesagt, thunlichste Garantie haben, dass sie sich in gleichen Zeiten abspielen. Wir können etwa ganz gleiche Körper unter ganz gleichen Umständen fallen lassen oder ganz gleiche Pendel um gleiche Strecken aus der Ruhelage entfernen. Wenn das erste die Ruhelage erreicht, lassen wir das zweite seine Bewegung beginnen etc. Ob wir gegenseitige Störungen wirklich genügend vermieden haben, kann natürlich nur der Vergleich mit verschiedenen analogen Versuchen zeigen. Wir sehn natürlich bald, dass auch ein Pendel die verschiedenen sich folgenden Schwingungen nahe unter den gleichen Umständen vollzieht und können diese zur Zeitmessung benutzen. Freilich ist der absolute Isochronismus der Schwingungen wieder ein Ideal, Temperatur, Barometerstand, Sonne und Mond haben darauf Einfluss, aber wie alle diese störenden Umstände bei gut gearbeiteten Chronometern möglichst vermieden werden, wie durch eine treibende Kraft die Schwingungen sehr lange erhalten werden, dass man, wenn ein bestimmtes Chronometer endlich unbrauchbar wird, dafür ein anderes möglichst gleichbeschaffenes substituiren kann, das alles ist nicht mehr Sache unserer gegenwärtigen allgemeinen Betrachtungen.

Wir wählen einen bestimmten Zeitmoment z. B. den, der einem bestimmten willkürlich gewählten Durchgang durch die Ruhelage entspricht, als Zeitmoment Null, den des nächsten Durchgangs durch die Ruhelage als Zeit 1, die weiter folgenden als die Zeiten 2, 3 u. s. w. Die Unterabtheilungen können wir durch schneller schwingende Stimmgabeln oder durch Bewegungen bestimmen, die sich für grössere Intervalle unter allen Umständen als genügend gleichförmig erwiesen und von denen wir Ursache haben dies auch für kleinere Intervalle zu vermuten. So gewinnen wir die Zeiten $\frac{1}{2}$, $\frac{1}{4}$ u. s. w und es lässt sich keine Grenze der Unterabtheilung feststellen. Die negativen Zahlen bezeichnen die Schwingungen vor derjenigen der wir die Zeit Null zugeordnet haben. In dieser Weise können wir alle Zeiten durch positive, negative, ganze, gebrochene, irrationale Zahlen darstellen, wie wir die Längen durch die Zahl darstellen, welche angibt, wie oftmals sie die Längeneinheit enthalten. Die Differenz der Zahlen, welche zwei gegebene Zeiten darstellen heisst das dazwischen liegende Zeitintervall oder die Zeitdifferenz auch die inzwischen verflossene Zeit. Unsere gewöhnliche Zeiteinheit leiten wir von der Umdrehungszeit der Erde ab, deren Gleichförmigkeit aber bei Ableitung der Principien der Mechanik wol besser durch einfachere Vorgänge controlirt wird, da es ohne Kenntnis der mechanischen Gesetze nicht so ohne weiters evident ist, dass die Umdrehungsgeschwindigkeit an allen Stellen der Erdbahn dieselbe bleibt.

Wir kehren nun zurück zu unserem Körper *K*, den wir auf ein mit dem gewählten Bezugssysteme fest verbundenes Coordinatensystem Ox, Oy, Oz beziehen. Ein auf demselben hervorgehobener Punkt befände sich zu einer bestimmten Zeit t in A und habe die rechtwinkeligen Coordinaten x, y, z. Wir verbinden ihn durch die Gerade OA mit dem Coordinatenursprunge: Diese Gerade heisst der Lagenvector des Punktes A, ihre Projectionen auf die drei Coordinatenaxen sind die drei Coordinaten x, y, z. Wenn nun der Körper eine gewisse gegebene Bewegung macht, so müssen wir zunächst jeden Zeitmoment der Bewegung etwa durch Vergleichung der gleichzeitigen Bewegung unseres Chronoskops durch eine Zahl darstellen. Es wird zu jeder Zeit eine bestimmte Lage des Körpers gehören, daher auch des Punktes A desselben, daher auch bestimmte Werte der Coordinaten y, x, z, welche wir uns ebenfalls durch reine Zahlen (ganze oder gebrochene Vielfache der Längeneinheit) dargestellt denken. Zu jedem Zahlenwerte der Zeit t gehört also ein eindeutig bestimmter Zahlenwert der Coordinate x, x ist eine eindeutige

Funktion von t, ebenso y und z. Wir schreiben dies so $x = \phi(t)$, $y = \chi(t)$, $z = \psi(t)$ und nennen t das Argument oder die independente Variabele, x, y, z aber die dependenten Variabeln. Wir können es zunächst als hinlänglich sicher gestellte Erfahrungsthatsache betrachten, dass ein Körper nie aus einer Lage plötzlich verschwindet und im nächsten Zeitmomente in einer andern um Endliches davon Verschiedenen wieder zum Vorschein kommt und dass dies auch von jedem Theile eines Körpers gilt, dass also ϕ, χ, ψ continuirliche Functionen der Zeit sind, d. h. ihre Zuwächse verschwinden um so mehr je kleiner der entsprechende Zuwachs der Zeit ist. Die von den verschiedenen Lagen des Punktes A zu den verschiedenen Zeiten gebildete Curve nennen wir die Bahn dieses Punktes, denjenigen Theil derselben, welcher allen Lagen, die während einer gegebenen Zeit durchlaufen werden entspricht den während dieser Zeit zurück gelegten Weg.

Nicht ganz so sicher als die Continuität der Functionen ϕ, χ, ψ ist es, ob sie auch differenzirbar sind. Man drückte sich in der alten Mechanik folgendermassen aus. Es lege ein Punkt eines Körpers, während einer sehr kleinen Zeit δt einen sehr kleinen Weg δs zurück. Es sei nun a priori evident, dass sich während dieser kleinen Zeit, die Umstände, unter denen sich der Körper befindet nur sehr wenig geändert haben können, dass es daher, während der nächst folgenden Zeit δt wieder einen sehr nahe gleichen und gleich gerichteten Weg δs zurücklegen muss, so dass also für kleine Zeiten sowohl der Weg als auch die Coordinatenzuwächse der verstrichenen Zeit proportional sein müssen. Man glaubte damals überhaupt, dass jede überall endliche continuirliche Function einen Differenzialquotienten haben muss. Weierstrass hat bekanntlich gezeigt, dass dies ein Irrthum ist. Bezeichnen wir z. B. mit y die Weierstrass'sche Reihe so nähert sich der Zuwachs des y, der irgend einem Zuwachse des x entspricht an allen Stellen immer mehr der Nulle, wenn sich der betreffende Zuwachs des x der Nulle nähert und trotzdem nähert sich der Quotient beider Grössen niemals einer bestimmbaren Grenze. Bei der deductiven Darstellung ergibt sich hieraus wieder nicht die mindeste Schwierigkeit. Wir können ja dann unser Bild formen, wie wir wollen und einfach die Differenzirbarkeit von vornherein in dasselbe aufnehmen, es damit rechtfertigend, dass das Bild hinterher mit der Erfahrung stimmt. Aber jetzt ist es unsere Absicht von der Erfahrung auszugehn. Nun lehrt uns zwar diese, dass sehr häufig, während kleiner noch beobachtbarer Zeiten der Weg eines Punktes eines Körpers um so genauer der verflossenen Zeit proportional ist, je kürzer diese ist, woraus wir wohl auf die Differenzirbarkeit der Functionen ϕ, χ, ψ schliessen können. Allein wir kennen auch Beispiele sehr rascher Oscillationen und können nicht exact beweisen, ob nicht in gewissen Fällen Bewegungen vorhanden sind, wie z. B. die Wärmebewegungen der Moleküle, welche durch eine der Weierstrass'schen Function ähnliche besser als durch eine Differenzirbare dargestellt werden. Doch sind dies allerdings Dinge von geringerer Wichtigkeit und wir wollen daher die Differenzirbarkeit der Coordinaten nach der Zeit unsern weitern Überlegungen zu Grunde legen. Unter dieser Voraussetzung existiren die Ableitungen der Functionen ϕ, χ, ψ nach der Zeit. Wir nennen sie die Componenten der Geschwindigkeit des Punktes A des Körpers. Die Geschwindigkeit selbst können wir in folgender Weise construiren: Es befinde sich der markirte Punkt des Körpers zur Zeit t in A zur Zeit $t + \delta t$ in B, so dass also OA, und OB die dazu gehörigen Lagenvectoren sind. Die Gerade AB ist dann das, was man die Differenz der beiden Vectoren nennt. Wir construiren nun einen Vector, welcher die Richtung AB hat und dessen Länge der Quotient AB dividirt durch δt ist. Ferner suchen wir die Grenze, welcher sich dieser Vector in Grösse und Richtung nähert, wenn δt immer mehr abnimmt. Die so bestimmte Länge ist die Geschwindigkeit, die Richtung aber, der sich der Vector nähert, die Geschwindigkeitsrichtung. Wir wollen hier noch eine Bemerkung anfügen. Damit wir den Weg durch die verflossene Zeit dividiren können, müssen beide durch reine Zahlen ausgedrückt sein und wir haben gesehen wie dies geschieht. Wählen wir die Längeneinheit a mal so gross, so wird die Zahl, welche nun eine gewisse Länge ausdrückt a mal kleiner. Es ist möglich, dass auch andere Grössen dieselbe Eigenschaft haben, dass sie durch a mal kleinere Zahlen ausgedrückt erscheinen, sobald wir die Längeneinheit a mal vergrössern. Von allen so beschaffenen Grössen sagen wir dann, dass sie die Dimension einer Länge haben. Jede Länge, (der Weg, die Coordinaten etc.) hat daher selbstverständlich die Dimension einer Länge. Die Zahl, welche uns die Zeit t ausdrückt, ist natürlich unabhängig von der gewählten Längeneinheit, wird aber a mal kleiner, wenn wir die Zeiteinheit a mal grösser wählen und wir sagen von jeder Grösse, welche durch eine Zahl von dieser Eigenschaft ausgedrückt wird, sie habe die Dimension einer Zeit. Die Geschwindigkeit wird durch den Quotienten zweier Zahlen gemessen, wovon der Zähler die Dimension einer Länge, der Nenner die einer Zeit hat. Sie ist also sowohl von der Wahl der

Längen als auch von der Zeiteinheit abhängig, und wird a mal kleiner, wenn die erstere a mal grösser, dagegen a mal grösser, wenn die letztere a mal grösser gewählt wird. Wir sagen daher ihre Dimensionen sind: Länge dividirt durch Zeit, was aber hiemit jeder geheimnisvollen oder metaphysischen Bedeutung entkleidet ist. Man redet vielfach statt von dem Quotienten der Zahl welche die Zeit ausdrückt in die, welche die Länge ausdrückt, einfach von dem Quotienten einer Zeit, in eine Länge. Man hat da den Begriff der Division erweitert und muss den Quotienten einer Zeit in eine Länge ganz neu definiren, geradeso wie man den Begriff einer negativen oder gebrochenen Potenz neu definirt und darunter einen Bruch respektive eine Wurzel versteht. Der Vortheil dieser neuen Definition besteht darin, dass man vielfach Rechnungsregeln, welche für die frühere Definition bewiesen wurden auf die neue Definition übertragen kann. Man darf aber nicht a priori schliessen, dass dies von allen Rechnungsregeln gilt; es muss vielmehr die Übertragbarkeit von jeder Rechnungsregel besonders bewiesen werden. Ebenso ist es eine vollständig neue Definition, wenn wir unter der zweiten oder dritten Potenz eines Centimeters die geometrische Figur eines Quadrats oder Würfels von 1 cm. Seitenlänge verstehen und es muss gerechtfertigt werden, in wie weit diese neue Definition zweckmässig ist. Die Fixirung des Begriffs der Beschleunigung und ihrer Componenten nach den drei Coordinatenrichtungen hat nun nicht mehr die mindeste Schwierigkeit. Sei AC der Vector, welcher in Grösse und Richtung die Geschwindigkeit zur Zeit t, OD der, welcher sie zur Zeit $t + \delta t$ darstellt. Wir ziehen die Gerade CD, also die Differenz der beiden Vectoren. Dieselbe wird sehr klein sein, wenn δt sehr klein ist. Wir erhalten aber eine endlich bleibende Gerade, wenn wir sie im Verhältnis der Zeiteinheit zur Zeit δt vergrössern, wobei ihre Richtung unverändert bleiben soll. Die Grenze, welcher sich der so vergrösserte Vector CD mit abnehmendem δt nähert, heisst der Beschleunigungsvector, seine Länge stellt die Grösse, seine Richtung die Richtung der Beschleunigung dar. Seine Componenten in den drei Coordinatenrichtungen heissen die Componenten der Beschleunigung. Man überzeugt sich in bekannter Weise, dass es die zweiten Ableitungen der früher mit χ, ϕ, ψ bezeichneten Functionen sind. Wir müssen daher die Voraussetzung machen, dass diese Functionen auch zweite Ableitungen haben. Man überzeugt sich auch leicht, dass die Zahl, welche die Grösse der Beschleunigung ausdrückt wieder sowohl von den gewählten Längen als von der gewählten Zeiteinheit abhängt und a mal kleiner wird, wenn ersteres a mal so gross, dagegen a^2 mal grösser, wenn die Zeiteinheit a mal so gross gewählt wird. Wir werden daher sagen, die Beschleunigung hat die Dimensionen: Länge dividirt durch das Quadrat der Zeit. Wir können wieder die Beschleunigung als solche definiren als den Quotienten einer Zeit in eine Geschwindigkeit oder des Quadrats einer Zeit in eine Länge; dürfen aber die letzteren Definitionen nur mit einer gewissen Vorsicht anwenden, da sie Erweiterungen des Begriffs der allgebraischen Division darstellen, für welche die Anwendbarkeit der verschiedenen in der Algebra bewiesenen Rechnungsregeln erst neu erprobt werden muss.

Nachdem wir diese Begriffe möglichst an die Erfahrung anknüpfend entwickelt haben, müssen wir zur Aufstellung der Gesetze übergehn, nach welchen die Bewegung der Körper geschieht. Wir werden da natürlich wieder nicht mit Aufstellung der Gesetze für die Bewegung eines materiellen Punktes beginnen, da dieser eine reine Abstraction ist. Wir werden uns natürlich auch nicht der Illusion hingeben, dass wir ohne alle Abstractionen auskommen. Wir können nach meiner Ansicht nicht einen einzigen Satz aussagen, welcher wirklich nur eine reine Erfahrungsthatsache wäre. Die einfachsten Worte wie gelb, süss, sauer etc., welche blosse Empfindungen anzugeben scheinen, drücken schon Begriffe aus, die bereits aus vielen Erfahrungsthatsachen durch Abstraction gewonnen worden sind. Wenn Göthe sagt, die Erfahrung ist nur zur Hälfte Erfahrung so will er mit diesem scheinbar paradoxen Satze sicher ausdrücken, das wir bei jeder begrifflichen Auffassung der Erfahrung oder Darstellung derselben durch Worte schon über die Erfahrung hinausgehen müssen. Die oft aufgestellte Forderung, dass die Naturwissenschaft nie über die Erfahrung hinausgehen dürfe, sollte daher nach meiner Ansicht dahin ausgesprochen werden, dass man nie zu weit über die Erfahrung hinaus gehen dürfe und nur solche Abstractionen einführen solle, die sich bald wieder an der Erfahrung prüfen lassen. Wir werden auch nicht das Trägheitsgesetz an die Spitze stellen. Dieses mag theoretisch das einfachste Gesetz der Mechanik sein, physikalisch ist es keineswegs das einfachste, da es eine ganze Reihe von Abstractionen zur Voraussetzung hat, worauf ich schon früher hingewiesen habe. Als die beiden physikalisch einfachsten Fälle erscheinen uns vielmehr erstens der der relativen Ruhe zweitens, der freie Fall eines schweren Körpers. Wie wir sahen, können wir einen Körper niemals ganz den äussern Einflüssen entziehen. Wenn nun solche Einflüsse vorhanden sind, von denen jeder für sich allein eine Bewegung erzeugen würde, wenn aber unter dem vereinten Einflusse aller relative Ruhe gegen das Bezugssystem Platz greift, so sagen wir alle Ursachen der Relativbewegung compensiren sich. Ich könnte mich auch des gebräuchlichsten Ausdruckes bedienen, die Kräfte halten sich das Gleichgewicht, allein ich will absichtlich die gewohnten Ausdrücke vermeiden, weil wir mit denselben unwillkürlich eine Menge von Vorstellungen verbinden, die sich dann, ohne dass wir es wollen, unkontrolirt in unsere Schlussweise einschmuggeln und so den Schein erwecken, als hätten wir etwas bewiesen, was wir nur gemäss unserer alten Denkgewohnheit und Ideenassociation ohne Begründung beigefügt haben. Ich will ausserdem das Wort Kraft vermeiden, ehe ich gleichzeitig auch von der Masse sprechen kann. Endlich betrachten wir hier nur die relative Bewegung. Es kann aber ein Körper relativ gegen seine Umgebung ruhen, ohne dass sich die auf ihn wirkenden Kräfte das Gleichgewicht zu halten brauchen wie ein Körper, der relativ gegen einen mit Beschleunigung sich bewegenden Lift ruht.

Wir betrachten nun einen bestimmten Fall, wo die Ursachen der relativen Bewegung compensirt sind. Ein schwerer Körper sei an einen dünnen Faden aufgehängt. Wir könnten da meinen, dass gar keine Bewegungsursachen vorhanden sind. Doch finden wir, dass sofort Bewegung eintritt, wenn wir den Faden entfernen. Es müssen also mindestens zwei Bewegungsursachen vorhanden gewesen sein, welche sich gegenseitig compensirten.

Wenn wir die nach Entfernung des Fadens eintretende Bewegung analysiren, so finden wir, dass sie, wenn gewisse allgemeine Bedingungen erfüllt sind, sehr angenähert immer in derselben Weise vor sich geht. Diese allgemeinen Bedingungen sind folgende. Die Oberfläche des Körpers darf nicht zu gross gegen dessen Gewicht sein, es darf keine heftige Luftbewegung um den Körper herum stattfinden, der Faden muss ohne Erschütterung durchgeschnitten oder ruhig durch Verbrennung oder sonst wie vernichtet worden sein. Dieselbe Bewegung tritt auch ein, wenn wir den Körper anfangs mit der Hand oder einer Zange oder einer sonstigen Vorrichtung halten und plötzlich ohne Erschütterung sich selbst überlassen. Das Charakteristische aller dieser Anfangsbedingungen besteht darin, dass sämmtliche Punkte des Körpers in den ersten Momenten der Bewegung sehr kleine Geschwindigkeiten haben. Wir können daher annähernd voraussetzen, dass sämmtliche Punkte des Körpers im ersten Momente der Bewegung keinerlei Anfangsgeschwindigkeit hatten. Wenn diese Bedingungen erfüllt sind, so lehrt die Erfahrung, dass der Körper stets fast genau nach denselben Gesetzen sich bewegt, wo immer er in der Nähe der Erdoberfläche sich selbst überlassen worden sei. Die Bewegung bestimmen wir dabei natürlich einstweilen relative gegen die Erde. Wenn wir uns noch auf einen nicht zu grossen Theil der Erdoberfläche beschränken, so ist auch die Richtung der Bewegung überall dieselbe; es ist die des Fadens, der früher den Körper trug. Die Erfahrung lehrt nun für diese Bewegung die folgenden Gesetze. Erstens der Körper bewegt sich parallel zu sich selbst, d. h. alle Punkte desselben legen in gleichen Zeiten, gleiche und gleichgerichtete Wege zurück. Da also die Bahn für jeden Punkt dieselbe ist, so kann man sie als die Bahn des ganzen Körpers bezeichnen. Zweitens, alle diese Wege sind geradlinig. Drittens, die Geschwindigkeit wächst fortwährend, die Beschleunigung ist jedoch überall, zu allen Zeiten und sogar für alle Körper dieselbe. Dass diese Gesetze in der Natur nur mit grösserer oder geringerer Annäherung realisirt sind, wurde bereits besprochen.

Wir können nun dasselbe Experiment wiederholen, nur dass wir dem Körper im Momente, wo wir ihn sich selbst überlassen einen Stoss geben, oder sonst wie bewirken, dass er schon anfangs eine Geschwindigkeit hat. Da wir die Sätze vom Schwerpunkt und der Drehung der Körper noch nicht kennen gelernt haben, so müssen wir uns dabei auf die Fälle beschränken, wo sich der Körper wieder parallel zu sich selbst bewegt. Es wird dies zwar nicht immer eintreten und wir können die Bedingungen dafür, dass es eintritt noch nicht angeben, aber in vielen Fällen wird dies stattfinden und diese Fälle wollen wir vorläufig allein betrachten. In allen diesen Fällen legen wieder alle Punkte des Körpers gleiche Bahnen zurück, welche wir also als die Bahn des Körpers bezeichnen können. Die ganze Bewegung kann wieder dahin beschrieben werden, dass die Beschleunigung immer vertikal nach abwärts gerichtet und überall zu allen Zeiten und für alle Körper dieselbe ist. Da wir nun gesehen haben, dass die Bewegung, wenn wir sie an verschiedenen Stellen im Zimmer oder in dessen Umgebung beginnen lassen, immer in ganz gleicher Weise vor sich geht, so müssen wir schliessen, dass die Bewegungsursache, welche wir Kraft nennen, daselbst überall unveränderlich dieselbe ist. Andererseits ist auch die Beschleunigung unveränderlich dieselbe, wir können daher schliessen, dass wenigstens in diesem speziellen Falle die Beschleunigung das für die Kraft Massgebende ist und weil erstere überall vertikal nach abwärts gerichtet ist, so sagen wir auf den Körper wirkt eine constante vertikal nach abwärts gerichtete Kraft die Schwere.

Dritte Vorlesung.

Um tiefer in die Gesetze der Bewegungen einzudringen, müssten wir jetzt die nächst einfachsten Fälle betrachten. Ein naives Gemüt könnte da wohl meinen, dass wir nun die Gesetze nach denen ein Grashalm wächst, untersuchen sollten. Leider aber wissen wir über diese noch heute fast gar nichts. Besser wäre es schon die Gesetze der Wirkung gespannter Schnüre, Federn etc. zu betrachten. Allein auch da treten die Bewegungsgesetze nicht in grösster Einfachheit hervor. Der historische Gang war vielmehr der folgende. Nachdem Galilei die Bewegungsgesetze soweit wir sie bisher betrachtet haben, gefunden hatte, suchte Newton sie vor allem auf die Bewegung der Gestirne anzuwenden und auch von ihm gilt, was Schiller von Wallenstein sagte: „Fürwahr ihn hat kein Wahn betrogen als er aufwärts zu den Sternen sah." Dem Laufe der Sterne hat er die Bewegungsgesetze abgelauscht, auf denen alle heute in der Technik und Machinenlehre benutzten Formeln ja überhaupt unsere ganze moderne Naturkenntnis basirt. Freilich bringt der Übergang zur Sternenwelt manche Unbequemlichkeit mit sich. Erstens müssen wir um einfache Gesetze zu erhalten, unser altes Bewegungssystem, als welches der Erdkörper diente, verlassen und ein relativ gegen den Fixsternhimmel sich nicht drehendes Coordinatensystem wählen. Zweitens ist auch die Bedingung, das die Planeten sich parallel zu sich selbst bewegen nicht erfüllt. An ihre Stelle tritt der Umstand, dass ihre Entfernungen vom Beobachter so gross sind, dass ihre einzelnen Theile überhaupt nur schwer unterschieden werden können, so dass wir also in der ersten Annäherung mit welcher wir uns wieder begnügen, überhaupt die Bahnen der verschiedenen Punkte eines und desselben Planeten gar nicht unterscheiden können. Wir können also wohl auch annehmen, dass die Gesetze dieselben wären, wenn die Himmelskörper sich parallel zu sich selbst bewegten. Wir kommen also hier einestheils dem Begriffe des materiellen Punktes sehr nahe, da die Ausdehnung der bewegten Körper so klein gegen die Länge ihrer Bahn ist, dass letztere für alle Punkte der Körpers merklich gleich wird. Andererseits aber sind wir von dieser Idee so weit entfernt als möglich, da wir es mit Körpern zu thun haben, die nichts weniger als materielle Punkte, vielmehr oft grösser als unser ganzer Erdkörper sind.

Die Beobachtung und Messung lehrt, dass sich im Weltraume häufig um einen Centralkörper ein System von Himmelskörpern bewegt, welche wir die Trabanten nennen. Wir erhalten die einfachsten Gesetze, wenn wir die Bewegung der Trabanten auf ein Coordinatensystem beziehen, dessen Anfangspunkt im Mittelpunkte des betreffenden Centralkörpers liegt und dessen Axen dreien fest mit dem Fixsternhimmel verbundenen Geraden stets parallel bleiben. Für die Bewegung der Trabanten gelten erfahrungsgemäss die drei Keppler'schen Gesetze. Da beim freien Falle die Beschleunigung eine so wichtige Rolle spielte, so wollen wir auch in diesem Falle die Beschleunigung berechnen, welche irgend ein Trabant in seiner Bewegung erfährt. Diese Rechung ist sehr bekannt und ganz leicht. Es hat sie Kirchhoff in seinen Vorlesungen über Mechanik in sehr eleganter Form durchgeführt. Man findet aus dem ersten und zweiten Keppler'schen Gesetze, dass sie für jeden Trabanten zu jeder Zeit gegen den Centralkörper gerichtet und dem Quadrate des Abstandes r von demselben verkehrt proportional, also in der Form $\frac{k}{r^2}$ darstellbar ist. Aus dem dritten Keppler'schen Gesetze ergibt sich ausserdem, dass die Constante k von Centralkörper zu Centralkörper verschieden ist, aber für alle Trabanten eines und desselben Centralkörpers denselben Wert hat. Da wir schon bei der Schwere die Beschleunigung als das massgebende für die Bewegungsursache oder Kraft erkannt haben, so wollen wir auch hier sagen, der Centralkörper übt auf jeden Trabanten eine Kraft aus, welche die Richtung der vom Mittelpunkte des Trabanten gegen den des Centralkörpers gezogenen Geraden hat und der Länge dieser Geraden verkehrt proportional ist. Diese ist einstweilen sonst nichts als ein anderer Ausdruck für die Thatsache des Vorhandenseins dieser Beschleunigung. Newton hat diesen Satz sofort enorm verallgemeinert indem er annahm, dass überhaupt jeder Himmelskörper auf jeden andern ja jedes materielle Theilchen auf jedes andere eine solche Kraft ausübt. Wenn daher ein Himmelskörper mehreren andern so nahe ist, dass er von ihnen eine merkliche Einwirkung erfährt, so haben wir den Fall, dass er gleichzeitig aus verschiedenen Ursachen verschiedene Beschleunigungen nach verschiedenen Richtungen erfährt. Da wir die Beschleunigung durch einen Vector dargestellt haben, so ist es nicht die einzig notwendige, aber doch bei weitem die nahe liegendste, einfachste Annahme, dass sich diese Beschleunigungen wie Vectoren addiren. In der That zeigt sich, dass man unter dieser Annahme immer Übereinstimmung mit der Erfahrung erhält. Es ergeben sich die Störungen der Planeten untereinander, der Monde durch die Sonne und durch die Planeten in genauer Übereinstimmung mit der Erfahrung. Man kann jetzt auch den Horizont erweitern und alle Himmelskörper auf ein und dasselbe mit dem Fixsternhimmel fest verbundene Coordinatensystem beziehen und erhält auch die Bewegung der Centralkörper gegen dieses Coordinatensystem in Übereinstimmung mit der Erfahrung. Die Schwere erweist sich als identisch mit der Anziehung des Erdkörpers auf den schweren Körper. Schliesslich zeigen die Erscheinungen der Ebbe und Flut, die Versuche von Cavendish, Maskelyne, Airy etc. die Richtigkeit der Ausdehnung des Newton'schen Gesetzes auf die irdischen Körper. Da die wirkliche Beschleunigung immer die Vectorsumme der verschiedenen von den wirkenden Körpern erzeugten Beschleunigung ist, so folgt jetzt als spezieller Fall des Newton'schen Gesetzes, dass ein Körper, welcher von allen übrigen so weit entfernt wäre, dass keiner derselben eine Wirkung auf ihn ausüben würde, zu allen Zeiten die Beschleunigung Null erführe. Wir erhalten also erst jetzt das Trägheitsgesetz. Selbstverständlich ist hiemit über die Ursache der Newton'schen Kraft, ob dieselbe eine direkte Fernwirkung ist oder durch ein Medium vermittelt wird, nicht das mindeste präjudicirt. Wir könnten auch jetzt schon den Begriff der Masse ableiten. Die Massen zweier Centralkörper würden sich ja wie die ihnen entsprechenden Werte der Constanten k des Gravitationsgesetzes verhalten und durch den Cavendish'schen Versuch könnte diese Definition auch auf irdische Körper ausgedehnt werden. Allein wir würden da die Proportionalität der Constante k mit der als Trägheitswiderstand definirten Masse vorwegnehmen, was offenbar ein logischer Fehler wäre. Wir müssen daher zum Begriffe der Masse auf ganz anderem Wege zu gelangen suchen. Wir haben bisher als das Massgebende für die Kraft die Beschleunigung betrachtet. Es könnte nun als das einfachste erscheinen, die Grösse der Beschleunigung, welche ein Körper durch einen andern erfährt, einfach als die Grösse der Kraft zu bezeichnen, welche der letztere auf den ersteren ausübt. Es geschieht dies auch manches Mal und man bezeichnet die so definirte Kraft als die beschleunigende Kraft. Allein im Allgemeinen ist es besser einen andern Begriff einzuführen. Wir denken nämlich beim Worte Kraft in erster Linie an die Muskelanstrengungen, welche wir ausüben können. Nun liegt freilich kein Grund vor, ja es wäre ganz verkehrt anzunehmen, dass jedes Mal, wenn unbelebte Körper Kräfte aufeinander ausüben etwas vorhanden sein müsse, was diesen Muskelanstrengungen irgendwie entspricht. Allein es wird sich doch empfehlen, wenn wir die Bezeichnungen so wählen, dass sie sich den durch diese Muskelanstrengungen erworbenen Begriffen möglichst gut anschliessen. Wir sahen, dass alle Körper durch die Schwere die gleiche Beschleunigung erfahren. Würden wir nun diese ohne weiteren Factor als Mass der Kraft wählen, so wäre die Kraft, welche die Schwere auf sie ausübt, (das Gewicht) für alle Körper dasselbe. Nun lehrt aber die tägliche Erfahrung, dass die Muskelanstrengung welche wir brauchen, um den Fall aufzuheben, für verschiedene Körper sehr verschieden ist. Wollen wir daher mit unseren Vorstellungen im Einklang bleiben, so müssen wir sagen, dass auch die Schwere auf die verschiedenen Körper sehr verschiedene Kräfte ausübt, dass aber die Körper von grösserem Gewichte dieser beschleunigenden Wirkung der Schwere einen grösseren Widerstand, den Trägheitswiderstand, die Masse, entgegensetzen, so dass erst in folge beider Umstände zusammen alle Körper die gleiche Beschleunigung erfahren. Um die Masse in dieser Weise als Trägheitswiderstand zu definiren, müssen wir an verschiedene Körper die gleiche Kraft anbringen. Das Verhältnis ihrer Massen können wir dann als das verkehrte Verhältnis der Beschleunigungen definiren, die sie durch gleiche Kräfte erhalten. Aber darin liegt eben die grösste Schwierigkeit wie man die Gleichheit der Kräfte, wenn diese auf verschiedene Körper wirken, ohne logischen Fehler feststellen soll. Man könnte zwei Körper dem Zuge gleich beschaffener gleich gespannter Schnüre oder elastischer Federn unterwerfen. Allein da müsste man erst durch complicirte der Erfahrung entnommene Argumente als wahrscheinlich hinzustellen suchen, dass gleich beschaffene Schnüre auf zwei ganz verschiedene Körper dieselben Kräfte ausüben, was gewiss nicht a priori evident ist. Wir könnten auch nach Mach einfach den Satz der Gleichheit der Wirkung und Gegenwirkung postuliren. Wenn dann bloss zwei Körper in Wechselwirkung begriffen sind, so wäre die Gleichheit der Kräfte, welche auf beide Körper wirken evident. Wenn sie sich zudem nur Parallelverschiebungen ertheilen, so wäre das Verhältnis ihrer Massen einfach zu definiren, als das verkehrte Verhältnis der Beschleunigungen, welche an ihnen zu beobachten sind. Allein bei der Wirkung dazwischen gebrachter Schnüre, Fäden etc. haben wir eigentlich schon immer mehr als zwei in Wechselwirkung begriffene Körper und es würde auch die Deformation dieser Zwischenkörper in Betracht zu ziehen sein. Der von Mach angenommene Fall könnte also in reiner

Weise eigentlich nur bei directer Fernwirkung vorkommen und es wäre sehr misslich, wenn man vom rein empirischen Standpunkte aus die directe Fernwirkung a priori annehmen müsste. Streintz sucht eine einwurfsfreie Definition in folgender Weise zu gewinnen. Er denkt sich irgend ein System beliebiger Körper. In demselben kommen zwei Körper K_1 und K_2 vor. Diese ruhen im ersten Augenblicke und beginnen sich dann mit Beschleunigung aber jeder parallel zu sich selbst zu bewegen. Es soll nun die Bewegung beider Körper dadurch aufgehoben werden können, dass man sie starr mit einander verbindet. Dies verwendet er als Kriterium, dass früher auf jeden genau die gleiche Kraft wirkte, weil sich beide Kräfte durch blosse starre Verbindung jetzt aufheben. Er nennt diese Begriffsbestimmung der Gleichheit der Kraft die statische. Sie hat das für sich, dass sie das Princip der Gleichheit der Wirkung und Gegenwirkung involvirt, wie man sofort sieht, wenn man den speziellen Fall betrachtet, dass das ganze System bloss aus den zwei auf einander wirkenden Körpern K_1 und K_2 besteht. Sie hat aber doch auch manches Willkürliche. Dass durch die starre Verbindung die Wirkung der übrigen Kräfte nicht gestört wird, kann wieder höchstens erfahrungsmässig wahrscheinlich gemacht werden. Dass die Verbindungskräfte sich zu den übrigen addiren, setzt schon gewisse Sätze der Statik voraus. Noch grösser würden die Schwierigkeiten, wenn, die Körper K_1 und K_2 anfangs in Bewegung begriffen wären. Wollte man da nicht von vornherein annehmen, dass die Kräfte bloss von der relativen Lage abhängen, durch den aus der plötzlichen starren Verbindung resultirenden Stoss nicht gestört werden und Ähnliches, so müsste ihre Beschleunigung durch eine die Bewegung gestattende und auf beide Körper bloss beschleunigend wirkende plötzlich eingeschaltete Feder aufgehoben werden. Hält man einmal an der Streintz'schen Vorstellung fest, so hat die Definition der Massenverhältnisse weiter keine Schwierigkeit. Die Massen der beiden Körper K_1 und K_2 verhalten sich dann umgekehrt wie die Beschleunigungen, die sie im ersten Falle, wo keine starre Verbindung vorhanden war, erhielten, da ja damals auf beide gleiche Kräfte wirkten. Natürlich ist sowohl bei der Mach'schen als bei der Streintz'schen Definition noch immer erforderlich, sich auf besondere Erfahrungssätze zu berufen, vermöge welcher das Massenverhältnis zweier Körper immer gleich ausfällt, unter was immer für Umständen man den hiezu dienenden Versuch angestellt haben mag und vermöge welcher das Verhältnis der Massen der Körper K_1 und K_2 stets gleich dem Producte der beiden Massenverhältnisse der Körper K_1, K_2 und K_1, K_3 ist.

Zu bemerken ist noch, dass wir nur das Verhältnis zweier Massen bisher definirt haben. Um die Masse durch eine Zahl auszudrücken, müssen wir irgend eine Masse willkürlich als eine neue Einheit wählen. Von allen Grössen, welche daher durch Zahlen ausgedrückt werden, deren Grösse von der Wahl der Masseneinheit abhängig ist, werden wir sagen dass sie gewisse Dimensionen bezüglich der Masse haben. Haben wir den Begriff der Masse in der einen oder andern Weise festgestellt, so hat die Definition der Kraft im gewöhnlichen Sinne oder wie man auch sagt, der bewegenden Kraft keine Schwierigkeit mehr. Dieselbe ist das Product der Masse in die Beschleunigungen und hat daher bezüglich der Masse die Dimension eins. Da sich die Beschleunigungen wie Vectoren addiren, so gilt dies auch von den Kräften, wenigstens insoweit wir diese bisher betrachtet haben. Dieser Satz vom Kräftenparallelogramm sowie die übrigen bisher entwickelten Sätze, können nun auch auf die Statik und Dynamik der durch gespannte Fäden oder durch Federn erzeugten Druck und Zugkräfte übertragen werden. Natürlich zunächst bloss in dem idealen Falle, dass die Bewegung der einzelnen Theile der Fäden und Federn nicht betrachtet wird und dass die bewegten Körper sich stets parallel zu sich selbst bewegen. Es könnte so z. B. die Mechanik der Atwood'schen Fallmaschine mit Hilfe des bisher Entwickelten ohne weiteres discutirt werden.

Aus dem Umstande, dass sich das Newton'sche Gravitationsgesetz in symetrischer Weise bezüglich beider wirkender Körper aussprechen muss und dass die Anziehungsconstante K für alle Trabanten desselben Centralkörpers gleich ist, leitet man leicht ab, dass diese gleich dem Producte der Massen der beiden wirkenden Körper in eine für das ganze Universum constante Grösse sein muss, während die Thatsache, dass alle Körper durch die Schwere die gleiche Beschleunigung erhalten, schon lehrt, dass das Gewicht der Masse proportional sein muss.

Wir sind aber noch sehr weit davon entfernt aus den bisher entwickelten Grundlagen sämmtliche Sätze der Mechanik ableiten zu können. Wir haben ja bisher bloss die Bewegung eines festen Körpers parallel zu sich selbst betrachtet und haben den wichtigen Begriff des Angriffspunktes einer Kraft noch gar nicht gewonnen. Um diesen zu erhalten, um die Drehung der starren Körper, die Deformationen der elastischen und die Bewegungen der flüssigen behandeln zu können, müssen wir von neuem

Thatsachen ausgehen. Wenn ein Faden an einem Körper befestigt ist oder eine Feder auf eine einzige Stelle desselben drückend wirkt, so gibt es stets eine ganz kleine Partie des Körpers, welche zunächst von der Kraft afficirt wird. Lösen wir diese los und stellen einen kleinen Zwischenraum zwischen ihr und den übrigen Theilen des Körpers her, so wird derselbe erst wieder afficirt, wenn dieser Zwischenraum durch die Bewegung des kleinen abgetrennten Theiles sich ausgefüllt hat. Wir nennen daher diesen Theil die Angriffstelle und können sie wieder zu einem Angriffspunkte idealisiren. Wir müssen nun noch die bekannten Sätze über die Versetzbarkeit von Kräften an starren Körpern als idealisirte Erfahrungsthatsachen beifügen. Mittelst derselben können wir dann in ebenfalls hinlänglich bekannter Weise die Sätze über das Gleichgewicht von beliebigen Kräften, welche auf einen starren Körper wirken, die Sätze von den statischen Momenten ableiten. Wir schlagen hier insoferne einen analogen Weg ein, wie Streintz bei der Definition der Masse, als wir von der Statik ausgehen und erst von dieser zur Dynamik gelangen. Die Sätze von den statischen Momenten haben wir da freilich zunächst bloss für eine begrenzte Zahl von Kräften bewiesen, von denen jede nur auf einen einzelnen Punkt des Körpers wirkt. Wir müssen dann noch die Annahme hinzufügen, dass man im Falle, wo die Kräfte den Körper oder einen ausgedehnten Theil desselben als Ganzes anfassen die Sache immer so ansehen kann, als ob sie auf sehr viele respective unendlich viele Punkte seiner Oberfläche oder seines Innern gerade so wirken würden, als ob an jedem dieser Punkte eine ein wenig gespannte Schnur oder eine ein wenig drückende Feder befestigt wäre. So muss mann z. B. von der Schwere annehmen, das sie gleichmässig auf alle Punkte des schweren Körpers wirkt. Einen andere Weg, auf welchem man den Übergang von der Bewegung parallel zu sich selbst zur Drehbewegung versuchen könnte, will ich hier nur ganz kurz andeuten. Wir können aus dem Principe der Erhaltung der lebendigen Kraft folgenden Satz ableiten. Wenn auf einen festen Körper eine Kraft wirkt, die ihn nur parallel zu sich selbst zu bewegen sucht, so muss immer eine ihrer Richtung parallele Gerade, welche wir die Angriffslinie nennen wollen, von solcher Beschaffenheit existiren, dass wenn man einen beliebigen Punkt des festen Körpers, welcher auf derselben liegt, festhält, der Körper ins Gleichgewicht kommen muss. In gleicher Weise kann man beweisen, dass, wenn zwei feste Körper K_1 und K_2 so in Wechselwirkung begriffen sind, dass jeder dem andern nur eine Bewegung parallel zu sich selbst ertheilt, Wirkung und Gegenwirkung gleich sein muss und die Angriffslinien zusammenfallen müssen. Denkt man sich dann einen Punkt A der gemeinsamen Angriffslinien festgehalten, so muss das ganze System ins Gleichgewicht kommen. Jeden solchen Punkt können wir als Angriffspunkt der Kraft betrachten. An diesen Begriff des Angriffspunktes, können dann ebenfalls die Sätze von den statischen Momenten geknüpft werden.

Hat man einmal diese Sätze so oder so gewonnen, so muss man zur Zerlegbarkeit der Körper in Volumelemente übergehen. Man führt wieder als Erfahrungssatz an, dass sehr viele Körper, wenigstens mit genügender Annäherung in zwei Körper von je der halben Masse zerlegt werden, wenn man sie in zwei Theile von gleichem Volumen zerschneidet. Analog, wenn man sie in drei gleiche Theile theilt u. s. f. Denkt man sich dies ins Unendliche fortgesetzt, so gelangt man zu einem Satze, den man dahin aussprechen kann dass diese Körper aus unendlich vielen Volumelementen $d\tau$ bestehen und die in jedem Volumelemente enthaltene Masse $dm = \rho d\tau$ ist. Bei andern inhomogenen Körpern gilt dies wenigstens nahezu für jeden kleinen Volumtheil des Körpers, so dass wir dieselbe Formel anwenden können, wenn wir ρ als von Punkt zu Punkt veränderlich betrachten.

Was nun die Kräfte anbelangt, welche die Volumelemente fester Körper aufeinander ausüben, so muss man annehmen, dass jedes Volumelement nur auf die unmittelbar benachbarten wirkt und dass es auf alle der Trennungsfläche anliegenden Punkte Kräfte ausübt, welche gerade so wirken, als ob daran siebende gespannte Fäden oder drückende, aufgestützte Stäbe befestigt wären. Wenn die Trennungsfläche eben und genügend klein ist, so muss man zudem annehmen, dass diese Kräfte gleichmässig auf alle der Trennungsfläche anliegenden Punkte wirken. Diese Sätze können wol kaum direct erfahrungsmässig bestätigt werden und finden ihre Rechtfertigung nur in der nachherigen Übereinstimmung der aus ihnen entwickelten Sätze mit der Erfahrung. Wendet man den Satz von den statischen Momenten auf ein Volumelement an, so findet man, dass im Falle des Gleichgewichtes die auf ein zur x-axe senkrechtes Flächenelement in der y-Richtung wirkende Kraft gleich sein muss der auf ein gleiches zur y-Richtung senkrechtes Flächenelement in der x-Richtung wirkenden Kraft, was wir den Satz X nennen wollen. Zu den bisher aufgestellten Annahmen welche wir uns als durch die Erfahrung genügend motivirt dachten, sind noch die folgenden hinzuzunehmen.

Erstens, die elastische Kraft ist bloss von der augenblicklichen Gestaltveränderung des betreffenden Körpers, nicht von den früheren Zuständen desselben, noch auch von der Geschwindigkeit seiner Theilchen abhängig. Zweitens, jedes Volumelement bewegt sich nach den Gesetzen, welche wir bisher bloss für die Bewegung parallel zu sich selbst abgeleitet haben. Unter diesen Annahmen erhält man dann sofort die Gleichungen der gewöhnlichen Elasticitätslehre. Dieselben gelten natürlich wieder nur für einen idealen festen Körper, alle festen Körper zeigen innere Reibung und elastische Nachwirkung, welche wir bisher ausgeschlossen haben. Auch der Satz, welchen wir den Satz X nannten, ist keineswegs a priori evident. Lord Kelvin hat sich einmal den Lichtäther, sonst ganz mit den Eigenschaften begabt gedacht, welche wir an festen Körpern wahrnehmen, nur dass er die Richtigkeit dieses Satzes X fallen liess. Wir wollen uns hier nicht in eine Discussion einlassen ob durch die Annahme Lord Kelvins das Verhalten des Lichtäthers erklärt werden kann. Es genügt uns, dass derselbe ohne alle inneren Widersprüche Bewegungsgleichungen für die Volumelemente eines festen Körpers ausarbeiten konnte, für welchen der Satz X nicht gilt. Wir wollen jedoch vorläufig bei Körpern stehen bleiben, welche den idealen Gleichungen der Elasticitätslehre genügen. Wenn solche Körper so wenig deformirbar sind, dass man sie als starr betrachten kann und wenn durch beliebige Systeme derselben beliebige Bedingungsgleichungen realisirt sind, so kann man jetzt leicht nachweisen, dass für dieselben das vereinigte Princip der virtuellen Geschwindigkeiten und d'Alembert's gelten muss. Denn wenn man alle Kräfte auch die elastischen ins Auge fasst, so verschwindet jedenfalls die Summe

$$\sum\left[\left(m\frac{d^2x}{dt^2}-X\right)\delta x+\left(m\frac{d^2y}{dt^2}-Y\right)\delta y+\left(m\frac{d^2z}{dt^2}-Z\right)\delta z\right],$$

da jedes Glied dieser Summe einzeln verschwindet. Da aber die Wirkung immer gleich der Gegenwirkung ist, so müssen die Glieder dieser Summe, welche sich auf die Wechselwirkung der Volumelemente beziehen separat verschwinden, wenn diese starren Körpern angehören also keiner relativen Lagenänderung fähig sind, während bei bloss einseitigen Verbindungen die bekannten Ungleichungen abgeleitet werden können. Dies kann auch auf Verbindungen übertragen werden, die nur theilweise starr sind z. B. unausdehnsame Flächen, Fäden etc.; denn diese können immer als Grenzfall sehr dünner elastischer Körper betrachtet werden. Man erhält so das vereinigte Princip der virtuellen Verschiebungen und d'Alembert's in der gewöhnlichen Form. Erst aus diesem Principe können wir jetzt die Sätze von der Bewegung des Schwerpunkts, vom Trägheitsmomente etc. ableiten. Diese Sätze erscheinen daher in unserem Systeme erst an dieser Stelle. Es kann dies nicht anders sein; denn darin besteht ja das Wesen der inductiven Methode, dass wir nicht den Begriff des materiellen Punktes als eines unausgedehnten mit Masse begabten Körpers postuliren, sondern die Schlüsse, welche man sonst mit Hilfe dieses Begriffes macht, erst ausführen, wenn wir zur Vorstellung des Volumelementes gekommen sind, welche wir eher der Erfahrung entnehmen zu können glauben, als die des materiellen Punktes. Wir können dann diese Sätze erst erhalten, wenn wir die Wechselwirkung der Volumelemente behandelt haben. Wir mussten freilich schon früher an zwei Stellen vom Begriffe des mathematischen Punktes Gebrauch machen, nämlich als wir die Bewegung eines einzigen hervorgehobenen Punktes eines Körpers betrachteten und als wir Kräfte fingirten, welche an einem einzigen Punkte eines Körpers angreifen. Allein da war die Abstraction doch viel einfacher und klarer, als wenn wir das Ideal eines unausgedehnten mit Masse begabten Körpers bilden und dessen Drehung einfach vernachlässigen, ohne dass wir die Gesetze der Drehung vorher kennen gelernt haben. Manche Sätze könnten wir allerdings auch auf einem andern als dem eingeschlagenen Wege gewinnen. Ein Analogon des Schwerpunktsatzes könnten wir z. B. ableiten, indem wir ein System von ausgedehnten Körpern betrachten würden, zwischen denen innere Kräfte thätig sind und auf welche auch äussere Kräfte wirken, welche ihnen aber alle nur Bewegungen parallel zu sich selbst ertheilen. Nimmt man dann noch die Annahme, dass für die innere Kräfte Wirkung und Gegenwirkung immer gleich ist, so würde ein dem Schwerpunktsatze ähnlicher Satz für ein solches System in Wechselwirkung begriffener ausgedehnter Körper folgen.

Die Kräfte, welche in Flüssigkeiten wirken, können als ein spezieller Fall, der in elastischen Körpern wirkenden betrachtet werden und sie können daher ebenfalls nach der im bisherigen auseinandergesetzten Methode gewonnen werden. Die Gestaltänderungen der Flüssigkeiten können dann durch die Bewegung der Volumtheile derselben dargestellt werden, welche die entwickelten Gesetze befolgt; nur dass die Deformation des Körpers als Ganzes jetzt eine beliebig grosse sein kann.

Wir haben hiemit das Gebiet der eigentlichen mechanischen Erscheinungen erschöpft. Bei den dissipativen Erscheinungen (elastische Nachwirkung, Reibung etc.) spielt bereits die entwickelte Wärme eine Rolle. Wir können natürlich die Form der frühern Gleichungen wahren, indem wir zu den bisher abgeleiteten Kräften noch Glieder von solcher Beschaffenheit hinzu addiren, dass deren Summe genau gleich dem Werte der mit der Masse multiplicirten Beschleunigung wird. Diese Zusatzglieder können wir dann immer als Reibungskraft, Mittelswiderstandskraft etc. bezeichnen, doch hat diese Darstellung einen rein formalen Wert, wenn die Zusatzglieder in ganz complicirter Weise von der Bewegungsgeschwindigkeit, den frühern Zuständen etc. abhängen. Es bietet die Molekulartheorie da entschieden mehr Anschaulichkeit, da sie die Zusatzglieder doch durch langsame Drehung der Moleküle in neue Ruhelagen, Umsetzung der sichtbaren Bewegung in Molekularbewegung etc. einigermassen versinnlichen kann. Das Princip der virtuellen Verschiebung behält dann natürlich, so lange es auf das Gleichgewicht ruhender Körper angewendet wird, seinen Sinn, da bei der Ruhe dissipative Vorgänge fehlen. Aber das d'Alembert'sche Princip ist auch zu einer leeren Formel herabgesunken, so bald sich in den Ausdrücken für die Kräfte Glieder finden, welche selbst wieder von der Bewegung, von den vorhergegangenen Zuständen der Körper etc. abhängen. Über die Darstellung der elektrischen und magnetischen Erscheinungen will ich hier nur bemerken, dass dieselbe ebenfalls in die Form der mechanischen Gleichungen gebracht werden kann und muss, sobald diese Erscheinungen von Bewegungen ponderabler Körper begleitet sind. Des Näheren hierauf einzugehn, ist jedoch nicht meine Absicht.

Ich wollte in dem Bisherigen keineswegs eine consequente in sich abgeschlossene Darstellung der Mechanik vom inductiven Standpunkt geben. Ich wollte vielmehr bloss die Wege andeuten, auf denen eine solche vielleicht gewonnen werden könnte und namentlich die Schwierigkeiten aufdecken, mit denen ihre Durchführung verknüpft ist, wenn man sich bestrebt, das innere Bild ebenso klar hervortreten zu lassen und consequent durchzuführen, wie dieses bei der deductiven Behandlung möglich ist. Ich komme daher zu dem Resultate, dass unter den bisherigen Darstellungsversuchen der Mechanik die deductiven, wie die von Hertz und die von mir in meinem citirten Buche gemachte vorzuziehen seien. Da aber diese deductive Darstellung wie schon zu Anfang gezeigt wurde, den Mangel hat, dass sie so lange Zeit hindurch gar nicht an die Erfahrung anknüpft und vielfach den Schein des Willkürlichen erweckt, so würde es mich sehr freuen, wenn es jemanden gelänge, der deductiven Darstellung eine inductive an die Seite zu stellen, welche

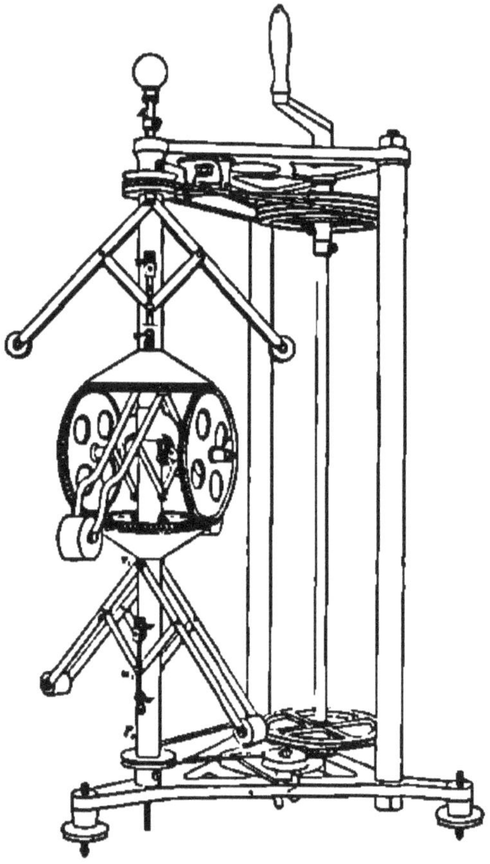

gleich einfach und naturgemäss vorginge und doch das innere geistige Bild in gleicher Deutlichkeit und Consequenz hervortreten liesse. Es wäre dies wohl in einer kurzen Abhandlung kaum möglich, sondern nur in einem grösseren Buche, wo man den Grundprincipien sogleich die Anwendung auf alle speziellen Fälle folgen lassen könnte. Denn erst an der Möglichkeit der exacten Darstellung aller möglichen speziellen Fälle erprobt sich die Klarheit und Consequenz der Bilder, wie sich das am besten an der Hertz'schen Darstellung zeigt, wo diese Anwendung auf spezielle Fälle fehlt. Sollten sich aber die Lücken, die sich in meiner gegenwärtigen Darstellung finden, nicht ausfüllen lassen, so würde mich auch dies freuen, denn es würde den definitiven Sieg der deductiven über die inductive Behandlungsweise bedeuten. Ich möchte gewissermassen die Vertreter der inductiven Richtung einladen, alle Fehler, die sich in meiner gegenwärtigen Darstellung finden aufzudecken, die Möglichkeit der genauen Durchführung aller Schlussweisen, die ich hier nur kurz angedeutet habe, zu zeigen und ihre besten Kräfte einzusetzen in dem Wettkampfe mit der deductiven Darstellung, damit beide mit einander verglichen werden können und sich im Wettstreite stets ausbilden und vervollkommnen.

Da der Energiebegriff nicht nur in der Mechanik, sondern in der ganzen Naturwissenschaft eine so wichtige Rolle spielt, so wären auch consequente Darstellungen der Grundprincipe der Mechanik vom Standpunkte der Energetik höchst erwünscht, welche also nicht von den Begriffen der Beschleunigung und Kraft sondern von denen der lebendigen Kraft und des Potentiales auszugehen hätten. Doch müssten die betreffenden Bilder auch nach der deductiven oder inductiven Methode durchaus klar consequent und einwurfsfrei entwickelt werden und es müssten vollkommen präcise Regeln gegeben werden, wie dieselben eindeutig auf alle speziellen Fälle anzuwenden sind, ohne dass die Kenntnis der alten Mechanik dabei vorausgesetzt wird.

Vierte Vorlesung.

Die vierte Vorlesung begann der Vortragende mit der Vorzeigung des Modells für die Maxwell'sche Theorie der Elektricität und des Magnetismus, welches in dessen Buch „Vorlesungen über Maxwells Theorie der Elektricität und des Lichtes erster Theil" beschrieben ist. Es wurden alle dort erwähnten Experimente mit gutem Erfolge durchgeführt. Hierauf gab er noch folgende Übersicht über die das Princip der kleinsten Wirkung und das Hamilton'sche Princip umfassenden Gleichungen.

Wenn wir die Fälle einseitiger Verbindungen ausschliessen, so wird das vereinigte Princip der virtuellen Verschiebungen und d'Alemberts, wie wir sahen durch eine Gleichung ausgedrückt, welche wir erhalten, wenn wir den Ausdrück auf Seite 36 gleich Null setzen. Führt man darin generalisirte Coordinaten ein und setzt Einfachheit halber voraus, dass eine Kraftfunction V besteht, welche aber die Zeit enthalten kann, so transformirt sich dieselbe in folgende Gleichung

$$\frac{dq}{dt} - \frac{\partial T}{\partial p} + \frac{\partial V}{\partial p} = 0,$$

wobei p irgend eine generalisirte Coordinate, q das dazu gehörige Moment, T die gesammte kinetische Energie ist. Wenn jede beliebige Coordinate p zu jeder beliebigen Zeit t eine beliebige Variation δp erfährt, so kann man die letzte Gleichung mit δp multipliciren und bezüglich aller p summiren. Im speciellen Falle, dass alle δp integrable Functionen der Zeit sind, kann man noch mit dt multipliciren und über eine beliebige Zeit (von t_0 bis t) integriren; nach partieller Integration der dq/dt enthaltenden Glieder folgt in dieser Weise:

$$\delta \int_{t_0} (T - V) dt = \Sigma(q\delta p - q_0 \delta p_0) \qquad (1)$$

wobei sich rechts die erstern Grössen auf die obere die letztern auf die untere Integrationsgrenze beziehen.

1. *Hamiltons Princip der stationären Wirkung.*

Aus der Fundamentalgleichung 1) folgt das Princip der stationären Wirkung, wenn man die Grenzen des Integrals und die Coordinatenwerte für dieselben als unveränderlich voraus setzt. Dann ergibt sich, wenn man setzt

$$T - V = W, \quad \int_{t_0} W dt = \Omega, \quad \frac{\Omega}{t - t_0} = \overline{W}$$

folgende Gleichung:

$$\delta\Omega = 0 \text{ oder } \delta\overline{W} = 0.$$

Ω oder $\overline{W}$ haben also für die Bewegung dieselbe Bedeutung, wie V für das Gleichgewicht in der Ruhe. Die Bedingungen, welche den Grenzwert von Ω oder $\overline{W}$ unter den geschilderten Umständen angeben, sind mit den Bewegungsgleichungen identisch, weshalb Helmholtz diese Grösen als kinetisches Potential bezeichnet. Für das Gleichgewicht in der Ruhe, bestimmen diese Bedingungen einen Grenzwert von V, da dann $T = 0$ und V von der Zeit unabhängig ist. Der Satz, dass für das Gleichgewicht, V ein Grenzwert ist, ist also ein ganz specieller Fall des Satzes vom kinetische Potentiale oder des Hamilton'schen Princip der stationären Wirkung, wie dieser auch genannt wird.

2. *Hamiltons Princip der variirenden Wirkung.*

Wir setzen in Gleichung 1) einmal nur die untere dann nur die obere, dann nur den Wert einer Coordinate für die untere, endlich diesen Wert für die obere Grenze des Integrales als veränderlich voraus; es folgen sofort die Hamilton'schen partiellen Differentialgleichungen:

$$\frac{\partial\Omega}{\partial t_0} = -W, \quad \frac{\partial\Omega}{\partial t} = W, \quad \frac{\partial\Omega}{\partial p_0} = -q_0, \quad \frac{\partial\Omega}{\partial p} = q.$$

Es soll nun V die Zeit nicht enthalten, also die Energie $T + V$ sich mit der Zeit nicht ändern. Wenn man dann in Gleichung 1) die Grenzen als variabel betrachtet, so transformirt man sie nach einigen Zwischenrechnungen leicht in die folgende:

$$2\delta\int_{t_0} T dt = \int_{t_0} \delta(T + V) dt + \Sigma(q\delta p - q_0 \delta p_0) \qquad (2)$$

wobei aber die δp jetzt unter gleichzeitiger Variation der Grenzen für die Zeit und der Bewegung zu bilden sind.

3. *Das alte Princip der kleinsten Wirkung.*

Setzt man in Gleichung 2) die Coordinatenvariationen für die Grenzen von t gleich Null und nimmt ausserdem an, dass die Variation der Bewegung ohne Energiezufuhr geschieht also $\delta(T + V) = 0$ ist, so folgt

$$\delta\int_{t_0} T dt = 0,$$

also die alte Form des Princips der kleinsten Wirkung, welches in mancher Beziehung specieller, in so fern aber wieder allgemeiner ist, als das Princip der stationären Wirkung, als es die Bewegungszeit als veränderlich betrachtet.

4. *Analogien mit dem zweiten Hauptsatze.*

Wir wollen annehmen, dass das letzte Glied der Gleichung 2) verschwindet. Es gilt dies nicht bloss, wenn an den Grenzen für die Zeit $\delta p = \delta p_0 = 0$ ist, sondern auch wenn die Bewegung periodisch ist und $t - t_0$ die Dauer dieser Periode ist. Es gilt auch wenn die Verschiebungen sämmtlicher materiellen Punkte des Systemes in folge der Variation der Bewegung senkrecht auf der augenblicklichen Geschwindigkeitsrichtung derselben steht. Bisher waren die δp ganz willkürliche Variationen. Wir wollen sie nun in folgender Weise erzeugt denken. 1. Mit dem Systeme, auf welches sich die Gleichung 2) bezieht, soll ein zweites System verbunden sein, welches mit dem ersten in Wechselwirkung steht und letzteres soll eine unendlich kleine Bewegung machen. 2. Ausserdem soll dem ersten Systeme eine unendlich kleine lebendige Kraft δQ zugeführt werden. Die in der Gleichung vorkommende Grösse δV ist bloss die Veränderung von V in folge der Lagenänderung der Punkte des ersten Systems. Sei $\delta' V$ die in Folge der Lagenänderung des zweiten Systems, so ist $\delta' V$ die Arbeit der vom ersten auf das zweite System wirkenden Kräfte. Sie muss mit der zugeführten Energie δQ zusammen die gesammte Änderung δE der Energie des ersten Systems geben. Es ist also $\delta E = \delta Q + \delta' V$. Anderseits ist $\delta E = \delta T + \delta V + \delta' V$, da δT die Änderung der kinetischen, $\delta V + \delta' V$ die Gesammtänderung der potentiellen Energie ist. Aus beiden Gleichungen folgt $\delta Q = \delta\,(T + V)$. Setzen wir

$$\overline{\delta Q} = \frac{\int_{t_0}^{t} \delta Q\,dt}{t - t_0} \quad \text{und} \quad \bar{T} = \frac{\int_{t_0}^{t} T\,dt}{t - t_0},$$

so folgt aus Gleichung 2) unter den gemachten Annahmen sofort

$$\frac{\overline{\delta Q}}{\bar{T}} = \delta\left[\text{lognat.}\left(\int_{t_0}^{t} T\,dt\right)^2\right]$$

wo die Analogie mit dem zweiten Hauptsatze deutlich zu Tage tritt. Thermodynamisches Beispiel: Unter dem ersten Systeme verstehen wir die Moleküle eines Gases, unter dem zweiten einen das Gas begrenzenden beweglichen Stempel, δQ ist die dem Gase zugeführte Wärme. Mechanisches Beispiel: Das erste System ist ein mit einer punktförmigen Masse verbundener Magnetpol der gezwungen ist, sich in einer Ebene zu bewegen, das zweite System ein kurzer Magnet, um welchen der Magnetpol eine Centralbewegung macht. Nun erfährt der Magnet eine kleine Drehung wodurch sich das Wirkungsgesetz der Centralbewegung ändert und ausserdem der Magnetpol einen kleinen Stoss. Das Gesagte soll gewissermassen ein Schema sein, in welchem die verschiedenen dem Principe der kleinsten Wirkung verwandten Principe zusammengestellt sind. Es zeigt sich, dass die Analogien mit dem zweiten Hauptsatze weder einfach mit dem Principe der kleinsten Wirkung, noch auch mit dem Hamilton'schen identisch sind, aber sowohl zum einen, wie auch zum andern in sehr naher Beziehung stehen.

Ich habe zu Anfang betont, dass die Entwicklung der Wissenschaft nicht immer in stetiger Verfolgung der alten Wege vor sich geht, sondern sehr häufig durch plötzliche Einführung ganz neuer Methoden und Ideen gefördert wird. Wo könnte für letztere Art der Entwicklung ein fruchtbarer Boden sein als in Amerika, wo alles neu ist, wo die Geschicklichkeit des Geistes, Ungewöhnliches zu unternehmen, die grössten unvorhergesehenen Schwierigkeiten zu besiegen stete Übung findet, während wir in Europa wolgedrillt in den Bahnen der alten wissenschaftlichen Methode uns zwar mit grösserer Leichtigkeit und Sicherheit bewegen, als die Bewohner der neuen Welt, aber dem Ungewohnten und Neuen gegenüber verblüfft und unbehülflich sind. Sicher werden daher nicht bloss die Amerikaner aus ihren rastlosen Bestrebungen die Pflege der reinen Wissenschaft zu fördern den grössten Nutzen ziehen, sondern auch die Wissenschaft wird durch die Mitwirkung der Amerikaner stets mehr und grossartiger gefördert werden. Auch ich fühle den hohen bildenden Wert, den es für mich hatte meinen engbegrenzten heimatlichen Horizont durch die Bekanntschaft mit der grossartigen Natur und Cultur Amerikas zu erweitern, wol das fruchtbringendste Experiment, das ich je angestellt habe. Ich sage Ihnen daher meinen besten Dank für die hohe Ehre, welche Sie mir durch die Berufung zu diesen Vorträgen erwiesen, und wünsche nur, dass das von mir gebotene nicht ganz hinter der Grösse dieser Auszeichnung zurückstehen möge.

S. Ramon Cajal

STUDY ... SORY AR... OF THE HU...

By Santiago Ra...

...pond worthily to the ...
... honored me, I ...
... synthesis, a general ...
... minute anatomy of the ...
... professorships every ...
... necessary for the accomp...
... moderate my ambition ...
... analytical contribution ...
... of the sensory centres of ...
a subject ... I have devoted the leis...

...ct is so vast and ... ficult that, in spite of my ...
...ed to it, I have ... to clear up ... a
... contribution ... to my ...
... teresting, as it ...
... and some of ...
... ations on the stru...
... study of the sense...
... our knowledge, presents ...
... logists who have ...
... brain are divided at present ...

... trine, proclaimed by Mey...
... Kölliker, supposes that ...
... same structure, functio...
... afferent or sensory nerves ...
... energy of nerves is the ...

S. Ramon Cajal

COMPARATIVE STUDY OF THE SENSORY AREAS OF THE HUMAN CORTEX.

By Santiago Ramón y Cajal.

In order to respond worthily to the gracious invitation with which Clark University has honored me, I ought to offer you, as was my original intention, a work of synthesis, a general summary of the present state of our knowledge of the minute anatomy of the nervous system. Unfortunately, the duties of my professorship, every day more pressing, have deprived me of the time necessary for the accomplishment of such a task, and have compelled me to moderate my ambition, and to limit it to presenting to you a modest analytical contribution to our knowledge of the microscopical structure of the sensory centres of the human cerebral cortex, a subject to which I have devoted the leisure of the past months.

This subject is so vast and so difficult that, in spite of my efforts and the time devoted to it, I have been able to clear up only a *few* points. Consequently, my contribution will be, to my utmost regret, a very incomplete one, treating, as it does, only the visual cortex as I have made it out in man and some of the higher mammals. I shall add, however, a few observations on the structure of other sensory regions.

This anatomical study of the sensory areas of the cortex, at the present state of our knowledge, presents points of special interest, since, as you well know, neurologists who have interested themselves in the histology of the brain are divided at present into two camps, the unicists and the pluralists.

The unicist doctrine, proclaimed by Meynert and reaffirmed quite recently by Golgi and Kölliker, supposes that all regions of the cortex possess essentially the same structure, functional diversity being due to diversity of origin of afferent or sensory nerves. This amounts to saying that cerebral specific energy of nerves is the necessary effect of the particular organization of each sense as well as of the special character of the stimuli received by the peripheral sensory surfaces, skin, retina, organ of Corti, etc.

The pluralist doctrine, upheld recently by Flechsig, without rejecting the particular influence of connections with different nerves, maintains that diversities of function result also from the particular structure of each cortical area.

It is this latter opinion, as we shall presently see, that presents a closer agreement with the observed facts. In fact, my researches tend to prove that the topographical specialization of the brain depends not only on the quality of the stimuli analyzed and gathered up by the sensory mechanisms, but also on the structural adaptations which the corresponding cerebral areas undergo; since it is very natural to suppose, even if one were to form an *a priori* judgment, that the cortical areas connected with the special senses sight and touch, which form exact images of the exterior world with fixed relations of space and intensity, have by accommodation to the stimuli received an organization different from that existing in cortical areas attached to the chemical senses of taste or smell, and from that which is appropriate to the chronological sense hearing, which gives only relations of succession, free from every spacial quality.

We may add that if there exist in the human cerebral cortex, as Flechsig supposes, besides the sensori-motor centres, other regions, association centres, characterized by absence of direct sensory or motor connections, it seems very natural also to associate to these important regions of the brain, with which are connected the highest activities of psychic life, a special organization corresponding to their supremacy in the hierarchy of functions.

But we must not carry to an extreme the structural plurality of the brain. In fact, our researches show that while there are very remarkable differences of organization in certain cortical areas, these points of difference do not go so far as to make impossible the reduction of the cortical structure to a general plan. In reality, every convolution consists of two structural factors: one, which we may call a factor of a general order, since it is found over the whole cortex, is represented by the molecular layer and that of the small and large pyramids; the other, which we may call the special factor, particularly characteristic of the sensory areas, is represented by fibre plexuses formed by afferent nerve fibres and by the presence at the level of the so-called granular layer of certain cell types of peculiar form.

But, before proceeding to outline the general conclusions of an anatomico-physiological order, that result from all our researches taken together, permit me to present very briefly the facts of observation.

Visual Cortex.

The minute anatomy of the visual cortex (region of the calcarine fissure, sulcus cornu lobulus lingualis) has been already explored by several investigators, among whom we may make particular mention of Meynert, Vicq d'Azyr, Gennari, Krause, Hammarberg, Schlapp, Kölliker, *et al.* But their very incomplete researches have been performed by such insufficient methods as staining with carmine, the Weigert-Pall method, or that of Nissl with basic anilines — methods which, as is well known, do not suffice at all to demonstrate the total morphology of the elements and the organization of the most delicate nerve plexuses. They led, however, in spite of the difficulties which stood in the way of these first analytical attempts, toward a precise differentiation of the visual cortex from other regions of the brain. At the outset two characteristic differences attracted the attention of the first investigators into the structure of the visual cortex: first, the existence of a very thick stratum of granules, subdivided into accessory strata by laminæ of molecular appearance; and, second, the presence in the intermediate layers of the cortex of a white lamina formed of medullated fibres — which lamina may be seen with the unaided eye. This lamina, appearing in cross-section as a white line, has been named, in honor of the writers who first described it, the line of Gennari or Vicq d'Azyr.

For the sake of brevity, we shall omit a detailed description and discussion of the various layers admitted by the authorities on this region; suffice it to mention in order the eight layers described by Meynert for the human cortex: First, molecular; the second, layer of small pyramidal cells; third, layer of nuclei or granules; fourth, layer of solitary cells; fifth, layer of intermediate granules; sixth, layer similar to the fourth, containing nuclei and scattered cells; seventh, deep nuclear layer; eighth, layer of fusiform cells. We may also mention the arrangement of layers recently described by Schlapp for the occipital cortex of the monkey: (1) layer of tangential fibres; (2) layer of exter-

nal polymorphic cells; (3) layer of pyramidal cells; (4) layer of granules; (5) layer of small solitary cells; (6) second layer of granules; (7) layer poor in cells; (8) layer of internal polymorphic cells.

The investigations which I have made on the human cortex as well as on that of the dog and cat, by both the Nissl and Golgi methods, have led me to distinguish the following layers: —

1. Plexiform layer (called molecular layer by authors generally and cell-poor layer by Meynert).
2. Layer of small pyramids.
3. Layer of medium-sized pyramids.
4. Layer of large stellate cells.
5. Layer of small stellate cells (called layer of granules by the authors).
6. Second plexiform layer, or layer of small pyramidal cells with arched axon.
7. Layer of giant pyramidal cells (solitary cells of Meynert).
8. Layer of medium sized pyramidal cells with arched ascending axon.
9. Layer of fusiform and triangular cells (fusiform cell layer of Meynert).

You see that we have modified current nomenclature by introducing terms which call to mind cellular morphology. For we believe that such trite expressions as "molecular layer," "granular layer," must be

Fig. 1. — Vertical section of the visual cortex of man, calcarine sulcus, stained by Nissl's method — semi-schematic. 1. Plexiform layer. 2. Layer of small pyramids. 3. Layer of medium-sized pyramids. 4. Layer of large stellate cells. 5. Layer of small stellate cells. 6. Second plexiform layer, or layer of small pyramids with arched axon. 7. Layer of giant pyramids. 8. Layer of medium-sized pyramidal cells with ascending axon. 9. Layer of fusiform and triangular cells.

banished once for all from scientific language, and they must be replaced by terms which point out dominant morphological characters in the nerve structures of each layer or some interesting peculiarity relative to the course and connections of the axis cylinder processes. The number of layers could be easily increased or diminished, because they are not separated by well-marked boundaries, particularly in Nissl's preparations. Thus the number of layers which I adopt is somewhat arbitrary. By distinguishing, however, nine layers, I have followed a criterion of individualization which seems to me the most convenient and suitable for my exposition of the cortex as a mechanism composed of elements at a certain level which differ in special morphological features from those of neighboring levels. Besides, the number, extent, and size of cells in these layers vary a little in the different median occipital convolutions, as does also the degree of definite nidification, according as we study the convex or concave aspect of the gyri. Our description relates generally to the cortex of the margin of the calcarine fissure, the region where structural differentiation of the visual cortex is most pronounced.

Plexiform Layer.

The plexiform or molecular layer is one of the oldest cerebral formations in the phylogenetic series. It presents characters similar to those of the human cortex in all vertebrates except the fishes. This has been fully demonstrated by the researches of comparative histology undertaken by Oyarzun (batrachia), by myself (batrachia, reptilia, and mammalia), by my brother (batrachia, reptilia), by Eddinger (batrachia, reptilia, aves), by Cl. Sala (aves). In the visual cortex of man, the structure of this layer coincides perfectly with that which my own researches, as well as those of G. Retzius, have revealed in the motor region. The only modification which may be noted, visible even by Nissl's method, is its notable thinness in the margins of the calcarine fissure (except in the sulci, and here it appears somewhat thinned). This diminution in thickness, noted by authors generally, depends probably on the small number of medium-sized and giant pyramidal cells in the underlying layers, because it is well known that each pyramidal cell is represented in the plexiform layer by a spray of dendrites. A similar opinion has been expressed by Bevan Lewis in order to explain irregularities in thickness of this layer in different regions of the cortex of the rabbit and guinea-pig. The structure of the plexiform layer is very complex. From my own researches, confirmed largely by those of Retzius, Schäfer, Kölliker, and Bevan Lewis, it follows that it consists of an interweaving of the following elements: (*a*) the radial branches of the small, medium-sized, and giant pyramidal cells, with which we must include in addition those of the so-called polymorphic cells; (*b*) layer of terminal ramifications of the ascending axons of Martinotti; (*c*) layer formed by the arborizations of the nerve fibres, terminal or collateral, which come from the white matter; (*d*) layer of special or horizontal cells of the first layer (Cajal's cells, of Retzius); (*e*) layer of small and medium-sized stellate cells with short axons; (*f*) layer of neuroglia cells, well described by Martinotti, Retzius, and Andriesen.

a. **Terminal Arborizations of the Pyramidal Cells** (Fig. 4). — As my observations have shown in case of the mammalian cortex, and those of Retzius for the human fœtus, the radial trunk of the pyramidal cells does not end, as Golgi and Martinotti supposed, in a point entwined by neuroglia elements in connection with the blood-vessels, but in a spray of varicose dendrites covered with contact granules, spreading out sometimes over a considerable area of the plexiform layer. In my first work on the cerebral cortex, I thought that the only cells whose terminal dendrites reached up to the first layer were the medium-sized, small, and giant pyramidal cells; but my latest researches have enabled me to discover that all cells possessing a radial stem, without exception, including even those of the deeper layers, are represented in the plexiform layer by a terminal dendritic arborization. It is without doubt an important structural law whose physiological import must be very considerable. We may observe that large trunks which arise from the giant pyramids divide into a spray with very long and thick branches having their distribution in the deeper level, while the slender stems emanating from the medium and small sized pyramids form an arborization of numerous slender branches of limited extension and distributed particularly through the superficial laminæ of the plexiform layer. This distribution, which is not absolutely constant, leads us to surmise that the terminal arborizations of each kind of pyramidal cell come into contact with special neuritic terminal arborizations in traversing this first layer.

The trunk and end brush intended for the first layer appear not only in preparations made by the chromate of silver method; for I have stained them perfectly with methylene blue (method of Ehrlich-Bethe) in case of young animals, and also in adult gyrencephalous mammals, such as the dog and cat. Besides, in good preparations by Ehrlich's method, particularly when fixation has been made a short time after the impregnation, one may see very distinctly the contact granules of the dendrites, processes which I was first to describe and whose existence has been confirmed by many investigators since. With methylene blue they present the same appearance as in Golgi preparations, *i.e.* they are slender and short, stand out at a right angle, are sometimes divided, and end freely in a rounded knob. This proves, accordingly, how groundless are all the gratuitous objections which have been brought against the preëxistence of these appendages, as well as against their mode of termination. Among the entirely arbitrary conjectures which have been made as to the disposition of these appendages we include also W. Hill's opinion, who considers them the fibres of a reticulum that is incompletely stained by means of the chromate of silver. We must proclaim emphatically that at present there is no method of staining cellular processes that is capable of disproving the agreeing results of the methods of Golgi, Ehrlich, and Cox. Whoever, having as a foundation the revelations of any one of these methods, has considered it possible to demonstrate the existence of such a reticulum has only exposed to view his own lack of experience in handling these important means of analysis.

b. **Special or Horizontal Cells of the Plexiform Layer.**—These interesting elements, which I discovered in the cortices of the small mammals (rat, rabbit, guinea-pig), have been successfully investigated by Retzius in case of man, as well as by my brother in batrachians and reptiles, and by Veratti in the rabbit's embryo. They present in the visual cortex, where I have stained them very often, the same characters as in other regions of the brain. As I have already described these elements elsewhere, I shall give here only an outline, to which I may add a few remarks derived from my recent observations upon man (Fig. 2).

Following the example of Retzius, when we study the horizontal cells by Golgi's method in a human fœtus from the seventh to the ninth month, or in case of a newborn babe, we notice that they are distributed throughout the entire thickness of the plexiform layer, but are especially numerous in close proximity to the pia. Their form is very variable, sometimes fusiform or triangular, and again stellate, with the angles extending out into the long processes. But the characteristic feature of these elements is due to the fact that their processes, which are variable

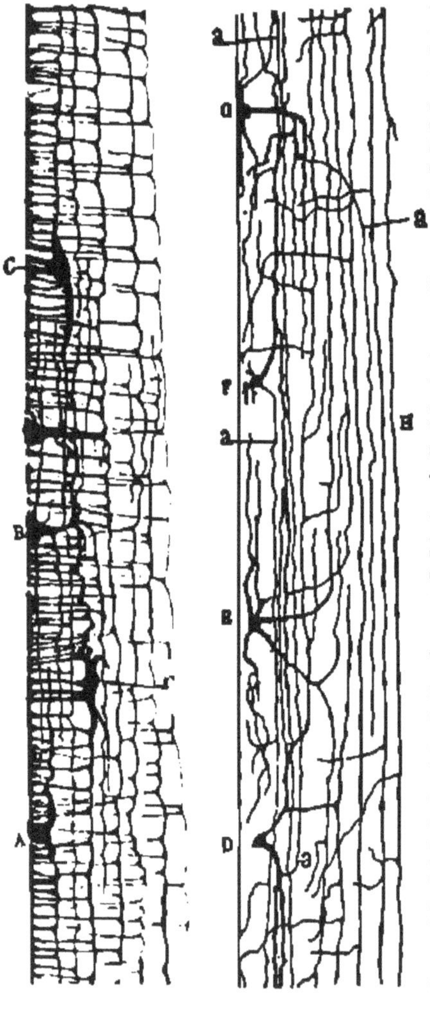

FIG. 2. — Cells of the 1st lamina of the plexiform layer. *A*, *B*, *C*, horizontal cells of the visual cortex of infant at birth; *D*, *E*, *F*, *G*, cells of visual cortex of infant at twenty days; *H*, horizontal fibres arising from cells of the same kind situated at a great distance within the first lamina; *a*, delicate processes having the appearance of axons.

in number and very large at their origin, give rise, after a few divisions, to an extraordinary number of varicose horizontal fibres, extremely long, from which spring at right angles numberless ascending secondary branches terminating in rounded knobs near the cerebral surface. Very often the superior surface of the cell body also gives rise to some of these ascending branches, which sometimes have a considerable thickness.

In what way do these tangential fibres terminate? Is it possible to discern among them certain processes possessing the characters of axons?

Upon careful examination of the best preparations obtained from cortices of human embryos, we discover easily that these processes, when they become very fine, have all the appearances peculiar to axons. There is no morphological distinction which would enable us to distinguish the two classes or species of cellular processes. That which most strikes one is the enormous length of their horizontal fibres (tangential fibres of Retzius). One can follow them for two or three tenths of a millimeter without being able to discover their true termination. However, in certain cases it is possible to demonstrate that the tangential fibres, after having given rise to a great number of vertical twigs, become thinner and finer, and finally subdivide into terminal branchlets, which spread out under the pia or in the superficial laminæ of the first layer.

On comparing these cells of the human brain with their homologues in the higher mammals (rabbit, cat, etc.), we discover that among the latter they give rise to a relatively small number of tangential branches, and that these extend a much shorter distance. This is the reason we consider the remarkable profusion and the extreme length of the horizontal fibres as one of the most characteristic features of the human cortex.

Retzius did not succeed in staining the horizontal cells in man except in the fœtal period. Accordingly, it was impossible to know what becomes of these elements in the adult, and whether, as Retzius is inclined to think, all the processes that we find in the embryonic period persist. My recent researches on the cortex of infants fifteen months and even fifteen and twenty days old, in which I have been successful in staining the horizontal cells, suffice to furnish a few data which, if they do not solve the problem once for all, at any rate place the question in a somewhat more favorable light.

When we examine the plexiform layer of a babe fifteen days old, we find considerable changes in the horizontal cells. First of all, we notice that they have become smaller, and that the tangential processes have diminished in diameter while they have become notably lengthened. But the peculiarity which most strikes the attention is the almost total disappearance of the ascending collateral branches. This atrophy begins in a progressive thinning of the processes and in the reabsorption of their terminal varicosities; then the whole branch disappears, so that the only structures left are the horizontal fibres, whose ensemble forms throughout the thickness of the plexiform layer a system of parallel fibres of enormous length. There are places, however, where the ascending branches persist, but very much changed as to their direction, having become oblique instead of vertical, becoming branched several times, and terminating in the plexiform layer without reaching so far up toward the pia as before. In a word, most of the vertical branches seem to me to represent an embryonic arrangement corresponding to the interstices, for the most part vertical, between the epithelial cells of the cerebral cortex of the fœtus, which proves once more, as I have demonstrated in other nerve centres, that during the period of evolution the neuron is the locus of a double series of functions: on the one side a vegetative building up of the dendrites; on the other, reabsorptions and transformations of the cells which persist.

Have the horizontal cells with which we are now concerned a true functional process? In case this is so, what is the part played by these elements in the vast system of nervous relations established in the plexiform layer?

In preparations of the human brain stained with chromate of silver, it must be confessed, it is not easy to solve this important question, since the purely morphological criterion, which is sufficient to distinguish the axon in other neurons, cannot be applied to horizontal cells, all the processes of which, on becoming finer, have the form of true axons. Thus, in spite of Veratti's affirmation, we believe that this method will shed no light upon the subject, even when applied to embryos. In order to approximate to any solution of the problem, we must use a method capable of staining nerve prolongations in a manner to differentiate them from dendrites. It was only after using Ehrlich's methylene-blue method upon the motor and visual cortex of the cat that I became convinced that the horizontal cells have in reality a very long axon, which is provided with a medullary sheath. The other processes, which we have called horizontal fibres, represent true dendrites, as is shown by two peculiarities: the great facility with which they take methylene blue, and their pronounced varicosity after fixation with ammonium molybdate. We must repeat that this varicose alteration, which is a striking modification in the form of cellular prolongations, presents itself only in dendrites. The neurites maintain perfectly, with methylene blue, their normal contours, unless exposure to the air, necessary to obtain the selective staining, has been too long.

As to the axon, it may be sufficiently well demonstrated in horizontal sections of the plexiform layer in the form of a pale blue fibre, except the initial portion and the nodes, which present a dark blue staining. This is a property of all parts of a fibre not surrounded with a medullary sheath. At the point of certain constrictions we may succeed in discovering a few collaterals springing out at right angles, provided also with myeline sheaths. Finally, one is sometimes so fortunate as to discover in an axon of this kind true bifurcations situated at a great distance from the cell of origin, but always in the plane of the plexiform layer. Unfortunately, the methylene blue does not stain the terminal nerve arborizations. This has prevented me from learning in just what way these axons terminate and with what axons they are dynamically associated. It is possible that certain heavy horizontal fibres come into contact with the horizontal cells, since they never bend downward toward the underlying layers, as do the medium-sized and finest medullated fibres. They belong probably to the terminal arborizations of Martinotti's ascending axons and, perhaps, also to the collaterals and terminals coming in from the white matter.

c. **Cells with a Short Axon** (Fig. 3, *G*, *E*, *F*).— A few years ago, while studying the cerebral cortex of the small mammals, I discovered, besides the gigantic horizontal cells, other elements which I called polygonal cells. These are characterized by their stellate form and by their short axon, which ramifies and ends within the limits of the plexiform layer. These cells, whose existence neither Schäfer nor Lewis seem to have been able to confirm,—no doubt on account of the insufficiency of their attempts to obtain an impregnation of them,—are much more abundant than might have been supposed from my first observations. However, I must acknowledge that, they are not at all easily impregnated with chromate of silver and that, in order to find a sufficient number for study, we must make a great many attempts at staining them. On the other hand, Ehrlich's method stains them very readily in the dog and rabbit. In these animals

— and I think that it holds true also in man — the plexiform layer of the cerebrum is as richly supplied with elements with a short axon as the molecular layer of the cerebellar cortex. They occur in all levels of the layer and differ remarkably in size and shape. The majority of them are stellate and are comparable in size to other cells with short axons

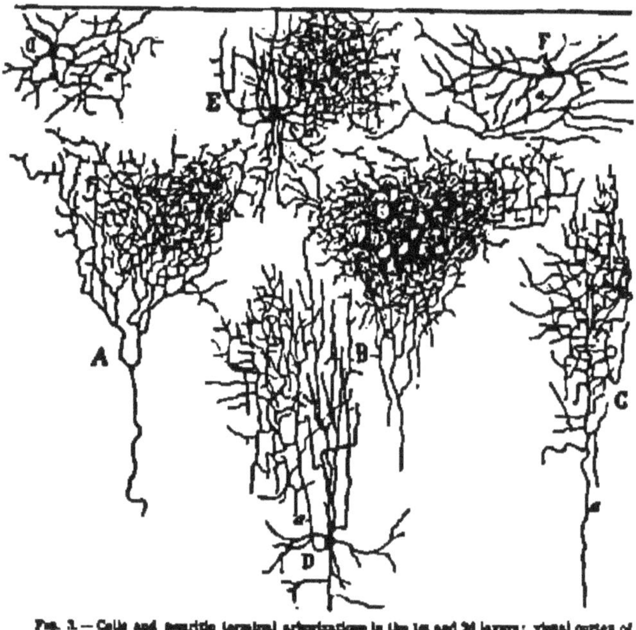

FIG. 3. — Cells and neuritic terminal arborizations in the 1st and 2d layers; visual cortex of infant 20 days old. *A* and *B*, neuritic plexus, extremely fine and dense, situated in the layer of small pyramids; *C*, an analogous arborization, but not so dense; *D*, a small cell whose ascending axon forms a similar arborization; *E*, spider-shaped stellate cell of the 1st layer; *F*, *G*, cells with short axon branching loosely in the plexiform layer; *a*, axon.

that occur in the deeper layers of the cortex. Others are smaller, resembling in their minuteness the granules of the cerebellum. But whether large or small, the morphological characters of these elements are very similar. Their dendrites are divergent, extremely branched, and distributed exclusively to the plexiform layer. Their neurites are usually very short, subdivide in a most complicated manner in the neighborhood of the cell, but never cross the deep boundary of the first layer.

From the point of view of the direction and length of their neurites all these elements may be classified into three varieties: (1) Stellar cells with horizontal neurite which becomes resolved after a varying distance, generally very long, into a terminal arborization which has the appearance of being connected with the terminal branches of the remote pyramids. (2) Cells of generally smaller size whose neurite branches either laterally or vertically from the cell body, but always at a moderate distance (Fig. 8, *G*, *F*). (3) Very small cells (which I discovered recently in the human cerebral cortex) provided with numerous fine, divergent, and slightly branched dendrites, whose neurite, extremely slender, breaks up near its origin into a dense arborization, exceedingly fine and complicated. We shall designate these elements dwarf or spider-shaped cells. They may be found, as we shall see, in all the layers of the cortex (Fig 8, *E*).

To sum up: bearing in mind the form of cell bodies and formation and connection of axons, all the stellate cells of the plexiform layer, including the horizontal or special cells, seem to me similar to the stellate cells of the molecular layer of the cerebellum and to those which occur in the layers of the same name in the *cornu ammonis* and *fascia dentata*. Their function is probably to establish connections between terminal arborizations as yet imperfectly made out, possibly those formed by the ascending axons of Martinotti, or the association fibres coming up from the white matter with the terminal branches of the pyramidal cells. The function of the great horizontal cells would seem to be to establish connections between elements, that is to say between terminal neuritic arborizations and radial dendrites, separated by very considerable distances; while the medium-sized and small elements, with their short axons, would perform the same associative function at short or moderate distances.

d. **Martinotti's Ascending Fibres.** — There is no lack of these in the visual cortex, although it has seemed to me that they are not so numerous as in other regions of the brain. Their terminal ramifications, well known from the researches of Martinotti as well as my own, occupy really the whole plexiform layer, where they extend over wide areas, distributing themselves preferably into its deeper levels and coming in contact with cells with short axons and, possibly, also with the large horizontal cells.

Granting that the cells of origin for these fibres lie in layers of the cortex that contain sensory fibres, we might suppose that Martinotti's ascending axons represent intermediate links placed vertically between these sensory fibres and cells with short axon in the plexiform layer. And as these are connected, perhaps, with the dendrites of the pyramidal cells, the result would be that the sensory stimuli, entering the cortex in this indirect way, would be compelled to traverse two intercalated nerve cells before reaching the pyramids.

e. **Neuroglia Cells.** — These conform in the visual cortex to the well-known types of other cerebral regions. We find accordingly: (1) Cells with long radii, the marginal cells well described by Martinotti, which lie just under the pia. They emit long, smooth, descending processes radiating across the plexiform layer, ending at different levels both of this and of the layer of small pyramids; (2) Cells with short radii. These elements, long since described by Golgi, and described in detail by Retzius, by myself, Andriesen, Kölliker, and others, are characterized by their form, very often stellate or fusiform, by their location in all levels of the plexiform layer, and by the great number of their processes, short, spongy, branching, and bristling with innumerable contact granules, which penetrate into the spaces lying between the neuro-protoplasmic plexus and are well spread over the interstices of the elements which must not come into contact. It is in virtue of this intricate relation between these appendages and the cell bodies and dendrites, as well as for other reasons which we have not time to dilate upon here, that we attribute to the neuroglia elements with short processes an insulating rôle. According to my view, they prevent inopportune contacts, while their processes exercise due regard to all points of cells or fibres where contacts exist and nerve currents pass.

Layer of Small Pyramids.

This layer is well separated from the 1st, but blends by insensible gradations with the 3rd, or layer of medium-sized pyramidal cells (Fig. 4, *B*).

Examined in Nissl preparations this layer presents a great number of small pyramids, very poor in chromatic granules and separated by a plexus of fibrils much more dense than in the case of cells of the deeper layers. We find also, scattered irregularly, stellate or triangular cells larger than the pyramids. These are the giant cells with short axon, as is shown in good chromate of silver preparations (Fig. 5, *D*, *C*). We shall now discuss the cells of this layer, beginning with the pyramids.

Pyramids. — The morphology and relations of these cells being well

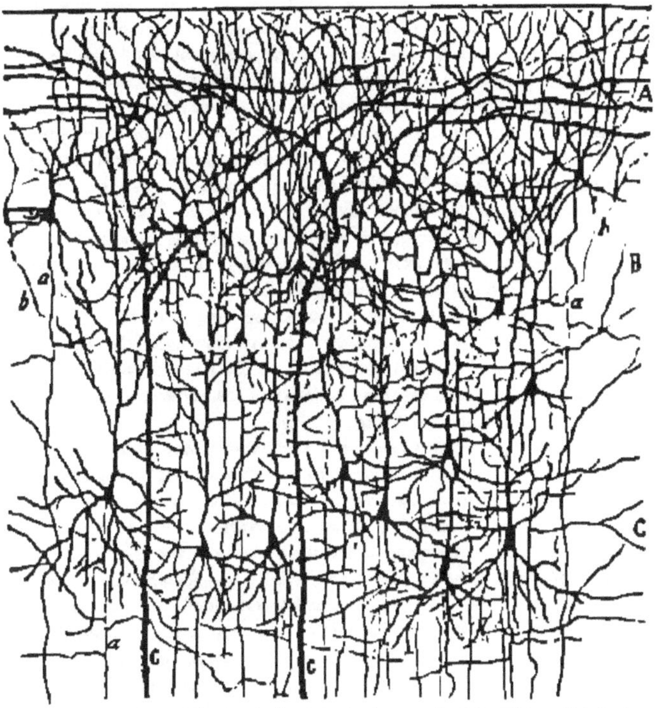

FIG. 4. — Small and medium-sized cells of the visual cortex of an infant 20 days old (calcarine sulcus). *A*, Plexiform layer; *B*, layer of small pyramids; *C*, layer of medium-sized pyramids; *a*, descending axon; *b*, recurrent collateral; *c*, dendritic trunk of giant pyramid.

known since the researches of Golgi, Retzius, and myself, I shall limit my remarks to a bare mention of a few peculiarities of their disposition in the visual cortex.

It will be noticed that these cells are generally smaller and more numerous in the visual centres than in other cortical areas. Sometimes the more superficial cells are arranged in one or two regular files and separated from those beneath by a fine dense plexus of fibres.

The small pyramids give rise to the following processes: an axial dendrite, often bifurcated near its origin, which runs to the plexiform layer and terminates in a spray of fine branches, which often ascend to the neighborhood of the pia; basilar divergent dendrites, rather long and repeatedly branched; and, finally, a fine descending axon, which, in most favorable specimens, can be followed down to the neighborhood of the white matter. From the initial portion of its course spring three, four, or a larger number of collateral processes, which traverse, with many subdivisions, in a horizontal or oblique direction, a very considerable extent of the second layer. From the small pyramids lying close to the plexiform layer, and even from some cells more deeply situated, the first two collaterals recurve, ascending sometimes, as Schäfer has discovered, up to their termination in the first layer. However, this termination in the first layer is much less frequent than might be inferred from this authority's descriptions and drawings. In our preparations of the visual and motor cortex of a child a few days old and of a cat twenty-five days old, the great majority of the recurrent collaterals do not cross the boundary of the second layer. Here, in conjunction with many neurites belonging to cells with short axons, they assist in forming a very dense plexus, which contains in its meshes the primary dendrites of the small pyramids. Generally, — and this may be considered as an answer to the authorities who strive to convert the recurrent course of the collaterals into an argument for the doctrine of the cellulipetal conduction of these fibres (v. Lenhossék, Schäfer), — I may affirm that the vast majority of the initial neuritic collaterals — and I consider such all those that arise within the gray matter — always come into contact with some of the dendrites belonging to homologous nerve cells situated at different levels of the same cortical formation. When the cells to which they correspond lie in the same or a deeper plane, the collaterals intended for them take a horizontal, descending, or oblique course; but if the cells of the same category are situated in a more superficial plane than the point of origin of the collateral, they must describe a recurrent arc in order to reach their destination.

Layer of Medium-sized Pyramids.

Being a continuation by insensible gradations of the small pyramidal layer, it contains cells of precisely similar form, differing from the cells of the second layer only in their somewhat greater size, their longer radial dendrite, and, ordinarily, by a larger number of neuritic collaterals (Fig. 4, *C*). In the deeper level of this layer may be observed — very seldom, however — large pyramidal cells, but not so large as those situated in the seventh layer.

Cells with Short Axon of the Second and Third Layers. — These elements, almost as numerous as the pyramidal cells themselves, may be seen scattered irregularly throughout the entire thickness of the two layers. They are generally more numerous near the limits of these layers, that is to say, in the superficial portion of the second and in the deeper level of the third layer.

Although in form and size these elements are very variable, and although there are transitional forms which make it often difficult to distinguish between them and to subdivide them into well-pronounced types, still, by considering the size of the cell body and the character of the axon, they may be divided into the following five classes: (*a*) cells with short ascending axon; (*b*) cells with short descending axon; (*c*) cells with horizontal or oblique axon; (*d*) dwarf or spider-shaped elements; (*e*) fusiform or bipanicled cells, whose axon breaks up into a fibrillar arborization.

a. Cells with Ascending Axon (Fig. 5, *a*, *B*). — As may be seen in Fig. 5, these cells belong to two principal varieties: (*a*) Gigantic cells, with long dendrites (Fig. 5, *A*, *C*). These are quite numerous in the visual cortex, where they occupy preferably the deep portion of the third layer. Their form is stellate, sometimes fusiform or triangular. From their angles arise several varicose, thick, and very long dendrites, often disposed as two brushes, the one ascending, the other descending. The axon takes its origin either from the cell body or from a dendrite. Sometimes it describes an arc, whose concavity is toward the surface, on its way outward to become resolved into an arborization of very few branches. The characteristic feature of this arborization is the enormous length and the horizontal or oblique direction of its terminal twigs. These traverse a very considerable portion of the second and third layers, where they make contact with numberless pyramidal cells. It

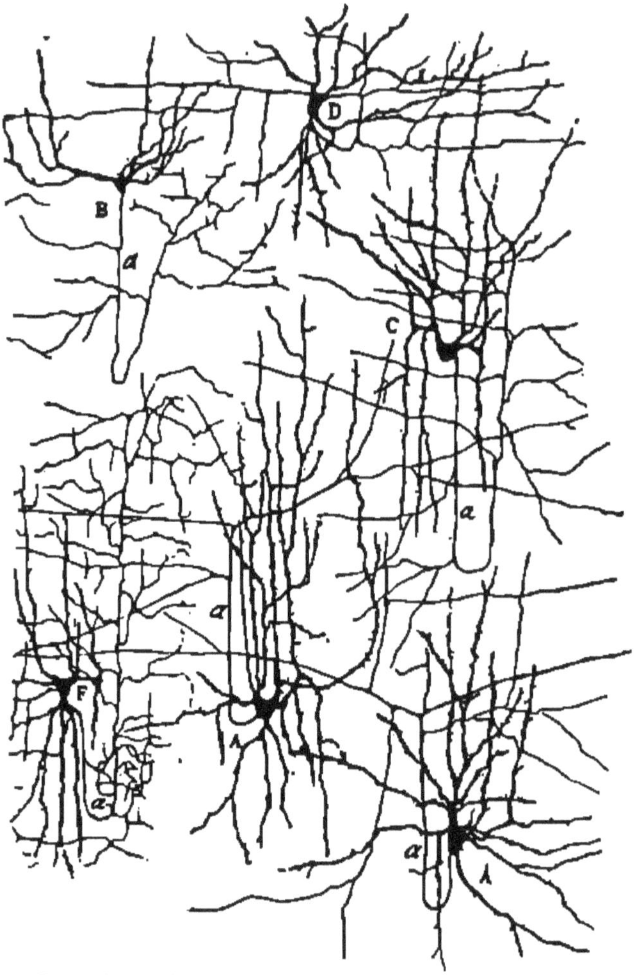

Fig. 5.—Large stellate cells having short ascending axons, 2d and 3d layers, visual cortex, infant 15 days old. *A*, elements of the 3d layer with axons divided into long horizontal branches; *B*, small cell with arched axon from the layer of small pyramids; *C*, large cell with arched axon; *D*, large cell from the boundary of the 1st layer; *F*, cell with arched ascending axon branching in a most complicated manner; *a*, *a*, *a*, axons.

may be added that these gigantic cells may be recognized even in Nissl preparations by their stellate form and considerable size. They correspond, probably, to the globular cells of Bevan Lewis and other writers. (*b*) Medium-sized type: This is a fusiform or stellate cell, whose size does not exceed that of the small or medium-sized pyramids. It is characterized above all by its axon, which is slender and ascending, and which terminates in a complicated arborization with many varicose branches and with relatively small spread at varying levels of the second and third layers. As to the dendrites, they appear varicose and diverge in all directions, but usually do not extend to the first layer (Fig. 5, *F*, and Fig. 8, *D*).

b. Cells with Descending Axons. — These are stellate, triangular, or fusiform, of medium size, and provided with many ascending and descending dendrites. They occur chiefly, as has been pointed out by Schäfer for other regions of the cortex, along the superficial boundary of the layer of small pyramids (Fig. 5, *B*, and 6, *C*). Their axons descend through the second and sometimes through the third layer, giving off to them a few collaterals, and terminate in a diffuse arborization throughout the different levels of these layers. Very frequently this axon, after descending a certain distance, emitting a few collaterals to the layer of small or medium-sized pyramids, traces an arc with concavity toward the surface and ascends to terminate in an arborization, very complicated and with exceedingly varicose branches, in the layer of small pyramids close to the plexiform layer (Fig. 5, *B*). As seen in Fig. 6, which reproduces certain cells of short axons from the visual cortex of the cat, these elements with descending axons are very numerous in other gyrencephalous mammals. We also find a variety of cell, recognized in man, pyriform, uni-polar, whose single descending process gives rise to a bouquet of varicose dendrites and an axon (Fig. 6, *a*, *b*). The collaterals and terminal arborizations of these axons form in the cat a dense plexus throughout the superficial plane of the layer of small pyramids.

The great number of cells with short axons which occur in the most superficial lamina of the layer of small pyramids has induced certain writers, such as Schäfer and Schlapp, to consider this transitional region as a special layer, which they call the layer of superficial polymorphic cells. We cannot subscribe to this innovation because, in spite of the great number of these cells, this transitional lamina contains also a large number of small pyramids, that is to say, cells which, in addition to their morphological varieties, have the same connections as ordinary pyramidal cells. Of course, if for the subdivision of the cortex into layers we take

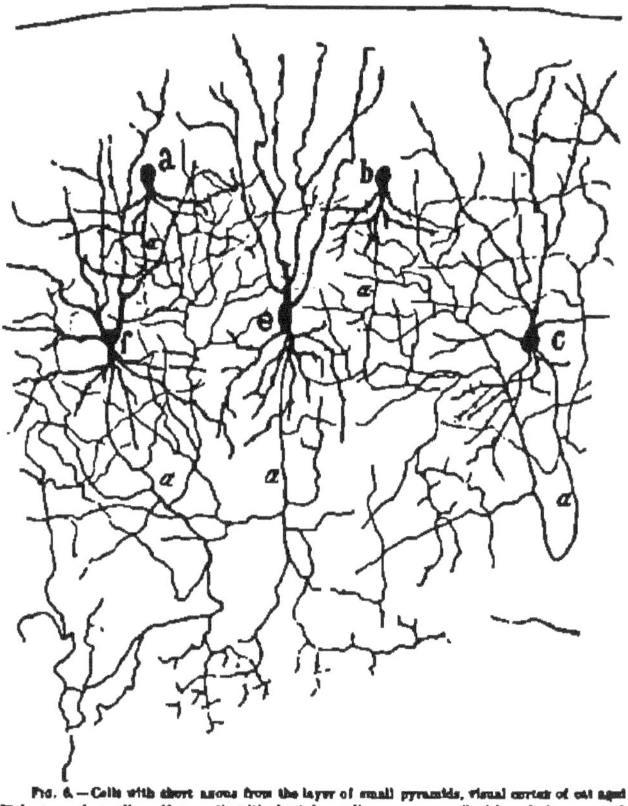

FIG. 6.—Cells with short axons from the layer of small pyramids, visual cortex of cat aged 25 days. *a*, *b*, small pyriform cells with short descending axons; *c*, cell with arched axon; *e*, *f*, cells with descending axons distributed to the medium-sized pyramids of 2d layer.

as our basis of classification the form of cell bodies, independently of other characters, we might be entitled to differentiate between the first and second layer consisting chiefly of stellate cells; because in this region, as is well known, the small pyramids have a stellate or triangular form. But, in assigning to an element a place in his classification, one must not decide from the form alone, which in case of superficially placed pyramids is a function of their position. In fact, we find that the form of these cells varies according to their proximity to the plexiform layer. The true characteristic of a pyramidal cell consists in the presence of a long axon extending down to the white matter and of a spray of dendrites (supported or not by an intermediate trunk) spreading up into the plexiform layer. Now, in the light of such a criterion, it is easy to see that sufficient reason does not exist for making out of the most superficial pyramids a distinct category of cells to be used as a basis for the creation of a new cortical layer.

c. Cells with Horizontal or Oblique Axon (Fig. 7). — These elements, which are angular or fusiform, with their long axes more or less horizontal, possess few, but rather long, dendrites. Their axon arises generally from the lateral aspect of the cell body or from a thick polar dendrite, takes from the first a horizontal or oblique direction and, after giving off a few collaterals, terminates, sometimes after extending to a considerable distance, in an arborization widely spread but with few branches. In certain cells of this category, it is shorter and subdivides in the immediate neighborhood of the cell body (Fig. 7, *E, C*).

d. Dwarf or Spider-shaped Cells. — Brought to our attention by Cl. Sala in the corpus striatum of birds, mentioned also by my brother in the cerebral cortex of batrachians and reptiles, these strange elements are notably abundant and of very pronounced character in the cerebral cortex of man and gyrencephalous mammals. They are found irregularly scattered in all layers of the visual area. Their soma is very small, not exceeding the diameter of the nucleus by more than five or six μ. About the nucleus is a thin lamina of protoplasm which is drawn out into a great number of dendrites, delicately varicose, radiating, slightly branched and short. The appearance of these dendrites is such that one might mistake the cell, at first sight, for a neuroglia corpuscle with short processes. But, examining them with a high power, we recognize at once that their slender dendrites do not possess collateral appendages (contact granules), so characteristic of processes of neuroglia cells. Finally, attentive examination reveals the axon, a delicate fibre, which becomes resolved immediately into a very dense varicose arborization of incomparable fineness. Often this terminal plexus is so extremely fine that it appears through an ordinary objective as a yellowish or brownish spot in the neighborhood of the cell and resembling somewhat a granular precipi-

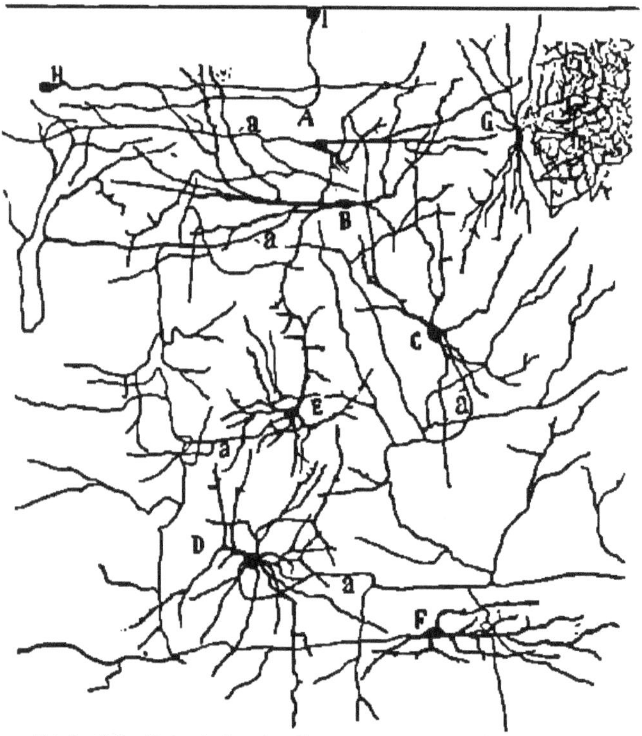

FIG. 7.—Cells with short horizontal or oblique axons situated in the 2d and 3d layers, visual cortex of infant a few days old. *A*, *B*, cells with axons almost horizontal from 2d layer; *C*, *D*, *E*, cells with short axon diffusely branched; *F*, *H*, *I*, pyriform cells of the 1st layer, whose significance is still uncertain; *G*, small cell with very short axon diffusely branching within the 1st layer.

tate. In some cases this arborization is coarser and can be seen with a Zeiss objective D or E. At the level of the superior boundary of the layer of small pyramids, in the visual cortex of the child and even of other mammals, may often be seen a dense plexus of exceedingly slender branching fibrils. Their original fibre appears to come from the deeper levels of the 2d layer (Fig. 8, *A*, *B*, *C*). These terminal plexuses often take the impregnation irregularly, which gives the appearance of brownish or coffee-colored spots scattered and sometimes arranged in a row just underneath the plexiform layer. At first I was not successful in tracking satisfactorily the fibres of origin and, therefore, hesitated as to stating the significance of these interesting arborizations. Very recently, however, in two or three fortunate specimens I have been able to demonstrate the connection between this plexus and the fine ascending axons of certain small cells situated in the deeper level of the 2d or outer level of the 3d layer. I am, therefore, now inclined to consider this intermediate, or subplexiform, nerve plexus as consisting of terminal arborizations intended for the small pyramids. The fibres of origin spring from more deeply situated spider-shaped cells very hard to impregnate. I may add that these plexuses are not lacking in the cat and dog, although in these animals the fibrillæ are not so numerous nor so extremely fine as in the human brain. Permit me also to add that they occur in all regions of the cortex, although up to the present we have obtained the best impregnation of them in the visual area.

e. Small Bipanicled Cells. — In the visual region, as well as in other areas, of the human cortex we find in profusion certain small cells vertically elongated. Their axon presents the very singular feature of breaking up into long slender brushes of terminal fibrillæ. At first, I thought that these singular cells were forms characteristic of the acoustic area, for here they are remarkably developed and very numerous. Further investigation, however, has convinced me that they occur in all parts of the cortex, disposed in greatest numbers along the lower level of the 2d and 3d layers (Fig. 8 and Fig. 11, *E*, *F*).

As stated above, we are discussing the small spindle-shaped cells with poles radially disposed, which give rise to groups of dendrites, slender, unprovided with contact granules, very finely varicose, and often arranged in long ascending and descending brushes. In some cases these are so fine that on superficial examination they might be mistaken for delicate neuritic arborizations. But the most striking peculiarity of these cells concerns the subdivisions and course of their axons. This process is very delicate. It ascends or descends a certain distance, then generally gives off a few collaterals at right angles which soon subdivide into

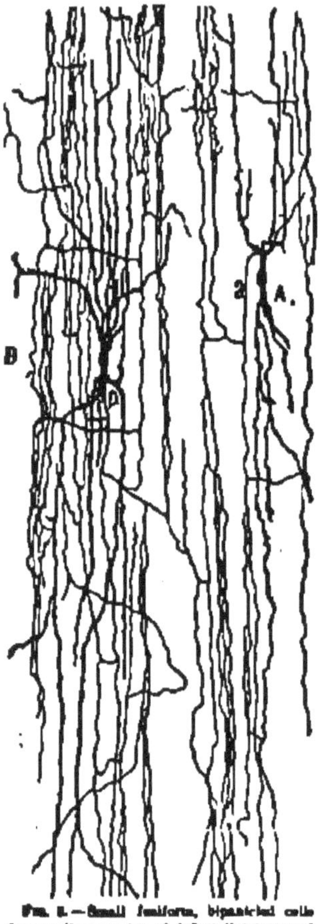

Fig. [illegible].—Small fusiform, bipanicled cells from auditory cortex of infant (1st temporal convolution). *A*, cell giving origin to a descending axon moderately branched; *B*, cell whose axon breaks up into a number of pencils of very long ascending and descending fibrils; *a*, axon. (Examined with Zeiss apochromatic obj. 1.30.)

ascending or descending fibrillæ, and finally it breaks up into brushes of very slender filaments which run radially, extending throughout almost the entire thickness of the cortex. As a whole this arborization with its initial collaterals forms one or several parallel brushes, the fibrils of which skirt the trunks of the pyramids and adapt themselves to the cell bodies, over which they appear to creep, like the creeping fibres of the cerebellum on the branches and bodies of the Purkinje cells.

In the brain of the human infant at birth these arborizations have not attained complete development and present but few vertical branchlets. It is not until twenty or thirty days after birth that we can observe the long and complicated terminal brushes. In certain areas, the acoustic, for example, each neurite may form as many as five ascending or descending brushes. The fibrils of which they consist are so delicate that in order to see them well we must use the highest apochromatic objectives.

If now we consider all the different kinds of cells having short axons, of which we have given a somewhat fastidious description, from the point of view of their connections and their probable functions, we may characterize them as special cells of association. The form of their cell body and the disposition of the axon vary according to the number, form, and position of the cells to which they must convey nerve stimuli. Thus cells with a horizontal axon must be intended to transmit impulses to elements, probably pyramidal cells, which occur at the same level in the cortex. Those whose axon is vertical, ascending or descending, would naturally transmit impulses to elements of different layers. Those which are bipanicled would serve to associate dynamically a great number of pyramids in vertical series. Finally, the small, spider-shaped cells may have for their function association of groups of pyramids very close together. Unfortunately for this theory, we do not know from which nerve fibres all these elements of association receive their initial stimuli. Accordingly, we must be resigned to remain in ignorance as to the path of the afferent impulses and, as well, in regard to the special influence which these elements must exercise. It seems very probable, however, that their function consists not only in facilitating the spread of incoming stimuli, but also in adding to it something new, some specific modification which cannot now be determined. We shall return to this point in our general conclusions upon this work. But we may see from the above how many paths nature has opened up to render association of nerve impulses possible in every direction and through any distance. That which proves the importance of these association cells and leads us to surmise that they play an important psychic rôle is the fact that they are extremely numerous in the human brain. They are found in the animal brain as well, but are not numerous and are usually confined to the boundary of the 1st layer.

I conclude here my exposition of the prosy topics that I chose as the theme of this lecture. And nothing remains except to thank you for the attention and good will which you have shown me in spite of the extreme dryness of the subject-matter.

LECTURE II.

Layer of the Large Stellate Cells.

My recent researches in the visual cortex of man have led to the unexpected discovery of certain large cells of stellate form possessing an axon which descends to the white matter. Figs. 9 and 10 represent very clearly the most common forms of these strange elements. They are differentiated immediately from pyramidal cells by their lack of a radial trunk. Generally speaking, the cell body is stellate, but there is no lack of semilunar, triangular, and even mitral forms. Their dendrites are thick and much branched, and extend in all directions, especially horizontally, without ever leaving the territory of the 4th layer. In man these processes are sparsely provided with contact granules, while they are very numerous in the homologous cells of the mammalia (cat and dog).

As to the axon, it is rather large, arises from the inferior surface of the cell body, descends through the 4th layer, sometimes tracing here accommodation curves, and after crossing the 5th, 6th, 7th and 8th layer, passes into the white matter and is there continued as a medullated nerve fibre. In passing through the 4th and 5th layers it gives off three, four, or a larger number of, often, very large collaterals which end in arborizations extending over a considerable area in these layers. It is not uncommon to see these collaterals taking a recurrent course to become distributed in planes above the point of origin; but in this they never trespass on the boundaries of the 4th and 5th layers. Finally, and this is a very frequent disposition in the adult cortex, this axon, after having given off its collaterals, becomes notably finer. Taking into consideration its diameter, sometimes less than that of its first collateral, we might be led to mistake it for the latter rather than a true continuation of the axon. We shall return to this peculiarity, which is presented by many cells in the visual cortex. The stellate cells present a similar character in the adult human cortex, and I reproduce in Fig. 10 their principal types impregnated (long method of Golgi) in the case of a man thirty years old. The only difference that we remark between these cells in the adult and infant brain is the greater development of the dendrites, which extend long distances in horizontal planes in the adult. The volume of the soma also

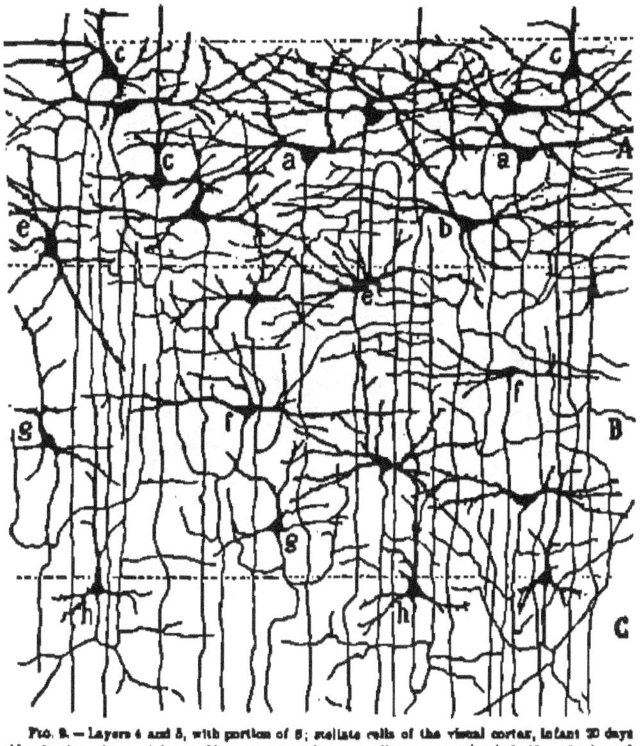

FIG. 9. — Layers 4 and 5, with portion of 6; stellate cells of the visual cortex, infant 20 days old, calcarine sulcus. *A*, layer of large stellate cells; *a*, semilunar corpuscle; *b*, fusiform horizontal cell; *c*, cell with radial trunk; *e*, cell with arched axon; *B*, layer of small stellate cells; *f*, horizontal fusiform cells; *g*, triangular cells with heavy arching collaterals; *C*, layer of small pyramids with arched axon; *h*, cells of this type.

increases with age, which shows that growth of dendrites does not depend solely on the lengthening out of the initial or primitive protoplasm of the cell, but also on an actual augmentation of cell substance.

Cells with Short Axon. — As it happens in other cortical layers, the 4th contains a large number of cells with short axon. The following three types may be distinguished: —

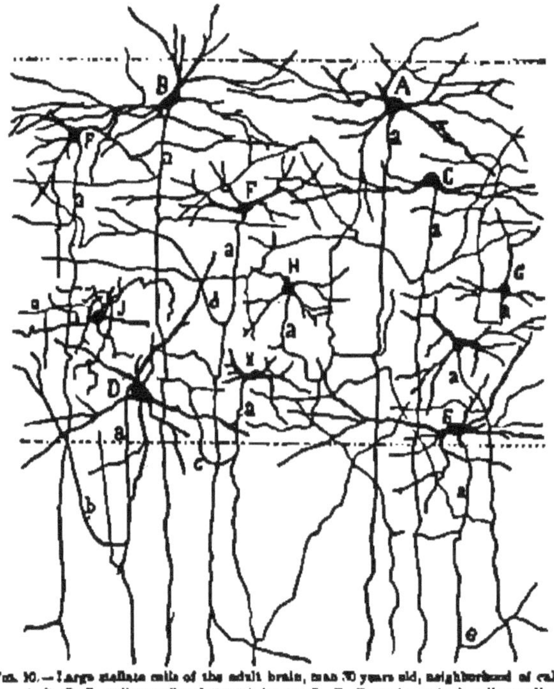

Fig. 10. — Large stellate cells of the adult brain, man 30 years old, neighborhood of calcarine sulcus. *A*, *B*, *C*, *F*, stellate cells of the 4th layer; *D*, *E*, *E*, medium-sized stellate cells of 5th layer; *G*, *H*, *J*, cells with short axon. (Golgi's slow method.)

(*a*) Cells, stellate, fusiform, or triangular, whose axon ascends to be distributed in the superficial plane of the 4th layer (Fig. 11, *A*, *C*, *D*).

(*b*) Cells of similar form and position, but whose axon distributes itself to the layer of medium-sized pyramids (Fig. 11, *B*).

(*c*) Spider-shaped cells with a notably short axon, as may be seen in Fig. 13, *E*.

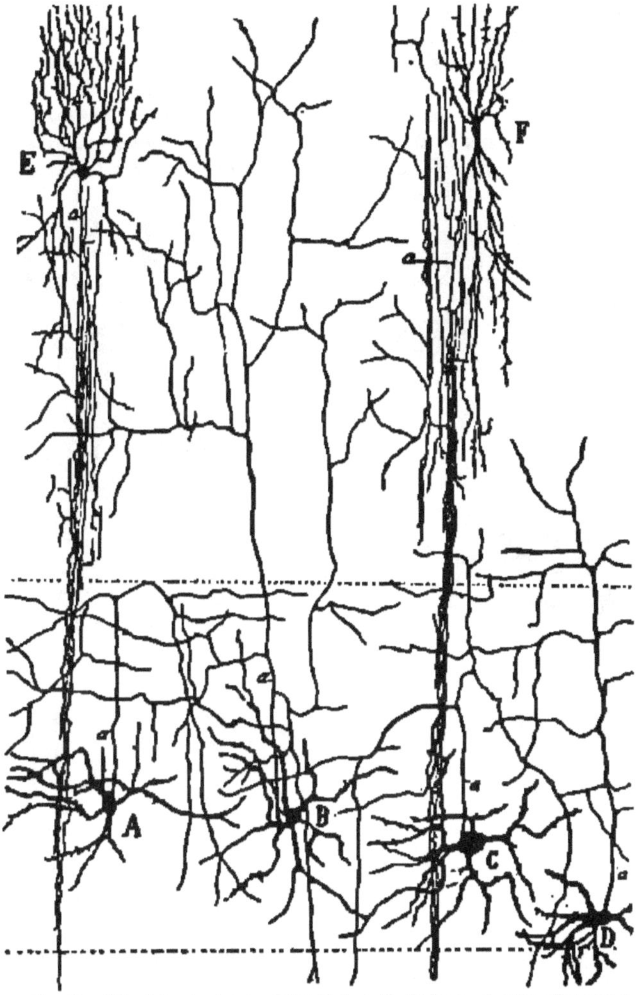

FIG. 11.—Cells of the visual cortex, infant 15 days old, 4th layer. *A*, cell sending axon to superior portion of 4th layer; *B*, cell whose axon branches to the 3d and 4th layers; *C*, another cell sending branches into the 3d, 4th, and 5th layers; *E*, *F*, very small bipanicled cells from layer of medium-sized pyramids; *a*, axon.

The cells with ascending axon are remarkable on account of the curious arched course of the latter. It has in some cases initial collaterals.

The stellate cells as well as other cells with the short axon are also found in the cortex of the cat and dog, where they form a well-defined layer of their own, corresponding, considering the character of its elements, to the 4th, 5th, and 6th in the visual cortex of the child, Fig. 12. Cells

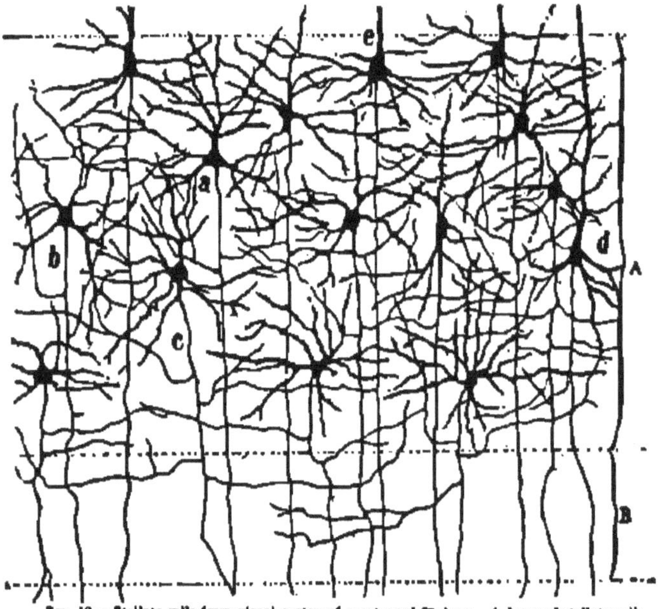

FIG. 12.—Stellate cells from visual cortex of a cat aged 25 days. *A*, layer of stellate cells corresponding to the 4th and 5th layers in man; *B*, layer of giant pyramids; *a*, *b*, *c*, stellate cells having long descending axons; *d*, *e*, medium-sized pyramids among the stellate cells.

with short ascending axon are especially numerous and are characterized by being fusiform in shape and by the contact granules which cover the cell body and principal dendrites. Besides the existence of cells in the cerebral cortex whose axons ascend, but do not make their way into the first layer as do those from Martinotti's elements, is the fact that I long since discovered while working upon the motor cortex of the small mammals; this is, as my latest observations show, that these elements are very numerous, and that each cortical layer, or better, that each layer of a plexiform aspect, contains a special kind of this element. In addition, as we shall see in a moment, these cells form a constant factor in all the cortical layers in which nerve fibres incoming from the white matter make their terminal arborizations.

Fifth Layer, or Layer of Small Stellate Cells.

This layer, which corresponds to the greater part of the stripe of Vicq d'Azyr, when examined in Nissl preparations appears to contain an enormous number of small rounded elements which might be mistaken for scattered nuclei not surrounded by protoplasm. But in these same preparations we may still detect, beside these corpuscles, a few others, scattered here and there, of stellate or triangular form and medium or large size, very similar to the great stellate cells of the 4th layer. Golgi's method reveals to us the great complexity of the 5th layer, and by this means we have succeeded in differentiating as many as five kinds of elements. The following are the most common types: —

(*a*) *Stellate Cells of Medium Size.* — These are exactly similar to the stellate cells of the 4th layer. They are not numerous, and lie irregularly scattered in all levels of the 5th layer. Their dendrites diverge, but run for the most part horizontally, and do not pass beyond the layer of their cells of origin. Their axons descend and, after emitting a few collaterals to the 5th layer, make their way to the white matter. In some cases their collaterals are given off lower down, in the 6th layer, and then their course is recurrent, because they must make their terminal arborizations between homonymous cells (Fig. 9, *g*, *f*).

(*b*) *Cells with Ascending Axon.* — These are fusiform or triangular, disposed with long axis vertical. Their axon is similar to that of cells of this type in the 4th layer. That is to say, after ascending a certain distance it forms a terminal arborization of arching branches distributed among the elements of the overlying layer. From its initial portion spring a few collaterals which are distributed to the 5th layer (Fig. 18, *A*, *B*, *C*).

(*c*) *Ovoid or Stellate Corpuscles (properly designated, Granules).* — These rarely exceed in diameter more than ten or twelve μ. They are the most numerous element of the 5th layer. Their soma is ovoid, spheroidal, and even polygonal in form and gives rise to three, four, or more fine, smooth dendrites, which terminate, after a short, wavy course, within the limits of the 5th layer. Their axons are very delicate and

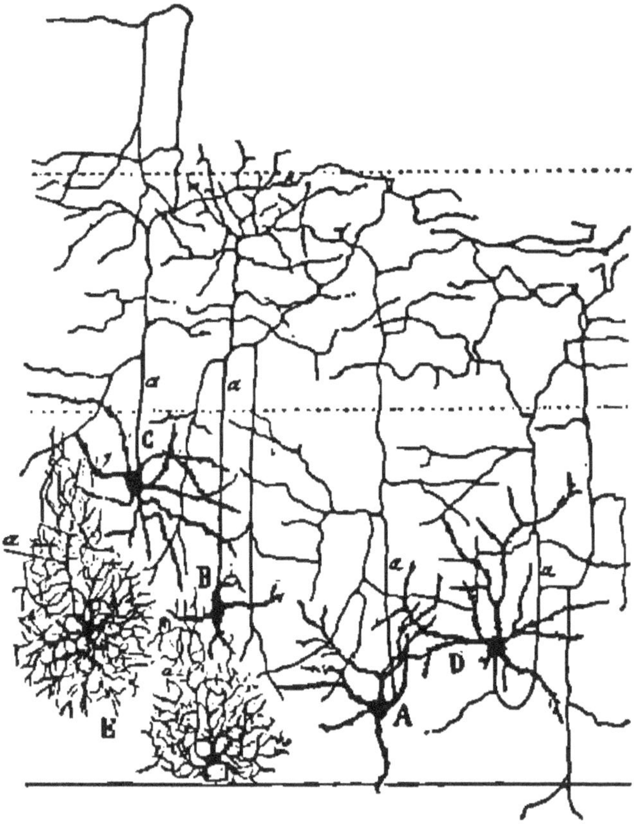

FIG. 13.—Cells in the 6th layer with ascending axon, visual cortex of infant aged 15 days. *A*, *B*, cells whose axons subdivide in the layer of large stellate cells; *C*, cells whose axons give rise to branches destined for the layer of medium-sized pyramids; *D*, cell with arched axon, the initial portion of which gives rise to branches for the 4th, 5th, and even 6th layers; *E*, very small cells, arachniform, with delicate ascending axons; *a*, axon.

take a great variety of directions, — ascending, descending, or horizontal, — and finally end in an extended arborization of few branchlets distributed exclusively to the very midst of the 5th layer (Fig. 14).

(*d*) *Dwarf or Spider-shaped Corpuscles.* — Of these there is no lack in

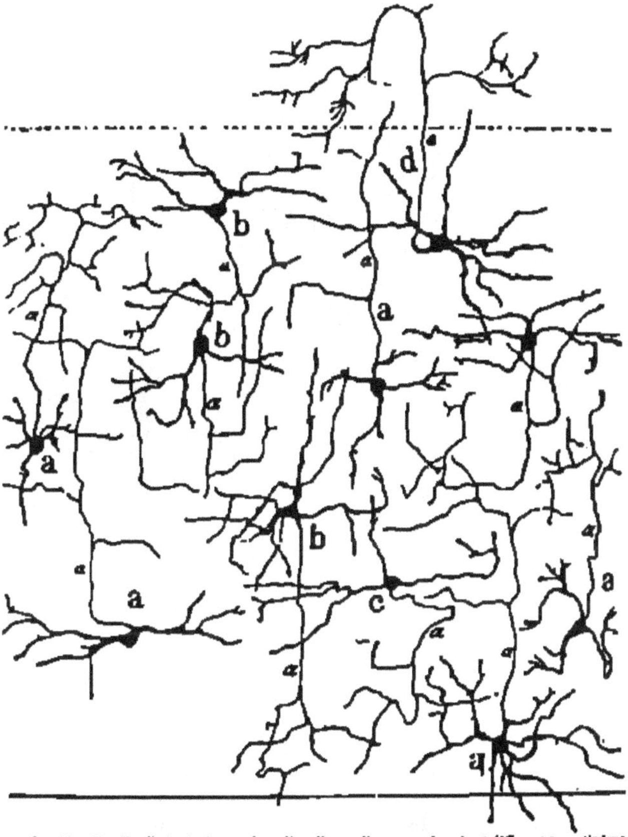

Fig. 14. — Small cells in the layer of small stellate cells, possessing short diffuse axons (infant 20 days). a, cells with delicate ascending axons; b, c, cells with descending axons; d, larger cell whose axon forms its terminal arborization in the 4th layer; α, axon.

this layer, whose nerve plexus they help to bewilder. Their very tiny, often ascending, axon resolves itself very soon into an extremely dense,

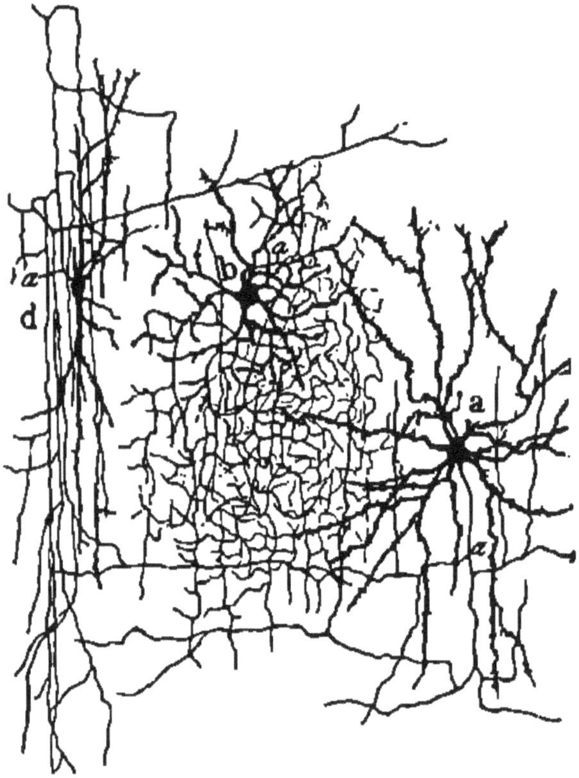

FIG. 15. — Cells with short axons of the layer of stellate cells from the visual cortex of a cat aged 25 days. *a*, large cell whose descending axon subdivides in the deeper level of the 4th layer (4th and 5th of man); *b*, arachniform cell whose axon forms a fine and very dense plexus; *d*, fusiform cell whose axon is resolved into vertical branches.

fine arborization close to the cell. In the dense masses of these arborizations we notice spaces, which probably correspond to groups of granules.

The cells with short axons are very abundant in the visual cortex of the cat, as may be observed by examining Figs. 15 and 16. Among them the more abundant types are: *a*, fusiform cells whose ascending axon is distributed to the superior levels of the layer in question (4th and 5th in man) (Fig. 16, *D*); *b*, large stellate cells with descending axon forming their terminal arborizations in the deeper levels of this layer (Fig. 15, *a*);

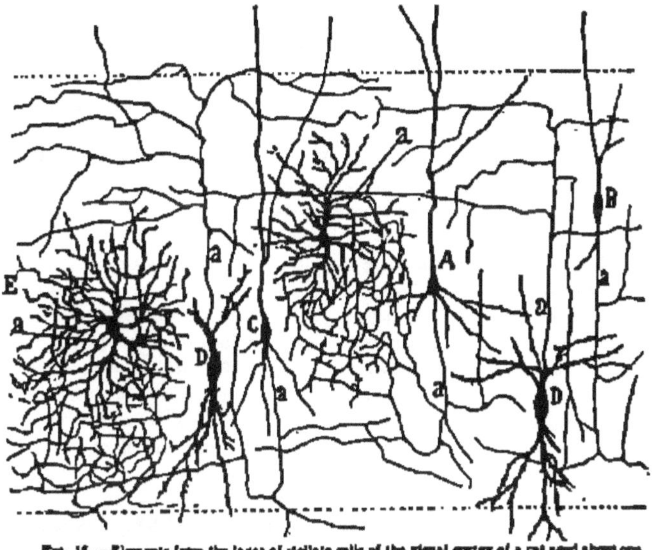

FIG. 16. — Elements from the layer of stellate cells of the visual cortex of a cat aged about one month. *A*, *B*, *C*, small pyramids with axons arched and ascending; *D*, large fusiform cells with ascending axons; *E*, arachniform cells with short axon; *a*, axon.

c, stellate-arachniform cells whose axon forms a most complicated arborization (Figs. 15, *b*, and 16, *E*); *d*, bipanicled cells larger than corresponding cells in the human brain (Fig. 15, *d*).

Nerve Plexus of the 4th and 5th layers of the Cortex. One of the chief characteristics of these layers consists in the very dense plexus of medullated fibres extending among their nerve cells. This is formed by two kinds of fibres: (1) Exogenous fibres, that is to say those coming from the white matter, probably continuations of the cerebro-optic tract. (2) Endogenous fibres, formed by the terminal arborizations of the axons which come from cells of the 4th and 5th or the underlying layers.

Exogenous Fibres. — I have already stated that Gennari's or Vicq d'Azyr's stripe corresponds chiefly to the 5th layer, but also includes part of the 4th. However, the true composition of this stripe cannot be seen in Weigert-Pal preparations, because the hematoxylin stains only the large or medium-sized fibres which possess a myeline sheath. Now these fibres, as we shall presently see, represent but a very small portion of the components of Gennari's stripes. Very fortunately Golgi's method, applied to the brain of an infant at birth or but a few days old, affords us a very clear view of the medullated and unmedullated fibres which make up this plexus. This method accordingly furnishes us a means of analyzing its origin and manner of termination. Permit me to state at the outset that the principal contingent of exogenous fibres is represented by a considerable number of fibres from the white matter, which I shall henceforth call, in virtue of their physiological significance, optic fibres.

The optic fibres are easily distinguished from the axons of the pyramids by their direction, which is oblique (in some cases they are tortuous or even stair-shaped), by their large calibre, often exceeding that of axons of the giant pyramids; finally by the fact that, instead of going to a cell as its axon, they repeatedly divide dichotomously, each branch resolving itself into a perfectly free terminal arborization spreading almost horizontally through the extent of the 4th and 5th layers. Fig. 17 reproduces the appearance of the optic plexus in a preparation in which it was impregnated almost alone. I call your attention to the fact that these optic fibres send off no collaterals, or very few, in passing through the deeper layers (9th, 8th, 7th, 6th), but immediately on reaching the 5th layer their final ramification begins. This occurs in many ways. Some fibres divide at different levels of the 5th layer into two equal or unequal branches which run horizontally to great distances, becoming resolved into a great number of collaterals which ramify throughout the entire thickness of the layer. Other fibres may be seen which, after giving off a few long collaterals during their ascent through the 5th layer, reach up to the extreme limit of the 5th layer and here become horizontal. There is no lack of fibres which ascend directly up to the limit of the layer of medium-sized pyramids and there describe arcs, and even very long wavy courses, and end by descending, dividing as they descend, through the 4th and 5th layers. Finally, from the arching portion of some of these latter fibres fine collaterals may be seen to spring on their way to the layer of medium-sized pyramids, where they disappear after a few divisions. To sum up, the optic fibres terminate almost exclusively within the 4th and 5th layers. In only two instances have I discovered collaterals of optic fibres which appeared to form their terminal arborizations within the 1st layer.

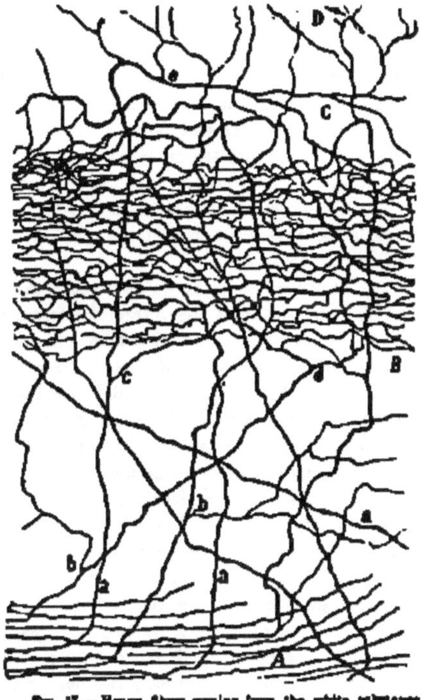

FIG. 17.—Heavy fibres coming from the white substance and subdividing in Gennari's stripe; visual cortex of infant aged three days. *A*, white substance; *B*, layer of small stellar cells; *C*, arched fibres of 4th layer; *D*, border of layer of medium-sized pyramids; *a*, trunks of the incoming fibres; *b*, collaterals for the deeper layers; *c*, ascending collaterals destined for the more superficial layers.

This plexus of optic fibres is one of the richest and densest to be found in the gray matter of the brain. If it is completely impregnated, which frequently occurs in an infant brain fifteen or twenty days old, it appears as a bewildering meshwork of wavy fibres, besprinkled with vacant spaces corresponding to the cell bodies of these layers (Fig. 18, *B*).

I may add that the appearance of this plexus differs a little in the two layers (Fig. 18). In the 4th layer its fibres are larger and often disposed in arches or horizontal bars, its arborizations are loose and separated by ample spaces in conformity to the size of the great stellate cells; while in the 5th layer it consists of fine varicose fibrils arranged in an extremely dense lattice work with small spaces, corresponding to the small size of the medium-sized stellate cells (Fig. 18, *B*).

In the preceding brief description I have called the large exogenous fibres optic fibres. But what reasons have we to suppose that these fibres actually come in from the primary optic centres? We must acknowledge, at the outset, that the proof of their optical origin is not perfect; but there is no lack of facts which favor such a view. Some of these facts are the following: —

(*a*) In the minute brains, as, for example, that of a newborn mouse, we can follow these fibres in some cases to the radiation of Gratiolet.

(*b*) The fibres which are on their way to Gennari's plexus are very large, larger than the axons of the giant pyramids or those of cells of intercortical association.

(*c*) In the motor cortex we have found that large fibres distributed in a similar way actually come in from the corona radiata.

(*d*) In the visual cortex of a man who became blind I have discovered, by using Nissl's method, a perceptible atrophy of the stellate cells of the 4th and 5th layers. A similar case has been recently reported by Cramer; and this fact would seem to point to an intimate union between these elements and the act of visual perception, a union whose material bond is probably represented by the exogenous fibres of Gennari's plexus.

(*e*) Granted that the visual cortex must receive a great number of fibres from the radiation of Gratiolet, it is natural to refer to this source the fibres which form Gennari's plexus; since this is the distinctive plexus of this region of the brain.

From the probable fact that the plexus of Gennari's stripe is the terminus of the optic fibres, we may draw the important conclusion that the cells of the 4th and 5th layers represent histologically the principal substratum for visual sensation; because up to this point in the cortex sensory impulses heap up on the centripetal side, and here begin to become centrifugal.

Another conclusion not less interesting follows from it: for an ensemble of anatomico-physiological facts seem to show that the region of the calcarine fissure is not the locus of visual memories, but only that of sensations of luminosity, and that the residues of the latter must go (in order to become transformed into latent images) to other nerve centres. We are naturally led to consider the long axon of the 4th and 5th layers as the principal, if not the only, path joining these two kinds of centres.

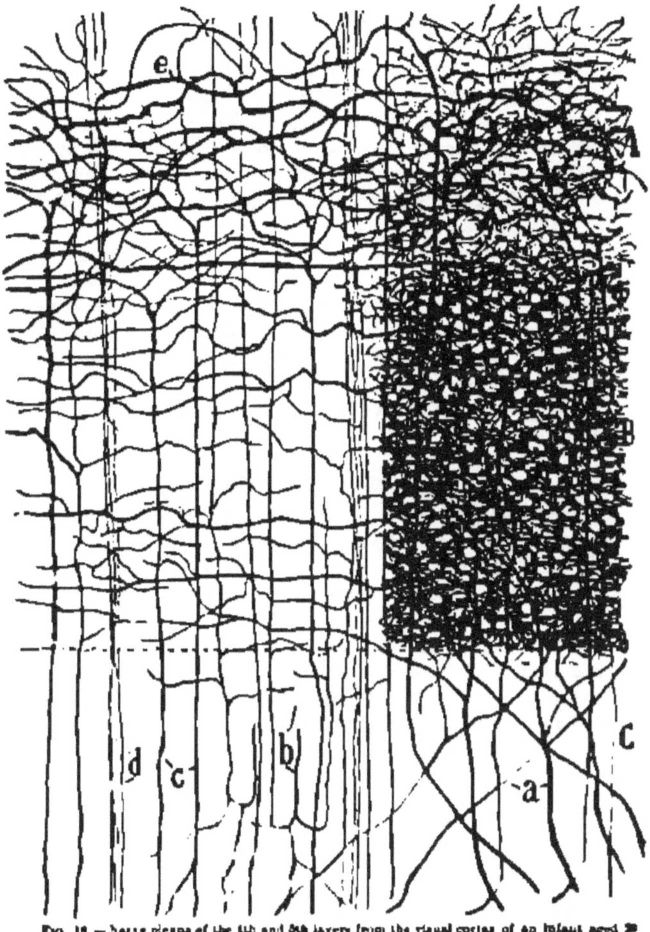

FIG. 18 — Nerve plexus of the 4th and 5th layers from the visual cortex of an infant aged 20 days. *A*, *B*, *C*, respectively, layers 4th, 5th, and 6th; *a*, trunks of optic fibres; *b*, axons of cells of the 6th layer; *c*, ascending axons of cells in the 5th layer; *d*, bundle of axons descending from the medium-sized pyramids; *e*, transverse arches of the optic fibres giving rise to ascending collaterals.

These fibres would function, accordingly, in carrying the copy, or the sensory residue, received in Gennari's plexus, to appropriate association areas of the brain. Their psychic rôle is thus a very important one, and we should suppose that their interruption would produce psychic blindness as certainly as the destruction of the occipital lobe itself.

The plexus of Gennari is well developed in other mammals, but the terminal arborizations are never as complicated as in man (Fig. 19). Further than this I have not been able to demonstrate any definite differences in arrangement at various levels of the layer of stellate cells. However, it has seemed to me that the terminal branches, which are very varicose, tend to be especially dense in the superficial planes of this layer.

Endogenous Fibres. — In addition to the large nerve fibres entering from the white matter, Gennari's plexus contains either terminal or collateral ramifications of fibres which arise in the cells proper of the visual cortex. Such are: —

(1) The very numerous branches from the small cells with short axon of the 5th layer.

(2) The terminal neuritic arborizations of cells with ascending axon lying in the 6th, 7th, and 8th layers.

(3) Arborizations of collateral branches supplied to the 4th and 5th layers by the long descending axons of the stellate cells.

(4) Terminal arborizations from the fusiform or triangular cells of the 4th and 5th layers which have ascending axons, etc.

The plexus formed by all the above fibrils is usually finer than that of the optical fibres. In order to make out to the best advantage its extreme complication throughout its whole extent, we must study it in the cortex of an infant from fifteen to twenty-five days old, a period at which the terminal arborizations of the visual cells are completely developed. It has seemed to me that the endogenous arborizations are more numerous in the 4th than in the 5th layer. We may notice also that they show a tendency to form true nests surrounding the stellate cells of these two median layers.

Sixth Layer.

Plexiform and poor in cells in Nissl preparations, it contains a large number of small pyramidal or ovoid elements with long axis vertical and provided, as may be seen in good Golgi specimens, with a radial trunk extending up to the first layer. They have also a few short basilar

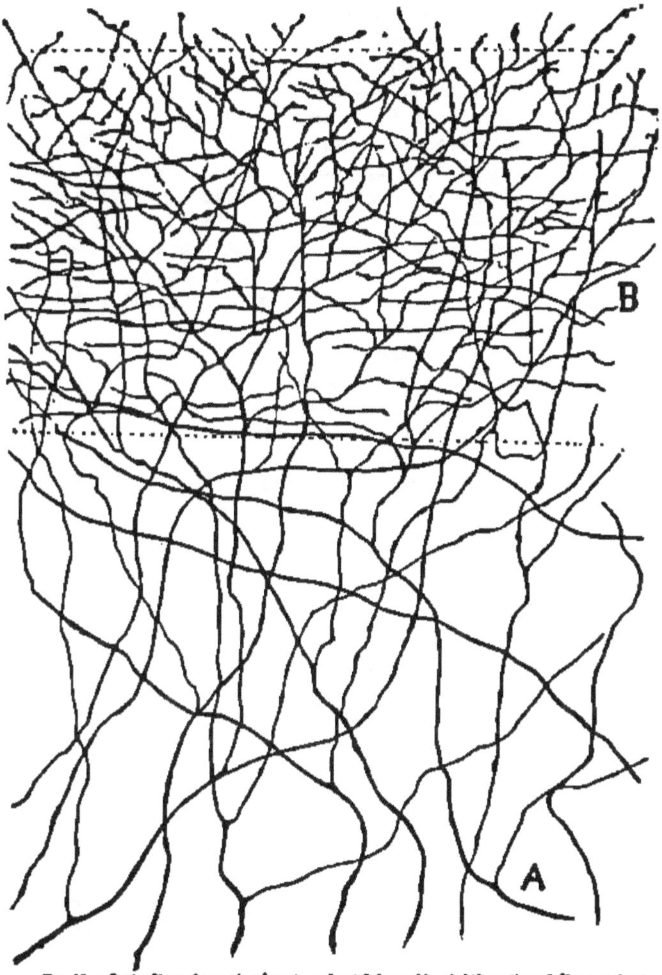

FIG. 19. — Optic fibres from visual cortex of cat 8 days old. *A*, bifurcation of fibres a short distance from the white matter; *B*, nerve plexus in layer of stellate cells (4th and 6th layers in man).

dendrites, descending or oblique and little branched. But the most distinctive character of these small elements consists in the course of their axons. These descend a short distance, then curve upward and ascend through the 6th, 5th, and 4th layers, to which they give a few collaterals, and end in a manner which I have not been able to discover. In some cases these axons have branched close to their origin and, instead of one, describe two arcs continued by ascending fibres. Other axons, moreover, make even a greater number of loops. From the convex aspect of these curves, as well as from the ascending portion of the axons, within the 6th layer spring numerous collaterals which branch throughout the entire thickness of the layer. Some descend still further and subdivide in the plexus of the 7th layer, that is to say, at the level of the giant pyramids (Fig. 20, *B*).

Besides these small cells, which are certainly the most abundant, we find two other cellular types: (*a*) Cells of stellate form and medium size. They possess radiating dendrites which do not usually pass beyond the 6th layer. Their axons ascend and form an arborization throughout the extent of the 6th, 5th, and 4th layers. (*b*) Ordinary pyramidal cells, very scarce, of medium or large size. They have precisely the same characters as the pyramids of the 7th layer.

Seventh Layer or Layer of Giant Pyramids.

Solitary Cells of Meynert.—This layer contains one or two irregular and discontinuous files of giant pyramids, which appear, here and there, lost as it were in a dense and extended plexus. To this plexus the layer owes its finely granular appearance, which may be seen even in preparations stained by Nissl's method (Fig. 20, *C*, and Fig. 22, *B*).

The cells in question, like other pyramidal cells, possess a very large radial trunk which ends in a flattened spray of horizontal branches in the lower levels of the plexiform layer. The cells are also provided with a few many-branched basilar dendrites which distribute themselves throughout the layer and, finally, with a great number of horizontal dendrites forming a plexus which would seem to provide connections between these cells through long distances. This is such a characteristic feature that by its presence alone we are able to distinguish the visual from all other cortical areas. The axon of the giant pyramids is very large, extends almost vertically through the 8th and 9th layers, and is continued as a fibre of the white matter. Collaterals spring from its initial portion which ramify in the 7th and even the superficial levels of the 6th layer.

In addition to the giant pyramids, which in some cases are not at all

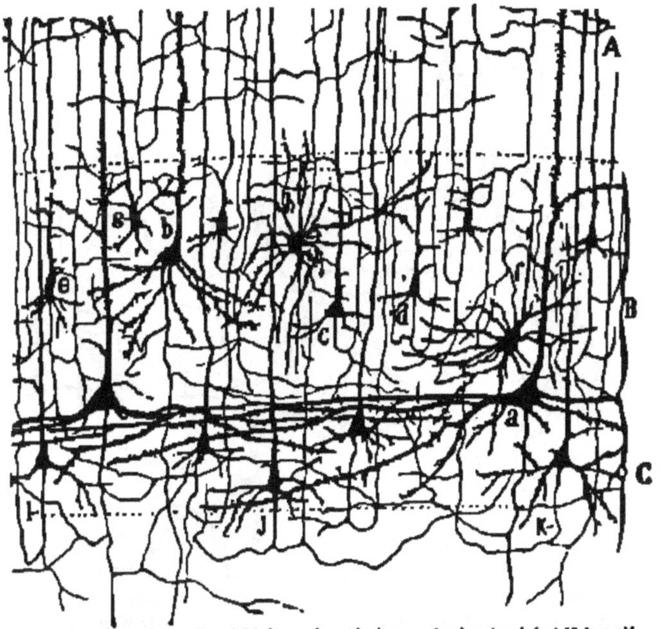

FIG. 20.—Cells of the 6th and 7th layers from the human visual cortex, infant 15 days old. *A*, 5th layer; *B*, 6th layer; *C*, 7th layer; *a*, giant pyramid; *b*, medium-sized pyramid with descending axon; *c*, small pyramid with arched ascending axon; *d*, pyramid whose axon presents two arches; *e*, pyramid whose axon gives rise to several arched fibres; *h*, *f*, *g*, stellate cells with ascending axons ramified in the 5th and 6th layers; *i*, *J*, *K*, pyramids whose axons arch and subdivide in the 7th and 8th layers.

numerous, the 7th layer contains: (*a*) a number of medium-sized pyramids possessing the same characters; (*b*) several small elements exactly similar to those of the 6th layer, the cells with the complicated forked and arched axons distributed in the manner above described (Fig. 20, *K*, *i*, *J*); (*c*) in addition may be found medium-sized stellate cells situated in the

7th and 8th layers (Fig. 21, *A*, *B*). The very remarkable feature of the latter cells consists in their terminal arborizations. Their neurites take at first an ascending or oblique course, divide into two, and then give rise to a large number of oblique or horizontal branches which occupy

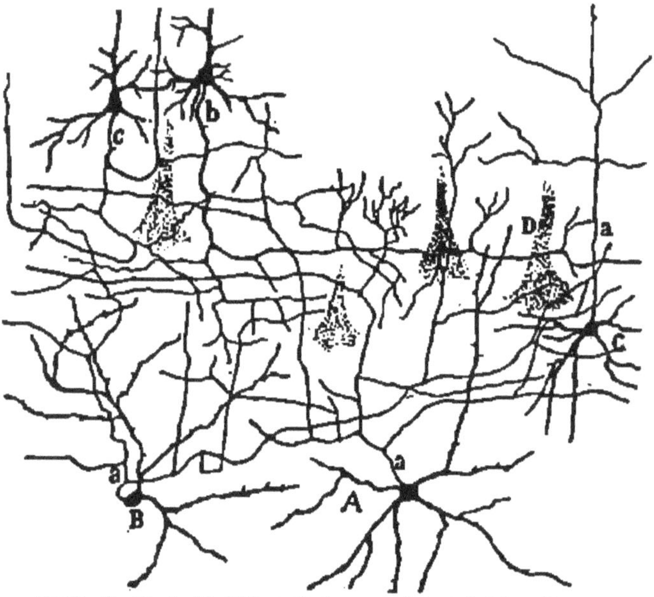

FIG. 21. — Special cells of the 7th layer, visual cortex of infant. *A*, *B*, stellate cells whose axons form terminal arborizations in the layer of giant pyramids; *C*, cell with long ascending axon distributed to the 6th and 5th layers; *D*, giant pyramid of 7th layer; *c*, *b*, axons of small pyramids of 6th layer.

a good part of the 7th layer. In the brain at birth their terminals present no special peculiarities; but in one twenty days old I have found that a number of these arborizations surround the giant pyramids, forming terminal nests. Only their arrangement is not so definite here as in the motor region, where we find it wonderfully developed. (Compare with description below.)

Eighth Layer.

Examined in Nissl preparations this layer presents a mass of medium-sized pyramids and a remarkably dense formation of granules. This is the reason Meynert and other writers have called this the layer of deep granules or inferior granular layer.

Golgi's method reveals in this formation elongated cells of pyramidal form. They have the radial trunk continued, up to the plexiform layer and also descending basilar dendrites which become subdivided and end within the 8th layer. Among these there is no lack of fusiform or triangular cells, but they always present the long radial trunk which we find over the whole cortex (Fig. 22, *C*).

In general form, it will be observed that these cells resemble true pyramids. However, the peculiar behavior of their axons establishes a very clear distinction between them. As may be seen in the figure (22, 1), this axon at first descends, then describes an arc, ascends into the 7th, 6th, and 5th layers, and finally ends in a horizontal arborization chiefly distributed to the layer of stellate cells, but a few of its branches go to the 5th layer. From the loop of the axon, and in the course of its ascent, spring several collaterals, which ramify in different planes of the 8th layer. In a few of these cells we may observe that, at the bend of the axon, a slender branch, similar to a collateral, is given off, which crosses the 8th and 9th layers and enters the white matter as a medullated fibre (Fig. 22, g). The great majority of these collaterals, however, terminate completely within the 8th and 9th layers. At any rate, we must distinguish, considering the morphology of their axons, two kinds of cells: (*a*) cells with arched axon none of whose collaterals extend to the white matter; (*b*) cells whose neurite divides, at the arch, into a fine descending branch, which becomes a medullated fibre of the white matter, and into a larger ascending branch with its terminal arborization in the 4th or 5th layers.

This arched arrangement of the axon in cells of the 8th layer appears very strange. It occurs not only in the infant brain, but in the visual cortex of the adult as well. It seems, at first sight, to violate all laws that govern the length and direction of the axons in other sections of the nervous system. And, what seems still more remarkable, all these whimsical windings seem to subserve solely the purpose of shortening the stretch between the cell body and the first collaterals given off by the arch. This same phenomenon occurs in many other nerve cells. Were

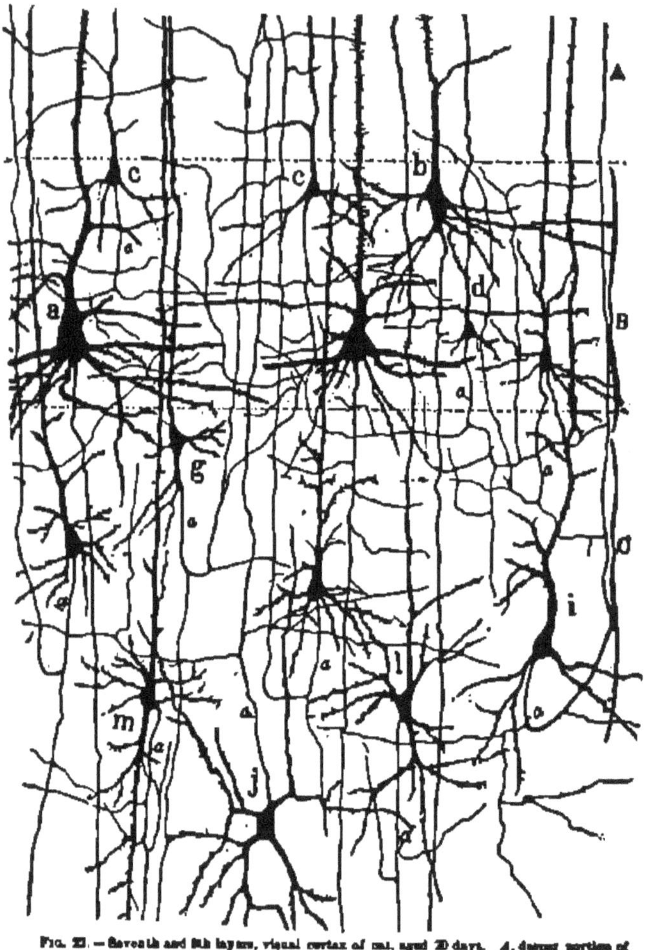

FIG. 23. — Seventh and 8th layers, visual cortex of cat, aged 20 days. *A*, deeper portion of layer of stellate cells; *B*, layer of giant pyramids; *C*, layer of medium-sized pyramids with arched axons; a, b, pyramids; c, d, small pyramids with axons distributed to 1th layer; g, triangular cell, whose axon gives rise to a large ascending collateral; l, another whose axon forms an arch and ascends; i, pyramid with axon descending to white matter; j, element from the deepest levels of the layer of medium-sized pyramids (corresponding to layer of fusiform cells in man) which gives origin to a large axon that ascends possibly to the 1st layer.

it not for a deviation from our present theme, I might adduce very convincing instances of this tendency of the axon to take the direction most favorable for the nerve impulses which arise in the cell to very quickly reach the elements connected with their initial collaterals.

Permit me also to add that the 8th layer contains giant stellate cells with ascending axon (Martinotti's cells), which runs to the plexiform layer (Fig. 22, j), and also a similar but smaller cell, whose axon gives rise to an arborization between the neighboring cells.

Ninth Layer.

Coinciding closely with the so-called polymorphic layer of other authors, this layer contains elongated elements, fusiform, triangular, or ovoid, possessing a radial dendrite, extending up to the plexiform layer, and also one or several basal dendrites, which take a descending or oblique direction. Finally, these cells have an axon which descends in a straight line to the white matter; where, after giving off several collaterals, it continues as a medullated fibre. There are also in the 9th layer a few fusiform cells with short radial dendrites and ascending axon and a number of stellate cells with short axon of the so-called Golgi type.

In addition, the arrangement of the cells of the 9th layer varies greatly in different parts of a convolution. In the convex portion they are very numerous, fusiform, and slender, elongated and perfectly radial; while opposite the sulcus they have a quite different form, are stouter, more variable, and frequently lie with long axis parallel to the white matter, *i.e.* perpendicular to their ordinary direction. Their peripheral processes perform the most whimsical contortions in order to become radial and reach the plexiform layer. Their axon appears frequently horizontal, describing a very open curve on its way to the white matter. All these forms and many others represent adaptations of the cells to the foldings of the cortex and to its varying thickness in different parts of a convolution.

I will not impose further upon your indulgent attention with these tiresome enumerations of layers and forms of cells, in the mazes of which nature herself seems to have intended to lose the investigator and put his patience to the test. And I will close this tedious lecture with a succinct exposition of the anatomico-physiological inductions that seem to follow from my observations on the minute structure of the visual cortex of man and the mammalia.

1. The visual cortex of man and gyrencephalous mammals possesses a special structure very different from that of any other cortical area.

2. The visual region is characterized, above all, by fewness of giant pyramids and by presenting, at the level of the granular layer of other cortical areas, three distinct layers of cells of special form, to wit: the layer of large stellate cells, the layer of small stellate cells, and the layer of pyramids with arched ascending axon.

3. Gennari's or Vicq d'Azyr's stripe contains principally terminal arborizations of certain very large fibres, originating probably in the primary optic centres (external geniculate body, pulvinar, anterior corpora quadrigemina).

4. Since these optic fibres are distributed chiefly to the stellate cells of the 4th and 5th layers, it seems natural to consider these elements the substratum of visual sensation.

5. The innumerable cells with short axons in the 4th and 5th layers represent, probably, the intermediate links between the optic fibres on the one side and the stellate cells of the 4th and 5th layers and the pyramidal cells on the other.

6. As these intermediate cells are often very small and have short axons, it may be that, besides their function of diffusing the incoming impulses through the cortex, they play also the special rôle of augmenting the visual impulses by fresh discharges of nerve force, in order that they may reach, in sufficient strength, the cortical regions in which the function of commemorative recording of optical images occurs. The pathways for conveyance of visual residues from the median occipital region to the association centres in the parietal cortex are possibly represented by axons of the stellate cells of the 4th and 5th layers.

7. Granting that the giant pyramids of other cortical regions give rise to motor fibres, it would follow that in the 7th layer they possess the same function. These cells, whose dendritic trunks come into contact with the optical plexus, 4th and 5th layers, serve probably to mediate the reflexes of the eyeball and head (conjugate movements of the eyes) occasioned by elective stimulation of the visual cortex, a theory which would seem to be supported by the physiological experiments of Schäfer, Danillo, Munk, and others.

8. Granting that each giant pyramid comes into contact in the 4th and 5th layers, as well as in the first layer, with fibres that are probably associative, we may suppose that motor discharges of these cells can be effected by two kinds of impulses: by ordinary optical stimulation and by stimuli of a volitional order, possibly coming from the association centres and reaching, finally, the plexiform layer.

My own researches do not furnish grounds for further conclusions. Many points still remain to be cleared up; but their complete elucidation will be the fruit of researches more detailed and exact than those I have been able to undertake.

LECTURE III.

THE SENSORI-MOTOR CORTEX.

AFTER the study that we have just made of the visual cortex, we can be more concise in our examination of the motor area. In all cortical regions we notice general structural characters and special features which constitute the physiognomy proper of each cerebral area. Naturally, the latter will be of more interest to us, and they will form the subject of the present lecture.

I shall not stop here to give any history of researches undertaken upon the minute anatomy of the psycho-motor areas. A bibliography of the subject would be very long, tedious, and altogether superfluous, since it has already been provided in the recent studies of Retzius, Hammarberg, and Kölliker. It will suffice to name, among those to whom we are most indebted for a knowledge of the structure of the motor cortex, Meynert, Baillarger, Kölliker, Krause, Betz, Lewis, Golgi, Martinotti, Retzius, Flechsig, Kaes, Hammarberg, Nissl, etc. All these writers have selected the psycho-motor cortex for special study; and it is safe to assert that all our knowledge of the minute structure of the entire cortex has taken its character from this region, which some writers have denominated "typical." They have done this because it was thought at the time when the fundamental works of Meynert and Golgi appeared that in histological structure the whole cortex corresponded to a uniform design, presenting only unimportant variations in different regions.

Neither have I time to enumerate the layers which have been described for this cerebral region. Their number has varied under the pen of each writer with the animal and the method he has happened to employ. Thus Meynert, who made his observations on man, distinguished five layers; Stieda, Henle, Boll, and Schwalbe limited their number to four; while writers like Krause admitted as many as seven. I myself, at the time of my investigations upon the small mammals, recognized four, naming them: (1) molecular layer; (2) layer of small and medium-sized pyramids;

(3) layer of large pyramids; (4) layer of polymorphic cells. This number, derived particularly from study of the small mammals, is not valid in the more complicated human cortex. To the four classical layers of smooth-brained mammals we must add one at least, the so-called granular layer of Meynert and other writers. This layer, situated in its very midst, divides the layer of giant pyramids into two, which we may call respectively the external, or superficial, and the internal, or deep, layers of giant pyramids.

To sum up, the following are the layers which it is possible to recognize by Nissl's method in the human motor cortex (ascending frontal and ascending parietal convolutions). To conform to our scheme in the visual cortex, we have altered the terminology for this region also.

1. Plexiform layer (layer poor in cells of Meynert, molecular layer of some writers).

2. Layer of small and medium-sized pyramids.

3. External layer of giant pyramids.

4. Layer of small stellate cells (granular layer of the authors).

5. Internal, or deep, layer of giant pyramids.

6. Layer of polymorphic cells (fusiform and medium-sized pyramids of certain writers).

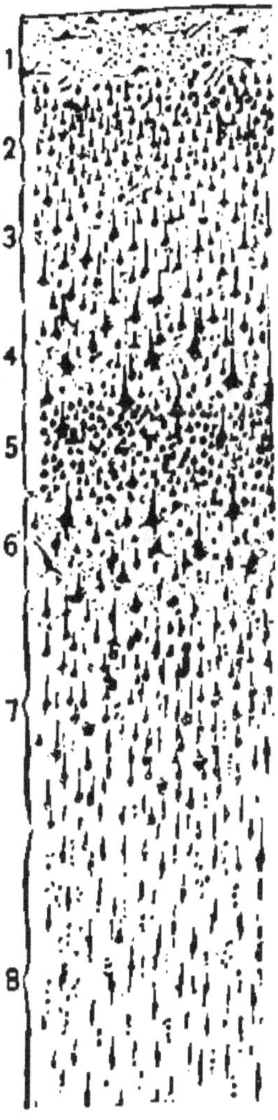

FIG. 23.—Section of adult human motor cortex, stained by Nissl's method (semischematic). 1, plexiform layer; 2, layer of small pyramids; 3, layer of medium-sized pyramids; 4, external layer of giant pyramids; 5, layer of small stellate cells; 6, internal layer of giant pyramids; 7, layer of polymorphic cells or deep pyramidal layer of medium-sized cells; 8, layer of fusiform cells.

These layers correspond particularly to the concave portions of the motor convolutions. Over the convexities the gray matter is thickened especially at the level of the polymorphic layer, which here appears divided into two sub-layers: an external, very rich in pyramidal and triangular cells (Fig. 23, 7); the other, internal, presenting, besides the heavy bundles of white fibres, fusiform cells disposed in parallel series (Fig. 23, 8).

1. **Plexiform Layer.** — This is similar in structure in the motor and visual areas. It contains, therefore: (1) dendritic arborizations of the pyramidal and polymorphic cells, that is to say, of all the cells of deeper layers (2, 3, 4, 5, 6) except stellate cells of the 4th layer and the cells with short axons scattered through the entire cortex; (2) terminal arborizations of the ascending axons of Martinotti; (3) the ramifications of the recurrent collaterals which come up from the axons of certain small and medium-sized pyramids; (4) the fibres, terminal and collateral, which arise from the white matter; (5) stellate cells of variable size with short axon which ramifies within the 1st layer; (6) the special, or horizontal, cells with long tangential dendrites; (7) finally, neuroglia cells of the two well-known types, with long radiating processes close underneath the pia (Martinotti, Retzius, Andriesen, Bevan Lewis, *et al.*), and type with short processes, located at all levels of the plexiform layer (Golgi, Cajal, Retzius, Martinotti).

We shall not enter upon their descriptive details, since all the structures present the same characters here as in the visual cortex. We shall merely add that in the motor cortex the plexiform layer is notably thick. It also contains a greater number of horizontal cells and terminations of the trunks of pyramidal cells (Fig. 25, *A*, *B*, *C*). Its greater thickness arises probably, as Lewis remarks, from the extraordinary number of pyramidal cells in the underlying layers.

2. **Layer of Small and Medium-sized Pyramids** (Fig. 24, 2 and 3). — We shall not stop upon these, because they are so well known. Permit me merely to call to mind the fact that their radial trunk, often forked near its origin, makes its arborization in the plexiform layer; while from the base springs a fine neurite which, in case of the small mammals, we can trace into the white matter. In the child's cortex this is made difficult by the distance, but I have been fortunate on two occasions in following this axon into the medullary substance, where it was continued as a medullated fibre. The neuritic collaterals are also very numerous

and a number of them may be seen to recur and make their arborizations in the superficial lamina of the plexiform layer.

Cells with Short Axons.—These are numerous, although it does not seem to me that they are so extremely abundant as in the visual region. In Fig. 25 I have reproduced some of these elements which habitually occur in my preparations. We remark especially: *a*, a large stellate type, whose ascending axon subdivides into horizontal or oblique branches covering a great extent of the layer of small and medium-sized pyramids (Fig. 25, *E*); *b*, a second type of similar form but whose axon forms its terminal arborization very close to the cell (Fig. 25, *E*); *c*, still another form with horizontal axon the superficial branches of which penetrate into the plexiform layer (Fig. 25, *D*); *d*, arachniform cells with axons subdivided into dense plexuses (Fig. 25, *F*, *G*); *e*, fusiform, bipanicled cells, which have been sufficiently described.

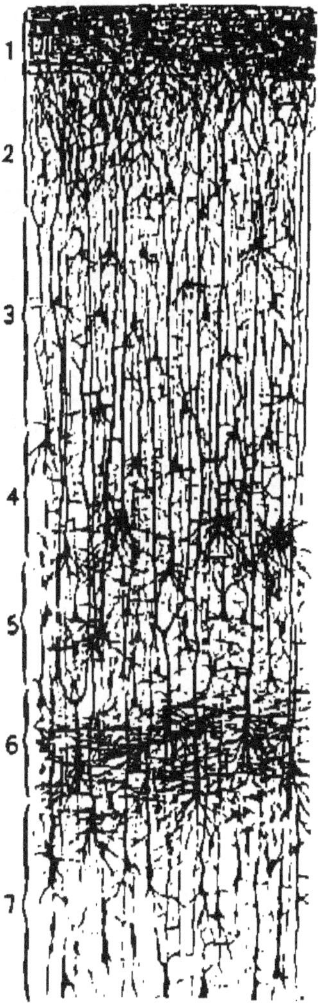

FIG. 24. — Ensemble of layers of motor cortex of infant aged one and a half months; Golgi's method (semischematic). Layers are numbered as follows: 1, plexiform; 2 and 3, small and medium-sized pyramids; 4, superficial giant pyramids; 5, granular or small stellate cells; 6, deep giant pyramids; 7, polymorphic cells, or deep medium-sized pyramids. (In this figure I have not represented the deepest portion of the 7th layer.)

Having studied all these types and many others in the visual cortex, it is unnecessary here to enter upon a more detailed description. One

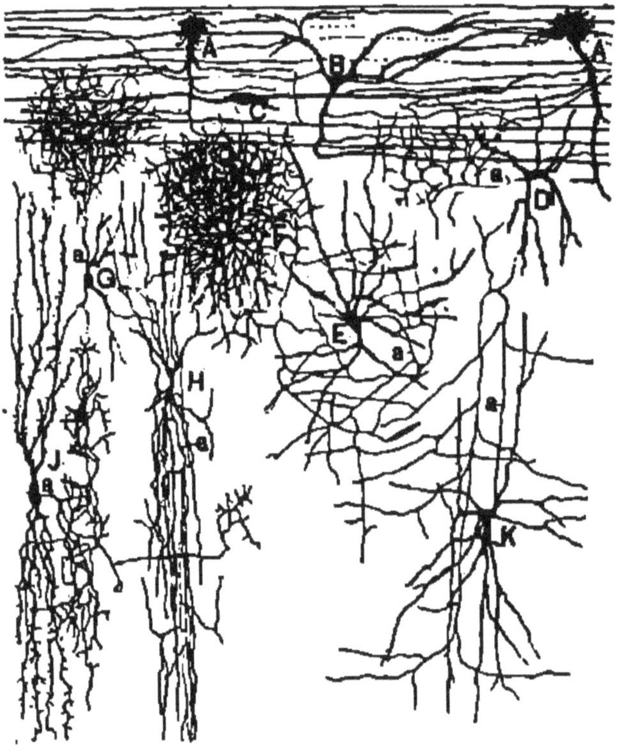

FIG. 25. — Cells with short axons of the plexiform and small and medium-sized pyramidal cell layers from motor cortex of infant aged one month and a few days. *A*, *B*, *C*, horizontal cells of the plexiform layer; *D*, cell with horizontal axon; *E*, large cell with very short diffusely subdivided axon; *F*, *G*, spider-shaped cells whose delicate axons form a dense plexus (*G*) up to the plexiform layer; *H*, *J*, bipanicled cells.

thing concerning the bipanicled cells I may add, viz., that in the motor cortex there appear to be two kinds: one, small cells provided with slender axon disposed in very delicate vertical pencils (Fig. 25, *H*); the other consisting of relatively large cells having very long and thick dendrites and with an ascending or descending axon giving rise to terminal arborizations of extreme complexity, producing nests or terminal baskets about the bodies of the small and medium-sized pyramidal cells (Fig. 25, *J*). Possibly this type, which I take to be a variety of the common bipanicled cell, is present over the whole cortex; but as yet I have succeeded in finding it only in the motor convolutions of the infant at over one month of age.

8. **Superficial Layer of Giant Pyramids.** — Being a continuation by imperceptible gradations of the above, this layer contains the well-known large pyramids of the writers. In addition to the observations of Betz, Lewis, Golgi, and myself, however, I must add a single detail to their classical description. The radial process varies greatly as to the extent of surface it covers in the plexiform layer. When its dendrites must cover a large surface, the trunk forks near the cell, and the two trunks, deviating at an acute angle, ascend to give rise to two or more terminal sprays, in some cases at considerable distances apart. This amounts to saying that certain medium-sized and large pyramids stand related to a large number of nerve fibres in the 1st layer, while other cells of the same size have more limited connections (Fig. 24).

In gyrencephalous mammals, dog and cat, the superficial large pyramids are smaller than in the infant. They might be considered as a subordinate element in the layer of medium-sized pyramids. Most frequently the only giant pyramids in the cat occur below the granular layer, — a layer which, I may add, is very slightly developed in this animal, being often blended with the layer of medium-sized pyramids.

The number of superficial, medium-sized, and giant pyramids is very large in the motor area both in animals and man; and this is one of its characteristic features. However, the regions designated by Flechsig as association centres possess also a notable number of large pyramids. From this feature alone it would be quite difficult to distinguish the frontal and parietal from the motor convolutions.

The axon of the large and medium-sized pyramids descends, as is well known, to the white matter and is continued as one or two nerve fibres. I must call special attention to the fact that, as shown by my own researches, this fibre may fork usually into a fine branch which goes, probably, to the corpus callosum and a larger branch to the corpus striatum. This may be easily observed in the brain of a newborn mouse or in one a few days old. It may also be seen that the fibre entering the corona radiata passes beyond the corpus striatum, giving off to it a few collaterals. It is thus well established that the axon of the large pyramids is true projection fibre which takes part in forming the pyramidal tract. But we must be on our guard about accepting the view of certain writers, — v. Monakow, for example, — who ascribe this rôle, participation in the motor tract, exclusively to the giant pyramids, because I have demonstrated beyond all doubt, in the motor region of the mouse and rabbit, that a number of the axons of medium-sized pyramids and many from polymorphic cells also penetrate the corpus striatum. I therefore consider as wholly arbitrary all the opinions which tend to attribute an exclusive function to elements in each distinct cortical layer. In the cortical layers, as well as in the ventral horn of the spinal cord, there occur together elements with axons of very diverse character and connections. The motor cell takes its place beside the associational cell along with the element whose axon or collateral goes to the corpus callosum. There are, accordingly, in the cortex no "sensory layers" nor "motor layers"; because, as we shall see in a moment, the great majority of the cells are related, either by their cell bodies or by their radial trunks, to the plexus of sensory fibres. We find thus reproduced the arrangement of the spinal cord, where all the cells, or almost all, come into contact with sensory fibres of the first or second order, and all represent links in the chain of reflex connections.

4. **Layer of Small Stellate Cells** (*Granular Layer of the Authors*). — Stained by Nissl's method the layer of small stellate cells appears as a great number of nuclei surrounded with little protoplasm which contains a few fine granules of chromatin (Figs. 23, 5, and 24, 5). Most of these elements, the granules proper, are very small and globular or stellate in form. Others, I have observed, are comparable to small pyramids, being of triangular form and having a fine radial trunk. Nor is there any lack of stellate or fusiform cells of considerable size, which call to mind those of the visual cortex. All these elements appear to be mingled. However, in certain places I thought I could discover that the small globular cells are situated chiefly in the external plane of the layer, while the minute pyramids were more numerous in the deeper levels, but there are exceptions to this.

But Nissl's method does not enable us to study the fine processes of these elements. To this end we must have recourse to the chromate of silver method, and by its application—especially in case of an infant fifteen to thirty days old, a time at which the reaction is easily obtained—I have been able to demonstrate the extreme complexity of the granular layer. Good preparations show that it consists of elements with very diverse characters, which in spite of their minor differences may be classed into two groups: (1) cells with long axons which extend down to the white matter; (2) cells with short axons which end within the granular layer or in layers above it.

Cells with Long Axons.—These may be classed into two varieties, small pyramidal cells and medium-sized stellate cells.

(*a*) The small pyramid is specially numerous in the deep level of the 4th layer (Fig. 28, *A*, *B*). It has been figured by various writers, notably by Kölliker, although even he does not give us any information on the character of its axon. The cells are ovoid-pyramidal in form. They possess a radial trunk which extends up to the plexiform layer, where it ends in a few very slender varicose twigs without contact granules. It also has a few tiny descending or oblique dendrites which divide repeatedly. Finally, I have very often traced its axon to the white matter, in which it is continued as a slender medullated fibre. From its initial portion arise two, three, or four collaterals, some of which curve upward to distribute themselves through the 4th layer. In some cases the diameter of these collaterals is so large, compared with that of the axon, that they might be considered the real axons.

(*b*) Stellate Cells. Very hard to stain, and possibly quite scarce. Their dendrites arise from the angles of the cell body and run in all directions, but are distributed exclusively to the 4th layer (Fig. 28, *D*). Their axons spring from the inferior surface, descend almost in a straight line, and, after giving off a few large collaterals, very frequently arched and recurrent, are lost in the white matter. These interesting cells, exactly similar to the stellate cells of the visual cortex, are also found in the motor cortex of gyrencephalous mammals, although, to judge from my own preparations, only in small numbers. Their presence would seem to indicate distinctively sensory regions of the brain.

Elements with Short Axons.—These are also very numerous in the infant brain, representing, perhaps, the chief morphological factor of the 4th layer. Several varieties have been distinguished, of which the most common are the following:—

(*a*) Stellate or Fusiform Cells of Medium Size. Their dendrites diverge in all directions, but chiefly above and below, and end in the midst of the 4th layer. Their axon springs from the superior surface, ascends for a variable distance, and at varying levels of the layer of stel-

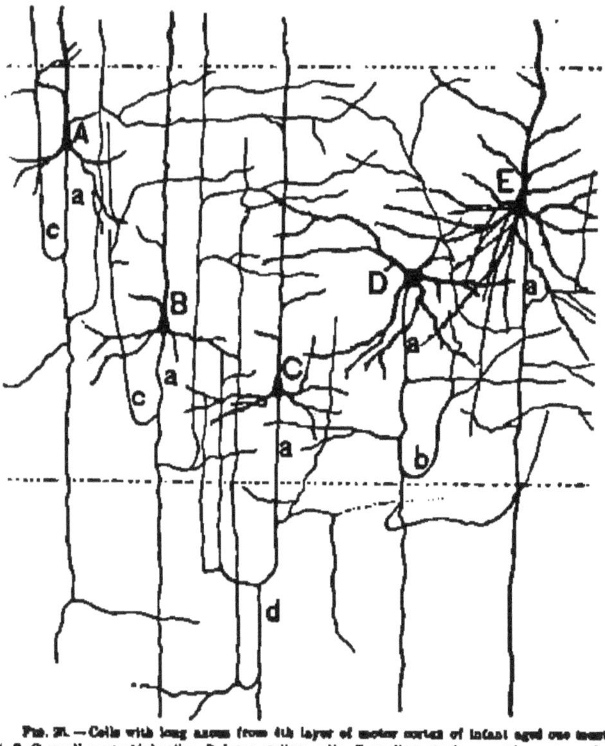

FIG. [illegible]. — Cells with long axons from 4th layer of motor cortex of infant aged one month. *A, B, C,* small pyramidal cells; *D,* large stellate cell; *E,* medium-sized pyramid; *a,* axon; *b, c,* large descending collaterals.

late cells forms an arborization of horizontal or oblique branches of considerable length and distributed exclusively to the 4th layer. Very often the axon branches in the form of a T before proceeding to its terminal arborization, and from its initial part arise collaterals whose course and terminations resemble those of the terminal branches. These cells, we may add, correspond in all points to the cells with ascending axons described for the 4th and 5th layers of the visual cortex (Fig. 27, *A*, *C*, *D*).

(*b*) Fusiform, Triangular, or Stellate Cells. These are somewhat

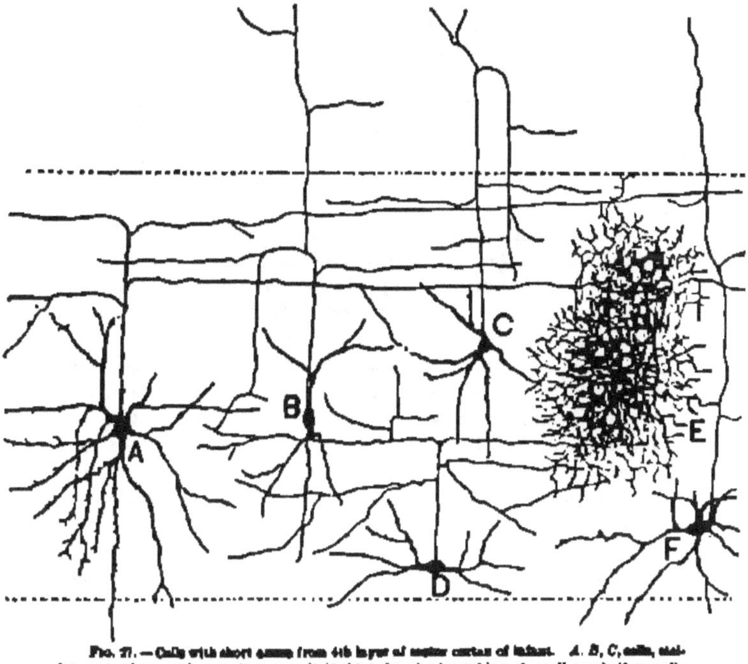

FIG. 27. — Cells with short axons from 4th layer of motor cortex of infant. *A*, *B*, *C*, cells, stellate or fusiform, with ascending axon divided into long horizontal branches; *E*, arachniform cell; *F*, cell with axon distributed to layer of medium-sized pyramids.

larger than the preceding. Their axon ascends to the plexiform layer, in which it subdivides and terminates. In its ascent it supplies a few collaterals to the 4th and 3d layers. These elements, as we see, correspond to the so-called cells of Martinotti. In a few cells of this class the axon possibly does not reach the first layer, becoming lost in the layers below (Fig. 27, *A*).

(*c*) Small Stellate or Spider-shaped Cells. These possess fine and richly subdivided dendrites and also a neurite, which forms a very rich arborization close to the cell (Fig. 27, *E*).

(*d*) Bipanicled Cells. These have the characteristics already described in our study of the visual cortex.

(*e*) Finally, in the cat and dog I have found a few stellate cells with very numerous dendrites, whose descending neurite forms a very dense and complicated arborization, for the most part in the 4th layer, but in some cases extending down to the deep layer of giant pyramids. Possibly these cells are homologous to the spider-shaped cells in man, which they resemble in the extraordinary richness of the plexus formed by the axon. It would then be necessary to suppose, however, that in the cat and dog these cells are much larger than in man.

In order to complete my description, permit me to add that there is no lack of ordinary pyramidal cells, in some cases large, scattered irregularly in the 4th layer (Fig. 26, *E*). In mammals like the cat and dog, and to a much greater degree in the rabbit, the profusion of pyramidal cells obscures our picture of the granular layer.

Sensory Nerve Plexus of the 4th Layer. — One of the most significant facts which I have discovered in the motor cortex is a plexus of very large fibres whose numerous subdivisions occupy the 4th layer and extend even into the 2d and 3d. They probably enter the cortex from the corona radiata. As early as in my first work I called attention to these fibres as being different in diameter, direction, and origin from axons of pyramidal cells, but at that time I had not succeeded in determining the region to which they are peculiar or the precise place of their termination in the cortex. My recent researches upon the brain of man and also small mammals enable me to add a few details to my description of some years ago (Fig. 28).

First of all, I have been able to determine exactly their origin and position in the brain. These are both easy to observe in the brain of a rabbit at birth and still better in that of a mouse a few days old. In the mouse it may be seen especially well that certain large fibres (called by Kölliker, who has confirmed their existence, fibres of Cajal) proceed from the corpus striatum, enter the white matter, and often extend horizontally in it for great distances. In their course they throw off long collaterals, which penetrate into the overlying gray matter. All these collaterals, as well as finally the original axon itself, ascend through the

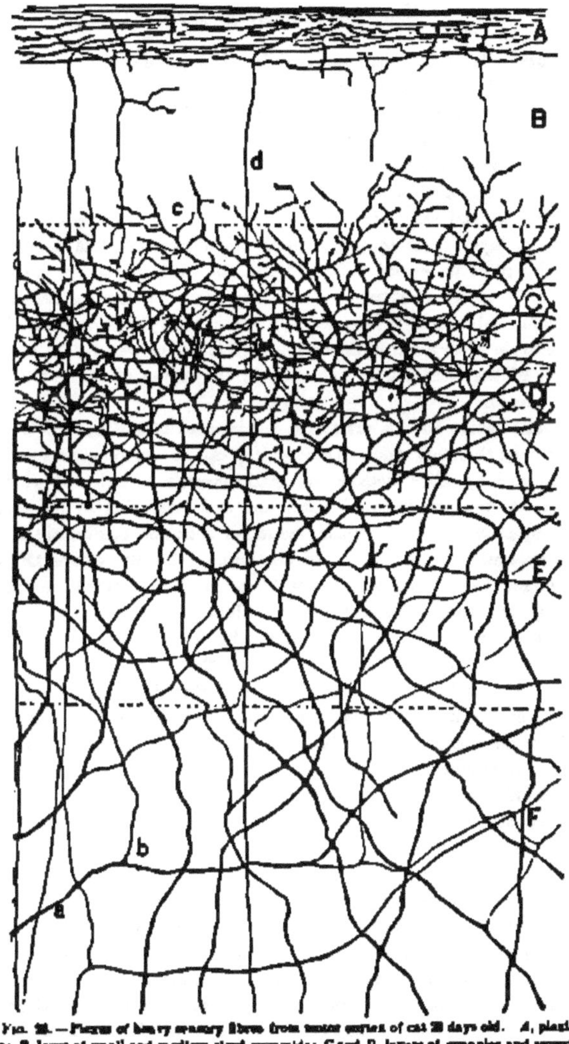

Fig. [illegible].—Plexus of heavy sensory fibres from motor cortex of cat [illegible] days old. *A*, plexiform layer; *B*, layer of small and medium-sized pyramids; *C* and *D*, layers of granules and superficial layer of giant pyramids; *E*, deep layer of giant pyramids; *F*, layer of polymorphic cells; *a*, fibre from white matter; *b*, ascending collateral; *c*, varicose terminal arborisation; *d*, fibre directed to the plexiform layer, which appears to be distinct from the large fibres.

polymorphic layer, dividing once or twice, then, passing obliquely through intervening layers, form an arborization of heavy fibres within the layers of small, medium-sized, and large pyramidal cells. However, in the rat and rabbit these branches are most numerous in a relatively superficial plane, which corresponds probably with the granular layer of the human brain, — a layer that is not differentiated in the small mammals. We also find a relatively small number of branches that ascend to the plexiform layer. As to the cortical distribution of this plexus, we may also place on record a fact of interest. It never covers the whole cortex. It begins to appear some distance from the median fissure and disappears below long before reaching the olfactory area or limbic lobe. I have never observed it in the cortex of this sulcus, nor in the anterior portion of the frontal lobe, nor even in the region of the auditory or visual centres.

I shall return to this matter in a future investigation, for I think it merits most thorough study; because, if it can be confirmed in a positive manner and by other methods, we shall possess a criterion by which to distinguish between areas of association and projection in the cortex. The projection areas will probably be found to be not, as Flechsig thinks, those possessing fibres that go to the corpus striatum (since Déjerine and others have discovered these fibres in the so-called association centres) but those receiving sensory fibres. At the same time, the association centres will be characterized by the absence of these direct sensory connections. At any rate, I believe that even in the brain of the smallest mammal there are areas, of small extent it may be, specialized to store up the images or residues of the sensory projection centres. It would be most astounding if the brains of the small mammals possessed a different architecture from that of man, taking into consideration the fact that all the senses have the same essential structure in all mammals and that memory — visual, tactile, muscular, etc. — is just as necessary to their lives as to our own.

The sensory plexus is highly developed in gyrencephalous mammals and in man. I have found it well impregnated in the brains of infants at birth and a few days old. Here it appears made up of large fibres having an oblique direction and a flexuous or even staircased course. After dividing several times in the 6th and 5th layers they give rise to a singularly extended arborization of horizontal fibres distributed chiefly to the layer of granules or small stellate cells. We thus see in the motor cortex, as was the case in the visual, that the layer of granules is the principal focus of sensory impressions. From this terminus they are propagated by the numberless cells with short ascending axons to the layers above and especially to the medium-sized and giant pyramids. However, it must be acknowledged that the sensory plexus is not so narrow and well defined as the optic. For, although its greatest density occurs in the 4th layer, its terminal branches divide in their ascent to the superficial layer of medium-sized and giant pyramids. The fibres which extend up to the small pyramids in man are not numerous. It is for this reason that I cannot agree with Bevan Lewis in ascribing to them sensory functions. I do not wish to be understood to deny the sensory function of the small and medium-sized pryamids. According to my view, all the cells of the motor cortex are sensory because they all, possibly, come into contact either directly (cells of the 3d, 4th, and 5th layers) or indirectly, through the intervention of cells with short axons, with sensory terminal arborizations. But, since some cells send their axons to the pyramidal tracts, we are able to distinguish them as *sensori-motor cells of the first order*. The others, which send their neurites to other motor areas of the brain, possibly effect contact with sensori-motor cells of the first order located elsewhere. These cells of indirect sensori-motor communication we may be warranted in calling *sensori-motor cells of the second order*. It goes without saying that this distinction is purely hypothetical; for no method enables us to determine the precise point within the brain where the axons of the pyramidal tracts of the corpus callosum or of bands of association fibres form their terminal arborizations.

5. **Layer of the Giant and Medium-sized Pyramids.**—In the adult human brain stained by Nissl's method, a section of the motor cortex reveals, below the granular layer, a layer of plexiform or granular aspect filled very thickly, but in no particular order, with a few giant and a great number of medium-sized pyramids (Fig. 29).

Usually the giant pyramids are located near the 4th layer, forming there a few irregular ranks. Impregnated by Golgi's method, they appear similar to the same cells in other regions of the cortex, but differ in a few particulars. The body is generally conical, very much elongated, giving rise at the apex to a large trunk, often dividing near the cell, which terminates in the 1st layer in the usual manner. A group of long complicated dendrites diverges from its base, and from the sides spring several very long horizontal processes which subdivide into terminal brushes, and these, intertwining with similar structures from neighboring cells of the same level, form a dense and very characteristic

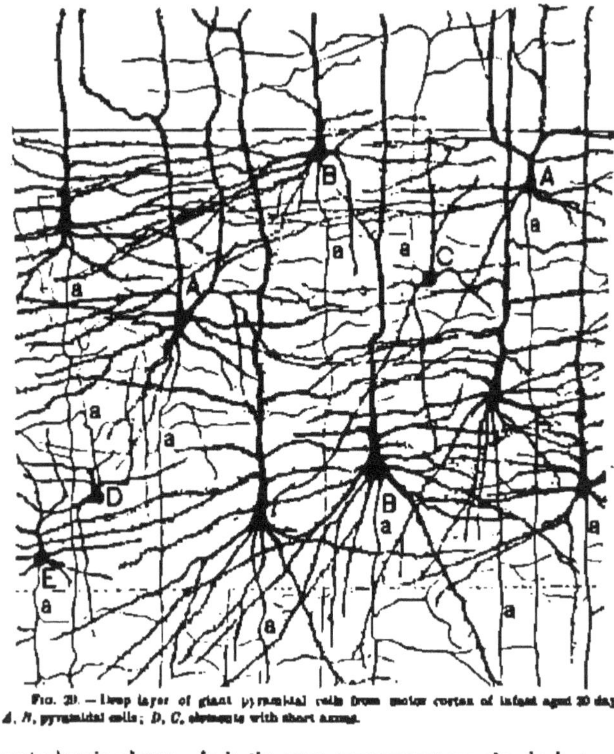

FIG. 20. — Deep layer of giant pyramidal cells from motor cortex of infant aged 20 days. *A, B*, pyramidal cells; *D, C*, elements with short axons.

protoplasmic plexus. It is the same arrangement we already know so well in the visual cortex, except that, instead of one plexus, there are many. The axon is large and, after giving off very long collaterals to the 5th and 6th layers, it passes on to become a medullated fibre of the white matter.

The medium-sized pyramids are very numerous, much scattered, and occur in greatest profusion in the lower levels of the layer. They do not differ in character from the giant pyramids, except as to the lateral somatic dendrites, which are few and not characteristic.

Besides the pyramidal cells the 5th layer contains a few other kinds of elements. From the point of view of their morphology the following are the more striking types.

(*a*) *Cells which form Terminal Nests.* — These cells, very similar to those which give rise to the basket fibres of the cerebellum, are most numerous in the 5th layer between or below the giant pyramids. I have found them also in the layer of granules or small stellate cells.

Their volume is small, similar to that of a small pyramid, and in form they appear stellate or triangular with very long and much-branched varicose dendrites. The neurite, however, presents the most distinctive feature. It ascends, forking close to its origin, and breaks up into a ramification of very many branches, ascending, oblique, or horizontal. After a few subdivisions, all these branches make their way to the giant and medium-sized pyramids to form very complicated varicose arborizations close around their cell bodies and principal processes, after the manner of the terminal baskets of the cerebellum or the nests found in Deiter's nucleus. Each nest contains arborizations from several cells, and each basket cell helps to form a large number of nests (Fig. 80, *d*).

(*b*) *Cells with a Diffusely Branched Ascending Axon.* — This is a fusiform or stellate cell located at different levels of the 5th layer, to which it sends its dendrites. The axon ascends to the superior limits of the layer where it forks, and its terminal branches form a loose horizontal arborization of an enormous extent and connected probably with the deep giant pyramids (Fig. 29, *C*, *D*).

(*c*) *Small Pyramids with Arched Axons.* — This cell, which I have studied particularly in the motor cortex of the cat, is entirely similar to the element which we found in the 6th and 7th layers of the visual cortex. The cells possess a fine dendrite which ascends to the first layer, where it ends in a very modest and delicate arborization. Their axon descends and, after giving off a few relatively long recurrent collaterals, appears to fork and end in the midst of the 5th layer. The branches which spring from the bend of the arch descend in some cases, but I have not been able to trace them down to the white matter.

(*d*) *Cells with Long Ascending Axon.* — These are fusiform or triangular cells with long polar dendrites which never reach the first layer.

Their axon arises from the superior surface of the cell, and, after giving off a few branches to the 5th and 4th layers, it continues its ascent to the plexiform layer and there makes its terminal arborization.

6. **Layer of Polymorphic Cells.** — This layer contains the same elements as the layer of the same name (9th) in the visual cortex (Fig. 81), that

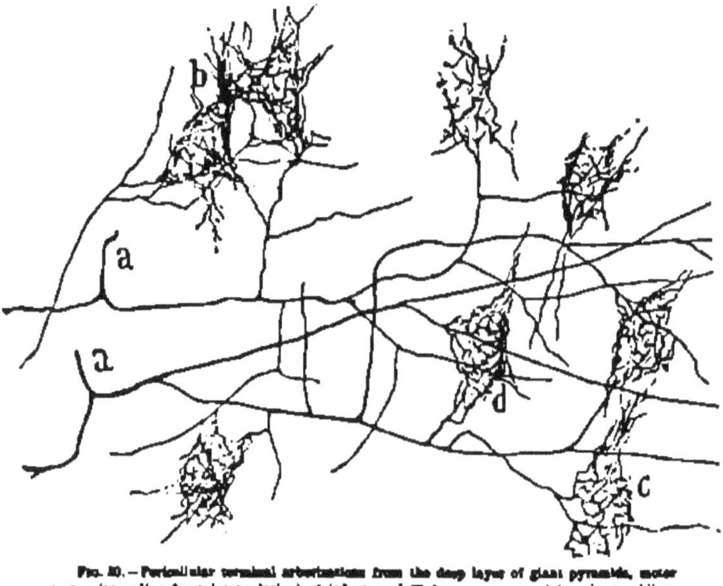

FIG. 80. — Pericellular terminal arborizations from the deep layer of giant pyramids, motor cortex (ascending frontal convolution) of infant aged 25 days. *a*, axons giving rise to oblique and horizontal branches; *b*, *c*, *d*, terminal nests.

is to say, fusiform cells with two long polar dendrites, triangular cells, and true pyramids. Their axons all go to the white matter. Their ascending trunks, which are never lacking, become very attenuated on account of the branches given off while passing through the 4th layer and reach the 1st layer as an exceedingly delicate fibril, which ends in a fine, slightly extended, notably varicose dendritic spray.

In Fig. 81, I have reproduced the principal types of cells found in the polymorphic layer. Besides the medium-sized pyramidal and triangular types having long descending axons (Fig. 81, *A*, *B*), there occur other forms in great numbers. These are fusiform or triangular cells whose axons penetrate into the superposed layers, furnishing to them a great

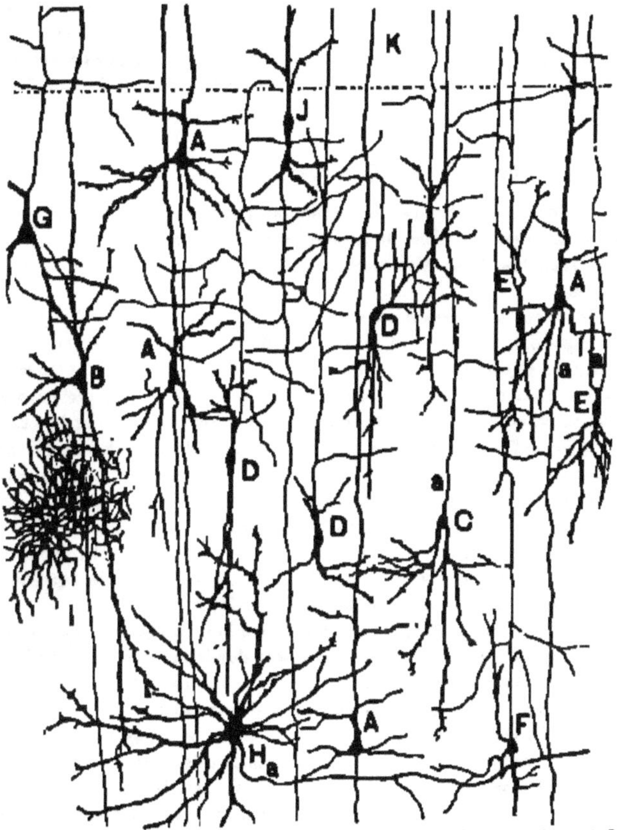

FIG. 21.—*Principal types of polymorphic cells from motor cortex of infant aged 20 days. A, B, cells with long axons extending to white matter; C, D, E, fusiform cells with ascending axon; H, giant stellate cell.*

number of branches. Some of these axons seem to end in the deep layer of giant pyramids, but others appear to pass beyond this. Finally, there is no lack of arachniform cells (Fig. 81, *I*), cells with short axon of the sensory type of Golgi, whose axons form terminal arborizations in the layer under consideration. I may add that I have found in two cases giant stellate cells with heavy horizontal axon which gives off collaterals (Fig. 81, *H*). I do not know the ultimate fate of this process and am unable to say whether these scattering cells form a constant feature of the motor cortex.

Cortex of Acoustic, Olfactory, and Associational Areas.

Unfortunately, my own researches are not as yet in a very advanced state in regard to these important cortical centres. So that any information that I can give must necessarily be fragmentary and of little value.

The acoustic resembles exactly the motor cortex as to general arrangement of cells and layers, but differs from it in a few peculiarities: (1) by the fineness of the fibres forming the plexus at the level of the layer of granules or small stellate cells; (2) in the profusion of bipanicled cells with their very delicate and complicated neuritic brushes; (3) above all, by the presence of certain special cells scattered irregularly through the entire thickness of the cortex. The very large axon of these special cells extends in a horizontal or oblique direction, but I have not yet been able to determine exactly its manner of termination. These large cells are fusiform and lie horizontally. From their polar dendrites spring a number of fine ascending branches, which subdivide repeatedly but do not extend up as far as the plexiform layer.

The olfactory cortex, that of the limbic lobe, is characterized by the following peculiarities: (1) the enormous development of the plexiform layer and the presence in it, in addition to its usual structures, of the antero-posterior fibres that come from the external root of the olfactory tract; (2) the absence of the layers of small pyramids and granules; (3) the presence of certain large horizontal cells below the plexiform layer; (4) the peculiar form of the medium- and large-sized pyramids which emit from the deep end of the cell body a brush consisting of numerous much subdivided dendrites; (5) above all, the fact that the sensory plexus, i.e. the fibres which come from the olfactory bulb, makes its terminal arborization exclusively in the plexiform layer and in the most superficial portion of that layer, corresponding to that of the small pyramids. This significant fact, brought to light by the studies of Calleja, shows us that the sensory fibres do not end in the same level of the cortex in all regions. Hence, the layer specialized to serve as substratum for the phenomena of sensation may change its position in different sensory areas.

Our task is now drawing to its close. My work upon the topographical structure of the cortex has been fragmentary and leaves much to be desired. Many things, in fact, are still undiscovered. But, despite the very incomplete state of my researches and the narrow limits of the field they cover, I may draw a few anatomico-physiological conclusions, of which the chief are the following: —

And first, as to the hierarchy of centres in the cortex of the human brain, comparing it with the mammalian brain, we may call to mind that, while it does not contain wholly new elements, it presents very distinctive characteristics, to wit: —

1. The enormous development of the horizontal cells of the plexiform layer and the considerable length of their so-called tangential fibres.

2. The great abundance of cells with short axons scattered throughout the whole cortex, cells which form special varieties by reason of differences in their forms and the directions of their axons.

3. The presence of cells with short axons, very slender (bipanicled spider cells), with terminal arborizations whose delicacy is not approached by anything found in any animal.

4. The considerable development of basilar dendrites of the pyramidal cells.

5. The presence among the mid-layers of the cortex of a formation of so-called granular cells, a kind of focus occupied by enormous numbers of pyramids with short axons descending, arched, and ascending. This granular formation is present in gyrencephalous mammals, but in them it is very poor in cells with short axons and in small pyramids. In the smooth-brained animals it is almost wholly lacking.

The human cortex has evolved, accordingly, along three different lines: by multiplying cells with long axons and, above all, those with short axons; by decreasing the volume of cells and the diameter of certain fibres in order to make possible within the limits of space a delicate and greatly improved organization; finally, by varying and infinitely complicating the external morphology of the nerve elements, undoubtedly with the purpose of multiplying, in correspondence with their complexity, functional associations of all kinds.

As to differences and analogies in regional structure, the following propositions may be regarded as established: —

1. The sensory as well as the so-called associational areas are made up by a combination of two orders of structural factors. The first order consists of common factors, which show very little modification. They are represented by the plexiform layers and the layers of pyramidal and polymorphic cells. The second order comprises special factors, structures peculiar to each cortical area. Their chief anatomical feature resides especially in the granular layer and is related mainly to the presence of particular centripetal fibres and of special types of cells with long axons (stellate cells of different kinds).

2. It seems probable that the common factors perform functions of a general order concerned, possibly, with ideas of representations of all kinds of movements related to the special sensations of which the cortical region is the seat. It seems also probable that the special anatomical factors of the sensory areas perform the function of elaborating specific sensations (sensation of seeing, hearing, etc.) and also of conveying sensory residues to the so-called association centres, where they may be transformed into latent images.

3. Each sensory cortical centre receives a special category of nerve fibres (fibres of central sensory tracts). Their cells of origin, as has been shown by the researches of v. Monakow, Flechsig, v. Bechterew, and many others, reside in the particular nuclei of the medulla, corpora quadrigemina, and optic thalami. It is precisely the presence of these sensory fibres of the second order that constitutes the prime anatomical characteristic of the centres of sensation or projection.

4. The absence of these sensory fibres, which come from the corona radiata, may be used in all mammals to distinguish the so-called association centres. These centres, which exist even in the mouse, also have a nerve fibre plexus distributed among their median layers (layer of granules in the association areas in man). The fibres, however, which constitute them are very fine and appear to come from sensory centres of the brain. Possibly the cells about which these sensorio-ideational fibres terminate represent the substratum or, at any rate, the first link in the chain of nerve elements whose function is the representation of ideas.

5. Since we have seen that each afferent fibre in the sensory cortex comes into contact with an extraordinary number of nerve cells apparently scattered without any order, we must suspect that these relations conform to the preconceived design of a well-determined and constant organization.

As, at present, it seems to be impossible to discover these relations, we may surmise that each sensory fibre comes into contact, directly or through other cells, solely with those pyramids whose stimulation is necessary in order to effect, after the manner of the reflex arc, movements coördinated and intentional. We may also surmise (supposing that the stellate cells of the tactile and visual cortex form the link between the sensory and ideational centres) that each sensory afferent fibre, bringing a unit of sensation (the impression received by a cone of the retina or by the terminal arborization of any peripheral nerve fibre), enters into relation exclusively with the group of nerve cells entrusted with the function of conveying this impression to a particular point in the associational cortex.

Many other hypotheses are possible, but I must conclude for fear of tiring your kind and sympathetic attention and exhausting your patience. I fear that I have already made too free use of hypotheses and have pretended to fill the gaps of possible observations with arbitrary suppositions.

It is a rule of wisdom, and of nice scientific prudence as well, not to theorize before completing the observation of facts. But who is so master of himself as to be able to wait calmly in the midst of darkness until the break of dawn? Who can tarry prudently until the epoch of the perfection of truth (unhappily as yet very far off) shall come? Such impatience may find its justification in the shortness of human life and also in the supreme necessity of dominating, as soon as possible, the phenomena of the external and internal worlds. But reality is infinite and our intelligence finite. Nature and especially the phenomena of life show us everywhere complications, which we pretend to remove by the false mirage of our simple formulæ, heedless of the fact that the simplicity is not in nature but in ourselves.

It is this limitation of our faculties that impels us continually to forge simple hypotheses made to fit, by mutilating it, the infinite universe into the narrow mould of the human skull, — and this, despite the warnings of experience, which daily calls to our minds the weakness, the childishness, and the extreme mutability of our theories. But this is a matter of fate, unavoidable because the brain is only a savings-bank machine for picking and choosing among external realities. It cannot preserve impressions of the external world except by continually simplifying them, by interrupting their serial and continuous flow, and by ignoring all those whose intensities are too great or too small.

I cannot conclude this, my third and last lecture, without a word of tribute to this great people of North America, — the home of freedom and tolerance, — this daring race whose positive and practical intelligence, entirely freed from the heavy burdens of tradition and the prejudices of the schools, which weigh still so heavily on the minds of Europe, seems to be wonderfully endowed to triumph in the arena of scientific research, as it has many times triumphed in the great struggles of industrial and commercial competition.

Ai suoi cari Colleghi della Clark
University di Worcester in segno
di amicizia A. Mosso
Nov. 1899.

ssion to [illegible]
ble for ma[illegible]
of psycholog[illegible] in Europe
[illegible] of the development of [illegible], we are all
[illegible] a fertile field where philosophers and
[illegible], a field, indeed, where they [illegible]
[illegible] the idealists and the [illegible]
[illegible], laboring, as they all are, at the
most difficult of all problems — the [illegible]

[illegible] pedagogy
[illegible] to perfect
[illegible], to make
[illegible], the [illegible] of [illegible] which
[illegible] between the psychic [illegible] and

I.

[illegible] our brain has at birth a grayer hue, and
[illegible]. This whitish color originates from
[illegible] fibres, after their complete development,
[illegible] this color.
[illegible] great credit of having shown that our
[illegible] at birth, and that the [illegible]
[illegible] extending from the [illegible] the

PSYCHIC PROCESSES AND MUSCULAR EXERCISE.

By Professor Angelo Mosso.

First, let me give expression to my gratitude to Clark University, whose invitation made it possible for me to take part in this celebration.

To the American schools of psychology, a subject which in Europe forms so characteristic a branch of the development of science, we are all deeply indebted. Psychology is a fertile field, where philosophers and scientists can unite for common labor, a field, indeed, where they cannot be separated from each other, for here the idealists and the empiricists are held together by a common bond, laboring, as they all are, at the solution of the greatest and the most difficult of all problems — the investigation of the human mind.

Clark University, moreover, can boast of having given to pedagogy also a new impulse. Many excellent teachers come hither to perfect themselves for their profession. I may be permitted, therefore, to make both fields, psychology and pedagogy, the subject of my lectures, which will treat of the relations existing between the psychic processes and muscular exercise.

I.

It had long been known that our brain has at birth a grayer hue, and only later takes on a whitish color. This whitish color originates from the fact that the cerebral nerve fibres, after their complete development, are surrounded by a sheath which has this color.

To Paul Flechsig[1] is due the great credit of having shown that our cerebral nerve fibres are not complete at birth, and that the white nerve-paths come from the medulla, extending from the periphery toward the centre.

In man, the brain develops later than in all the other animals, because his muscles also develop later. The striped muscles are more incomplete at birth in man than in any other animal. For this fact, that the human brain develops so slowly, I am able to discover no other reason than this, that at birth the organs which effect movement, over which the brain later exercises its authority, are not yet complete.

The muscles of the adult human being are thirty-seven times as heavy as those of the newborn child, while the brain of the *former* is only 3.76 times as heavy as that of the latter.

It had been long known also that the brain of man slowly increases in weight up to the fortieth year. Recently Kaes[2] has shown that, up to the fortieth year, there are formed in the cerebral convolutions new plexuses of nerve fibres, which are lacking in younger brains.

Excitation of the senses and impulses to movement hasten the development of the nerves in question. The experiments of Ambronn and Held[3] have shown that, if one eye of a newborn kitten is opened to the light, the other remaining closed, the optical fibres of the eye which is stimulated by the light are more quickly surrounded with myelin than those of the other. Another important fact is that the motor nerve fibres are complete earlier than the sensory.

These facts we must apply to pedagogy. Only that science can show how injurious is precocious instruction for the development of the child.

If we wish to hasten the maturity of the brain, we must decide whether the formation of the myelin can better be hastened by stimulations of the senses and intellectual work, or better by muscular exercises. The latter way seems to me the more natural. We must, therefore, to begin with, consolidate the motor nerve paths which develop first, and after that seek to develop the portion of the brain concerned with intellectual work. Modern views show a tendency to confirm what the great philosophers of Greece already recognized, viz., that children ought to begin to read and write only with the tenth year. The conviction is again slowly maturing that our children begin to learn too early, that it is injurious for the development of the brain to be fettered to the school-desk when only five or six years old. The conviction is slowly making its way that no more time should be devoted to intellectual work than to muscular exercise. The modern education of youth, however, resembles more an artificial hothouse culture than a natural training of the human plant.

II.

The fact observed by me that in man the phenomena of intellectual fatigue are identical with those of muscular fatigue, caused me to inquire whether or not the conscious processes and those of movement are identical processes, which take place in like cells, or, perhaps, alternately in one and the same cell.

The new phrenology exhibits a tendency to localize the mental functions, but the old idea, which distributed the nervous functions over the whole cerebral cortex, does not yet acknowledge its defeat, and what I have to say to-day will show that there exists an intimate connection between the conscious processes and muscular exercise.

Doubtless, there are regions known in the brain which are traversed by the will impulse which sets certain muscle groups in motion, but they are the junctions of roads, they are the tracks upon which the trains run, not the stations where the trains are formed, and where they receive the will impulse. In fact, in cases where it was possible to stimulate electrically the motor region of the human cerebral cortex, the subject declared that he felt, in that part of the body in which the current caused a muscular contraction, sensations which resembled the creeping or running of ants.

If the so-called motor region of the brain is destroyed, it is found that a change of sensibility also takes place. These facts suffice to show that, up to the present, no absolute local separation of movement and sensibility is demonstrable. Moreover, all agree that every will impulse is joined to the idea of the movement to be executed.

If, in a monkey, the roots of the sensory nerves which go to the arm are severed, the animal no longer moves the hand spontaneously, although the voluntary nerve paths are uninjured, because the *ubi consistam* of sensibility is lacking. Our mechanisms are so complete that the movement-command is never given by the cells without a clear idea of the place where it is to be carried out.

In every voluntary movement there exists between the periphery and the centre such an intimate connection that patients who have lost the muscle sense can contract the muscles of the hand around an object and keep them contracted, as long as they look at the object. So soon, however, as they turn their eyes away, the muscles instantaneously relax. For a movement impulse to express itself, it must be controlled by the sensory nerves; for the will and the sensibility are functions inseparably connected with each other.

III.

Attention, which has been called an internal sense, shows really in the best way how isolation from the influence of the external world is possible in the study of psychic phenomena. Attention is the most intense activity of the mind, and yet we all know that we are not capable of absolutely controlling it. The more or less favorable disposition for intellectual work, which we perceive on certain days and at certain hours, awakes the suspicion that attention itself is, to a great extent, conditioned by internal reflex phenomena.

I have already shown in my writings[4] that, in a state of attention, the respiration becomes slower and deeper, the blood-vessels in the forearm and in the foot contract, the blood flows more abundantly to the centre, the form of the brain and arm pulse changes, and the activity of the heart is increased.

In the state of attention, moreover, there exist an increased secretion of sweat, a greater consumption of the organism — the blood is poisoned by the products of intellectual fatigue.[5]

Attention produces not only the same chemical effects and the same fatigue as muscular exertion does, but we feel also, when we are attentive to anything, the characteristic muscular strain on the occiput, the forehead, and other parts of the body.

One of the characteristic phenomena of attention is its periods, which have been so well studied by Wundt and his pupils, — periods which exhibit a great resemblance to those observed by Dr. W. P. Lombard[6] in the case of continued muscular contraction. Under the direction of Dr. G. Stanley Hall, Lindley[7] has investigated the involuntary movements which we make when we think of anything, muscular contractions of the face, hands, and feet. These movements are like those which we make during muscular exertion.

We cannot force the attention to fix itself upon one object continually, because it quickly becomes exhausted, and renews itself only when a new object is offered it, when new paths for its activity are opened. It is not *we* who direct the attention. We can only indicate to it the direction which it is to take according to our wishes. After that it is free and does what it pleases; it flits about like a butterfly on the path which we have pointed out for it.

The excitability of artists, the peculiarity of their character, show that in them the involuntary movements are more easily executed, and that intelligence and mobility increase together. But the fact that artists see objects in a particular way, and that the thing seen by artists, like that seen by littérateurs, is retained by the memory in very characteristic fashion, proves that attention works in a different way with them. The plastic talent of southern peoples, the ease of their movements, their more lively gestures, the more intense expression of their emotions, disclose to us the nature of the artists' genius. I believe, however, that there is also contained in attention an emotional factor.

IV.

Great impressionability and the capacity to fix the attention for a longer time are, doubtless, two of the chief conditions for artistic genius. But I believe also that the exercise of the hands exerts an influence upon the development of the mind.

During the first epoch of the Renaissance, the greatest artists of Florence were all apprentices in the workshops of the goldsmiths. Luca della Robbia, Lorenzo Ghiberti, Filippo Brunelleschi, Francia, Domenico Ghirlandajo, Sandro Botticelli, Andrea del Sarto, — to mention only a few examples, — performed, during their apprenticeship, the simplest labors in the workshop of a goldsmith. But the exercise with which they gained their manual dexterity surely influenced also the development of their genius.

In the beginning of the sixteenth century this school ended, but from the pedagogical standpoint it is still worth studying. If I may be permitted to express an opinion, I would say that the manual dexterity favored by this labor contributed much to the development of the great masters of genius.

A fact which cannot be doubted is the manysidedness of genius which some Italians of the Renaissance possessed, and which has never again appeared with like copiousness.

Giotto was painter, sculptor, and architect. Leonardo da Vinci was a celebrated musician, a great painter, an engineer, an architect, a man of letters and of science. Andrea del Verrocchio was goldsmith, sculptor, engraver, architect, painter, and musician. These facts are to be read in many histories of art. An incomparable example, however, is Michelangelo. For twelve years he studied anatomy on the cadaver, and afterwards painted the Sixtine Chapel and executed the tombs of the Medici and the dome of St. Peter's.

In the artist, better than in other human beings, is seen the intimate connection between the psychic processes and muscular exercise. Power of resistance against fatiguing labors, dexterity, and capacity for concentration, are the secret of their marvellous life. I am convinced that muscular movements have formed the omnipotence of genius, just as, *vice versâ*, intellectual exercises effect advantageously the development of the muscles. Michelangelo ground his colors himself. Raphael, while as an engineer in Rome he carried on excavations and painted the rooms of the Vatican, wrote a treatise on how the smoking of the chimney in the kitchen of a prince might be prevented. As Vasari relates, Perino del Vaga made every mechanical object; he fabricated often trumpeters' pennons, portières, drapery, flags, embroidery, and carving, and painted sarcophagi. He was a great painter, and his stucco works belong to the most valuable of the Renaissance period. Even if the genius of these mighty men will remain a secret for all time, yet we can say this much, that their hand was just as dexterous as their mind was lofty.

These men, who are the greatest representatives of our race, have carried the dexterity of their hands to the highest degree of perfection. They were simple workers, who, laboring untiringly with their hands, lifted the human mind to the highest ideals of beauty.

If the Greeks excelled all other peoples in genius, it was because they paid more attention than did the others to bodily exercises; they brought gymnastics, the study of bodily positions and bodily exercise, to a height which has never been reached by other peoples since their day.

V.

Our brain possesses probably more substance than we generally use, so that a not inconsiderable part of it may be looked upon as an organ of luxury. The fact observed by me, that we breathe in more air than is necessary, together with the fact observed much earlier, that we eat much more than we need, allows us to designate as luxury all that is not absolutely necessary.

Our brain has on the average about a milliard of nerve cells. Many men have more, and others less brain substance, without it being possible to detect a difference in the intensity of their psychic processes.

Large and heavy brains are often found in men who do not make full use of them. Such a brain was that of Rustan, which Rudolphi has described. It weighed 2222 gr., while that of Helmholtz[4] weighed only 1420 gr. The brain of the unknown, commonplace individual, Rustan, was therefore 802 gr. heavier than that of Helmholtz. The great facility with which, in the case of partial destruction of the brain, the individual parts can substitute one another has been demonstrated by Flourens and Goltz.

Not all the brain cells work simultaneously, but they relieve one another probably with such punctuality that only under certain conditions do we notice that some groups are fatigued.

That this relief process exists can be argued from the fact that the nerve cells offer only a very small resistance to fatigue.

The attention itself works in periods of activity and rest. These periods have been observed in the case of the sense of sight, as well as in the senses of hearing, taste, and touch. Since, as Bowditch has shown, the nerves, as such, do not become fatigued, we must ascribe such fluctuations to the centre.

If we close one eye, and with the other look at an equally illuminated wall or the sky, we notice that the visual field now darkens, now lights up again.[9] The dark color becomes green, yellowish, or blue, and appears in regular intervals, 5 - 12 times a minute. These periods vanish as soon as the eye in attention is directed towards a certain object. I do not believe that this phenomenon arises from the movement of the blood-vessels, for it appears only when we look with *one* eye. I am of the opinion that it points to a relief-process in cerebral activity, and to a period during which a slight fatigue of the brain cells takes place, if the latter are not incited by the attention to more intense labor. Our attention turns automatically now to one, now to the other eye.[10]

There exists a remarkable agreement between the periods of activity and rest of the brain cells and of the sympathetic system. If we investigate the movements of the blood-vessels with the plethysmograph,[11] and also the movements of the bladder,[12] we notice great undulations, coinciding with some respiratory movements. In the curves also, observed in man and animals when the blood pressure is investigated, these fluctuations, which were first described by Traube, are seen. I myself have shown that the respiratory curve exhibits periods of greater and less activity. These fluctuations are particularly characteristic in mountain sickness. With each period of rest the excitability of the nervous centres is decreased.

From all these phenomena it seems to follow that the nerve cells have only a small power of resistance, and that they show on the average every ten seconds a tendency to rest.

I have further been able to show, by means of the ergograph, that to strongly contract the hand suffices to induce in the brain the first symptoms of fatigue, and that a few seconds of rest are enough to make the nerve cells capable of functioning again.

The very short duration of the capacity to resist in the nerve cells makes it plain that the brain must necessarily possess a great number of cells. It is the task of pedagogy to show how the brain cells can most fitly be employed for the welfare of the individual and of society.

It is already well known that the barbarians were able to learn foreign languages with greater facility than the Greeks and Romans.[23] When we say of young peoples that they will some day excel us in literature, as in art and in science, we, unconsciously perhaps, intimate thereby that their brain still possesses tracts of virgin soil, which, with later cultivation, will become fertile.

VI.

The more mobile the extremities of an animal are, the more intelligent it is. Among all birds the parrot is the most intelligent, because it makes more use than do other birds of its legs, beak, and tongue. The elephant is more intelligent than all other wild animals, because he makes use not only of his legs, but also of his snout, as organs of movement.

Another consideration: The most mobile parts of the body are at the same time the most sensitive, *e.g.* the tongue, the hand, the snout. This increased sensitiveness depends neither on a more numerous ramification of nerves, nor on the more complicated character of the end organs, but arises from the fact that the brain itself is more irritable, as shown by the passions of animals, which are more violent the more mobile the creature is.

Romanes[24] has already said that the higher intelligence of monkeys and the highest intelligence of man are related to a more perfect instrument of motion, viz. the hand, in which the ideal of perfection seems to have been reached.

The cephalopods, which have eight arms, formed of muscle-substance and provided with suckers, stand, among the mollusca, nearest to the vertebrates on account of their strength and power of movement. It was movement, probably, that developed their brain-ganglia, for these are larger in the cephalopods than in the other mollusca. As they possess a good memory and a high intelligence, so they also exhibit more intense emotions, as may be seen from the great facility with which the color of their skin changes.

The mutual relation of intelligence and movement is one of the most constant factors in nature. The movements always change when the intelligence changes. We need only consider the gait of the Indians in order to convince ourselves of the truth of my assertion. Their walk is characteristic, being heavier and slower than ours. Microcephalic individuals have an awkward gait, and an inconsiderable dexterity in the movement of the hands. This change in movement is still more striking in the case of idiots.

In some parts of Italy and of Switzerland there are many cretins. On my frequent Alpine excursions, I was often able to recognize by their gait the degree of intelligence of persons who were near me. I have convinced myself of the fact that the first signs of cretinism can be detected in the heavy gait, the arched vertebral column, and the manner of moving the arms in walking.

VII.

Neither anatomy nor physiology has hitherto been able to decide whether like brain cells have different functions, or whether all cells perform the same service.

Since neither chemically nor by the use of the strongest microscopes can we demonstrate differences in the nerve cells of the cerebral cortex, it is therefore probable that none such exist. Hence, I believe that the psychic functions cannot be separated from the motor, that rather the psychic phenomenon and that which imparts the movement impulse both have their seat in the same cell. How closely connected thought and movement, consciousness and muscular activity, are, is best seen in the phenomena of sleep. If, shortly before going to sleep, we hold a book or some other object in the hand, we notice that the object falls, the muscles relaxing, the moment consciousness ceases. The significance of the fact emphasized here is not decreased by the phenomena of movement observed in somnambulists and individuals who have been hypnotized. It is well known that one can ride and walk when asleep. By practice one can learn to play the pianoforte without distinguishing the individual finger-movements. Some can play an instrument when asleep. But these are not voluntary, but instinctive and reflex movements.

In a diseased arm, in which the muscles have been atrophied, the sensitiveness of the fingers is simultaneously improved if one seeks to remove the atrophied condition of the muscles by exercises in contraction.

When the brain has been fatigued by exclusively intellectual activity, the sensitiveness of the hand and direct irritability of the muscles are also decreased. These observations force us to the assumption that the intelligence, the sensitiveness, and the movement are phenomena which cannot be separated from each other, that their fusion and their connection belong to the conditions which permit us to comprehend the nature of the mind.

Imbecile signifies weak in body, but particularly weak in mind. In Latin, however, *in bacillum* means "leaning on a staff." The ancients have thus understood the relations in question better than I am able to express them in words.

VIII.

It is well known that an injury on a certain spot in the left temporal lobe of the brain carries with it the loss of speech. Forty years ago Broca first described a case of this kind. At the autopsy of a man who had lost his speech, whose right arm and leg were paralyzed, and who, besides, exhibited disturbances of intelligence, there was found a broad and deep depression of the brain substance, extending from the Sylvian fissure to that of Rolando. Afterward appeared the celebrated treatises of Broca, which form an imperishable monument in the history of cerebral localization. It is the merit of James to have shown that the motor impulse develops itself before the appearance of language in the convolutions of the left cerebral hemisphere.

In our development gestures and other movements appear first; then, later, the sounds of language.

It is not the process of consciousness which makes our hands dexterous, but perhaps the movements of the right extremities which effect the higher psychic development of the left cerebral hemisphere.

The influence of the hand upon the development of language is evident from the fact that an aphasic patient is made to write in order that he may gradually regain the power of speech.

The relation between muscular movements and conscious processes is so intimate that when the arms and hands of a hypnotized person are brought into certain positions and certain muscles by external contact made to contract, certain emotions are induced corresponding to those muscular contractions. Here, then, intellectual processes are certainly effected by external muscular activity.

There is no doubt that the first human beings were dumb, and that men for a long time made use of gesture-language for purposes of mutual understanding before they discovered sound-language. The child, too, before it is able to speak, expresses itself by gestures. It observes the looks of its parents and of the persons who speak to it, in order to comprehend the meaning of the words heard. Pantomime is the heightened expression of the involuntary movements which accompany the individual phases of mental activity. In the hieroglyphs of the Egyptians and in the representations on Greek vases we recognize the gestures and the involuntary movements which men made more than three thousand years ago.

III.

Leonardo da Vinci, in his treatise on painting, had already attempted to describe the passions by detailing how to represent a man in a state of rage and despair. The first men who were able to make themselves intelligible to each other must also have been the most excitable, and in them the motor ideas must have been very active. The word and the language of a people, superhuman gifts, according to the ancients, are produced by reflex movements, gestures, and interjections. Even now artists still feel more keenly than others the intimate relation between muscular movements and psychic functions; they have the gift of representing the effects of the emotions upon bodily posture and of idealizing them.

The great, picturesque mode of representation of the human body, which was the glory of the Renaissance, had its basis in this physiological law.

A pleiad of the greatest artists, who perceived the internal power of the emotions, popularized the study of bodily postures by representing in sacred and profane creations the feelings that thrilled the soul. They glorified the naked body, busying themselves with showing through the study of bodily forms and their movements the perfection and the philosophy of art.

We need here neither to think of the heroic figures of Michelangelo and their powerful musculature, nor of the pleasing, feeling, and directly perceived figures of Botticelli, nor yet of the sublimely sensual, passion-stirred figures of the Venetian school, in order to comprehend how in works of art the mind is revealed in muscular contractions. It suffices to recall the sublime figures of Perugino, the teacher of Raphael, which compel us to admiration with their expression of the devotion, the enthusiasm, and the ardor of faith. Everything here is kept calm; in these figures we find nothing exciting, the expression of the face alone mirroring the mood which the artist himself felt during the production.

In my next lecture I will speak further of the basic conditions of the emotions. Here, however, I will close.

The nervous system, as you know, consists of an intimate union between sense-surface and muscles. Golgi and Cajal, the greatest discoverers in the structure of the nervous system, tell us now that there is no difference to be found in the cells of the central organs, that there is no evidence of a morphological distinction between motor and sensory cells in the brain.

The structure of the nervous cells is the same; the relations alone are different. Probably there is but one nervous substance, which is active for all functions. The immense number of the brain cells is easily explained, since the cells can relieve one another and the nervous activity go on uninterruptedly from one series of cells to another. The greatest complication lies in the life of a single brain cell.

In this lecture I have sought to show how intimately related are mental processes and movements. If we desired to make a pedagogical application, we might say that physical education and gymnastics serve not only for the development of the muscles, but for that of the brain as well.

---

1. P. Flechsig. Die Leitungsbahnen im Gehirn und Rückenmark des Menschen. Leipzig, 1896.

2. Th. Kaes. Ueber die markhaltigen Nervenfasern in der Gehirnrinde des Menschen. Neurologisches Centralblatt, 1894, p. 410.

3. H. Ambronn und Held. Ueber experimentelle Reifung des Nervenmarks. Arch. f. Anat. u. Entwicklungsgesch. Leipzig, 1896, p. 227.

4. A. Mosso. Periodische Athmung und Luxusathmung. Archiv f. Anat. u. Physiol. 1886.

—— Die Diagnostik des Pulses. Leipzig, 1879.

—— Ueber den Kreislauf des Blutes im menschlichen Gehirn. Leipzig, 1881.

5. —— Die Ermüdung. Leipzig, 1892.

6. W. P. Lombard. Alterations in the Strength which occur during Fatiguing Voluntary Muscular Work. Journal of Physiology, Vol. XIV., 1893, pp. 97–124.

7. Lindley, E. H. A Preliminary Study of Some of the Motor Phenomena of Mental Effort. Amer. Journ. Psychol., Vol. VII., pp. 491–517.

8. D. Hansemann. Ueber das Gehirn von H. v. Helmholtz. Ztschr. f. Psychol. u. Physiol. d. Sinnesorgane, 1899, p. 921.

9. H. v. Helmholtz. Physiologische Optik., p. [illegible].

10. Schön und Mosso. Eine Beobachtung betreffend den Wettstreit der Sehfelder. Arch. f. Ophth., Berlin, 1874, pp. [illegible]–277.

11. A. Mosso. Ueber den Kreislauf des Blutes im menschlichen Gehirn. Leipzig, 1881, p. 101.

12. A. Mosso et Pellacani. Sur les fonctions de la vessie. Arch. ital. de Biol., Tome I., p. 97.

13. Max Müller. Vorlesungen über die Wissenschaft der Sprache. Leipzig, 1866, p. 79.

14. G. J. Romanes. L'évolution mentale chez les animaux. Paris, 1884, p. 4.

THE MECHANISM OF THE EMOTIONS.

BY PROFESSOR ANGELO MOSSO.

I.

TO-DAY I may be permitted to express my own ideas about the mechanism of the emotions.

We are sometimes surprised by a sad or a joyful piece of news. We all know what happens in a state of fear and distress. Physiological phenomena occur that cannot be described. But when we learn suddenly that the news which has troubled us is false, that our fear and distress had no foundation, the internal disturbance does not cease, the physiological phenomena continue in the organism in spite of all efforts of the will to suppress them.

The investigation of these processes has shown that the seat of the emotions lies in the sympathetic nervous system.

Before we were born, and for a long time after birth, our life was entrusted to the activity of the sympathetic system and the reflex movements derived from the spinal cord. We need not be surprised at this, when we reflect how great an importance nature has attributed to the vegetative and generative life processes in the formation of the organism.

In decisive moments of life, when the emotions are most violent, it is just the sympathetic nervous system that comes into action. The intestines and the smooth muscular fibres contract in order to raise the pressure of the blood, and to utilize the blood better for the brain and the muscles.

The first observations concerning this subject were made by me more than twenty years ago. I was able to see that in sleep a contraction of the blood-vessels always takes place as soon as the sense organs and the skin are stimulated, even when the stimulation is so weak that the subject does not wake up.[1] These changes, which result without our knowledge, form one of the most remarkable arrangements which we can observe among the perfections of our organization. During the interruption of consciousness our body does not remain helplessly exposed to the influences of the external world, or in danger of becoming the prey of its enemies. Even in sleep a portion of the nerve centres watches over the operations of the external world, and prepares in good time the material conditions for the awaking of consciousness. If we glance back at the unconscious processes which we saw take place in sleep under external influences, we shall see that they are all coördinated in correspondence with a final object; they all coincide in favoring the circulation of the blood in the brain, and thereby making it possible that, in case of danger, the organ may awake to full activity.

I do not believe myself far from the truth in maintaining that the totality of the reflex movements to be observed during sleep forms a real defensive apparatus for the organism.

Other investigators have since demonstrated the same thing. Two years later, in 1881, Dr. Pellacani and I found that even very weak sensations caused a contraction of the bladder.[1] These facts had, in general, been already known, for these contractions have become proverbial in connection with fear and other emotional conditions; but no one had previously observed that this organ reacts with such facility to all sense impressions that its tonicity changes in consequence of attention and inconsiderable psychic processes.

II.

The organs of the abdomen and the pelvic cavity are just as sensitive to the emotions as the heart. I have studied the movements of the abdominal organs, the stomach, and the rectum. In the smallest emotions movements of the intestines and stomach always occur.

In the movements of the bladder, we must distinguish between active and passive, *i.e.* between such as are peculiar to the bladder itself, and such as are transferred to it from the diaphragm and from the walls of the abdomen.

In order to investigate with exactness these movements of the bladder itself, I have carried on experiments both on the dog and on woman. I shall first explain the construction of the apparatus employed, and then give an account of the experiments performed.

The instrument made use of was my plethysmograph, which has the advantage of maintaining the pressure constant and of registering the slightest movements of contraction and relaxation of the bladder.

A catheter for female use (Fig. 1) *A* is in communication with a glass tube *BC* which, with a rectangular curve, sinks to the depth of 1 or 2 cm. below the level *ab* of the liquid contained in the large receptacle, *P*. This descending tube must be put into a perfectly vertical position before

Fig. 1.—Arrangement of the plethysmograph for tracing the movements of the bladder.

every experiment, and fixed firmly in that position by the iron support *DE*. The pressure-screws at the foot of the support facilitate this necessary arrangement. A test-tube *F*, like those used for chemical reactions, with very thin walls, and suspended by two silk threads from a pulley *G*, is held in equilibrium by means of a piece of lead *H*, which has the same weight as the cylinder *F*. To this counterpoise is fixed a pen for tracing on a smoked cylinder, or on the continuous roll of a Ludwig kymograph.

The cylinder *F* is suspended in such a manner that it has the vertical glass tube *C* in perfect correspondence to its axis and so that it can move up and down without touching it.

In order to avoid the attraction of the cylinder by adhesion to the tube running down its axis, and the consequent development of resistance, it is advisable to furnish the lower end of the tube with a little ring of sealing-wax, or of india-rubber, cut from a tube of corresponding diameter.

The cylinder *F* is drawn up until its bottom touches the lower end of the vertical tube; the jar *P*, for the time being, we suppose to be full of water.

The catheter *A* and the bladder of the animal or human being into which it is introduced must be on the same level *ab* as the liquid in the large vessel. The true level is easily found by placing the plethysmograph and the cylinder on which the tracing is done on a strong iron table, which may be raised or lowered by means of a screw; a photographer's table serves the same purpose.

The tube *AIBC* and part of the cylinder *F* being filled with water, the catheter is introduced into the bladder, and the clip *I* opened. If a contraction of the bladder takes place, a quantity of water corresponding to the diminution of the capacity of the bladder will flow into the cylinder *F*. The cylinder *F*, becoming heavier through this afflux of water, is bound to sink into the liquid of the jar below until it has displaced a volume of liquid corresponding to the increase of water received. If a dilatation of the bladder takes place, a certain volume of water will flow into it, and the cylinder becoming lighter will rise to a corresponding height above its original level.

Had the walls of the cylinder neither volume nor weight, and were the jar full of water *P* so wide that the immersion of the cylinder would not sensibly alter the level of the water contained, it is clear that the cylinder might rise or sink without any change taking place in the level of the water, either in the cylinder or in the jar *P*. But since the walls of a glass cylinder, however thin they may be, have nevertheless a certain weight and volume, the immersion of the cylinder in water will cause a loss of so much of its weight as would correspond to the weight of a cylinder precisely similar with walls of water. This diminution of weight at the side *F* of a system *FH*, which is held in equilibrium by means of the pulley *G*, must produce a displacement. The counterpoise *H*, which has remained constant, will repair the loss in weight of the cylinder *F* in raising above the level *ab* a weight of water in the cylinder which will equal the loss in weight of the cylinder in its immersion.

A column of water being raised in this manner above the level *ab*, there is of necessity an augmentation of pressure within the bladder corresponding to the height of the column. In order to remedy this defect, which as a rule is not more than a column of 2 cm. of water, we fill the jar *P* with a liquid which is less dense than water, that is, with alcohol and water. At every contraction of the bladder a corresponding quantity of water will pass into the cylinder, and the latter will sink into the diluted alcohol in the jar *P*. As, however, the density of this liquid is less than that of water, the cylinder *F* will not only, in its descent, displace a volume of alcohol equal to that of the water which it contains, but will tend to sink lower, thus carrying the level of the water it contains below the level *ab* of the surrounding alcohol.

Then, again, we have already noticed that the cylinder in plunging into the liquid loses gradually in weight, in accordance with the well-known principle of Archimedes, and that the counterpoise, which remains constant, seeks to repair this loss by raising the inner level of the water *ab* above the level of the surrounding alcohol, until the equilibrium is reëstablished.

We have, therefore, in this case two forces acting in opposition: that is, gravity, which tends to bring the water level below the alcohol level *ab*, and the loss in weight undergone by the cylinder *F* during immersion, which gives it an upward impetus. If these two forces are equal they will cancel each other and the cylinder *F* will be able to rise and fall to the extent of its entire length, the level *ab* of the water contained in it remaining meanwhile unaltered.

In order to obtain the exact degree of density necessary to this end we make use of an empirical method; that is, we prepare a mixture of water and absolute alcohol if the cylinder has thickish walls. The liquid will have the required degree of density when the cylinder is filled to the top with water or empty; in other words, when the cylinder is immersed up to its neck in the liquid or has its base merely touched by it, the level *ab* of the water contained in it remains constant on the plane *ab* of the surrounding liquid.

For all these necessary operations of filling, emptying the cylinder, adding or taking away water from the bladder, a glass tube *L* graduated in cubic centimetres is made use of. This tube communicates by means of another of india-rubber closed by a clip *K* and of a T-tube with the horizontal tube *BC*. In order to empty the cylinder *F* or take water from the bladder, an inward breath is drawn at the mouth of the tube *N*, the tube *L* meanwhile being closed with the stopper *M*, which has a glass tube running through it; in order to add water, one need only open the nipper *K*.

For the experiments explained in the sequel a graduated and calibrated cylinder which contained 30 cc. to 18 cm. length was made use of, therefore every centimetre measured on the ordinates of our tracings corresponds to a little less than 2 cc.

Care must be taken that the pulley *G* be sensitive enough and so well balanced that it remains in equilibrium in every position. A description of the apparatus that puts the cylinder *S* in movement, its velocity being constant or variable as required, is here unnecessary, as it is a piece of clockwork with a Foucault regulator which is to be found in all laboratories.

When a certain pressure was to be exercised on the bladder in order to dilate it, it sufficed to raise the table on which the plethysmograph stood, so that the level *ab* was above the plane of the bladder, and to add water with the tube *L* or to lower the animal or human being.

In order to measure exactly the pressure exercised on the bladder during our experiments, we made use of a water level consisting of a simple india-rubber tube with an inner diameter of 5 mm., 1 m. in length, which had at its end two pointed glass tubes about 20 cm. in length. One of these tubes being placed near the symphysis pubis, the other was put against the jar *P*, and the difference of level between the bladder and the plane *ab* was read on a double decimetre measure. This height is the pressure exercised on the bladder.

Six days after a fistula had been applied to a male dog the bladder was connected through it with my plethysmograph, and the curve thus obtained recorded on a rotating cylinder. Simultaneously I had the thoracic and the abdominal respiration registered. The movements of the bladder and of the abdomen are by this means directly fixed upon the cylinder, while the thoracic respiration is represented reversed upon it, *i.e.* a sinking of the curve corresponds in the latter case to expiration, a rise to inspiration. Since the three curves were recorded exactly over each other, the movements could be studied independently and compared (Fig. 2).

The curve for the bladder showed, as was to be expected, also the respiratory movements. In this curve we see that the bladder begins to contract before the abdomen rises. This comes from the fact that the sinking of the diaphragm depresses the intestines, and, with them, also the bladder. The effect must first appear in the very place where the resistance is least, *i.e.* in the open bladder; then the abdominal walls

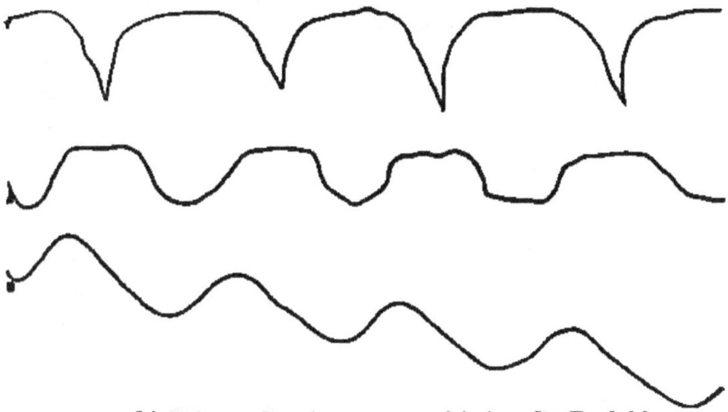

FIG. 2.—Relation between the respiratory movement of the thorax (line *T*) and of the abdomen (line *A*) with the passive movements of the bladder (line *B*).

are forced forward. Some time after the contraction of the diaphragm the expansion of the chest begins.

But, besides these respiratory movements, there can be perceived in the bladder curve a slight sinking, and, after it, again a rising of the whole curve. These are active movements proper to the bladder itself. They are easily distinguished from the passive movements, since they occur less quickly.

Another day while we were recording the movements of the bladder, a servant, to whom the dog was much attached, entered the laboratory. Immediately the curve showed an active contraction of the bladder, as may be seen in Fig. 3 at *G*. In *abc* we see passive movements of the bladder, which have become weaker because the respiration is more superficial.

When, shortly before, another person, whom the dog did not know so well, had entered the room, we had also noticed another, but stronger, contraction of the bladder. In order to keep the dog quiet, one of us laid his hand on his head. (See *P* in the curve of Fig. 6.) When the hand was taken away, and the servant laid his upon the dog, there occurred again an active, but less marked, contraction of the bladder. As soon as the respiration became more superficial, the passive movements of the bladder became also less distinct.

After these observations, the dog lay with eyes half-closed, as if he was about to go to sleep. His tail was touched, and immediately afterward the curve showed an active contraction of the bladder, while — what is noteworthy — the rhythm and depth of the respiratory movements did not change. After the bladder had again assumed its full volume, and while the dog was perfectly quiet, his skin was touched, and the curve record showed at once a stronger, active contraction of the bladder. In like manner, sensations of pain, which we produced by pulling the dog's ears, caused strong, active contractions of the bladder.

Such experiments were many times repeated. They were also carried on with bitches, the bladder being directly connected with the plethysmograph by the introduction of a catheter, without previous establishment of a fistula. The results which we obtained were always the same. It was sufficient to speak kindly to the animals, or to caress them, to make the curve express the psychic influence upon their active movements.

But I could not rest content with these results obtained from animals. I needed to corroborate them by experiments on human beings. Naturally this can be done better with woman, since with her the bladder can be easily brought into connection with the plethysmograph by the introduction of a catheter. My clinical colleagues were kind enough to place at my disposal some girls from the hospitals, who readily offered themselves for the purposes of these experiments.

Fig. 6.

I may be permitted to give an account of these experiments also. These experiments were carried on, otherwise, as the first. Again I had the thoracic and abdominal respiration and the movements of the bladder independently recorded. The subject lay comfortably on a bed. Here, in a state of complete rest, the whole curve of the bladder was, at times, horizontal, showing, at others, slight active undulations. To touch the hand of the subject lightly sufficed, however, to produce at once an active contraction of the bladder. (See *T* in the curve of Fig. 4.)

Fig. 4.

While the subject was lying quietly on the bed, the clockwork of the kymograph was wound up (see *C*). The noise resulting was entirely unknown to the subject, but the impression sufficed to cause itself to be reflected in the bladder, and to induce a contraction, visible in the curve. When the subject was addressed (see *P*), it could be seen that the bladder contracted immediately, while, if she herself spoke (see *R*), a series of such contractions took place. All these contractions are movements proper to the bladder. As was shown by other experiments as well, they were not transferred to the bladder from the abdominal walls or from the diaphragm, and were not, therefore, passive movements *F*. The lower line *T* marks the seconds.

I was particularly interested in the movements produced in the bladder by purely psychic influences. These are shown, *e.g.*, by the following experiment. While the girl lay quietly on the bed, and respiration was quiet and normal, — this is always shown by the curves, — some one said to her, "Now I'm going to pinch you," but without doing so. Immediately the bladder contracted, without the slightest change being noticed in the thoracic and abdominal respiration. After rest had been again restored, a jest was spoken to the girl, and again we perceived a contraction of the bladder on the curve, without seeing any modification whatever of the two respiratory curves.

Beyond all doubt, then, the contractions of the bladder which we observed were movements proper to that organ itself.

All these phenomena may be considered the most delicate reflex movements which occur in the organism. I was particularly interested to know what influence a direct activity of the brain would exercise upon the movements of the bladder, and I carried on experiments to that end. The subject had only a slight education; she was especially a bad mental arithmetician, very easy problems in arithmetic causing her difficulties. She needed, therefore, in such work to exert her brain very much.

While she lay quietly on the bed and her respiration was quite normal, she was given the following example in arithmetic: "How many eggs are seven dozen?" Immediately the bladder was seen to contract (Fig. 5). After this problem was solved (see *W*), we had her multiply in her head thirteen by twelve, and then a relaxation of the bladder was to be seen.

I noticed, also, that merely speaking to the girl, without her answering, was sufficient to produce a contraction of the bladder.

III.

The preponderating activity of the sympathetic system in the emotions is so great that the brain effort is not able to suppress it. Many men feel a contraction in the abdomen when they look down from a tower or other high place. These troublesome sensations, which are connected with the idea of a possible fall, are simply caused by the contraction of the bladder and the intestines.

When we investigate, by means of the plethysmograph, the movements of the intestines during emotional states, we obtain the same curves as we receive from the movements of the blood-vessels of the extremities or of the brain, or from the movements of the bladder. All these facts enable us to understand the mechanism of the emotions better. *Emotio* signifies movement. We understand now that the constant and fundamental movements taking place in emotions are the movements of the internal organs of vegetative life.

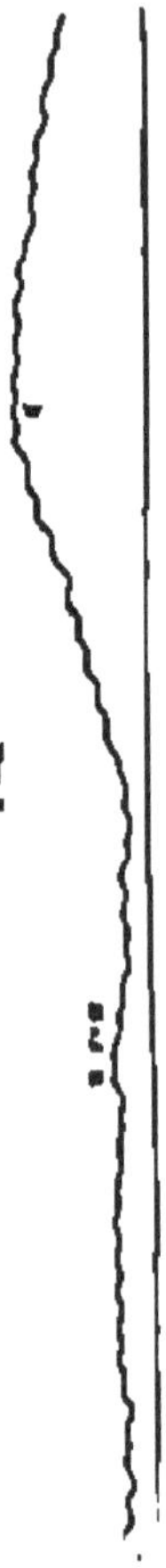

Fig. 5.

The investigations carried on in my laboratory by Dr. Kiesow have convinced me that in certain emotions the blood pressure increases, and the blood-vessels and smooth muscular fibres contract in order to prevent the blood from being dammed up in the abdominal cavity.

In order to increase the circulation of the blood in the brain and muscles our bodily machine has to work under a higher blood pressure. This end could be attained only through the sympathetic system, which sends its fibres every where to the smooth musculature. During blushing a paling of the skin can be noticed before the blood-vessels expand, and the blush proper takes place.

In the study of the emotions the reflex movements of the striped musculature of the face, the extremities, and the trunk are of secondary significance to the physiologist. They are simply accompanying phenomena and, just because they are more complicated, less fundamental.

However useful the first reactions of the nervous system are, yet we all know that they do not suffice for the defence of the organism in strong emotions. The nerve substance is so irritable that a small shock is enough to disturb the equilibrium. I will not enter into detail here, since I have already shown in my book on "Fear," how unstable is the equilibrium of the nervous system, and how easily the brain and the sympathetic system go beyond the proper measure in their activity when danger threatens, and existence is at stake.

Even a practiced observer is often unable to decide from the gestures and facial expression of an individual whether he is enraged or in a state of the greatest joy.

To recall the expressions of two so opposite emotional conditions suffices to convince us that the reflex phenomena accompanying them are not only useless, but even injurious. Indeed, in great pain and great pleasure we have the same phenomena: trembling of the muscles, secretion of tears, expansion of the pupils, decrease of visual acuity, buzzing in the ears, oppression of the breathing, palpitation of the heart, inability to speak, exclamations, convulsive movements of the diaphragm, etc. All these phenomena are injurious. After the emotion is over we feel nervous fatigue, have headache, and suffer from insomnia. I am sorry to find myself in this matter in disagreement with Darwin, but I cannot concede that the unconscious processes occurring during the emotions (at least the best known and most characteristic) have always a physiological purpose.

If we compare the expressions of pleasure and satisfaction in their highest degrees with those of pain, it will be seen that there is one and the same mechanism for both. In my book on "Fear" I have shown that it is the quantity and not the quality of the excitation which disturbs the equilibrium of our organism. Only the processes which take place in the system of the great sympathetic are purposive and advantageous for the preservation of life. And it cannot be otherwise. The animals, whose involuntary movements preserved them from destruction in danger, won in the struggle for existence over others who possessed in less marked degree this capacity.

Whatever the emotions may be, we always see that in these states the blood pressure increases, the heart beats become stronger, and the respiration deeper. These advantageous effects are the same in man as in animals, when they fix the attention, are passionately excited, curious or jealous, or when they run at play or in pursuit of prey.

But as soon as the emotion becomes more intense, the equilibrium of the organs ceases. The condition of excitability is increased and becomes more complicated, contractions of the muscles and changes in the sense organs take place, from which it results that the capacity for resistance of the organism is lowered. In strong emotions, as in rage and anger, we are overpowered by unconscious and discoördinated movements, and a penetrative and irresistible transformation occurs in us, as if the influence of education had been extinguished, as if our reason had suffered an eclipse. We are no longer able to suppress the internal excitement, the voice refuses its office, and we utter a wild cry. Many persons in such states gnash their teeth like wild beasts, others act foolishly, like children.

These disturbances occur not only in the reflex movements, but also in the conscious processes, and more even in the latter than in the former. Education has taught us that we must seek to master and to calm ourselves during this internal excitement, for in these states we lack mental clearness and power of judgment, and consciousness cannot again regain control until these discoördinated reflex movements have ceased. Even the ancients knew that strong emotions resembled a suddenly occurring sickness. The legend of ancient Rome idealized a king in order to represent war. They gave him the name *Hostilius*, which is derived from *hostis*. Tradition further informs us that this king erected a temple to "Pallor and Fear," for *pallor* and *fear* were looked upon as malevolent, destructive deities who must be appeased in order that the soldiers might be victorious in battle.[3]

---

1. A. Mosso. Ueber den Kreislauf des Blutes im menschlichen Gehirne. Leipzig, 1881.
2. A. Mosso e Pellacani. Sulle funzioni della vescica. Mem. d. R. Accad. dei Lincei, 1881.
3. E. Pais. Storia di Roma. Torino, 1898. Vol. I., Parte I., p. 304.

HYPN[illegible]

By [illegible]

[illegible] I beg to pr[illegible] [illegible] to go[illegible] as far [illegible] [illegible]lation of the present state [illegible] of course [illegible] along with no [illegible] we must [illegible] that everything [illegible] to phenom[illegible] of brain activit[illegible] [illegible] over [illegible] [illegible] as it could [illegible] [illegible] activity. W[illegible] [illegible] and to the fam[illegible] [illegible]. Should these be [illegible] not belong here [illegible] certainly [illegible] better evidence than so far [illegible] [illegible] is yet unexplained is [illegible] [illegible] of human know[illegible] [illegible] facts [illegible] be ignored, [illegible] [illegible] respect [illegible] [illegible] and cerebral [illegible] I beg [illegible] myself [illegible]

ANA[illegible] F[illegible]

[illegible] difficult[illegible] to this [illegible] of the [illegible] [illegible] we show [illegible] and [illegible] [illegible] stands in [illegible] [illegible]

We know [illegible] there is only

HYPNOTISM AND CEREBRAL ACTIVITY.

BY PROFESSOR AUGUST FOREL.

GENTLEMEN: — I beg to present to you as few hypotheses as possible, and to put together as far as feasible merely the facts which must form the foundation of the present state of the doctrine of hypnotism. We cannot, of course, get along with no explanatory theory at all. Before all, we must maintain that everything that is known can be traced altogether to phenomena of brain activity. Everything that one has tried (and still tries) to bring over from the field of mysticism, or so-called occultism, has, as far as it could be controlled, turned out to be mistaken phenomena of brain activity. We may calmly leave the rest to metaphysical speculators and to the famous breadth of the imaginary knowledge of the ignorant. Should there be anything in telepathy, for instance, it would not belong here; certainly its representatives would have to furnish better evidence than so far exists.

That much is yet unexplained is perfectly evident — as obvious as in any other domain of human knowledge. It does not follow, however, that facts should be ignored, even if their connections present many obscurities; nor can we respect here the famous dogmatic line of division between psychology and cerebral physiology with the traditional awe, and for this I beg to excuse myself at the outset.

ANATOMICAL FOUNDATION.

However difficult it may be to this day to grasp even the rudiments of the relation of the brain as an organ to the physiological and psychological aspect of its function, we should not cease one moment to work on this problem. Nearer and nearer we must get to it, and, truly, what has already been reached stands inspection well and need not cause us, in the least, to despair.

We know to-day that there is only one kind of nervous elements, that is, the neurone, the cell with its fibre and branched processes. When, in 1886–87, about the same time as His, I first put forth this view as a probable hypothesis on the ground of numerous facts, I had no idea that three years later my illustrious colleague, S. Ramón y Cajal, would establish the matter histologically in such a beautiful and conclusive manner. The nerve elements do not anastomose, as was formerly believed, but touch one another by ramifying branches, end-baskets, arborizations, etc. Every nerve fibre (axone), together with its ramifications, is merely a part of the protoplasm of a certain cell. Further, Schiller showed in my laboratory that the number of nerve elements in the newborn (oculomotor nerve of the cat) was approximately as large as in the adult, and that only the caliber of the medullary fibres differed enormously. Since it appears certain that, in a lifetime, destroyed elements of the central nervous system are never replaced by newly formed ones, we may draw the conclusion that the nerve elements of an old person are the same as those of his childhood, a point very important for the theory of memory.

A matter of further importance is the relation of chromatic reaction of the nerve cell, established by Nissl, to the details of its finer structure. The fibrils, already recognized by v. Kupffer, Schultze, Leydig, and others, and the chromatic bodies present, as it were, elements of a second order, which increase considerably the complication of nerve structure and open new perspectives. The same holds for the change of cell structure after exhausting activity, demonstrated first by Dr. Hodge of this University, and for the grave changes due to the use of alcoholic beverages established by many investigators — an additional reason why we should banish those abominable social and individual nerve poisons from human diet.

Hand in hand with the progress mentioned, we notice the advances in the recognition of local structural conditions in the brain of man and animals, of systems of neurones, etc., especially through v. Gudden's method of experimental atrophy; but also by direct anatomical study. The works of Déjerine and Mme. Déjerine-Klumpke, and of Kölliker, are encyclopædic monuments of those researches. I mention further the doctrine of localization built up by Broca, Hitzig, Ferrier, Munk, etc., which can only lead slowly to a clear and objective understanding of the whole in connection with an accurate knowledge of anatomy, of pathology, and of the experimental method of v. Gudden. At the same time, we must always guard ourselves against speculations built on insufficient and unsafe ground, such as the recent doctrines of Flechsig. While it is possible to establish, to a great extent, the function of the peripheral nerves and their nuclei of origin by direct observation and experiment, and while we have also a certain direct access to the study of the spinal cord, we recognize the function of the cerebral cortex in two ways: (*a*) by physiological experiments and investigations; (*b*) by so-called introspective or psychological observation and experiments. But the mutual relations of sensory stimulation and muscular action to the hemispheres must also be observed both psychologically and physiologically. If I prick some one, the subsequent reflex contraction is observed by me physiologically; whereas the character and intensity of the pain which the person claims to feel can only be measured by him on the psychological side. I see and hear his answers physiologically only, but make out their sense psychologically only, etc.

If we consider more accurately this continual interaction between psychological and physiological phenomena in the light of our knowledge of the brain, we are bound to become sure of one thing, viz. that there is a dark field between the subjectively accessible, psychological, sentient, and perceptive parts of the hemisphere cortex, and those representing the physiologically accessible, sensory receiving stations and the motor, or efferent, mechanisms of motion. In this dark, intermediate field, powerful accumulations of stimuli of an unconscious nature must go on, and obscure, instinctive automatic mechanisms, inherited from our animal ancestors, must work and influence us unconsciously to a great extent in the shape of impulses and feelings. We are driven to assume that the great ganglionic nerve centres of the base of the brain, corpora striata, thalami, pons, tegmentum, cerebellum, must play a part utterly obscure, which perhaps might clear up many points, if we could penetrate more deeply. Unfortunately this point is still far from accessible, since the fragments furnished by physiology are hardly fit to be digested.

We should not forget in this whole question what recent investigations have demonstrated, viz. that the field of expansion of a single nerve element, a neurone, may be very large. Just think of a Betz-cell of the central convolutions, the nerve process of which reaches through the corona radiata, the crus, pons, and pyramid, as far as the spinal cord, or of a cell of the anterior horn of the lumbar cord, whose process reaches muscles of the foot. Thus, neurones of varied significance and destination cross and interweave in a thousand ways in the central and in the peripheral nervous systems, in order to form the wonderful machinery. One sees, from this alone, how brutal and defective the physiological experiments in the brain must be, and how indefinite the physiological concept of a "centre" is.

Physiological Remarks.

There is but little in the old nerve physiology that can be used to-day, because it rested, to a great extent, on erroneous histological concepts. We must accept the well-known fundamental facts concerning stimulation, inhibition, reflexes, etc., and also the results of the pioneers of brain physiology, Flourens, Magendie, Vulpian, Duchenne, etc. We may conceive that the brain is a powerful accumulator, a kind of very highly complicated dynamo, in which a still enigmatical physico-chemical wave-like power prevails, for which I have used the expression "neurokyme," (the "force neurique" of the French). This force does not cause any motion of the masses, and consequently belongs to the type of molecular motion, or vibration, as is shown by its great velocity of conduction. Its action leaves in the cell visual changes in the form of material signs of exhaustion. It may be accumulated as energy by so-called mechanisms of inhibition, and again be discharged in definite channels by what Exner calls "Bahnung." In this connection, O. Vogt has justly insisted on the important fact that in excessive stimulation the effect is often suddenly stopped because a radiation of neighboring centres of neurones takes place, which is apt to lead away the entire neurokyme, if those centres are more easily excitable. In this way it is in a manner possible to understand associative activity. To enter upon detail would lead too far; but I beg to say, in a general way, that it is well known that certain functions become much easier and stronger after a while through practice; whereas, in an obscure but very frequent manner, on the other hand, certain single impulses may leave behind lasting inhibitions, or stimuli, and perhaps disorders of function which may take a pathological character, and seriously tantalize the victim. Such points were used, a few years ago, by Breuer and Freud in Vienna, for the foundation of their doctrine of arrested emotions, which, unfortunately, was developed into a one-sided system, although it started from correct facts. Thus especially violent affects are apt to leave behind all sorts of nervous disorders (convulsions, paralysis, pains, dyspepsia, menstrual disorders). Breuer and Freud tried to lead the patients in a hypnotic condition to the causative, frequently forgotten, and frequently sexual moment of the trouble, to make them dream over that moment and to give, once and forever, a counter suggestion, curing the disorder. In many cases this works; but by no means always.

Before all, we must acknowledge with Isidore Steiner that the greatest nerve centre has the dominant position in this interaction of the neurokymes, owing to its greater mass. It becomes the guide and director of the whole, and the activity of the other centres is brought into subjection. Steiner proved this by a clever experiment on a fish, and showed that in those animals the mid-brain, and not the fore-brain, is the director and the soul of the animal; consequently it is not the morphological homology which decides the absolute anatomical size or physiological strength, and hence the eminently important fact that the relative size of the individual part of the central nervous system is of great importance for the relative independence or dependence. We see the proof for this fact in the comparative physiology of the animal series. The spinal cord and ganglia are far more independent in the lizard than in the rabbit; much more independent in the latter than in the dog; and in the dog, much more independent than in man. In man these organs have become the subordinated servants of the hemispheres and totally dependent, although their structure is much more complicated than in the lizard.

We need not wonder, therefore, if the function of these lower centres is governed and influenced most powerfully by the dynamics of the fore-brain just named, even when, as in the sympathetic, only loose connection exists, such as would suggest, ordinarily, a greater independence.

How is a neurokyme, which spreads over an axone, transferred from one neurone to the others by the contact of dendritic ramifications? Duval thinks, by an amœboid motion of the dendrites, and we read that lately such motions have been directly observed in transparent animals. This hypothesis seems, however, quite immature as yet. It does not explain the extreme rapidity of the conduction of the neurokyme. The functional play of the neurones is better explained by pure molecular motion, as, for instance, in electricity. It would seem that these hypotheses are quite premature, and we must wait for actual progress in observations.

Finally, we must maintain the fundamental fact of memory, conscious or unconscious, viz. the residual of a dynamic trace of every nerve activity. Such a trace always facilitates the repetition of a corresponding activity, even if it should be forgotten subsequently, and the entire activity may be called forth again by the effect of the stimulus merely associated with the first one; for instance, ordinary remembrance. Organic memory is independent of consciousness and is the same for motor as for sensory and central activities, and even for reflexes and functions of the sympathetic.

Sleep and Waking State—Consciousness.

Man is normally limited to two states of his brain life: sleep and waking condition. Physiologically considered sleep means a relative rest from cerebral activity with recuperation of the exhausted neurones by chemical synthesis, whereas in the waking state processes of oxidation predominate. This is certain beyond doubt, but to draw the conclusion that sleep is called forth by the formation of fatigue products, such as lactic acid, or that sleeplessness could be cured by swallowing lactic acid, as Preyer did, is to become a victim of fallacies.

It does not take much acuteness of observation to see that there is a form of sleep which is not rest, and that the brain can rest fairly well even in the waking state. Further, one may sleep much and excessively though not exhausted, and again may keep awake in a state of cerebral exhaustion. Again, every unprejudiced observer must be struck with the usually rather sudden qualitative change in the attitude of a waking and of a sleeping person. That sleep is readily called forth by certain associations, regular hours, etc., is also obvious. Finally, dreams give us a chance to look into the life of sleep from the psychological side.

All these factors tend to present sleep as a state of qualitatively modified cerebral activity. This is, however, only intelligible in connection with the concept of consciousness.

It was a fundamental mistake of practically all physicians and most psychologists, to think of consciousness as a something, as a form of cerebral activity, *i.e.* to confuse the plastic concentrative activity of our *attention* with the purified phenomenon of *subjectiveness*. We will not quarrel over words. I, for one, am satisfied to be able to rest my view on such a psychologist as Spencer. If any one cares to use the word "consciousness" in any other sense, he may do so as long as he gives us another word for that which I understand to be consciousness, viz. the phenomenon of the inner reflection of the ego, the subjective side of the phenomena. Slight activities of the brain, as well as violent ones, are reflected by it and become "conscious"; but equally violent activities seem not to become conscious; they remain "unconscious." Consequently we are forced to distinguish between a conscious and an unconscious life of the brain.

The entire discord of the phenomena rests on the peculiar facts: (1) that the activity of the brain does not take place in one single continuity and connection, that, for instance, two subjective reflexes may occur simultaneously without being connected or "associated," so that the one does not know of the other and one is unconscious in reference to just that other reflex; (2) that everything which is subjectively "forgotten" drops out of the connection of consciousness so that amnesia and unconsciousness are continually confused.

The resulting fallacies are evident; we always call unconscious such actions or states of the brain as were conscious and appear to us to be forgotten, or which were illuminated by a consciousness other than our ordinary remembered consciousness.

In order to be concise, I venture to offer a hypothesis which agrees very well with all the facts: Every nerve activity is conscious, *i.e.* possesses internal reflection; but these reflections are by no means all capable of remaining in a synthetical connection with one another. For this we need a more intense associated activity, especially where the connection is to be fixed by memory. Everything which appears no longer, or not at all, in this connection, loses the subjective connection with our memory ego, and we erroneously deem it unconscious, whether it be a past or actual activity of the hemisphere, or only one of the sympathetic or of the spinal cord. In order to express such a view consistently we must: —

a. Eliminate the word "unconscious," and replace it by "subconscious" or "otherwise conscious."

b. Accept a multiplicity of fields of consciousness, or consciousnesses, the contents, *i.e.* the illuminated cerebral activities, of which are physiologically connected and influence one another subjectively, according to the kinds of activities underlying them; they are only rarely, or partially, or never connected (associated). That subjective associations require higher intensity and more synthesis than the objective (physiological) ones has been shown by psychology (Höffding).

c. Consider all brain activity as completely independent of the accompanying (subjective) illuminations by consciousness, whether it appears to us psychological or physiological. This is theoretically possible, at least for psychological phenomena.

d. Consider the word "consciousness" as the expression of an inner aspect of life, not as the name for any special thing, an activity, a peculiarity. We use the words "energy" and "matter" in a similar way; there is no energy without matter, as little as matter without energy. In the same way consciousness in our sense is nothing in itself, but merely the subjective aspect of brain life, an aspect probably common to all life.

If we adhere to what is said, we find sleep intelligible. We observe the following in the condition of sleep: —

1. The cerebral activity is highly dissociated. The ideas follow one another in a chaos which does not correspond any longer to the connection of things in the actual world. Things which exclude one another in reality appear identical, and the reverse. My friend may be at once a dog, water, or a piece of wood. I may be simultaneously dead and married, or simultaneously in Europe and America, or see my head before me at a distance of twenty yards. If you study this dissociation more closely, you readily see that it affects not only the logical sequence of higher concepts, but the very make-up, even the constituents, of perceptions. The notion of time and place, the single (usually subconscious) sensations constituting a perception, are frequently disjointed, and dance together a veritable Walpurgis dance. Again, there prevail powerful inhibitions which prevent all orderly association and keep us in an oppressive despair and impotence. The same chaos prevails in the field of emotions and of volitions, but here the inhibition, or, in the emotions, powerful ebullitions predominate.

2. The conceptions of dream life are hallucinations. When asleep we no longer distinguish between perception and spontaneous conception. The sensory stimuli either do not become conscious at all or they are allegorized; on the other hand, all perceptions appear as actual happenings. Moreover, the concept of a motion is usually not capable of eliciting the

corresponding actual muscular contraction. It is merely represented by a motor hallucination.

8. Since there are no corrective concepts, some emotions and ideas may, in this condition, obtain an enormous power, overcome obstacles unsurmountable in the waking condition, and hence produce especially intense consequences. Just think of the evil after-effects of dreams, of nocturnal pollutions, etc.

Duval has lately ventured to make a new hypothesis of sleep. He believes that all the terminations of the neurones are in active contact during the waking state by some kind of amœboid activity. During sleep he thinks they simply withdraw, so that the contact ceases. What a beautiful and simple explanation for all the dissociations and eliminations of all the senses! For the time being this view is a mere hypothesis.

Nothing demonstrates so thoroughly the deficiencies of Weber's and Fechner's psycho-physical law as sleep. There are too many intermediate forces between the "subject" and the measurable external stimuli. Heerwagen, for instance, tried to measure the intensity of sleep by the intensity of a noise necessary to wake the sleeping person! These two quantities are practically without any connection. Everything depends on the kind of association. The same sleeping person can be aroused by a very slight unusual sound, while the greatest noise need not disturb the sleep. Heerwagen further tried to make statistics on dreams by asking people for them; but he forgot that most dreams are forgotten, and that the forgetting of dreams and the "not dreaming" are two utterly different things. I am convinced that everybody dreams all the night through. I, myself, if I observe myself at all, cannot be aroused at any time of the night without just having dreamed.

Finally, there are all degrees of sleep, from the lightest, best associated, to the deepest. The former shows all transitions to the waking state. The difference in the cerebral activity during the sleeping and the waking condition implies a corresponding difference of the contents of consciousness. We consequently have two alternating conscious states every day and every night, and our ego is quite characteristic in each. A good trustworthy man may become a thief, a murderer, and a licentious person, a courageous man may be cowardly during sleep, etc. We usually forget our dreams owing to the dissociation, so that our two states of consciousness in sleeping and waking condition show only a slight and fragmentary connection. Not infrequently we find somnambulists who act in a coördinate manner during sleep. One who did all sorts of housework in her sleep was very tired after it, but did not remember anything. This is also the rule in the very frequent somnambulism of children. Out of such an orderly activity of a sleeping brain, *i.e.* out of the spontaneous somnambulism, originates an extraordinary and especially instructive form of double consciousness, such as has been described by McNish, Azam, Dessoir, and myself.

In my case (see *Zeitschrift für Hypnotismus*, 1898), a German made an eight months' journey to Australia and back without in the least remembering it. The amnesia of retrograde and antegrade character came on after dengue fever. Later I was able to revive the memory by suggestions. It was, however, impossible to establish a connected association between the two visits to Melbourne on his journey out and back. Those two Melbournes remained for him two entirely different cities.

The Data of Hypnotism.

At all times in the history of mankind, hypnotism has played a great rôle. Magicians, miracles, miraculous cures, sorcerers, the fakirs of India, are so many proofs of this. The principal fact was always the apparent and subsequently also actual power of certain persons over others, the ecstatic catalepsy or sleep produced by them, the asserted prophecies of the hypnotized, the cure of diseases, the miracles, etc. A magnificent instance of hypnotic influence may be found in the history of King Zoroaster (cf. Stoll's book on this topic). In the beginning of this century Mesmer thought to have discovered a new natural law in those phenomena, a new "fluid," which he assumed to be magnetism. Especially in living beings he called it animal magnetism. He produced hysterical convulsions usually by contact of men, finally "magnetized" trees and did other absurd things; but also cured a number of patients. Condemned by the French Academy as an obvious fraud, he came to a sad end. But he retained adherents. One of them, Puységur, discovered the quiet hypnotic sleep. They all adhered to the belief in a mysterious magnetic fluid. Braid, an English physician, was the first to take a great step toward a scientific elucidation of the question. He found that the whole series of phenomena depended not on a fluidum coming from the outside, but on the brain and nervous system of the person influenced. The very title of his book, "Neurohypnology," shows this. He found that certain stimuli and also certain ideas could produce this changed cerebral state, hypnotism. By this he had established the principal fact, but he made a mistake in the method by ascribing a capital rôle to the peripheral stimuli, just as Charcot did later on. He hypnotized with brilliant objects, and, therefore, did not obtain thoroughgoing results. These we owe to Liébault, at Nancy, and to his medically and philosophically highly educated friend, Professor Bernheim. The doctrine of Liébault and Bernheim has placed hypnotism among the fields for scientific research, from which it will not disappear again. ' This doctrine reduces hypnotism to the concept of suggestion. In this light we shall mention briefly the principal manifestations.

The fact that in falling asleep or awaking the entire mode of brain activity is suddenly altered, gives us, I believe, the key to an understanding of hypnotism. Conceive some means by which we are able to produce those two kinds of activity according to our needs, and, moreover, to localize, — to limit them to certain fields, — and you see before you almost the entire series of hypnotic phenomena. For this purpose you should merely be able to direct the cerebral activity of your neighbor, inhibit and facilitate, associate and dissociate. This actually happens by means of evoking certain concepts, which are known to lead most easily to dissociation. *A priori*, this may appear peculiar and improbable. As a matter of fact, it is exceedingly simple and common. All human beings are naturally more or less suggestible and, therefore, hypnotizable, although not all are equally influenced by others. Everything that produces the concept of sleep, everything that makes man passive, or throws him into ecstasy, admiration, or confidence, may be used by the rapid and concentrated action of the hypnotizer to dissociate, inhibit, or stimulate, any activity of his subject, — it may produce the desired and foretold effect, the mechanism of which remains subconscious in the person influenced. It is especially advantageous to begin with such effects as are readily obtained. This is the principle of Liébault's method.

For instance, I yawn; it becomes "infectious." Another yawns; with him it has the effect of a suggestive influence. He yawns because I yawned; however, he remains subconscious of the mechanism which produces the yawning. Now, I use the beginning dissociation, and tell him rapidly and with assurance: "You are quite sleepy, you cannot keep your eyes open, you cannot open them, you have a warm feeling in your feet; look at me; you are already asleep, your arms are heavy," etc. Quite frequently the subject will feel and even show the one or the other of these phenomena. If he is very suggestible, he will, perhaps, be asleep in a few seconds, to the surprise of those around. This sleep is, however, distinguished from ordinary sleep by remaining under my direction, i.e. by my remaining in connection with the sleeper through his hearing. As soon as I have reached this point a further mastership over his cerebration is an easy matter. I take his arm, lift it, and declare that he cannot lower it; and he cannot with all his efforts. I put both hands into a rotating motion, and he cannot stop without my permission. I declare that his hand, which I touch, is not sensitive, and no prick of a needle is felt any longer. I give him water to drink, declaring that it is chocolate; he tastes the chocolate. I tell him to open his eyes, make the dead appear before him, make him hear music which does not exist, assure him that he is a piece of wood, another person; in short, any fantastic nonsense; he feels it, believes it, lives through it. I awake him when I want to, put him asleep by another word in a quarter of a second, and allow him to either remember or forget everything that has been said or done to him. In short, I make his cerebration play as in a dream, but following my orders, surprise himself and all the spectators, and gain with the public the name of an accomplished magician. The whole trick consists in getting, to start with, an easily suggestible person, readily passing into somnambulism. If one is shown to be hypnotized, the others follow like the sheep of Panurge. The case described was that of a person easily put into artificial somnambulism. He need not be a spontaneous somnambulist for this purpose. The latter are rather rare, whereas fully twenty-five per cent of mankind can be thrown into artificial somnambulism. The spontaneous somnambulism, however, usually represents the autohypnosis of a hysterical person.

With others the matter is slower and more difficult, although it is facilitated by example (imitation). Many suggestions may at first be without effect; but with patience and practice one obtains at least a partial influence in ninety-six per cent of men. The person to be hypnotized must be neither insane nor in a state of emotion, of excitement, or fear. He must before all be treated in a friendly and quieting manner. Flies are caught with honey. First you must gain his confidence. Put him into a comfortable easy-chair, the head resting; put the right hand on the forehead, tell him to look into your eye, and explain to him that you are going to let him fall asleep, or, at least, to influence him. According to Bernheim, you have him look at two fingers of the left hand, after a few seconds lower them slowly in order to make the eyelids sink and, if the eyes do not close by themselves, you order them to be shut. Then you begin with easy suggestions, and pass to more difficult ones as soon as the others succeed. By no means all suggestions succeed with all people. According to the success of the more important categories, one may distinguish three or four degrees of hypnotism, of course with numerous transitions:—

1. Somnambulism, in which practically everything succeeds.

2. Deep sleep, in which at least amnesia for the time of the hypnosis is obtained.

3. Hypotaxia, in which the hypnotized yield to most suggestions, but have the subjective feeling of being awake and remember everything afterward.

4. Somnolence, in which only few suggestions succeed, and in which the hypnotized can resist with some effort.

There are, however, cases of deep sleep with little suggestibility and, again, others of simple hypotaxia with very great suggestibility, but without amnesia. Moreover, the hypnotizer can at any time transfer a somnambulist into one of the other degrees, according to suggestion.

The following are a few especially interesting phenomena which succeed chiefly in somnambulists:—

Posthypnotic Suggestions.

You declare that a certain phenomenon will take place after awaking, during the waking condition; for instance, he will feel, do, see, or think some particular thing. This actually occurs as foretold in the suggestion.

Suggestion *à échéance* (to take effect at a definite time).

You suggest the same thing for a later time; for instance, the next day or a week afterward, or even later. This, too, usually succeeds in somnambulists with a little patience and practice.

Suggestion in the Waking Condition.

After a little practice of the subject almost every suggestion succeeds nearly as well in the waking condition as during sleep or a somnolent state.

Not only laymen, but also many physicians, have imagined that hypnosis and wake-suggestion are totally different things. Nobody can show his ignorance of this question more thoroughly than by such a statement. Sleep, *i.e.* the subjective sensation of sleep of the person hypnotized, is merely a generalization of the suggested dissociation in the sense of ordinary sleep. When this generalization becomes too broad and the hypnotizer leaves the subject, he may at times lose the "rapport" with the subject, and when he tries to give further suggestions he may fail to succeed or he awakes the subject, just as out of ordinary sleep. It requires some precaution to reëstablish the connection or "rapport" without putting an end to the sleep. On the other hand, in a circumscribed suggestion, in a completely waking state, it is easiest to show the symptom of localized dissociation. As soon, however, as you increase the number of suggestions, *i.e.* of dissociations, in a perfectly waking condition, you see how the looks of the hypnotized change, become more dreamy; in other words, how the dissociations become more generalized and produce a state resembling general sleep. Beaunis and others tried to make out that this condition in complicated wake-suggestions and that of execution of post-hypnotic suggestions — practically the same thing — is something peculiar, a "veille somnambulique." This is quite unnecessary. We are dealing merely with a more or less localized or generalized condition of dissociations or sleep. It is true it differs from ordinary hypnosis, because in the latter a great part of brain-activity is not influenced by the hypnotizer, *viz.* the spontaneous impulses of the hypnotized; whereas in the intentional wake-suggestions everything is governed by the hypnotizer. Spontaneous is, of course, not to be taken in the sense of undetermined free will, which does not exist. What we understand by "spontaneous" is merely the resultant of all actual and past plastic and automatic brain activities as they are inherited and developed under the external influences during life.

Suggested Falsifications of Memory.

This is one of the most surprising illusions produced by suggestion, described in a masterly manner by Bernheim. You suggest to some one that he remembers accurately to have done, experienced, seen, or heard something, while there is absolutely no truth in it. This succeeds remarkably well. If external conditions make it possible very dangerous false witnesses might be produced in this way. Children especially are surprisingly disposed to such suggestions; also hysterical women, and even normal persons. For this it does not take a professional hypnotizer. Ordinary attorneys, and also physicians, obtain sometimes unknowingly such suggested confessions or symptoms. Curiously enough it is sufficient to suggest the chief points of the situation, and to leave the rest to the imagination of the subject. He completes himself everything that was missing in the suggestion given, and furnishes a mass of precise details, which he makes up, and believes in, and by which the deception is increased. Conscientious judges will, of course, find that the statement does not agree with the facts; but unfortunately sufficient pains are not always taken. We cannot say that the witness lies; he speaks with the greatest conviction, and makes a deep impression on the audience, especially on the jury.

Thus we see a series of phenomena, the beginning of which is insignificant, and which all occur, more or less, in normal sleep and in certain people, which, however, when called forth rapidly and in a condensed form, makes a very baffling, confusing, and almost miraculous impression. Especially confusing are the mass-suggestions, which take hold of a great number of enthusiastic believers, produce hallucinations of all senses, even of the tactile sense, and thus create convincing witnesses for apparitions, even for "materialized" spirits. Such is indeed the great tendency of our brain toward illusions. Only the more thorough psychologists are less surprised by these phenomena, because normal psychology has led them already to similar concepts.

The essential feature of suggestion is evidently the production of a sleeplike dissociation of brain activity by the means of ideas. Dissociation is used to call forth inhibition, facilitations, hallucinations, reënforcement of stimuli, decisions, impulses, affects, etc. A further characteristic feature is that the person influenced is never really conscious of the mechanism of the actual realization of a suggestion. In a general way suggestion makes it possible to eliminate consciousness, *i.e.* conscious memory, from any phenomenon whatever, and to bring it into the circuit again. You may make the "skin" (or rather the parts of the brain connected with it) totally insensitive to pricks, and yet later make conscious the sensation which was not actually present at the moment of the prick. Or you may produce the sensation of a prick and later make the subject amnesic for the pain felt, so that he will emphatically assure you that he did not feel anything, although this is not true. Again, you may suggest the pain of a prick which never occurred. In short, a weird play is possible with memory, consciousness, motion, and sensation in somnambulists.

The effect of facilitating or inhibiting suggestions goes even further. It may involve the sympathetic, and call for, or arrest, menstrual hemorrhages, and influence blushing, bleeding from the nose, peristalsis, etc. Constipation, as well as menorrhagia, can be cured as if by miracle; perspiration and even the pains of labor can be influenced. Surgical anæsthesia is quite often easily obtained. Even blistering of the skin has been produced by Wetterstrand beyond doubt.

All these things are continually doubted, especially by our esteemed colleagues, the physicians, and the *bona fides* of the hypnotized is continually denied. They cry: Mystification! Illusion! I hardly care to mention as a proof that I had several women controlled to whom I suggested menstruation to take place on a definite day of each month, exactly at 7 A.M., to last three days exactly, not merely once, but after the suggestion had had its regular effect for months. After all, theoretical criticisms can always be made against all such controls. If, however, I submit to your consideration the fact that the many thousands who were hypnotized by Liébault, Bernheim, Wetterstrand, van Renterghem, Vogt, and myself, almost all came in order to be cured of some disorder, and certainly not in order to deceive me, the objection that it might be humbug falls naturally, especially if you consider the regularity of the phenomena. It would be inconceivable that thousands of independent people, who come to a physician in order to be cured, should agree on the same story to deceive the physician *in the same manner*, and to simulate both hypnosis and cure. These considerations alone demonstrate the absurdity of the objection. Yet if I mention cases of perfectly honorable and loyal men and friends whom I have cured of constipation and similar things, if I mention a professor of surgery whom I made anæsthetic and again sensitive in a quarter of a second, not only in hypnosis but also in the waking state, such a hackneyed objection might finally be dropped. It is chiefly traceable to a fundamental ignorance of psychology and of the life of the brain on the part of the majority of physicians. Universities ought to put an end to this. It is, after all, by no means astonishing that a dynamo weighing three pounds, as the brain does, should be able to produce strong effects on the circulation, peristalsis, etc., by means of the neurokyme current through the peripheral nerves and ganglia. And if we are obliged to admit that an affect or a dream may have grave and lasting psychological consequences, such as paralysis, convulsions, pains, etc., why should not a suggestion be able to undo such consequences?

We cannot help admitting that, so far, we have greatly underrated the dynamic effects of the neurokyme in the brain, both on its evil and on its good side. We must go farther and declare that many diseases which internal medicine, gynecology, etc., have been in the habit of treating from a local point of view are nothing but affections of the brain which ought to be treated by suggestion alone. I merely speak of habitual constipation, of sleeplessness, of chlorosis, of most dyspepsias, and of most menstrual disorders. And further, we must claim that a larger number of our so-called remedies, such as electro-therapeutics, balneotherapy, many prescriptions, etc., cure merely by suggestion, and by no means through some imaginary specific action. The irregularity of their results, indications, and application prove this sufficiently. It must be admitted that such a remedy gives, in many cases, a stronger suggestion than mere verbal suggestion. In America, we ought not to forget the famous Keeley Gold Cure for inebriates, as a beautiful instance. Since Keeley suggested total abstinence, he was bound to have lasting results.

Let us not forget that therapeutic results of suggestion are nothing but lasting post-hypnotic effects, which, however, like everything normal, have a tendency to become lasting. We do not put anything new into the body; we merely lead the nerve paths back to the normal dynamic course.

It is rarely possible to hypnotize a person against his will, because confidence is the first condition of success. As soon as the hypnotized loses confidence in the hypnotizer, the influence of the latter is usually over. The brain does not submit any longer to voluntary dissociation, but it associates and concentrates all its energy against the lightly built dynamic structure.

There remain a few special points: —

Autosuggestion. — By this we mean suggestions which arise spontaneously, or at least without intention.

Hypnosis and Hysteria. — It was a serious blunder of Charcot, and especially of his pupils, to mistake hypnotism for hysteria, *i.e.* a normal fundamental quality of the human brain for a pathological condition. It was, therefore, inevitable that the Paris school of hypnotism had to yield to that of Nancy. Bernheim showed quite correctly that the so-called great hypnosis of Charcot, with its supposed three phases appearing on definite stimuli, was nothing but an *artefact* by suggestion in pathological hysterical subjects.

Nevertheless, hysteria deserves special mention here, *because its fundamental symptom consists precisely in a pathological exaggeration and degeneration of dissociability or autosuggestibility.* The hysterical, men and women, are, moreover, known to be much predisposed to convulsions, so that the hysterical react peculiarly to hypnosis. They are, as a rule, very sensitive to all hypnotic procedures, but exceedingly difficult to direct. They add to every suggestion a mass of autosuggestions, begin to get convulsions or headaches, or all sorts of other disorders which their brain adds on account of its oversensitiveness and excessive dissociability. So it easily happens that for one pathological symptom removed by suggestion, autosuggestion favors one with three new ones. Hence, hypnosis is an excellent, though double-edged, reagent for testing a hysterical subject. As a rule, however, it will be possible to see after one attempt how an unobtrusive and well-calculated suggestion may suffice in a conversation without the title "hypnosis," and in a perfect waking state. An awkward hypnotizer, or one ignorant of hysteria, will usually do harm to the hysterical, produce hysterical attacks, etc. The hysterical are apt to pass into deep cataleptic, and even lethargic, conditions from which they are difficult to rouse. In short, to play on them with hypnotism is playing with fire. All the unintentional damage which is attributed to hypnotism concerns hysterical subjects. I therefore tell every physician who wants to hypnotize: "Beware especially of the hysterical, and do not run any risk before you sit well in the saddle." Suggestion can do much good in the hysterical, but the physician must proceed exceedingly cautiously, individualizing, without even mentioning the word hypnotism.

Crime and Hypnosis.

This chapter was exaggerated to the extreme by Liégeois, and dealt with too lightly by Delbœuf. That misuse, especially sexual misuse, of hypnotized persons, may occur once in a while, is certain and possible, especially in deep hypnosis, in hysterical lethargy, etc. Even more dangerous is, however, the blackmailing by hysterical impostors. Hence the rule: Never hypnotize a woman alone, without a witness. That the hypnotized might be used for crime is theoretically possible and experimentally proved. But no such case has really occurred yet. False testimony through suggested falsifications of memory is about the most serious possibility. Abnormal love-affairs of pathological persons, especially of the hysterical or of pathological impostors in which hypnotism plays a rôle (case of Czinsky, etc.) rather belong to psychiatry. Of late those suffering from paranoia and other forms of insanity show a predilection for the delusion that they are secretly hypnotized.

Crimes through hypnosis are probably so rare because, as is said above, *confidence* is the first condition of hypnosis.

The insane can usually not be hypnotized, because the instrumental dynamo, the brain, fails to work properly, attention is defective, etc.

One can hypnotize only in one's mother tongue, or in another language which one knows very well, for it takes, before all, great certainty and rapidity, and a blunder in a foreign language which makes it difficult to understand, disturbs the "rapport" considerably.

For the purpose of watching patients dangerous to themselves, I have hypnotized the watching nurses with great success, and in this way produced a "sleeping night watch," who watches much better than a waking person, and does not become exhausted or overtired. I hear that my successor at Zürich, Professor Bleuler, continues the matter with equally good success. I give the nurse the suggestion to sleep quite well, but to notice during his sleep every unusual action of the patient, so that he awakes at once when the patient makes an attempt at suicide, and at once falls asleep again when the danger is averted. In artificial somnambulism this succeeds remarkably well.

Therapy of Nervous Diseases by Work.

General Psychotherapy.

Starting from the experience that agricultural occupation is the best for the insane, and that the natural man does not work as one-sidedly as the "civilized," but always has, as the condition of getting along, depended on a combination of mental occupation with muscular activity, I have tried for a number of years to treat severe cases of so-called nervous diseases (neurasthenia, etc.), *i.e.* psychopathias, with such occupations. A severe case which I thus cured by agricultural work encouraged me. Mr. Grohmann, a civil engineer, himself a patient, had recovered his health by gardening, and was much interested in the matter. I encouraged him in his attempt to occupy nervous patients in his gardens. This was the beginning of his institution for the occupation of nervous cases, which increased from year to year. Carpentry was added among other occupations, and very good results were obtained in severe cases. P. J. Moebius later gave the method much support, and the data were published in the dissertation of Menier (Zürich), and later more fully by Grohmann himself.

Grohmann emphasizes the observation that a combination of his treatment with suggestions by Dr. Ringier in Zürich led very frequently to good results.

My principal idea in the matter was that not the muscular labor as such, but especially the centrifugal concentration of attention on determined muscular innervation for an occupation, mentally satisfying and with a purpose, diverts the brain from pathological activities, and acts as a cure. Stupid muscular labor, as gymnastics, dumb-bells, and turning of the ergostat, does not give any satisfaction, and, above all, does not keep the mind or attention from going astray. Moreover, such useless activities cannot be pursued for any length of time as a real pursuit.

Now I should like to go a step farther to-day, and to sketch with a few cases a partially new chapter of psychotherapy, not touched upon by me so far.

Not all neuropaths are fit patients for horticultural, agricultural, or other work, nor is the pathology of brain life done justice to merely by the ordinary suggestions of sound sleep, appetite, and like functions. You further know that *genius* and *insanity* are somewhat related. Whereas, however, it is well known that many a genius perished with insanity, it is perhaps less clear to many physicians that under the picture of hysteria or other psychopathias, many a genius, or at least many a talent, may slumber and fret like a bird in a cage, and also that the therapeutic cant of neurologists paralyzes the wings of the bird instead of liberating them. Here, if anywhere, a correct diagnosis and individualizing treatment is necessary. To be sure, not everybody who feels himself to be a genius is a genius. The experience of the alienist must find out of the hundreds of defective brains suffering from exaltation and mental weakness, the few which are not really defective, but contain a wealth of high talent, the development of which is inhibited or paralyzed by certain disorders. If, however, you have discovered such a hidden, tied-down treasure among the numerous nervous patients (brain-patients or encephalopaths), it is your grand duty to leave the path of cant, and to restore the wings to the eagle. Hypnosis and occupation with manual labor may be a very helpful accessory remedy; but they are not the chief thing. It is necessary to gain the full confidence of the patient by affection and by penetrating into all the sides of his mental life, to make every fibre of his emotional life vibrate. Let the patient tell you the story of his entire life, live it over again with him, and allow yourself to be thoroughly penetrated by his feelings. In this you should, of course, never forget the sexual feeling which varies so strongly from one case to another. But it should not be examined after the ordinary medical routine, which usually considers only the seminal emissions and the coitus; but with full consideration of all the loftier vibrations connected with the sexual life. This being done, you search for the real definitive aim in the life of the patient, and lead him with determination and confidence. It is a cause of much surprise to see all the psychopathological disorders disappear as if by witchcraft, and to watch how the unhappy, incapable, nervous wreck becomes an energetic, efficient person, who may amaze others by his working capacity, and remains a warm friend to the physician who understood him. A miserable person becomes happy; a "failure," a "talent" or even a "genius"; a patient, a healthy being.

Allow me to give briefly a few instances. My friends may recognize themselves, but will pardon this publication in the interest of mankind.

1. A highly educated young lady, the daughter of a talented father and a very nervous mother, had the reputation of being less endowed than her sisters, was nervous, and became more and more hysterical. She finally developed very marked paralysis, and was brought to the hospital for the Insane. At first she was almost completely cured by ordinary hypnosis; but after a number of months she had a relapse, with almost total inability to walk. She was again cured by continual agricultural work with farmers. But she felt unhappy over not having an aim in life. Not without hesitation I allowed her to yield to her anxious desire to become a nurse; her parents were much afraid of the night service. But the latter was endured without trouble with the help of a few suggestions regarding it. She took up her work enthusiastically, carried it out with all its trials and fatigues, and became more and more active in every

direction, and to-day she is one of the most active members of a committee of philanthropic ladies, doing remarkable work.

2. A physician suffered for some time with "severe neurasthenic disorders," and tried in vain to cure himself with all sorts of remedies. He came to me with his complaints. I encouraged him, advised him not to consider all those disorders, and insisted on the higher ideals of his life. We agreed on a definite plan and he left. Later he wrote me that by that one conversation he had been cured.

3. A young man with some hereditary taint, from a very religious family, very talented, became "neurasthenic" and nearly insane. He attempted suicide, and was taken to various saniturium with complete interruption of his studies and very gloomy prognosis. He was absolutely unable to work any longer, suffered from headache, sleeplessness, and inability to keep his attention on any mental activity. Gloomy and in despair, he did not show any symptoms of melancholy inhibition, etc. He was quite clear concerning his "psychopathia" and "absolute failure in life." He also had suffered from various imperative ideas and actions which had played him many a trick. Sexually he was perfectly calm. He was brought to me as a case given up. Before long the talent of the young man struck me. More intimate relations showed him to be in a totally dissatisfied state of mind. Brought up in strict orthodoxy, he never could believe in those religious dogmata, and therefore thought himself to be an outcast and lost. The forced formal training, too, with which he was brought up was a source of disgust to him. Life seemed aimless to him. First I calmed him concerning his religion, and showed him that one can be a happy and valuable man without any positive belief. Further, I showed him that learning by heart is the "mind of the mindless," and that a mere understanding with interest stands much higher. I told him not to try to learn anything further, but to merely read with interest what interested him, and not to care whether he kept it or not. In this way I revived some confidence and some pleasure in life. He began to read his books with interest and pleasure, instead of learning them with disgust. As a philosopher and freethinker he returned to life, became an enthusiastic abstainer and a member of the Independent Order of Good Templars. He helped me found new lodges. My patient, who at first required watching for fear of suicide, soon became my friend and associate in the work. The nervous symptoms disappeared, one after another. Finally he made a rather long

journey alone in a tropical country, returning completely cured and with perfect self-confidence. He resumed his studies, passed his final examination *summa cum laude* a few years later, was admired by all his colleagues for his enormous working capacity, and gives every promise of a splendid career.

4. An hysterical lady consulted me — highly talented, but psychopathic from childhood, with attacks of "grande hystérie," and greatly excited by her living together with her mother. Notwithstanding numerous opportunities, she did not want to get married for a number of intellectual reasons. I tried hypnosis. Deep hysterical sleep came on and convulsions began to show. I waked her up with much trouble, told her boldly the result was deep beyond expectation, that she would be cured in a short time, and that she had been only too deeply influenced. From that time I gave her merely wake-suggestions. In a few days almost all the disorders had gone, also the constipation, and especially the convulsions (*sapienti sat!*). I explained to her that she was most in need of work and of a definite aim in life. She did not care to found a family, with some justification, but was interested in depraved youth. Now she started out. Instead of cures in watering places, electricity, and massage, I gave her a number of books on criminal anthropology and introductions to the directors of prisons, of asylums, of the reformatories for children, etc. She took up the work with enthusiasm, joined the prohibition movement and the Independent Order of Good Templars, visited prisoners, the insane, destitute children, showed great interest in everything, an equally good judgment, and an astonishing working capacity. She improved every day, and left in a few weeks for a larger city, where she wishes to continue her studies.

In such cases, I should formerly have prescribed mental rest, inactivity, manual labor, or what not. My patients did not improve. In such cases the brain is not exhausted, as one might suppose at first sight. It is merely *misled*, and works in abnormal paths; its natural talents starve, are inhibited, and the activity offered it does not agree with it, or certain scruples of a religions or sentimental kind paralyze its activities, and paths for pathological brain activity are created. This we must recognize and change by a bold diversion.

But beware of believing every psychopath who poses as a mistaken genius and wants to study higher philosophy. There are fifty cases of these to one of those described above. For these, agriculture is as good as for imbeciles and the insane. True inhibited greatness is not wont to brag or to think too highly of itself. We must look after it, must seek it and find it. Then we can go to the root of the matter and not remain content with mere trivial suggestions about gardening or carpentry.

A SKETCH OF THE BIOLOGY OF ANTS.

BY PROFESSOR AUGUST FOREL.

TOGETHER with the bees and the wasps, the real ants belong to the insect family of hymenoptera, whereas the termites, or white ants, belong, like the dragon-flies, to the neuroptera. All these insects live in social organizations. More than all the rest, the ants have developed social life most highly and variedly. This is why they deserve our special interest. They not only present an innumerable array of individuals, but also a magnificent variety of forms. Nearly 3000 species, divided into 154 genera, are already described from the five continents, and this number continues growing every year.

The social state of ants has brought about a peculiar phenomenon called polymorphism of the species. Just as the difference of sex in man and animals is generally marked by so-called correlative differences of organization (as, for instance, the beard in man), so we find in certain animals that these differences become especially pronounced (compare, for instance, the cock and the hen). In the ants, the difference of the sexes becomes so excessive that the females and the males look like different animals. But that is not all. An additional differentiation takes place in the species, in the female germs; a certain number develop into a second category of females with totally different shape of the body, much diminished ovaries, without wings, but with a more highly developed brain. This specialized category of females is called the "working ant." In many species, even a third specialization of the female sex has formed, with powerful head and strong jaws, called "soldiers." The females and the males are usually winged, the workers and the soldiers always without wings. Consequently, a family or a state of ants of any kind consists of three or four different forms of adult individuals. In rare instances, additional forms exist. Moreover, there are many species in which an incomplete division of the workers into two categories with transition forms occurs (large, medium, and small workers). To these we must add the young brood, which consists of eggs, the footless and eyeless, white and tender larvæ or maggots of all sizes, according to age and sex; and, finally, the antlike nymphs or chrysalides. In many species, the larva spins a fine silk cocoon, which is erroneously called the egg. The real ant eggs are extremely small, and look almost like a white powder.

The architecture of the ant body shows several important social peculiarities. The real brain, independent of the sense organs, is relatively very large in the worker and the soldier, smaller in the female, and almost rudimentary in the male, in accordance with the fact that the male ant plays a pitiably transient and good-for-nothing rôle, notwithstanding its powerful eyes and strong wings. Its immense imbecility and helplessness, in contrast with the well-developed senses, are a clear expression of its lack of brain. The real brain, Dujardin's pediculated body, possesses a highly developed, small-celled cerebral cortex, especially in the worker.

The ants possess a social stomach or crop. It is situated at the entrance to the abdomen, is very elastic (when it is overfed, the cubic contents of the abdomen may be ten times enlarged), and does not digest, since it has no glands. Its undigested contents can be vomited forth at any time by the ant and distributed to its fellows, or to the larvæ by feeding from mouth to mouth. The mutual feeding is one of the vital conditions of the state of ants. Behind the crop lies the chewing, or pumping, stomach. It has four hard valves, which usually close hermetically the digestive tract of the ant. When the ant wants to eat, it opens the valves and pumps some of the contents of the crop into its peculiar, individual stomach, which is lined with digestive glands and where digestion begins. I have demonstrated these conditions by an experiment. I gave some honey stained with Berlin blue to a hungry ant. After it had eaten very eagerly, I put it with a few equally hungry companions, who at once surrounded it, begging. They all were filled with blue droplets before long. I then dissected one after another and found that the first stomach, filled with the blue mass, had not at first allowed a trace of the blue fluid to pass into the chewing stomach and into the digestive stomach. Only, during the following days, the digestive stomach slowly became stained more and more blue.

On the fore legs the ants have a fine, spurlike comb which they use to clean the rest of the body. This is very necessary in the busy workers.

In the mouth, too, they have a comb with which they clean the combs of the legs, the larvae, and their companions.

Of great importance are further the mandibula, or upper jaws, which are usually dentated and serve as grasping tongue, biting weapon, mortar spoon, carrying instrument, scissors, etc. They replace our hands, our weapons, our scissors and knives. In the mouth they have, further, a tongue for licking, with fine organs of taste.

The most important social organs of the ant are, however, the antennæ, or feelers. They contain exceedingly delicate and numerous sense-organs for the tactile sense and odor, terminating in hairlike structures. The function of these sense-organs is experimentally established. It is especially remarkable that this protruding and mobile olfactory organ not only gives the ant information on the chemical constitution of bodies, through contact (I called this contact-odor of the insects), but also makes possible an appreciation of space by olfaction, owing to position and motility, an ability which we, with our invaginated, rudimentary olfactory organs, can form no conception of. This appreciation of space is possible, since the different nerve endings may convey to the brain simultaneously, or in successive moments, the impression of the various chemical properties (odors) of various objects or parts of objects, lying side by side. Numerous relations of space are perceived for this reason, and especially, owing to the high mobility of the feelers, not merely by contact but already at a certain distance, at which the differences of behind and before, of right and left, can readily be furnished by smell. This ability must produce a knowledge of space which lies between that of our tactile sense and that of the senses of hearing and seeing. When lately Bethe imagined he had discovered a "polarization" of the olfactory traces of the ants, he mistook and overlooked these conditions completely. Moreover, the ants perceive odor from a distance with their antennæ. It is experimentally established that ants recognize one another as friends or foes merely by the means of the feelers, as Huber supposed as early as 1810; and that, in their migration, they are largely oriented, or guided, by the feelers, although the eyes, too, help considerably in the orientation outside of the nest. An ant without feelers is lost, and at once excluded from the social life; whereas without eyes it may go on working, recognizing its companions from its enemies, and find its way, although with more difficulty, at least in the nest and in its near neighborhood.

Lubbock has proved that ants feel the ultra violet rays of the solar spectrum which we do not see. With the help of complicated experiments (by varnishing the eyes, or by the application of aesculin which absorbs the ultra violet rays) on the known instincts of ants, I have demonstrated that they see the ultra violet rays with the eyes, not photodermatically, *i.e.* with the skin, as many lower animals do. The flying females, and especially the males, have good eyes, with very distinct vision; the workers, however, see usually but poorly.

The workers form the most important social elements of the ant community, whereas the soldiers serve for certain special functions, and the females and males solely for the propagation of the species.

The socialism of the ants is limited to the solitary state of the ant colony. All the individuals of one colony live up to complete solidarity, whereas the rest of the world — with but few exceptions — and especially all the other states of ants, even of the same species, are rather consistently treated as enemies. Each state builds one or more nests. In these the immense wealth of instinct in ants shows itself. Almost every single species has some peculiarity in its architecture; yes, the same species knows how to adapt itself to the varying conditions, and to build accordingly. Our most common European ant, occurring also in North America, the small dark brown *Lasius niger* Linné, builds in the meadows large, regular labyrinth-like hills of earth. In stony ground it makes its nests under stones; in the woods, in rotten stumps; in houses, in rotten frames. Most European and North American species mine in the earth labyrinth-like complexes of galleries and rooms, where they nurse their brood. Many build a dome of earth on it, serving, like flat stones, to take up the radiating heat of the sun. When the sun shines in cool weather, the ants carry their whole brood under the cupola or under the stone. During the night, or in rain or in hot weather, everything is carried into the depth. The ants build with their jaws and forelegs, working up moist earth into little lumps, during or after a rain, and making walls with them. They are splendid masons and know how to use a blade of grass as timber or a leaf for a roof. Occasionally a little stalk is sawed with the teeth of the upper jaw wholly or partly bent, pulled sideways, etc. I recommend every friend of nature to watch this activity after a warm rain in a meadow.

Other ants with strong, hard jaws mine their nest in hard wood. In a species living in trunks of trees (*Camponotus s. Colobopsis truncatus*) a very narrow hole leads out. It is constantly watched by a peculiarly transformed soldier — its big head just fills the hole and is trimmed flat anteriorly, so that it closes the hole flush, like a cork. Even a trained eye has difficulty to find the hole stuffed in this manner. A closely related species lives in North America. Yet other species nest under the bark of trees, under stones, in rocks or cracks of walls, even in walls of our houses. In tropical America I found a great number of the species in hollow, dry sticks of the brush, also in the thorns of acacia and in hollow trees. The ant of our woods, *Formica rufa*, and its next European and North American cousins cover a dome of fir needles, small fragments of wood, etc., which keep warm the nest, built as a hollow labyrinth. The gates are opened by the ants in the morning and closed in the evening, in excessive heat frequently the reverse. Other ants evidently use a resin-like secretion of the maxillary gland, and cement with it meal of wood, earth, plant-fibres, and similar material to form a sort of cardboard or pulp out of which they make wonderful nests, either in hollow trees, as our European *Lasius fuliginosus* and *Liometopum microcephalum* (and the North American *Liometopum apiculatum*), or outside on branches of trees or on trunks, as we have found it in many Central American species of *Azteca* and *Cremastogaster*.

Finally there are ants which build nests spun between the leaves of the trees out of a fine, silk-like texture, as the species *Polyrhachis* and *Oecophylla*, and in Costa Rica the *Camponotus senex s. textor*. According to the most recent observations they are said to use their larvæ, which furnish the thread, and which they use with the jaws as a spinning instrument. Certain species (*Formica exsecta* in Europe and *exsectoides* in the Alleghanies) form powerful states or colonies, which, according to McCook, may consist in the Alleghanies of up to 1600 nests, which are all in friendly relations with one another and are able to govern a whole forest.

How does a colony form? Huber, McCook, Blochmann, and Lubbock have established the following facts: At a certain season, the mature young brood, the winged females and males, fly out from all the nests of the same species. In the air, on trees, or on the tops of hills, a wild mass-wedding takes place in which I was able to establish mutual, but especially female, polygamy. Shortly afterward the stupid males perish on account of inability to feed themselves. The females remove with their own legs the loosely attached wings and creep into the earth or into wood, singly or several together. They build a little room, lay a few eggs, and sparingly nurse the larvæ, or maggots, out of their own body juice (they are very stout and fat) until three or four very small workers have grown up. These begin to work at once and to feed and care for their mother or mothers, which have nothing to do after this. The wonderful feature is that the mother or the mothers keep so many spermatozoa in their seminal pocket from the one multiple copulation or wedding, that they remain fertile for many years and are able to lay millions of eggs. They evidently remain as a rule the mothers of the entire colony as long as it exists. At least Lubbock kept alive fertilized females in artificial nests for eight and even eleven years, and the existence of most colonies of ants probably does not last much longer. It is, however, not impossible that once in a while, later on, a female brought home by the workers, or a female of their own progeny fertilized already within the nest, may be added to their number. Except in parasitic species, strange females are always killed by the workers of a colony. The mothers or queens are well cared for and fed by the workers. Their sole work consists in laying eggs. A court of workers constantly surrounds the fertilized female, takes charge of the eggs, etc.

The interior life of an ant colony represents the purest anarchistic socialism. Each individual works for the community. Some build the nest; others clean every corner of it; yet others nurse the brood, feed it, clean it, and carry it, according to the temperature, into various parts of the dwelling. Others, again, leave the nest and see to the food supply of the community by filling first their social crop, or first stomach. The workers serve one another attentively, feed, clean, and carry one another, and have a mutual understanding by means of the feelers and certain butts. The understanding, as well as the motor impulse, of that language of signs, evidently depends on inherited instincts, and is decidedly quite limited, but must be sufficient for the social requirements. The males, and usually also the females, are inactive, and are, the former wholly, the latter largely, fed and cared for by the workers. Toward the outside world the whole number is usually hostile to everything living, which leads to offensive and defensive wars and expeditions, the study of which is uncommonly interesting for the comparative psychologist.

As I said before, the workers find their way outside with the help of their sense of smell and of touch, and partly, also, with their eyes. But this is frequently very difficult for them, and they help one another in two ways. Individuals with especially good sense of smell (with stronger olfactory bulbs of the antennæ) which have found something useful or dangerous, come home, butt impetuously against many companions, turn round, and are accompanied by a number of workers to the place of the finding or of the danger, guided by means of their sense of smell. On the way they often turn round to find out whether they are followed. Ants with relatively poorer sense of smell return home after having found something; take hold of a companion with the upper jaws, and induce him to have himself carried to the new place, motionless and partly rolled up. The carried, apparently motionless, ant sees and smells the way all the same, even if it amounts to thirty or forty yards. She returns to the nest herself and again brings new companions to the place of emigration. In this way, ants which have lost their way have themselves carried home when they meet a companion. If for any reason a colony of ants becomes tired of its old nest, the same course is chosen. The most enterprising workers search for new places, and the most fortunate and active ones among them finally bring the entire colony, with its brood, to the new site selected by them. These migrations are exceedingly instructive, since there are competitions between two or three new sites until one is victorious, because the ants come back from the others and reëmigrate.

Every working ant is capable of doing all the labors mentioned in turn, although many individuals, especially always the partially dimorphous forms of workers, usually have their preference for the one or the other. Huber has shown, and I have found it corroborated several times, that ants completely separated recognized one another after weeks and months, and saluted one another as friends, merely by the help of the peculiar olfactory organs of the antennæ. This kind of memory varies according to the species.

There are immense variations in the mode of nutrition of the ants, and this is one of the most important causes of variety of the habits, as a few instances will show.

The plant-lice are well known. On most of our plants we find these tiny, succulent parasites, imbibing with their trunks the juice of the plants, but digesting their rich and ever-present meals quite insufficiently, so that their excrements are a clear fluid containing sugar. It is anatomically demonstrable that these clear droplets are not secretions of special glands, but really the excrements of the lice. Most ants of our regions are in the habit of considering the plant-lice as a kind of cattle, to look for them everywhere, to tickle them with their feelers until the louse passes the clear drop, which is at once eagerly sipped by the ant. When no ants are present, the louse waits longer, and finally kicks like a horse, at the same time spurting forth the drop. By this the leaves get a brilliant coating of sugar, the so-called honey dew. In the manner described the ants fill their social stomach for the community. Certain species build a dainty mason-work of stables for the lice on the roots of the plants in their underground dwellings, and even take care of the eggs of the root-lice. Other species build stables above ground with moist earth, and galleries around the stalks of plants which bear leaf-lice, in order to protect their wealth in cattle against attacks by strangers. In other regions, especially in the tropical countries, little larvæ of cicadas and caterpillars of butterflies are used in a similar way as cattle for ants. The ants always know enough to unite their efforts, in order to lug home both pieces of prey and larger pieces for the construction of the nest. In America, Africa, and India there are ants (Dorylides) whose enormous colonies live as nomads above or beneath the surface. They usually nest for a while in the ground or in a hollow tree, whence they make enormous expeditions for prey, in which they attack, kill, cut to pieces, and carry home everything alive: cockroaches, rats, mice, spiders, etc. When they attack a human habitation, all the inhabitants are forced to leave at once; and they are glad to do so, because within a few hours all the vermin, big and small, are chopped up and carried away. Small children in the cradle must be protected against the intruders and taken away. But in return the house is free of vermin, and very soon all the ants, together with their prey, have disappeared. In the Dorylides the huge females are always devoid of wings and eyes; the males, also very large, are winged, however, and in possession of powerful eyes. In a short excursion through Colombia, I could watch the expeditions of the Dorylides species, in part at least.

Far more remarkable even is the mode of life of the ants which raise fungi. They belong to the South American tribe of the *Attini*. In their frequently very large nests these animals form caves which reach the size of a fist. The workers climb the trees in long processions, every worker cuts out a spherical piece of a green leaf with its strong jaws, and thousands of them return laden with such leaves. They have three sizes of workers: big-headed giants, minute dwarfs, and between them a scale of medium-sized individuals. The latter are the leaf-cutters, whereas the giants are at the same time defenders of the nests and crushers of the leaves. The harvest of leaves is prepared into a kind of a hashed pulp, which is built up in the form of a labyrinth, or rather sponge. This pulp of leaves serves as culture medium for the spores of the fungus (*Rhozites gongylophora* Möller), which are present in the nest in large quantities. The leaf-pulp rapidly becomes covered with a white film. The army of working dwarfs watch that the fungus does not fill the nest and stifle its inhabitants. Every growing twig or thread is at once cut off by these pigmies, hardly two millimetres long, until the fungus gets ready to produce its second form, which Möller has called ant-kohlrabi, because they are little nodes resembling miniature kohlrabi. The fungus produces immense quantities of these kohlrabi, and the whole ant-colony lives on them. But the nutritive power of the pulp for the fungi is not infinite. As soon as a part of a sponge-like fungus garden is exhausted and becomes brownish, it is torn down by the ants and thrown in small brown grains, out of the nest, around which they form wall-like hills. In return, these parts are continually replaced by the fresh supplies of leaves. Thus they work continually, day and night, throughout the year, the leaf-cutters, the leaf-crushers, and the weeders of the fungus garden, in busy harmony, for this magnificent culture of fungi destroying the forest. They are so numerous that they give the life of the virgin forests of South America a peculiar stamp. At every step you come across processions of leaf-carrying ants and their nests. I myself was able in a short trip through Colombia to corroborate a great part of the beautiful and careful scientific discoveries of Professor Möller, and to discover the as yet unknown gardens of fungi of several species and genera. Certain *Attini* have a rudimentary instinct of horticulture, and merely use the excrements of caterpillars, wood pulp, etc. They raise another fungus. The final form of fungus of *Rhozites* is a large, beautiful agaric, which grows on the nests of the ants. My attack with spades on a nest of *Atta sexdens* L., one metre high and six metres in diameter, turned into a real battle. The Indian who helped me took to his heels. In a few seconds my hands bled all over from the sharp bites of the large warriors. But I succeeded in uncovering about twenty gardens in a corner of the nest. Almost every bite of a warrior bleeds. The natives use these animals for suturing wounds; they have the ant bite together the two wound margins, and then they sever the body from the head. The head remains fastened with the jaws, and closes the wound like a small forceps. v. Jhering has shown that the fertilized females of *Attini* carry in the mouth a piece of the fungus taken from the nest. In this manner they have the germs from which their brood raises a new garden. North America has a small horticultural ant, *Atta (Trachymyrmex) Tardigrada* Buckley, var. *septentrionalis* McCook.

The habits of other species of ants were well known to, and interpreted by, King Solomon. I speak of the subgenus *Messor*, which lives in masses around the Mediterranean Sea. These animals also make large caves in the ground. They collect the seeds from all kinds of plants, and accumulate their subterraneous granaries. There they know how to prevent the sprouting until it is convenient for them. Then, in the moment of beginning germination, when the starch changes into diastase and sugar, they eat the grains, both in summer and in winter. There are no real winter provisions, as Solomon thought.

In Texas there is an ant (*Pogonomyrmex molefaciens*) which allows just one kind of grass, *Aristida oligantha*, to grow around its nest, while all the other plants are weeded out. It feeds on the seeds, and is the famous agricultural ant of Lincecum. A closely related form (*P. barbatus*) makes peculiar pavements on the surface of its nest with little stones. Other ants (*Myrmecocystus melliger* and *Mexicanus*) use part of their workers as provision-pots. These ants are so overfed by the other workers that their first stomach or crop reaches the size of a wine-grape, and correspondingly distends the abdomen. These so-called "nurses" cannot walk any longer, and hang in the subterraneous spaces as provision-pots for the community. Types of this kind live in Mexico, Colorado, and Texas, and are dug out and eaten by children. McCook has studied their habits.

A topic worthy of admiration is the so-called symbiosis of a South American ant, *Azteca Mülleri*, with the Cecropia tree Imbauba (*Cecropia peltata*). The tree is hollow inside. On peculiar cushions of the shoulders of its leaves it produces granules rich in albuminous substance and not present in other Cecropias (Müller's granules). The ant lives in the hollow space of the Cecropia, where the mother of the colony digs into an apparently specially adapted, thinner portion. In this tree the *Azteca* finds a home and its food in the granules of Müller. But it is very bellicose. As soon as the leaf-cutting ants, just mentioned, attack the Cecropia, the furious Aztecas defend the tree and throw them back.

With what fury the *Azteca* species defend their trees with the help of a very odorous, resinous substance secreted by the anal glands, I have been able to see repeatedly in Columbia, where some live in self-made pulp-nests, hanging on the branches of trees, others in the Cecropias and other hollow trees, and one even under the flat leaves of a kind of ivy. The symbiosis of *Azteca Mülleri* with the *Cecropia peltata* is, however, incomplete, inasmuch as a complete mutual dependence of the two organisms does not exist; the Cecropia, at least, can live without the ants, at least in its first years. But the symbiosis of the fungus *Rhozites gongylophora* with the *Atta* species is complete. Neither fungus nor ant can live by itself; each is absolutely dependent on the other.

The ant nests have their parasites and domestic animals like the dwellings of man. Certain lice and worms trouble the ants, and lay their eggs into their brood. There also exist very wonderful relations between certain beetles, lepismas, centipedes, etc., and the colonies of ants. They are called guests, although as a rule they are rather harmful lodgers for the ants. They are tolerated or even loved by the ants on account of a certain odor or pleasant secretion of their hairs, which the ant licks passionately. They live as members of the colony in the ant nest, and, as Wasmann has so well described and Janet corroborated, take the habits of ants. They are fed by the ants from mouth to mouth, and even feed each other. They communicate by means of their feelers with the ants, and with one another. Even their brood is usually fed and raised mostly by the ants as if they were their own. Long ago I observed the feeding, transportation, and nursing of the larvæ of *Atemeles* (a beetle living with the ants), and wondered why the ants cared for these strangers just as for their own brood, without, however, knowing then that these larvæ belonged to the same beetle which is a guest of the ants as an adult. Wasmann has proved this; he also has demonstrated the harmful influence of these guests on the ant colony which begins to produce pathological malformations between the worker and female, described by me formerly without a knowledge of the cause.

Other guests are rather mischievous thieves, which creep into the nests and eat the ants or their brood (*Myrmedonia*), or merely in order to eat the excrements of ants (*Dinarda*). The excellent biologist, Wasmann, knew that in migrations of a colony of ants to a new nest the whole gang of little guests (beetles, centipedes, epismas) know how to follow the ants into the nest, following the trace by their sense of smell.

I myself have corroborated this observation. This is, however, not the case with the small, round *Thorictus Foreli* living in the nests of the large and long-legged *Myrmecocystus megalocola* in Algeria. It is too small and too slow to be able to follow the swift ant. Consequently this beetle (discovered by me in Algeria, and called after me by Wasmann) always clings to the shaft of the feeler of the ant, and is carried in this way. A peculiar notch in the head-shield allows it to wholly embrace with its jaws the feeler of the ant without hurting it. Lately Wasmann believed that he found that the beetle bores a hole into the shaft of the feeler of the ant with its lower jaws and suck its blood. But Escherich denies this, and the matter is not settled.

Even more remarkable than the relations of these guests are the slaves and the friendly relations of some species of ants to one another. Many years ago I accidentally discovered that some of our ants (for instance, *Formica rufa*, the common ant of our forests), which usually live by themselves and work hard, in very exceptional cases, probably after a war in which they were victorious, let the chrysalides of other weaker species (*Formica fusca*) hatch, rear them, and consider them as members of their community. This is the origin of the rare mixed colonies which give the explanatory history of evolution in the animal series for the following long-known fact. Charles Darwin had theoretically surmised that mode of origin of the instinct of slavery in ants.

The *Formica sanguinea*, as Huber first discovered, is almost always in the habit of making irregular raids in June, July, and August, in which they surround the nests of *Formica fusca*, attack this weaker species, and chase away after a violent struggle the inhabitants of the nest, whose brood they seize and carry home. The larvæ and chrysalides, kidnapped in this manner, hatch in the nests of the *sanguinea*, where they feel at home very much as kidnapped infants. There they render the greatest service as workers to the robbers, so that the latter, although also relatively active, lead an easier and more insolent life of prey than their nearest relations. This gives the *Formica sanguinea* a very peculiar, enterprising, and intelligent biological stamp. It is taken up by the daily labor much less than other species. The so-called slaves, or better, helpers, feel themselves so well at home that they do not recognize their real brothers and sisters from the robbed nest, and treat them as enemies. It is established that the ability of ants to recognize begins only a few days after the hatching of the chrysalis, when the soft chitine is getting harder. In order to show this, I have put together larvæ and new-born ants of various species and genera, and raised a mixed but peaceable colony. In North America there are families of *Formica sanguinea* (*rubicunda* Emery, etc.) which have similar habits.

The Amazon ant of Huber (*Polyergus rufescens*) has developed further the system of slaves. Their dagger-shaped, bent jaws are already unfit for work. Like a Macedonian phalanx, its rust-colored army, consisting of usually from 300 to 1200 ants, rushes from its nest on summer afternoons. In a close array and forced march it follows the path previously reconnoitred by a few robbers, and in one half to one hour it covers distances of from fifty to one hundred metres. It is true the army often loses its way or stops until a few ants have found it again, rapidly butt with their heads against the others, and give them the sign to follow. If not, the swarm returns unsuccessfully. As a rule, however, they reach a nest of *Formica fusca* or *rufibarbis*, rush with an incredible haste into the entrances of the nest, and sack in a few minutes the entire brood of the unfortunate, overpowered ants in order to run home, and to throw the prey simply to their helpers. The observation of such an expedition is probably the most interesting zoölogical spectacle I ever have witnessed. I have observed them very often in the canton of Vaud, and kept statistics on the number of expeditions, of the soldiers, of the robbed nests, and the rapidity of the march. The Amazon ant completely depends on its helpers. Their entire brood is fed and cared for by them. Yes, the robber cannot even eat without help, and starves, as Huber and I have shown, in presence of the richest food, if it is not poured into its mouth by the helpers. It is able to swallow if its mouth happens to get into honey; but the instinct to eat has been lost. The North American *Polyergus lucidus* (which robs *Formica pallida fulva*) and *breviceps* have the same habits.

The little genus *Strongylognathus* shows how the instinct of robbing slaves can slowly develop into parasitism. In 1871, I discovered a new species in Wallis, *Strongylognathus Huberi*, and I was able to show on the spot by an experiment that it can rob like *Polyergus*. The more frequent and smaller *Strongylognathus testaceus*, however, cannot do this any longer. This small and weak animal, in which the workers are dying out, according to my observations, still shows ridiculous remnants of the fighting tactics of its relatives. Wasmann has proved that the fertilized female of this ant sneaks into the nests of another kind,

Tetramorium cæspitum, is received by the workers beside the *Tetramorium* mother, and lives beside her. For some cause the Tetramoriums raise from that time on the workers of their own species only; whereas they allow the larvæ of the males and females of their own species to perish; instead of this they raise the whole brood of the *Strongylognathus* mother, perhaps merely since it causes less trouble and work.

At last the parasitism of the *Anergates atratulus* goes even further, they having become totally devoid of workers. Here the fertilized female of *Tetramorium cæspitum* is received; whereas the own mother of the colony of this species disappears in a manner not yet explained. As long as the existing workers live, they nurse the entire brood of the *Anergates* female, consisting merely of winged females and wingless males. The *Tetramorium* workers from that time merely work for the parasites. The females of *Anergates* are fertilized in the nest by their own brothers; not till then do they fly out to found new nests. In this manner the species is subject to continued inbreeding, since there is always only one mother in a nest; but it does not seem to suffer from it. In North America, *Epœcus Pergandei* lives as a parasite with *Monomorium minutum*. But nothing definite is known of its biology as yet.

Another ant, *Formicoxenus nitidulus* Nyl., lives as a small but active tolerated guest with its entire brood in the partitions of the nests of the common wood ant. It also lives in the Rocky Mountains.

The northern *Tomognathus sublævis*, however, according to Adlerz, penetrates as a brutal, uncalled-for guest into the nest of a weaker ant (*Leptothorax acervorum*), and forces its brood on these animals, moreover allowing itself to be lazy and comfortable and fed by the host. The wingless worker of Tomognathus is at the same time female; the male is winged. *Tomognathus Americanus* from Washington probably lives in a similar manner.

The tiny but warlike *Solenopsis fugax* lives in very small rooms and channels, which it burrows into the partitions of the nests of larger ants; but it lives there as an enemy, robber, and thief, sneaking among the brood of the larger kind and eating it up. Since my first publication of this point in 1869, it has become known that this manner of living occurs in a large group of the *Solenopsis* species and related genera, such as *Æromyrma*, certain *Monomorium* species, etc., which all represent, in this manner, small robbers hidden in the walls of the nests of larger species.

It seems that in North America *Solenopsis modera*, *pollux*, and *molesta* live in a similar manner. In Africa and India the *Carebara* species live in the same way in the nest of *Termites*, also *Æromyrma* in Madagascar.

In the Colombian virgin forests, I discovered in 1896 a new, previously unknown relation of two ant-colonies, which I called *parabiosis*. A small *Dolichoderus* and a still smaller *Cremastogaster*, both of a deep black and glossy, live usually, though not always, together in the following manner: They inhabit the same nest, probably robbed from a species of *Termites*. The cavities and galleries are all in open connection, and are inhabited by the two species in a mix-up, almost inextricable to the human eye. This much is certain, that the two species do not mix. Each occupies definite rooms and galleries, and cares for its own brood only, notwithstanding the open communication. But there is peace, never war; in common expeditions, the two species leave the nest in order to find food on plants and trees, but only to the point where the final aims divide; there they separate, and each species goes on to its special aim (the plant-lice or flowers). Thus we have a peaceable symbiosis without mixing and without any intimate relations. The relation of guests might well be called "Xenobiosis," the helpers' relation "bothobiosis." These expressions would be preferable not only among ants, but also for analogous relations of other animals. Wasmann's expressions ("Symphilia," etc.) are, however, preferable. Apart from the raids and the other conditions described, the ant colonies, even those of the same species, have warfare usually about the source of nutrition. We men believe ourselves the sovereigns of the earth. Obviously, the ants do the same in their little world, since the larger colony considers a certain district around its nest as its property. This district comprehends trees, plants, and the soil; whoever enters it is attacked, and, if possible, slain. Hence the wars between neighboring colonies, wars which are often carried to the annihilation of the weaker part. A victory is accounted for by the number and courage of the warriors, and also by certain weapons, as stings, poison-sacks, hardness of body, swiftness, resinous secretions of the anal glands which are spurted out, certain tricks, as for instance in *Polyergus* the piercing of the brain of the enemy, in *Formica exsecta* the sawing off of the neck, or the like. The smaller kinds usually take hold of the legs of the larger ones, seize them this way, and finally kill them by the number of their pricks or bites; whereas the big ones cut or crush the small with their jaws. Whole chains of combatants are formed, of which few may survive the battle. Slowly the victor gains ground, until the enemy either faces about or finally is surrounded in its own nest, chased away, or killed with its entire brood. Besides such larger wars, which may last days or weeks, there are innumerable skirmishes along the frontiers, especially about the possession of plant-lice.

Yet ants do not merely murder and carry on warfare; they also can make peace. This does not only happen because two exhausted colonies often give up fighting and avoid a certain strip of contested land, but also, in rare cases, by coalition and complete union. I have produced this experimentally by mixing rather large parts of nests of various colonies of *Formica fusca* with their inhabitants, or at least putting them close together in a strange place, where they were forced to build a new nest. Necessity and circumstances, the mutual need for food and habitation, reduced the warlike impulses. After usually insignificant threats, taunts, and weak attempts at fighting, the ants began to work together, and in the course of one or two days formed one harmonious colony. If, however, you bring part of a colony near the nest of another one, it is driven away and often annihilated.

Once (1871) I poured the inhabitants of two colonies of very hostile different kinds (*Formica sanguinea* and *pratensis*) into one bag and allowed them to struggle one hour, in order to put them into connection with an artificial glass-nest. Fighting, with the greatest excitement and total confusion, the ants reached the glass-nest where they carried their larvæ. Necessity gradually reduced the fever of the battle. The next day several hundred had killed one another; the survivors began to work together, though defiant and threatening. A few kept up the fighting spirit. After five days the union was perfect. Ten days later I allowed them to get out on the meadow, where they built a common nest and after that lived in undisturbed friendship. When, however, I put a few ants from the original nest of the *pratensis* with the new allies, the new arrivals were kindly received by their former sisters, but fiercely attacked and partly killed by the *sanguinea*. This case is very instructive, and shows that the *sanguinea* had closed friendship with only the definite set of *pratensis*, and were quite well able to distinguish them from the, as yet, unknown sisters.

The instinctive feeling of duty of the workers has been illustrated by me in the following manner: One meter from a nest of *Formica pratensis*, I placed a strong portion of a strange colony of the same kind.

They soon began the attack, and a great battle began, lasting several hours and costing nearly a thousand lives on the two sides. While the inhabitants of the nest rushed out to the defence of their home, I poured honey quite close to the soldiers running into the battle. Under ordinary circumstances the honey would have become black with ants in a short time. But the workers passing by sipped for only one or two seconds, could not be tempted any longer, and rushed into the combat — as a rule into death — although the ants have neither criminal law nor court-martial. Whoever wants to be a coward or egoist may do so without any interference. But the ant cannot act or will antisocially, and this is the secret of their socialism. In the struggle between the individual instincts and impulses against social ones the latter usually have the upper hand. There are, of course, short hesitations which are very instructive to observe.

As has been said already, the community of ants realizes the purest ideals of our modern anarchists. No government, no king, no laws, no bureaucracy, no officials. Nobody commands, nobody obeys. Even the so-called slaves are perfectly free and work voluntarily, from mere instinct. Hence, absolute freedom with absolute solidarity. When a worker wants to be lazy, he is cared for none the less (this is seen in the Amazon ant, which is totally dependent on its "slaves"). But this laziness does not occur at all, except with the slave-makers and the parasitic species. Consequently there are no 'cracies, no parties, no rebellions, no crimes; at least almost none (and we must remember no alcoholism either); at the most only occasional individual differences which, however, are almost always quite short and insignificant.[1] And yet, there is the most perfect order, indeed, a wonderful skill to create order by harmonious, energetic work in a short time, in the most difficult and confused situations possible. If, for instance, you demolish brutally a nest of ants, take all the inhabitants into a bag, and throw them in a completely unknown region amidst

[1] I have described one exception in my "Fourmis de la Suisse"; a mixed colony of Amazon ants suffered for lack of food, owing to prolonged drought. There I saw how a few helpers (slaves), importuned for food by the Amazons, would bite their "masters," and finally carry them as far as possible to throw them away. The hard Amazons took it good-naturedly, but always returned home at once. Tired of such a Sisyphus labor, one of the helpers began to bite, so that an Amazon lost patience, pierced the brain of the rebellious slave, and thereby killed it promptly. This fact is quoted by the famous criminal anthropologist, C. Lombroso, and has been interpreted as a case of crime among ants. This interpretation stands discussion, and the case is certainly instructive.

enemies, they reconnoitre rapidly, gather the brood, find a place for a nest, hide the brood provisionally under leaves or in the hole of a cricket; the enemies are kept away, the nest built, food, especially plant-lice, is sought for and found, etc.

The wonderful and manifold social instincts of ants have called forth many erroneous views, and produced a sort of anthropomorphism of the ant's mind. There are, indeed, enough analogies and points of contact between the society of man and of ants,—slavery, raising of cattle, horticulture, war, treaties, etc. These are phenomena of convergence, the complicated connection of which in both ant and man is brought about by the fact of social community of living brains. The chief difference lies in the inherited automatism of instinct in the ant, and the immensely individual plasticity of the human brain. You may ask how it is that the brain of an ant, only the size of a pin-head (Charles Darwin calls it the most wonderful atom of substance of the world), can do as complicated things as the human brain, which weighs two and one-half to three and one-quarter pounds; but you must consider the other side of the matter, namely, the immense limitation of an ant as soon as it ought to do something that does not lie in its inherited instinct. We see the Amazon ant, which has such complicated ways of plundering, perish beside ample food although it can lick and swallow, because it has lost the instinct to eat. Every species has its special tricks, but only those, and it never devises anything else. It is true, that ants adapt themselves to new conditions to some extent, and better than other insects, because their brain is relatively a little larger; but this is the case only in a very limited manner. In its whole life, an ant learns almost nothing apart from a certain knowledge of places, and the ability to distinguish other ants; shortly after it comes forth from its chrysalis it knows almost all it will ever know, innate and inherited; whereas the mammals, and even the birds, learn very much during their lives, have far more memories, and combine and use them. Hence, it follows that mental or cerebral activities which are one-sidedly complicated, fixed in the brain and inherited, necessitate far fewer brain elements than the ability to learn individually to combine, to adapt itself, to practise new activities, and to make them become secondarily automatic by practice. This ability, which may be called plastic in comparison with the automatism of instinct, especially distinguishes the human brain, although even we think and feel and act far more from inheritance than we believe. Still there is no actual contrast between instinct and the plasticity of reason. There rather are thousands of transitions, especially the so-called hereditary dispositions, which are, so to speak, rudimentary, not completely developed instincts, and which, for instance, distinguish a Mozart or a Koczalski, who were able to become virtuosi and composers as children, from unmusical persons over whom all the teachers labor for years in vain.

The animals with complicated high instincts are, therefore, by no means more stupid than those which have only slight instincts. All depend on two different modalities of brain activity which may go, side by side, to a varying height, without excluding one another mutually.

As I wrote over twenty-five years ago, the community of ants teaches us further that the social state of man cannot be arranged after the pattern of the ants. Man has too much and too little for this. He lacks the sexless workers, the social first stomach, and, above all, the high social instinct which, without any legal compulsion, works much rather for the community than for itself. In return, he can receive, digest, and combine in his powerful brain a world of plastic concepts, which the little ant, with her automatic, one-sided, though extremely well-built and remarkably well-used, brain is unable to do. The highly developed human brain contains an unlimited number of plastic powers, capable of development, connected with overpoweringly strong inherited egoistic instincts and passions of animals of prey, but capable of being influenced in manifold manners by selections and by individual adaptations. Man and his brain cannot be forced into one single collective or anarchistic dogma, because overwhelming impulses lead him forcibly toward a higher evolution, which cannot be defined beforehand. We are, of course, in a position to recognize, to some extent, the laws of this psychical evolution, especially by the help of history, of ethnology, of psychology, connected with anatomy and physiology of the brain, and to remove, in a negative manner at least, that which deranges and inhibits it, as the use of alcohol, of opium, the cult of the golden calf and of illusory gods, and other causes of degeneration, and to try positively to increase the number of the fittest germs at the expense of the unfit. But, unfortunately, the higher insight of man has to meet continually the obstinate narrowness of prejudice, so that the victory of truth is not easy.

Notwithstanding the difference of their physical organizations and size from ours, with all their relatively low rank in the animal series, the ants, with their social biology and psychology, are an extremely valuable and interesting object of comparison, both of living nature and of the social relations of man, and for human psychology generally. They prove how the eternal, divine powers of nature produce equal or similar phenomena in completely different ways, whether they be those of living beings in their various combinations, or those which are called the physico-chemical powers of inorganic and organic nature. Have not slavery, the raising of cattle, and horticulture been practised by ants long before there were any men on earth? These ants very probably have acquired these arts in the way of natural selection, automatically, in the course of innumerable generations, with the helps of inherited combinations, without there ever having existed an ant which could have got a perspective of the adequacy of the process, individually. Man, however, invents individually, with the help of innumerable combinations of plastic impulses, and he often devises, individually, things which long before had been produced by natural powers, or living beings before him. Let me mention the sail long used by the nautilus, electricity, etc.

In Proverbs vi. 6–8, we read: "Go to the ant, thou sluggard; consider her ways, and be wise; which having no guide, overseer, or ruler, provideth her meat in the summer and gathereth her food in the harvest." To this sentence, which is scientifically true, word for word, I add the following: She gives man the social doctrines of work, of harmony, of courage, of sacrifice, and of a spirit of solidarity.

DEGREES CONFERRED.

Following are the degrees conferred by the University during its first decade. In case of the degree of Doctor of Philosophy, the subject of the dissertation and the date of the examination are given.

DOCTORS OF PHILOSOPHY.

MATHEMATICS.

J. W. A. Young, Sept. 16, 1892.
On the Determination of Groups whose Order is a Power of a Prime.
American Journal of Mathematics, April, 1893, Vol. 15, pp. 124–178.

William H. Metzler, Jan. 4, 1893.
On the Roots of Matrices.
American Journal of Mathematics, Oct., 1892, Vol. 14, pp. 326–377.

Thomas F. Holgate, May 9, 1893.
On Certain Ruled Surfaces of the Fourth Order.
American Journal of Mathematics, Oct., 1893, Vol. 15, pp. 344–386.

John E. Hill, June 17, 1895.
On Quintic Surfaces.
Mathematical Review, July, 1896, Vol. 1, pp. 1–59.

L. Wayland Dowling, June 19, 1895.
On the Forms of Plane Quintic Curves.
Mathematical Review, April, 1897, Vol. 1, pp. 97–119.

Thomas F. Nichols, June 20, 1895.
On Some Special Jacobians.
Mathematical Review, July, 1896, Vol. 1, pp. 60–80.

Warren G. Bullard, June 17, 1896.
On the General Classification of Plane Quartic Curves.
Mathematical Review, Vol. 1, pp. 193–208, 3 plates.

Frederick C. Ferry, June 15, 1898.
Geometry of the Cubic Scroll of the First Kind.
Archiv for Mathematik og Naturvidenskab, B. 21, Nr. 3.

ERNEST W. RETTGER, June 16, 1899.
On Lie's Theory of Continuous Groups.
American Journal of Mathematics. (In press.)

JOHN S. FRENCH, March 28, 1899.
On the Theory of the Pertingents to a Plane Curve. (In press.)

PHYSICS.

T. PROCTOR HALL, June 19, 1893.
New Methods of Measuring the Surface-Tension of Liquids.
Philosophical Magazine, Nov., 1893, Vol. 36, pp. 385–413.

CLARENCE A. SAUNDERS,[1] July 6, 1895.
The Velocity of Electric Waves.
Physical Review, Sept.–Oct., 1896, Vol. 4, pp. 81–105.

THOMAS W. EDMONDSON, July 11, 1896.
On the Disruptive Discharge in Air and Liquid Dielectrics.
Physical Review, Feb., 1898, Vol. 6, pp. 65–97.

SAMUEL N. TAYLOR, July 31, 1896.
A Comparison of the Electromotive Force of the Clark and Cadmium Cells.
Physical Review, Sept.–Oct., 1898, Vol. 7, pp. 149–170.

ALBERT P. WILLS, June 21, 1897.
On the Susceptibility of Diamagnetic and weakly Magnetic Substances.
Physical Review, April, 1898, Vol. 6, pp. 223–238.

WILLIAM P. BOYNTON, June 23, 1897.
A Quantitative Study of the High-Frequency Induction Coil.
Physical Review, July, 1898, Vol. 7, pp. 35–63.

CHEMISTRY.

THOMAS H. CLARK, June 13, 1892.
The Addition-Products of Benzo- and of Toluquinone.
American Chemical Journal, Dec., 1892, Vol. 14, pp. 553–576.

JOHN L. BRIDGE, Jan. 8, 1894.
Ueber die Aether des Chinonoxims. (p-Nitrosophenols.)
Liebig's Annalen, Sept., 1893, Vol. 277, pp. 79–104.

JULIUS B. WEEMS, June 20, 1894.
On Electrosyntheses by the Direct Union of Anions of Weak Organic Acids.
American Chemical Journal, Dec., 1894, Vol. 16, pp. 569–588.

[1] Died Dec. 19, 1898.

BIOLOGY.

HERMON C. BUMPUS, Sept. 29, 1891.
The Embryology of the American Lobster.
Journal of Morphology, Sept., 1891, Vol. 5, pp. 215–262, 6 plates.

WILLIAM M. WHEELER, May 10, 1892.
A Contribution to Insect Embryology.
Journal of Morphology, April, 1893, Vol. 8, pp. 1–160, 6 plates.

EDWIN O. JORDAN, May 11, 1892.
The Habits and Development of the Newt.
Journal of Morphology, May, 1893, Vol. 8, pp. 269–366, 5 plates.

JAMES R. SLONAKER, June 20, 1896.
A Comparative Study of the Area of Acute Vision in Vertebrates.
Journal of Morphology, May, 1897, Vol. 13, pp. 445–502, 5 plates.

COLIN C. STEWART, June 19, 1897.
Variations in Daily Activity Produced by Alcohol and by Changes in Barometric Pressure and Diet, with a Description of Recording Methods.
Journal of Physiology, January, 1898, Vol. 1, pp. 40–56.

PSYCHOLOGY.

HERBERT NICHOLS, Sept. 29, 1891.
The Psychology of Time, Historically and Philosophically Considered with Extended Experiments.
American Journal of Psychology, Feb., 1891, Vol. 3, pp. 453–529; April, 1891, Vol. 4, pp. 60–112.

ALEXANDER F. CHAMBERLAIN, March 9, 1892.
The Language of the Mississaga Indians of Skūgog. A Contribution to the Linguistics of the Algonkian Tribes of Canada.
MacCalla & Co., Philadelphia, 1892. 84 pp.

WILLIAM L. BRYAN, Dec. 13, 1892.
On the Development of Voluntary Motor Ability — with a Preface on the Requirements of Work in Experimental Psychology.
American Journal of Psychology, Nov., 1892, Vol. 5, pp. 125–204, 3 charts.

FREDERICK TRACY, May 29, 1893.
The Psychology of Childhood.
D. C. Heath & Co., Boston, 1893. 94 pp.

ARTHUR H. DANIELS, June 21, 1893.
The New Life: A Study of Regeneration.
American Journal of Psychology, Oct., 1893, Vol. 6, pp. 61–106.

John A. Bergström, May 14, 1894.
An Experimental Study of Some of the Conditions of Mental Activity.
American Journal of Psychology, Jan., 1894, Vol. 6, pp. 247–274.

Fletcher B. Dresslar, June 14, 1894.
Studies in the Psychology of Touch.
American Journal of Psychology, June, 1894, Vol. 6, pp. 313–368.

Thaddeus L. Bolton, April 30, 1895.
Rhythm.
American Journal of Psychology, Jan., 1894, Vol. 6, pp. 145–238.

Frank Drew, July 29, 1895.
Attention: Experimental and Critical.
American Journal of Psychology, July, 1896, Vol. 7. pp. 533–573.

James H. Leuba, July 29, 1895.
A Study in the Psychology of Religious Phenomena.
American Journal of Psychology, April, 1896, Vol. 7, pp. 309–385.

Colin A. Scott, June 30, 1896.
Old Age and Death.
American Journal of Psychology, Oct., 1896, Vol. 8, pp. 67–122.

Ellsworth G. Lancaster, June 11, 1897.
The Psychology and Pedagogy of Adolescence.
Pedagogical Seminary, July, 1897, Vol. 5, pp. 61–128.

Ernest H. Lindley, June 12, 1897.
A Study of Puzzles with Special Reference to the Psychology of Mental Adaptation.
American Journal of Psychology, July, 1897, Vol. 8, pp. 431–493.

A. Caswell Ellis, June 18, 1897.
The History of the Philosophy of Education. (In press.)

George E. Dawson, August 2, 1897.
Psychic Rudiments and Morality.
American Journal of Psychology. (In press.)

Edwin D. Starbuck, August 3, 1897.
Some Aspects of Religious Growth.
American Journal of Psychology, Oct., 1897, Vol. 9, pp. 70–124.

Frederic Burk, June 8, 1898.
From Fundamental to Accessory in the Development of the Nervous System and of Movements.
Pedagogical Seminary, Oct., 1898, Vol. 6, pp. 5–64.

Linus W. Kline, June 10, 1898.
The Migratory Impulse *vs.* Love of Home.
American Journal of Psychology, Oct., 1898, Vol. 10, pp. 1–81.

J. Richard Street, June 11, 1898.
A Genetic Study of Immortality.
Pedagogical Seminary, Sept., 1899, Vol. 6, pp. 267–313.

Daniel E. Phillips, June 13, 1898.
The Teaching Instinct.
Pedagogical Seminary, March, 1899, Vol. 6, pp. 188–245.

Frederick W. Colegrove, June 13, 1898.
Individual Memories.
American Journal of Psychology, Jan., 1899, Vol. 10, pp. 228–255.

Henry S. Curtis, June 16, 1898.
Inhibition.
Pedagogical Seminary, Oct., 1898, Vol. 6, pp. 65–113.

Frederick E. Bolton, Aug. 15, 1898.
Hydro-Psychoses.
American Journal of Psychology, Jan., 1899, Vol. 10, pp. 171–227.

Henry H. Goddard, June 12, 1899.
The Effects of Mind on Body as evidenced by Faith Cures.
American Journal of Psychology, April, 1899, Vol. 10, pp. 431–502.

The following gentlemen have taken the examination for the doctor's degree, but have not yet completed all the formal requirements.

Eugene W. Bohannon,
Edmund B. Huey,
Cephas Guillet,
George E. Partridge,
Charles H. Walker.

DOCTORS OF LAWS.

HONORIS CAUSA.

Ludwig Boltzmann, July 10, 1899.
Professor of Theoretical Physics, University of Vienna.

Santiago Ramón y Cajal, July 10, 1899.
Professor of Histology, and Rector of the University of Madrid.

August Forel, July 10, 1899.
Late Director of the Burghölzli Asylum, Switzerland.

Angelo Mosso, July 10, 1899.
Professor of Physiology, and Rector of the University of Turin.

Émile Picard, July 10, 1899.
Professor of Mathematics, University of Paris.

TITLES OF PAPERS

Published by Past and Present Members of the Staff, Fellows, and Scholars.

H. AUSTIN AIKINS:—

B.A., University of Toronto, 1887; Instructor, University of Southern California, 1888; Graduate Student, Yale University, 1888–91; Lecturer on History of Philosophy, *ibid.*, 1890–91; Ph.D., Yale University, 1891; Professor of Logic and Philosophy, Trinity College, North Carolina, 1891–93; Fellow in Psychology, Clark University, Oct., 1893–Jan., 1894; Professor of Philosophy, College for Women, Western Reserve University, Cleveland, O., Jan., 1894–.

Author of:—

The Philosophy of Hume, in extracts, with introduction. (Sneath's *Series of Modern Philosophers.*) Henry Holt & Co., N. Y., 1893. 176 pp.

From the Reports of the Plato Club. *Atlantic Monthly*, Sept. and Oct., 1894, Vol. 74, pp. 340–353; 470–480.

The Daily Life of a Protozoan (with C. F. Hodge). *Am. Jour. of Psy.*, Jan., 1895, Vol. 6, pp. 524–533.

Education of the Deaf and Dumb. *Educational Review*, Oct., 1896, Vol. 12, pp. 236–251.

The Field of Pedagogy. *Western Reserve University Bulletin*, April, 1897, Vol. 3, pp. 15–31.

S. AKIYAMA:—

School of Science, Tokio, Japan, 1888–90; College of Pharmacy, San Francisco, Cal., 1890–91; Student in Chemistry, University of California, 1891–93; Scholar in Chemistry, Clark University, 1893–94.

ERNEST ALBEE:—

A.B., University of Vermont, 1887; Scholar in Philosophy, Clark University, 1889–90; Fellow in Philosophy, 1890–91; Fellow Sage School of Philosophy, Cornell University, 1891–92; Instructor in Philosophy, *ibid.*, 1892–; Ph.D., Cornell University, 1894; Member of the Am. Psy. Ass'n.

Author of:—

The Ethical System of Richard Cumberland. *Philosophical Review*, May and July, 1895, Vol. 4, pp. 264–290; 371–393.

The Relation of Shaftesbury and Hutcheson to Utilitarianism. *Ibid.*, Jan., 1896, Vol. 5, pp. 24–35.

Gay's Ethical System. *Ibid.*, March, 1897, Vol. 6, pp. 132–145.

Hume's Ethical System. *Ibid.*, July, 1897, Vol. 6, pp. 337–345.

ARTHUR ALLIN:—

A.B., Victoria University, Toronto, 1889 (Double Gold Medalist in Classics and Philosophy); University of Heidelberg, 1892; University of Breslau, 1892–93; Ph.D., Berlin University, 1895; Honorary Fellow in Philosophy, Clark University, 1895–96; Professor of Psychology and Education, Ohio University, 1896–97; Professor of Psychology and Education, University of Colorado, 1897–;

Consulting Psychologist, State Industrial School of Colorado.

Author of: —

Ueber das Grundprincip der Association, Berlin, 1895.

The Recognition-Theory of Perception. *Am. Jour. of Psy.*, Jan., 1896, Vol. 7, pp. 237–248.

Recognition. *Ibid.*, Jan., 1896, Vol. 7, pp. 249–273.

The Psychology of Tickling, Laughing, and the Comic (with G. S. Hall). *Ibid.*, Oct., 1897, Vol. 9, pp. 1–41.

Pedagogy in Ohio. *Trans. Ohio College Ass'n*, 1897.

Extra-Organic Evolution. *Science*, Feb. 25, 1898, N. S., Vol. 7, pp. 267–269.

Extra-Organic Evolution and Education. *Northwestern Monthly*, May and June, 1899, Vol. 9, pp. 400–403; 436–439.

LOUIS W. AUSTIN: —

A.B., Middlebury College, 1889; Student, University of Strassburg, 1889–90 and 1891–93; Fellow in Physics, Clark University, 1890–91; Ph.D., University of Strassburg, 1893; Instructor in Physics, University of Wisconsin, 1893–96; Assistant Professor, *ibid.*, 1896–; Member of the Wisconsin Academy of Sciences.

Author of: —

Experimentaluntersuchungen über die elastische Längs- und Torsionsnachwirkung in Metallen. *Annalen der Physik und Chemie*, 1893, N. F., Bd. 50, pp. 659–677.

The Effect of Extreme Cold on Magnetism. *Physical Review*, March–April, 1894, Vol. 1., pp. 381–382.

An Experimental Research on the Longitudinal and Torsional Elastic Fatigue. *Ibid.*, May–June, 1894, pp. 401–425.

On Gravitational Permeability. (With Charles B. Thwing.) *Ibid.*, Nov.–Dec., 1897, Vol. 5., pp. 294–300.

Exercises in Physical Measurement. (With Charles B. Thwing.) Allyn and Bacon, Boston, 1896. 208 pp.

H. P. AVERY: —

A.B., Amherst College, 1891; Principal, Yates Academy, Chittenango, N. Y., 1891–95; Scholar in Psychology, Clark University, Oct., 1895–Jan., 1896; admitted to the Massachusetts bar, June, 1896.

FRANK K. BAILEY: —

S. B., Colorado College, 1898; Scholar in Physics, Clark University, 1898–99.

THOMAS P. BAILEY, JR.: —

A.B., South Carolina College, 1887; Principal Winyah School, Georgetown, S. C., 1887–88; Tutor in English and History, University of South Carolina, 1888–89; A.M., University of South Carolina, 1889; Secretary, *ibid.*, 1889–91; Ph.D., University of South Carolina, 1891; Adjunct Professor of Biology, South Carolina College, 1891–92; Fellow in Psychology, Clark University, 1892–93; Lecturer, South Carolina College for Women, 1893–94; Superintendent of Schools, Marion, S. C., 1894–95; Assistant Professor of Science and Art of Teaching, University of California, 1894–98; Associate Professor of Education as related to Character, *ibid.*, 1898–.

Author of: —

The Development of Character (Doctor's Thesis), 1891.

Humanity of the Spiritual Life. *Christian Thought*, Oct., 1892.

Ejective Philosophy. *Am. Jour. of Psy.*, July, 1893, Vol. 5, pp. 465–471.

Herbart and Character Culture. *So. Ed. Jour.* Dec. 1893–Jan. 1894.

Psychology for Teachers. *Proc. S. C. Teachers' Ass'n*, 1893.

The Practice of Medicine and the Practice of Teaching. *Ibid.*, 1894.

Comparative Child-study Observations. *Handbook Ill. Soc. for Child-study*, 1895.

The Teaching Force — its General Culture. *Proc. Cal. Teachers' Ass'n*, 1894.

Child-study for "Naturalists." *Pacific Ed. Jour.*, April–May, 1896.

The Education of the Human Animal. *Proc. Cal. Teachers' Ass'n*, 1895.

Adolescence. *Ibid.*, 1896.

Child-study Notes. *Overland Monthly* (School Edition), 1896–97.

Work and Play. *Proc. Cal. Teachers' Ass'n*, 1896.

Ethological Outlines. *Oakland School Report*, 1896–97.

Ethology and Child-study. *Northwestern Monthly*, Nov., 1897, Jan., 1898.

Ethology and Child-study. *Proc. S. Cal. Teachers' Ass'n*, 1898.

Reformers in Ethology. *Bul. No. 13, Library Univ. of Cal.*, 1899.

Ethology: Standpoint, Method, Tentative Results. *University Chronicle* (University of California), Dec., 1898, Feb., 1899.

HENRY ROLFE BAKER:—

A.B., Iowa College, 1883; A.M., 1886; B.D., Yale University, 1886; Congregational Ministry, 1887; Graduate Student, Andover Theological Seminary, 1889–90; Hopkins Graduate Student in Philosophy and Comparative Religion, Harvard Divinity School, 1890–91; Student in Psychology, Clark University, 1894–95; Fellow, 1895–97; Honorary Fellow, 1898–99.

Author of:—

The Position of Myth, Science, and Nature Study in the Philosophy of Education.

FRANKLIN W. BARROWS:

A.B., Amherst College, 1885; Instructor in Sciences, Worcester Academy, 1885–88; A.M., Amherst College, 1888; Instructor in Natural Sciences, Central High School, Buffalo, N. Y., 1888–Jan. 1894; M.D., University of Buffalo, 1893; Fellow in Physiology, Clark University, Jan.–June, 1894; Instructor in Zoölogy and Physiology, Central High School, Buffalo, N. Y., 1894; Instructor in Histology and Biology, Medical Department of University of Buffalo, 1894–97; Professor, *ibid.*, 1897–.

GEORGE H. C. L. BAUR:—

Academy of Hohenheim, 1878–79; University of Munich, 1879–81; University of Leipzig, 1881–82; Ph.D., University of Munich, 1882; Assistant to Professor C. Kupffer, Munich, 1882–84; Assistant to Professor O. C. Marsh, Yale University, 1884–90; Docent in Osteology and Palæontology, Clark University, 1890–92; In charge of the Salisbury Expedition to the Galapagos Islands, May–Oct., 1891; Assistant Professor, Osteology and Palæontology, University of Chicago, 1892–95; Associate Professor, *ibid.*, 1895–97.

Died June 25, 1898.

Author of:—

Der Tarsus der Vögel und Dinosaurier. Eine Morphologische Studie. Inaugural-dissertation. Univers. München. Leipzig, 1882, Wilh. Engelmann, pp. 1–44, 2 taf. *Same* in *Morph. Jahrb.*, 1883, Bd. 8, pp. 417–456, Taf. XIX and XX.

Der Carpus der Paarhufer. Eine Morphogenetische Studie. (Vorl. Mittheil.) *Morph. Jahrb.*, 1884, Bd. 9, pp. 597–603.

Dinosaurier und Vögel. Eine Erwiederung an Herrn Prof. W. Dames in Berlin. *Ibid.*, 1885, Bd. 10, pp. 446–454.

Note on the Pelvis in Birds and Dinosaurs. *American Naturalist*, Dec., 1884, Vol. 18, pp. 1273–1275.

Bemerkungen über das Becken der Vögel und Dinosaurier. *Morph. Jahrb.*, 1885, Bd. 10, pp. 613–616.

Zur Morphologie des Tarsus der Saugethiere. *Ibid.*, 1885, Bd. 10, pp. 458–461.

On the Morphology of the Tarsus in the Mammals. *American Naturalist*, Jan., 1885, Vol. 19, pp. 86–88.

Ueber das Centrale Carpi der Saugethiere. *Morph. Jahrb.*, 1885, Bd. 10, pp. 455–457.

On the Centrale Carpi of the Mammals. *American Naturalist*, Feb., 1885, Vol. 19, pp. 195–196.

Das Trapezium der Cameliden. *Morph. Jahrb.*, 1885, Bd. 10, pp. 117–118.

The Trapezium of the Camelidae. *American Naturalist*, Feb., 1885, Vol. 19, pp. 196–197.

A Second Phalanx in the Third Digit of a Carinate-Bird's Wing. *Science*, May 1, 1885, Vol. 5, p. 355.

A Complete Fibula in an Adult Living Carinate-Bird. *Ibid.*, May 8, 1885, Vol. 5, p. 375.

On the Morphology of the Carpus and Tarsus of Vertebrates. *American Naturalist*, July, 1885, Vol. 19, pp. 718–720.

Zur Morphologie des Carpus und Tarsus der Wirbelthiere. *Zool. Anz.*, 1885, No. 196, pp. 326–329.

Zur Vögel-Dinosaurier-Frage. *Ibid.*, 1885, No. 200, pp. 441–443.

Nachträgliche Bemerkungen zu: Zur Morphologie des Carpus und Tarsus der Wirbelthiere (*Zool. Anz.*, 1885, No. 196). *Ibid.*, 1885, No. 202, pp. 486–488.

Zum Tarsus der Vögel. *Ibid.*, 1885, No. 202, p. 488.

Note on the Sternal Apparatus in Iguanodon. *Ibid.*, 1885, No. 204, pp. 561–562.

Einige Bemerkungen über die Ossification der "langen" Knochen. *Ibid.*, 1885, No. 205, pp. 580–581.

Bemerkungen über den "Astragalus" und das "Intermedium tarsi" der Säugethiere. *Morph. Jahrb.*, 1885, Bd. 11, pp. 468–483, Taf. XXVII.

Zur Morphologie des Carpus und Tarsus der Reptilien. (Vorl. Mittheil.) *Zool. Anz.*, 1885, No. 208, pp. 631–638.

Ueber das Archipterygium und die Entwicklung des Cheiropterygium aus dem Ichthyopterygium. (Vorl. Mittheil.) *Ibid.*, 1885, No. 209, pp. 663–666.

Preliminary Note on the Origin of Limbs. *American Naturalist*, Nov. 1885, Vol. 19, p. 1112.

Historische Bemerkungen. *Internat. Monatschr. f. Anat. u. Hist.*, 1886, Bd. 3, pp. 5–7.

Der älteste Tarsus (Archegosaurus). *Zool. Anz.*, 1886, No. 216, pp. 104–106.

The Oldest Tarsus (Archegosaurus). *American Naturalist*, Feb., 1886, Vol. 20, pp. 173–174.

W. K. Parker's Bemerkungen über Archaeopteryx, 1864, und eine Zusammenstellung der hauptsächlichsten Litteratur über diesen Vogel. *Zool. Anz.*, 1886, No. 216, pp. 106–109.

The Intercentrum of Living Reptilia. *American Naturalist*, Feb., 1886, Vol. 20, pp. 174–175.

The Proatlas, Atlas and Axis of the Crocodilia. *Ibid.*, March, 1886, Vol. 20, pp. 288–293, 5 figs.

Die zwei Centralia im Carpus von Sphenodon (Hatteria) und die Wirbel von Sphenodon und Gecko verticillatus Laur (G. verus Gray). *Zool. Anz.*, 1886, No. 219, pp. 188–190.

Herrn Prof. K. Bardeleben's Bemerkungen über "Centetes madagascariensis." *Ibid.*, 1886, No. 220, pp. 219–220.

Ueber die Kanäle im Humerus der Amnioten. *Morph. Jahrb.*, Bd. 12, pp. 299–305.

Bemerkungen über Sauropterygia und Ichthyopterygia. *Zool. Anz.*, 1886, No. 221, pp. 245–252.

Ueber das Quadratum der Säugethiere. *Sitzungsber. Gesell. Morph. u. Physiol.*, München, 1886, pp. 45–47.

On the Quadrate in the Mammalia. *Quart. Journ. Micr. Sci.*, 1886, Vol. 28, new ser., pp. 169–180.

Ueber die Morphogenie der Wirbelsäule der Amnioten. *Biol. Centralbl.*, 1886, Bd. 6, Nos. 11, 12, pp. 332–342, 353–363.

The Intercentrum in Sphenodon (Hatteria). *American Naturalist*, May, 1886, Vol. 20, pp. 465–468.

Berichtigung. *Zool. Anz.*, 1886, No. 223, p. 322.

The Ribs of Sphenodon (Hatteria). *American Naturalist*, Nov., 1886, Vol. 20, pp. 979–981.

Ueber die Homologien einiger Schädelknochen der Stegocephalen und Reptilien. *Anat. Anz.*, 1886, Jahrg. 1, pp. 348–350.

Osteologische Notizen über Reptilien. *Zool. Anz.*, 1886, No. 238, pp. 685–690.

Osteologische Notizen über Reptilien. Fortsetzung I. *Ibid.*, 1886, No. 240, pp. 738–745.

On the Morphogeny of the Carapace of the Testudinata. *American Naturalist*, Jan., 1887, Vol. 21, p. 89.

Osteologische Notizen über Reptilien. Fortsetzung II. *Zool. Anz.*, 1887, No. 244, pp. 96–102.

Erwiederung an Herrn Dr. A. Günther. *Ibid.*, 1887, No. 245, pp. 120–121.

Ueber Lepidosiren paradoxa Fitzinger. *Zool. Jahrb.*, 1887, Bd. 2, pp. 575–583.

Nachträgliche Notiz zu meinen Bemerkungen: "Ueber die Homologien einiger Schädelknochen der Stegocephalen und Reptilien" in No. 13 des ersten Jahrgangs dieser Zeitschrift. *Anat. Anz.*, 1887, Jahrg. 2, No. 21, pp. 657–658.

On the Phylogenetic Arrangement of the Sauropsida. *Jour. of Morph.*, Sept., 1887, Vol. 1, pp. 93–104.

Ueber die Abstammung der Amnioten Wirbelthiere. *Biol. Centralbl.*, 1887, Bd. 7, No. 16, pp. 481–493.

On the Morphology and Origin of the Ichthyopterygia. *American Naturalist*, Sept., 1887, Vol. 21, pp. 837–840.

On the Morphology of Ribs. *Ibid.*, Oct., 1887, Vol. 21, pp. 942–945.

Beiträge zur Morphogenie des Carpus und Tarsus der Vertebraten. I Theil. Batrachia. Jena, Gustav Fischer, 1888, pp. 1–86, Taf. I.–III.

Ueber den Ursprung der Extremitäten der Ichthyopterygia. *Bericht über die 20. Versamm. d. Oberrhein. Geolog. Vereins*, Jan. 16, 1888, 4 pp., 1 taf.

Dermochelys, Dermatochelys oder Sphargis. *Zool. Anz.*, 1888, No. 270, pp. 44–45.

Unusual Dermal Ossifications. *Science*, March 23, 1888, Vol. 11, p. 144.

Notes on the American Trionychidae. *American Naturalist*, Dec., 1888, Vol. 22, pp. 1121–1122.

The Theory of the Origin of Species by Natural Selection. *Ibid.*, Dec., 1888, Vol. 22, p. 1144.

Osteologische Notizen über Reptilien. Fortsetzung III. *Zool. Anz.*, 1888, No. 285, pp. 417–424.

Osteologische Notizen über Reptilien. Fortsetzung IV. *Ibid.*, 1888, No. 291, pp. 592–597.

Osteologische Notizen über Reptilien. Fortsetzung V. *Ibid.*, 1888, No. 296, pp. 736–740.

Osteologische Notizen über Reptilien. Fortsetzung VI. *Ibid.*, 1889, No. 298, pp. 40–47.

Revision meiner Mittheilungen im zoologischen Anzeiger, mit Nachträgen. *Ibid.*, 1889, No. 306, pp. 238–243.

Neue Beiträge zur Morphologie des Carpus der Säugethiere. *Anat. Anz.*, 1889, Jahrg. 4, No. 2, pp. 49–51, 4 figs.

The Systematic Position of Meiolania, Owen. *Ann. Mag. Nat. Hist.*, (6) Jan., 1889, Vol. 3, pp. 54–62.

On "Aulacochelys," Lydekker, and the Systematic Position of Anosteira, and Pseudotrionyx, Dollo. *Ibid.*, 1889, (6) Vol. 3, pp. 273–276.

On Meiolania and Some Points in the Osteology of the Testudinata: a Reply to Mr. G. A. Boulenger. *Ibid.*, 1889, (6) Vol. 4, pp. 37–45, Pl. vi.

Mr. E. T. Newton on Pterosauria. *Ibid.*, 1889, pp. 171–174.

Die systematische Stellung von Dermochelys Blainv. *Biol. Centralbl.*, 1889, Bd. 9, Nos. 5 and 6, pp. 149–153, 180–191.

Nachträgliche Bemerkungen über die systematische Stellung von Dermochelys Blainv. *Ibid.*, 1889, Bd. 9, Nos. 20 and 21, pp. 618–619.

Palaeohatteria Credner and the Proganosauria. *Am. Jour. of Sci.*, April, 1889, Vol. 37, pp. 310–313.

Kadaliosaurus priscus Credner, a new Reptile from the Lower Permian of Saxony. *Ibid.*, Feb., 1890, pp. 166–168.

Bemerkungen über den Carpus der Proboscidier und der Ungulaten im Allgemeinen. *Morph. Jahrb.*, 1889, Bd. 15, Heft 3, pp. 478–482, 1 fig.

On the Morphology of Ribs and the Fate of the Actinosts of the Median Fins in

Fishes. *Jour. of Morph.*, Dec., 1889, Vol. 3, pp. 463–466, 7 figs.

On the Morphology of the Vertebrate-Skull. *Ibid.*, 1889, Vol. 3, No. 3, pp. 467–474.

A Review of the Charges against the Paleontological Department of the U. S. Geological Survey, and of the Defence made by Prof. O. C. Marsh. *American Naturalist*, March 26, 1890, Vol. 24, pp. 298–304.

Note on Carettochelys, Ramsay. *Ibid.*, Nov., 1889, Vol. 23, p. 1017.

The Gigantic Land Tortoises of the Galapagos Islands. *Ibid.*, Dec., 1889, Vol. 23, pp. 1039–1057.

The Relationship of the Genus Dirochelys. *Ibid.*, Dec., 1889, Vol. 23, pp. 1099–1100.

The Genera of the Podocnemididae. *Ibid.*, May, 1890, Vol. 24, pp. 482–484.

Note on the Genera Hydraspis and Rhinemys. *Ibid.*, May, 1890, Vol. 24, pp. 484–485.

The Genera of the Chelonidae. *Ibid.*, May, 1890, Vol. 24, pp. 486–487.

On the Classification of the Testudinata. *Ibid.*, June, 1890, Vol. 24, pp. 530–536.

Professor Marsh on Hallopus and Other Dinosaurs. *Ibid.*, June, 1890, Vol. 24, pp. 569–571.

An Apparently New Species of Chelys. *Ibid.*, Oct. 1890, Vol. 24, pp. 967–968.

On the Characters and Systematic Position of the Large Sea Lizards, Mosasauridae. *Science*, Nov. 7, 1890, Vol. 16, No. 405, p. 262.

Two New Species of Tortoises from the South. *Ibid.*, Nov. 7, 1890, Vol. 16, No. 406, pp. 262–263.

The Problems of Comparative Osteology. *Ibid.*, 1890, Vol. 16, No. 407, pp. 281–282.

Das Variiren der Eidechsen-Gattung Tropidurus auf den Galapagos Inseln und Bemerkungen über den Ursprung der Inselgruppe. *Biol. Centralbl.*, 1890, Bd. 10, Nos. 15 und 16, pp. 475–483.

The Very Peculiar Tortoise, Carettochelys Ramsay, from New Guinea. *Science*, Apr. 3, 1891, Vol. 17, No. 426, p. 190.

American Box Tortoises. *Ibid.*, Apr. 3, 1891, Vol. 17, No. 426, pp. 190–191.

The Horned Saurians of the Laramie Formation. *Ibid.*, Apr. 17, 1891, Vol. 17, No. 428, pp. 216–217.

The Lower Jaw of Sphenodon. *American Naturalist*, May, 1891, Vol. 25, pp. 489–490.

Notes on the Trionychian Genus Pelochelys. *Ann. Mag. Nat. Hist.*, May, 1891, (6) Vol. 7, pp. 445–446.

Remarks on the Reptiles generally called Dinosauria. *American Naturalist*, May, 1891, Vol. 25, pp. 434–454.

On the Origin of the Galapagos Islands. *Ibid.*, March and April, 1891, Vol. 25, pp. 217–229, 307–326.

On the Relations of Carettochelys, Ramsay. *Ibid.*, July, 1891, Vol. 25, pp. 631–639, Pls. x.–xvi.

On Intercalation of Vertebrae. *Jour. of Morph.*, Jan., 1891, Vol. 4, pp. 331–336.

The Pelvis of the Testudinata, with Notes on the Evolution of the Pelvis in General. *Ibid.*, 1891, Vol. 4, No. 3, pp. 345–359, 13 figs.

Notes on Some Little-known American Fossil Tortoises. *Proc. Acad. Nat. Sci. Phil.*, 1891, pp. 411–430.

[Dr. Baur's Trip to the Galapagos Islands.] *American Naturalist*, Oct., 1891, Vol. 25, pp. 902–907.

The Galapagos Islands. *Proc. Am. Ant. Soc.*, Oct. 21, 1891, pp. 3–8.

Das Variiren der Eidechsen-Gattung Tropidurus auf den Galapagos-Inseln. *Festschr. z. 70. Geburtstage R. Leuckarts.* Leipzig, 1892, Wilhelm Engelmann, pp. 259–277.

Professor Alexander Agassiz on the Origin of the Fauna and Flora of the Galapagos Islands. *Science*, March 25, 1892, Vol. 19, No. 477, p. 176.

Der Carpus der Schildkröten. *Anat. Anz.*, 1892, Jahrg. 7, Nos. 7 und 8, pp. 206–211, 4 figs.

On the Taxonomy of the Genus Emys, C. Duméril. *Proc. Am. Phil. Soc.*, 1892, Vol. 30, pp. 40–44.

Addition to the Note on the Taxonomy of the Genus Emys, C. Duméril. *Ibid.*, 1892, Vol. 20, p. 245.

On Some Peculiarities in the Structure of the Cervical Vertebræ in the Existing Monotremata. *American Naturalist*, Jan., 1892, Vol. 26, p. 72.

[Visit to the Galapagos Islands.] *Proc. Bost. Soc. Nat. Hist.*, March, 1892, Vol. 25, p. 317.

The Cervical Vertebræ of the Monotremata. *American Naturalist*, May, 1892, Vol. 26, p. 435.

Bemerkungen über verschiedene Arten von Schildkröten. *Zool. Anz.*, 1892, No. 389, pp. 155–159.

Ein Besuch der Galapagos-Inseln. *Biol. Centralbl.*, 1893, Bd. 13, pp. 221–250.

On the Morphology of the Skull in the Mosasauridæ. *Jour. of Morph.*, Oct., 1892, Vol. 7, pp. 1–22, Pls. I and II.

Notes on the Classification and Taxonomy of the Testudinata. *Proc. Am. Phil. Soc.*, May 5, 1893, Vol. 31, pp. 210–225.

Notes on the Classification of the Cryptodira. *American Naturalist*, July, 1893, Vol. 27, pp. 672–675.

Two New Species of North American Testudinata. *Ibid.*, July, 1893, Vol. 27, pp. 675–677.

Further Notes on American Box-Tortoises. *Ibid.*, July, 1893, Vol. 27, pp. 677–678.

G. Jäger und die Theorie von der Continuität des Keimprotoplasmas. *Zool. Anz.*, 1893, No. 425, p. 300.

Ueber Rippen und ähnliche Gebilde und deren Nomenclatur. *Anat. Anz.*, 1893, Jahrg. 9, No. 4, pp. 116–120.

The Discovery of Miocene Amphisbænians. *American Naturalist*, Nov., 1893, Vol. 27, pp. 998–999.

The Relationship of the Lacertilian Genus Anniella Gray. *Proc. U. S. Nat. Mus.*, Vol. 17, No. 1006, pp. 345–351.

Bemerkungen über die Osteologie der Schläfengegend der höheren Wirbelthiere. *Anat. Anz.*, Dec., 1894, Bd. 10, No. 10, pp. 315–330.

Ueber den Proatlas einer Schildkröte (Platypeltis spinifer Les.). *Ibid.*, Jan., 1895, Bd. 10, No. 11, pp. 349–354, 6 figs.

Die Palatingegend der Ichthyosauria. *Ibid.*, 1895, Bd. 10, No. 14, pp. 456–459, 1 fig.

The Differentiation of Species on the Galapagos Islands and the Origin of the Group. *Biol. Lect. M. B. L. Woods Holl*, 1895, pp. 67–78.

Pithecanthropus erectus. *Jour. Geol.*, Feb. and March, 1895, Vol. 3, No. 2, pp. 237–238.

The Fins of Ichthyosaurus. *Ibid.*, Feb. and March, 1895, Vol. 3, No. 2, pp. 238–240.

The Experimental Investigation of Evolution. *The Dial*, May 1, 1895, p. 275.

Cope on the Temporal Part of the Skull, and on the Systematic Position of the Mosasauridæ. A Reply. *American Naturalist*, Nov., 1895, Vol. 29, pp. 998–1002.

Ueber die Morphologie des Unterkiefers der Reptilien. *Anat. Anz.*, 1895, Bd. 11, No. 13, pp. 410–415, 4 figs.

Das Gebiss von Sphenodon (Hatteria) und einige Bemerkungen über Prof. Rud. Burckhardt's Arbeit über das Gebiss der Sauropsiden. *Anat. Anz.*, 1895, Bd. 11, No. 14, pp. 436–439.

The Paroccipital of the Squamata and the Affinities of the Mosasauridæ Once More. A Rejoinder to Prof. E. D. Cope. *American Naturalist*, Feb., 1896, Vol. 30, pp. 143–147, Pl. iv.

Nachtrag zu meiner Mittheilung über die Morphologie des Unterkiefers der Reptilien. *Anat. Anz.*, 1896, Bd. 11, Nos. 18 and 19, p. 569.

Review of Dr. A. E. Ortmann's "Grundzüge der marinen Thiergeographie." *Science*, March 6, 1896, Vol. 3, No. 62, pp. 356–357.

The Stegocephali. A Phylogenetic Study. *Anat. Anz.*, 1896, Bd. 11, No. 22, pp. 657–673, 8 figs.

Mr. Walter E. Collinge's "Remarks on the Preopercular Zone and Sensory Canal of Polypterus." *Ibid.*, 1896, Bd. 11, Nos. 9 and 10, pp. 247–248.

Professor Cope's Criticisms of my Drawings of the Squamosal Region of Conolophus subcristatus Gray (*American*

Naturalist. Feb., 1898, pp. 148–149), and a Few Remarks about his Drawings of the Same Object from Steindachner. *Ibid.*, April, 1896, Vol. 30, pp. 327–329.

Bemerkungen zu Prof. Dr. O. Böttger's Referat über: Seeley, H. G. on Thecodontosaurus and Palaeosaurus. *Zool. Centralbl.*, Jahrg. 3, No. 11, 1896, p. 395.

Der Schädel einer neuen, grossen Schildkröte (Adelochelys) aus dem zoologischen Museum in München. *Anat. Anz.*, 1896, Bd. 12, Nos. 12 und 13, pp. 314–319, 4 figs.

Bemerkungen über die Phylogenie der Schildkröten. *Ibid.*, 1896, Bd. 12, Nos. 24 und 25, pp. 561–570.

On the Morphology of the Skull of the Pelycosauria and the Origin of Mammals. (With E. C. Case.) *Ibid.*, 1897, Bd. 13, Nos. 4 und 5, pp. 109–120, 3 figs.

Remarks on the Question of Intercalation of Vertebræ. *Zoological Bulletin*, Aug., 1897, Vol. 1, No. 1, pp. 41–55.

Birds of the Galapagos Archipelago: A Criticism of Mr. Robert Ridgway's Paper. *American Naturalist*, Sept., 1897, Vol. 31, pp. 777–784.

Archegosaurus [Review of O. Jäkel's "Die Organisation von Archegosaurus"]. *Ibid.*, Nov., 1897, Vol. 31, pp. 975–980.

New Observations on the Origin of the Galapagos Islands, with Remarks on the Geological Age of the Pacific Ocean. *Ibid.*, Aug., 1897, Vol. 31, pp. 661–680, and Oct., 1897, pp. 864–896 (incomplete).

HENRY BENNER: —

B.S., State Normal School, West Chester, Pa., 1885; M.S., *ibid.*, 1887, and University of Michigan, 1889; **Fellow in Mathematics, Clark University, 1889–90**; Instructor in Mathematics, Preparatory School, Northwestern University, 1890–92; Instructor in Mathematics, Chicago Manual Training School, 1892–.

JOHN A. BERGSTRÖM: —

A.B., Wesleyan University, Middletown, Conn., 1890; **Fellow in Psychology, Clark University, 1891–94; Ph.D., Clark University, 1894**; Assistant Professor of Psychology and Pedagogy, Indiana University, 1894–96; Associate Professor of Psychology and Pedagogy, *ibid.*, 1896–.

Author of: —

Experiments upon Physiological Memory by Means of the Interference of Associations. *Am. Jour. of Psy.*, April, 1893, Vol. 5, pp. 356–369.

An Experimental Study of Some of the Conditions of Mental Activity. *Ibid.*, Jan., 1894, Vol. 6, pp. 247–274.

The Relation of the Interference to the Practice Effect of an Association. *Ibid.*, June, 1894, Vol. 6, pp. 433–442.

School Hygiene. (Translation of Dr. Ludwig Kotelmann's *Ueber Schulgesundheitspflege*. With Edward Conradi.) Bardeen, Syracuse, N. Y., 1899, 391 pp.

ADOLF BERNHARD: —

A.B., Johns Hopkins University, 1889; Teacher of Mathematics and Science, National German-American Teachers' Seminary, Milwaukee, Wis., 1889–91; **Fellow in Chemistry, Clark University, 1891–92**; Fellow in Chemistry, University of Chicago, 1892–94; Ph.D., University of Chicago, 1894; Laboratory Assistant in Chemistry, *ibid.*, 1894–96.

Author of: —

Ueber die Einführung von Acylen in den Benzoylessigäther (Thesis). Chicago, 1894, pp. 43.

FRANZ BOAS: —

Ph.D., Kiel, 1881; Expedition to Baffin Land, 1883–84; Privatdocent, University of Berlin, Assistant Royal Ethnographical Museum of Berlin, 1884–86; Expedition to British Columbia, 1886–87; Assistant editor of *Science*, 1887–89; **Docent in Anthropology, Clark University, 1889–92**; Chief Assistant, Department of Anthropology, World's Columbian Exposition, Chicago, 1892–94; Expedition to Alaska, British Columbia, and California, 1895; Assistant Curator, Department of Anthropology, American Museum of Natural History, New York, 1896–; Lecturer on Anthropology, Columbia University, 1896–99; Professor of Anthropology, *ibid.*, 1899–; Member of: the New York Academy of Sciences, the American Statistical Association, the American Psychological Association, the American Folk-Lore Society, the Berlin Anthropological Society, the Berlin Geographical Society; Corresponding member of the Anthropological Society of Vienna, the Imperial Society of Friends of Natural Sciences, Anthropology, and Ethnology at Moscow, the Roman Anthropological Society, the Anthropological Society of Paris, the Anthropological Society at Washington, the American Antiquarian and Numismatic Society of Philadelphia; Past Vice-President of the Anthropological Section of the American Association for the Advancement of Science; Associate Editor of the *Internationales Archiv für Ethnographie*, and of the *American Anthropologist*, N. S.

Author of:—

Beiträge zur Erkenntniss der Farbe des Wassers. Inaugural Dissertation. Kiel, 1881.

Ein Beweis des Talbot'schen Satzes. *Annalen der Physik und Chemie*, 1881, pp. 359–362.

Ueber eine neue Form des Gesetzes der Unterschiedsschwelle. *Pflüger's Archiv*, 1882, pp. 493–500.

Ueber die verschiedenen Formen des Unterschiedsschwellenwerthes. *Ibid.*, 1882, pp. 214–222.

Ueber die Berechnung der Unterschiedsschwelle nach der Methode der richtigen und falschen Fälle. *Ibid.*, 1882, pp. 84–94.

Die Bestimmung der Unterschiedsempfindlichkeit nach der Methode der übermerklichen Unterschiede. *Ibid.*, 1882, pp. 562–566.

Ueber die Grundaufgabe der Psychophysik. *Ibid.*, 1882, pp. 566–576.

Ueber den Unterschiedsschwellenwerth als das Maass der Intensität psychischer Vorgänge. *Philosophische Monatshefte*, 1882, pp. 367–375.

Ueber die ehemalige Verbreitung der Eskimos im arktisch-amerikanischen Archipel. *Zeitschrift der Gesellschaft für Erdkunde*, 1883, pp. 118–136.

Die Wohnsitze der Neitchillik Eskimos. *Ibid.*, 1883, pp. 161–172.

Arctic Exploration and its Object. *Pop. Sci. Mon.*, May, 1885, Vol. 27, pp. 78–81.

Bemerkungen zur Topographie der Hudson Bay. *Petermann's Mittheilungen*, 1884, pp. 424–426.

Baffin Land. Geographische Ergebnisse einer in den Jahren 1883 und 1884 unternommenen Forschungsreise. Gotha, 1885. 104 pp., 2 maps.

Die Sprache der Bella Coola Indianer. *Verh. Anthrop. Ges.*, Berlin, 1886, pp. 202–206.

Zur Ethnologie von Britisch Columbien. *Petermann's Mittheilungen*, 1887.

Mittheilungen über die Bilqula Indianer. Originalmittheilungen aus dem *K. Museum für Völkerkunde*, Berlin, 1886, pp. 177–182.

On certain songs and dances of the Kwakiutl Indians. *Jour. Am. Folk-Lore*, April–June, 1888, Vol. 1, pp. 49–64.

Meteorologische Beobachtungen im Cumberland Sunde. *Annalen der Hydrographie*, 1885, pp. 311–363.

The Game of Cat's Cradle. *Internationales Archiv für Ethnographie*, 1888.

Chinook Songs. *Jour. Amer. Folk-Lore*, 1888, pp. 220–226.

Das Fadenspiel. *Mittheilungen der Anthropologischen Gesellschaft*, Vienna, 1888, p. 85.

Sagen der Eskimos von Baffin Land. *Verh. der Berliner Anthropologischen Gesellschaft*, 1885, pp. 398–405.

The Study of Geography. *Science*, 1887, Vol. 9, p. 137.

Arrangement of Ethnological Collections. *Ibid.*, 1887, Vol. 9, pp. 485, 587, 614.

Ice and Icebergs. *Ibid.*, 1887, Vol. 9, p. 294.

Formation and Dissipation of Sea-water Ice. *Ibid.*, Vol. 10, p. 118.

The Eskimo Tribes. Review of Rink's Eskimo Tribes. *Ibid.*, Vol. 10, p. 271.

Eskimo and Indian. *Ibid.*, Vol. 10, p. 273.

The Central Eskimo. *Sixth An. Rep. Bur. Ethn.*, Washington, 1888, pp. 399–669.

Die Eisverhältnisse des südöstlichen Theiles von Baffin-Land. *Petermann's Mittheilungen*, 1888, pp. 296–298, 16 plates.

Eskimo Tales and Songs (Texts). H. Rink and F. Boas. *Jour. Am. Folk-Lore*, Vol. 2, pp. 123–131.

Notes on the Snanaimuq. *American Anthropologist*, 1889, pp. 321–328.

Die Ziele der Ethnologie. New York, 1889, 30 pp.

Fourth Report of the Committee on the Northwestern Tribes of Canada. *British Ass'n Adv. Science*, 1888, pp. 1–10.

Fifth Report of the Committee, 1889, pp. 1–98.

Sixth Report, 1890, pp. 1–163.

Seventh Report, 1891, pp. 1–40, 4 tables.

Ninth Report, 1894, pp. 1–16.

Tenth Report, 1895, pp. 1–74, 11 tables.

Eleventh Report, 1896, pp. 1–23.

A Critique of Psycho-Physic Methods. *Science*, Vol. 11, p. 119.

The Indians of British Columbia. *Pop. Sci. Mon.*, March, 1888, Vol. 32, pp. 628–636.

Is Stanley Dead? *Nor. Am. Rev.*, 1888.

On Alternating Sounds. *American Anthropologist*, 1889, pp. 47–53.

On the Census Maps of the United States. *Science*, Vol. 12.

Cranium from Yucatan. *Am. Antiq. Soc.*, 1890, pp. 350–357.

The Use of Masks and Head Ornaments in British Columbia. *Intern'l Arch. Eth.*, 1890.

Mixed Races. *Science*, 1891, Vol. 17, p. 179.

Dissemination of Tales in America. *Jour. Am. Folk-Lore*, 1891, pp. 13–20.

Petroglyph in Vancouver Island. *Verh. der. Berliner Ges. für Anth.*, 1891, pp. 158–160.

Sagen der Kootenay. *Ibid.*, pp. 160–172.

Notes on the Chemakum Language. *American Anthropologist*, 1892, pp. 37–44.

Vocabularies from the North Pacific Coast. *Trans. Am. Phil. Soc.*, 1891, pp. 20.

Chinook Jargon. *Science*, Vol. 19, p. 474.

The Growth of Children. *Ibid.*, Vol. 19, pp. 256–268, 281–283.

Anthropologie in Amerika. *Correspondenzblatt deutsch. Anth. Gesellschaft*, 1893, pp. 114–116.

Notes on the Chinook Language. *American Anthropologist*, 1893, pp. 55–63.

The Growth of Children. *Science*, 1892, Vol. 20, p. 351.

Vocabulary of the Kwakiutl Language. *Am. Phil. Soc.*, 1892, pp. 34–82.

Eskimo Songs and Tales. *Jour. Am. Folk-Lore*, 1894, pp. 45–50.

Correlation of Anatomical and Physiological Measurements. *American Anthropologist*, 1894, pp. 313–324.

Linguistische Resultate einer Reise in Baffin Land. *Mittheilungen der Anthropologischen Gesellschaft*, Vienna, 1894, pp. 97–114.

Anthropology of the North American Indians. *Intern'l Cong. Anth.*, Chicago, 1894, pp. 37–49.

Classification of Languages of the North Pacific Coast. *Ibid.*, pp. 339–346.

Omaha Music. Review. *Jour. Am. Folk-Lore*, 1894, pp. 169–170.

Remarks on the Theory of Anthropometry. International Statistical Congress, Chicago. *Quar. Jour. Amer. Stat. Soc.*, 1893.

The Half-blood Indian. *Pop. Sci. Mon.*, October, 1894.

Human Faculty as Determined by Race. *A. A. A. S.*, 1894. Reprint, pp. 1–37.

Chinook Texts. *Bulletin, Bureau of Ethnology*, Washington, D.C., 1894, pp. 1–278.

Salishan Texts. *Am. Philos. Soc.*, 1895, pp. 31–48.

Notes on the Eskimo of Port Clarence, Alaska. *Jour. Am. Folk-Lore*, 1894, pp. 205–208.

Zur Mythologie der Indianer von Washington und Oregon. *Globus*, 1893, Nos. 10–12.

Dr. W. T. Porter's Investigations on the Growth of the School Children of St. Louis. *Science*, March 1, 1895, pp. 225–230. *Correspondenzblatt der deutschen Anth. Ges.*, 1895.

The Growth of First-born Children. *Science*, April 12, 1895.

Zur Ethnologie von Britisch Columbien. *Verh. d. Ges. für Erdkunde*, Berlin, May 4, 1895.

Indianische Sagen von der Nordpacifischen Küste. A. Asher, Berlin, 1895. vi + 364 pp.

The Relations Between Length-breadth and Length-height Index of the Skull. *Verh. Berliner Ges. für Anthropologie.*

The Growth of United States Naval Cadets. *Science*, N. S., Vol. 2, pp. 344–346.

Anthropometry of the Indians of Southern California. *Am. Ass'n for the Adv. Sci.*, 1896, pp. 261–269, 9 tables.

Zur Anthropologie der Indianer Nord Amerikas. *Verh. der Berliner Anth. Ges.*, 1895, pp. 366–411.

Sprachen Karte von Britisch Columbien. *Petermann's Mittheilungen*, 1896, No. 1, 3 plates.

The Growth of Indian Mythologies. *Jour. Am. Folk-Lore*, 1896, pp. 1–11.

Livi, Antropometria Militare. Review. *Science*, N. S., Vol. 3, pp. 829 ff.

The Growth of the Head. *Ibid.*, N. S., Vol. 4, No. 82.

Songs of the Kwakiutl Indians. *Int. Archiv für Ethnographie*, IX., 1896, pp. 1–9.

The Limitations of the Comparative Method of Anthropology. *Science*, Dec. 18, 1896, pp. 901–908.

Traditions of the Ts'ets'ā'ut. *Jour. Am. Folk-Lore*, Vol. 9, pp. 257–268; Vol. 10, pp. 35–48.

The Growth of Children. *Science*, Vol. 5, pp. 570–573.

The Decorative Art of the Indians of the North Pacific Coast. *Bull. Amer. Mus. Nat. His.*, 1897, pp. 123–176.

Eskimo Songs. *Jour. Am. Folk-Lore*, 1897, pp. 109–115.

Northern Elements in the Mythology of the Navaho. *American Anthropologist*, 1897, pp. 371–376.

Social Organization and Religious Ceremonials of the Kwakiutl Indians. Report of the U. S. National Museum for 1895. Washington, 1897, pp. 311–738.

Traditions of the Tillamook. *Jour. Am. Folk-Lore*, 1898, pp. 23–38, 133–150.

Ehrenreich; Die Ureinwohner Brasiliens. *Science*, N. S., Vol. 6, pp. 880–883.

Introduction to James Teit. Traditions of the Thompson River Indians of British Columbia, 1898, pp. 1–18.

The Growth of the School Children of Toronto. *Annual Report of the Commissioner of Education*, 1896–97. Washington, 1898, Vol. 2, pp. 1541–1599.

Cathlamet Texts. *Nineteenth Annual Report of the Bureau of Ethnology*, 280 pp.

[illegible] Texts. *Ibid.*, 100 pp.

Facial Paintings of the Indians of Northern British Columbia. *Memoirs Am. Mus. Nat. His.*, Vol. 2, pp. 1–24.

Mythology of the Bella Coola Indians. *Ibid.*, pp. 25–127.

A Precise Criterion of Species. *Science*, Vol. 7, No. 182, pp. 860–861.

Twelfth Report of the Committee of the British Association for the Advancement of Science on the Northwestern Tribes of Canada (with Dr. Livingston Farrand). *Proc. of the B. A. A. S.*, Bristol Meeting, 1898, pp. 1–61, 13 tables.

Anthropologie in Nord Amerika. *Correspbl. der deuts. Ges. f. Anthrop.*, 1898.

Mittheilungen aus Amerika. *Ibid.*, 1898, Jahrg. 29, pp. 121–122.

Some Recent Criticisms of Physical Anthropology. *American Anthropologist*, Jan., 1899, N. S., Vol. 1, pp. 98–106.

The Cephalic Index. *Ibid.*, July, 1899, N. S., Vol. 1, pp. 448–461.

EUGENE W. BOHANNON :—

Graduate, Indiana State Normal School, 1887; Superintendent of Schools, Brownsburg, Ind., 1887–89; A.B., Indiana University, 1890; Superintendent of Schools, Plainfield, Ind., 1889–91; Principal, High School, Pekin, Ill., 1891–92; A.M., Indiana University, 1892; Superintendent of Schools, Rensselaer, Ind., 1892–95; **Scholar in Pedagogy, Clark University, 1895–96; Fellow in Psychology, 1896–98**; Professor of Psychology, Pedagogy, and Practice, State Normal School, Mankato, Minn., 1898–.

Author of:—

Peculiar and Exceptional Children. *Pedagogical Seminary*, Oct., 1896, Vol. 4, pp. 3–60.

The Only Child in a Family. *Ibid.*, April, 1898, Vol. 5, pp. 475–496.

The Undue Emphasis of Method. *Ind. School Jour.*, Jan., 1899, pp. 1–7.

FREDERICK E. BOLTON :—

Graduate, State Normal School, Milwaukee, Wis., 1890; Principal, High School, Fairchild, Wis., 1890–91; B.S., University of Wisconsin, 1893; Principal of Schools, Kaukauna, Wis., 1893–95; M.S., University of Wisconsin, 1896; University of Leipzig, Germany, 1896–97; **Honorary Fellow in Psychology, Clark University, 1897–98; Ph.D., Clark University, 1898**; Professor of Psychology and Pedagogy, State Normal School, Milwaukee, Wis., 1898–; Member, Wisconsin Educational Club; Past Vice President, Wisconsin Child Study Society; Member, Wisconsin State Teachers' Association.

Author of:—

The Accuracy of Recollection and Observation. *Psychological Review*, May, 1896, Vol. 3, pp. 286–295.

The Development of School Curricula in the United States. Thesis deposited in Library of University of Wisconsin, 1896, pp. 206.

Apperception in the Study of Geography. *Wis. Jour. Ed.*, Aug., 1896.

The Importance of Higher Education to the Teacher. *Ibid.*, Sept., 1896.

The Training of Elementary Teachers in Germany. *Ibid.*, April, 1896.

Elementary Schools in Germany. *Ibid.*, June, 1897.

A Contribution to the Study of Illusions. *Am. Jour. of Psy.*, Jan., 1898, Vol. 9, pp. 167–182.

Hydro-Psychoses (Doctorate Dissertation). *Ibid.*, Jan., 1899, Vol. 10, pp. 171–227.

Scientific and Practical Child-study: The Province and the Limitations of Each. *Wis. Jour. Ed.*, May, 1899, and *Child Study Monthly*, May, 1899, Vol. 5, pp. 7–24.

The Secondary School System of Germany. *The Internat. Ed. Series.* D. Appleton & Co. (In press.)

THADDEUS L. BOLTON :—

A.B., University of Michigan, 1889; Principal, Public Schools, Vulcan, Mich., 1889–90; **Scholar in Psychology, Clark University, 1890–91; Fellow and Assistant, 1891–92; Fellow and Demonstrator, 1892–93**; Assistant in Ethnology, World's Columbian Exposition, 1893; Teacher in Psychology, State Normal School, Worcester, Mass., 1893–1896; **Ph.D., Clark University, 1893**; Professor of Psychology and Pedagogy, State Normal School, San José, Cal., 1896–97; Professor of Philosophy and Education, University of Washington, Seattle, Wash., 1897–98; University of Heidelberg, 1898–99.

Author of:—

Brain Model on a Large Scale, by Dr. Auzoux. Translation. (With H. H. Donaldson.) *Am. Jour. of Psy.*, April, 1891, Vol. 4, pp. 135–141.

The Size of the Several Cranial Nerves in Man, as indicated by the Areas of their Cross-sections. (With H. H.

Donaldson. (*Ibid.*, Dec., 1891, Vol. 4, pp. 224–229.

The Growth of Memory in School Children. *Ibid.*, April, 1892, Vol. 4, pp. 362–370.

A Study of the Spinal Cord of a Springhalt Horse. *Jour. of Nervous and Mental Diseases*, Jan., 1893, N. S., Vol. 18, pp. 7–12.

On the Discrimination of Groups of Rapid Clicks. *Am. Jour. of Psy.*, April, 1893, Vol. 5, pp. 294–310.

Rhythm. *Ibid.*, Jan., 1894, Vol. 6, pp. 145–238.

Asymmetry of Body. *Report of Cal. State Teachers' Ass'n*, June, 1897.

Modern Psychology in its Relation to Training of Teachers. *Ibid.*, June, 1897.

What is the New Psychology and what are its Claims? *Teacher and Student*, San José, Cal., June, 1897, Vol. 4, pp. 121–128.

Knowledge from the Standpoint of Association. (With E. M. Haskell.) *Ed. Rev.*, May, 1898, Vol. 15, pp. 474–499.

Die Zuverlässigkeit einiger Methoden für die Messung des Ermüdungsgrades in Schulkindern. *Psychol. Arbeiten*, herausg. v. E. Kraepelin. (In press.)

OSKAR BOLZA.

Ph.D., University of Göttingen, 1886; Reader in Mathematics, Johns Hopkins University, 1888–89; Associate in Mathematics, Clark University, 1889–92; Associate Professor of Mathematics, University of Chicago, Jan., 1893–Jan., 1894; Professor of Mathematics, *ibid.*, Jan., 1894–.

Author of:—

Ueber die Reduction Hyperelliptischer Integrale auf Elliptische. Sitzungsberichte der Freiburger Naturforschenden Gesellschaft, 1886. Dissertation, Gottingen, 1886. *Math. Annalen*, 1887, Vol. 28, pp. 447–456.

Darstellung der Invarianten der Binärform sechster Ordnung durch die Nullwerte der zugehörigen Theta-Functionen. *Ibid.*, 1887, Vol. 30, pp. 478–495.

On Binary Sextics with Linear Transformations into Themselves. *Am. Jour. of Math.*, 1888, Vol. 10, pp. 47–70.

On the Construction of Intransitive Groups. *Ibid.*, 1889, Vol. 11, pp. 195–214.

On the Theory of Substitution-Groups and its Applications to Algebraic Equations. *Ibid.*, 1891, Vol. 13, pp. 1–61.

Ueber Kronecker's Definition der Gruppe einer Gleichung. *Math. Annalen*, 1892, Vol. 42, pp. 253–256.

Ueber die linearen Relationen zwischen den zu verschiedenen singulären Punkten gehörigen Fundamentalsystemen von Integralen der Riemannschen Differentialgleichung. *Ibid.*, 1893, Vol. 42, pp. 526–536.

Netto's Theory of Substitutions, translated by Dr. Cole. *Bull. of the N. Y. Math. Soc.*, 1893, Vol. 2, pp. 83–106.

On the Transformation of Linear Differential Equations of the Second Order with Linear Coefficients. *Am. Jour. of Math.*, 1893, Vol. 15, pp. 264–273.

On Weierstrass' Systems of Hyperelliptic Integrals of the First and Second Kind. *Chicago Math. Congress Papers*, 1893, pp. 1–12.

On the First and Second Logarithmic Derivatives of Hyperelliptic Sigma Functions. *Am. Jour. of Math.*, 1895, Vol. 17, pp. 11–36.

Die cubische Involution und die Dreitheilung und Transformation dritter Ordnung der Elliptischen Functionen. *Math. Annalen*, 1897, Vol. 50, pp. 68–102.

Zur Reduction hyperelliptischen Integrale auf elliptische mittels einer Transformation dritten Grades. *Ibid.*, 1898, Vol. 50, pp. 314–324.

The Partial Differential Equations for the Hyperelliptic θ– and σ– Functions. *Am. Jour. of Math.*, April, 1899, Vol. 21, pp. 107–125.

Proof of Brioschi's Recursion Formula for the Expansion of the Even σ– Functions of Two Variables. *Am. Jour. of Math.*, April, 1899, Vol. 21, pp. 175-190.

JAMES W. BOYCE :—

B.S., University of Vermont, 1898; Fellow in Mathematics, Clark University, 1898-99.

WILLIAM P. BOYNTON :—

A.B., Dartmouth College (with honors in Physics), 1890; Professor of Physics and Chemistry, University of Southern California, 1890-93; A.M., Dartmouth College, 1893; Graduate Scholar and Assistant in Physics, *ibid.*, 1893-94; Scholar in Physics, Clark University, 1894-95; Fellow, 1895-97; Ph.D., Clark University, 1897; Instructor in Physics, University of California, 1897-.

Author of :—

A Quantitative Study of the High-Frequency Induction-Coil. *Physical Review*, July, 1898, Vol. 7, pp. 35-64; *Philosophical Magazine*, Sept., 1898, 5th ser., Vol. 46, pp. 312-328.

JOHN L. BRIDGE :—

B.S., Wesleyan University, Middletown, Conn., 1888; Assistant in Chemistry, *ibid.*, 1890-91; Fellow in Chemistry, Clark University, 1891-92; Fellow in Chemistry, University of Chicago, 1892-93; Ph.D., Clark University, 1894; Instructor in Science, Connecticut Literary Institution, 1893-96; Instructor in Science, Waterbury High School, 1896-.

Author of :—

The Ethers of Nitroso-phenol. *Am. Chem. Jour.*, 1892, Vol. 14, pp. 276-294.

Ueber die Aether des Chinonoxims. *Liebig's Annalen*, Vol. 277, pp. 79-105.

The Ethers of Toluquinoneoxime and their bearing on the Space Isomerism of Nitrogen. (With Wm. Conger Morgan.) *Am. Chem. Jour.*, Nov., 1898, Vol. 20, pp. 761-776.

CHARLES L. BRISTOL :—

B.S., New York University, 1883; Teacher of Natural Sciences, Riverview Academy, Poughkeepsie, N.Y., 1883-87; M.S., New York University, 1886; Professor of Zoölogy, State University, South Dakota, 1888-91; Fellow in Morphology, Clark University, 1891-92; Fellow in Biology, University of Chicago, 1892-93; Associate Professor of Biology, New York University, 1893-98; Professor of Biology, *Ibid.*, 1898-; Ph.D., University of Chicago, 1894; Member of American Naturalists; Member of Morphologists' Society; Member of New York Zoological Society; Fellow of New York Academy of Sciences.

Author of :—

The Metamerism of Nephelis, a contribution to the morphology of the nervous system, with a description of Nephelis Lateralis. *Journal of Morphology*, Oct., 1898, Vol. 15, pp. 17-72.

ERNEST NICHOLSON BROWN :—

B.A., Dalhousie University, Halifax, N.S., 1889; Scholar in Psychology, Clark University, 1892; Assistant in Ethnology, World's Columbian Exposition, 1893; Principal, Model School, Levis, Quebec, 1894-95; Principal, Model School, Lachute, Quebec, 1895-; Convener of Committee on Child Study of the Provincial Association of Protestant Teachers of Quebec, 1897-.

Author of :—

Child Study. *Educational Record of the Province of Quebec*, March, 1898, Vol. 18, pp. 81-85.

The Spelling Problem. *Ibid.*, May-June, 1899, Vol. 19, pp. 73-80.

ELMER B. BRYAN :—

Graduate of Indiana State Normal School, 1889; A.B., Indiana University, 1893; Principal of High School, Kokomo, Ind., 1893-94; Teacher of History, Industrial Training School, Indianapolis, 1894-95; Professor of Pedagogy, Butler College, 1895-97; Assistant Professor of Pedagogy, Indiana University, 1897-99; Associate Professor, 1899-; Graduate Student in Philosophy, Harvard University, Oct.,

1888–Jan., 1889; Scholar in Philosophy, Clark University, Jan.–June, 1889.

Author of: —

School Hygiene. *Indiana School Journal*, July, 1889, Vol. 44, pp. [illegible].

School Diseases. *Ibid.*, Aug., 1889, Vol. 44, pp. [illegible].

The Hygiene of Instruction. *Ibid.*, Sept., 1889, Vol. 44, pp. [illegible].

The Care of the Senses. *Ibid.*, Oct., 1889, Vol. 44, pp. [illegible].

Child Life. *Ibid.*, Nov., 1889, Vol. 44, pp. 647–648.

WILLIAM LOWE BRYAN: —

A.B., Indiana University, 1884; A.M., 1886; Student, University of Berlin, 1886–87; Instructor in Philosophy, Indiana University, 1885; Associate Professor in Philosophy, *ibid.*, 1885–87; Professor in Philosophy, *ibid.*, 1887; Fellow in Psychology, Clark University, Oct., 1891–Jan., 1892; Ph.D., Clark University, 1892; Vice-President, Indiana University, 1893–.

Author of: —

Psychology at Indiana University. *Am. Jour. of Psy.*, April, 1890, Vol. 3, pp. 283–284.

On the Development of Voluntary Motor Ability. *Ibid.*, Nov., 1892, Vol. 5, pp. 125–204.

Auditory and Visual Memory in School Children. *Proc. Internat. Ed. Ass'n*, 1893.

Suggestions on the Study of Children by Teachers. *Pamphlet*, 8 pp.

Child Study: Systematic and Unsystematic. *Proc. Dept. of Supt.*, 1895. *Proc. N. E. A.*, 1895, pp. 418–419.

On the Methods and Results of Child Study. Article in Johnson's *Encyclopædia*.

Syllabus on Imitation of Teacher by Pupil. (With U. J. Griffith.) *Handb. Ill. Soc. for Child Study*, May, 1895, Vol. 1, pp. 44–45.

Science and Education. *Proc. N. E. A.*, 1896, pp. 161–166.

Report on Work in Child Study in Indiana. *Ibid.*, 1896, pp. [illegible].

Scientific and Non-Scientific Methods of Child Study. *Ibid.*, 1896, pp. [illegible].

Studies on the Physiology and Psychology of the Telegraphic Language. (With Noble Harter.) *Psychological Review*, Jan., 1897, Vol. 4, pp. 27–53.

Hygiene of Motor Development. *Proc. Dept. of Supt., N. E. A.*, 1897.

Report of Special Committee on the Organization of a Committee on School Hygiene. National Council of Education, 1897.

Plato the Teacher. Being Selections from the Apology, Euthydemus, Protagoras, Symposium, Phædrus, Republic, and Phædo of Plato. Edited with Introduction and Notes. (With Charlotte Lowe Bryan.) Charles Scribner's Sons, New York, 1897. xii. + 434 pp.

The Republic of Plato. With Studies for Teachers (with Charlotte Lowe Bryan). Charles Scribner's Sons, New York, 1898. 313 pp.

Studies on the Telegraphic Language. The Acquisition of a Hierarchy of Habits. (With Noble Harter.) *Psychological Review*, July, 1899. Vol. 6, pp. 345–375.

WARREN G. BULLARD: —

A.B., Brown University, 1888; Instructor in Mathematics, Free Academy, Elmira, N.Y., 1888–93; Scholar in Mathematics, Clark University, 1893–96; Ph.D., Clark University, 1896; Instructor in Mathematics, University of Vermont, 1896–; Member of the American Mathematical Society.

Author of: —

On the General Classification of Plane Quartic Curves. *Math. Review*, Vol. 1, pp. 193–208. (Reprint.)

HERMON C. BUMPUS: —

Ph.B., Brown University, 1884; Instructor in Zoölogy, *ibid.*, 1884–86; Professor in Zoölogy and Geology, Olivet College, 1886–89; Fellow in Animal Morphology, Clark University, 1889–90; Ph.D., Clark University, 1891; Assistant Professor, 1890–91, and Associate Professor of Zoölogy, Brown University, 1891–92; Professor of Comparative Anatomy, *ibid.*, 1892–; Assistant Director, Marine Biological Laboratory, Woods Holl, Mass., 1893–95; Director Biological Laboratory of the U. S. Fish Commission, 1898–; Secretary of the American Society of Naturalists, 1895–99; Vice-President American Society of Naturalists, 1899–.

Author of: —

Studies in Zoölogy. *Am. Teacher*, 1886.

Reptiles and Batrachians of Rhode Island. *Random Notes on Nat. Hist.*, 1885–86, Vols. 2, 3.

Reptilia. *Stand. Nat. Hist.*, 1885, Vol. 3.

An Inexpensive Self-registering Auxanometer. *Bot. Gaz.*, 1887, Vol. 12.

The Embryology of the American Lobster. *Jour. of Morph.*, 1891, Vol. 5, pp. 215–262.

A New Method of using Celloidin for Serial Section Cutting. *Amer. Nat.*, Jan., 1892, Vol. 26, pp. 80–81.

A Laboratory Course in Invertebrate Zoölogy. Henry Holt & Co., 1893. 157 pp.

The Median Eye of Adult Crustacea. *Zool. Anz.*, 1894, p. 447.

Laboratory Teaching of Large Classes in Zoölogy. *Science*, March 8, 1895, N. S., Vol. 1, pp. 260–263.

Instinct and Education in Birds. *Ibid.*, August 21, 1896, N. S., Vol. 4, pp. 216–217.

Report of the Fourteenth Annual Meeting of the American Society of Naturalists. *Ibid.*, Feb. 28, 1896, N. S., Vol. 3, pp. 297–299.

A Review of "The American Lobster, a Study of its Habits and Development," by F. H. Herrick. *Ibid.*, Oct. 9, 1896, N. S., Vol. 4, pp. 536–537.

A Contribution to the Study of Variation. *Jour. of Morph.*, Feb. 1897, Vol. 12, pp. 455–484.

Records of the American Society of Naturalists for the Meeting of 1898.

A Review of Lloyd Morgan's "Habit and Instinct." *Science*, Dec. 17, 1897, N. S., Vol. 6, pp. 918–920.

Report of the Fifteenth Annual Meeting of the American Society of Naturalists. *Ibid.*, Jan. 7, 1898, N. S., Vol. 7, pp. 21–23.

The Result of the Suspension of Natural Selection as Illustrated by the Introduced English Sparrow. *Ibid.*, March 12, 1897, N. S., Vol. 5, pp. 423–424.

A Recent Variety of the Flatfish, and its Bearing upon the Question of Discontinuous Variation. *Ibid.*, Feb. 11, 1898, N. S., Vol. 7, pp. 197–198.

Certain Results from a Study of the Variation of Littorina. *Ibid.*, Feb. 11, 1898, N. S., Vol. 7, p. 198.

The Breeding of Animals at Woods Holl during the Month of March, 1898. *Science*, April 8, 1898, N. S., Vol. 7, pp. 485–487.

The Breeding of Animals at Woods Holl during the Month of May, 1898. *Ibid.*, July 15, 1898, N. S., Vol. 8, pp. 58–61.

The Breeding of Animals at Woods Holl during the Months of June, July, and August, 1898. *Ibid.* Dec. 16, 1898, N. S., Vol. 8, pp. 850–858.

The Variations and Mutations of the Introduced Sparrow (*Passer domesticus*). Biological Lectures of the Marine Biological Laboratory, 1896–97. Ginn & Co., Boston, 1898, pp. 1–15.

The Variations and Mutations of the Introduced Littorina. *Zoölogical Bulletin*, Feb., 1899, Vol. 1, pp. 247–259.

A Possible Case of Mutation. *Jour. Boston Soc. Med. Sci.*, Dec. 21, 1897, Vol. 2, pp. 25–28.

The Work of the Biological Laboratory of the U. S. Fish Commission at Woods Holl. *Science*, July 22, 1898, N. S., Vol. 8, p. 96.

The Identification of Adult Fish that have been Artificially hatched. Proceedings American Fisheries Society for 1898. *American Naturalist*, June, 1898, Vol. 32, pp. 407–412.

Professor James Ingraham Peck. (An Account of his Life and Work.) *Sci-*

ence, Dec. 2, 1898, N. S., Vol. 8, p. 763.

The Elimination of the Unfit as Illustrated by the Introduced Sparrow (*Passer domesticus*). Biological Lectures of the Marine Biological Laboratory. (In press.)

The Return of the Tilefish. *Bulletin U. S. Fish Commission.* (In press.)

FREDERIC BURK:—

B.L., University of California, 1883; Instructor in Literature and History, California Military Academy, 1889-90; Graduate Student in Literature, University of California, 1890-91; Instructor in Mathematics, Berkeley Gymnasium, 1890-91; Graduate Student in Philosophy, Stanford University, 1891-92, and A. M., 1892; Supervising Principal of Schools, Santa Rosa, Cal., 1892-94; Fellow in Psychology, Clark University, 1894-96; Honorary Fellow, 1896-98; Ph. D., Clark University, 1898; Supt. of Schools, Santa Barbara, Cal., 1898-99; President, State Normal School, San Francisco, 1899-; President of the Cal. State Teachers' Ass'n, 1899; Chairman of the Department of Child Study of the N. E. A., 1899.

Author of:—

Magic Wand. (Alumni Address at Stanford University, 1894, pamphlet).

Report upon the Pedagogical Methods in the Schools of Santa Rosa (pamphlet), 1894.

Modern Changes in Superintendency. *Pacific Ed. Jour.*, March and April, 1895.

Teasing and Bullying. *Pedagogical Seminary*, April, 1897, Vol. 4, pp. 336-371.

The Training of Teachers; "The Old View of Childhood and the New." *Atlantic Monthly*, Oct., 1897, Vol. 80, pp. 547-561.

The Graded System vs. Individual Pupils. *Northwestern Monthly*, March, 1898, Vol. 8, pp. 481-484.

Growth of Children in Height and Weight. *Am. Jour. of Psy.*, April, 1898, Vol. 9, pp. 253-326.

Normal Schools and the Training of Teachers. *Atlantic Monthly*, June, 1898, Vol. 81, pp. 769-779.

From Fundamental to Accessory in the Development of the Nervous System and of Movements. *Pedagogical Seminary*, Oct., 1898, Vol. 6, pp. 5-64.

The Evolution of Music and the Pedagogical Application. *Proc. Cal. Teachers' Ass'n*, 1898.

A Curriculum for the Kindergarten from a Child's Standpoint. *Ibid.*, 1898.

A Study of the Kindergarten Problem. (With Caroline Frear Burk.) The Whitaker and Ray Co., San Francisco, 1899. 128 pp.

The Kindergarten Child Physically. *Proc. N. E. A.*, 1899.

Child Study Application to the Curricula of the Primary School and Kindergarten. *Ibid.*, 1899.

The Influence of Exercise upon Growth. *Am. Phys. Ed. Rev.*, Dec., 1899, Vol. 4, and *Proc. N. E. A.*, 1899.

WILLIAM H. BURNHAM:—

A.B., Harvard University (with Honors in Philosophy), 1882; Instructor in Wittenberg College, 1882-83; Instructor in State Normal School, Potsdam, N. Y., 1883-85; Fellow, Johns Hopkins University, 1885-86; Ph.D., Johns Hopkins University, 1888; Instructor in Psychology, *ibid.*, 1888-89; Docent in Pedagogy, Clark University, 1890-92; Instructor, 1892-; Member of American Psychological Association.

Author of:—

Memory, Historically and Experimentally Considered. I. The Older Conceptions of Memory; II. Modern Conceptions of Memory; III. Paramnesia; IV. Recent Theories. *Am. Jour. of Psy.*, Nov., 1888, Feb., May, Aug., 1889, Vol. 2, pp. 39-90; 225-270; 431-464; 568-622.

The Stage and the Pulpit. *Christian Union*, April 19, 1888, Vol. 37, pp. 485-487.

Training the Memory. *Nation*, Dec. 19, 1888, Vol. 47, pp. 490–491.

Economy in Intellectual Work. *Scribner's Magazine*, March, 1889, Vol. 5, pp. 306–314.

Examination and Education. *Nineteenth Century*, Am. Suppl., March, 1889, Vol. 25, pp. 23–34.

Recent Educational Literature. *Nation*, Aug. 15, 1889, Vol. 49, pp. 130–132.

The New German School. *Pedagogical Seminary*, Jan., 1891, Vol. 1, pp. 13–18.

The Study of Adolescence. *Ibid.*, June, 1891, Vol. 1, pp. 174–195.

Observation of Children at the Worcester Normal School. *Ibid.*, June, 1891, Vol. 1, pp. 219–224.

Higher Pedagogical Seminaries in Germany. *Ibid.*, Dec. 1891, Vol. 1, pp. 390–408.

Illusions of Memory. *Scribner's Magazine*, Feb., 1892, Vol. 11, pp. 185–195.

Outlines of School Hygiene. *Pedagogical Seminary*, June, 1892, Vol. 2, pp. 9–71.

La nuova scuola tedesca. (Translation of "The New German School" by Paolo Vecchia). *Saggi Pedagogici*. Turin, 1893, pp. 103–129.

A Scheme of Classification for Child-study. *Pedagogical Seminary*, March, 1893, Vol. 2, pp. 191–198.

Individual Differences in the Imagination of Children. *Ibid.*, pp. 204–225.

Some Recent German Literature on Physical Education. *Ibid.*, pp. 226–230.

Child-study as the Basis of Pedagogy. *Proc. Int. Cong. of Ed.*, Chicago, 1893, pp. 718–720.

Motor Ability in Children: Development and Training. *Proc. Am. Inst. of Instruction*, Boston, 1894, pp. 127–140.

Un esquema de clasificación para el estudio del niño. (Translation of "A Scheme of Classification for Child-study). *Boletín de la Institución libre de Enseñanza*, Madrid, April 30, 1894, Vol. 18, pp. 107–112.

Bibliographical Notes to Lectures in School Hygiene. Worcester, Mass., 1897. 11 pp.

Impurities in the Air of Schoolrooms. *Northwestern Monthly*, July, 1897, Vol. 8, pp. 15–20.

Suggestions from the Psychology of Adolescence. *School Review*, Dec. 1897, Vol. 6, pp. 14–37.

Some Aspects of the Teaching Profession. *The Forum*, June, 1898, Vol. 25, pp. 481–495.

Bibliography of School Hygiene. *Proc. N. E. A.*, 1898, pp. 505–523.

El estudio del niño como base de la pedagogía. (Translation of "Child-study as the Basis of Pedagogy" by Manuel Valdés Rodríguez). *Ensayos sobre Educación Teórica Práctica y Experimental*, Tomo Segundo, Habana, 1898, pp. 160–162.

Mental Hygiene. Johnson's *Universal Cyclopaedia*, New Edition, 1899, Vol. 10.

School Diseases. *Ibid.*

School Hygiene. *Ibid.*

The Child in Education. *Nation*, Jan. 26, 1899, Vol. 68, pp. 72–73.

B. C. BURT: —

A.B., University of Michigan, 1875; Professor, Indiana State Normal School, 1875–78; A.M., University of Michigan, 1879; Fellow in Philosophy, Johns Hopkins University, 1881; Assistant Professor, University of Michigan, 1881–87; Fellow by Courtesy, Johns Hopkins University, 1887; Docent in Philosophy, Clark University, 1889–90; Ph.D., University of Michigan, 1894; Professor (*ad interim*) of Philosophy and Pedagogy, University of Colorado, 1894–95; Agent, "Northwestern Line" and "Santa Fé Route," Superior, Nebraska, 1895–.

Author of: —

Shakespeare in the Opinion of the 17th Century. *New Englander*, 1881.

Watson's Kant and his English Critics. *Unitarian Review*, 1882.

Series of Articles on Greek Philosophy. *Unity*, Chicago, 1885–86.

Some Relations between Philosophy and Literature. *Pub. of Phil. Soc.*, University of Michigan, 1888.

References for Students in English Literature. Pamphlet, 1887.

Philosophical Works of Professor George S. Morris. *Chronicle*, 1889.

A Brief History of Greek Philosophy. Ginn & Co., Boston, 1889. xiv. + 296 pp.

Translation of Erdmann's History of Philosophy from Kant to Hegel. Swan, Sonnenschein & Co., London.

German Philosophy since Hegel. *Education*, April and May, 1890.

Natural Science and the Philosophy of Nature. *Philosophical Review*, May, 1892, Vol. 1, pp. 284–291.

History of Modern Philosophy. 2 vols. McClurg & Co., Chicago, 1892, 323, 321 pp.

Translation of Hegel's Rechts-Pflichten und Religionslehre.

Translation of Erdmann's *Logik und Metaphysik*. Macmillan & Co., New York.

JOHN CHEBAN CARDWELL :—

M.D., University of the City of New York, Medical Department, 1888; Assistant in the Physiological Laboratory, *ibid.*, 1888–89; Fellow in Physiology, Clark University, 1889–91; Instructor in Physiology, Harvard Medical School, 1891–93; Lecturer on Physiology, Brooklyn College of Pharmacy, 1894–98; Assistant to the Chair of Nervous Diseases, Long Island College Hospital, 1897–; Chief of Clinic for Nervous Diseases, Polhemus Clinic, Brooklyn, N. Y., 1898–; Demonstrator of Physiology, Long Island College Hospital, 1899–; Associate Director of Department of Physiology, Hoagland Laboratory, 1899–.

ALEXANDER F. CHAMBERLAIN :—

A.B., University of Toronto (with Honors in Modern Languages and Ethnology), 1886; A.M., University of Toronto, 1889; Fellow in Modern Languages, University College, Toronto, 1887–90; Examiner in French and German, Department of Education, Toronto, 1888–89; Librarian Canadian Institute, Toronto, 1889–90; Examiner in German, University of Toronto, 1888–91; Examiner in Modern Languages, Trinity University, Toronto, 1889–91; Anthropological Researches in British Columbia, under the auspices of the British Association for the Advancement of Science, Summer of 1891; Secretary Anthropological Section, American Association for the Advancement of Science, 1894; Secretary Anthropological Section, British Association for the Advancement of Science, 1897; Fellow in Anthropology, Clark University, 1890–92; Ph.D., Clark University, 1892; Lecturer in Anthropology, 1892–.

Author of :—

The Relationship of the American Languages. *Proc. Canad. Inst.* (Toronto), 3d ser., Vol. 5, 1886–87, pp. 57–76.

Prehistoric Ethnology. [Brief Abstract.] *Ibid.*, Vol. 5, 1886–87, p. 144.

The Catawba Language. [Abstract.] *Ibid.*, Vol. 6, 1887–88, p. 23.

The Eskimo Race and Language. *Ibid.*, Vol. 6, 1887–88, pp. 261–337.

A First Contribution to the Bibliography of the Archæology of the Dominion of Canada and Newfoundland. *Ann. Rep. Canad. Inst.*, 1887–88, pp. 54–59.

The Catawba Language. Toronto, 1888. 4 pp., 8vo.

The Mississaguas of Scugog. [Abstract.] *Proc. Canad. Inst.*, 3d ser., Vol. 7, 1888–89, pp. 2–3.

Deluge Myths of Canadian Indians. [Abstract.] *Ibid.*, pp. 11–13.

Archæology of Scugog Island. [Abstract.] *Ibid.*, pp. 14–16.

The Language of the Mississaguas of Scugog. [Abstract.] *Ibid.*, pp. 213–216.

The Origin and Development of Grammatical Gender. [Abstract.] *Ibid.*, pp. 216–217.

A Second Contribution to the Bibliography of the Archæology of Canada. *Ann. Rep. Canad. Inst.*, 1888–89, pp. 102–118.

Notes on the Negro Words lagniappe, bucra, goober. *Science*, July 13, 1888, p. 23.

Mississagua Etymology. *Ibid.*, Sept. 14, p. 132.

The Archæology of Scugog Island. Port Perry, 1889. 4 pp., 8vo.

Notes on the History, Customs, and Beliefs of the Mississagua Indians. *Jour. Am. Folk-Lore*, Vol. 1, 1888, pp. 150–160.

Tales of the Mississaguas. I. *Ibid.*, Vol. 2, pp. 141–147.

A Mohawk Legend of Adam and Eve. *Ibid.*, Vol. 2, pp. 228, 311.

Algonkin Onomatology, with some Comparisons with Basque. [Abstract.] *Proc. Am. Ass'n Adv. Sci.*, Vol. 38, 1889, pp. 351–352.

The Two Brothers: A Mississagua Legend. [Abstract.] *Ibid.*, pp. 352–353.

Words of Indian Origin in the French Canadian Dialect and Literature. *Am. Notes and Queries* (Philadelphia), Vol. 1, 1888, pp. 220–221, 232–233, 258–259, 270–271, 278–279, 293–294, 305–306; Vol. 2, 1888–89, pp. 2–3, 16–17, 30–31, 52–53, 62–63, 76–77, 87–88, 99–100, 124–125; Vol. 4, 1889, pp. 77–78.

Who was "Etowokoam," mentioned in *Spectator*, No. 50? *Ibid.*, Vol. 2, pp. 287–288.

The Etymology of Terrapin. *Ibid.*, Vol. 3, pp. 210–211.

The Etymology of Tuxquan. *Ibid.*, Vol. 3, pp. 262–263; Vol. 4, p. 234.

The Derivation of Chicago. *Ibid.*, Vol. 4, pp. 35, 91–92.

The Names of the Humming Bird. *Ibid.*, Vol. 4, pp. 276–288.

New York Dialect Forms. *Ibid.*, Vol. 3, pp. 295–296.

Slav Proverbs. *'Varsity* (University of Toronto), April 7, 1888.

Etymology of Horse-Radish. *Am. Notes and Queries*, Vol. 2, 1889, pp. 119–120.

Etymologies of Acadia, gorr, andera, goober, Saginaw, Key West, cockle, Gal, [illegible], Manhattan, moccasin, hurrah, chipmunk, pisquesolve. *Ibid.*, Vol. 1, p. 285; Vol. 2, pp. 62, 310, 311; Vol. 3, pp. 8, 9, 10, 102, 107; Vol. 4, pp. 34, 164, 165, 214.

Hiawatha in Flemish. *Ibid.*, Vol. 3, pp. 85–87.

Etymology of Fad. *Ibid.*, Vol. 3, pp. 164–165.

Mississagua Place Names. *Jour. Am. Folk-Lore*, Vol. 3, 1890, p. 74.

Tales of the Mississaguas. II. *Ibid.*, pp. 149–154.

A Negro Creation Legend. *Ibid.*, p. 302.

The Indians of Canada. [Abstract.] *Trans. Canad. Inst.*, Vol. 1, 1890–91, pp. 18–19.

The American Indian in Literature. [Abstract.] *Ibid.*, pp. 33–34.

Mohawk Folk-Lore. *Science*, Vol. 16, 1890, p. 289.

The Prehistoric Naturalist. *Univ. Quart. Rev.* (University of Toronto), Vol. 1, 1890, pp. 179–197.

Dialect Research in Canada. *Dialect Notes*, Vol. 1, 1890, pp. 43–56.

Contributions toward a Bibliography of the Archæology of the Dominion of Canada and Newfoundland. III. *Ann. Rep. Canad. Inst.*, 1890–91, pp. 76–82.

The Algonkian Indians of Baptiste Lake. *Ibid.*, pp. 83–89.

The Aryan Element in Indian Dialects. I. *Canadian Indian*, Vol. 1, 1890–91, pp. 148–153.

The Thunder-Bird amongst the Algonkins. *American Anthropologist*, Vol. 3, 1890, pp. 51–54.

Note on the Os Incæ. *Ibid.*, Vol. 3, p. 104.

Notes on Indian Child Language. *Ibid.*, Vol. 3, pp. 237–241.

The Maple amongst the Algonkian Tribes. *Ibid.*, Vol. 4, 1891, pp. 39–43.

Maple Sugar and the Indians. *Ibid.*, Vol. 4, pp. 381–383.

Folk-Etymology in Canadian French. *Modern Language Notes*, Vol. 6, 1891, 203–206.

Notes of French Canadian Folk-Lore. *Dominion Illustrated* (Montreal), Vol. 4, 1891, pp. 12–13.

Nanibozhu amongst the Otchipwe, Mississagas, and other Algonkian Tribes.

Jour. Am. Folk-Lore, Vol. 4, 1891, pp. 193–213.

Words of Algonkian Origin in the Chinook Jargon. *Science*, Vol. 18, 1891, pp. 260–261.

African and American. The Contact of the Negro and the Indian. *Ibid.*, Vol. 17, 1891, pp. 85–90.

Classics and Modern Languages in Europe and America since 1880, or Ten Years of the New Learning. Toronto, 1891, 60 pp.

Some Points in Linguistic Psychology. *Am. Jour. of Psy.*, Vol. 5, 1892–93, pp. 116–119.

Notes on the Canadian French Dialect of Granby, P. Q. I. Vocabulary. *Modern Language Notes*, Vol. 7, 1892, pp. 324–327.

Der Wettlauf: Eine Sage der Kitonaqa. *Am Ur-Quell*, III. Bd., 1892, S. 212–213.

A Mississaga Legend of Nāniboʒū. *Jour. Am. Folk-Lore*, Vol. 5, 1892, pp. 291–292.

The Use of Diminutives in -ing by Some Writers in Low German Dialects. *Pub. Mod. Lang. Ass'n Am.*, Vol. 7 1892, pp. 212–217.

The Language of the Mississaga of Skūgog. A Contribution to the Linguistics of the Algonkian Tribes of Canada. [Thesis.] Philadelphia, 1892. 84 pp., 8vo.

British Association for the Advancement of Science. Edinburgh Meeting, 1892. Eighth Report on the Northwestern Tribes of Canada. Report on the Kootenay Indians of Southeastern British Columbia. (With introduction by Horatio Hale.) London, 1892. 71 pp., 8vo.

Human Physiognomy and Physical Characteristics in Folk-Lore and Folk-Speech. *Jour. Am. Folk-Lore*, Vol. 6, 1893, pp. 13–24.

The Canadian-French Dialect of Granby, Province of Quebec. II. Phonetics. *Modern Language Notes*, Vol. 8, 1893, 31–35.

Einige Wurzeln aus der Sprache der Kitonaqa-Indianer von Britisch-Columbien. *Verh. der Berl. Gesellsch. f. Anthr., Ethn. u. Urgesch.*, 1893, S. 419–425.

Ueber den Zauber mit menschlichem Blut und dessen Ceremonial-Gebrauch bei den Indianern Amerikas. *Am Ur-Quell*, IV. Bd., 1893, I., S. 1–3, II., S. 34–37, III., S. 64–65.

Sagen vom Ursprung der Fliegen und Moskitos. *Ibid.*, S. 201–202.

Die Natur und die Naturerscheinungen in der Mythologie und Volkskunde der Indianer Amerikas. I. Der Regenbogen. *Ibid.*, S. 281–282.

The Physical Education of Woman. By Prof. Mosso. [Translation.] *Pedagogical Seminary*, Vol. 2, 1892–93, pp. 226–228.

Notes on the Kootenay Indians. I. The Name. *Am. Antiq. and Orient. Jour.*, Vol. 15, 1893, pp. 292–294.

Further Notes on Indian Child Language. *American Anthropologist*, Vol. 6, 1893, pp. 321–322.

Colour-Comparisons in the Low-German Poets. [Abstract.] *Trans. Canad. Inst.*, Vol. 3, 1892–93, pp. 43–44.

"Ch'nal-Cay." *Nation*, Vol. 56, p. 83.

Sulle significazioni nelle lingue degli indigeni americani detti Kitonaqa (Kootenay) dei termini che denotano gli anni e le condizioni del corpo e dell' animo. Saggio di psicologia filologica. *Arch. per l' antrop. e la etnol.* Firenze, Vol. 23, 1893, pp. 393–399.

Primitive Woman as Poet. [Abstract.] *Proc. Am. Ass'n Adv. Sci.*, Vol. 42, 1893, p. 317.

Syllabus of Lectures on the Mythology of the North American Indians. *Report of President Clark Univ.*, 1893, pp. 133–140.

Bibliography to accompany a Syllabus of Lectures on the Mythology of the North American Indians. *Ibid.*, pp. 141–158.

The Coyote and the Owl (Tales of the Kootenay Indians). *Mem. Intern. Cong. Anthrop.*, Chicago, 1894, pp. 282–284.

A Kootenay Legend: The Coyote and the Mountain Spirit. *Jour. Am. Folk-Lore*, Vol. 7, 1894, p. 195.

Words Expressive of Cries and Noises in the Kootenay Language. *American Anthropologist*, Vol. 7, 1894, pp. 68–70.

New Words in the Kootenay Language. *Ibid.*, pp. 186–192.

Life and Growth of Words in the French Dialect of Canada. I. *Modern Language Notes* (Baltimore), Vol. 9, 1894, pp. 78–87.

Life and Growth of Words in the French Dialect of Canada. II. *Ibid.*, pp. 135–141.

Ueber die Benennung des Pferdes in den Sprachen amerikanischer Indianer. *Am Ur-Quell*, V. Bd., 1894, S. 5–6.

Notes on the Kootenay Indians. Second Paper. Linguistic Data. *American Antiq.*, Vol. 17, 1894, pp. 271–274.

Anthropology in Universities and Colleges. *Pedagogical Seminary*, Vol. 3, Oct., 1894, pp. 48–60.

Primitive Anthropometry and its Folk-Lore. [Abstract.] *Proc. Am. Ass'n Adv. Sci.*, Vol. 43, 1894, pp. 348–349.

Incorporation in the Kootenay Language. [Abstract.] *Ibid.*, pp. 346–348.

Translation into Primitive Languages; Errors and Pitfalls; with Illustrations from Algonkian dialects. [Abstract.] *Ibid.*, p. 346.

Bayou (Etymology). *Nation*, Nov. 22, 1894, Vol. 59, p. 381.

La Belle Nivernaise, par Alphonse Daudet, and Le Chien du Capitaine, par Louis Énault. Edited, with Lives of the Authors, Notes, and Vocabulary, by John Squair, B.A., and A. F. Chamberlain, M.A. Toronto, 1895, 6 + 184, and 199 + 133 pp.

Notes on the Kootenay Indians. III. Mythology and Folk-Lore. *Am. Antiq. and Orient. Jour.*, Vol. 17, 1895, pp. 68–72.

On Words for "Anger" in Certain Languages. A Study in Linguistic Psychology. *Am. Jour. of Psy.*, Vol. 6, 1894–95, pp. 585–592.

Mutation of Gender in the French Dialect of Canada. *Modern Language Notes*, Vol. 10, pp. 232–236.

The Child and Childhood in Folk-Thought (The Child in Primitive Culture). Macmillan's, N. Y., 1896, x. + 474 pp., 8vo.

Indian Legends and Beliefs about the Squirrel and the Chipmunk. *Jour. Am. Folk-Lore*, Vol. 9, 1896, pp. 48–50.

The Poetry of American Aboriginal Speech. *Ibid.*, pp. 43–47.

Record of American Folk-Lore. *Ibid.*, pp. 204–209.

Beitrag zur Pflanzenkunde der Naturvölker America's. *Verh. d. Berl. Ges. f. Anthr.*, 1896, S. 551–556.

Childhood. Address before Conference of Lend-a-Hand Clubs, Lowell, Mass., Feb. 1, 1896. *Ten Times One Record* (Boston), Vol. 8, 1896, pp. 7–8.

Anthropology at the Toronto Meeting of the British Association. *Science*, N. S., Vol. 6, 1897, pp. 476–483.

Record of American Folk-Lore. *Jour. Am. Folk-Lore*, Vol. 10, 1897, pp. 67–75.

In Memoriam: Horatio Hale. *Ibid.*, pp. 60–66.

The Mythology and Folk-Lore of Invention. *Ibid.*, pp. 89–100.

Record of American Folk-Lore. *Ibid.*, pp. 149–154.

The Unitarian Church as a Social Institution *versus* Alcoholism. Boston, 1897, 16 pp.

The Lesson of the "Little Child." *Northwestern Monthly* (Lincoln, Neb.), Vol. 7, 1898, pp. 435–439.

Record of American Folk-Lore. *Jour. Am. Folk-Lore*, Vol. 10, 1897, pp. 232–239.

Darwin and Lincoln. An Anniversary Address. *Worcester* (Mass.) *Gazette*, Feb. 8, 1898.

Record of American Folk-Lore. *Jour. Am. Folk-Lore*, Vol. 11, 1898, pp. 61–66.

The Kootenays and their Salishan Neighbours. *Rep. Brit. Ass'n Adv. Sci.*

(Toronto, 1897), Vol. 47, London, 1898, p. 792.

Kootenay Indian Drawings. *Ibid.*, pp. 797–798.

Record of American Folk-Lore. (Jointly with I. C. C.) *Jour. Am. Folk-Lore*, Vol. 11, 1898, pp. 151–158.

Record of American Folk-Lore. (Jointly with I. C. C.) *Ibid.*, pp. 293–297.

On the Words for Fear in Certain Languages. A Study in Linguistic Psychology. *Am. Jour. Psy.*, Vol. 10, 1898–99, pp. 302–305.

Ethnology of the Aborigines. In British Association for the Advancement of Science (Toronto Meeting, 1897). *Handbook of Canada* (Toronto, 1897), pp. 103–120.

American Indian Names of White Men and Women. *Jour. Am. Folk-Lore*, Vol. 12, 1899, pp. 24–31.

The Child. A Study in Human Evolution. (Volume of about 400 pages. In press.)

Art of the Kootenay Indians. (In preparation.)

Mythology of the Kootenays. (In preparation.)

Dictionary of the Kootenay Indian Language. I. Kootenay-English. II. English-Kootenay. (In preparation.)

Three Shapers of Childhood's Genius — Society, Opportunity, Travel. *Northwestern Monthly*, June, 1899, Vol. 9, pp. 439–443.

Record of American Folk-Lore. (With I. C. C.) *Jour. Am. Folk-Lore*, Vol. 12, 1899, pp. 135–143.

Numerous reviews of books and articles in *Journal of American Folk-Lore*, *Review of Historical Publications relating to Canada*, *American Journal of Psychology*, *Pedagogical Seminary*, etc.

WILL GRANT CHAMBERS:—

Graduate, Pennsylvania State Normal School, Lock Haven, 1887; Instructor in Mathematics, *ibid.*, 1887–90; A.B., Lafayette College (Honors in English and Philosophy), 1894; Instructor in Mathematics, State Normal School, Indiana, Pa., 1894–97; B.S., State Normal School, Indiana, Pa., 1896; M.S., *ibid.*, 1897; A.M., Lafayette College, 1897; Scholar in Psychology, Clark University, 1897–99; Instructor in Mathematics and Pedagogy, State Normal School, Indiana, Pa., 1899–.

WALTER CHANNING:—

Student, Massachusetts Institute of Technology, 1867–68; M.D., Harvard University, 1872; Honorary Scholar, Clark University, 1889–90; Honorary Fellow, 1890–92; Professor of Mental Diseases, Tufts College Medical School, 1896–; Assistant Physician Asylum for Insane Criminals, New York, 1873–75; First Assistant Physician, Insane Hospital, Danvers, Mass. 1876–78; Superintendent, Private Hospital Mental Diseases, Brookline, Mass., 1879–; Chief, Department Mental Diseases, Boston Dispensary; Consulting Physician, Boston Aid Society; Member of: American Medical Association, Massachusetts Medical Society, American Medico-Psychological Society, American Neurological Society, New England Psychological Society, Boston Medical Improvement Society, Boston Medical Library Association, Corporation Massachusetts School for Feeble-minded; Honorary Member, Association Institutions for Feeble-minded; Member of Council American Association Advancement Physical Education, Boston Society of Physical Education, Massachusetts Prison Association, National Conference of Charities; Ex-president, Brookline Education Society, and Boston Medico-Psychological Society; Trustee, New England Conservatory of Music; Member, Brookline School Board.

Author of:—

Case of Helen Miller. Self-mutilation. Tracheotomy. *Am. Jour. of Insanity.*

A Case of Feigned Insanity. *Boston Med. and Surg. Jour.*, 1878, Vol. 98, p. 666.

Buildings for Insane Criminals. *Proc. of Conference of Charities*, Chicago, June, 1879.

Care of the Insane in Massachusetts. *Boston Med. and Surg. Jour.* 1879, Vol. 101, p. 760.

The Study of Psychological Medicine. *Ibid.*, 1880, Vol. 102, p. 316.

Note on the Construction of Hospitals for Insane Paupers. *Proc. of Conference of Charities*, Cleveland, June, 1880.

Recent Progress in Insane Asylum Management. *Boston Med. and Surg. Jour.*, 1880, Vol. 102, p. 343.

The Treatment of Insanity in its Economic Aspect. *Proc. of Am. Social Sci. Ass'n*, Saratoga, N. Y., Sept. 9, 1880.

The Use of Mechanical Restraint in Insane Hospitals. *Boston Med. and Surg. Jour.*, 1880, Vol. 103, p. 178.

Recent Progress in Insane Asylum Management and Care of the Insane. *Ibid.*, 1881, Vol. 104, p. 272.

The Care of Insane Criminals. *Ibid.*, 1881, Vol. 104, p. 172.

Medical Expert Testimony. *Ibid.*, 1881, Vol. 105, p. 1.

The Mental Status of Guiteau, the Assassin of President Garfield. *Ibid.*, 1882, Vol. 106, p. 290.

Recent Progress in Insane Asylum Management and Construction. *Ibid.*, 1882, Vol. 106, p. 297.

Recent Progress in the Management of Lunatic Asylums and Care of the Insane. *Ibid.*, 1882, Vol. 107, p. 441.

Non-Restraint in Lunatic Asylums. *Ibid.*, 1882, Vol. 107, p. 582.

Medical Treatment of the Insane with Special Reference to Opium. *Ibid.*, 1883, Vol. 108, p. 85.

Report on Recent Progress in the Construction of Insane Hospitals and Management of the Insane. *Ibid.*, 1883, Vol. 109, p. 403.

A Consideration of the Causes of Insanity. *Fifth Ann. Rep. Mass. Board of Health, Lunacy, and Charity*, 1884.

Recent Progress in the Construction of Insane Hospitals and Management of the Insane. *Boston Med. and Surg. Jour.*, 1884, Vol. 110, pp. 296 and 321.

Report on the Care of the Insane. *Ibid.*, 1885, Vol. 112, p. 349.

Temperature of the Insane, Especially in Acute Mania and Melancholia. *Ibid.*, 1885, Vol. 113, pp. 1 and 29.

The Connection between Insanity and Crime. Rep. of the Com. on Bibliography of Insanity. *Proc. of Am. Ass'n of Med. Supts. of Am. Institutions for the Insane*, Saratoga, N. Y., June, 1885.

Recent Progress in the Care of the Insane. *Boston Med. and Surg. Jour.* 1886, Vol. 114, pp. 291 and 315.

Report of a Case of Epilepsy of Forty-five Years' Duration, with Autopsy. *Ibid.*, 1886, Vol. 115, p. 4.

Recent Progress in Care of the Insane. *Ibid.*, 1887, Vol. 116, pp. 351–372.

Progress in the Care of the Insane. *Ibid.*, 1888, Vol. 118, p. 424.

An International Classification of Mental Diseases. *Am. Jour. of Insanity*, Jan., 1888.

Massachusetts Lunacy Laws. *Boston Med. and Surg. Jour.*, 1888, Vol. 119, p. 97.

Lunacy Legislation as Proposed by Dr. Stephen Smith and Others. *Am. Jour. of Insanity*, Jan., 1889.

Physical Training of the Insane. *Ibid.*, Oct., 1889.

Physical Education. *Boston Med. and Surg. Jour.*, 1891, Vol. 125, p. 4.

Physical Education of Children. *Proc. of the Ann. Meeting of the Social Sci. Ass'n*, Sept. 1891.

Evolution of Paranoia. (Rep. of a Case.) *Jour. of Nervous and Mental Diseases*, 1893, p. 192.

Some Remarks on the Address Delivered to the American Medico-Psychological Association by S. Weir Mitchell, M.D., May 16, 1894. *Am. Jour. of Insanity*, Oct. 1894.

Tuberculosis in Mental Disease. *Boston Med. and Surg. Jour.*, 1894, Vol. 131, p. 62.

Physical Training in Childhood. *Educational Review*, Oct., 1895, Vol. 10, pp. 262–279.

The Importance of Frequent Observations of Temperature in the Diagnosis of

Chronic Tuberculosis. *Boston Med. and Surg. Jour.*, Oct. 21, 1886.

A Case of Tumor of the Thalamus, with Remarks on the Mental Symptoms. *Jour. of Nervous and Mental Diseases*, Aug., 1882.

The Significance of the Palatal Deformities of Idiots. *Jour. Mental Sci.*, London, Jan., 1897.

Beginnings of an Education Society. *Educational Review*, Nov., 1897.

Characteristics of Insanity. *Boston Med. and Surg. Jour.*, Dec. 9 and 16, 1897.

The Relation of the Medical Profession to School Education. *Annals of Gynecology and Pediatry*, Jan. 25, 1897.

Physical Training in the Boston Public Schools. *Am. Physical Ed. Review*, June, 1897.

Medical Expert Testimony in the Kelly Murder Trial. *Am. Jour. of Insanity*, No. 3, 1898, Vol. 54.

The New Massachusetts Board of Insanity. *Charities Review*, Oct., 1898.

OSCAR CHRISMAN :—

Teacher and Principal in Public Schools, (Owen County, Gosport, Peru, Kokomo, Logansport), Indiana, 1876–86; Graduate, Indiana State Normal School, 1887; A.B., Indiana University, 1888; Principal (Third Ward), Public School, Houston, Texas, 1888–89; Supt. Public Schools, Gonzales, Texas, 1889–92; Fellow in Pedagogy, Clark University, 1892–94; A.M., Indiana University, 1893; Student in Philosophy and Pedagogy, University of Jena, 1894–95; Ph.D., University of Jena, 1895; Professor of History of Education and Child-study, Kansas State Normal School, 1895– ; Secretary, 1896, and President, 1898, of the Kansas Society for Child-study.

Author of :—

The Hearing of Children. *Pedagogical Seminary*, Dec., 1893, Vol. 2, pp. 397–441.

Secret Language of Children. *Science*, 1893, Vol. 22, p. 303; 1894, Vol. 23, p. 18.

The Science of the Child. *South Dakota Educator*, Feb., 1894, p. 11.

Vertical Writing. *Texas School Jour.*, 1894.

Child-study, a New Department of Education. *Forum*, Feb., 1894, Vol. 16, pp. 728–736.

Contribution to a Symposium on Child-study. *Interstate School Review*, Illinois, June, 1894, p. 226.

One Year with a Little Girl. *Educational Review*, Jan., 1895, Vol. 9, pp. 52–71.

Paidologie, Entwurf zu einer Wissenschaft des Kindes. Inaugural-Dissertation der philosophischen Fakultät der Universität Jena zur Erlangung der Doktorwürde. Jena, 1896. 96 pp.

Children's Secret Language. *Child-study Monthly*, Sept., 1896, Vol. 2, pp. 202–210.

How a Story Affected a Child. *Ibid.*, April, 1897, Vol. 2, pp. 650–651.

The Hearing of School Children. *Northwestern Monthly*, July, 1897, Vol. 8, pp. 31–35.

Motor Control: Its Place in the Physical and Psychical Life of the Child. *State Normal Monthly*, Oct., 1897, Vol. 10, p. 8.

Child-study in Texas. *Child-study Monthly*, Nov., 1897, Vol. 3, p. 347. (Report of the Child-study Section of the Texas State Teachers' Association held at Waco, June 29–July 2, 1897.)

The Secret Language of Children. *Northwestern Monthly*, Vol. 8, Oct., 1897, p. 187; June, 1898, p. 649; and Jan., 1899, p. 376.

Exceptionals. *State Normal Monthly*, Jan., 1898, Vol. 10, p. 61.

Results of Child-study. *Education*, Feb., 1898, Vol. 18, pp. 323–331.

Religious Ideas of a Child. *Child-study Monthly*, March, 1898, Vol. 3, pp. 516–528.

How to use the Library. *Western College Magazine*, March, 1898, Vol. 19, p. 603.

Paidology, the Science of the Child. *Educational Review*, March, 1898, Vol. 15, pp. 269–284.

The Secret Language of Childhood. *Century*, May, 1898, Vol. 56, pp. 54–58.

Religious Periods of Child-growth. *Educational Review*, June, 1898, Vol. 16, pp. 40–48.

Child and Parent. *Northwestern Monthly*, Vol. 9, Nov., 1898, p. 185; Dec., 1898, p. 150.

The Pubescent Period. *Education*, Feb., 1899, Vol. 19, pp. 342–347.

Opening Remarks as President of the Kansas Society for Child-study. *Child-study Monthly*, Feb., 1899, Vol. 4, p. 461.

Editorial for the Child-study Department. *Northwestern Monthly*, Feb., 1899, Vol. 9, p. 275.

Child and Teacher. *Jour. of Pedagogy*, May, 1899, Vol. 12, pp. 118–125.

Courses of Study for Normal Schools. *Arena*, July, 1899.

ARTHUR L. CLARK:—

B.S., Worcester Polytechnic Institute, 1894; Instructor in Mathematics and Physics, Bridgton Academy, Me., 1895–96; Scholar in Physics, Clark University, 1896–97; Fellow, 1897–99; Instructor in Science, Worcester Academy, 1899–.

Author of:—

A Method of Determining the Angle of Lag. *Phil. Mag.*, April, 1896, Vol. 41, pp. 369–372.

On the Specific Inductive Capacity of Certain Oils. *Physical Review*, Feb., 1898, Vol. 6, pp. 120–125.

ROBERT CLARK:—

A.B., Amherst College, 1892; Teaching, 1892–97; Scholar, Clark University, 1897–99.

THOMAS H. CLARK:—

B.S., Worcester Polytechnic Institute, 1880; Assistant Superintendent Pennsylvania Land Co., 1881–84; Student, Johns Hopkins University, 1884–85; Assistant in Chemistry, Wesleyan University, 1885–89; Fellow in Chemistry, Clark University, 1889–92; Ph.D., Clark University, 1892; Assistant in Chemistry, 1892–93; Instructor in Quantitative Analysis, Tufts College, 1894–95; Instructor in Chemistry and Physics, Clinton Liberal Institute, 1895–97; Instructor in Chemistry and Physics, State Normal School, Plymouth, N. H., 1897–; Member Am. Institute of Mining Engineers, and German Chem. Society.

Author of:—

The Addition-Products of Benzo- and of Toluquinone. *Am. Chem. Jour.*, Dec., 1892, Vol. 14, pp. 553–576.

Relative Leichtigkeit der Kohlendioxydabspaltung aus den Silbersalzen der β-Chlorcrotonsäuren. (With Professor Arthur Michael.) *Jour. für prakt. Chemie*, 1895, N. F., Bd. 52, pp. 326–339.

CHARLES W. CLINTON:—

Principal of Public Schools in Wisconsin and Minnesota; County Superintendent, Wisconsin; Visitor to the State Normal Schools, Wisconsin; Professor, Shattuck School, Faribault, Minn., 1880–88; Principal, St. John's Military Academy, Kansas, 1888–90; Head Master, Peekskill Military Academy, 1891–93; Principal, Marmaduke (Mo.) Military Academy, 1893–94; Ph.D., Ottawa University, 1895; Principal, Clinton Classical School, 1895–97; Fellow in Psychology, Clark University, 1897–99; Professor of Mathematics and Latin, Stamford (Ct.) Preparatory School, 1899.

HERBERT OTIS CLOUGH:—

A.B., Bowdoin College, 1895; Scholar in Mathematics, Clark University, 1895–97; Assistant in Mathematics, Bowdoin College, 1897–98; Principal Kennebunkport (Me.) High School, 1898–.

FREDERICK W. COLEGROVE:—

A.B., Colgate University, 1883; A.M., *ibid.*, 1886; Student, Hamilton Theological Seminary, 1883–84; Principal, Collegiate Institute, Marion, N. Y., 1884–89; Professor of Latin, Colgate University, 1889–93; President, Ottawa University, Kansas,

1892–95; D.D., University of Rochester, 1893; Honorary Fellow in Psychology, Clark University, 1896–99; Ph.D., Clark University, 1898; Honorary Fellow in Psychology, Oct.–Dec., 1899; Student in Universities of Europe, 1899; Professor of Philosophy, University of Washington, Seattle, Sept., 1899–; Member of the American Philological Association, and Kansas Historical Society.

Author of:—

Freedom of Worship. *Our Young People*, April, 1897.

Individual Memories. *Am. Jour. of Psy.*, Jan., 1899, Vol. 10, pp. 228–255.

The Time required for Recognition. *Ibid.*, pp. 286–292.

Notes on Mental Standards of Length. *Ibid.*, pp. 292–296.

LEVI L. CONANT:—

A.B., Dartmouth College, 1879; Principal of High Schools, Minnesota and Indiana, 1880–83; Superintendent of Schools, Deadwood and Rapid City, So. Dak., 1883–87; A.M., Dartmouth College, 1887; Professor of Mathematics, Dakota School of Mines, 1887–90; Scholar in Mathematics, Clark University, 1890–91; Assistant Professor of Mathematics, Worcester Polytechnic Institute, 1891–93; A.M. and Ph.D., Syracuse University, 1893; Associate Professor of Mathematics, Worcester Polytechnic Institute, 1893–98; Professor of Mathematics, *ibid.*, 1898–.

Author of:—

Historical Development of Arithmetical Notation; and Text Books in Arithmetic. *Pedagogical Seminary*, June, 1892, Vol. 2, pp. 149–152.

Primitive Number Systems. *Smithsonian Report*, 1892, pp. 583–594.

The Teaching of Mathematics. *School Review*, April, 1893, Vol. 1, pp. 210–217.

Note on the Translation of Certain Memoirs on Infinite Series. *Bull. of the N. Y. Math. Soc.*, 1894.

The Origin of Numeral Words. *Proc. A. A. A. S.*, 1894.

English Folk Tales in America. *Jour. of Am. Folk-Lore*, April–June, 1895, Vol. 8, pp. 143–144.

The Number Concept. Macmillan and Company, New York, 1896. vi + 218 pp.

An Application of the Theory of Substitutions. *Am. Math. Soc.*, Aug., 1898.

ALFRED COOK:—

A.B., Northwestern University, 1877; Ph.D., University of Halle, 1886; Fellow by courtesy, Johns Hopkins University, 1887; Superintendent of Schools, Nimonk, Ill., 1887–88; Instructor in Philosophy, Bryn Mawr College, 1888–89; Docent and Lecturer on History of Philosophy, Clark University, 1889–90; Independent University Extension Lecturer on Psychology and on the Philosophy of History, 1890–.

Author of:—

Ueber die Berkeleysche Philosophie. C. A. Kaemmerer & Co., Halle, 1886. 48 pp.

Harmony of Natural Law and Free Will, a Dissertation on the Kantian Philosophy. Bloomington, Ill., 1888. 16 pp.

L. P. CRAVENS:—

A.B., Carthage College, 1876; A.M., *ibid.*, 1879; Professor of Mathematics, Mt. Morris Academy, 1880–84; Professor of Mathematics, Carthage College, 1884–86; Superintendent of Schools, Carthage, Ill., 1886–89; Scholar in Mathematics, Clark University, 1889–90; Professor of Mathematics, State Normal School, Winona, Minn., 1890–91; Student in Mathematics, University of Halle, 1891–92; Professor of Mathematics, Fort Worth University, Texas, 1892–94; Student in Mathematics, University of Chicago, 1894–95; Principal of Academic Department of Coe College, 1895–96; Principal of High School, Lake City, Minn., 1896–97; Superintendent of Schools, Lake City, Minn., 1897–.

T. R. CROSWELL:—

A.B., Bowdoin College, 1891; Principal, Wilton Academy, 1891–94; Student in Pedagogy, Columbia College, 1894–95; Scholar in Pedagogy, Clark University, 1895–97; Teacher in Public Schools of Chicago, 1897–99; Teacher in Stevens Point (Wis.) Normal School, 1899.

Author of:—

Courses of Study in the Elementary Schools of the United States. *Pedagogical Seminary*, April, 1897, Vol. 4, pp. 294–335.

A Study of the Ungraded Schools of Maine. *Maine School Report*, 1897, Appendix II., pp. 1–16.

Amusements of Worcester School Children. *Pedagogical Seminary*, Sept., 1899, Vol. 6, pp. 314–371.

HENRY S. CURTIS:—

A.B., Olivet College, 1894; A.B., Yale University, 1895 (Honors in Philosophy); Fellow in Psychology, Clark University, 1895–97; Ph.D., Clark University, 1898; Teacher, N. Y. Public Schools, 1898–.

Author of:—

Learning without Books. *Jour. of Pedagogy*, Jan., 1898, Vol. 11, pp. 56–60.

Inhibition. *Pedagogical Seminary*, Oct., 1898, Vol. 6, pp. 65–113.

Child-study in Connection with the Vacation Schools. (With G. E. Partridge.) Report on the Vacation Schools and Playgrounds, N. Y. City, Boroughs of Manhattan and the Bronx, 1898, pp. 51–67.

Child-study in Vacation Schools. *Educational Foundations*, May, 1899.

Child-study in the Playgrounds. *Ibid.*, June, 1899.

Plays and Playgrounds. (In press).

ARTHUR HILL DANIELS:—

B.A., Olivet College, 1887; Student, Yale Divinity School, 1887–90; B.D., Yale University, 1890; Student in Philosophy and Psychology, Yale University, 1890–92; Fellow in Psychology, Clark University, 1892–93; Ph.D., Clark University, 1893; Instructor in Philosophy, University of Illinois, 1893–96; Assistant Professor of Philosophy, *ibid.*, 1896–99; Professor of Philosophy, *ibid.*, 1899–.

Author of:—

The New Life: A Study of Regeneration. *Am. Jour. of Psy.*, Oct., 1893, Vol. 6, pp. 61–103.

The Memory After-image and Attention. *Ibid.*, Jan., 1895, Vol. 6, pp. 558–564.

SCHUYLER C. DAVISSON:—

A.B., Indiana University, 1890; A.M., *ibid.*, 1892; Instructor in Mathematics, *ibid.*, 1890–93; Associate Professor in Mathematics, *ibid.*, 1893–. Fellow in Mathematics, Clark University, 1895–96; Student, University of Tübingen, Germany, 1898–99.

GEORGE E. DAWSON:—

A.B., University of Michigan, 1887; Professor of Greek and English Literature, Carleton Institute, Farmington, Mo., 1887–88; Student, University of Leipzig, 1888–89; Principal, Oil City, Pa., High School, 1889–91; Professor of English and Literature, State Agricultural College, So. Dak., 1891–93; Instructor in English, University of Michigan, 1893–95; Fellow in Psychology, Clark University, 1895–97, Ph.D., Clark University, 1897; Professor of Psychology, Bible Normal College, Springfield, Mass., 1897–.

Author of:—

A Study in Youthful Degeneracy. *Pedagogical Seminary*, Dec., 1896, Vol. 4, pp. 221–258.

Series of Twelve Papers on Child-study. *International Evangel*, Sept., 1897–Sept., 1898.

The Study of Man as Related to Religious Work. *Biblical World*, March, 1899.

Interest, the Material of Instruction. *Biblical World*, June, 1899.

Suggestions as to the Basis of a Sunday School Curriculum. *Trans. Ill. Soc.*

for Child-Study, Apr.–July, 1899, Vol. 4, pp. 10–17.

Psychic Rudiments and Morality. *Am. Jour. of Psychology*. (In press.)

ALFRED T. DE LURY:—

B.A., University of Toronto (with Honors and Medal in Mathematics), 1890; **Fellow in Mathematics, Clark University, 1890–91**; Mathematical Master, Whetham College, Vancouver, 1891; Mathematical Master, Collegiate Institute, Toronto, 1892; Lecturer in Mathematics and Dean of the Residence, University of Toronto, 1892–; Member of the American Mathematical Society.

Author of:—

On Certain Deductions from the Theorem of Dr. Graves. *Papers Math. and Phys. Soc., Toronto Univ., Year 1890–91*, pp. 23–30.

Clark University. *The Varsity*, Toronto, Jan. 27, 1891, Vol. 10, pp. 150–151.

HENRY H. DONALDSON:—

A.B., Yale University, 1879; Sheffield Scientific School, 1880; College of Physicians and Surgeons, N. Y. City, 1881; Fellow, Johns Hopkins University, 1881–83; Ph.D., Johns Hopkins University, 1885; Associate in Psychology, *ibid.*, 1887–89; **Assistant Professor of Neurology, Clark University, 1889–92**; Professor of Neurology, University of Chicago, 1892–.

Author of:—

On the Detection and Determination of Arsenic in Organic Matter. (Under Prof. R. H. Chittenden.) *Am. Chem. Jour.*, Oct., 1880, Vol. 2, pp. 235–241.

The Influence of Digitaline on the Work of the Heart and on the Flow through the Blood Vessels. (With Dr. L. T. Stevens.) *Jour. of Phys.*, Jan., 1883, Vol. 4, pp. 165–197. (See also note in Vol. 5, p. 45.)

On the Temperature-Sense. *Mind*, July, 1885, Vol. 10, pp. 399–416.

Motor Sensations of the Skin. (With Dr. G. Stanley Hall.) *Ibid.*, Oct., 1885, Vol. 10, pp. 557–572.

On the Relation of Neurology to Psychology. *Am. Jour. of Psy.*, Feb., 1888, Vol. 1, pp. 210–221.

Anatomical Observations on the Brain and Several Sense-Organs of the Blind Deaf-Mute, Laura Dewey Bridgman. Part I. *Ibid.*, Sept., 1890, Vol. 3, pp. 293–342. Part II. Dec., 1891, Vol. 4, pp. 248–294.

Cerebral Localization. *Ibid.*, April, 1891, Vol. 4, pp. 113–130.

Notes on Models of the Brain. *Ibid.*, April, 1891, Vol. 4, pp. 130–131.

The Size of Several Cranial Nerves in Man as Indicated by the Areas of their Cross-sections. (With T. L. Bolton.) *Ibid.*, Dec., 1891, Vol. 4, pp. 224–229.

The Extent of the Visual Area of the Cortex in Man as deduced from the Study of Laura Bridgman's Brain. *Ibid.*, Aug., 1892, Vol. 4, pp. 503–513.

Preliminary Observations on Some Changes caused in Nervous Tissues by Reagents, commonly used to harden them. *Jour. of Morph.*, Jan., 1894, Vol. 9, pp. 123–166.

The Education of the Nervous System. *Educational Review*, Feb., 1895, Vol. 9, pp. 105–121.

The Growth of the Brain. (Contemporary Science Series.) Walter Scott, London. Chas. Scribner's Sons, New York, 1895. 374 pp.

Central Nervous System. Chapter X., *Howell's Am. Text-Book of Physiology*, W. B. Saunders, Philadelphia, 1896, pp. 605–743.

Observations on the Weight and Length of the Central Nervous System and of the Legs in Bull-frogs of Different Sizes. *Jour. of Comp. Neurol.*, Dec., 1898, Vol. 8, pp. 314–335.

D. ELLIS DOUTY:—

B.S., University of Washington, 1893; Assistant in Physics Laboratory, *ibid.*, 1896–99; Tutor in Physics, *ibid.*, 1899–

98; Scholar in Physics, Clark University, 1898-99.

L. WAYLAND DOWLING:—

Adrian College, 1886-90; Principal of Schools, Clayton, Mich., 1891-92; Fellow in Mathematics, Clark University, 1892-95; Ph.D., Clark University, 1895; Instructor in Mathematics, University of Wisconsin, 1895-98; Assistant Professor of Mathematics, *ibid.*, 1898-; Member of the American Mathematical Society; Member of the Wisconsin Academy of Sciences, Arts, and Letters.

Author of:—

On the Forms of Plane Quintic Curves. *Mathematical Review*, April, 1897, Vol. 1, pp. 97-119.

FLETCHER B. DRESSLAR:—

Instructor, Vincennes University, 1885; A.B., Indiana University, 1889; Principal, High School, Princeton, Ind., 1889-90; Superintendent of Schools, Princeton, Ind., 1890-91; Scholar in Psychology, Clark University, 1891-92; Instructor in Psychology, Indiana University, Sept.-Dec., 1892; Fellow in Psychology, Clark University, Jan., 1893-July, 1894; Ph.D., Clark University, 1894; Professor of Psychology and Pedagogy, State Normal School, Los Angeles, Cal., 1894-97; Assistant Professor of the Science and Art of Education, University of California, 1897-.

Author of:—

A Review of the Genus [illegible]. (With Ernest P. Bicknell.) *Proc. Acad. of Nat. Sci.*, Philadelphia, 1884.

A Review of the Family Scombridae (Illinois). (With Bert Fesler.) *Bull. of U. S. Fish Com.*, 1887.

Temperance Legislation in Indiana. (Prize Essay, University of Indiana.) *Indiana Student*, March, 1887.

Evils of Modern Immigration. (Prize Oration, University of Indiana.) *Ibid.*, Dec., 1888.

Fatigue. *Pedagogical Seminary*, June, 1892, Vol. 2, pp. 102-106.

A Sketch of Old School-Houses. *Ibid.*, June, 1892, Vol. 2, pp. 115-128.

Some Influences which affect the Rapidity of Voluntary Movements. *Am. Jour. of Psy.*, Aug., 1892, Vol. 4, pp. 514-527.

On Facial Vision and the Pressure Sense of the Drum of the Ear. *Ibid.*, April, 1893, Vol. 5, pp. 344-350.

A New Illusion for Touch and an Explanation for the Illusion of Displacement of Certain Cross Lines in Vision. *Ibid.*, Vol. 6, pp. 274-276.

A New and Simple Method for Comparing the Perception of Rate of Movement in the Direct and Indirect Fields of Vision. *Ibid.*, Vol. 6, p. 312.

Psychology of Touch. *Ibid.*, June, 1894, Vol. 6, pp. [illegible].

Outline for a Study of Habit-Degeneration. *Teachers' Handbook for Child-Study.* Published by Illinois Society for Child-Study, May, 1895, Vol. 1, pp. 31-33.

Preparation for History in the Grades. *Normal Exponent*, 1895.

The New Psychology and its Pedagogical Significance. *Proc. Cal. Teachers' Ass'n*, Dec., 1895.

Experiments in Psychology. *Overland Monthly*, Aug., Sept., Nov., Dec., 1896; Feb., March, April, June, 1897.

Education in Hawaii. *Educational Review*, Jan., 1897, Vol. 13, pp. [illegible].

Genetic Psychology. *Northwestern Monthly*, April, 1899, Vol. 9, pp. 346-352.

Counting, as influenced by Number Preferences. *Pop. Sci. Mo.*, April, 1899, Vol. 54, pp. 751-758.

FRANK DREW:—

Superintendent of Schools, Geneva, Ill., 1887-89; A.B., Indiana University, 1890; A.M., *ibid.*, 1891; Scholar in Psychology, Clark University, 1892-93; Fellow, 1893-95; Ph.D., Clark University, 1895; Instructor in Psychology, Indiana University, 1895-96; Teacher in State Normal School, Worcester, Mass., 1896-.

Author of: —

Adenoids in Children. *Pedagogical Seminary*, March, 189[illegible], Vol. [illegible], pp. 297–308.

Love Forms of College Students. *Ibid.* Dec. 18[illegible], Vol. [illegible], pp. 604–608.

Attention: Experimental and Critical. *Am. Jour. of Psy.*, July, 1896, Vol. 7, pp. 533–572.

LINDSAY DUNCAN: —

B.S., University of Maine, 1897; Scholar in Mathematics, Clark University, 1897–99; Instructor in Mathematics and Engineering, Union College, Schenectady, N. Y., 1899–.

ROBERT K. DUNCAN: —

A.B., University of Toronto, 1888; Fellow in Chemistry, Clark University, 1892–93; Instructor in Physics and Chemistry, Auburn, N. Y., High School, 1893–95; Instructor in Physics and Chemistry, Dr. Julius Sach's Collegiate Institute, New York, 1895–98; Non-Resident Student, Columbia University, 1897–98; Instructor in Physics and Chemistry, The Hill School, Pottstown, Pa., 1898–.

WILLIAM FREDERICK DURAND: —

Graduate, U. S. Naval Academy, 1880; Graduate, Course at Sea, 1882; Assistant Engineer, U. S. Navy, 1880–87; Graduate Student, Lafayette College, 1883–85; Ph.D., Lafayette College, 1888; Professor of Mechanics, Michigan State Agricultural College, 1887–91; Scholar in Physics, Clark University, Nov. and Dec., 1890; Professor of Marine Engineering, Cornell University, 1891–.

Author of: —

A Practical Method of Finding the Optical Centre of an Objective and its Focal Length. *Am. Mo. Micro. Jour.* Aug., 1885, Vol. 6, p. 161.

The Fundamental Conceptions of Mechanics. Privately published, 1889.

The Path of the Point of Contact of the Teeth of Gear Wheels. *Sci. Am. Supplement*, April 26, 1890, Vol. 29.

An Interesting Experiment with the Microscope. *Am. Mo. Micro. Jour.*, June, 1890, Vol. [illegible], p. [illegible].

The Behavior of Wood under Repeated and Varying Stress. *Trans. Mich. Eng. Soc.*, 1891, p. 41.

A New Form of Contour Caliper. *Ibid.* 1891, p. 62.

Decimal Subdivision by the Eye. *Sibley Jour. of Eng.*, Jan., 1892, Vol. 6, p. 132.

Study of the Element of a Screw Propeller. *Jour. of Am. Soc. of Naval Engineers*, 1892, Vol. 4, p. 72.

Treatment of Non-Algebraic Curves for Maxima and Minima by Use of Ordinates. *Ibid.* p. 71.

The Influence of Shock on Propeller Efficiency. *Ibid.* p. 611.

Some Points in the Philosophy of the Steamship. *Cassier's Magazine*, Nov., 1892, Vol. 3, p. 65.

Marine Engine Design. *Marine Review*, 1892, Vol. 6, Dec. 1, p. 6, and Dec. 8, p. 12.

Relative Weight of Water and Fire Tube Boilers. *American Shipbuilder*, June 20 and 27, 1893.

Planning and Equipment of Modern Ship and Engine Building Plants. *Rep. of Internat. Eng. Cong., Columbian Exposition, Div. of Marine Eng.*, Vol. 1, No. 29.

The Limit of Propeller Efficiency as Dependent on the Surface Form of the Propeller. *Trans. Am. Soc. of Mechanical Engineers*, 1893, Vol. 14, p. 65.

The Analysis of Certain Curves arising in Engineering Investigation. *Jour. of Am. Soc. of Naval Engineers*, 1893, Vol. 5, p. 543.

On the Law of Frictional Resistance. *Trans. of Am. Soc. of Naval Architects and Marine Engineers*, 1893, Vol. 1, p. 810.

A Planimeter for Averaging Radial Ordinates. *Sibley Jour. of Eng.* 1893, Vol. 7, p. 64.

Uses of Logarithmic Paper. *Engineering News*, Sept. 28, 1893.

New Rules for Approximate Integration. *Ibid.*, Jan. 18, 1894.

Mathematical Treatment of Continuous Functions by Approximate Methods. *Sibley Jour. of Eng.*, Jan., 1894, Vol. 8, p. 138.

An Approximate Formula for the Wetted Surface of Ships. (With G. R. McDermott). *Trans. Am. Soc. of Naval Architects and Marine Engineers*, 1894, Vol. 2, p. 897.

Water Tube Boilers for Marine Purposes. *Sibley Jour. of Eng.*, Feb., 1895, Vol. 9, p. 181.

Electricity for Marine Propulsion. *Cassier's Magazine*, Jan., 1896, Vol. 9, p. 143.

Curves showing the Relation between Equivalent Hollow and Solid Shafts. *Jour. of Am. Soc. of Naval Engineers*, 1896, p. 807.

The Number of Longitudinal Intervals in Ship Computations as Affecting the Accuracy of Integration for Displacement. *Trans. Am. Soc. of Naval Architects and Marine Engineers*, 1896, Vol. 4, p. 179.

Note on Different Forms of the Entropy Function. *Physical Review*, Vol. 4, p. 343.

Determination of the Current Curve Corresponding to any Form of Alternating Electromotive Force in a Circuit without Iron. *Sibley Jour. of Eng.*, 1897, p. 182.

Method of Determining a Continuous Record of the Performance of a Marine Engine. *Jour. Am. Soc. of Naval Engineers*, 1897, p. 1.

Graphical Determination of the Index of the Power according to which one quantity varies relative to another. *Jour. of Franklin Inst.*, March, 1897.

An Experimental Study of the Influence of Surface on the Performance of Screw Propellers. *Trans. Am. Soc. of Naval Architects and Marine Engineers*, Vol. 5, p. 107.

Steamship Vibrations and the Balancing of Marine Engines. *Marine Engineering*, June, July, August, 1897.

Resistance and Propulsion of Ships. J. Wiley & Sons, New York, 1898. ix + 431 pp.

The Approximate Treatment of Differential Equations. *Annals of Math.*, July, 1898, p. 110.

Entropy and Temperature Entropy Diagrams. *Jour. Soc. Naval Engineers*, 1898, p. 829.

Electrical Propulsion for Torpedo Boats. *Ibid.*, 1899, p. 68.

FREDERICK EBY :—

A.B., McMaster University, 1895; Graduate Student, University of Chicago, 1896–97; Assistant Instructor, Morgan Park Academy, Morgan Park, Ill., 1897–98; Scholar in Pedagogy, Clark University, 1898–99.

Author of :—

Suggestions for Work which can be done by Teachers. *43d Annual Report State Supt. of Ed., Albany, N. Y.*, 1897, Vol. 2, pp. 959–972.

Study of the Use of Secret Languages (Syllabus). *Ibid.*, pp. 972–976.

Preliminary Study of Child-Mathematics (Syllabus). *Ibid.*, p. 976.

Educational Value of Manual Constructive Work. *Education*, April, 1898, Vol. 18, pp. 491–495.

Translation of Pestalozzi's "Meine Nachforschungen." (With Dr. Julia E. Bulkley.) (In press.)

THOMAS W. EDMONDSON :—

B.A., London, Eng., 18[illegible] (first in Honors and Senior Exhibitioner at Matriculation, June, 18[illegible]); Akroyd Scholar, 18[illegible]–90; Senior Mathematical Scholar, Pembroke College, Cambridge University, Eng., 1886–91; B.A., Cambridge University (10th Wrangler in Mathematical Tripos), 1891; Graduate Student in Chemistry, Physics, and Botany, ibid., 1891; Assistant Tutor in Mathematics and Physics, University Corr. College, Cambridge, Eng., 1889–93; First Class in Intermediate Science Examination, London, 1893; Fellow in Physics, Clark University, 1894–96; Ph.D., Clark University.

1896; Assistant Professor of Physics, New York University, 1896–; Member of the American Mathematical Society, and American Physical Society.

Author of:—

Key to Briggs and Bryan's Coördinate Geometry. W. B. Clive & Co., London, New York, and Sydney, 1891. 196 pp.

Worked Examples in Coördinate Geometry. W. B. Clive & Co., London, New York, and Sydney, 1891; 16 Exam. Papers + 62 pp.

Mensuration and Spherical Geometry. (In collaboration with W. Briggs, M.A., LL.B., etc.) W. B. Clive & Co., London, New York, and Sydney, 1893. vi. + 112, ii. + 48 pp.

Key to Briggs and Bryan's Elementary Text-book of Mechanics. (In collaboration with Ethos Reynolds, M.A.) W. B. Clive & Co., London, New York, and Sydney, 1895. viii. + 173 pp.

On the Disruptive Discharge in Air and Liquid Dielectrics. *Physical Review*, Feb., 1898, Vol. 6, pp. 65–87.

CHARLES L. EDWARDS:—

B.S., Lombard University, 1884; B.S., Indiana University, 1886; A.M., *Ibid.*, 1887; Student, Johns Hopkins University, 1887–89; Ph.D., University of Leipzig, 1890; Fellow in Morphology, Clark University, 1890–91; Honorary Fellow, Clark University, 1891–92; Assistant Professor of Biology, University of Texas, 1892–93; Adjunct Professor of Biology, *Ibid.*, 1893–94; Professor of Biology, University of Cincinnati, 1894–; Member of the American Society of Naturalists; Morphological Society; President of the American Folk-Lore Society, 1899; Socio Correspondal, La Sociedad de Geografia y Estadistica, Mexico; Socio Honorario, La Sociedad Mexicana de Historia Natural; Socio Honorario, La Sociedad Antonio Alzate.

Author of:—

The Relation of the Pectoral Muscles in Birds to the Power of Flight. *American Naturalist*, Jan., 1886, Vol. 20, pp. 25–29.

A Review of the American Species of the Tetraodontidæ. (With President David S. Jordan.) *Proc. of U. S. Nat. Mus.*, 1886, p. 231.

The Influence of Warmth upon the Irritability of Frog's Muscle and Nerve. *Studies from Biol. Lab.*, *Johns Hopkins University*, July, 1887.

Winter Roosting Colonies of Crows. *Am. Jour. of Psy.*, May, 1888, Vol. 1, pp. 436–459.

Notes on the Embryology of Mülleria Agassizii Sel., a Holothurian common at Green Turtle Bay, Bahamas. *Johns Hopkins University Circular*, 1889, Vol. 8, p. 37.

Folk-Lore of the Bahama Negroes. *Am. Jour. of Psy.*, Aug., 1889, Vol. 2, pp. 519–542.

Beschreibung einiger neuen Copepoden und eines neuen copepodenähnlichen Krebses, Leuckartella paradoxa. *Archiv f. Naturgeschichte*, Berlin, 1891, Jahrg. 57, Bd. 1, 85 pp.

Some Tales from Bahama Folk-Lore. *Jour. of Am. Folk-Lore*, 1891, Vol. 4, pp. 47–54.

Some Tales from Bahama Folk-Lore. Fairy Tales. *Ibid.*, pp. 247–252.

Bahama Songs and Stories. (Vol. 3 of *Memoirs of the Am. Folk-Lore Society*.) Houghton, Mifflin & Co., Boston, 1895. 111 pp.

Notes on the Biology of Phrynosoma Cornutum Harlan. *Zool. Anzeiger*, 1896.

STAFFORD C. EDWARDS:—

Classical Graduate, Oneonta, N. Y., Normal, 1891; A.B., Brown University, 1895; A.M., Philosophy and Pedagogy, *Ibid.*, 1896; Student Teacher of History and English, High School, Providence, R. I., 1895–96; Principal of Greenport, N. Y., Union School, 1896–97; Scholar in Pedagogy, Clark University, Oct., 1897–March, 1899; Teacher of Mathematics, Jamaica, N. Y., Normal School, March–June, 1899; Principal Union School, Schuylerville, N. Y., 1899–.

ALEXANDER CASWELL ELLIS:—

Head Master, Classical High School, Chapel Hill, N. C., 1891-93; A.B., University of North Carolina, 1894; **Scholar in Pedagogy, Clark University, 1894-95; Fellow in Psychology, 1895-97; Ph.D., Clark University, 1897**; Adjunct Professor of Pedagogy, University of Texas, 1897-; Member of American Association for the Advancement of Physical Education; Member of Illinois Child-Study Society; Fellow, Texas Academy of Science.

Author of:—

Sunday School Work and Bible Study in the Light of Modern Pedagogy. *Pedagogical Seminary*, June, 1896, Vol. 3, pp. 363-412.

A Study of Dolls. (With G. Stanley Hall.) *Ibid.*, Dec., 1896, Vol. 4, pp. 129-175.

Suggestions for a Philosophy of Education. *Ibid.*, Oct., 1897, Vol. 5, pp. 159-201.

Play in Education. *Northwestern Monthly*, Nov., 1898; and *Rep. of Ad. and Proc. Texas State Teachers' Ass'n*, 1898.

Reading and Literature in the Schools. *Rep. of Ad. and Proc. Texas State Teachers' Ass'n*, 1898.

The Science of Education in the University of Texas, and Some of its Problems. *University Record*, University of Texas, Vol. 1, No. 2.

BENJAMIN F. ELLIS:—

A.B., Dartmouth College, 1889; Instructor in Physics and Mathematics, High School, Peoria, Ill., 1889-92; **Scholar in Physics, Clark University, 1892-93**; Instructor, High School, Peoria, Ill., 1893-.

PERCY NORTON EVANS:—

B.A.Sc., McGill University, Montreal, 1890; Assistant in Chemistry, *ibid.*, 1890-91; Student, University of Leipzig (McGill Exhibition of 1851 Science Scholar), 1891-93; Ph.D., University of Leipzig, 1893; **Honorary Fellow in Chemistry, Clark University, 1894**; Assistant in Chemistry to Professor Atwater, Wesleyan University, 1894-95; Instructor in Chemistry, Purdue University, 1895-96; Associate Professor of Chemistry, *ibid.*, 1896-; Member of the Indiana Academy of Science.

Author of:—

Condensation von β-Diketonen mit Harnstoff und Thioharnstoff. *Jour. für praktische Chemie*, Vol. 46, p. 353.

Condensationsprodukte der β-Diketone mit Harnstoff, Guanidin, und Thioharnstoff. *Ibid.*, Vol. 48, pp. 489-517.

Food Adulteration. *Purdue University Monographs*, 1898. 17 pp.

An Introductory Course in Quantitative Analysis. Ginn & Co., Boston, 1897. iv.+53 pp.

Note on Some Combustion Products of Natural Gas. *Proc. Ind. Acad. of Science*, 1897, pp. 183-184.

Note on the Iodine Number of Linseed Oil. *Ibid.*, 1898, pp. 160-162.

E. L. EVERETT:—

A.B., Brown University, 1886; A.M., Harvard University, 1889; Student, Berlin University, 1889-90; Professor, Utah Agricultural College, 1890-96; **Scholar in Psychology, Clark University, 1896-97; Honorary Fellow in Psychology, 1897-98**; Instructor, Mackenzie College, S. Paulo, Brazil, 1898-.

ALBERT C. EYCLESHYMER:—

Assistant in Animal Morphology, University of Michigan, 1888-89; Assistant in Botany, *ibid.*, 1889-90; Chief Assistant, Allis Lake Laboratory, 1890-91; B.S., University of Michigan, 1891; **Fellow in Morphology, Clark University, 1891-92**; Fellow in Biology, University of Chicago, 1892-93; Assistant in Anatomy and Histology, *ibid.*, 1893-95; Ph.D., University of Chicago, 1895; Tutor in Anatomy and Histology, *ibid.*, 1896-.

Author of:—

Celloidin Imbedding in Plant Histology. *Botanical Gazette*, Vol. 18, pp. 372-[illegible].

Notes on Celloidin Technique. *American Naturalist*, Vol. 26, pp. 554–558.

Club-root (*Plasmodiophora brassicae* Wor.) in the United States. *Journal of Mycology*, Vol. 7, pp. 79–90.

Paraphysis and Epiphysis in Amblystoma. *Anatomischer Anzeiger*, April 7, 1892, Vol. 7, pp. 815–817.

The Cleavage of the Amphibian Ovum. (With E. O. Jordan.) *Ibid.* Sept. 15, 1892, Vol. 7, pp. 622–624.

The Development of the Optic Vesicles in Amphibia. *Jour. of Morph.*, April, 1893, Vol. 8, pp. 189–194; Figs. 1–6.

On the Cleavage of Amphibian Ova. (With E. O. Jordan.) *Ibid.*, Sept., 1894, Vol. 9, pp. 407–416; Pl. xxvi.

The Early Development of Amblystoma with Observations on some other Vertebrates. *Ibid.*, Feb., 1895, Vol. 10, pp. 343–416; Pls. xviii–xxii.

FREDERICK C. FERRY :—

A.B., Williams College, 1891; Instructor in Latin and Mathematics, *ibid.*, 1891–94; A.M., *ibid.*, 1894; Graduate Student in Mathematics, Harvard University, 1894–95; A.M., *ibid.*, 1895; Fellow in Mathematics, Clark University, 1895–98; Ph.D., Clark University, 1898; Assistant Professor of Mathematics, Williams College, 1899–.

Author of:—

Geometry on the Cubic Scroll of the First Kind. *Archiv for Mathematik og Naturvidenskab*, B. xxi, Nr. 2.

DANIEL FOLKMAR :—

A.B., Western College, 1884; A.M., *ibid.*, 1888; Student, Harvard Divinity School, 1888–89; Fellow in Psychology, Clark University, 1889–90; Professor of Political Science and Psychology, Indiana Normal University, 1890–91; President and Professor of Social Science, *ibid.*, 1891–92; Professor of Social Science, Western Michigan College, 1892–93; President, *ibid.*, 1893; Lecturer in Sociology, University of Chicago, 1893–95; Professor of Psychology and Pedagogy, State Normal School, Milwaukee, Wis., 1895–98; Student, University of Paris, 1898–99; Professor of Anthropology, Université Nouvelle, Brussels, Belgium, 1898; Docteur ès sciences sociales, *ibid.*, June, 1899; Fellow of the Royal Statistical Society, London; Member of: Anthropologische Gesellschaft in Wien, Anthropological Society of Washington, American Association for the Advancement of Science, American Academy of Political and Social Science, American Statistical Association, American Institute of Sociology, Wisconsin Academy of Sciences, Arts, and Letters.

Author of:—

Instruction in Sociology in Institutions of Learning. Reprint from *Proc. of Nat. Conf. of Charities and Correction*, Boston, 1894. 19 pp. Also reprinted as Chapter XXVII of the *Report of U. S. Com. of Ed.* for 1894–95, Vol. 2, pp. 1211–1231.

A Sociological Ideal View of Normal Schools. *Proc. of Inter. Cong. of Ed. of the World's Columbian Exposition*, 1893, pp. 422–428. Published by Am. Ed. Ass'n, New York, 1893.

New Views in Social Science, etc. *The Interrogator*, Feb.–June, 1895.

The Ideal in Professional Training. *Education*, April, 1896.

The Duration of School Attendance in Chicago and Milwaukee. *Proc. Wisconsin Academy of Sciences, Arts, and Letters*, 1897, Vol. 12, pp. 255–305.

Anthropology, not Sociology, as an adequate Philosophy of Human Life. *Proc. A. A. A. S.*, 1898.

Sociology as based upon Anthropology. *Am. Jour. of Soc. Sci.*, 1898.

Anthropologie Philosophique. (In press.)

CLEMENS JAMES FRANCE:—

A.B., Hamilton College, 1898; Scholar in Psychology, Clark University, 1898–99.

Author of:—

The Psychology of Ownership. (With L. W. Kline.) *Pedagogical Seminary*. (In press.)

JOSEPH IRWIN FRANCE:—

A.B., Hamilton College (Root Scientific Fellowship, with Honors in Biology), 1895; Student, University of Leipzig, 1895–96; **Scholar in Psychology, Clark University, 1896–97**; A.M. (honorary), Hamilton College, 1898; Supervisor and Instructor in Science, Jacob Tome Institute, Port Deposit, Md., 1897–; Student, College of Physicians and Surgeons, Baltimore, Md., 1898–99.

Author of:—

The Conservation of Common. An Essay. Greasner & Schramm, Leipzig, 1896. 18 pp.

Nature-Study. *Educational Review*, March, 1899, Vol. 17, pp. 273–284.

ALEXANDER FRASER:—

A.B., Dalhousie College, 1889; Graduate Student, Harvard University, 1889–90; **Fellow in Psychology, Clark University, 1891–92**; Student in Medicine, Dalhousie University, 1893–97; M.D., C.M., *ibid.*, 1897; Lecturer in Psychology, Halifax Ladies' College, 1893–94; Instructor in Psychology, Halifax School for the Blind, 1894–96; House Surgeon, Victoria General Hospital, Halifax, N. S., 1897–98; Practising Physician and Surgeon, New Glasgow, N. S., 1898–.

Author of:—

Visualization as a Chief Source of the Psychology of Hobbes, Locke, Berkeley, and Hume. *Am. Jour. of Psy.*, Dec., 1891, Vol. 4, pp. 230–247.

The Psychological Foundation of Natural Realism. *Ibid.*, April, 1892, Vol. 4, pp. 429–450.

The Psychological Basis of Hegelism. *Ibid.*, July, 1893, Vol. 5, pp. 472–495.

JOHN S. FRENCH:—

A.B., Bowdoin College, 1895; **Scholar in Mathematics, Clark University, 1895–96; Fellow, 1896–98; Ph.D., Clark University, 1898**; Supervisor and Instructor in Mathematics, Jacob Tome Institute, 1898–.

Author of:—

On the Theory of the Pertingents to a Plane Curve. (In press.)

JOHN PHELPS FRUIT:—

A.B., Bethel College, Ky., 1876; Instructor of Latin and Mathematics, High School, Parker's Grove, Ky., 1876–79; Professor of Latin and Greek, Bardstown Institute, Ky., 1879–81; A.M., Bethel College, 1881; President, Liberty Female College, Glasgow, Ky., 1881–83; Professor of English Literature, Bethel College, 1883–97; **Scholar in Psychology, Clark University, 1891**; Graduate Student, University of Leipzig, 1894–95; Ph.D., University of Leipzig, 1895; Professor of English Language and Literature, William Jewell College, 1897–; Member of: Modern Language Association, American Dialect Society, American Statistical Association, Southern History Association.

Author of:—

The Evolution of Figures of Speech. *Modern Language Notes*, Dec., 1888.

Browning and Tennyson. *Ibid.*, May, 1890.

A Plea for the Study of Literature from the *Æsthetic* Standpoint. *Pub. of the Modern Language Ass'n*, 1891, Vol. 6, No. 1.

Shakespeare's Egoism. *Poet Lore*, Sept., 1889, Vol. 1, pp. 406–407.

The Destiny of Marriage: Portia and the Caskets. *Ibid.*, Feb., 1891, Vol. 3, pp. 69–74.

Uncle Remus in Phonetic Spelling. *Dialect Notes*, Boston, 1892, Part 4, pp. 196–198.

The Ideal the Need of the People. *Southern Magazine*, May, 1894.

John Milton. *Seminary Magazine* (Louisville, Ky.), March, 1899.

The Mind and Art of Poe's Poetry. A. S. Barnes & Co., New York, 1899. 144 pp.

HOMER GAGE:—

A.B., Harvard University, 1882; A.M., *ibid.*, 1887; M.D., *ibid.*, 1887; Physician and Surgeon, Worcester, Mass., 1888–;

Honorary Scholar in Anatomy, Clark University, 1889-90; Surgeon to Memorial, St. Vincent, and Worcester City Hospitals; Consulting Surgeon to Baldwinville Cottage Hospital.

BENJAMIN IVES GILMAN:—

A.B., Williams College, 1872; A.M., *ibid.*, 1880; Fellow, Johns Hopkins University, 1881-83; Lecturer at Princeton, Harvard, and Columbia, 1890-91; Instructor in Psychology, Clark University, 1892-93; Curator, Museum of Fine Arts, Boston, Mass., 1893-.

Author of:—

On Propositions and the Syllogism. On Propositions called Spurious. *J. H. U. Circular*, Aug., 1882, pp. 240-241.

On Operations in Relative Number. *Johns Hopkins Studies in Logic*, 1883.

A Study of the Inductive Theories of Bacon, Whewell, and Mill. *Colorado College Studies*, 1890, pp. 17-38.

Zuñi Melodies. *Jour. of Am. Arch. and Eth.*, Vol. 1, 1891, pp. 65-91.

On some Psychological Aspects of the Chinese Musical System. *Philosophical Review*, Jan. and March, 1892, Vol. 1, pp. 54-71, 154-178.

On the Properties of a One-dimensional Manifold. *Mind*, Oct., 1892, N. S., Vol. 1, pp. 518-526.

Report on an Experimental Test of Musical Expressiveness. *Am. Jour. of Psy.*, Vols. 4 and 5, Aug. and Oct., 1892.

Syllabus of Lectures on the Psychology of Pain and Pleasure. *Ibid.*, Oct., 1893, Vol. 6, pp. 1-60.

HENRY H. GODDARD:—

A.B., Haverford College, 1887; A.M., *ibid.*, 1889; Instructor in Latin and History, University of Southern California, 1887-88; Graduate Student, Haverford College, 1888-89; Principal, Damascus Academy, Ohio, 1889-91; Instructor in Latin and Greek, Oak Grove Seminary, Vassalboro, Me., 1891-93; Principal, *ibid.*, 1893-96; Scholar in Psychology, Clark University, 1896-97; Fellow, 1897-99; Ph.D., Clark University, 1899; Professor of Psychology and Pedagogy, State Normal School, West Chester, Pa., 1899-.

Author of:—

The Effects of Mind on Body as evidenced by Faith Cures. *Am. Jour. of Psy.*, April, 1899, Vol. 10, pp. 431-502.

JOHN H. GRAY, JR.:—

B.S., University of California, 1887; Assistant to State Analyst, California, 1887-90; Assistant in Chemistry, University of California, 1889-90; Instructor in Chemistry, *ibid.*, 1890-92; Fellow in Chemistry, Clark University, 1892-94; Instructor in Physics and Chemistry, State Normal School, Chico, Cal., 1894-95; Assistant in Chemistry, University of California, 1895-96; Instructor in Chemistry, *ibid.*, 1896-.

CEPHAS GUILLET:—

A.B., Victoria University, Cobourg, Ont. (Honors in English, French and German Literature), 1887; Modern Language Master, Perth, Ont., 1887-90; Modern Language Master, Ottawa, Ont., 1890-94; Student at Law, Osgoode Hall, Toronto, 1894-95; Scholar in Psychology, Clark University, 1895-96; Fellow, 1896-98.

R. R. GURLEY:—

United States Naval Academy, 1877-79; Assistant Resident Physician, Children's Hospital, Washington, D. C., 1882-84; M.D. (First Honor), National Medical College, Washington, D. C., 1884; Resident Physician, United States Soldiers' Home Hospital, Washington, D. C., 1884-85; Scientific Assistant, United States National Museum, Washington, D. C., 1886-90; Scientific Assistant, Biological Laboratory, United States Fish Commission, Washington, D. C., 1890-95; M. Sc., Columbian University, 1895; Fellow in Biology, Clark University, 1895-96; Junior Assistant Physician, Worcester Insane Hospital, 1896-97; Assistant Physician, *ibid.*, 1897-.

Author of: —

The Geologic Age of the Graptolite Shales of Arkansas. *Ann. Rep. Geol. Survey*, Arkansas, 1890, Vol. 3, pp. 401–416, Pl. 9.

Some Recent Graptolite Literature. *American Geologist*, 1891, pp. 35–43.

The Classification of the Myxosporidia, a Group of Protozoan Parasites infesting Fishes. *Bull. U. S. Fish Com.*, 1891, pp. 407–420.

The Myxosporidia, or Psorosperms of Fishes, and the Epidemics produced by them. *Rep. U. S. Fish Com.*, 1892, pp. 65–304, Pl. 1–47.

The North American Graptolites. *Journal of Geology*, 1896, Vol. 4, pp. 63–102; 291–311. Pl. 4–5.

G. STANLEY HALL: —

A.B., Williams College, 1867; A.M., 1870; Union Theological Seminary, N. Y., 1867–68; Universities Berlin and Bonn, 1869–70; Union Theological Seminary, N. Y., 1870–71; Universities of Berlin and Heidelberg, 1871–72; Professor of Philosophy, Antioch College, 1872–76; Instructor, Harvard University, 1876–78; Ph.D., Harvard University, 1878; Universities of Berlin and Leipzig, 1878–80; Lecturer in Harvard University and Williams College, 1880–81; Professor of Psychology, Johns Hopkins University, 1881–88; LL.D., University of Michigan, 1888, and Williams College, 1889; President, and Professor of Psychology, Clark University, 1888–; Editor and Founder of *American Journal of Psychology* (Founded in 1887), and *Pedagogical Seminary* (Founded in 1891); Resident Fellow of the American Academy of Arts and Sciences; Resident Member of the Massachusetts Historical Society; Member of American Antiquarian Society.

Author of: —

John Stuart Mill. *Williams Quarterly*, Williamstown, Mass., Aug., 1867.

Digest of Dorner's Theology. *Presbyterian Review*, Jan., 1873, pp. 60–68.

Hegel as the National Philosopher of Germany. (Translated from the German of Dr. Carl Rosenkranz.) Gray, Baker, & Co., St. Louis, 1874. 159 pp.

Hegel: His Followers and Critics. *Jour. of Spec. Philos.*, 1878, Vol. 12, pp. 93–103.

Color Perception. *Proc. Am. Acad. of Arts and Sciences*, March, 1878, Vol. 5, pp. 402–413.

The Muscular Perception of Space. *Mind*, Oct., 1878, Vol. 3, pp. 433–450.

The Philosophy of the Future. *Nation*, Nov. 7, 1878, Vol. 27, pp. 283–284.

Philosophy in the United States. *Mind*, Jan., 1879, Vol. 4, pp. 89–105; also *Pop. Sci. Mo.*, Suppl. No. 1, 1879, p. 57.

Ueber die Abhängigkeit der Reactionszeiten vom Ort des Reizes. (With J. v. Kries.) *Archiv f. Physiol.* (Du Bois-Reymond), Suppl. Band, 1879, pp. 1–10.

Die willkürliche Muskelaction. (With Hugo Kronecker.) *Ibid.*, pp. 11–47.

Laura Bridgman. *Mind*, April, 1879, Vol. 4, pp. 149–172.

Recent Researches in Hypnotism. *Ibid.*, Jan., 1881, Vol. 6, pp. 98–104.

Aspects of German Culture. James R. Osgood & Co., Boston, 1881. 320 pp.

Moral and Religious Training of Children. *Princeton Review*, Jan., 1882, Vol. 10, pp. 26–48.

Chairs of Pedagogy in our Higher Institutions of Learning. *N. E. A.*, March, 1882; *U. S. Bur. of Ed.*, Circular of Information, No. 2, 1882, pp. 35–44.

Optical Illusions of Motion. (With Dr. H. P. Bowditch.) *Jour. of Phys.*, Aug., 1882, Vol. 3, pp. 297–307.

The Education of the Will. *Princeton Review*, Nov., 1882, Vol. 10, pp. 306–325. Reprinted in *Pedagogical Seminary*, June, 1893, Vol. 2, pp. 72–89.

Methods of Teaching History. (Edited.) Ginn, Heath & Co., Boston, 1883. xii. + 296 pp.

Educational Needs. *N. A. Rev.*, March, 1883, Vol. 136, pp. 284–290.

Reaction-Time and Attention in the Hypnotic State. *Mind*, April, 1883, Vol. 8, pp. 170–182.

Contents of Children's Minds on entering School. *Princeton Review*, May, 1883, Vol. 11, pp. 249–272; *Pedagogical Seminary*, June, 1891, Vol. 1, pp. 139–173. Issued in pamphlet form by E. L. Kellogg & Co., New York, 1893, 56 pp.

Education and Theology. *Nation*, July 26, 1883, Vol. 37, pp. 81–82.

The Study of Children. (Privately printed.) N. Somerville, Mass., 1883, 13 pp.

Report of the Visiting Committee of the Alumni of Williams College, Williamstown, Mass., 1884. 11 pp.

Bilateral Asymmetry of Function. (With E. M. Hartwell.) *Mind*, Jan., 1884, Vol. 9, pp. 93–109.

New Departures in Education. *N. Am. Rev.*, Feb. 1885, Vol. 140, pp. 144–152.

The New Psychology. *Andover Review*, Feb. and March, 1885, Vol. 3, pp. 120–135, 239–248. Opening lecture, Johns Hopkins University, Oct., 1884.

Experimental Psychology. *Mind*, April, 1885, Vol. 10, pp. 245–249.

Children's Collections. *Nation*, Sept. 3, 1885, Vol. 41, p. 190; reprinted in *Pedagogical Seminary*, June, 1891, Vol. 1, pp. 234–237.

Overpressure in Schools. *Nation*, Oct. 22, 1885, Vol. 41, pp. 338–339.

Motor Sensations of the Skin. (With Dr. H. H. Donaldson.) *Mind*, Oct., 1885, Vol. 10, pp. 557–572.

Studies of Rhythm. (With Joseph Jastrow.) *Ibid.*, Jan., 1886, Vol. 11, pp. 55–62.

Hints toward a Select and Descriptive Bibliography of Education. (With John M. Mansfield.) D. C. Heath & Co., Boston, 1886. 309 pp.

Psychical Research. *Am. Jour. of Psy.*, Nov., 1887, Vol. 1, pp. 128–146.

Psychology. (Reviews.) *Am. Jour. of Psy.*, Nov., 1887, Vol. 1, pp. 146–164.

Dermal Sensitiveness to Gradual Pressure-Changes. (With Y. Motora.) *Ibid.*, Nov., 1887, Vol. 1, pp. 72–98.

The Story of a Sand Pile. *Scribner's Magazine*, June, 1888, Vol. 3, pp. 690–696. Reprint, E. L. Kellogg & Co., N. Y., 1897. 20 pp.

Introduction to American Edition of Preyer's Senses and Will. (Translated by H. W. Brown.) New York, 1888.

Address Delivered at the Opening of Clark University, Opening Exercises, pp. 9–32, Worcester, Mass., Oct. 2, 1889. (Published by the University.)

A Sketch of the History of Reflex Action. *Am. Jour. of Psy.*, Jan., 1890, Vol. 3, pp. 71–86.

How to teach Reading, and What to Read in School. D. C. Heath & Co., Boston, 1890. 40 pp. (First edition, 1886.)

Children's Lies. *Am. Jour. of Psy.*, Jan., 1890, Vol. 3, pp. 59–70. Reprinted in *Pedagogical Seminary*, June, 1891, Vol. 1, pp. 211–218.

The Training of Teachers. *Forum*, September, 1890, Vol. 10, pp. 11–22.

First Annual Report to the Board of Trustees of Clark University, Worcester, Mass., Oct. 4, 1890. 53 pp.

University Study of Philosophy. Discussion. *Regents' Rep.* Univ., State of New York, 1891, Vol. 104, pp. [illegible].

Boy Life in a Massachusetts Country Town Thirty Years Ago. *Proc. Am. Antiq. Soc.*, Worcester, Mass., 1891, N. S., Vol. 7, pp. 107–128.

Educational Reforms. *Pedagogical Seminary*, Jan., 1891, Vol. 1, pp. 1–12. Appeared also as Riforme Pedagogiche in *Il Risveglio Educativo*, Aprile 15–16, 1892, Anno 8, pp. 307–308, 310–311.

The Principles of Psychology. By William James. (Review.) *Am. Jour. of Psy.*, Feb., 1891, Vol. 3, pp. 578–591.

Contemporary Psychologists. I. Eduard Zeller. *Ibid.*, April, 1891, Vol. 4, pp. 156–175.

Enseignement des Sciences. *Revue Scientifique*, April 4, 1891, Vol. 47, pp. 430–432.

Notes on the Study of Infants. *Pedagogical Seminary*, June, 1891, Vol. 1, pp. 127–138.

The Moral and Religious Training of Children and Adolescents. *Ibid.*, pp. 196–210.

Second Annual Report to the Board of Trustees of Clark University, Worcester, Mass., Sept. 29, 1891. 56 pp.

The New Movement in Education. An address delivered before the School of Pedagogy of the University of the City of New York, Dec. 29, 1891. Published by the Women's Advisory Committee, New York, 1891. 20 pp.

The Outlook in Higher Education. *Academy*, Boston, Mass., Jan., 1892, Vol. 6, pp. 543–562.

Health of School Children as affected by School Buildings. *Report of Proc. Dept. of Superintendence*, held in Brooklyn, N. Y., Feb., 1892, pp. 163–172. Also *Proc. N. E. A.*, 1893, pp. 682–691.

Moral Education and Will Training. *Pedagogical Seminary*, June, 1892, Vol. 2, pp. 72–89.

Child-study as a Basis for Psychology and Psychological Teaching. *Report of Com. of Ed.*, 1892–93, Washington, D.C., 1895, Vol. 1, pp. 357–358, 366–370.

Third Annual Report to the Board of Trustees of Clark University, Worcester, Mass., April, 1893. 158 pp.

Psychological Progress. The Liberal Club, Buffalo, N. Y., Nov. 16, 1893.

Child-study: The Basis of Exact Education. *Forum*, Dec., 1893, Vol. 16, pp. 429–441.

American Universities and the Training of Teachers. *Ibid.*, April, 1894, Vol. 17, pp. 148–159.

Universities and the Training of Professors. *Ibid.*, May, 1894, Vol. 17, pp. 297–309.

Scholarships, Fellowships, and the Training of Professors. *Ibid.*, June, 1894, Vol. 17, pp. 443–454.

Research the Vital Spirit of Teaching. *Ibid.*, July, 1894, Vol. 17, pp. 558–570.

Child-study in Summer Schools. *Regents' Bulletin*, University of the State of New York, No. 28, July, 1894. Albany, N. Y., 1895, Vol. 1, pp. 333–336.

The New Psychology as a Basis of Education. *Forum*, August, 1894, Vol. 17, pp. 710–720.

Address at the Bryant Centennial, Aug. 16, 1894. *Bryant Memorial*, Cummington, Mass., 1894, pp. 67–69.

Address. Dedication of the Haston Free Public Library Building, North Brookfield, Mass., September 20, 1894. pp. 11–31.

On the History of American College Text-Books and Teaching in Logic, Ethics, Psychology, and Allied Subjects. *Proc. Am. Antiq. Soc.*, Worcester, Mass., 1894, N. S., Vol. 9, pp. 137–174.

Remarks on Rhythm in Education. *Proc. N. E. A.*, 1894, pp. 84–85.

Child-study. *Ibid.*, 1894, pp. 173–179.

Practical Child-study. *Jour. of Ed.*, Dec. 13, 1894, Vol. 40, pp. 391–393.

Topical Syllabi for 1894–1895. These were one- or two-page leaflets, prepared by Dr. Hall, and privately printed at Worcester, Mass. They covered: I. Anger; II. Dolls; III. Crying and Laughing; IV. Toys and Playthings; V. Folk-Lore Among Children; VI. Early Forms of Vocal Expression; VII. The Early Sense of Self; VIII. Fears in Childhood and Youth; IX. Some Common Traits and Habits; X. Some Common Automatisms, Nerve Signs, etc.; XI. Feeling for Objects of Inanimate Nature; XII. Feeling for Objects of Animate Nature; XIII. Children's Appetites and Foods; XIV. Affection and its Opposite States in Children; XV. Moral and Religious Experiences.

Laboratory of the McLean Hospital, Somerville, Mass. *Am. Jour. of Insanity*, Jan., 1895, Vol. 51, pp. 358–364.

Psychic Research. *Am. Jour. of Psy.*, Oct., 1895, Vol. 7, pp. 135–142.

Results of Child-study applied to Education. *Trans. Ill. Soc. for Child-study*, 1895, Vol. 1, No. 4, p. 13.

Introduction to the Psychology of Childhood. By Frederick Tracy. Boston, 1895.

Address at Union College Centennial Anniversary, June 24, 1895. Printed by the College. N. Y., 1897, pp. 230–244.

Topical Syllabi for 1895–96. I. Peculiar and Exceptional Children, with E. W. Bohannon; II. Moral Defects and Perversions, with G. E. Dawson; III. The Beginnings of Reading and Writing, with Dr. H. T. Lukens; IV. Thoughts and Feelings about Old Age, Disease, and Death, with C. A. Scott; V. Moral Education, with N. P. Avery; VI. Studies of School Reading Matter, with J. C. Shaw; VII. Courses of Study in Elementary Grammar and High Schools, with T. R. Croswell; VIII. Early Musical Manifestations, with Florence Marsh; IX. Fancy, Imagination, Reverie, with E. H. Lindley; X. Tickling, Fun, Wit, Humor, Laughing, with Dr. Arthur Allin; XI. Suggestion and Imitation, with M. H. Small; XII. Religious Experience, with E. D. Starbuck; XIII. Kindergarten, with Miss Anna E. Bryan and Miss Lucy Wheelock; XIV. Habits, Instincts, etc., in Animals, with Dr. R. R. Gurley; XV. Number and Mathematics, with D. E. Phillips; XVI. The Only Child in the Family, with E. W. Bohannon.

The Case of the Public Schools. *Atlantic Monthly*, March, 1896, Vol. 77, pp. 402–413.

Psychological Education. *Proc. of the Am. Medico-Psychological Ass'n.* 52d Annual Meeting, Boston, May 26–29, 1896, Transactions, Vol. 3, pp. 87–100; also, *Am. Jour. of Insanity*, Oct. 1896, Vol. 53, pp. 228–241.

Generalizations and Directions for Child-study. *Northwestern Jour. of Ed.*, July, 1896, Vol. 7, p. 8.

Address at Mount Holyoke College, Founder's Day, Nov. 5, 1896. *Mount Holyoke*, S. Hadley, Mass. Nov., 1896, Vol. 6, pp. 64–71.

A Study of Dolls. (With A. C. Ellis.) *Pedagogical Seminary*, Dec., 1896, Vol. 4, pp. 129–175. Reprint, E. L. Kellogg & Co., N. Y., 1897, 69 pp.

Nature Study. *Proc. N. E. A.*, 1896, pp. 156–158.

The Methods, Status, and Prospects of the Child-study of To-day. *Trans. Ill. Soc. for Child-study*, May, 1896, Vol. 2, pp. 178–191.

Topical Syllabi for 1896–97. I. Degrees of Certainty and Conviction in Children, with Maurice H. Small; II. Sabbath and Worship in General, with J. P. Hylan; III. Migrations, Tramps, Truancy, Running Away, etc., vs. Love of Home, with L. W. Kline; IV. Adolescence, and its Phenomena in Body and Mind, with E. C. Lancaster; V. Examinations and Recitations, with John C. Shaw; VI. Stillness, Solitude, Restlessness, with H. S. Curtis; VII. The Psychology of Health and Disease, with Henry H. Goddard; VIII. Spontaneously Invented Toys and Amusements, with T. R. Croswell; IX. Hymns and Sacred Music, with Rev. T. R. Peede; X. Puzzles and their Psychology, with Ernest H. Lindley; XI. The Sermon, with Rev. Alva R. Scott; XII. Special Traits as Indices of Character and as Mediating Likes and Dislikes, with E. W. Bohannon; XIII. Reverie and Allied Phenomena, with G. E. Partridge; XIV. The Psychology of Health and Disease, with H. H. Goddard.

A Study of Fears. *Am. Jour. of Psy.*, Jan., 1897, Vol. 8, pp. 147–249.

Some Practical Results of Child-study. First National Congress of Mothers, Washington, D. C., 1897. D. Appleton and Co., New York, 1897, pp. 165–171.

The Psychology of Tickling, Laughing, and the Comic. (With Arthur Allin.) *Am. Jour. of Psy.*, Oct., 1897, Vol. 9, pp. 1–41.

Topical Syllabi for 1897–98. I. Immortality, with J. Richard Street; II. Psychology of Ownership vs. Loss, with Linus W. Kline; III. Memory, with F. W. Colegrove; IV. Humorous and Cranky Side in Education, with L. W. Kline; V. The Psychology of Shorthand Writing, with J. O. Quantz; VI. The Teaching Instinct, with D. E. Phillips; VII. Home and School Punlishments and Penalties, with Chas. H. Sears; VIII. Straightness and Uprightness of Body; IX. Conventionality, with Albert Schinz; X. Local Voluntary Association among Teachers, with Henry D. Sheldon; XI. Motor Education, with E. W. Bohannon; XII. Heat and Cold; XIII. Training of Teachers, with W. G. Chambers; XIV. Educational Ideals, with Lewis Edwin York; XV. Water Psychoses, with Frederick E. Bolton; XVI. The Institutional Activities of Children, with Henry D. Sheldon; XVII. Obedience and Obstinacy, with Tilmon Jenkins; XVIII. The Sense of Honor Among Children, with Robert Clark.

Some Aspects of the Early Sense of Self. *Am. Jour. of Psy.*, April, 1898, Vol. 9, pp. 351–395.

Initiations into Adolescence. *Proc. of Am. Antiq. Soc.*, Worcester, Mass., Oct. 21, 1898, N. S. Vol. 12, p. 367–400.

The Love and Study of Nature: A Part of Education. *Agriculture of Massachusetts*, for 1898, pp. 134–154.

Topical Syllabi for 1898–99. I. The Organizations of American Student Life, with Henry D. Sheldon; II. Mathematics in Common Schools, with E. B. Bryan; III. Mathematics in the Early Years, with E. B. Bryan; IV. Unselfishness in Children, with Willard S. Small; V. The Fooling Impulse in Man and Animals, with Norman Triplett; VI. Confession, with Erwin W. Runkle; VII. Pity; VIII. Perception of Rhythm by Children, with Chas. H. Sears.

Résumé of Child-study. *Northwestern Monthly*, March–April, 1899, Vol. 9, pp. 347–349. *Paidologist*, Cheltenham, Eng., April, 1899, Vol. 1, pp. 5–8.

The Kindergarten. *School and Home Education*, Bloomington, Ill., June, 1899, Vol. 18, pp. 507–509.

A Study of Anger. *Am. Jour. of Psy.*, July, 1899, Vol. 10, pp. 516–591.

The Line of Educational Advance. *Outlook*, Aug. 5, 1899, Vol. 62, pp. 768–770.

T. PROCTOR HALL: —

B.A., University of Toronto, 1882; Fellow and Instructor in Chemistry, *ibid.*, 1882–84; B.A., McMaster University, Toronto, 1884; M.A., and Ph.D., Illinois Wesleyan University, 1885; Science Master, Woodstock College, Woodstock, Ont., 1885–90; Fellow in Physics, Clark University, 1890–93; Ph.D., Clark University, 1893; Professor of Natural Sciences, Tabor College, Iowa, 1893–96; Professor of Physics, Kansas City University, 1896–; President Society of Economics, Kansas City; Vice-President Ex-Canadian Society, Kansas City.

Author of: —

The Projection of Four-fold Figures upon a Three-flat. *Am. Jour. of Math.*, April, 1893, Vol. 15, pp. 179–189.

The Possibility of a Realization of Four-fold Space. *Science*, May 13, 1892.

New Methods of Measuring the Surface Tension of Liquids. *Philosophical Magazine*, Nov., 1893, Vol. 36, pp. 385–413.

Graphic Representation of the Properties of the Elements. *Proc. Iowa Acad. of Sci.*, 1894.

A Mad-Stone. *Ibid.*, 1896.

Physical Theories of Gravitation. *Ibid.*, 1896.

Unit Systems and Dimensions. *Electrical World*, Feb. 7, 1896.

A Physical Theory of Electricity and Magnetism. *Ibid.*, July 3, 1897, Vol. 30, pp. 10–12.

The Vortex Theory of Electricity and Magnetism. *Home Study for Electrical Workers*, Sept., 1898, pp. 34–39.

Complex Algebra of the Plane Extended to Three-fold Space. *Proc. Iowa Acad. of Sci.*, 1898, Vol. 6.

JOHN A. HANCOCK: —

B.S., Baker University, 1877; Principal of Schools, Indiana and Wisconsin, 1877–89; Graduate Student in Pedagogy, University of Wisconsin, 1889–90; M.L., *ibid.*, 1890; City Superintendent, Green Bay, Wis., 1890–92; Graduate Student in Pedagogy, Leland Stanford Jr. University, 1892–93; M.A., *ibid.*, 1893; Fellow in Pedagogy, Clark University, 1893–94; Superintendent of Schools, Durango, Col., 1894–97; Temporary Assistant Professor of Psychology, University of Colorado, 1897–98; Superintendent of Schools, Santa Barbara, Cal., 1898–.

Author of: —

Secularization of Education. *Wis. Jour. of Ed.*, March, 1890.

Preliminary Study of Motor Ability. *Pedagogical Seminary*, Oct., 1894, Vol. 3, pp. 9–29.

The Kindergarten and Child Study. *Col. School Jour.*, Feb., 1896.

The Relation of Strength to Flexibility in the Hands of Men and Children. *Pedagogical Seminary*, Oct., 1896, Vol. 4, pp. 306–318.

Children's Ability to Reason. *Educational Review*, Oct., 1896, Vol. 12, pp. 251–265.

An Early Phase of the Manual Training Movement — the Manual Labor School. *Pedagogical Seminary*, Oct., 1897, Vol. 5, pp. 237–252.

Mental Differences of School Children. *Proc. N. E. A.*, 1897, pp. 851–857.

Children's Tendencies in the Use of Written Language Forms. *Northwestern Monthly*, June, 1898, Vol. 8, pp. 646–649.

ROLLIN A. HARRIS: —

Ph.B., Cornell University, 1885; Fellow in Mathematics, *ibid.*, 1885–87; Ph.D., *ibid.*, 1888; Fellow in Mathematics, Clark University, 1889–90; Computer, United States Coast and Geodetic Survey, Washington, D.C., 1890–.

Author of: —

The Theory of Images in the Representation of Functions. *Annals of Math.*, 1888, Vol. 4, pp. 65–86, 138.

On the Expansion of sn u. *Ibid.*, Vol. 4, pp. 87–90.

Design for a Cosinograph. *Scien. Am. Supp.*, 1890, No. 740.

On the Invariant Criteria for the Reality of the Roots of the Quintic. *Annals of Math.*, 1891, Vol. 5, pp. 217–228.

On Certain Bicircular Quartics Analogous to Cassini's Oval. *Mathematical Magazine*, Vol. 2, pp. 77–79.

Note on Isogonal Transformations; Particularly on obtaining Certain Systems of Curves which Occur in the Statics of Polynomials. *Annals of Math.*, 1891, Vol. 6, pp. 77–80.

Note on the Use of Supplementary Curves in Isogonal Transformation. *Am. Jour. of Math.*, 1892, Vol. 14, pp. 291–300.

Some Connections between Harmonic and Non-harmonic Quantities, Including Applications to the Reduction and Prediction of Tides. *U. S. Coast and Geod. Sur. Report*, 1894, Appendix, No. 7 (Manual of Tides, Part III.).

Introduction and Historical Treatment of the Subject, *Ibid.*, 1897, Appendix, No. 8 (Manual of Tides, Part I.).

Tidal Observations, Equilibrium Theory, and the Harmonic Analysis, *Ibid.*, 1897, Appendix, No. 9 (Manual of Tides, Part II.).

A Proposed Tidal Analyzer. *Physical Review*, 1899, Vol. 8, pp. 54–60.

JAMES N. HART: —

B.C.E., Maine State College, 1885; Principal of High School, Dennysville, Me., 1885; Instructor in Mathematics and Drawing, Maine State College, 1887–90; C.E., *ibid.*, 1890; Scholar in Mathematics, Clark University, 1890–91; Professor of Mathematics and Astronomy, University of Maine, 1891–; Graduate Student in Mathematics and Astronomy, University of Chicago, 1894–96; M.S., *ibid.*, 1897; Member of American Mathematical Society.

S. B. HASLETT: —

Graduate, Edinboro, Pa., State Normal School, 1885; Principal, Creighton Public Schools, 1887–89; A.B., Grove City

College, Pa., 1889; Principal, Braddock High School, 1891-93; Graduate, Allegheny Theological Seminary, 1893; Presbyterian Ministry, 1893-; A.M., Grove City College, 1895; **Scholar in Psychology, Clark University, 1898-99.**

W. B. HELLER:—

B.S., University of Pennsylvania, 1884; Professor of Mathematics, Boys' High School, Reading, Pa., 1887-91; **Scholar in Mathematics, Clark University, 1891-92**; Fellow in Mathematics, University of Chicago, 1893-93; Assistant Professor in Mathematics, Drexel Institute, Philadelphia, 1893-.

CLARK WILSON HETHERINGTON:

A.B., Leland Stanford Jr. University, 1895; Instructor, Encina Gymnasium, Stanford University, 1893-96; Statistician and Director of Physical Training, Whittier State Reform School, 1896-98; **Fellow in Psychology, Clark University, 1898-99.**

JOHN E. HILL:—

Ph.B., Sheffield Scientific School (Yale), 1885; Resident Engineer, C. M. and St. Paul R.R., 1885-86; Professor of Mathematics, Military Academy, Louisville, Ky., 1888-89; Superintendent of Schools, Pleasantville, N. Y., 1889-90; Professor of Mathematics and Civil Engineering, Highland Park College, 1890-92; **Fellow in Mathematics, Clark University, 1892-95; Ph.D., Clark University, 1895**; Tutor in Mathematics, Columbia University, 1895-97; Teacher of Mathematics, Manual Training High School, Brooklyn, N. Y., 1897-98; Teacher of Science, High School, Stamford, Ct., 1898-99.

Author of:—

On Quintic Surfaces. *Mathematical Review*, July, 1896, Vol. 1, pp. 1-69.

Bibliography of Surfaces and Twisted Curves. *Bull. Am. Math. Soc.*, Jan., 1897, Vol. 3, pp. 133-146.

On Three Septic Surfaces. *Am. Jour. of Math.*, Oct., 1897, Vol. 19, pp. 289-311.

BENJAMIN C. HINDE:—

A.B., Central College, Missouri, 1881; A.M., *ibid.*, 1883; Instructor in Physical Sciences, Howard College, 1883-85; Graduate Student, Johns Hopkins University, 1886-90; Professor of Physics and Chemistry, State Normal College, Mo., 1890-91; Professor of Physics, Trinity College, N. C., 1891-92; **Fellow and Assistant in Physics, Clark University, 1892-93**; Professor of Physics, Trinity College, N. C., 1893-94.

Died Feb. 6, 1894.

CLIFTON F. HODGE:—

A.B., Ripon College, 1882; Civil Engineer, Montana, 1882-86; Graduate Student, Johns Hopkins University, 1886-88; Fellow in Biology, *ibid.*, 1888-89; Ph.D., Johns Hopkins University, 1889; **Fellow in Psychology and Assistant in Neurology, Clark University, 1889-91**; Instructor in Biology, University of Wisconsin, 1891-92; **Assistant Professor of Physiology and Neurology, Clark University, 1892-**; Member of: American Physiological Society, Society American Naturalists, Massachusetts Forestry Association, Boston Society of Medical Sciences.

Author of:—

Some Effects of Stimulating Ganglion Cells. *Am. Jour. of Psy.*, May, 1888, Vol. 1, pp. 479-486.

Some Effects of Electrically Stimulating Ganglion Cells. *Ibid.*, May, 1889, Vol. 2, pp. 376-402.

A Study of the Oyster Beds of Long Island Sound with Reference to the Ravages of Starfish. *J. H. U. Circular*, Sept., 1889, No. 75, Vol. 8, p. 102.

A Sketch of the History of Reflex Action. *Am. Jour. of Psy.*, April and Sept., 1890, Vol. 3, pp. 149-167, 343-363.

The Process of Recovery from the Fatigue occasioned by the Electrical Stimulation of Cells of the Spinal Ganglia. *Ibid.*, Feb., 1891, Vol. 3, pp. 530-543.

Homing Pigeons. *Ægis*, June, 1892.

A Microscopical Study of Changes due to Functional Activity in Nerve Cells. *Jour. of Morph.*, Nov., 1892, Vol. 7, pp. 95–168.

The Method of Homing Pigeons. *Pop. Sci. Mo.*, April, 1894, Vol. 44, pp. 758–775.

Changes in Ganglion Cells from Birth to Senile Death. Observations on Man and Honeybee. *Jour. of Phys.*, 1894, Vol. 17, pp. 129–134.

Botanical Gardens. *Wor. Co. Hort. Soc. Rep.*, 1894–95, pp. 103–117.

Die Nervenzelle bei der Geburt und beim Tode an Altersschwäche. *Anat. Anzeiger*, Aug. 1, 1894, Vol. 9, pp. 706–710.

A Microscopical Study of the Nerve Cell during Electrical Stimulation. *Jour. of Morph.*, Sept., 1894, Vol. 9, pp. 449–463.

The Daily Life of a Protozoan: A Study in Comparative Psycho-Physiology. (With H. A. Aikins.) *Am. Jour. of Psy.*, Jan., 1895, Vol. 6, pp. 524–533.

The Vivisection Question. *Pop. Sci. Mo.*, Sept. and Oct., 1896, Vol. 49, pp. 614–624, 771–785.

Experiments on the Physiology of Alcohol, made under the Auspices of the Committee of Fifty. *Ibid.*, March and April, 1897, Vol. 50, pp. 594–603, 796–812.

Horticultural Interests in Relation to Public Education. *Wor. Co. Hort. Soc. Rep.*, 1898, pp. 62–81.

The Common Toad. Nature Study Leaflet. *Biology Series*, No. 1, 1898. Worcester, Mass. 16 pp.

Our Common Birds. *Biology Series*, No. 2, 1899. Worcester, Mass. 24 pp.

FREDERICK H. HODGE:—

A.B., Boston University, 1894; A.M., *Ibid.*, 1899; Special Student, Bridgewater Normal School, 1894–95; Professor of Mathematics, J. B. Stetson University, 1895–96; Graduate Student in Mathematics, University of Chicago, 1896–97; Scholar in Mathematics, Clark University, 1897–98; Fellow, 1898–99; Professor of Mathematics and History, Bethel College, Russellville, Ky., 1899–.

THOMAS FRANKLIN HOLGATE:—

B.A., Victoria University, Toronto, 1884; Mathematical Master, Albert College, Belleville, Ont., 1884–90; M.A., Victoria University, 1890; Fellow in Mathematics, Clark University, 1890–93; Ph.D., Clark University, 1893; Instructor in Mathematics, Northwestern University, 1893–94; Professor of Applied Mathematics, *Ibid.*, 1894–; Member of the American Mathematical Society.

Author of:—

On the Cone of the Second Order which is Analogous to the Nine Point Conic. *Annals of Math.*, 1893, Vol. 7, pp. 73–76.

On Certain Ruled Surfaces of the Fourth Order. *Am. Jour. of Math.*, Oct., 1893, Vol. 15, pp. 344–386. Additional Note on same. *Ibid.* (In press.)

Correction of an Error in Salmon's "Geometry of Three Dimensions." *Bull. N. Y. Math. Soc.*, 1894, Vol. 3, p. 224.

A Geometrical Locus connected with a System of Coaxial Circles. *Bull. Am. Math. Soc.*, Nov., 1897, 2d ser., Vol. 4, pp. 63–67.

A Second Locus connected with a System of Coaxial Circles. *Ibid.*, Dec., 1898, Vol. 5, pp. 135–143.

Reye's "Lectures on the Geometry of Position" (translation), Part I. Macmillan Company, New York, 1898. 248 pp.

RICHARD J. HOLLAND:—

B.A., Victoria College, Toronto, 1887; Certificate Specialist in Science, Teachers' Training Institute, Kingston, Ont., 1887–88; Science Master, Morrisburg Collegiate Institute, 1888–90; Graduate Student, University of Leipzig, 1890–92; Ph.D., University of Leipzig, 1893; Honorary Fellow in Physics, Clark University, 1893–94; with Westinghouse Electric Company, Pittsburg, Pa., 1894–96; with

Electric Power Storage Company, N. Y. City, April, 1898–.

Author of:—

Ueber die Aenderung der electrischen Leitfähigkeit einer Lösung durch Zusatz von kleinen Mengen eines Nichtleiters. *Wied. Annalen*, Sept., 1893, Vol. 50, pp. 361–372.

Ueber die electrische Leitfähigkeit von Kupferchloridlösungen. *Ibid.*, pp. 549–550.

E. C. HOLLENBAUGH:—

A.B., Bucknell University, 1885; Principal, Cross Creek Academy, 1888–89; A.M., Bucknell University, 1891; Ph.D., Wooster University, 1891; Graduate Student, Johns Hopkins University, 1891–92; **Scholar in Psychology, Clark University, 1892.**

Died July 6, 1893.

WILLIAM A. HOYT:—

A.B., Bates College, 1880; Principal High School, Rockport, Me., 1881–82; Principal Greeley Institute, Cumberland, Me., 1882–83; Cornwall Heights School, Cornwall, N. Y., 1883–86; A.M., Bates College, 1884; Principal High School: Medway, Mass., 1886–88, North Brookfield, Mass., 1888–92, Augusta, Me., 1892–93; **Scholar in Pedagogy, Clark University, 1893–94**; Superintendent of Schools, Brookfield, Mass. (District), 1894–.

Author of:—

The Love of Nature as the Root of Teaching and Learning the Sciences. *Pedagogical Seminary*, Oct., 1894, Vol. 3, pp. 61–86.

EDMUND B. HUEY:—

A.B., Lafayette College (First Honors in Philosophy and Anglo-Saxon), 1895; Instructor in Latin, Harry Hillman Academy, Wilkesbarre, Pa., 1896–97; **Scholar in Psychology, Clark University, 1897–98; Fellow, 1898–99**; Professor of Psychology, State Normal School, Moorhead, Minn., 1899–.

Author of:—

Preliminary Experiments in the Physiology and Psychology of Reading. *Am. Jour. of Psy.*, July, 1898, Vol. 9, pp. 575–586.

D. D. HUGH:—

A.B., Dalhousie College, 1891; A.B., Harvard University, 1893; A.M., Cornell University, 1893; **Fellow in Psychology, Clark University, 1895–96**; Principal of High School, La Junta, Col., 1896–98; Professor of Psychology, Colorado State Normal School, Greeley, Col., 1898–99; Professor of Pedagogy and English, State Agricultural College, Logan, Utah, 1899–.

Author of:—

Formal Education from the Standpoint of Physiological Psychology. *Pedagogical Seminary*, April, 1898, Vol. 5, pp. 599–605.

The Animism of Children. *Northwestern Monthly*, June, 1899, Vol. 9, pp. 450–453.

LORRAIN S. HULBURT:—

A.B., University of Wisconsin, 1883; A.M., *ibid.*, 1886; Professor of Mathematics, University of So. Dakota, 1887–91; Graduate Student, University of Göttingen, 1889–90; **Fellow in Mathematics, Clark University, 1891–92**; Instructor in Mathematics, Johns Hopkins University, 1892–94; Ph.D., Johns Hopkins University, 1894; Associate in Mathematics, *ibid.*, 1894–97; Collegiate Professor of Mathematics, *ibid.*, 1897–; Member of American Mathematical Society.

Author of:—

Theorems on the Number and Arrangement of the Real Branches of Plane Algebraic Curves. *Am. Jour. of Math.*, July, 1892, Vol. 14, pp. 246–250.

Topology of Algebraic Curves. *Bull. of the N. Y. Math. Soc.*, 1892, Vol. 1, pp. 197–202.

JOHN I. HUTCHINSON:—

A.B., Bates College, 1889; **Scholar in Mathematics, Clark University, 1890–**

91; Fellow, 1891-92; Fellow in Mathematics, University of Chicago, 1892-94; Instructor in Mathematics, Cornell University, 1894-; Ph.D., University of Chicago, 1895; Member of American Mathematical Society.

Author of:—

A Special Form of a Quartic Surface, *Annals of Math.*, June, 1897, Vol. 3, pp. 158-160.

On the Reduction of Hyperelliptic Functions, ($p = 2$) to Elliptic Functions by a Transformation of the Second Degree. (Dissertation.) Göttingen, 1897. 40 pp.

Note on the Tetrahedroid. *Bull. of the Am. Math. Soc.*, April, 1898, 2d ser., Vol. 4, pp. 327-329.

The Hessian of the Cubic Surface. *Ibid.*, March, 1899, 2d ser., Vol. 5, pp. 283-292.

The Asymptotic Lines of the Kummer Surface. *Ibid.*, July, 1899, 2d ser., Vol. 5, pp. 466-467.

JOHN P. HYLAN:—

Student, Harvard University, 1891-95; Fellow in Psychology, Clark University, 1895-97; Instructor in Psychology, University of Illinois, 1897-98; Assistant Professor, *ibid.*, 1898-99; Member of Executive Commission of Illinois Society of Child Study.

Author of:—

Fluctuation of Attention. (Studies from the Harvard Psy. Lab.) *Psychological Review*, Jan., 1896, Vol. 3, pp. 56-63.

The Fluctuation of Attention. *Psychological Review*, Monograph Supplement, March, 1898, Vol. 2, No. 2. 78 pp.

MASSUO IKUTA:—

Student, University of Tokio, Japan, 1880-86; University of Berlin, 1886; University of Erlangen, 1887-88; Ph.D., University of Erlangen, 1888; Consulting Chemist, Tokio, Japan, 1889-90; Assistant in Chemistry, Clark University, 1890-92; Assistant in Chemistry, University of Chicago, 1892-96; Instructor, *ibid.*, 1896-.

Author of:—

Ueber die Einwirkung von Acetessigäther auf Chinone; Synthese von Benzofurfuran-Derivaten. *Jour. für praktische Chemie*, 1892, Vol. 45, pp. 65-82.

Metamidophenol and its Derivatives, *Am. Chem. Jour.*, Jan., 1893, Vol. 15, pp. 39-44.

JAMES EDMUND IVES:—

Jessup Student, Academy of Natural Sciences, 1887-91; Assistant Curator, *ibid.*, 1887-93; Instructor in Physics, Drexel Institute, 1893-97; Student in Histology and Embryology, University of Pennsylvania, 1888-89; Student in Mathematics, *ibid.*, 1893-95; Student in Physics, Cavendish Laboratory, Cambridge, Eng., 1896; Scholar in Physics, Clark University, 1897-98; Fellow, 1898-99.

Author of:—

On Two New Species of Starfishes. *Proc. Acad. Nat. Sci. of Phila.*, 1888, pp. 421-424.

Linguatula Diesingii, from the Sooty Mangabey. *Ibid.*, 1889, p. 31.

Variation in Ophiura Panamensis and Ophiura teres. *Ibid.*, 1889, pp. 76-77.

On a New Genus and Two New Species of Ophiurans. *Ibid.*, 1889, pp. 143-145.

Catalogue of the Asteroidea and Ophiuroidea in the Collection of the Academy of Natural Sciences of Philadelphia. *Ibid.*, 1889, pp. 169-179.

Mimicry of the Environment in Pterophryne histrio. *Ibid.*, 1889, pp. 344-345.

On Arenicola cristata and its Allies. *Ibid.*, 1890, pp. 73-75.

Echinoderms from the Northern Coast of Yucatan and the Harbor of Vera Cruz. *Ibid.*, 1890, pp. 317-340.

Crustacea from the Northern Coast of Yucatan, the Harbor of Vera Cruz, the West Coast of Florida and the Bermuda Islands. *Ibid.*, 1891, pp. 176-207.

Echinoderms and Arthropods from Japan. *Ibid.*, 1891, pp. 210-223.

Echinoderms from the Bahama Islands. *Ibid.*, 1891, pp. 337–341.

Reptiles and Batrachians from Northern Yucatan and Mexico. *Ibid.*, 1891, pp. 458–463.

Echinoderms and Crustaceans collected by the West Greenland Expedition of 1891. *Ibid.*, 1891, pp. 479–481.

A New Species of Pycnogonum from California. *Ibid.*, 1892, pp. 143–144.

TILMON JENKINS:—

B.A., National Normal University, 1882; Professor of Didactics, Salina, Kan., Normal University, 1883–85; Superintendent of Schools, Kingman, Kan., 1885–87; M.A., National Normal University, 1891; Educational work in Colorado, 1887–96; Assistant State Superintendent of Public Instruction, Colorado, 1894; Superintendent of Schools, Santa Fé, New Mexico, 1896–97; Scholar in Pedagogy, Clark University, 1897–98; Special Student, University of Colorado, 1898–99.

GEORGE ELLSWORTH JOHNSON:—

A.B., Dartmouth College, 1887; A.M., *ibid.* 1891; Principal, Colebrook Academy, N. H., 1887–88; Principal of Schools, Springfield, Vt., 1888–92; Student, Hartford Theological Seminary, 1892–93; Scholar in Pedagogy, Clark University, 1893–94; Fellow, 1894–95; Superintendent of Schools, Andover, Mass., 1895–.

Author of:—

Education by Plays and Games. *Pedagogical Seminary*, Oct., 1894, Vol. 3, pp. 97–133.

Contribution to the Psychology and Pedagogy of Feeble-minded Children. *Ibid.*, Oct., 1895, Vol. 3, pp. 246–301.

Play in Education. *Northwestern Monthly*, July, 1897, Vol. 8, pp. 3–8.

Games and Play. First of Series of Twelve Monographs on Social Work. Issued by Lincoln House, Boston, Mass., and The Commons, Chicago, Ill. The Co-operative Press, Cambridge, 1898. 29 pp.

Play in Physical Education. *Am. Phys. Ed. Rev.*, Sept., 1898, Vol. 3, pp. 179–187.

The New Education. Address delivered before the Andover Burns Club, March 19, 1898. The Andover Press, Andover, Mass., 1898. 15 pp.

HERBERT P. JOHNSON:—

A.B., Harvard University (with Honors in Natural History), 1889; A.M., *ibid.*, 1890; Assistant in Biology, Williams College, 1890–91; Fellow in Morphology, Clark University, 1891–92; Fellow in Morphology, University of Chicago, 1892–94; Ph.D., University of Chicago, 1894; Instructor in Biology, Des Moines College, 1894; Assistant Professor of Zoology, University of California, 1894–; Member of: American Society of Naturalists; California Academy of Sciences; San Francisco Microscopical Society.

Author of:—

Amitosis in the Embryonal Envelopes of the Scorpion. *Bull. Museum Comparative Zoöl.*, Harvard College, 1892, Vol. 22, pp. 127–161; 3 pls.

A Contribution to the Morphology and Biology of the Stentors. *Jour. of Morph.*, Aug., 1893, Vol. 8, pp. 467–562; 4 pls.

The Plastogamy of Actinosphaerium. *Ibid.* April, 1894, Vol. 9, pp. 269–276.

A Preliminary Account of the Marine Annelids of the Pacific Coast, with Descriptions of New Species. Proc. California Academy of Sciences, Third Series. Zoölogy, 1897, Vol. 1, pp. 153–198; 6 pls.

EDWIN O. JORDAN:—

S.B., Massachusetts Institute of Technology, 1888; Chief Assistant Biologist, Massachusetts State Board of Health, 1888–90; Lecturer in Biology, Massachusetts Institute of Technology, 1889–90; Fellow in Morphology, Clark University, 1890–92; Ph.D., Clark University, 1892; Associate in Biology, University of Chicago, 1892–93; Instructor in Biology, *ibid.*, 1893–95; Assistant Professor of Bacteriology, *ibid.*, 1895–.

Author of: —

Phagocytosis and Immunity. *Boston Med. and Surg. Jour.*, 1890, Vol. 122, p. 463.

Recent Theories on the Function of the White Blood-Cell. *Technology Quarterly*, 1890, Vol. 3, p. 170.

Certain Species of Bacteria observed in Sewage. *Report of the Mass. State Board of Health on Water Supply and Sewerage*, 1888–90, Vol. 2, p. 821.

Investigations on Nitrification and the Nitrifying Organism. (With Mrs. Ellen H. Richards.) *Ibid.*, Vol. 2. Volume on Water Supply and Sewerage, 1890, p. 865.

The Spermatophores of Diemyctylus. *Jour. of Morph.*, Sept., 1891, Vol. 5, pp. 263–270.

The Cleavage of the Amphibian Ovum. (With A. C. Eycleshymer.) *Anat. Anzeiger*, Sept. 16, 1892, Vol. 7, pp. 622–624.

The Habits and Development of the Newt. *Jour. of Morph.*, May, 1893, Vol. 8, pp. 270–366, 5 Plates.

On the Cleavage of Amphibian Ova. (With A. C. Eycleshymer.) *Ibid.*, Sept., 1894, Vol. 9, pp. 407–416, 1 Plate.

The Identification of the Typhoid Fever Bacillus. *Jour. Am. Med. Ass'n*, Dec. 22, 1894.

On Some Conditions affecting the Behavior of the Typhoid Bacillus in Water. *Medical News*, Sept. 28, 1895.

The "Inheritance" of Certain Bacterial Diseases. *Chicago Med. Recorder*, Aug., 1895, Vol. 16, p. 82.

The Production of Fluorescent Pigment by Bacteria. *Botanical Gazette*, Jan., 1899, Vol. 27, p. 19.

Translation of the Principles of Bacteriology by Professor F. Hueppe. Open Court Publishing Co., Chicago. 467 pp.

The Death-rate from Diphtheria in the Large Cities of the United States. *Philadelphia Med. Jour.*, Feb. 18, 1899.

F. C. KENYON: —

B.Sc., University of Nebraska, 1890; Instructor in Zoölogy, *ibid.*, 1891–93; Assistant and Fellow in Biology, Tufts College, 1893–95; A.M. and Ph.D., Tufts College, 1895; Fellow in Biology, Clark University, 1895–96; Fellow, American Association for the Advancement of Science; Member of: American Morphological Society, American Society of Naturalists, National Geographic Society.

Author of: —

The Morphology and Classification of the Pauropoda. *Tufts College Studies*, 1895.

In the Region of the New Fossil; Dæmonelix. *American Naturalist*, 1895.

Formal as a Preserving Agent. *Ibid.*, 1895.

The Meaning and Structure of the So-called Mushroom Bodies of the Hexapod Brain. *Ibid.*, 1896.

The Brain of the Bee. *Jour. Comp. Neurology*, 1896.

The Optic Lobes of the Bee's Brain in the Light of Recent Neurological Methods. 1897.

Delarvation. *American Naturalist*, 1897.

The Chætognaths of American Waters. *Ibid.*

The Regeneration of an Antenna-like Structure instead of an Eye. *Ibid.*

The Regeneration of the Lens of the Eye of Triton. *Ibid.*

Formol or Formalin. *Ibid.*

Effect of Lithium Chloride upon the Development of the Frog and Toad Egg. *Ibid.*, 1896.

The Terminology of the Neurocytes. *Science*, 1897.

HERBERT G. KEPPEL: —

A.B., Hope College, Holland, Mich., 1889; Instructor in Mathematics, Northwestern Classical Academy, Orange City, Ia., 1891–92; Scholar in Mathematics, Clark University, 1892–93; Fellow, 1893–95; Instructor in Mathematics, Academy of Northwestern University, Evanston, Ill., 1895–96; Instructor in

Mathematics, Northwestern University, Evanston, Ill., 1896–; Member of the American Mathematical Society; Member of Het Wiskundig Genootschap, Amsterdam.

E. A. KIRKPATRICK:—

B.Sc., Iowa Agricultural College, 1887; M.Ph., *Ibid.*, 1889; **Scholar in Psychology, Clark University, 1889–90; Fellow, 1890–91**; Professor of Psychology and Pedagogy, State Normal School, Winona, Minn., 1893–97; Professor of Psychology and Child Study, State Normal School, Fitchburg, Mass., 1898–; Member of American Psychological Association.

Author of:—

Observations on College Seniors and Electives in Psychological Subjects. *Am. Jour. of Psy.*, April, 1890, Vol. 3, pp. 166–178.

Number of Words in an Ordinary Vocabulary. *Science*, Aug. 21, 1891, Vol. 18, pp. 107–108.

How Children learn to Talk. *Ibid.*, Sept. 25, 1891, Vol. 18, pp. 175–176.

Mental Images. *Ibid.*, Oct. 27, 1893, Vol. 22, pp. 227–230.

An Experimental Study of Memory. *Psychological Review*, Nov., 1894, Vol. 1, pp. 602–609.

Inductive Psychology: An Introduction to the Study of Mental Phenomena. E. L. Kellogg & Co., New York, 1895, 208 pp.

Child Study in the Training of Teachers. *Review of Reviews*, Dec., 1896, Vol. 14, pp. 686–692.

Handbook of Minnesota Child-Study Association. Jaques and Kroeger, Winona, Minn., 1897. 80 pp.

Continuous Sessions of Schools. *Review of Reviews*, July, 1897, Vol. 16, pp. 190–191.

Play as a Factor in Social and Educational Reforms. *Ibid.*, Aug., 1899, Vol. 20, pp. 192–196.

Children's Reading. *Northwestern Monthly*, June, 1898, Vol. 8, pp. 651–654; Dec., 1898, Jan., March–April, 1899, Vol. 9, pp. 185–191, 229–233, 338–342.

Learning Voluntary Movements. *School and Home Education*, March, 1899, Vol. 18, pp. 337–344.

The Development of Voluntary Movement. *Psychological Review*, May, 1899, Vol. 6, pp. 275–281.

MILTON S. KISTLER:—

Graduate, West Chester, Pa., State Normal School, 1885; Principal, High School, Honey Brook, Pa., 1888–89; Principal, Blaine Normal Institute, Pa., 1889–90; Ph.B., Dickinson College, 1894; A.M., *Ibid.*, 1897; Professor of Latin and English, Edinboro, Pa., State Normal School, 1894–97; **Scholar in Pedagogy, Clark University, 1897–98**; Teacher, N. Y. City Schools, 1898–.

Author of:—

John Knox's Services to Education. *Education*, Boston, Mass., Oct. 1898, Vol. 19, pp. 106–116.

LINUS W. KLINE:—

Student, University of Virginia, 1886–87; L.I., Peabody Normal College, 1889; Principal, Hamilton Grammar School, Houston, Texas, 1891–93; B.S., Harvard University, 1895; **Scholar in Psychology, Clark University, 1896–97; Fellow, 1897–98; Ph.D., Clark University, 1898; Honorary Fellow and Assistant in Psychology, 1898–99**; Professor of Psychology and Pedagogy, State Normal School, Mankato, Minn., 1899–.

Author of:—

Truancy as Related to the Migrating Instinct. *Pedagogical Seminary*, Jan., 1898, Vol. 5, pp. 381–420.

The Migratory Impulse vs. Love of Home. *Am. Jour. of Psy.*, Oct. 1898, Vol. 10, pp. 1–81.

Methods in Animal Psychology. *Ibid.*, Jan., 1899, Vol. 10, pp. 256–279.

Suggestions toward a Laboratory Course in Comparative Psychology. *Ibid.*, April, 1899, Vol. 10, pp. 399–430.

The Psychology of Ownership. (With C. J. France.) *Pedagogical Seminary.* (In press.)

WILLIAM O. KROHN :—

A.B., Western College, 1887; Ph.D., Yale University, 1889; Instructor in Philosophy and Psychology, Western Reserve University, 1889-91; Inspecting Psychological Laboratories in German Universities, July, 1891–Feb. 1892; **Fellow in Psychology, Clark University, March–June, 1892**; Professor of Psychology, University of Illinois, 1892-97; Psychologist, Illinois Eastern Hospital, Kankakee, Ill., 1897–; Editor of *Child-Study Monthly.*

Author of :—

Facilities in Experimental Psychology at the Various German Universities. *Am. Jour. of Psy.*, Aug., 1892, Vol. 4, pp. 585-594.

Pseudo-Chromesthesia, or the Association of Colors with Words, Letters, and Sounds. *Ibid.*, Oct., 1892, Vol. 5, pp. 20-41.

An Experimental Study of Simultaneous Stimulation of the Sense of Touch. *Jour. of Nervous and Mental Disease*, March, 1893; N. S., Vol. 18, pp. 169-184.

Practical Lessons in Psychology. The Werner Co., Chicago and New York. 400 pp.

Laboratory Psychology as applied to the Study of Insanity. *Psychiater*, Vol. 1, No. 1.

Minor Mental Abnormalities in Children as occasioned by Certain Erroneous School Methods. *Proc. N. E. A.*, 1898, pp. 162-172.

ELLSWORTH G. LANCASTER :—

B.A., Amherst College, 1885; M.A., *ibid.* 1888; Teacher, Elocution and Physical Culture, Williston Seminary, Easthampton, Mass., 1885-86; Student, Auburn Theological Seminary, 1886-87; Teacher, Physical Culture, Latin, and German, Morgan Park Military Academy, 1887-88; Student, Chicago Baptist Seminary, 1887-88; Student, Andover Theological Seminary, 1888-89; B.D., *ibid.*, 1889; Pastor, Congregational Church, Ashby, Mass., 1889-90; Principal, Southern Kansas Academy, 1890-95; **Scholar in Psychology, Clark University, 1895-96; Fellow, 1896-97; Ph.D., Clark University, 1897**; Instructor in Philosophy and Pedagogy, and President's Assistant, Colorado College, 1897-98; Assistant Professor, *ibid.*, 1898–.

Author of :—

Psychology and Pedagogy of Adolescence. *Pedagogical Seminary*, July, 1897, Vol. 5, pp. 61-128.

Warming Up. *Colorado College Studies*, Nov., 1898, Vol. 7, pp. 16-29.

JAMES STEPHEN LEMON :—

B.A., Wesleyan University, 1853; M.A., *ibid.*, 1856; Principal of High School, Brownville, New York, 1859; Assistant on McClintock and Strong's *Cyclopædia of Biblical, Theological, and Ecclesiastical Literature*, 1859-61; Assistant on Strong's *Concordance of the Bible*, 1859-65; Professor of Physics, Marion, N. Y., Institute, 1863-65; Principal, Almond Collegiate Institute, 1866; Principal, Macedon, N. Y., Academy, 1867; Rector, Protestant Episcopal Church, 1877–; **Scholar in Psychology, Clark University, 1891-93; Student in Psychology, 1893-94**; Lecturer in Psychophysics, Columbian University, Washington, D.C., 1894–; Ph.D., Columbian University, 1896; Lecturer in Physiological Psychology, Howard University, 1897–; Member Society for Philosophical Inquiry, Washington, D.C.; Member American Anthropological Society.

Author of :—

Signalling by Flashlights. Troy, Pa., 1874. 10 pp.

The Body Considered in its Relation to the Intellectual Processes. Union Springs, N. Y., 1875.

Lists of Questions to be Asked as to Defectives, etc., admitted to Cottage

Hospitals for Children. Athol, Mass. 7 pp.

Psychic Effects of the Weather. *Am. Jour. of Psy.*, Jan., 1894, Vol. 6, pp. 277–311.

Requirements Demanded for Official Recognition as Teachers. Templeton Press, Templeton, Mass., 1898. 13 pp.

The Skin considered as an Organ of Sensation. Journal Publishing Co., Gardner, Mass., 1898. 77 pp.

The Weather Idea. Journal Publishing Co., Gardner, Mass., 1899. 80 pp.

Numerous reviews and articles in *Healthy Home*, *Cottager*, and *National Tribune*, 1880–.

JAMES E. LEROSSIGNOL:—

B.A., McGill University, 1888; Teacher in Berthelet School, Montreal, 1888–89; Student in Philosophy, University of Leipzig, 1889–92; Ph.D., University of Leipzig, 1892; Fellow in Psychology, Clark University, May–July, 1892; Professor of Psychology and Ethics, Ohio University, Athens, 1892–94; Professor of History and Political Economy, University of Denver, 1894–; Member of: American Economic Association, American Academy of Political and Social Science, American Historical Association.

Author of:—

The Ethical Philosophy of Samuel Clarke. G. Kreysing, Leipzig, 1892. 97 pp.

The Training of Animals. *Am. Jour. of Psy.*, Nov., 1892, Vol. 5, pp. 205–213.

Malevolence in the Lower Animals. *Ohio University Bulletin*, Sept., 1893, Vol. 1, pp. 1–8.

The Expression of Anger. *Transactions of the Ohio College Association*, 1894, pp. 40–49.

Spinoza as a Biblical Critic. *Canadian Methodist Review*, Jan.–Feb., 1894, Vol. 7, pp. 53–60.

JAMES H. LEUBA:—

B.S., University of Neuchâtel, Switzerland, 1886; Ph.B., Ursinus College, 1888; Instructor in French and German, St. Mark's School, Southborough, Mass., 1891–92; Scholar in Psychology, Clark University, 1892–93; Fellow, 1893–95; Ph.D., Clark University, 1895; Professor of Psychology and Pedagogy, Bryn Mawr College, 1897–; Universities of Leipzig, Göttingen, Heidelberg, and Paris, 1897–98; Member of the American Psychological Association.

Author of:—

A New Instrument for Weber's Law; with Indications of a Law of Sense Memory. *Am. Jour. of Psy.*, April, 1893, Vol. 5, pp. 370–384.

National Destruction and Construction in France as seen in Modern Literature and in the Neo-Christian Movement. *Ibid.*, July, 1893, Vol. 5, pp. 496–539.

A Study in the Psychology of Religious Phenomena. *Ibid.*, April, 1896, Vol. 7, pp. 309–385.

The Psycho-Physiology of the Moral Imperative. *Ibid.*, July, 1897, Vol. 8, pp. 528–559.

On the Validity of the Griesbach Method of Determining Fatigue. *Psychological Review*, Nov., 1899, Vol. 6, pp. 573–598.

FRANK R. LILLIE:—

Assistant in Biology, University of Toronto, 1890–91; B.A., *ibid.*, 1891; Fellow in Morphology, Clark University, 1891–92; Fellow in Zoölogy, University of Chicago, 1892–93; Reader in Embryology, *ibid.*, 1893–94; Ph.D., University of Chicago, 1894; Instructor in Zoölogy, University of Michigan, 1894–99; Professor of Biology, Vassar College, 1899–; Member American Society of Morphologists; Member Michigan Academy of Sciences.

Author of:—

Preliminary Account of the Embryology of Unio complanata. *Jour. of Morph.*, Aug., 1893, Vol. 8, pp. 569–578, 1 plate.

The Embryology of the Unionidæ, a Study in Cell-Lineage. *Ibid.*, Jan., 1895, Vol. 10, pp. 1–100, 6 plates.

On the Smallest Parts of Stentor Capable of Regeneration. A Contribution on the Limits of Divisibility of Living Matter. *Ibid.*, May, 1896, Vol. 12, pp. 239-249.

On the Effect of Temperature on the Development of Animals. (With F. P. Knowlton.) *Zoölogical Bulletin*, Dec., 1897, Vol. 1, pp. 179-193.

On the Origin of the Centres of the First Cleavage Spindle in Unio complanata. *Science*, March 5, 1897, N. S., Vol. 5, pp. 389-390.

Centrosome and Sphere in the Egg of Unio. *Zoölogical Bulletin*, May, 1898, Vol. 1, pp. 265-274.

Hertwig's "Zelle und Gewebe," Vol. 2. *Science*, Oct. 14, 1898, N. S., Vol. 8, pp. 517-520.

Adaptation in Cleavage. Woods Holl Biological Lectures, 1898. Ginn & Co., Boston. (In press.)

ERNEST H. LINDLEY :—

A. B., Indiana University, 1893; A. M., *ibid.*, 1894; Instructor in Philosophy, *ibid.*, 1893-95; Fellow in Psychology, Clark University, 1895-97; Ph.D., Clark University, 1897; Universities of Jena, Leipzig, and Heidelberg, 1897-98; Associate Professor of Psychology, Indiana University, 1898-; Member American Psychological Association.

Author of :—

A Preliminary Study of Some of the Motor Phenomena of Mental Effort. *Am. Jour. of Psy.*, July, 1896, Vol. 7, pp. 491-517.

Some Mental Automatisms. (With G. E. Partridge.) *Pedagogical Seminary*, July, 1897, Vol. 5, pp. 41-60.

A Study of Puzzles with Special Reference to the Psychology of Mental Adaptation. *Am. Jour. of Psy.*, July, 1897, Vol. 8, pp. 431-493.

Ueber Arbeit und Ruhe. *Psychologische Arbeiten*, herausg. von E. Kraepelin. Heidelberg. (In press.)

C. E. LINEBARGER :—

A.B., Northwestern University, 1888; Student, Chicago Medical College, 1888-89; Student, Universities of Tübingen and Paris, 1889-91; Fellow in Chemistry, Clark University, 1891; Instructor in Chemistry, North Division High School, Chicago, 1891-93; Student, University of Göttingen, 1893-94; Student, School of Mines, Paris, 1894; Instructor in Chemistry and Physics, South Division High School, Chicago, 1894-96; Instructor in Chemistry and Physics, Lake View High School, Chicago, 1896-99; Member of American Chemical Society, Chemical Society of Paris, German Electro-chemical Society.

Author of :—

An Examination of Fusel Oil. (With J. H. Long.) *Jour. of Anal. Chem.*, 1890, Vol. 4, p. 4.

Sur l'Hydroxanthranol. *Bull. d. l. Soc. Chimique*, 1891, Vol. 6, p. 21.

The Action of Benzene on Benzal Chloride in the Presence of Aluminium Chloride. *Am. Chem. Jour.*, 1891, Vol. 13, p. 556.

The Reaction between Triphenylmethane and Chloroform in the Presence of Aluminium Chloride. *Ibid.*, p. 553.

On Dinaphtotetraphenylene. *Jour. Am. Chem. Soc.*, Vol. 13, p. 270.

A Rapid Dialyser. *Jour. of Anal. Chem.*, 1892, Vol. 6, p. 91.

On the Nature of Colloid Solutions. *Am. Jour. of Sci.*, 1892, Vol. 43, p. 218.

The Molecular Masses of Dextrine and Gum Arabic as determined by their Osmotic Pressures. *Ibid.*, p. 426.

On the Formation of Layers in Solutions of Salts in Mixtures of Water and Organic Liquids. *Am. Chem. Jour.*, 1892, Vol. 14, p. 380.

On the Relations between the Surface Tensions of Liquids and their Chemical Constitution. *Am. Jour. of Sci.*, 1892, Vol. 44, p. 83.

On the Influence of the Concentration of the Ions on the Intensity of Color of Solutions of Salts in Water. *Ibid.*, p. 416.

The Dissociation of Salts into their Ions by Water of Crystallization. *Am. Chem. Jour.*, 1892, Vol. 14, p. 604.

On the Application of the Friedel-Crafts Reaction to Syntheses in the Anthracene Series. *Ibid.*, p. 602.

On the Preparation and Constitution of Paranthracene. *Ibid.*, p. 567.

A Definition of Solutions. *Science*, 1892, Vol. 20, p. 352.

The Solubility of Triphenylmethane in Benzene. *Am. Chem. Jour.*, 1893, Vol. 15, p. 45.

The Hydrates of Manganous Sulphate. *Ibid.*, 1893, Vol. 15, p. 225.

On the Existence of Double Salts in Solution. *Ibid.*, 1893, Vol. 15, p. 337.

An Isothermal Curve of Solubility of Mercuric and Sodium Chlorides in Acetic Ether. *Ibid.*, 1894, Vol. 16, p. 215.

The Benzoyl Halogen Amides. *Ibid.*, 1894, Vol. 16, p. 216.

Ueber die Bestimmung kleiner Dissociationsspannungen speciell Krystallwasserhaltiger Salze. *Zeits. f. phys. Chemie*, 1894, Vol. 13, p. 500.

Some Modifications of Beckmann's Ebullioscopic Apparatus. *Chemical News*, 1894, Vol. 69, p. 279.

The Boiling Points of Dilute Solutions of Water in Alcohol and in Ether. *Ibid.*, p. 312.

On the Application of the Schroeder-Le Chatelier Law of Solubility to Solutions of Salts in Organic Liquids. *Am. Jour. of Sci.*, 1895, Vol. 49, p. 48.

The Combination of Sulphur with Iodine. *Am. Chem. Jour.*, 1895, Vol. 17, p. 33.

On Some Experiments in the Anthracene Series. *Jour. Am. Chem. Soc.*, 1895, Vol. 17, p. 351.

On the Reaction between Zinc Sulphate and Potassium Hydroxide. *Ibid.*, p. 358.

On Some Relations between Temperature, Pressure, and Latent Heat of Vaporization. *Am. Jour. of Sci.*, 1895, Vol. 49, p. 380.

On the Vapor Tensions of Mixtures of Volatile Liquids. *Jour. Am. Chem. Soc.*, 1895, Vol. 17, p. 580.

On the Formation of Layers in Mixtures of Acetic Acid and Benzene. *Ibid.*, p. 603.

On the Heat Effect of mixing Liquids. *Physical Review*, 1896, Vol. 3, p. 418.

On the Specific Gravities of Mixtures of Normal Liquids. *Am. Chem. Jour.*, 1896, Vol. 18, p. 429.

A Rapid Method of determining the Molecular Masses of Liquids by Means of their Surface Tensions. *Jour. Am. Chem. Soc.*, 1896, Vol. 18, p. 514.

On the Reaction between Carbon Tetrachloride and the Oxides of Niobium and Tantalum. (In collaboration with M. Delafontaine.) *Ibid.*, p. 53.

Ueber die Dielektricitätskonstanten von Flüssigkeitsgemischen. *Zeitschr. f. phys. Chemie*, 1896, Vol. 20, p. 131.

An Apparatus for the Rapid Determination of the Surface Tensions of Liquids. *Am. Jour. Sci.*, 1896, Vol. 2, p. 108.

On the Surface Tension of Mixtures of Normal Liquids. *Ibid.*, p. 226.

On the Viscosity of Mixtures of Liquids. *Ibid.*, p. 331.

The Phase Rule. By Wilder D. Bancroft. Review. *Monist*, 1897, Vol. 7, p. 624.

Grundzüge einer thermodynamischen Theorie elektrochemischer Kräfte. By Alfred H. Bucherer. Review. *Ibid.*, p. 635.

The Phase Rule. By Wilder D. Bancroft. Review. *Jour. Am. Chem. Soc.*, 1897, Vol. 19, p. 767.

The Surface Tensions of Aqueous Solutions of Oxalic, Tartaric, and Citric Acids. *Ibid.*, 1898, Vol. 20, p. 128.

An Outline of the Theory of Solution and its Results. By J. Livingston R. Morgan. Review. *Ibid.*, 1898, Vol. 20, p. 163.

The Principles of Mathematical Chemistry. By J. Livingston R. Morgan. Review. *Ibid.*, 1898, Vol. 20, p. 164.

On the Speed of Coagulation of Colloid Solutions. *Ibid.*, 1898, Vol. 20, p. 375.

Text-book of Physical Chemistry. By Clarence L. Speyers. Review. *Ibid.*, 1898, Vol. 20, p. 259.

On a Balance for Use in Courses in Elementary Chemistry. *Ibid.*, 1899, Vol. 21, p. 31.

The Surface Tension of Aqueous Solutions of Alkaline Chlorides. *Ibid.*, 1899, Vol. 21, p. 327.

A Simple Volumenometer. *Ibid.*, 1899, Vol. 21, p. 435.

The Elements of Differential and Integral Calculus. (In collaboration with J. W. A. Young.) 1899, D. Appleton & Co.

SIDNEY J. LOCHNER:—

A.B., Union College, 1890; A.M., *ibid.*, 1892; First Assistant in Astronomy, Dudley Observatory, Albany, N. Y., 1890–92; **Fellow in Physics, Clark University, Oct., 1892–May, 1893**; Assistant, Harvard Observatory, 1893; Admitted as Attorney at Law, Detroit, Mich., Dec., 1893; Professor of Physics and Mathematics, Delaware Literary Institute, Franklin, N. Y., 1894–.

Author of:—

On the Elongation Produced in Soft Iron by Magnetism. *Phil. Magazine*, Dec., 1893, Fifth Series, Vol. 36, pp. 498–507.

Modern Scientific Investigations. *Union College Concordiensis*, 1894.

WILLIAM B. LOCKWOOD:—

Ph.B., Sheffield Scientific School, Yale University, 1883; M.D., *ibid.*, 1886; Instructor in Chemistry, *ibid.*, 1886–88; Instructor and Demonstrator in Physiology, *ibid.*, 1887–91; **Fellow in Physiology, Clark University, 1891–92.**

Died at Redlands, Cal., June 23, 1897.

Author of:—

The New Haven Water Supply: A Criticism of the Results of Analyses of this Water, as given by Dr. Arthur J. Wolff, in the Report of the Connecticut State Board of Health for 1886. (With Herbert E. Smith, M.D.) New Haven. 8 pp.

Report of the Analyses of One Hundred and Two Well Waters, collected in New Haven. (With Herbert E. Smith, M.D.) Report of the Connecticut State Board of Health, 1886, pp. 259–269.

Some Hints for the Physician concerning Urinary Analysis. *Medical Register*, Philadelphia, March 19, 1887, Vol. 1, pp. 169–174.

MORRIS LOEB:—

A.B., Harvard University, 1883; Ph.D., University of Berlin, 1887; Assistant to Professor Wolcott Gibbs, 1888–89; **Docent in Physical Chemistry, Clark University, 1889–91**; Professor of Chemistry, New York University, N. Y. City, 1891–.

Author of:—

Ueber die Einwirkung von Phosgen auf Anthranyldiphenyldiamin. *Ber. d. deut. chem. Gesellschaft*, Aug., 1885, Vol. 18, pp. 2427–2428.

Ueber Amidinderivate. *Ibid.*, Aug., 1886, Vol. 19, pp. 2340–2344.

Das Phosgen und seine Abkömmlinge. Berlin, March 16, 1887. 61 pp.

The Molecular Weight of Iodine in its Solutions. *Jour. of Chem. Soc.*, Trans., 1888, Vol. 53, pp. 805–812. Also *Zeits. f. physikalische Chemie*, July, 1888, Vol. 2, pp. 606–612.

The Use of Aniline for Absorbing Cyanogen in Gas Analysis. *Jour. of Chem. Soc.*, Trans., 1888, Vol. 53, pp. 812–814.

The Rates of Transference and the Conducting Power of Certain Silver Salts. (With W. Nernst.) *Am. Chem. Jour.*, Feb., 1889, Vol. 11, pp. 106–121. Also *Zeits. f. physikalische Chemie*, Nov., 1888, Vol. 2, pp. 948–963.

Is Chemical Action Affected by Magnetism? *Am. Chem. Jour.*, March, 1891, Vol. 13, pp. 145–153.

WARREN P. LOMBARD:—

A.B., Harvard University, 1878; M.D., Harvard Medical School, 1881; University of Leipzig, 1883–85; Assistant in Physiology, College of Physicians and Surgeons, New York City, 1885–89; **Assistant Professor of Physiology, Clark Univer-**

sity, 1889–92; Professor of Physiology, University of Michigan, 1892–; Member American Physiological Society.

Author of:—

Beiträge zur Theorie der Wärmeempfindung. Vorläufige Mittheilung. *Centralbl. f. d. Med. Wissensch.*, 1883, Vol. 21, pp. 577–579.

Die räumliche und zeitliche Aufeinanderfolge reflectorisch contrahirter Muskeln. *Arch. f. Anat. u. Physiologie*, Physiol. Abthl., 1885, pp. 408–489.

Is the "Knee-jerk" a Reflex Act? *Am. Jour. of Med. Sciences*, Jan., 1887.

The Variations of the Normal "Knee-jerk." *Am. Jour. of Psy.*, Nov., 1887, Vol. 1, pp. 5–71.

Die Variationen des normalen Kniestosses. *Arch. f. Anat. u. Physiologie*, Suppl. Band, 1889, pp. 292–334, 10 pls.

On the Nature of the "Knee-jerk." *Jour. of Physiology*, Feb., 1889, Vol. 10, pp. 122–148.

The Effect of Fatigue on Voluntary Muscular Contraction. *Am. Jour. of Psy.*, Jan., 1890, Vol. 3, pp. 24–42.

Effet de la fatigue sur la contraction musculaire volontaire. *Arch. Ital. de Biologie*, 1890, Vol. 13, pp. 371–381.

Alterations in the Strength which occur during Fatiguing Voluntary Muscular Work. *Jour. of Physiology*, Jan., 1893, Vol. 14, pp. 97–124.

General Physiology of Muscle and Nerve. Chapter II., Howell's *Am. Text Book of Physiology*. W. B. Saunders, Philadelphia, 1896. pp. 33–141.

FRANK H. LOUD:—

A.B., Amherst College, 1873; Walker Instructor in Mathematics, *ibid.*, 1873–76; Professor of Mathematics, Colorado College, 1877–; Director of State Weather Service, Colorado, 1889–90; **Scholar in Mathematics, Clark University, 1890–91.**

Author of:—

A Rigorous Elementary Proof of the Binomial Theorem. *Col. College Studies*, 1890, pp. 7–15.

On Certain Cubic Curves. *Ibid.*, 1890, p. 16.

The Elliptic Functions Defined Independently of the Calculus. *Ibid.*, 1891, pp. 45–61.

ELWYN E. LOVEWELL:—

Ph.B., University of Vermont, 1888 (Double Honors); **Scholar in Mathematics, Clark University, 1888–89.**

GEORGE W. A. LUCKEY:—

Teacher in Public Schools of Indiana, 1874–78; Superintendent of Schools, Adams Co., Ind., 1878–83; Superintendent of Schools, Decatur, Ind., 1883–87; Supervising Principal, Ontario, Cal., 1888–92; Non-Resident Student, University of City of New York, 1890–92; Student in Pedagogy and Psychology, Leland Stanford Jr. University, 1892–94; A.B., *ibid.*, 1894; **Fellow in Psychology, Clark University, 1894–95**; Associate Professor of Pedagogy, University of Nebraska, 1895–96; Professor of Pedagogy, *ibid.*, 1896–; Editor of the Child Study Department, *Northwestern Monthly*, 1895–99.

Author of:—

Comparative Observations on the Indirect Color Range of Children, Adults, and Adults Trained in Color. *Am. Jour. of Psy.*, Jan., 1895, Vol. 6, pp. 489–504.

Some Recent Studies of Pain. *Ibid.*, Oct., 1895, Vol. 7, pp. 108–123.

Child Study in its Effects upon the Teacher. *Child Study Monthly*, Feb., 1896, Vol. 1, pp. 230–247.

Children's Interests. *Northw. Monthly*, 1896–97, Vol. 7, pp. 67, 96, 152, 176, 221, 245, 306, and 335.

Practical Results Obtained through the Study of Children's Interests. *Proc. N. E. A.*, 1897, pp. 284–288; also *Jour. of Ed.*, Apr. 8, 1897, Vol. 45, p. 222.

Lines of Child Study for the Teacher. *Educational Review*, Nov., 1897, Vol. 14, pp. 340–347; also *Proc. N. E. A.*, 1897, pp. 826–833.

A Brief Survey of Child Study. *Northwestern Jour. of Ed.*, July, 1898, Vol. 7, pp. 2–9.

Methods Pursued in Child Study. *Ibid.*, pp. 33–35.

The Best Works on Child Study. *Ibid.*, pp. 46–48.

The Development of Moral Character. *Proc. N. E. A.*, 1899.

HERMAN T. LUKENS:—

A.B., University of Pennsylvania, 1885; A.M., *ibid.*, 1888; Student in Halle, Jena, and Berlin, 1888–91; Ph.D., University of Jena, 1891; Instructor in Biology, N. W. Division High School, Chicago, 1891–94; Honorary Fellow in Psychology, Clark University, 1894–95; Docent in Pedagogy, 1895–; Lecturer in Education, Bryn Mawr College, 1896–97; Visit to Europe to study Education, 1897–98; Head Training Teacher, S. W. State Normal School, California, Pa., 1898–.

Author of:—

Herbart's Psychological Basis of Teaching. Part II of Th. B. Noss's *Outlines of Psychology and Pedagogy*, Pittsburg, 1890.

Die Vorstellungsreihen und ihre pädagogische Bedeutung. Gütersloh, Prussia, 1892.

A Portion of the Translation of Lange's *Apperception*. Edited by Charles De Garmo. D. C. Heath & Co., Boston, 1893. 279 pp.

The Connection between Thought and Memory. Based on Dörpfeld's *Denken und Gedächtnis*. D. C. Heath & Co., Boston, 1895. 179 pp.

The Correlation of Studies. *Educational Review*, Nov., 1895, Vol. 10, pp. 364–383.

Correlation. *Jour. of Ed.*, May 9 and June 20, 1895, Vol. 41, pp. 311–313; Vol. 42, p. 15.

A Point of Difference between Race and Individual Development. *Second Herbartian Yearbook*, 1896.

Preliminary Report on the Learning of Language. *Pedagogical Seminary*, June, 1896, Vol. 3, pp. 424–460.

A Study of Children's Drawings in the Early Years. *Ibid.*, Oct. 1896, Vol. 4, pp. 79–110.

Child Study for Superintendents. *Educational Review*, Feb., 1897, Vol. 13, pp. 105–120.

Honorary Degrees in the United States. *Ibid.*, June, 1897, Vol. 14, pp. 8–16.

Language Defects. *Northw. Monthly*, July, 1897, Vol. 8, pp. 39–44.

The Vital Question in the Curriculum. *Education*, Sept., 1897, Vol. 18, pp. 19–29.

Die Entwickelungsstufen beim Zeichnen. *Kinderfehler*, Dec., 1897, Vol. 3, pp. 166–170.

Malendes Zeichnen. *Aus dem päd. Univ.-Seminar Jena*, VII., 1897.

The School Fatigue Question in Germany. *Educational Review*, March, 1898, Vol. 15, pp. 246–254.

The Method of Suggestion in the Cure of Faults. *Northwestern Monthly*, May, 1898, Vol. 8, pp. 593–595.

The School and Real Life. *N. Y. School Jour.*, Oct. 1, 1898, Vol. 57, pp. 377–379.

Notes Abroad. *Pedagogical Seminary*, Oct., 1898, Vol. 6, pp. 114–125.

A School-Garden in Thuringia. *Educational Review*, March, 1899, Vol. 17, pp. 237–241.

Mental Fatigue. *Am. Phys. Ed. Review*, March and June, 1899, Vol. 4, pp. 19–29, 121–138.

The Joseph Story. *N. Y. Teachers' Magazine*, April, 1899, Vol. 1, pp. 331–334.

Drawing in the Early Years. *Proc. N. E. A.*, 1899.

ALEXANDER G. McADIE:—

A.B., College of City of New York, 1881; A.M., *ibid.*, 1884; Student, Harvard University, 1882–85; A.M., *ibid.*, 1885; Physical Laboratory, U. S. Signal Office, 1886–87; Fellow in Physics, Clark University, 1889–90; U. S. Signal Office, Washington, 1890–91; U. S. Weather Bu-

rents, Washington, 1891-95; Hodgkins Medal and Honorable Mention, Smithsonian Institution, 1895; Local Forecast Official, New Orleans, 1898-99; Forecast Official, San Francisco, 1899-; Honorary Lecturer in Meteorology, University of California; Director, California Climate and Crop Service.

Author of: —

On the Aurora. *U. S. Signal Service Note*, No. 18, pp. 21, 5 maps, 12 charts.

Protection against Lightning. *Am. Met. Jour.*, June, 1885, Vol. 2, pp. 60-66.

Atmospheric Electricity at High Altitudes. *Proc. Am. Academy*, 1886, Vol. 18, pp. 129-134.

Electrometer Work. *Monthly Weather Review*, 1886-87, Vol. 14, pp. 166-167.

Observations of Atmospheric Electricity. *Am. Met. Jour.*, March, 1887, Vol. 3, pp. 523-531; April, 1887, Vol. 3, pp. 551-561; May, 1887, Vol. 4, pp. 21-31.

William Ferrel. *Ibid.*, Feb., 1888, Vol. 4, pp. 441-449.

Lightning and the Electricity of the Atmosphere. *Ibid.*, May, 1889, Vol. 6, pp. 1-4.

Tornadoes. Prize Essay. *Ibid.*, Vol. 7, pp. 179-192.

Mean Temperatures in the United States. Professional Paper, U. S. Signal Office, June, 1891. Washington, 1891. 45 pp.

Franklin's Kite Experiment. *Am. Met. Jour.*, July, 1891, Vol. 8, pp. 97-103.

Shall We erect Lightning Rods? *Ibid.*, July, 1892, Vol. 9, pp. 60-66.

Experiments in Atmospheric Electricity. *Annals of Observatory of Harvard College*, Vol. 40, Part 1, pp. 53-58.

Experiments in Atmospheric Electricity at Blue Hill, 1891. *Annals of Observatory of Harvard College*, Vol. 40, Part 2, pp. 120-124.

Energy of a Flash of Lightning. *Proc. of the Internat. Met. Congress*, Chicago, 1893, Paper 5, Part 1, pp. 18-21.

Utilization of Cloud Observations. *Ibid.*, Paper 6, Part 1, pp. 21-26.

Protection from Lightning. U. S. Weather Bureau. *Bulletin No. 15*, 1894.

A Colonial Weather Service. *Pop. Sci. Mo.*, July, 1894, Vol. 45, pp. 331-337.

The Storage Battery of the Air. *Harper's Magazine*, July, 1894, Vol. 89, pp. 216-219.

New Cloud Classifications. *Proc. Phil. Soc. of Washington*, March 2, 1895, Vol. 13, pp. 77-86.

The Work and Equipment of an Aëro-Physical Laboratory. Smithsonian Institution, 1896. 20 pp. *Smithsonian Miscellaneous Collections*, Vol. 39, No. 1077.

Fog Possibilities. *Harper's Magazine*, Jan., 1897, Vol. 94, pp. 262-266.

What is an Aurora? *Century Magazine*, Oct., 1897, Vol. 54, pp. 874-878.

Franklin's Kite Experiments. *Pop. Sci. Mo.*, Oct. 1897, Vol. 51, pp. 739-747.

Needless Alarm during Thunder-storms. *Century Magazine*, Aug., 1899, Vol. 58, pp. 604-606.

FRANK H. McASSEY: —

A.B., Ripon College, Ripon, Wis., 1897; Scholar in Psychology, Clark University, 1898-99.

J. F. McCULLOCH: —

A.B., Adrian College, 1883; A.M., *ibid.*, 1886; Ph.B., *ibid.*, 1884; Assistant Professor of Mathematics, *ibid.*, 1885-87; Instructor in Mathematics, University of Michigan, 1887-88; Assistant Professor of Mathematics, Adrian College, 1888-89; Fellow in Mathematics, Clark University, 1889-90; President, Adrian College, 1890-93; Pastor of M. P. Church, Fairmont, W. Va., 1893-94; Editor, *Our Church Record*, Greensboro, N. C., 1894-.

Author of: —

Rolle's Theorem extended. *Annals of Mathematics*, Vol. 4, p. 5.

A Theorem in Factorials. *Ibid.*, Vol. 4, p. 161.

ARTHUR MacDONALD: —

A.B., University of Rochester, 1879; A.M., *ibid.*, 1883; Union Theological Seminary, 1880-83; Graduate Student, Harvard University, 1883-85; Fellow, Johns Hopkins

University, 1885; Universities of Berlin, Leipzig, Paris, and Zürich, 1884-89; Docent in Ethics, Clark University, 1889-91; Specialist in Education as related to the Abnormal and Weakling Classes, U. S. Bureau of Education, 1891-; U. S. Delegate, International Criminal Congress, Brussels, 1892; International Psychological Congress, London, 1892; International Demographical Congress, Budapest, 1894.

Author of:—

Ethics as Applied to Criminology. *Jour. of Mental Science*, Jan., 1891, Vol. 37, pp. 10-16, and *Open Court*, July, 1891.

Alcoholism. *Medico-Legal Journal*, June, 1891.

Criminal Aristocracy, or the Maffia. *Medico-Legal Journal*, June, 1891, Vol. 9, pp. 31-35.

Criminology. With an Introduction by C. Lombroso, with Bibliography. Funk & Wagnalls Co., New York, 1893. 416 pp.

Abnormal Man. Being Essays on Education and Crime and Related Subjects, with Digests of Literature and a Bibliography. U. S. Bureau of Education, Washington, 1893. 445 pp.

Le Criminel-Type dans quelques formes graves de la Criminalité. Bibliographie de Sexualité Pathologique. Un volume in 8° illustré de Portraits. A Storck, Lyon et G. Masson, Paris, 1895. 300 pp.

Education and Patho-Social Studies. Reprint from *Annual Report of U. S. Commissioner of Education for 1893-94*, Washington, D. C., 1896. 57 pp.

Émile Zola: a Psycho-Physical Study of Zola's Personality. Reprint from *Open Court*, August, 1898. 16 pp.

Experimental Study of Children, including Anthropometrical and Psycho-Physical Measurements, with a Bibliography. Reprint from *Annual Report of U. S. Commissioner of Education for 1897-98*, Washington, D. C., 1899. 325 pp.

Ueber Körpermessungen an Kindern. *Deuts. Zeits. f. Ausländisches Unterrichtswesen*, July, 1899, Vol. 4, pp. 263-288.

Abnormal Children. (In press.)

JOHN McGOWAN:—

B.A., University of Toronto, 1889; Fellow in Mathematics, *ibid.*, 1889-91; Scholar in Mathematics, Clark University, 1891-92; Instructor in Mathematics, Princeton College, 1892-93; Graduate Student, University of Toronto, 1893-94; Lecturer in Mathematics and Physics, Toronto Technical School, 1894-95; B.S., University of Toronto (School of Practical Science), 1896.

J. PLAYFAIR McMURRICH:—

B.A., University of Toronto, 1879; M.A., *ibid.*, 1881; Assistant in Biological Laboratory, *ibid.*, 1880-81; Professor of Biology, Ontario Agricultural College, 1882-84; Instructor in Osteology, Johns Hopkins University, 1884-86; Ph.D., Johns Hopkins University, 1885; Professor of Biology, Haverford College, 1886-89; Docent in Morphology, Clark University, 1889-91; Assistant Professor, 1891-92; Professor of Biology, University of Cincinnati, 1892-94; Professor of Anatomy, University of Michigan, 1894-.

Author of:—

On the Origin of the So-called Test-cells in the Ascidian Ovum. *Studies from Biol. Lab. J. H. U.*, 1882, Vol. 2. Abstract in *Biol. Centralblatt*, 1882, Vol. 2; *Arch. de Zool. exp. et gén.*, 1882, Vol. 10.

Note on the Function of the "Test-cells" in Ascidian Ova. *Zool. Anzeiger*, 1882, Vol. 5. Abstract in *Jour. Roy. Micros. Soc.*, 1882, Vol. 2.

On the Osteology and Development of Syngnathus peckianus (Storer). *Quart. Jour. Micros. Sci.*, 1883, Vol. 23. Abstract in *J. H. U. Circular*, 1883, No. 27.

The Osteology and Myology of Amiurus catus (L.) Gill. *Proc. of the Canadian Inst.*, Toronto, 1884, Vol. 2. Preliminary Notice in *Zool. Anzeiger*, 1884, Vol. 7.

On the Structure and Affinities of Phytoptus. *J. H. U. Circular*, 1884, No. 33. Abstract in *Jour. Roy. Micros. Soc.*, 1885, Vol. 5.

On the Tape-worm Epidemic among Lambs (Taenia expansa). *9th Ann. Rep. of the Ont. Agricultural College*, Toronto, 1884.

The Cranial Muscles of Amia calva (L.), with a consideration of the Post-occipital and Hypoglossal Nerves in the various Vertebrate Groups. *Studies from Biol. Lab. J. H. U.*, 1885, Vol. 3. Preliminary Notice in *J. H. U. Circular*, 1885, No. 38.

On the Existence of a Post-oral Band of Cilia in Gasteropod Veligers. *J. H. U. Circular*, 1885, No. 43. Abstract in *Jour. Roy. Micros. Soc.*, 1886, Vol. 6.

A Contribution to the Embryology of the Prosobranch Gasteropoda. *Studies from Biol. Lab. J. H. U.*, 1886, Vol. 3. Preliminary Notice in *J. H. U. Circular*, 1886, No. 49. Abstract in *Jour. Roy. Micros. Soc.*, 1886, Vol. 6.

Notes on the Actiniæ obtained at Beaufort, N. C. *Studies from Biol. Lab. J. H. U.*, 1887, Vol. 4.

On the Occurrence of an Edwardsia Stage in the Free-swimming Embryos of a Hexactinian. *J. H. U. Circular*, 1889, No. 70. Abstract in *Jour. Roy. Micros. Soc.*, 1889, Vol. 9.

A Contribution to the Actinology of the Bermudas. *Proc. of the Acad. of Nat. Sciences*, Philadelphia, 1889. Abstract in *Jour. Roy. Micros. Soc.*, 1889, Vol. 9.

Note on the Structure and Systematic Position of Lebrunia neglecta, Duch. and Mich. *Zool. Anzeiger*, 1889, Vol. 12. Abstract in *Jour. Roy. Micros. Soc.*, 1889, Vol. 9.

Article "Reproduction" in Buck's *Reference Handbook of the Medical Sciences*, 1889, Vol. 6.

The Actiniaria of the Bahama Islands, W. I. *Jour. of Morph.*, 1889, Vol. 3. Abstract in *Jour. Roy. Micros. Soc.*, 1890, Vol. 10; *American Naturalist*, 1889; Preliminary Notice in *J. H. U. Circular*, 1889, No. 70.

Contributions on the Morphology of the Actinozoa. I. The Structure of Cerianthus americanus. *Jour. of Morph.*, Oct., 1890, Vol. 4, pp. 131–150.

Contributions on the Morphology of the Actinozoa. II. On the Development of the Hexactiniæ. *Ibid.*, Jan., 1891, Vol. 4, pp. 303–330.

Contributions on the Morphology of the Actinozoa. III. The Phylogeny of the Actinozoa. *Ibid.*, June, 1891, Vol. 5, pp. 125–164.

The Gastræa Theory and its Successors. *Biological Lectures*. Marine Biological Laboratory, Woods Holl. Ginn & Co., Boston, 1891, pp. 79–108.

The Formation of the Germ-layers in the Isopod Crustacea. *Zool. Anzeiger*, Jahrg. 15, 1892.

Report on the Actiniæ collected by the U. S. Fish Commission steamer *Albatross* during the winter of 1887–88. *Proc. U. S. National Museum*, 1893, Vol. 16, p. 119.

A Text-book of Invertebrate Morphology. New York, 1894.

Embryology of the Isopod Crustacea. *Jour. of Morph.*, May, 1895, Vol. 11, pp. 63–154.

Cell Division and Development. *Biological Lectures*, Marine Biological Laboratory, Woods Holl. Ginn & Co., Boston, 1895, pp. 125–147.

Notes on Some Actinians from the Bahama Islands, collected by the late Dr. J. I. Northrop. *Annals N. Y. Acad. of Science*, 1896, Vol. 9, p. 161.

The Yolk-lobe and Centrosome of Fulgur carica. *Anat. Anzeiger*, 1896, Bd. 12, p. 534.

Contributions on the Morphology of the Actinozoa. IV. On Some Irregularities in the Number of the Directive Mesenteries in the Hexactiniæ. *Zoöl. Bulletin*, 1897, Vol. 1.

The Epithelium of the So-called Midgut of the Terrestrial Isopods. *Jour. of Morph.*, 1897, Vol. 14, p. 83.

A Case of Crossed Dystopia of the Kidney with Fusion. *Jour. of Anat. and Phys.*, 1898, Vol. 32, p. 652.

Report on the Actiniaria collected by the Bahama Expedition of the State University of Iowa, 1896. *Bull. Lab. of Nat. Hist. State Univ. of Iowa*, 1896, Vol. 4, p. 326.

The Present Status of Anatomy. *American Naturalist*, 1889, Vol. 23, p. 188.

FRANKLIN P. MALL:—

M.D., University of Michigan, 1883; University of Heidelberg, 1883–84; University of Leipzig, 1884–86; Fellow, Instructor, and Associate in Pathology, Johns Hopkins University, 1886–89; Adjunct Professor of Vertebrate Anatomy, Clark University, 1889–92; Professor of Anatomy, University of Chicago, 1892–93; Professor of Anatomy, Johns Hopkins University, 1893–.

Author of:—

Entwickelung der Branchialbogen und -Spalten des Hühnchens. *Arch. f. Anatomie* (His u. Braune), 1887, pp. 1–34, 6 pls.

Die Blut- und Lymphwege im Dünndarm des Hundes. *Abhandl. d. K. S. Gesellsch. der Wissenschaften*, 1887, Vol. 24, pp. 153–189, 6 pls.

The First Branchial Arch of the Chick. *J. H. U. Circular*, Feb., 1888, Vol. 7, p. 39.

The Branchial Region of the Dog. *Ibid.*, Feb., 1888, Vol. 7, p. 39.

Development of the Eustachian Tube, Middle Ear, Tympanic Membrane, and Meatus of the Chick. *Studies from Biol. Lab. J. H. U.*, June, 1888, Vol. 4, pp. 185–192, 1 pl.

The Development of the Branchial Clefts of the Dog with Special Reference to the Origin of the Thymus Gland. *Ibid.*, pp. 193–216, 3 pls.

Reticulated and Yellow Elastic Tissues. *Anat. Anzeiger*, June 1, 1888, Vol. 3, pp. 397–401.

Die motorischen Nerven der Portalvene. *Du Bois-Reymond's Arch. f. Physiologie*, 1890, Supp. Band, pp. 57–58.

Development of the Lesser Peritoneal Cavity in Birds and Mammals. *Jour. of Morph.*, June, 1891, Vol. 5, pp. 165–179.

Das Reticulirte Gewebe. *Abhandl. d. K. S. Gesellsch. der Wissenschaften*, 1891, Vol. 17, pp. 299–338, 11 pls.

A Human Embryo Twenty-six Days Old. *Jour. of Morph.*, Dec., 1891, Vol. 5, 459–480, 2 pls.

Methods of preserving Human Embryos. *American Naturalist*, Dec., 1891, Vol. 25, pp. 1144–1146.

Der Einfluss des Systems der Vena portae auf die Vertheilung des Blutes. *Du Bois-Reymond's Arch. f. Physiologie*, 1892, pp. 409–453.

The Vessels and Walls of the Dog's Stomach. *J. H. Hospital Reports*, 1896, Vol. 1, pp. 1–36, 6 pls.

A Study of the Intestinal Contraction. *Ibid.*, pp. 37–75, 3 pls.

Healing of Intestinal Sutures. *Ibid.*, pp. 76–92.

Reversal of the Intestine. *Ibid.*, pp. 93–110.

A Human Embryo of the Second Week. *Anat. Anzeiger*, Aug. 5, 1893, Vol. 8, pp. 630–633.

Histogenesis of the Retina in Amblystoma and Necturus. *Jour. of Morph.*, May, 1893, Vol. 8, pp. 415–432.

Coelom, pp. 164–169; Human Embryos, pp. 268–269; The Heart, pp. 391–395; Development of the Thymus Gland, pp. 675–677; Development of the Thyroid Gland, pp. 679–683. *Ref. Handbook of Med. Sciences* (Supp. Vol.).

What is Biology? *Chautauquan*, Jan., 1894, Vol. 18, pp. 411–414.

Early Human Embryos and the Mode of their Preservation. *Bull. of J. H. Hospital*, Dec., 1893, Vol. 4, pp. 115–131.

The Preservation of Anatomical Material for Dissection. *Anat. Anzeiger*, April 9, 1896, Vol. 11, pp. 769–775.

The Contraction of the Vena Portae and its Influence upon the Circulation. *J. H. Hospital Reports*, 1896, Vol. 1, pp. 111–153.

Reticulated Tissue and its Relation to the Connective Tissue Fibrils. *Ibid.*, 1896, Vol. 1, pp. 171–208, 9 pls.

The Anatomical Course and Laboratory of the Johns Hopkins University. *Bull. of J. H. Hospital*, May–June, 1896, Vol. 7, pp. 85–100, 5 pls.

Development of the Human Cœlom. *Jour. of Morph.*, Feb., 1897, Vol. 12, pp. 395–453.

Ueber die Entwickelung des menschlichen Darmes und seiner Lage beim Erwachsenen. *His's Arch. f. Anatomie*, 1897, Supp. Band, pp. 403–434, 10 pls.

Development of the Ventral Abdominal Walls in Man. *Jour. of Morph.*, June, 1898, Vol. 14, pp. 347–366, 6 pls.

Development of the Human Intestine and its Position in the Adult. *Bull. of J. H. Hospital*, Sept.–Oct., 1898, Vol. 9, pp. 197–208, 5 pls.

The Lobule of the Spleen. *Ibid.*, pp. 218–219.

Development of the Internal Mammary and Deep Epigastric Arteries in Man. *Ibid.*, pp. 232–235.

The Value of Embryological Specimens. *Md. Med. Jour.*, Oct. 29, 1898, Vol. 40, p. 22.

Liberty in Medical Education. *Phila. Med. Jour.*, April 1, 1899, Vol. 3, p. 720.

CHARLES W. MARSH:—

Ph.B., Columbia College, School of Mines, 1879; Ph.D., Columbia College, 1882; Assistant in Chemistry, Green School of Science, Princeton, N. J., 1882–85; University of Berlin, 1885–87; Assistant in Chemistry, Lehigh University, 1887–89; Honorary Fellow in Chemistry, Clark University, 1889–90; Electrical Engineer, New York City, 1893–.

Author of:—

Note on the Ammonia-Process for Water Analysis. *Am. Chem. Jour.*, July, 1882, Vol. 4, pp. 189–192.

A Method for the Detection of Chlorine, Bromine, Iodine, and Sulphur in Organic Compounds. *Ibid.*, April, 1889, Vol. 11, pp. 240–244.

A New Form of Adapter. *Am. Jour. of Anal. Chem.*, Jan., 1889.

The Reduction of Barium Sulphate to Barium Sulphide on Ignition with Filter Paper. *Ibid.*, April, 1889.

ALFRED G. MAYER:—

M.E., Stevens Institute, Hoboken, N. J., 1889; Assistant in Physics, Clark University, 1889–90; Assistant in Physics, University of Kansas, 1890–92; Graduate Student in Zoölogy, Harvard University, 1892–95; Museum Assistant in Charge of Radiates, Echinoderms, and Polyps, and Assistant to Dr. Alexander Agassiz, 1895–; Sc.D., Harvard University, 1896; Member of: American Society of Naturalists, American Morphological Society, Boston Society of Natural History, American Association for Advancement of Science; President of the Cambridge Entomological Society.

Author of:—

Radiation and Absorption of Heat by Leaves. *Am. Jour. of Sci.*, April, 1893, Vol. 45, pp. 340–346.

Some New Medusæ from the Bahamas. *Bull. Mus. Comp. Zoöl.*, 1894, Vol. 25, pp. 235–242, 3 pls.

Color and Color-Patterns of Moths and Butterflies. *Ibid.*, 1897, Vol. 30, pp. 169–256, 10 pls.

The Development of Wing Scales and their Pigment in Butterflies and Moths. *Ibid.*, 1896, Vol. 29, pp. 209–236, 7 pls.

A New Hypothesis of Seasonal Dimorphism in Lepidoptera. *Psyche*, April–May, 1897, Vol. 8, pp. 47–50, 59–62.

On Dactylometra. (With A. Agassiz.) *Bull. Mus. Comp. Zoöl.*, 1898, Vol. 32, pp. 1–11, 13 pls.

On Some Medusæ from Australia. (With A. Agassiz.) *Ibid.*, 1898, Vol. 32, pp. 13–19, 3 pls.

Acalephs from the Fiji Islands. (With A. Agassiz.) *Ibid.*, 1899, Vol. 32, pp. 151–189, 17 pls.

On an Atlantic "Palolo" Worm. *Ibid.* (In press.)

Medusæ of the Atlantic Coast of North America. (With A. Agassiz.) *Mem. Mus. Comp. Zoöl.*

A. D. MEAD: —

A.B., Middlebury College, 1890; A. M., Brown University, 1891; Fellow in Morphology, Clark University, 1891-92; Fellow in Biology, University of Chicago, 1892-95; Ph.D., University of Chicago, 1895; Instructor in Comparative Anatomy, Brown University, 1895-97; Associate Professor of Embryology and Neurology, *ibid.*, 1897–.

Author of: —

Preliminary Account of the Cell-Lineage of Amphitrite and other Annelids. *Jour. of Morph.*, Sept., 1894, Vol. 9, pp. 465–473.

Some Observations on Maturation and Fecundation of Chaetopterus pergamentaceus Cuvier. *Ibid.*, Jan., 1895, Vol. 10, pp. 316–317.

The Origin of the Egg Centrosomes. *Ibid.*, Feb., 1897, Vol. 12, pp. 391–394.

The Early Development of Marine Annelids. (Thesis.) *Ibid.*, May, 1897, Vol. 13, pp. 227–326.

The Origin and Behavior of the Centrosomes in the Annelid Egg. *Ibid.*, June, 1898, Vol. 14, pp. 181–218, 4 pls.

The Rate of Cell Division and the Function of the Centrosome. *Woods Holl Biol. Lectures*, 1896-97. Ginn & Co., Boston, 1898, pp. 203-218.

The Breeding of Animals at Woods Holl during the Month of April, 1898. *Science*, May 20, 1898, N. S., Vol. 7, pp. 702-704.

Habits and Life History of the Starfish. I. *28th Rep. of the Com. of Inland Fisheries of R. I.*, 1898.

Habits and Life History of the Starfish. II. *29th Rep.*, *ibid.*, 1899.

Peridinium and the "Red Water" in Narragansett Bay. *Science*, Nov 18, 1898, N. S., Vol. 8, pp. 707-709.

The Cell Origin of the Prototroch. *Woods Holl Biol. Lectures*, 1899.

GEORGE F. METZLER: —

A.B., Albert College, Ontario, Can., 1880; Head Master, Port Dover High School, 1880-81; Professor of Mathematics, Albert College, 1881-84; A.M., Victoria College, 1888; Professor of Mathematics, Marietta College, 1889-90; Ph.D., Johns Hopkins University, 1891; Honorary Fellow in Psychology, Clark University, 1891-92; Docent in University of Chicago and Instructor in Mathematics, University of Michigan, 1892-93; University of Göttingen, 1893-94; University of Berlin, 1894-96; Associate in Mathematics, Queens College, 1896-97; Assistant Pastor Methodist Church, Newburgh, Can., 1897-98; Pastor of Methodist Church, Wilberforce, Canada, 1898–.

Author of: —

Equations and Variables Associated with the Linear Differential Equation. *Annals of Math.*, Vol. 9, pp. 171-178; Vol. 11, pp. 1-8.

Surfaces of Rotation with Constant Measure of Curvature and their Representation on the Hyperbolic (Cayley's) Plane. *Am. Jour. of Math.*, Jan., 1898, Vol. 20, pp. 76-86.

WILLIAM H. METZLER: —

A.B., University of Toronto, 1888; Science Master, Collegiate Institute, Ingersoll, Ont., 1888-89; Fellow in Mathematics, Clark University, 1889-92; Ph.D., Clark University, 1892; Instructor in Mathematics, Massachusetts Institute of Technology, 1892-94; Professor of Mathematics, Genesee Wesleyan Academy, 1894-95; Associate Professor of Mathematics, Syracuse University, 1895-96; Professor of Mathematics, *ibid.*, 1896–; Member of: American Association for the Advancement of Science; American Mathematical Society; Deutsche Mathematiker-Vereinigung; Mathematical Association (England); British Association for the Advancement of Science; London Mathematical Society.

Author of: —

On the Roots of Matrices. *Am. Jour. of Math.*, Oct., 1892, Vol. 14, pp. 326-377.

On Certain Properties of Symmetric, Skew Symmetric, and Orthogonal Matrices. *Ibid.*, July, 1893, Vol. 15, pp. 274–[illegible].

Homogeneous Strains. *Annals of Math.*, Vol. 8, No. 5.

On Compound Determinants. *Am. Jour. of Math.*, April, 1894, Vol. 16, pp. 131-160.

Matrices which Represent Vectors. *Technology Quarterly*, Vol. 6. No. 4.

Some Notes on Symmetric Functions. *Proc. London Math. Soc.*, March 11, 1897, Vol. 28, pp. [illegible].

Compound Determinants. *Am. Jour. of Math.*, July, 1898, Vol. 20, pp. [illegible]–373.

A Theorem in Determinants. *Ibid.*, July, 1898, Vol. 20, pp. 373–376.

On the Excess of the Number of Combinations in a set which have an even number of inversions over those which have an odd number. (In press.)

On the Roots of a Determinantal Equation. *Am. Jour. of Math.*, Oct., 1899, Vol. 21, pp. [illegible].

On a Determinant each of whose Elements is the Product of *K* Factors. (In press.)

On a Theorem in Determinants related to Laplace's. (In press.)

ADOLF MEYER:—

Maturitätsexamen, Gymnasium, Zürich, 1885; Medical Staatsexamen, Zürich, 1890; Graduate Student in Medicine, Paris, Edinburgh, and London, 1890–91; Neurological Work in the Laboratory of the Clinic of Psychiatry of Professor A. Forel, Zürich, 1891; Neurological Student, Vienna, 1892; M.D., University of Zürich, 1892; Docent in Neurology, University of Chicago, and Pathologist, Illinois Hospital for the Insane, 1893–95; Director of the clinical and laboratory work, Worcester Insane Hospital, 1895–; Docent in Psychiatry, Clark University, 1895–.

Author of:—

Medicinische Studien in Paris, Edinburgh, und London. *Correspondenz-Blatt für Schweizer Aerzte*, June 1, 1891, Vol. 21, pp. 350–351; June 15, pp. 381–[illegible]; July 1, pp. 417–420.

Ueber das Vorderhirn einiger Reptilien. *Zeitschrift für wissenschaftliche Zoologie*, 1892, Vol. 55, pp. 63–133, 2 pls.

Zur Homologie der Fornixcommissur und des Septum lucidum bei den Reptilien und Säugern. *Anatomischer Anzeiger*, March 16, 1895, Vol. 10, pp. 474–[illegible].

Neurological Work at Zürich. *Journal of Comparative Neurology*, 1893, Vol. 3, pp. 1–6, 41–44, 114–115.

How Can We Prepare Neurological Material to the Best Advantage? *Journal of Nervous and Mental Diseases*, May, 1894, Vol. 19, pp. 277–291.

Considerations on the Findings in the Spinal Cord of Three General Paralytics. *Am. Jour. of Insanity*, Jan., 1895, Vol. 51, pp. 374–378.

Mental Abnormalities in Children during Primary Education. *Trans. Ill. Soc. for Child Study*, Dec., 1894, Vol. 1, No. 1, pp. 48–58.

Schedule for the Study of Mental Abnormalities in Children. *Ibid.*, May, 1895, Vol. 1, No. 2, pp. 53–57.

On the Observation of Abnormalities of Children. *Child Study Monthly*, May, 1895, Vol. 1, pp. 1–12.

Report to the Governor of Illinois on the Treatment of the Insane. *Compilation of Special Reports, etc.*, Springfield, Ill., 1894, pp. 18–29.

A Few Demonstrations of Pathology of the Brain and Remarks on the Problems connected with Them. *Am. Jour. of Insanity*, Oct., 1895, Vol. 52, pp. 243–249, 5 pls.

On the Diseases of Women as a Cause of Insanity in the Light of Observations in Sixty-nine Autopsies. *Trans. of the Ill. State Med. Soc.*, 1895.

A Review of the Signs of Degeneration and of Methods of Registration. *Am. Jour. of Insanity*, Jan., 1895, Vol. 52, pp. 344–[illegible].

Pathological Report of the Illinois Eastern Hospital for the Insane at Kankakee, Ill. Chicago, 1895, pp. 1–[illegible], 16 pls.

A Case of Landry's Paralysis, with Autopsy. (With Dr. Th. Diller.) *Am. Jour. of the Medical Sciences*, April, 1898, Vol. 115, pp. 404–413.

Etiological, Clinical, and Pathological Factors in Diagnosis and Rational Classification of Infectious, Toxic, and Asthenic Diseases of the Peripheral Nerves, Spinal Cord, and Brain. *Medicine*, Detroit, Mich., Aug. 1896, Vol. 2, pp. 639–653.

A Short Sketch of the Problems of Psychiatry. *Am. Jour. of Insanity*, April, 1897, Vol. 53, pp. 538–549.

General Paralysis and Other Nervous and Mental Affections Following Syphilitic Infection. *Yale Medical Journal*, May, 1897, Vol. 3, pp. 311–317.

Demonstration of Various Types of Changes in the Giant Cells of the Paracentral Lobule. *Am. Jour. of Insanity*, Oct. 1897, Vol. 54, pp. 231–236, 3 pls.

Anatomical Findings in a Case of Facial Paralysis of Ten Days' Duration in a General Paralytic, with Remarks on the Termination of the "Auditory" Nerves. *Jour. of Experimental Medicine*, Nov. 1897, Vol. 2, pp. 607–610, 3 pls.

Special Report of the Medical Department of the Worcester Lunatic Hospital. Annual Report, Oct. 1898, pp. 30–37.

Critical Review of the Data and General Methods and Deductions of Modern Neurology. *Jour. of Comp. Neurology*, Nov.–Dec., 1898, Vol. 8, pp. 113–148; 249–313, 7 pls.

Critical Review of Recent Publications of Bethe and Nissl. *Ibid.*, March, 1899, Vol. 9, pp. 39–45.

Reviews in the *Neurologisches Centralblatt*, *Psychological Review*, *Am. Jour. of Insanity*, *Jour. of Nervous and Mental Disease*.

ARTHUR MICHAEL:—

University of Heidelberg, 1873–75; University of Berlin, 1875–78; École de Médecine, 1879–80; Professor of Chemistry, Tufts College, 1881–89; Ph.D. (Honorary), Tufts College, 1889; Professor of Chemistry, Clark University, Sept.–Dec., 1889; Research Work in England, 1890–94; Professor of Chemistry, Tufts College, 1894–.

Author of:—

Ueber die Einwirkung von Kaliumsulfhydrat auf Chloralhydrat. *Ber. d. deuts. chem. Gesellschaft*, 1876, Vol. 9, pp. 1267–1268.

Ueber die Darstellung und Eigenschaften des Trijodresorcins. (With T. H. Norton.) *Ibid.*, Vol. 9, pp. 1752–1753.

Ueber die Einwirkung von wasserentziehenden Mitteln auf Säureanhydride. (With S. Gabriel.) *Ibid.*, 1877, Vol. 10, pp. 391–393; 1551–1562, 2199–2210; 1878, Vol. 11, pp. 1007–1021, 1679–1683.

Zur Darstellung der Paramidobrombenzoesäure. *Ibid.*, 1877, Vol. 10, pp. 576–580.

Ueber die Diamidosulfobenzid-Dicarbonsäure. (With T. H. Norton.) *Ibid.*, Vol. 10, pp. 580–583.

Zur Kenntniss der aromatischen Sulfone. (With A. Adair.) *Ibid.*, Vol. 10, pp. 583–587.

Ueber die Einwirkung des Broms auf Aethylphtalimid. *Ibid.* Vol. 10, pp. 1644–1646.

Ueber die Einwirkung des Chlorjods auf aromatische Amine. (With L. M. Norton.) *Ibid.*, 1878, Vol. 11, pp. 107–116.

Zur Kenntniss der aromatischen Sulfone. (With A. Adair.) *Ibid.*, Vol. 11, pp. 116–121.

Ueber Benzylmethylglycolsäure. (With S. Gabriel.) *Ibid.*, 1879, Vol. 12, pp. 814–816.

On the Action of Iodine Monochloride upon Aromatic Acids. (With L. M. Norton.) *Am. Chem. Jour.*, 1879, Vol. 1, pp. 255–257.

On the Synthesis of Helicin and Phenolglucoside. *Ibid.*, Vol. 1, pp. 305–312.

On a New Formation of Stilbene and some of its Derivatives. *Ibid.*, Vol. 1, pp. 312–316.

On Mono-Ethylphthalate. *Ibid.*, 1880, Vol. 1, pp. 413–416.

On a New Formation of Ethyl-Mustard Oil. *Ibid.*, Vol. 1, pp. 416–418.

On the Preparation of Methyl Aldehyde. *Ibid.*, Vol. 1, pp. 418–420.

On the "Migration of Atoms in the Molecule" and Reimer's Chloroform Aldehyde Reaction. *Ibid.*, Vol. 1, pp. 420–426.

On α- and β-Monochlorcrotonic Acids. (With L. M. Norton.) *Ibid.*, Vol. 2, pp. 11–19.

Preliminary Note on the Synthesis of Methylconine and Constitution of Conine. (With Charles Gundelach.) *Ibid.*, Vol. 2, pp. 171–172.

Ueber die Einwirkung von aromatischen Oxysäuren auf Phenole. *Ber. d. deuts. chem. Gesellschaft*, 1881, Vol. 14, pp. 656–658.

Ueber die Synthese des Methylarbutins. *Ibid.* Vol. 14, pp. 2097–2102.

Zur Kenntniss des Paraconilins. *Ibid.*, Vol. 14, pp. 2105–2110.

Ueber die Synthese des Salicins und des Anhydrosalicylglucosids. *Ibid.*, 1882, Vol. 15, pp. 1922–1925.

On the Action of Aromatic Oxy-acids on Phenols. *Am. Chem. Jour.*, 1883, Vol. 5, pp. 81–97.

On Some Properties of Phenylsulphonacetic Ethers. (With A. M. Comey.) *Ibid.*, Vol. 5, pp. 116–119.

Synthetical Researches in the Glucoside Group. *Ibid.*, Vol. 5, pp. 171–182.

On the Formation of Crotonic and β-Oxybutyric Aldehydes from Ethyl Aldehyde. (With Adolph Kopp.) *Ibid.*, Vol. 5, pp. 182–191.

On the Action of Sodium Ethyl Oxide on Bromethylidenebromide. *Ibid.*, Vol. 5, pp. 192–197.

A New Synthesis of Allantoin and Some Suggestions on the Constitution of Uric Acid. *Ibid.*, Vol. 5, pp. 198–202.

On a Convenient Method for Preparing Bromacetic Acid. *Ibid.*, Vol. 5, pp. 202–203.

On Several Cases of Intermolecular Rearrangement. *Ibid.*, Vol. 5, pp. 203–206.

On a New Synthesis of Cinnamic Acid. *Ibid.*, Vol. 5, pp. 206–208.

On the Action of Aldehydes on Phenols. *Ibid.*, Vol. 5, pp. 338–349.

Action of Ethylaldehyde on Orcin and Resorcin. (With A. M. Comey.) *Ibid.*, Vol. 5, pp. 349–353.

Some Convenient Quantitative Lecture Apparatus. *Ibid.*, Vol. 5, pp. 353–359.

Observations on the Action of Acetylchloride and Acetic Anhydride on Corn and Wheat Starch. *Ibid.*, Vol. 5, pp. 359–360.

On the Constitution of Benzcyanin. *Ibid.*, Vol. 5, pp. 434–440.

Ueber die optisch-inactive Asparaginsäure. (With J. F. Wing.) *Ber. d. deuts. chem. Gesellschaft*, 1884, Vol. 17, p. 2984.

On the Action of Sodium Phenylsulphinate on Methylene Iodide. (With G. M. Palmer.) *Am. Chem. Jour.*, 1884, Vol. 6, pp. 253–257.

On the Conversion of Organic Isocyanates into Mustard Oils. (With G. M. Palmer.) *Ibid.*, Vol. 6, pp. 257–260.

Synthetical Researches in the Glucoside Group. *Ibid.*, Vol. 6, pp. 336–340.

On the Action of Methyl Iodide on Asparagine. (With J. F. Wing.) *Ibid.*, 1885, Vol. 6, pp. 419–422.

On Some Properties of Phenylsulphonacetic Ethers. (With G. M. Palmer.) *Ibid.*, Vol. 7, pp. 65–71.

Note on the Constitution of the Addition-Product of Chlorhydric Acid to Ethylcyanide. (With J. F. Wing.) *Ibid.*, Vol. 7, pp. 71–74.

On the Decomposition of Cinchonine by Sodium Ethylate. *Ibid.*, Vol. 7, pp. 182–189.

On Simultaneous Oxidation and Reduction by Means of Hydrocyanic Acid. (With G. M. Palmer.) *Ibid.*, Vol. 7, pp. 189–194.

On the Action of Alkyl Iodides on Amido Acids. (With J. F. Wing.) *Ibid.*, Vol. 7, pp. 195–198.

On Benzacetophenone. (With G. M. Palmer.) *Ibid.*, Vol. 7, pp. 275–277.

On Inactive Aspartic Acid. (With J. F. Wing.) *Ibid.*, Vol. 7, pp. 278–281.

Ueber die Einwirkung von Fünffach-Chlorphosphor auf die Aether organischer Säuren. *Ber. d. deuts. chem. Gesellschaft*, 1886, Vol. 19, pp. 845–847.

Ueber einen Zusammenhang zwischen Anilidbildung und der Constitution ungesättigter, mehrbasischer, organischer Säuren. *Ibid.*, Vol. 19, pp. 1372–1375.

Ueber einen Zusammenhang zwischen Anilidbildung und der Constitution ungesättigter, mehrbasischer, organischer Säuren. (With G. M. Palmer.) *Ibid.*, Vol. 19, pp. 1375–1376.

Ueber die Einwirkung des Anilins auf die Brommalein- und Chlorfumarsäure. *Ibid.*, Vol. 19, pp. 1377–1378.

Zur Isomerie in der Zimmtsäurereihe. (With G. M. Browne.) *Ibid.*, Vol. 19, pp. 1378–1381.

Zur Isomerie in der Fettreihe. *Ibid.*, Vol. 19, pp. 1381–1386.

Ueber die Nitrirung des Phenylhydrazins. *Ibid.*, Vol. 19, pp. 1386–1388.

Zur Kenntniss der Einwirkung von Aldehyden auf Phenole. (With J. P. Ryder.) *Ibid.*, Vol. 19, pp. 1388–1390.

Die Citraconsäure als Reagens zur Erkennung und Scheidung der aromatischen Amine. *Ibid.*, Vol. 19, pp. 1390–1392.

Ueberführung der α-Bromzimmtäther in Benzoylessigäther. (With G. M. Browne.) *Ibid.*, Vol. 19, pp. 1392–1393.

Zur Isomerie in der Zimmtsäurereihe. (With G. M. Browne.) *Ibid.*, 1887, Vol. 20, pp. 550–556.

Bemerkungen zu einer Abhandlung des Hrn. L. Claisen. *Ibid.*, Vol. 20, pp. 1572–1573.

On the Addition of Sodium Acetacetic Ether and Analogous Sodium Compounds to Unsaturated Organic Ethers. *Am. Chem. Jour.*, 1887, Vol. 9, pp. 112–124.

On Some New Reactions with Sodium Acetacetic and Sodium Malonic Ethers. *Ibid.*, Vol. 9, pp. 124–129.

On the Action of Aldehydes on Phenols. (With J. P. Ryder.) *Ibid.*, Vol. 9, pp. 130–137.

Researches on Alloisomerism. *Ibid.*, Vol. 9, pp. 180–183.

A Relation between the Constitution of Polybasic Unsaturated Organic Acids and the Formation of their Anilides. *Ibid.*, Vol. 9, pp. 183–197.

A Relation between the Constitution of Polybasic Unsaturated Organic Acids and the Formation of their Anilides. (With G. M. Palmer.) *Ibid.*, Vol. 9, pp. 197–204.

On the Action of Phosphorus Pentachloride on the Ethers of Organic Acids, and on some Derivatives of Acetic Acid. *Ibid.*, Vol. 9, pp. 205–217.

On the Action of Phosphorus Pentachloride on Acetanilide. *Ibid.*, Vol. 9, pp. 217–219.

Preliminary Notes. *Ibid.*, Vol. 9, pp. 219–223.

Researches on Alloisomerism. (With G. M. Browne.) *Ibid.*, Vol. 9, pp. 274–289.

Remarks on the Constitution of Levulinic and Maleic Acids. *Ibid.*, Vol. 9, pp. 364–372.

Ueber eine bequeme Darstellungsweise von bromirten Fettsäuren. *Jour. f. praktische Chemie*, 1887, Vol. 35, pp. 92–95.

Das Verhalten von Essigsäure und einigen Derivaten derselben gegen Fünffach-Chlorphosphor. *Ibid.*, Vol. 35, pp. 95–96.

Ueber die Constitution der Trimethylentricarbonsäure. *Ibid.*, Vol. 35, pp. 132–136.

Zur Kenntniss der Einwirkung des Fünffach-Chlorphosphors auf Acetanilid. *Ibid.*, Vol. 35, pp. 207–208.

Ueber die Bildung des Indigblaus aus Orthonitrophenylpropiolsäure mittelst Cyankalium. *Ibid.*, Vol. 35, pp. 254–256.

Ueber Alloisomerie in der Crotonsäurereihe. (With G. M. Browne.) *Ibid.*, Vol. 35, pp. 257–260.

Ueber die Addition von Natriumacetessig- und Natriummalonsäureäthern zu den Aethern ungesättigter Säuren. *Ibid.*, Vol. 35, pp. 349–356.

Die Reduction von Alpha- und Alloalpha-bromzimmtsäuren zu Zimmtsäure. *Ibid.*, Vol. 35, pp. 357–358.

Ueber aromatische Hydroxylamine. (With G. M. Browne.) *Ibid.*, Vol. 35, pp. 358–359.

Ueber neue Reactionen mit Natriumacetessig- und Natriummalonsäureäther. *Ibid.*, Vol. 35, pp. 449–459.

Ueber das Verhalten von Oxalsäureäther zu Resorcin. *Ibid.*, Vol. 35, pp. 510–512.

Antwort auf eine Bemerkung von L. Claisen. *Ibid.*, Vol. 36, pp. 113–114.

Zur Isomerie in der Crotonsäurereihe. (With G. M. Browne.) *Ibid.*, Vol. 36, pp. 174–176.

Zur Constitution des Natriumacetessigäthers. *Ibid.*, 1888, Vol. 37, pp. 473–530.

Ueber das Verhalten von Natriummalonäther gegen Resorcinol. *Ibid.*, Vol. 37, pp. 469–471.

Zur Alloisomerie in der Crotonsäurereihe. (With H. Pendleton.) *Ibid.*, Vol. 38, pp. 1–6.

Zur Kritik der Abhandlung von J. Wislicenus: "Ueber die räumliche Anordnung der Atome in organischen Molekülen." *Ibid.*, Vol. 38, pp. 6–39.

Preliminary Note on the Constitution of Sodium Acetacetic and Malonic Ethers. *Am. Chem. Jour.*, 1888, Vol. 10, pp. 158–160.

Bemerkung zu der Abhandlung von Otto und Rössing über die Ersetzbarkeit des Natriums im Natriumphenylsulfonessigäther durch Alkyle. *Ber. d. deuts. chem. Gesellschaft*, 1890, Vol. 23, pp. 669–671.

On the Constitution of Sodium Acetacetic Ether. *Am. Chem. Jour.*, 1892, Vol. 14, pp. 481–544.

On the Action of Acetic Anhydride on Phenylpropiolic Acid. (With J. E. Bucher.) *Ibid.*, 1898, Vol 20, pp. 89–120.

On the Formation of Imido-1, 2-Diazo Derivatives from Aromatic Azimides and Esters of Acetylenecarboxylic Acids. (With F. Luehn and H. H. Higbee.) *Ibid.*, Vol. 20, pp. 377–395.

Zur Schmelzpunktsbestimmung von hochschmelzenden und sogen. unschmelzbaren organischen Verbindungen. *Ber. d. deuts. chem. Gesellschaft*, 1895, Vol. 28, pp. 1629–1633.

Ueber die Addition von Schwefel an ungesättigten organischen Verbindungen. *Ibid.*, Vol. 28, pp. 1633–1637.

Ueber die Einwirkung von Essigsäureanhydrid auf Säuren der Acetylenreihe. (With J. E. Bucher.) *Ibid.*, Vol. 28, pp. 2511–2512.

Einwirkung v. Aethyljodid u. Zink auf α β-Fettsäuren. *Ibid.*, Vol. 29, p. 1791.

Zur Kenntniss der Additionsvorgänge bei den Natriumderivaten von Formyl- und Acetessigestern, und Nitroalkanen. *Ibid.*, Vol. 29, pp. 1794–1799.

Zur Constitution der Oxalessigsäure. (With J. E. Bucher.) *Ibid.*, Vol. 29, pp. 1792–1793.

Ueber die Regelmässigkeiten bei der Anlagerung von Halogenverbindungen an ungesättigten Säuren. *Jour. f. prakt. Chemie*, 1889, Vol. 40, pp. 171–179.

Ueber die Einwirkung von Jodwasserstoff auf die Krotonsäuren. *Ibid.*, Vol. 40, pp. 95–96.

Zur Kenntniss der Lävulinsäure und des Acetondiessigsäuredilaktons. *Ibid.*, Vol. 43, pp. 113–130.

Ueber die Addition von Natriumacetessig- und Natriummalonsäureäthern zu den Aethern ungesättigter Säuren. (With P. C. Freer.) *Ibid.*, Vol. 43, pp. 390–395.

Zur Kenntniss der Halogenwasserstoffentziehung bei organischen α β-Halogensäureäthern. (With O. Schulthess.) *Ibid.*, Vol. 43, pp. 587–595.

Ueber die Addition von Brom an Acetylendicarbonsäure und deren Alkyläther. *Ibid.*, Vol. 46, pp. 210–233.

Ueber die Einwirkung von Natriumäthylat auf Dibrombernsteinsäureäther. (With C. C. Maisch.) *Ibid.*, Vol. 46, pp. 233–238.

Ueber die Crotonsäure und Derivate derselben. (With O. Schnitzlein.) *Ibid.*, Vol. 46, pp. 256–265.

Ueber die Bildung von fester Crotonsäure bei der Reduction von allo-α-Brom- und-chlorcrotonsäure. *Ibid.*, Vol. 46, pp. 265–272.

Beiträge zur Kenntniss einiger Homologen der Aepfelsäure. (With G. Timot.) *Ibid.*, Vol. 46, pp. 285–304.

Ueber die Addition von Chlor an mehrbasischen, ungesättigten Fettsäuren. (With G. Timot.) *Ibid.*, Vol. 46, pp. 391–427.

Ueber die Addition von Natriumacetessig- und Natriummacetmalonäther zu den Aethern ungesättigter Säuren. *Ibid.*, Vol. 49, pp. 20–24.

Beiträge zur Kenntniss der Ringbildung bei organischen, stickstoffhaltigen Verbindungen. *Ibid.*, Vol. 49, pp. 26–43.

Untersuchungen über Alloisomerie. *Ibid.*, Vol. 49, pp. 259–272.

Ueber das Verhalten von Benzaldehyd gegen Phenol. *Ibid.*, Vol. 57, 634–636.

Ueber einige Gesetze und deren Anwendung in der organischen Chemie. *Ibid.*, Vol. 60, pp. 286–470.

ALBERT A. MICHELSON :—

Midshipman, U. S. Naval Academy, 1873; Instructor in Physics and Chemistry, *ibid.*, 1875–79; Nautical Almanac Office, Washington, 1880; University of Berlin, 1880; University of Heidelberg, 1881; Collège de France, École Polytechnique, 1882; Professor of Physics, Case School of Applied Science, Cleveland, O., 1883–89; Corresponding Member, British Association for the Advancement of Science, 1884; Associate Fellow of American Academy of Arts and Sciences, 1885; Ph.D. (Honorary), Western Reserve University, 1886; and Stevens Institute, 1887; Vice-President, American Association for the Advancement of Science, *ibid.*; Member of National Academy of Sciences, 1888; Rumford Medal, 1889; Professor of Physics, Clark University, 18[illegible]–9[illegible]; Head Professor of Physics, University of Chicago, 1892–; Bureau International des Poids et Mesures, 189[illegible]–93; Member, Société Française de Physique, 18[illegible]; Fellow, Royal Astronomical Society, 18[illegible]; Foreign Member, Société Hollandaise des Sciences, 1897; Honorary Member, Cambridge Philosophical Society, *ibid.*; Member (for the United States) of the International Committee of Weights and Measures, *ibid.*; Lowell Lecturer, 1899; Sc.D. (Honorary), University of Cambridge (England); Honorary Member Royal Institute, 1899.

Author of :—

Experimental Determination of the Velocity of Light. Papers I. and II. *Proc. A. A. A. S.*, 1879 and 1880.

The Relative Motion of the Earth and the Luminiferous Ether. *Am. Jour. of Sci.*, 1881, Vol. 2[illegible], pp. 120–129.

A New Sensitive Thermometer. *Jour. de Physique*, 18[illegible].

Interference Phenomena in a New Form of Refractometer. *Am. Jour. of Sci.*, May, 18[illegible], Vol. 2[illegible], pp. [illegible]–400.

A Method of Determining the Rate of Tuning-Forks. *Am. Jour. of Sci.*, Jan., 18[illegible].

Experimental Determination of the Velocity of Light. Third Paper. Astron. Papers, *Nautical Almanac*, Vol. 2.

Velocity of Light in Carbon Disulphide and Velocity of Red and Blue Light in Same. *Ibid.*

M. Wolf's Modification of Foucault's Apparatus for the Measurement of the Velocity of Light. *Nature*, May 7, 18[illegible], Vol. 32, pp. 6–7.

Influence of Motion of the Medium on the Velocity of Light. *Am. Jour. of Sci.*, May, 1886, Vol. 31, pp. [illegible]–[illegible].

On the Relative Motion of the Earth and the Luminiferous Ether. (With E. W. Morley.) *Philosophical Magazine*, 5th ser., Dec., 1887, Vol. 24, pp. 449–463.

On a Method for Making the Wave Length of Sodium Light the Actual and Practical Standard of Length. (With E. W. Morley.) *Am. Jour. of Sci.*, Dec., 1887, Vol. 34, pp. 427–430. *Philosophical Magazine*, 5th ser., Dec., 1887, Vol. 24, pp. 463–466.

On the Feasibility of Establishing a Light Wave as the Ultimate Standard of Length. (With E. W. Morley.) *Am. Jour. of Sci.*, 3rd ser., Sept., 1889, Vol. 38, pp. 181–186.

Measurement by Light Waves. *Ibid.*, Feb., 1890, Vol. 39, pp. 115–121.

A Simple Interference Experiment. *Ibid.*, March, 1890, Vol. 39, pp. 216–218.

Application of Interference Methods to Astronomical Measurements. *Philosophical Magazine*, 5th ser., July, 1890, Vol. 30, pp. 1–21.

Visibility of Interference Fringes in the Focus of a Telescope. *Ibid.*, March, 1891, Vol. 31, pp. 256–259.

Application of Interference Methods to Spectroscopic Measurements. *Ibid.*, April, 1891, Vol. 31, pp. 338–346.

Measurement of Jupiter's Satellites by Interference. *Mem. Astr. Soc. of the Pacific*, 1891.

Les méthodes interférentielles en métrologie et l'établissement d'une longueur d'onde comme unité absolue de longueur. *Rév. Gén. des Sciences*, 30 Juin, 1893. Translation in *Nature*, Nov. 16, 1893. Abstracts in *Comptes Rendus* and *Soc. de Physique*.

Détermination expérimentale de la valeur du mètre en longueur d'ondes lumineuses. *Travaux et Mémoires du Bureau International des Poids et Mesures*, Paris, 1894, Vol. 11, pp. 3–85.

On the Broadening of Spectral Lines by Temperature and Pressure. *Astrophysical Journal*, Nov., 1895.

On the Conditions which Affect the Spectrum Photography of the Sun. *Ibid.*, Jan., 1896.

On the Limit of Visibility of Fine Lines in a Telescope. *Ibid.*, June, 1896.

The Relative Motion of the Earth and the Ether. *Am. Jour. of Sci.*, 4th ser., 1897, Vol. 3, pp. 475–478.

Radiation in a Magnetic Field. *Philosophical Magazine*, 5th ser., July, 1897, Vol. 44, pp. 109–115.

A New Harmonic Analyser. (With S. W. Stratton.) *Am. Jour. of Sci.*, 4th ser., Jan., 1898, Vol. 5, pp. 1–13.

A Spectroscope without Prisms or Gratings. *Ibid.*, 4th ser., March, 1898, Vol. 5, pp. 215–217.

Radiation in a Magnetic Field. *Astrophysical Journal*, Feb., 1898.

The Echelon Spectroscope. *Ibid.*, June, 1898.

Nouvelle Méthode de tracer et d'observer des divisions de précision, formées par des traits lumineux sur fond noir. *Travaux et Mémoires du Bureau International des Poids et Mesures*, Paris, 1899.

DICKINSON SERGEANT MILLER:

University of Pennsylvania, 1885–89; Fellow in Philosophy, Clark University, 1889–90; Morgan Fellow, Harvard University, 1890–91; Walker Fellow, *ibid.*, 1891–92; A.B. and A.M., *ibid.*, 1892; University of Berlin, 1892–93; Ph.D., University of Halle, 1893; Associate in Philosophy, Bryn Mawr College, 1893–98; Instructor, Harvard University, for the year 1899–1900; Member of American Psychological Association.

Author of:—

The Meaning of Truth and Error. *Philosophical Review*, July, 1893, Vol. 2, pp. 408–425.

The Confusion of Function and Content in Mental Analysis. *Proc. Am. Psy. Ass'n*, Dec., 1893, and *Psychological Review*, Nov., 1895, Vol. 2, pp. 535–550.

The Relations of "Ought" and "Is." *Internat. Jour. of Ethics*, July, 1894, Vol. 4, pp. 499–512.

Desire as the Essence of Pleasure. *Proc. Am. Psy. Ass'n*, Dec., 1894. *Psychological Review*, March, 1895, Vol. 2, pp. 164–165.

"The Will to Believe" and the Duty to Doubt. *Internat. Jour. of Ethics*, Jan., 1899, Vol. 9, pp. 169–195.

Professor James on Philosophical Method. *Philosophical Review*, March, 1899, Vol. 8, pp. 165–179.

WILLIAM S. MILLER:—

M.D., Yale Medical School, 1879; Practising Physician, *ibid.*, 1879–86; College of Physicians and Surgeons, New York, 1886–87; Lecturer in Microscopical Technique, Mt. Holyoke College, 1887–88; Pathologist, City Hospital and Memorial Hospital, Worcester, Mass., 1888–91; Scholar in Anatomy, Clark University, 1889–91; Fellow, 1891–92; Instructor in Biology, University of Wisconsin, 1892–93; Instructor in Vertebrate Anatomy, *ibid.*, 1893–95; on leave of absence, University of Leipzig, 1895–96; Assistant Professor of Vertebrate Anatomy, University of Wisconsin, 1895–; Fellow, Massachusetts Medical Society, Fellow, A. A. A. S.; Member Anatomische Gesellschaft, Member Wisconsin Academy of Arts and Sciences.

Author of:—

The Lobule of the Lung and its Blood-Vessels. *Anat. Anzeiger*, 1892, Vol. 7, pp. 181–190.

The Structure of the Lung. *Jour. of Morph.*, April, 1893, Vol. 8, pp. 165–188.

On the So-called Inner Eyes. *Science*, Feb. 10, 1893, Vol. 21, pp. 74–75.

The Anatomy of the Lung. *Ref. Handbook of the Med. Sciences*, 1893, Vol. 9, pp. 671–678.

The Anatomy of the Heart of Cambarus. *Trans. Wis. Acad. of Sciences, Arts, and Letters*, 1895, Vol. 10, pp. 327–338.

The Relation between the Cortex and Medulla in the Cat's Kidney, and an Estimation of the Number of Glomeruli. *Ibid.*, pp. 525–538.

The Lymphatics of the Lung. *Anat. Anzeiger*, June 4, 1896, Vol. 12, pp. 110–114.

HALCOTT C. MORENO:—

A.B., University of Georgia, 1893; A.M., *ibid.*, 1894; B.L., *ibid.*, 1895; Tutor in Mathematics, *ibid.*, 1895–97; Scholar in Mathematics, Clark University 1897–98; Fellow, 1898–99.

SAMUEL P. MULLIKEN:—

S.B., Massachusetts Institute of Technology, 1887; Assistant in Chemistry, University of Cincinnati, 1887–88; Graduate Student, University of Leipzig, 1888–90; Ph.D., University of Leipzig, 1890; Fellow in Chemistry, Clark University, Jan.–June, 1891; Associate in Chemistry, Bryn Mawr College, 1891–92; Instructor in Chemistry, Clark University, 1892–94; Research Assistant to Professor Wolcott Gibbs, Newport, R. I., 1894–95; Instructor in Organic Chemistry, Massachusetts Institute of Technology, 1895–.

Author of:—

Ueber die Konstitution der Chlorzimmtsäuren. (Inaugural-dissertation der Universität Leipzig.) Leipzig, 1890. 57 pp.

The Geometrical Isomerism of the Chlorcinnamic Acids. *Technology Quarterly*, 1891, Vol. 4, pp. 170–177.

A New Class of Organic Electrosyntheses. *Am. Chem. Jour.*, June, 1893, Vol. 15, pp. 323–332.

Laboratory Experiments on the Class Reactions of Organic Substances and their Identification. (With A. A. Noyes.) First edition, 17 pp., Maclachlan, Boston, 1895; second edition, 69 pp., 1897, and third edition, 80 pp., 1898. Chem. Publishing Company, Easton, Pa.

A Simple Color Reaction for Methyl Alcohol. (With H. Scudder.) *Am. Chem. Jour.*, March, 1899, Vol. 21, pp. 266–271.

Reactions for the Detection of the Nitro-group. (With E. R. Barker.) *Ibid.*, pp. 271–276.

F. WILLIAM MUTHMANN:—

Assistant in Analytical Chemistry, University of Munich, 1884–86; Ph.D., University of Munich, 1886; Instructor in

Chemistry and Crystallography, *ibid.*, 1887–89; Docent in Chemistry, Clark University, 1889–91; Assistant in Chemistry, Academy of Science, Munich, 1891–94; Docent in Chemistry, University of Munich, 1894–95; Professor of Inorganic and Analytical Chemistry, *ibid.*, 1895–.

Author of:—

Ueber niedere Oxyde des Molybdäns. (Inaugural dissertation.) *Liebig's Annalen*, 1887, Vol. 238, pp. 108–137.

Ueber Polymorphie und Mischkrystalle einiger organischer Substanzen. *Zeits. f. Krystallographie*, 1889, Vol. 15, pp. 60–79.

Krystallographisch-chemische Notizen. *Ibid.*, 1889, Vol. 15, pp. 387–402.

Krystallographische Untersuchung der Phtalsäure, und einiger Derivate derselben. (With W. Ramsay.) *Ibid.*, 1889, Vol. 17, pp. 73–84.

Messelit, ein neues Mineral. *Ibid.*, 1889, Vol. 17, pp. 93–94.

Untersuchungen über den Schwefel und das Selen. *Ibid.*, 1890, Vol. 17, pp. 336–367.

Zur Frage der Silberoxydulverbindungen. *Ber. d. deuts. chem. Gesellschaft*, 1887, Vol. 20, pp. 983–990.

Krystallographische Untersuchung einiger Derivate der Terephtalsäure. *Zeits. f. Krystallographie*, 1890, Vol. 17, pp. 460–483.

Ueber Isomorphismus einiger organischer Substanzen. *Ibid.*, 1891, Vol. 19, pp. 357–367.

Bemerkung über den rothen Phosphor. *Zeits. f. anorg. Chemie*, 1893, Vol. 4, pp. 303–304.

Untersuchungen über das Selen. (With Dr. J. Schäfer.) *Ber. d. deuts. chem. Gesellschaft*, 1893, Vol. 26, pp. 1008–1016.

Eine bequeme Methode zur Darstellung von Baryumpermanganat. *Ibid.*, pp. 1016–1018.

Ueber die Reindarstellung von Rubidiumsalzen. *Ibid.*, pp. 1019–1020.

Berichtigung. *Ibid.*, pp. 1425–1426.

Beiträge zur Volumtheorie der krystallisirten Körper. *Zeits. f. Krystallographie*, 1894, Vol. 22, pp. 497–551.

Ueber die Löslichkeit der Mischkrystalle einiger isomorpher Salzpaare. (With Dr. O. Kuntze.) *Ibid.*, 1894, Vol. 23, pp. 368–378.

Ueber den sogenannten Schneebergit. *Ibid.*, 1895, Vol. 24, pp. 583–586.

Schwefelstickstoff. *Ber. d. deuts. chem. Gesellschaft*, 1896, Vol. 29, pp. 340–343.

Zur quant. Best. und Scheidung des Kupfers. *Zeits. f. anorg. Chemie*, 1896, Vol. 11, pp. 268–271.

Ueber einige Verbindungen des Phosphors und Selens. *Ibid.*, Vol. 13, pp. 191–199.

Stickstoffpentasulfid. *Ibid.*, Vol. 13, pp. 200–206.

Löslichkeit des Schwefels Caroxydals in Wasser. *Ibid.*, 1897, Vol. 16, pp. 460–462.

Zusammensetzung einiger Tellurmineralien. *Zeits. f. Krystallographie*, 1893, Vol. 22, pp. 140–145.

Ueber Permolybdate. *Zeits. f. anorg. Chemie*, 1898, Vol. 17, pp. 73–81. Also *Ber. d. deuts. chem. Gesellschaft*, 1898, Vol. 31, pp. 1836–1844.

Doppelthiosulfate von Kupfer und Kalium. *Ber. d. deuts. chem. Gesellschaft*, 1898, Vol. 31, pp. 1732–1734.

JOHN U. NEF:—

A.B., Harvard University (with Honors in Chemistry), 1884; Kirkland Fellow, *ibid.*, 1884–87; University of Munich, 1884–87; Ph.D., University of Munich, 1886; Professor and Director of Chemical Laboratory, Purdue University, 1887–89; Assistant Professor of Chemistry, Clark University, 1889–92; Professor of Chemistry and Director of the Kent Chemical Laboratory, University of Chicago, 1892–96; Head Professor of Chemistry and Director of the Kent Chemical Laboratory, ibid., 1896–.

Author of:—

The Volumetric Determination of Combined Nitrous Acid. (With Dr. Kinnicoll.) *Am. Chem. Jour.*, Nov. 1883, Vol. 5, pp. 388-389.

Ueber einige Derivate des Durols. *Ber. d. deuts. chem. Gesellschaft*, 1885, Vol. 18, pp. 2801-2807.

Ueber Benzochinoncarbonsäuren. *Ibid.*, pp. 3496-3499.

Ueber Benzochinoncarbonsäuren. *Liebig's Annalen*, 1887, Vol. 237, pp. 1-39.

Ueber Py-3-Phenylchinaldinsäure und Py-3-Phenylchinolin. (With Dr. Koenigs.) *Ber. d. deuts. chem. Gesellschaft*, 1886, Vol. 19, pp. 2427-2432.

Ueber das Py-3-Phenylchinolin und Py-3-B-Dichinolyl. (With Dr. Koenigs.) *Ibid.*, 1887, Vol. 20, pp. 622-628.

Notiz über die Cinchoninsäure. (With W. Meihmann.) *Ibid.*, 1887, Vol. 20, pp. 628-633.

Nitranilsäure aus Chloranil. *Ibid.*, 1887, Vol. 20, pp. 2027-2031.

On Tautomeric Compounds. Part I. *Am. Chem. Jour.*, Jan., 1889, Vol. 11, pp. 1-17.

The Constitution of the Anilic Acids. *Ibid.*, pp. 17-28.

Ueber tautomere Körper. *Liebig's Annalen*, 1890, Vol. 258, pp. 261-318.

Die Constitution des Benzochinons. *Jour. f. praktische Chemie*, 1890, Vol. 42, pp. 161-188.

On Tautomeric Compounds. Part II. *Am. Chem. Jour.*, June, 1890, Vol. 12, pp. 379-425.

The Constitution of Benzoquinone. Part I. *Ibid.*, July, 1890, Vol. 12, pp. 463-488.

Zur Kenntniss des Acetessigäthers. *Liebig's Annalen*, 1891, Vol. 266, pp. 52-138.

The Constitution of Benzoquinone. Part II. *Am. Chem. Jour.*, June, 1891, Vol. 13, pp. 422-428.

Ueber das zweiwerthige Kohlenstoffatom. Erste Abh. *Liebig's Annalen*, 1892, Vol. 270, pp. 267-335. Also in *Proc. of Am. Acad. of Arts and Sciences*, on Bivalent Carbon, for 1892, Vol. 27, pp. 102-162.

Zur Kenntniss des Acetessigäthers. *Liebig's Annalen*, 1893, Vol. 276, pp. 200-245.

Ueber die 1.3 Diketone. *Ibid.*, 1893, Vol. 277, pp. 59-78.

Ueber die Constitution der Salze der Nitroparaffine. *Ibid.*, 1894, Vol. 280, pp. 263-291. Also in *Proc. of Am. Acad. of Arts and Sciences*, 1894, Vol. 30, pp. 134-150.

Ueber das zweiwerthige Kohlenstoffatom. Zweite Abh. *Liebig's Annalen*, 1894, Vol. 280, pp. 291-342. Also in *Proc. of Am. Acad. of Arts and Sciences*, 1894, Vol. 30, pp. 151-193.

Ueber das zweiwerthige Kohlenstoffatom. Dritte Abh. Die Chemie des Cyans und des Isocyans. *Liebig's Annalen*, 1895, Vol. 287, pp. 265-359.

Ueber das zweiwerthige Kohlenstoffatom. Vierte Abh. Die Chemie des Methylens. *Ibid.*, 1897, Vol. 298, pp. 202-374.

Notiz über die Formhydroxamsäure. *Ber. d. deuts. chem. Gesellschaft*, 1898, Vol. 31, pp. 2720-2721.

Ueber das Phenylacetylen, seine Salze, und seine Halogen Substitutions Produkte. *Liebig's Annalen der Chemie*, 1899, Vol. 308, pp. 264-328.

Ueber das Verhalten der tri- und tetrahalogen-substituirten Methane. *Ibid.*, 1899, Vol. 308, pp. 329-333.

Dissociationsvorgänge bei den Alkyläthern der Salpetersäure, der Schwefelsäure und der Halogenwasserstoffsäuren. *Ibid.*, 1899, Vol. 309, pp. 126-189.

HERBERT NICHOLS :—

B.S., Worcester Polytechnic Institute, 1871; Fellow in Psychology, Clark University, 1889-91; Ph.D., Clark University, 1891; Instructor in Psychology, Harvard University, 1891-93; Lecturer in Psychology, Johns Hopkins University, 1895-96; Member American Society of Naturalists, 1890; Member American Psychological Association, 1892.

Author of :—

The Psychology of Time. *Am. Jour. of Psy.*, Feb., 1891, Vol. 3, pp. 453-529;

April, 1891, Vol. 4, pp. 60–119. Henry Holt & Co., N. Y., 1891, 140 pp.

The Origin of Pleasure and Pain. *Philosophical Review*, July, 1892, Vol. 1., pp. 403–432; Sept., 1892, Vol. 1., pp. 518–534.

Experiments upon Pain. *Report First An. Mtg. Am. Psy. Assn.*, Dec., 1892. Macmillan & Co., N. Y., 1894.

Perceptions of Rotation. *Ibid.*, Dec., 1892. Macmillan & Co., N. Y., 1894.

Primary Education. *Report Special Correspondence*, Feb., 1893. Educational Club, Philadelphia, 1893.

The Harvard Psychological Laboratory. *McClure's Magazine*, Oct., 1893, Vol. 1, pp. 399–409.

The Promise in Mental Science. *Ibid.*, Jan., 1894, Vol. 2, pp. 202–208.

Beiträge zur Psychologie des Zeitsinns, und Untersuchungen zur Psychologie und Æsthetik des Rhythmus. By Ernst Meumann. Review. *Psychological Review*, Nov., 1894, Vol. 1, pp. 638–641.

Our Notions of Number and Space. Ginn & Co., Boston, 1894. 201 pp.

The Motor Power of Ideas. *Philosophical Review*, March, 1895, Vol. 4, pp. 174–185.

William James. (Biographical Sketch.) *The Book Buyer*, March, 1895, Vol. 12, pp. 61–63.

The "Feelings." *Philosophical Review*, Sept., 1895, Vol. 4, pp. 506–530.

Pain Nerves. (Discussion.) *Psychological Review*, Sept., 1895, Vol. 2, 487–490.

Psychology and Education. *The Citizen*, Dec., 1895, Vol. 1, pp. 229–230. University Extension Study, Philadelphia.

Pain Nerves. (Discussion.) *Psychological Review*, May, 1896, Vol. 3, pp. 309–313.

Fear. By Angelo Mosso. Review. *Ibid.*, July, 1896, Vol. 3, pp. 446–447.

Ueber Raumwahrnehmungen im Gebiete des Tastsinnes. By Chas. Hubbard Judd. Review. *Ibid.*, Sept., 1896, Vol. 3, pp. 577–578.

Professor Baldwin's New Factor in Evolution. *The American Naturalist*, Sept., 1896, Vol. 30, pp. 697–710.

Further Comments on Professor Baldwin's New Factor in Evolution. *Ibid.*, Nov., 1896, Vol. 30, pp. 951–954.

The Biologic Origin of Mental Variety, or How We came to Have Minds. *Ibid.*, Dec., 1896, Vol. 30, pp. 963–975; Jan., 1897, Vol. 31, pp. 9–16.

The Psycho-Motor Problem. *Am. Jour. of Insanity*, July, 1897, Vol. 54, pp. 69–80.

Psychology and Physiology. *Ibid.*, Oct., 1897, Vol. 54, pp. 181–200.

The Psychology of the Emotions. By Th. Ribot. Review. *Ibid.*, Oct., 1897, Vol. 54, pp. 366–370.

Hallucinations and Illusions. By Edmund Parish. Review. *Ibid.*, Jan., 1898, Vol. 54, pp. 473–474.

The New Psychology. By E. W. Scripture. Review. *Ibid.*, Jan., 1898, Vol. 54, pp. 474–476.

The Psychology of Suggestion. By Boris Sidis. Review. *Ibid.*, April, 1898, Vol. 54, pp. 643–644.

The Genesis and Dissolution of the Faculty of Speech. By Joseph Collins. Review. *Ibid.*, July, 1898, Vol. 54, p. 184.

THOMAS F. NICHOLS:—

A.B., Bowdoin College, 1892; Scholar in Mathematics, Clark University, 1892–93; Fellow, 1893–95; Ph.D., Clark University, 1895; Assistant in Mathematics, University of Wisconsin, 1895–96; Assistant Professor of Mathematics, Hamilton College, 1896–.

Author of:—

On Some Special Jacobians. *Mathematical Review*, July, 1896, Vol. 1, pp. 60–80.

On the Generation of Certain Curves of the Fifth and Sixth Orders. *Ibid.*, April, 1897, Vol. 1, pp. 141–153.

ARTHUR A. NOYES:—

S.B., Massachusetts Institute of Technology, 1886; S.M., *ibid.*, 1887; Assistant in Chemistry, *ibid.*, 1887–88; Ph.D., University of Leipzig, 1890; Instructor in Chemistry, Massachusetts Institute of Technology, 1890–92; Non-resident Lecturer in Physical Chemistry, Clark University, 1892–94; Assistant Professor of Chemistry, Massachusetts Institute of Technology, 1893–97; Associate Professor of Organic Chemistry, *ibid.*, 1897–99; Professor of Theoretical and Organic Chemistry, *ibid.*, 1899–.

Author of: —

On the Action of Heat upon Ethylene. (With L. M. Norton.) *Am. Chem. Jour.* Oct., 1886, Vol. 8, pp. 362–364.

The Constitution of Benzol. *Technology Quarterly*, 1887, Vol. 1, pp. 79–80.

On the Action of Heat on Isobutylene. *Ibid.*, pp. 278–281.

Note on the Butines. (With L. M. Norton.) *Am. Chem. Jour.*, Nov., 1888, Vol. 10, pp. 430–433.

An Index to the Literature of the Butines and their Halogen Addition Products. *Technology Quarterly*, 1888, Vol. 2, pp. 119–123.

Ueber die Abweichungen von den Gasgesetzen in Lösungen. *Zeits. f. physik. Chemie*, 1890, Vol. 5, pp. 53–67.

Ueber die gegenseitige Beeinflussung der Löslichkeit von dissociirten Körpern. *Ibid.*, 1890, Vol. 6, pp. 241–267.

Ueber vermehrte Löslichkeit. Anwendung der Gefrierpunktsbestimmungen zur Ermittelung der Vorgänge in Lösung. *Ibid.*, 1890, Vol. 6, pp. 385–402.

Ueber die Bestimmung der elektrolytischen Dissociation von Salzen mittels Löslichkeitsversuche. *Ibid.*, 1892, Vol. 9, pp. 603–632. Translation in *Technology Quarterly*, 1891, Vol. 4, pp. 259–291.

Ueber die Wasserstoffionenabspaltung bei den sauren Salzen. *Ibid.*, 1893, Vol. 11, pp. 495–500. Translation in *Technology Quarterly*, 1892, Vol. 5, pp. 242–249.

Influence of the Introduction of a Sulphonic Acid Group upon the Power of a Developer. (With W. K. Gaylord.) *Technology Quarterly*, 1893, Vol. 6, pp. 60–61.

Ueber die elektrolytische Reduktion des Nitrobenzols in Schwefelsäurelösung. (With A. A. Clement.) *Ber. d. deutsch. chem. Gesellschaft*, 1893, Vol. 26, pp. 990–992. Translation in *Technology Quarterly*, 1893, Vol. 6, pp. 63–64.

Ueber die Bestimmung der elektrolytischen Dissociation von Salzen mittels Löslichkeitsversuche. *Zeits. f. physik. Chemie*, 1893, Vol. 12, pp. 162–166. Translation in *Technology Quarterly*, 1893, Vol. 6, pp. 237–240.

Löslichkeit des sauren Kaliumtartrats bei Gegenwart anderer Salze. (With A. A. Clement.) *Zeits. f. physik. Chemie*, 1894, Vol. 13, pp. 412–416.

Die Wasserstoffionenabspaltung bei dem sauren Kaliumtartrat. *Zeits. f. physik. Chemie*, 1894, Vol. 13, pp. 417–418.

Kryoskopische Untersuchungen mit Aluminaten und Boraten von Alkalimetallen. (With W. R. Whitney.) *Ibid.*, 1894, Vol. 14, pp. 694–698.

The Electrolytic Reduction of Paranitrobenzoic Acid in Sulphuric Acid Solution. (With A. A. Clement.) *Am. Chem. Jour.*, Nov., 1894, Vol. 16, pp. 511–512.

Eine Prüfung der Princips der Löslichkeitsbeeinflussung und ein Vergleich der daraus und aus der elektrischen Leitfähigkeit berechneten Dissociationswerte. (With C. G. Abbot.) *Zeits. f. physik. Chemie*, 1895, Vol. 16, pp. 125–138. Translation in *Technology Quarterly*, 1895, Vol. 8, pp. 47–63.

Die Geschwindigkeit der Reaktion zwischen Zinnchlorür und Eisenchlorid. Eine Reaktion dritter Ordnung. *Zeits. f. physik. Chemie*, 1895, Vol. 16, pp. 546–561.

Synthesis of Diphenyldiphenyl and its Identification as Benzerythrene. (With Rolfe M. Ellis.) *Am. Chem. Jour.*, Oct., 1895, Vol. 17, pp. 620–623. Also in *Technology Quarterly*, 1895, Vol. 8, pp. 176–180.

Die Geschwindigkeit der Hydrolyse des Salicins durch Säuren. (With W. J. Hall.) *Zeits. f. physik. Chemie*, 1895, Vol. 18, pp. 240–244. Translation in *Technology Quarterly*, 1895, Vol. 8, pp. 283–293.

Beitrag zur Kenntniss der Gesetze der Geschwindigkeit von polymolekularen Reaktionen. (With W. O. Scott.) *Zeits. f. physik. Chemie*, 1895, Vol. 18, pp. 118–132.

The Electrolytic Reduction of Paranitro Compounds in Sulphuric Acid Solution. (With J. T. Dorrance.) *Ber. der deuts. chem. Gesellschaft*, 1895, Vol. 28, pp. 2349–2352. Translation in *Jour. Am. Chem. Soc.*, 1895, Vol. 17, pp. 855–859.

The Occurrence of Trimethylene Glycol as a By-product in the Glycerine Manufacture. (With W. H. Watkins.) *Jour. Am. Chem. Soc.*, 1895, Vol. 17, pp. 890–891. Also *Technology Quarterly*, 1895, Vol. 8, pp. 361–363.

Die katalytische Wirkung der Wasserstoffjonen auf polymolekulare Reaktionen. *Zeits. f. physik. Chemie*, 1896, Vol. 19, pp. 599–606.

Bemerkung über das Gesetz der Geschwindigkeit der Reaktion zwischen Eisenchlorid und Zinnchlorür. *Ibid.*, 1896, Vol. 21, p. 16.

Die innere Reibung des Quecksilberdampfes. (With H. M. Goodwin.) *Ibid.*, 1896, Vol. 21, pp. 671–679. Translation in *Physical Review*, Nov.–Dec., 1896, Vol. 4, pp. 207–216.

Sind Diphenyljodonium- und Thalliumnitrat isomorph? (With C. W. Hapgood.) *Zeits. f. physik. Chemie*, 1896, Vol. 22, pp. 464–466.

Instruction in Theoretical Chemistry. *Technology Quarterly*, 1896, Vol. 9, pp. 323–335.

Formation of Diacetylenyl (Butadiine) from Copper Acetylene. (With C. W. Tucker.) *Am. Chem. Jour.*, Feb. 1897, Vol. 19, pp. 123–129.

Synthesis of Hexamethylene-Glycol Diethyl Ether and Other Ethers from Trimethylene Glycol. *Ibid.*, Nov., 1897, Vol. 19, pp. 766–781.

Die Reaktionsgeschwindigkeit zwischen Eisenchlorür, Kaliumchlorat und Salzsäure. (With R. S. Wason.) *Zeits. f. physik. Chemie*, 1897, Vol. 22, pp. 210–221. Translation in *Jour. Am. Chem. Soc.*, 1897, Vol. 19, pp. 199–212.

Bestimmung des osmotischen Druckes mittels Dampfdruckmessungen. (With C. G. Abbot.) *Zeits. f. physik. Chemie*, 1897, Vol. 23, pp. 56–77.

Ueber die Auflösungsgeschwindigkeit von festen Stoffen in ihren eigenen Lösungen. (With W. R. Whitney.) *Ibid.*, pp. 689–692. Translation in *Jour. Am. Chem. Soc.*, 1897, Vol. 19, pp. 930–934.

Bemerkung über die Kinetische Theorie der Lösungen. *Zeits. f. physik. Chemie*, 1897, Vol. 24, p. 366.

Qualitative Chemical Analysis. The Macmillan Co., N. Y., 1897. 89 pp. Third edition.

Laboratory Experiments on the Class Reactions and Identification of Organic Substances. (With S. P. Mulliken.) Chemical Publishing Co., Easton, Pa., 1897. 81 pp. Second edition.

Investigation of the Theory of Solubility Effect in the case of Tri-ionic Salts. (With E. H. Woodworth.) *Jour. Am. Chem. Soc.*, 1898, Vol. 20, pp. 194–201. Also *Zeits. f. physik. Chemie*, 1898, Vol. 26, pp. 152–158.

The Reliability of the Dissociation Values Determined by Electrical Conductivity Measurements. *Jour. Am. Chem. Soc.*, 1898, Vol. 20, pp. 517–528. Also *Zeits. f. physik. Chemie*, 1898, Vol. 26, pp. 699–710.

The Solubility of Salts of Weak Acids in Stronger Acids. (With David Schwartz.) *Jour. Am. Chem. Soc.*, 1898, Vol. 20, pp. 742–751. Also *Zeits. f. physik. Chemie*, 1898, Vol. 27, pp. 279–284.

Die Theorie der Löslichkeitsbeeinflussung bei zweiionigen Elektrolyten mit lauter verschiedenen Jonen. *Zeits.*

f. physik. Chemie, 1898, Vol. 27, pp. 267-278.

The Solubility of Acids in Solutions of the Salts of Other Acids. (With E. S. Chapin.) *Ibid.*, pp. 442-446. Translation in *Jour. Am. Chem. Soc.*, 1898, Vol. 20, pp. 751-756.

Die Löslichkeit von Jod in verdünnten Kaliumjodidlösungen. (With L. J. Seidensticker.) *Zeits. f. physik. Chemie*, 1898, Vol. 27, pp. 257-260. Translation in *Jour. Am. Chem. Soc.*, 1899, Vol. 21, pp. 217-220.

Die Geschwindigkeit der Reaktion zwischen Silberacetat und Natriumformiat. Eine Reaktion dritter Ordnung. (With G. T. Cottle.) *Zeits. f. physik. Chemie*, 1898, Vol. 27, pp. 579-584.

Die Beziehung zwischen osmotischer Arbeit und osmotischem Druck. *Ibid.*, 1899, Vol. 28, pp. 220-224.

C. A. ORR:—

A.B., University of Michigan, 1887; Student, Johns Hopkins University, 1887-88; Principal, High School, Salem, O., 1888-89; Anthropologist, Solar Eclipse Expedition, Clark University, 1889-90; Lecturer in Latin, University of Chicago, 1892-; Instructor, Chicago High Schools, 1894-.

VICTOR PÄPCKE:—

Ph.D., University of Göttingen, 1888; Assistant in Chemistry, Clark University, 1889-90; Medical Student, University of Leipzig, 1893.

GEORGE E. PARTRIDGE:—

Special Student in Philosophy, Clark University, 1893-96; Scholar in Psychology, 1896-98; Fellow, 1898-99.

Author of:—

Second Breath. *Pedagogical Seminary*, April, 1897, Vol. 4, pp. 372-381.

Blushing. *Ibid.*, April, 1897, Vol. 4, pp. 387-394.

Some Mental Automatisms. (With E. H. Lindley.) *Ibid.*, July, 1897, Vol. 5, pp. 41-60.

Reverie. *Ibid.*, April, 1898, Vol. 5, pp. 445-474.

Child Study in Connection with the Vacation Schools. (With H. S. Curtis.) Report on the Vacation Schools and Playgrounds, N. Y. City, Borough of Manhattan and the Bronx, 1898, pp. 51-97.

Experiments upon the Control of the Reflex. *Am. Jour. of Psy.* (In press.)

T. RICHARD PEEDE:—

Christian Biblical Institute, New York, 1881-84; Boston University, 1884-88; Special Student in Philosophy and Pedagogy, Clark University, 1895-96; Honorary Scholar in Philosophy, 1896-97; Pastor, South Baptist Church, Worcester, 1896-.

JOSEPH DE PEROTT:—

Universities of Paris and Berlin, 1877-80; Docent in Mathematics, Clark University, 1890-.

Author of:—

Sur la sommation des nombres. *Bull. des Sci. Mathématiques*, 1881, 2d ser., Vol. 5, pp. 37-40.

Sur l'infinité de la suite des nombres premiers. *Ibid.*, pp. 183-184.

Sur une arithmétique espagnole du 16me siècle. *Bull. di bibliografia e di storia delle scienze matematiche*, 1882, Vol. 15, pp. 163-170.

Sur la recherche des diviseurs des fonctions entières. *Bull. de la Soc. Mathématique*, 1882, Vol. 10, pp. 240-251.

Sur un théorème de Gauss. *Ibid.*, pp. 67-68.

Sur la formation des déterminants irréguliers. *Jour. f. Mathematik*, 1883, Vol. 95, pp. 232-237.

Sur le problème des fous. *Bull. de la Soc. Mathématique*, 1883, Vol. 11, pp. 173-186.

Sur la formation des déterminants irréguliers. Second Mémoire. *Jour. f. Mathematik*, 1884, Vol. 96, pp. 327-348.

Démonstration du théorème fondamental de l'algèbre. *Ibid.*, 1886, Vol. 99, pp. 141–160.

Démonstration de l'existence des racines primitives pour les modules égaux à des puissances de nombre premier impair. *Bull. des Sci. Mathématiques*, 1885, 2e sér., Vol. 9, pp. 21–24.

Sur les logarithmes à un grand nombre de décimales et en particulier sur les Tables de Steinhauser. *Ibid.*, 1887, 2e sér., Vol. 11, pp. 61–80.

Sur l'équation $t^2 - Du^2 = -1$. *Jour. f. Mathematik*, 1888, Vol. 102, pp. 185–223.

Remarque au sujet du théorème d'Euclide sur l'infinité du nombre des nombres premiers. *Am. Jour. of Mathematics*, 1889, Vol. 11, pp. 99–138; 1891, Vol. 13, pp. 235–308.

Sur une proposition empirique énoncée au Bulletin. *Bull. de la Soc. Mathématique*, 1889, Vol. 17, pp. 165–166.

On a Theorem of Gauss. *J. H. U. Circular*, 1889, No. 76, p. 30.

The Gaussian Interpolation Theory, formulæ for n = 7, 8, 9. *Quar. Jour. of Mathematics*, 1891, Vol. 25, pp. 200–202.

Sur les groupes de Galois. *Bull. de la Soc. Mathématique*, 1893, Vol. 21, pp. 61–66.

Démonstration de l'existence de racines primitives pour tout module premier impair. *Bull. des Sci. Mathématiques*, 1893, 2e sér., Vol. 17, pp. 66–68.

Démonstration de l'existence de racines primitives module premier impair. *Ibid.*, 1894, 2e sér., Vol. 18, pp. 64–66.

Mathematical Tables. *Sci. Am. Supplement*, July 7, 1894, Vol. 38, pp. 15436–15437.

The Theory of Numbers. (Review of M. Stieltjes's "Sur la théorie des nombres.") *Bull. of Am. Math. Soc.*, June, 1895, Vol. 1, pp. 217–232.

DANIEL EDWARD PHILLIPS:—

Graduate West Virginia State Normal School, 1890; Principal, Public Schools, Philippi, W. Va., 1890–91; A.B., University of Nashville, 1893; A.M., *ibid.*, 1894; **Scholar in Psychology, Clark University, 1894–March, 1895**; Professor of Pedagogy, Normal Department, University of Georgia, March, 1895–Jan., 1897; **Honorary Scholar in Psychology, Clark University, Jan.–June, 1897; Fellow, 1897–98; Ph.D., Clark University, 1898**; Professor of Philosophy and Education, University of Denver, 1898–.

Author of:—

The End of Education. 23 pp.

Religious Education. *Peabody Record*, Nov., 1898, Vol. 4, pp. 53–60.

Course of Study for Common Schools. *Southern Jour. of Ed.*, Oct., 1895, Vol. 9, pp. 472–478.

Genesis of Number Forms. *Am. Jour. of Psy.*, July, 1897, Vol. 8, pp. 506–527.

Number and its Application psychologically considered. *Pedagogical Seminary*, Oct., 1897, Vol. 5, pp. 221–281.

Some Remarks on Number and its Application. *Ibid.*, April, 1899, Vol. 6, pp. 590–598.

Some Aspects of the Child Study Movement. *Northwestern Monthly*, Jan., 1899, Vol. 9, pp. 333–337.

The Teaching Instinct. *Pedagogical Seminary*, March, 1899, Vol. 6, pp. 188–245.

Sunday-School Teaching. *Study*, March, 1899, Vol. 4, pp. 309–318.

JEFFERSON E. POTTER:—

A.B., Brown University, 1877; A.M., *ibid.*, 1887; Instructor, Vermont Academy, 1877–78; State Normal School, Castine, Me., 1878–85; Professor of Pedagogy, State College of Kentucky, 1885–88; Instructor in Natural Sciences, State Normal School, Farmington, Me., 1888–90; **Scholar in Psychology, Clark University, 1890–91**; Superintendent of Schools, Ashland and Hopkinton, Mass., 1891–93; Superintendent of Schools, Walpole, Foxboro, and Norfolk, Mass., 1893–95; Superintendent of Schools, Walpole and Foxboro, Mass., 1895–98; Member:

New England Conference of Educational Workers; New England Association of School Superintendents.

Author of:—

History of Methods of Instruction in Geography. *Pedagogical Seminary*, Dec., 1891, Vol. 1, pp. 416–424.

J. O. QUANTZ:—

B.A., University of Toronto (Honors in Philosophy and Psychology), 1894; Fellow in Psychology, University of Wisconsin, 1895–97; Ph.D., University of Wisconsin, 1897; **Honorary Fellow in Psychology, Clark University, 1897–98**; Honorary Fellow in Philosophy, Cornell University, 1898–99.

Author of:—

The Influence of the Color of Surfaces on our Estimation of their Magnitude. *Am. Jour. of Psy.*, Oct., 1895, Vol. 7, pp. 26–41.

Problems in the Psychology of Reading. *Psychological Review*, Monograph Supplement, Dec., 1897, pp. 1–51.

The Physiology of Shorthand. *Phonographic World*, March, 1898, Vol. 13, pp. 292–293.

Dendro-psychoses. *Am. Jour. of Psy.*, July, 1898, Vol. 9, pp. 449–506.

An Analysis of the Muscular Sensations involved in Drawing a Line.

ROLLA R. RAMSEY:—

Assistant in Shop, Indiana University, 1894–95; A.B., Department of Physics, *ibid.*, 1895; A.M., *ibid.*, 1896; Science Teacher, Decatur, Ind., High School, 1895–96; Laboratory Assistant, Indiana University, 1896–97; Professor of Physics, Westminster College, 1897–98; **Scholar in Physics, Clark University, 1898–99**; Assistant in Physics, Cornell University, 1899–.

Author of:—

A Photographic Study of Electrolytic Cells. *Physical Review*, Sept., 1899, Vol. 9, pp. 169–180, 1 pl.

JOHN F. REIGART:—

A.B., Dickinson College, 1886; Principal of High School, Chester, Pa., 1888–90; **Scholar in Psychology, Clark University, 1890–91**; Associate Professor in Education, Teachers' College, New York City, 1891–93; Professor of Psychology and History of Education, *ibid.*, 1893–97; Superintendent Workingman's School, New York City, 1897–.

Author of:—

The Training of Teachers in England. *Pedagogical Seminary*, Dec., 1891, Vol. 1, pp. 409–415.

ERNEST W. RETTGER:—

Graduate, Indiana State Normal School, 1891; A.B., Indiana University, 1893; Principal, Rensselaer, Ind., High School, 1893–94; Instructor in Mathematics, Indiana University, 1894–96; **Fellow in Mathematics, Clark University, 1896–98**; **Ph.D., Clark University, 1898**; Instructor in Mathematics, Indiana University, 1898–.

Author of:—

Note on the Projective Group. *Proc. Am. Acad. of Sci.*, July, 1898, Vol. 33, pp. 491–499.

On Lie's Theory of Continuous Groups. *Am. Jour. of Math.* (In press.)

ROBERT J. RICHARDSON:—

Teacher in Public Schools, Varna, Ont., 1887–90; Graduate, Ontario School of Pedagogy, 1891; Student at Toronto University, 1892–93; Teacher in High School, Prescott, Ont., 1893–94; B.A., University of Toronto, 1897; Graduate Student, *ibid.*, 1897–98; **Fellow in Psychology, Clark University, 1898–99.**

Author of:—

A case of Abnormal Color-Sense examined with Special Reference to the Space-Threshold of Colors. (With J. W. Baird.) *Univ. of Toronto Studies*, Psychological Series, 1898, pp. 87–100.

CAMILLE REID:—

Protestant School, Freiburg, Baden, 1856–59; Classical Gymnasium, Lahr, Baden, 1860–60; Student in Paris, 1862–63; Resident in Paris, 1863–65, and 1867–70; Resident in Spain, 1865–67; Student in Freiburg, 1870–71; Student in Boston, 1881–86; Head of School of Languages, Boston, 1887–90; Instructor in Modern Languages, Clark University, 1889–91; Instructor, Nautical School, U. S. S. *Enterprise*, 1891–94.

STANLEY H. ROOD:—

S.B., Worcester Polytechnic, in Mechanical Engineering, 1890; in Electrical Engineering, 1891; Instructor in Physics, *ibid.*, 1890–93; Scholar in Physics, Clark University, Sept., 1893–April, 1894; Instructor in Joinery, Mechanic Arts High School, Boston, April–June, 1894; Instructor in French, *ibid.*, 1894–95; Graduate Student, Harvard University, 1895–96; Instructor in Joinery, Manual Training High School, Worcester, 1896–.

EDWIN W. RUNKLE:—

A.B., Western College, 1890; Graduate Student in Psychology and Philosophy, Yale University, 1890–93; Lecturer in the History of Philosophy, *ibid.*, 1892–93; Ph.D., Yale University, 1893; Assistant Professor of Psychology and Ethics, Pennsylvania State College, 1893–99; Honorary Fellow in Psychology, Clark University, Jan.–June, 1899; Professor of Psychology and Ethics, Pennsylvania State College, 1899–.

Author of:—

Education and Life. *Free Lance*, State College, Pennsylvania, Jan., 1894, Vol. 12, pp. 96–98.

Why do we Dream? *Ibid.*, Oct. 1895, Vol. 14, pp. 5–8.

Factors in Education. *Ibid.*, May, 1896, Vol. 15, pp. 13–18.

Psychology and the Modern Novel. *School Gazette*, June, 1897, Vol. 8, pp. 8–12.

Review of Breuer and Freud: Studien über Hysterie. *Am. Jour. of Psy.*, July, 1899, Vol. 10, pp. 592–594.

G. EDWARD RYERSON:—

M.A., Queen's University, 1895; Fellow in Mathematics, Clark University, 1895–96.

Died, March 25, 1896.

EDMUND C. SANFORD:—

A.B., University of California, 1883; Teacher in Oahu College, Hawaiian Islands, 1883–85; Student, Johns Hopkins University, 1885–88; University Scholar, *ibid.*, 1887; Fellow, *ibid.*, 1887–88; Ph.D., Johns Hopkins University, 1888; Instructor in Psychology, *ibid.*, 1888–89; Instructor in Psychology, Clark University, 1889–92; Assistant Professor of Psychology, 1892–; Joint Editor, with President Hall and Professor Titchener, of the *American Journal of Psychology*; Member of the American Psychological Association.

Author of:—

The Writings of Laura Bridgman. (Two articles.) *Overland Monthly*, 1886–87.

The Relative Legibility of the Small Letters. *Am. Jour. of Psy.*, May, 1888, Vol. 1, pp. 402–435.

Personal Equation. *Ibid.*, Nov., 1888; Feb. and May, 1889, Vol. 2, pp. 3–38, 271–298, 403–430.

A Simple and Inexpensive Chronoscope. *Ibid.*, April, 1890, Vol. 3, pp. 174–181.

Psychology at Clark University. *Ibid.*, April, 1890, Vol. 3, pp. 284–285.

A Laboratory Course in Physiological Psychology. *Ibid.*, April and Dec., 1891; April, 1892, Vol. 4, pp. 141–155, 303–322, 474–490; April, 1893, Vol. 5, pp. 390–415; Jan., 1895, Vol. 6, pp. 593–616; April, 1896, Vol. 7, pp. 412–424.

A New Visual Illusion. *Science*, Feb. 17, 1893, Vol. 21, pp. 92–93.

On Reaction-Times when the Stimulus is Applied to the Reacting Hand. (With J. F. Reigart.) *Am. Jour. of Psy.*, April, 1888, Vol. 1, pp. 351–355.

A New Pendulum Chronograph. *Ibid.*, April, 1893, Vol. 5, pp. 385–389.

Some Practical Suggestions on the Equipment of a Psychological Laboratory. *Ibid.*, July, 1893, Vol. 5, pp. 429–438.

Notes on New Apparatus. *Ibid.*, Jan., 1895, Vol. 6, pp. 575–584.

The Philadelphia Meeting of the American Psychological Association. *Science*, Jan. 24, 1896, Vol. 3, pp. 119–124.

The Vernier Chronoscope. *Am. Jour. of Psy.*, Jan., 1898, Vol. 9, pp. 191–197.

A Course in Experimental Psychology. D. C. Heath & Co., Boston, Mass., 1898. 449 pp.

CLARENCE ARTHUR SAUNDERS:

B.A., King's College, Windsor, N. S., 1885; M.A., 1889; Graduate Student, Johns Hopkins University, 1889–92; Assistant, Smithsonian Institution, Washington, 1891–92; **Fellow in Physics, Clark University, 1892–95; Ph.D., Clark University, 1895**; Professor of Mathematics and Physics, Ursinus College, 1895–98.

Died Dec. 19, 1898.

Author of:—

The Velocity of Electric Waves. *Physical Review*, Sept.–Oct., 1896, Vol. 4, pp. 81–105.

ALBERT SCHINZ:—

B.A., Neuchâtel, 1888; M.A., *ibid.*, 1889; Licentiate in Theology, *ibid.*, 1892; Student, University of Berlin, 1892–93; Student, Tübingen, 1893; Ph.D., Tübingen, 1894; Collège de France et Sorbonne, Paris, 1894; Second Librarian, Library of Neuchâtel, and Associate Professor of Philosophy, University of Neuchâtel, 1896–97; **Honorary Fellow in Psychology, Clark University, 1897–98**; Instructor in French, University of Minnesota, 1898–99; Lecturer in French Literature, Bryn Mawr College, 1899–.

Author of:—

La nature du péché: étude psychologique. Delachaux et Niestlé, Neuchâtel, 1893. 124 pp.

Morale et déterminisme. *Revue Philosophique*, Jan., 1895, Vol. 39, pp. 67–75.

La philosophie de M. Ernest Naville. *Revue de Théologie et de Philosophie*, July, 1895.

Mysticisme et Magie. *Centralblatt des Zofingervereins*, Dec., 1895.

Le récent mouvement moral en Europe et en Amérique. Bridel et Cie, Lausanne, Suisse. (Imprimé d'abord dans *La Revue de Théologie et de Philosophie*, Sept., 1895.)

Essai sur la notion du miracle, considéré du point de vue de la théorie de la connaissance. Delachaux et Niestlé, Neuchâtel, 1897. 35 pp. (Reprint from *La Revue de Théologie et de Philosophie*, March, 1897.)

La moralité de l'enfant. *Revue Philosophique*, March, 1898, Vol. 45, pp. 259–286.

Die Moralität des Kindes. Translation by Ch. Ufer. Langensalza, 1898. 12 pp. (Heft I. der "Beiträge zur Kinderforschung.")

Le positivisme est un méthode et non un système. *Revue Philosophique*, Jan., 1899, Vol. 47, pp. 63–75.

Les bibliothèques publiques en Amérique. *Bibliothèque Universelle*, Lausanne, Suisse, Aug.–Sept., 1898.

Les sports dans les Universités Américaines. *La Suisse Universitaire*, Feb., 1899.

L'Université de Clark à Worcester, Mass. *Revue des Revues*, Paris, July, 1898.

L'église aux États Unis d'Amérique. (In press.)

Translation of Dr. E. C. Sanford's "A Course in Experimental Psychology." Schleicher frères, Paris, 1899. (In press.)

Chronique du féminisme aux États-Unis. *Revue de Morale Sociale*, Paris, June, 1899.

La langue internationale Esperanto. *La Semaine Littéraire*. Genève, Suisse, 29 Juillet, 1899.

La secte des Scientistes Chrétiens aux États-Unis d'Amérique. *Revue des Revues*, Paris. (In press.)

Un représentant de l'Agnosticisme aux États-Unis, Robert G. Ingersoll. (In press.)

L'éducation des nègres aux États-Unis d'Amérique. L'institut de Tuskegee en Alabama. *La Semaine Littéraire.* Genève. 21 Octobre, 1899.

Le culte d'Omar Khayyam. (In press.)

La Philosophie et le Sens Commun, *Revue Philosophique*, Paris. (In press.)

ALVA ROY SCOTT:—

A.B., De Pauw University, 1886; A.M., *ibid.*, 1889; Principal, Leavenworth Schools, 1886–87; Student, McCormick Theological Seminary, Chicago, 1888–91; Pastor, First Presbyterian Church, Hanover, Ill., 1891–93; Graduate Student, Harvard University, 1893–94; Honorary Scholar in Psychology, Clark University, 1894–95; Pastor, First Presbyterian Church, Worcester, Mass., 1894–98.

COLIN ALEXANDER SCOTT:—

Student, College of City of New York, 1877–78; Graduate, Toronto Normal School, 1879; Director of Instruction in Drawing, Kingston Schools, 1883–84; B.A., Queen's University, Kingston, Ont., 1885 (Gold Medalist with Honors in Chemistry, Biology, and Geology); Instructor in Chemistry, Ladies' Medical College, Kingston, 1885–86; Science Master, Ingersoll Collegiate Institute, 1886–87; Science Master, Ottawa Collegiate Institute, 1887–94; Fellow in Psychology, Clark University, 1894–96; Ph.D., Clark University, 1896; Head of Department of Physiological Psychology and Child Study, Chicago Normal School, 1896–.

Author of:—

Sex and Art. *Am. Jour. of Psy.*, Jan., 1896, Vol. 7, pp. 153–226.

Old Age and Death. *Ibid.*, June, 1896, Vol. 8, pp. 67–122.

Children's Fears as Material for Expression and a Basis of Education in Art. *Trans. Ill. Soc. for Child Study*, April, 1896, Vol. 2, pp. 12–17.

E. W. SCRIPTURE:—

A.B., College of the City of New York, 1884; A.M., *ibid.*, 1888; Universities of Leipzig, Berlin, and Zurich, 1888–90; Ph.D., University of Leipzig, 1891; Fellow in Psychology, Clark University, 1891–92; Instructor in Experimental Psychology, Yale University, 1892–98; Director of the Yale Psychological Laboratory, 1898–; Assistant Editor of *American Journal of Psychology*, 1891–98; Editor of *Studies from the Yale Psychological Laboratory*, 1893–; Member: American Psychological Association; American Society of Naturalists; Fellow, American Association for the Advancement of Science.

Author of:—

Vorstellung und Gefühl. *Philos. Studien*, 1890, Vol. 6, pp. 536–542.

Ueber den associativen Verlauf der Vorstellungen. (Inaugural Dissertation.) Leipzig, 1891, 101 pp., and *Philos. Studien*, 1891, Vol. 7, pp. 50–146.

Arithmetical Prodigies. *Am. Jour. of Psy.*, April, 1891, Vol. 4, pp. 1–59.

The Problem of Psychology. *Mind*, 1891, Vol. 16, pp. 305–326.

Zur Definition einer Vorstellung. *Philos. Studien*, 1891, Vol. 7, pp. 213–221.

Einige Beobachtungen über Schwebungen und Differenztöne. *Ibid.*, 1892, Vol. 7, pp. 630–632.

The Need of Psychological Training. *Science*, March 4, 1892, Vol. 19, pp. 127–128.

An Instrument for Mapping Hot and Cold Spots on the Skin. *Ibid.*, May 6, 1892, Vol. 19, p. 258.

Education as a Science. *Pedagogical Seminary*, June, 1892, Vol. 2, pp. 111–114.

Psychological Notes. *Am. Jour. of Psy.*, Aug., 1892, Vol. 4, pp. 577–584.

Tests on School Children. *Educational Review*, Jan., 1893, Vol. 5, pp. 52–61.

Ist eine cerebrale Entstehung von Schwebungen möglich? *Philos. Studien*, 1893, Vol. 8, pp. 638–640.

Systematised Graduate Instruction in Psychology. *Science*, July 28, 1893, Vol. 22, pp. 43–44.

A System of Color-teaching. *Educational Review*, Dec., 1893, Vol. 6, pp. 464–474.

Consciousness under the Influence of Cannabis indica. *Science*, Oct. 27, 1893, Vol. 22, p. 233.

Psychological Measurements. *Philosophical Review*, Nov. 1893, Vol. 2, pp. 677–689.

A New Reaction-key and the Time of Voluntary Movement. (With J. M. Moore.) *Studies from Yale Psy. Lab.*, 1892–93, Vol. 1, pp. 88–91.

Drawing a Straight Line: a Study in Experimental Didactics. (With C. L. Lyman.) *Ibid.*, pp. 92–96.

Some New Psychological Apparatus. *Ibid.*, pp. 97–100.

On the Measurement of Hallucinations. *Science*, Dec. 29, 1893, Vol. 22, p. 353.

Work at the Yale Laboratory. *Psychological Review*, Jan., 1894, Vol. 1, pp. 66–69.

Ueber die Aenderungsempfindlichkeit. *Zeits. f. Psy. u. Phys. d. Sinnesorgane*, 1894, Vol. 6, pp. 472–474.

Observation on the Use of the Terminal Verb in Infant Speech. *Science*, Feb. 2, 1894, Vol. 23, p. 62.

New Materials for Color-teaching. *Educational Review*, April, 1894, Vol. 7, pp. 382–383.

The Use of Antiphones. *N. Y. Med. Jour.*, April 7, 1894, Vol. 59, p. 45.

On the Adjustment of Simple Psychological Measurements. *Psychological Review*, May, 1894, Vol. 1, pp. 281–282.

The Kinesimeter. (With E. B. Titchener.) *Am. Jour. of Psy.*, June, 1894, Vol. 6, pp. 424–426.

Accurate Work in Psychology. *Ibid.*, pp. 427–430.

Some Psychological Illustrations of the Theorems of Bernoulli and Poisson. *Ibid.*, pp. 431–433.

Methods of Laboratory Mind-study. *Forum*, Aug., 1894, Vol. 17, pp. 721–728.

Aims and Status of Child Study. *Educational Review*, Oct., 1894, Vol. 8, pp. 236–239.

On Mean Values for Direct Measurements. *Studies from Yale Psy. Lab.*, 1894, Vol. 2, pp. 1–39.

Remarks on Dr. Gilbert's Article. *Ibid.*, pp. 101–104.

Experiments on the Highest Audible Tone. (With H. F. Smith.) *Ibid.*, pp. 105–113.

On the Education of Muscular Control and Power. (With T. L. Smith and E. M. Brown.) *Ibid.*, pp. 114–119.

A Psychological Method of determining the Blind-spot. *Ibid.*, pp. 120–121.

Tests of Mental Ability as Exhibited in Fencing. *Ibid.*, pp. 122–124.

Reaction-time and Time-memory in Gymnastic Work. *Rep. Ninth Meet. Am. Ass'n Physical Education*, 1894, pp. 44–49.

On the Measurement of Imaginations. *Sci. Am.*, Feb. 9, 1895, Vol. 72, p. 86.

The Nature of Science and its Relation to Philosophy. *Science*, March 29, 1895, N. S., Vol. 1, pp. 350–352.

Scientific Child Study. *Trans. Ill. Soc. for Child Study*, May, 1895, Vol. 1, pp. 32–37.

Simple but Accurate Tests for Child Study. *Ibid.*, pp. 57–60.

Practical Computation of the Median. *Psychological Review*, July, 1895, Vol. 2, pp. 376–379.

The Second Year at the Yale Laboratory. *Ibid.*, pp. 379–381.

A New Method of Computation. *Sci. Am. Supplement*, July 6, 1895, Vol. 4, p. 16210.

Thinking, Feeling, Doing. Flood & Vincent, Meadville, Pa., 1895. 304 pp.

A New Method of Making Lantern Slides. *Scientific American*, Aug. 24, 1895, Vol. 73, p. 123.

Some Principles of Mental Education. *School Review*, Nov., 1895, Vol. 3, pp. 533–547.

A Method of Stereoscopic Projection. *Scientific American*, Nov. 23, 1895, Vol. 73, p. 327.

Some New Apparatus. *Studies from Yale Psy. Lab.*, 1895, Vol. 3, p. 98–109.

The Red Eye Factory. *Outlook*, Feb. 29, 1896, Vol. 53, pp. 393–394.

Untersuchungen über die geistige Entwickelung der Schulkinder. *Zeits. f. Psy. u. Phys. der Sinnesorgane*, 1896, Vol. 10, pp. 161–182.

Measuring Hallucinations. *Science*, May 22, 1896, N. S., Vol. 3, pp. 762–763.

Child Study: Methods and Results. *Report 65th Meeting Am. Institute of Instruction*, pp. 161–166.

The Third Year at the Yale Laboratory. *Psychological Review*, July, 1896, Vol. 3, pp. 416–421.

The Law of Rhythmic Movement. *Science*, Oct. 9, 1896, N. S., Vol. 4, pp. 535–536.

My Pedagogic Creed. *School Journal*, Dec. 5, 1896, Vol. 53, pp. 621–623.

Nouveaux Instruments. *Année psychologique*, 1896, Vol. 3, pp. 658–664.

The Law of Size-Weight Suggestion. *Science*, Feb. 5, 1897, N. S., Vol. 5, p. 227.

Sources of the New Psychology. *Pop. Sci. Mo.*, May, 1897, Vol. 51, pp. 98–105.

Pleasure without Other Sensations. *N. Y. Med. Jour.*, July 17, 1897, Vol. 66, p. 99.

Cerebral Light. *Science*, July 23, 1897, N. S., Vol. 6, pp. 138–139.

The New Psychology. Walter Scott, London, 1897. 500 pp.

Researches on Reaction-time. *Studies from Yale Psy. Lab.*, 1897, Vol. 4, pp. 12–26.

Researches on Voluntary Effort. *Ibid.*, 1897, Vol. 4, pp. 69–75.

New Apparatus and Methods. *Ibid.*, 1897, Vol. 4, pp. 76–89.

Elementary Course in Psychological Measurements. *Ibid.*, 1897, Vol. 4, pp. 89–139.

On Binaural Space. *Ibid.*, 1898, Vol. 5, pp. 76–80.

Researches on the Memory for Arm Movements. (With W. C. Cooke and C. M. Warren.) *Ibid.*, 1898, Vol. 5, pp. 90–92.

Principles of Laboratory Economy. *Ibid.*, 1898, Vol. 5, pp. 93–102.

Reaction-time in Abnormal Conditions of the Nervous System. *Medical Record*, 1898, Vol. 53, p. 193.

Electrical Anaesthesia. *Science*, June 3, 1898, N. S., Vol. 7, p. 778.

The Anaesthetic Effects of a Sinusoidal Current of High Frequency. *Ibid.*, March 10, 1899, N. S., Vol. 9, p. 377.

Color Weakness and Color Blindness. *Ibid.*, June 2, 1899, N. S., Vol. 9, pp. 771–774.

Cerebral Light. *Ibid.*, June 16, 1899, N. S., Vol. 9, pp. 850–851.

Arousal of Instinct by Taste. *Ibid.*, June 23, 1899, N. S., Vol. 9, p. 878.

Anaglyphs and Stereoscopic Projection. *Ibid.*, Aug. 11, 1899, N. S., Vol. 10, pp. 185–187.

CHARLES H. SEARS:—

Graduate, State Normal School, Westfield, Mass. (four years' course), 1883; Principal of Public Schools, Cheshire, Mass., 1883–86; Teacher, Prospect Park Institute, Brooklyn, N. Y., 1886–88; Teacher of Latin, State Normal School, Edinboro, Pa., 1888–92; A.M., Allegheny College, 1893; Ph.D., Allegheny College, 1895; Principal, Normal Department, Claflin University, 1893–97; Honorary Fellow in Pedagogy, Clark University, 1897–99.

Author of:—

Home and School Punishments. *Pedagogical Seminary*, March, 1899, Vol. 6, pp. 159–187.

ALBERT H. SEGSWORTH:—

B.A., University of Toronto, 1890; Student, University of Leipzig, 1890–91; University of Toronto, 1891–92; Student, University of Leipzig, 1892–93; Honorary Fellow in Psychology, Clark University, 1893–94.

Author of:—

On the Difference Sensibility for the Valuation of Space Distances with the Help of Arm Movements. *Am. Jour.*

of Psy., June, 1894, Vol. 6, pp. 389–407.

Ueber Intervallempfindungen. (Privately printed.) 1894. 6 pp.

BENJAMIN F. SHARPE:—

A.B., Wesleyan University, 1887; A.M., *ibid.*, 1890; Adjunct Professor of Physics and Biology, Randolph-Macon College, 1887–91; Graduate Student and Scholar, Johns Hopkins University, 1891–94; **Fellow in Physics, Clark University, 1894–96;** Professor of Mathematics, State Normal School, New Paltz, N. Y., 1896–97; **Fellow in Physics, Clark University, 1897–99.**

Author of:—

A Double Instrument and a Double Method for the Measurement of Sound. *Science*, June 9, 1899, N. S., Vol. 9, pp. 808–811.

An Advance in Measuring and Photographing Sounds. U. S. Weather Bureau, No. 208, Washington, D. C., 1899. 16 pp., 1 pls.

JOHN C. SHAW:—

Graduate, State Normal School, Fairmont, W. Va., 1889; Principal of Graded Schools, Paw Paw, W. Va., 1889–90; B.S., University of Nashville, 1893; M.S., *ibid.*, 1894; L.I., Peabody Normal College, Nashville, 1893; Principal of Public School, Douglasville, Tex., 1893–94; Teacher of Mathematics, Marshall College, 1894–95; **Scholar in Pedagogy, Clark University, 1895–96; Fellow in Psychology, 1896–97;** Teacher in State Normal School, West Liberty, W. Va., 1897–.

Author of:—

Chairs of Pedagogy in the United States. *W. Va. School Journal*, April, May, and June, 1895.

A Test of Memory in School Children. *Pedagogical Seminary*, Oct., 1896, Vol. 4, pp. 61–78.

What Children like to Read. *W. Va. School Journal*, Charleston, W. Va., Oct., 1897, Vol. 17, pp. 4–6.

HENRY DAVIDSON SHELDON:—

A.B., Stanford University, 1896; A.M., *ibid.*, 1897; Instructor in Department of Education, *ibid.*, 1896–97; **Fellow and Assistant in Pedagogy, Clark University, 1897–99.**

Author of:—

The Institutional Activities of American Children. *Am. Jour. of Psy.*, July, 1898, Vol. 9, pp. 425–448.

FREDERIC D. SHERMAN:—

A.B., University of Michigan, 1887; Principal of Berrien Springs, Mich., School, 1887–88; Principal of Charlotte, Mich., High School, 1888–89; Principal of Bay City, Mich., High School, 1889–94; Universities of Bonn and Leipzig, 1894–97; Ph.D., University of Leipzig, 1897; Professor of Psychology and Pedagogy, State Normal School, Oshkosh, Wis., 1897–98; **Honorary Fellow in Psychology, Clark University, Oct.–Nov., 1898;** Lecturer in History of Education, Teachers College, Columbia University, Dec., 1898–June, 1899; Assistant in Latin, Erasmus Hall High School, Brooklyn, N. Y., 1899–.

Author of:—

Ueber das Purkinje'sche Phänomen im Centrum der Netzhaut. *Philosophische Studien*, 1897, Vol. 13, pp. 434–479.

TOSHIHIDE SHINODA:—

Graduate, Higher Normal School, Tokio, Japan; Graduate Student in United States and Europe, 1886–91; **Honorary Scholar in Pedagogy, Clark University, 1889–90;** Professor in Higher Normal School, Tokio, Japan, 1891–.

LOUIS SIFF:—

S.B., Cornell University (Special Mention in Mathematics), 1897; Graduate Student, Johns Hopkins University, Oct., 1897–Feb., 1898; **Scholar in Mathematics, Clark University, 1898–99;** Teaching Fellow in Mathematics, University of Nebraska, 1899–.

ERNEST B. SKINNER :—

A.B., Ohio University, 18[illegible]; Professor of Mathematics, Amity College, College Springs, Ia., 18[illegible]–91; Scholar in Mathematics, Clark University, 1891–92; Instructor in Mathematics, University of Wisconsin, 189[illegible]–95; Assistant Professor, *ibid.*, 1895–; Member American Mathematical Society.

STEPHEN E. SLOCUM :—

B.E., Union University (Honors in Mathematics and Physics), 1897; Scholar in Mathematics, Clark University, 1897–98; Fellow, 1898–99.

Author of :—

Note on the Chief Theorem of Lie's Theory of Continuous Groups. *Proc. Am. Acad.* (In press.)

JAMES R. SLONAKER :—

Graduate, Indiana State Normal School, 18[illegible]; Supervising Principal of Schools, Elroy, Wis., 18[illegible]–91; University of Wisconsin, 1891–93; B.S., *ibid.*, 1893; Fellow in Biology, Clark University, 1893–96; Ph.D., Clark University, 1896; Instructor in Zoölogy, Indiana University, 1896–; Member Indiana Academy of Science.

Author of :—

A Comparative Study of the Point of Acute Vision in the Vertebrates. *American Naturalist*, Jan., 1896, Vol. 30, pp. 24–32.

A Comparative Study of the Area of Acute Vision in Vertebrates. *Jour. of Morph.*, May, 1897, Vol. 13, pp. 445–502.

The Fovea. *Proc. Ind. Acad. of Science*, 1896, pp. 304–310.

A Method of Preserving the Eye for Sectioning, or for Demonstrating the Area of Acute Vision. *Jour. of Applied Microscopy*, Feb., 1898, Vol. 1, p. 18.

The Eye of the Mammoth Cave Rat. *Proc. Ind. Acad. of Science*, 189[illegible].

MAURICE H. SMALL :—

A.B., Colby University, 18[illegible]; Principal, High School, Norway, Me., 18[illegible]–[illegible]; *ibid.*, Westbrook, Me., 18[illegible]–95; Scholar in Psychology, Clark University, 1895–96; Fellow, 1896–98; Principal High School, Passaic, N.J., 189[illegible]–.

Author of :—

The Suggestibility of Children. *Pedagogical Seminary*, Dec., 1896, Vol. 4, pp. 176–220.

Methods of manifesting the Instinct for Certainty. *Ibid.*, Jan., 1898, Vol. 5, pp. 313–380.

An Experiment borrowed from the Schoolroom. *Northwestern Monthly*, Nov., 1898, Vol. 9, pp. 134–155.

WILLARD STANTON SMALL :—

A.B., Tufts College, 1894; A.M., *ibid.*, 1897; Tufts Divinity School, 1894–96; Professor of English Language and Literature, Lombard University, 1896–97; Scholar in Psychology, Clark University, 1897–98; Fellow, 1898–99.

Author of :—

Friedrich Nietzsche (Review). *Pedagogical Seminary*, April, 1898, Vol. 5, pp. 606–610.

Note on the Psychic Development of the Young White Rat. *Am. Jour. of Psy.*, Oct., 1899, Vol. 11, pp. 80–100.

WARREN R. SMITH :—

A.B., Bowdoin College, 1890; Instructor Leicester Academy, Leicester, Mass., 1890–91; Scholar in Chemistry, Clark University, 1891–92; Fellow in Chemistry, University of Chicago, 1892–94; Ph.D., *ibid.*, 1894; Assistant in Chemistry, Bowdoin College, 1894–95; Instructor in Science, New Bedford High School, 1895–96; Instructor in charge Department of Chemistry, Lewis Institute, Chicago, Ill., 1896–.

Author of :—

On the Addition Products of the Aromatic Isocyanides. *Am. Chem. Jour.*, May, 1894, Vol. 16, pp. 372–393.

HUGH A. SNIFF:—

A.B., Heidelberg College, 1893; Principal, High School, Germantown, O., 1893–94; Tutor in Mathematics, Heidelberg College, 1894–95; Scholar in Mathematics, Clark University, 1895–96; Instructor in Mathematics and Science, High School, Tiffin, O., 1896–98; Student in Mathematics, University of Chicago, Summer Quarter, 1897.

FRANK E. SPAULDING:—

A.B., Amherst College, 1889; Instructor, Military Academy, Louisville, Ky., 1889–90; Instructor and Associate Principal, *ibid.*, 1890–91; Student in Universities of Leipzig, Paris, and Berlin, 1891–94; Ph.D., University of Leipzig, 1894; **Honorary Fellow in Psychology, Clark University, Oct., 1894–May, 1895**; Superintendent of Schools, Ware, Mass., May, 1895–June, 1897; Superintendent of Schools, Passaic, N. J., September, 1897–; President, New Jersey Association for the Study of Children and Youth, 1899.

Author of:—

Richard Cumberland als Begründer der Englischen Ethik. Leipzig, 1894. xii + 101 pp.

The Province of the Elementary School. *Jour. of Pedagogy*, Sept., 1896, Vol. 9, pp. 129–137.

Mental Images. *Educational Foundations*, Sept., 1897, Vol. 9, pp. 15–21.

The Dynamics of Mental Images. *Ibid.*, Oct., 1897, Vol. 9, pp. 65–70.

Some Psychic Processes involved in Reading. *Ibid.*, Nov., 1897, Vol. 9, pp. 130–137.

The Psychology of Defective Reading. *Ibid.*, Dec., 1897, pp. 194–201.

Mental Economy in Reading. *Ibid.*, Jan., 1898, Vol. 9, pp. 257–262.

Psychic Aspects of Learning to Read. *Ibid.*, Feb., 1898, Vol 9, pp. 347–352.

Preventing and Correcting Defective Reading. *Ibid.*, March, 1898, Vol. 9, pp. 389–394.

What can One Read? *Ibid.*, April, 1898, Vol. 9, pp. 514–520.

Psychology in Geography. *Ibid.*, May and June, 1898, Vol. 9, pp. 572–577, 619–625.

The Elementary Character of Secondary Education. *Jour. of Pedagogy*, Jan., 1899, Vol. 12, pp. 11–24.

Immediate Educational Work. *Annual Report, Supt. of Schools*, Ware, Mass., Feb. 1, 1896, pp. 17–22.

Educational Policy and Aims. *Ibid.*, Feb. 1, 1897, pp. 14–32.

The Course of Study; Grading and Promotion, etc. *Annual Report, Supt. of Schools*, Passaic, N. J., 1897–98, pp. 9–64.

EDWIN D. STARBUCK:—

A.B., Indiana University, 1890; Teacher of Mathematics and Latin, Spiceland, Ind. Academy, 1890–91; Teacher of Mathematics, Vincennes College, 1891–93; Student in Psychology, Harvard University, 1893–95; A.B., *ibid.*, 1894; A.M., *ibid.*, 1895; **Fellow in Psychology, Clark University, 1895–97; Ph.D., Clark University, 1897**; Assistant Professor of Education, Stanford University, 1897–.

Author of:—

A Study of Conversion. *Am. Jour. of Psy.*, Jan., 1897, Vol. 8, pp. 268–308.

Some Aspects of Religious Growth. *Ibid.*, Oct., 1897, Vol. 9, pp. 70–124.

Child Study and its Possibility as a Science. *Northwestern Monthly*, March–April, 1899, Vol. 9, pp. 356–362.

Psychology of Religion. With an introduction by Professor William James. *Contemporary Science Series.* (In press.)

ORLANDO B. STETSON:—

Worcester Polytechnic Institute, 1895–98; **Scholar in Mathematics, Clark University, 1898–99.**

COLIN C. STEWART:—

B.A., University of Toronto, 1894; **Scholar in Physiology, Clark Uni-**

versity, 1894–95; Fellow, 1896–97; Ph. D., Clark University, 1897; Assistant in Physiology, Harvard Medical School, 1897–98; Tutor in Physiology, Columbia University, 1898–; Member American Physiological Society.

Author of:—

The Influence of Acute Alcohol Poisoning on Nerve Cells. *Jour. of Exp. Medicine*, Nov., 1896, Vol. 1, pp. 623–629.

Variations in Daily Activity produced by Alcohol and by Changes in Barometric Pressure and Diet, with a Description of Recording Methods. *Am. Jour. of Physiology*, Jan., 1898, Vol. 1, pp. 40–56.

On the Course of Impulses to and from the Cat's Bladder. *Ibid.*, Jan., 1899, Vol. 2, pp. 182–202.

A Simple Etherizing Bottle. *Ibid.* (Proc. Am. Physiol. Soc., Dec., 1898), Vol. 2, p. x.

The Relaxation of the Cat's Bladder. *Ibid.*, Aug., 1899, Vol. 3, pp. 1–8.

JULIUS STIEGLITZ:—

University of Berlin, 1886–89; University of Göttingen, 1888; Ph.D., University of Berlin, 1889; Scholar in Chemistry, Clark University, Jan.–June, 1890; Chemist, Parke, Davis & Co., Detroit, Mich., 1890–92; Docent in Chemistry, University of Chicago, 1892–93; Assistant in Chemistry, *ibid.*, 1893–94; Instructor in Chemistry, *ibid.*, 1894–97; Assistant Professor in Chemistry, *ibid.*, 1897–; Fellow of the American Association Advancement of Science; Member, Deutsche Chemische Gesellschaft.

Author of:—

Ueber das Verhalten der Amidoxime gegen Diazobenzolverbindungen. *Ber. d. deuts. chem. Gesellschaft*, 1889, Vol. 22, pp. 3148–3160.

On Benzoquinone Carboxylic Acids. *Am. Chem. Jour.*, 1891, Vol. 13, pp. 38–42.

Alkaloidwertbestimmung von Extrakten. *Pharmaceutische Rundschau*, 1892 and 1893, 8 papers.

Ferric Phosphate, U. S. P., and Ferric Pyrophosphate, U. S. P. *Journal of Pharmacy*, 1891.

Notes on Pyrophosphoric and Phosphoric Acid. *Ibid.*, 1891.

Derivatives of Nitrogen Halogen Compounds. (With F. Lengfeld.) *Am. Chem. Jour.*, 1893, Vol. 15, pp. 215–223, 504–518; Vol. 16, pp. 373–378.

The Action of Phosphorus Pentachloride on Urethanes. (With F. Lengfeld.) *Ibid.*, 1894, Vol. 16, pp. 70–76.

Ueber Alkylisoharnstoffe. (With F. Lengfeld.) *Ber. d. deuts. chem. Gesellschaft*, 1894, Vol. 27, pp. 926–927.

Ueber die Einwirkung von Natriumäthylat auf Carbodiphenylimid. *Ibid.*, 1895, Vol. 28, pp. 573–574.

Ueber Thiamine. (With F. Lengfeld.) *Ibid.*, 1895, Vol. 28, pp. 575–576, 3742–3744.

On Imidoethers of Carbonic Acid. (With F. Lengfeld.) *Am. Chem. Jour.*, 1895, Vol. 17, pp. 98–116.

On the "Beckmann Rearrangement." *Ibid.*, 1896, Vol. 18, pp. 751–761.

On the Constitution of the Salts of Imidoethers and other Carbimide Derivatives. *Ibid.*, 1899, Vol. 21, pp. 101–111.

F. E. STINSON:—

Iowa Agricultural College, 1884–85; Principal, Poplar Grove Institute, Ark., 1889–90; Instructor in Physics and Mathematics, Paris Academy, Ark., 1890–92; Scholar in Mathematics, Clark University, 1892–93; Fellow, 1893–95.

WILLIAM E. STORY:—

A.B., Harvard University, 1871; Parker Fellow, *ibid.*, 1874–75; Universities of Berlin and Leipzig, 1871–75; Ph.D., University of Leipzig, 1875; Tutor of Mathematics, Harvard University, 1875–76; Associate, Assistant Professor, and Associate Professor of Mathematics, Johns Hopkins University, 1876–89; Associate Editor in Charge, *American Journal of Mathematics*, 1878–82; Professor of Mathematics, Clark University,

1889–; Editor, *Mathematical Review*, 1896–.

Author of:—

On the Algebraic Relations existing between the Polars of a Binary Quantic. Dissertation approved for the degree of Ph.D., Leipzig, 1875. 55 pp.

On the Elastic Potential of Crystals. *Am. Jour. of Math.*, 1878, Vol. 1, pp. 177–183.

Note on Mr. Kempe's Paper on the Geographical Problem of the Four Colors. *Ibid.*, 1879, Vol. 2, pp. 201–204.

Note on the "15" Puzzle. *Ibid.*, 1879, Vol. 2, pp. 399–404.

On the Theory of Rational Derivation on a Cubic Curve (followed by a Note on Totients). *Ibid.*, 1880, Vol. 3, pp. 356–387.

On the Non-Euclidean Trigonometry. *Ibid.*, 1881, Vol. 4, pp. 332–335.

On the Non-Euclidean Geometry. *Ibid.*, 1883, Vol. 5, pp. 180–211.

On Non-Euclidean Properties of Conics. *Ibid.*, 1883, Vol. 5, pp. 358–381.

On the Absolute Classification of Quadratic Loci, and on their Intersections with each other and with Linear Loci. *Ibid.*, 1885, Vol. 7, pp. 223–246.

The Addition-Theorem for Elliptic Functions. *Ibid.*, 1886, Vol. 8, pp. 364–376.

A New Method in Analytic Geometry. *Ibid.*, 1887, Vol. 9, pp. 38–44.

On the Covariants of a System of Quantics. *Math. Annalen*, 1893, Vol. 41, pp. 469–490.

On an Operator that produces all the Covariants and Invariants of any System of Quantics. *Proc. London Math. Soc.*, 1892, Vol. 23, pp. 265–272.

Hyperspace and Non-Euclidean Geometry. I. *Mathematical Review*, April, 1897, Vol. 1, pp. 169–184.

J. RICHARD STREET:—

A.B., Victoria University, 1884; A.M., *Ibid.*, 1893 (with First Honors in English, French, German, and Italian); Modern Language Master, Smithville High School, 1885–86; Walkerton High School, 1886–87; Principal Caledonia High School, Ontario, 1887–95; Associate Member of the Board of Government Examiners, 1891–96; Member and Secretary of the County Board of Examiners for Professional Teachers' Certificates, 1890–95; Sometime Examiner in English, French, and German for Albert, Alma, and Brantford Colleges; Instructor in the Mechanics Institute, Caledonia, 1893–95; Scholar in Pedagogy, Clark University, 1895–96; Fellow in Psychology, 1896–98; Ph.D., Clark University, 1898; Professor of Pedagogy, Bible Normal College, Springfield, Mass., 1898–; also Professor of Theory and Practice of Teaching, Mount Holyoke College, 1899–.

Author of:—

A Study in Language Teaching. *Pedagogical Seminary*, April, 1897, Vol. 4, pp. 269–293.

A Study in Moral Education. *Ibid.*, July, 1897, Vol. 5, pp. 5–40.

A Genetic Study of Immortality. *Ibid.*, Sept., 1899, Vol. 6, pp. 267–313.

Linguistic Interpretation. (In press.)

CHARLES A. STRONG:—

A.B., University of Rochester, 1884; A.B., Harvard University, 1885; Rochester Theological Seminary, 1885–86; Fellow, Harvard University, 1886–87; University of Berlin, 1886–87; Instructor in Philosophy, Cornell University, 1887–89; Universities of Paris, Berlin, and Freiburg, 1889–90; Docent in Philosophy, Clark University, 1890–91; Associate Professor of Psychology, University of Chicago, 1892–95; Lecturer in Psychology, Columbia University, 1895–.

Author of:—

A Sketch of the History of Psychology among the Greeks. *Am. Jour. of Psy.*, Dec., 1891, Vol. 4, pp. 177–197.

Dr. Münsterberg's Doctrine of Mind and Body and its Consequences. *Philosophical Review*, March, 1892, Vol. 1, pp. 179–196.

Mr. James Ward on Modern Psychology. *Psychological Review*, Jan., 1894, Vol. 1, pp. 73–81.

The Psychology of Pain. *Ibid.*, July, 1895, Vol. 2, pp. 329–347.

Physical Pain and Pain Nerves. *Ibid.*, Jan., 1896, Vol. 3, pp. 64–68.

Consciousness and Time. *Ibid.*, March, 1896, Vol. 3, pp. 149–167.

CHARLES E. SWARTZ :—

A.B., Johns Hopkins University, 1888; University of Heidelberg, 1888–89; Fellow in Chemistry, Clark University, 1889–90; Gettysburg Theological Seminary, 1890–91; Oberlin Theological Seminary, 1891–93; B.D., *ibid.*, 1893; Pastor, Congregational Church, Bellevue, O., 1893–.

HENRY TABER :—

Ph.B., Yale University (Sheffield Scientific School), 1882; Johns Hopkins University, 1883–86 and 1886–88; Ph.D., Johns Hopkins University, 1888; Assistant in Mathematics, *ibid.*, 1888–89; Docent in Mathematics, Clark University, 1889–92; Assistant Professor of Mathematics, 1892–; Resident Fellow American Academy of Arts and Sciences; Member: London Mathematical Society; American Mathematical Society.

Author of:

On the Theory of Matrices. *Am. Jour. of Math.*, July, 1890, Vol. 12, pp. 337–396.

On the Application to Matrices of any order of the Quaternion Symbols *S* and *V*. *Proc. London Math. Soc.*, Dec. 11, 1890, Vol. 22, pp. 67–79.

On Certain Identities in the Theory of Matrices. *Am. Jour. of Math.*, Jan., 1891, Vol. 13, pp. 159–172.

On Certain Properties of Symmetric, Skew Symmetric, and Orthogonal Matrices. *Proc. London Math. Soc.*, June 11, 1891, Vol. 22, pp. 449–469.

On the Matrical Equation $\phi\Omega = \Omega\phi$. *Proc. A. A. A. S.*, 1891, Vol. 26, pp. 64–66.

On a Theorem of Sylvester's relating to Non-Degenerate Matrices. *Ibid.*, 1892, Vol. 27, pp. 46–56.

Note on the Representation of Orthogonal Matrices. *Ibid.*, 1892, Vol. 27, pp. 163–164.

On the Linear Transformations between Two Quadrics. *Proc. London Math. Soc.*, May 11, 1893, Vol. 24, pp. 290–306.

On Real Orthogonal Substitution. *Proc. A. A. A. S.*, 1893, Vol. 28, pp. 212–221.

On Orthogonal Substitution. Mathematical papers read at International Mathematical Congress, Chicago, 1893. Macmillan & Co., N. Y., 1896. pp. 395–400.

On Orthogonal Substitutions that can be expressed as a Function of a Single Alternate (or Skew Symmetric) Linear Substitution. *Am. Jour. of Math.*, Jan., 1894, Vol. 16, pp. 123–130.

On Orthogonal Substitutions. *Bull. N. Y. Math. Soc.*, July, 1894, Vol. 3, pp. 251–259.

On the Automorphic Linear Transformation of a Bilinear Form. *Proc. A. A. A. S.*, 1894, Vol. 29, pp. 178–179.

On the Group of Automorphic Linear Transformations of a Bilinear Form. *Ibid.*, pp. 371–381.

On those Orthogonal Substitutions that can be generated by the Repetition of an Infinitesimal Orthogonal Substitution. *Proc. London Math. Soc.*, May 9, 1895, Vol. 26, pp. 364–376.

On the Automorphic Linear Transformation of an Alternate Bilinear Form. *Math. Annalen*, 1895, Vol. 46, pp. 561–583.

On Certain Sub-Groups of the General Projective Group. *Bull. Am. Math. Soc.*, April, 1896, 2d ser., Vol. 2, pp. 221–233.

On a Twofold Generalization of Stieltje's Theorem. *Proc. London Math. Soc.*, June 11, 1896, Vol. 27, pp. 613–621.

Note on the Special Linear Homogeneous Group. *Bull. Am. Math. Soc.*, July, 1896, 2d ser., Vol. 2, pp. 336–339.

Note on the Automorphic Linear Transformation of a Bilinear Form. *Proc.*

A. A. A. S., 1896, Vol. 31, pp. 161–163.

On the Group of Real Linear Transformations whose Invariant is an Alternate Bilinear Form. *Ibid.*, pp. 336–337.

Notes on the Theory of Bilinear Forms. *Bull. Am. Math. Soc.*, Jan., 1897, 2d ser., Vol. 3, pp. 156–164.

On the Transformations between Two Symmetric or Alternate Bilinear Forms. *Mathematical Review*, April, 1897, Vol. 1, pp. 120–128.

On the Group of Linear Homogeneous Transformations whose Invariant is a Bilinear Form. *Ibid.*, pp. 164–168.

On the Group of Real Linear Transformations whose Invariant is a Real Quadratic Form. *Proc. A. A. A. S.*, 1897, Vol. 52, pp. 77–83.

ROBERT R. TATNALL:—

S.B., Haverford College, 1890; A.M., *Ibid.*, 1891; Graduate Student, Johns Hopkins University, 1891–93; Fellow and Assistant in Physics, Northwestern University, 1893–94; Graduate Student, Johns Hopkins University, 1894–96; Ph.D., Johns Hopkins University, 1896; Instructor in Physics, University of Pennsylvania, 1896–97; Honorary Fellow in Physics, Clark University, 1897–98; Instructor in Physics, Academy of Northwestern University, 1899–.

Author of:—

A New Proof of the Fundamental Equation of the Spectrometer. (Note by Professor Crew in *Astronomy and Astrophysics*, 1892, pp. 232–233.)

On a New Method for Mapping the Spectra of Metals. (With H. Crew.) *Philosophical Magazine*, Oct., 1894, 5th ser., Vol. 38, pp. 379–386.

The Arc-Spectra of the Elements. (With H. A. Rowland.) *Astrophysical Journal*, Jan., Feb., and Oct., 1895, and April, 1896.

SAMUEL N. TAYLOR:—

Ph.B., Wesleyan University, Middletown, Conn., 1887; In Charge of Experimental Laboratory, Thompson-Houston Electric Works, Lynn, Mass., 1887–91; Professor of Natural Sciences, Maine Wesleyan Seminary and Female College, 1891–93; Fellow in Physics, Clark University, 1893–96; Ph.D., Clark University, 1896; Instructor in Physics, Purdue University, 1896–99; Associate Professor of Physics, Syracuse University, 1899–; Member of Indiana Academy of Science.

Author of:—

A Comparison of the Electromotive Force of the Clark and Cadmium Cells. *Physical Review*, Sept.–Oct., 1898, Vol. 7, pp. 149–170.

CHARLES HUBBARD THURBER:—

Ph.B., Cornell University, 1886; A.M., Haverford College, 1890; Registrar and Secretary, Cornell University, 1886–88; Teacher, Haverford College Grammar School, 1888–90; Special Agent U. S. Bureau of Education in Germany, 1890–91; Student, Royal Polytechnicum, Dresden, 1890–91; Instructor in French, Cornell University, 1891–93; Professor of Pedagogy, Colgate University, and Principal, Colgate Academy, 1893–95; Director of Division of Child Study, Department of Public Instruction, State of New York, 1894–95; Assistant to Editor-in-chief, Johnson's "Universal Cyclopædia," 1893–94; Editor, *School Review*, 1893–; Editor, *Transactions of Illinois Society for Child Study*, 1898–99; Dean of the Morgan Park Academy, Sept., 1895–April, 1899; Associate Professor of Pedagogy, University of Chicago, 1895–; Director of Coöperating Work, *Ibid.*, April, 1899; Honorary Fellow in Pedagogy, Clark University, Jan.–April, 1899.

Author of:—

The Cohesive Forces in American Nationality. *Cornell Review*, 1886, Vol. 13, pp. 303–307.

The Higher Schools of Prussia and the School of Conference of 1890. *Rep. of the Com'r of Ed.*, 1889–90, Vol. 1, pp. 315–416.

School Reform in Germany. *Academy*, April, 1891, Vol. 6, p. [illegible].

A History Lesson in German. *Jour. of Education*, Sept. [illegible], 189[illegible], Vol. [illegible], pp. [illegible]-[illegible].

Editor, L'oro e l'orpello. (Heath's Modern Language Series.) Boston, 189[illegible]. 68 pp.

Summer Meetings. *School Review*, Sept., 1894, Vol. 2, pp. 430-43[illegible].

The N. E. A. at Denver. *School Review*, Sept., 1895, Vol. 3, pp. 42[illegible]-433.

Report of Child Study Division, Department of Public Instruction, State of New York, 1895.

Tabular Statement of Entrance Requirements to Representative Colleges and Universities of the United States. (With W. J. Chase.) *School Review*, June, 1896, Vol. 4, pp. 341-416.

College Entrance Requirements. *Proc. Ass'n Colleges and Preparatory Schools of the Middle States and Maryland*. Philadelphia meeting, 1896.

High School Self-Government. *School Review*, Jan., 1897, Vol. 5, pp. [illegible]-[illegible].

The Report of the Committee of Ten. *School Journal*, June, 1897.

Brennende Fragen in dem Unterrichtswesen der Vereinigten Staaten. *Deutsche Zeitschrift für Ausländisches Unterrichtswesen*, July, 1897, Vol. 2, pp. [illegible]-[illegible].

The Relation of Child Study to Sunday School Work. *Northwestern Monthly*, Sept., 1897, Vol. 8, pp. 137-141.

Is the Present High-School Course a Satisfactory Preparation for Business? If not, how should it be modified? *Proc. N. E. A.*, 1897, pp. [illegible]-81[illegible].

Die Sekundärschulen. *Rein's Encyklopädisches Handbuch der Erziehungs- und Unterrichtslehre*, 1897, Vol. 1, part II, pp. [illegible]-604.

Report of the Department of Child Study. *Rep. State Super. Pub. Instr.*, Albany, N. Y., 1897, Vol. [illegible], pp. [illegible]-[illegible].

English as it is taught. *School Review*, May, 1898, Vol. 6, pp. [illegible]-[illegible].

Plans for the Development of Child Study in the State through the State Department. *Trans. Ill. Soc. for Child Study*, Jan., 1899, Vol. 3, pp. 19[illegible]-19[illegible].

Vittorino da Feltre. *School Review*, May, 1899, Vol. 7, pp. [illegible]-[illegible].

The New Courses in Pedagogy. *Madisonensis*, Vol. 26, pp. 175-176.

The Field and Work of a College Christian Association. *New Era*, Vol. [illegible], p. 16.

Hints on Child Study. *Dep. Pub. Instr.*, State of New York.

Numerous signed biographical and educational articles in Johnson's "Universal Cyclopædia" (new edition), 189[illegible]-94; 1895-9[illegible].

Editor of "Twentieth Century" Text-Books.

FREDERICK TRACY: —

Pickering College, 1883-86; B.A., University of Toronto, 1890; Fellow in Philosophy, *ibid.*, 1890-91; Fellow in Psychology, Clark University, 1892-93; Ph.D., Clark University, 1893; Lecturer in Philosophy, University of Toronto, 1893-; Member Illinois Society for Child Study; President Ontario Child Study Association.

Author of: —

The Testimony of Consciousness. *Woodstock Col. Mon.*, March, 1891.

The Language of Children. *Proc. Int. Ed. Congress*, 1893.

The Psychology of Childhood. D. C. Heath & Co., Boston, 1893. 2d ed., 1894.

The New Psychology. *Can. Meth. Mag.*, Nov., 1894.

The Scottish Philosophy. *Univ. of Toronto Quar.*, Nov., 1895.

Hypnotism. *Can. Meth. Mag.*, Nov., 1895.

Results of Child Study applied to Education. *Trans. Ill. Soc. for Child Study*, 1895, Vol. 1, No. 4, p. 1[illegible].

Child Study and Pedagogy. *Proc. Ont. Ed. Ass'n*, 1895.

Character as a Product of Education in Schools. Overland Monthly Publishing Co., 1896.

A Syllabus of Psychology. Toronto, 1898.

The Culture of the Spiritual Life. *McMaster Univ. Mon.*, Jan., 1897.

Die Kinderpsychologie in England und Nord-America. *Die Kinderfehler*, April and July, 1897, Vol. 2, pp. 33–42, 72–87.

Results of Child Study. *N. Y. School Jour.*, July 10, 17, and 24, 1897.

Left-handedness. *Trans. Ill. Soc. for Child Study*, 1897, Vol. 2, pp. 68–76.

Child Study, its Practical Value. *Proc. Ont. Ed. Ass'n*, 1897.

Sully's "Studies of Childhood." *Ibid.*, 1898.

Psychologie der Kindheit. Translated by J. Stimpfl. E. Wunderlich, Leipzig, 1899. 168 pp.

NORMAN TRIPLETT: —

A.B., Illinois College, 1889; Principal New Berlin, Ill., School, 1889–91; Practised Law, *ibid.*, 1891–94; Instructor in Physics, Chemistry, and Psychology, Quincy, Ill., High School, 1894–97; A.M., Indiana University, 1898; Fellow in Psychology, Clark University, 1898–99.

Author of: —

The Dynamogenic Factors in Pacemaking and Competition. *Am. Jour. of Psy.*, July, 1898, Vol. 9, pp. 507–533.

FREDERICK TUCKERMAN: —

B.S., Boston University, 1878; M.D., Harvard Medical School, 1882; Student, London and Berlin, 1882–83; Lecturer in Anatomy and Physiology, Massachusetts Agricultural College, 1883–86; Fellow in Vertebrate Anatomy, Clark University, 1889–90; Student, Universities of Berlin, London, and Heidelberg, 1892–94; A.M. and Ph.D., University of Heidelberg, 1894; Private Laboratory at Amherst, Mass., 1894–; Fellow of the Massachusetts Medical Society, 1883–86; Member of: American Society of Naturalists, Boston Society of Natural History, Anatomical Society of Germany, etc.

Author of: —

Some Observations in Reference to Bilateral Asymmetry of Form and Function. *Jour. Anat. and Phys.*, 1884, Vol. 19, pp. 307–308.

Supernumerary Leg in a Male Frog (Rana palustris). *Ibid.*, 1886, Vol. 20, pp. 516–519, Pl. xvi.

The Tongue and Gustatory Organs of Mephitis mephitica. *Quar. Jour. Micr. Sci.*, 1887, Vol. 28, pp. 149–167, Pl. xi.

The Tongue and Gustatory Organs of Fiber zibethicus. *Jour. Anat. and Phys.*, 1888, Vol. 22, pp. 135–141, Pl. vii.

Note on the Papilla foliata and other Taste Areas of the Pig. *Anat. Anzeiger*, 1888, Vol. 3, pp. 69–73.

An Interesting Specimen of Taenia saginata. *Zool. Anzeiger*, 1888, Vol. 11, pp. 94–95.

The Anatomy of the Papilla foliata of the Human Infant. *Jour. Anat. and Phys.*, 1888, Vol. 22, pp. 499–501, Pl. xviii.

Antipyrine in Cephalalgia. *N. Y. Med. Record*, 1888, p. 180.

Observations on the Structure of the Gustatory Organs of the Bat (Vespertilio subulatus). *Jour. of Morph.*, 1888, Vol. 2, pp. 1–6, Pl. i.

Supplementary Note on Taenia saginata. *Zool. Anzeiger*, 1888, Vol. 11, pp. 475–476, figures.

Anthropometric Data Relating to Students of the Massachusetts Agricultural College. Amherst, 1888.

On the Gustatory Organs of Putorius vison. *Anat. Anzeiger*, 1888, Vol. 3, pp. 941–942.

On the Gustatory Organs of Vulpes vulgaris. *Jour. Anat. and Phys.*, 1889, Vol. 23, pp. 201–205.

On the Gustatory Organs of Arctomys monax. *Anat. Anzeiger*, 1889, Vol. 4, pp. 334–335.

On the Development of the Taste-Organs of Man. *Jour. Anat. and Phys.*, 1889, Vol. 23, pp. 559–582.

On the Gustatory Organs of Sciurus carolinensis. *Microscope*, 1889, Vol. 9, pp. 193–196, Pl. vii.

On the Gustatory Organs of Erethizon dorsatus. *Am. Mo. Micr. Jour.*, 1889, Vol. 10, p. 181.

An Hitherto Undescribed Taste Area in Perameles nasuta. *Anat. Anzeiger*, 1889, Vol. 4, pp. 411–412, figure.

On the Gustatory Organs of the American Hare (Lepus americanus). *Am. Jour. of Sci.*, 1889, Vol. 38, pp. 277–280.

Note on the Tongue of Chrysotis aestiva. *Microscope*, 1889, Vol. 9, pp. 289–290.

The Gustatory Organs of Belideus ariel. *Jour. Anat. and Phys.*, 1889, Vol. 24, pp. 85–88, Pl. v.

Further Observations on the Development of the Taste-Organs of Man. *Ibid.*, pp. 130–131.

The Gustatory Organs of Procyon lotor. *Ibid.*, pp. 156–159, Pl. x.

On the Gustatory Organs of the Mammalia. *Proc. Boston So. Nat. Hist.*, 1890, Vol. 24, pp. 470–482.

On the Gustatory Organs of some Edentata. *Internat. Monats. f. Anat. u. Phys.*, 1890, Vol. 7, pp. 335–339.

On the Gustatory Organs of some of the Mammalia. *Jour. of Morph.*, 1890, Vol. 4, pp. 151–193.

The Development of the Gustatory Organs in Man. *Am. Jour. of Psy.*, April, 1890, Vol. 3, pp. 195–197.

On the Gustatory Organs of Sciurus hudsonius. *Internat. Monats. f. Anat. u. Phys.*, 1891, Vol. 8, pp. 137–139, Pl. xi.

Observations on some Mammalian Taste-Organs. *Jour. Anat. and Phys.*, 1891, Vol. 25, pp. 505–508.

On the Terminations of the Nerves in the Lingual Papilla of the Chelonia. *Internat. Monats. f. Anat. u. Phys.*, 1892, Vol. 9, pp. 1–5, Pl. i.

The Gustatory Organs of Ateles ater. *Jour. Anat. and Phys.*, 1892, Vol. 26, pp. 391–393.

Further Observations on the Gustatory Organs of the Mammalia. *Jour. of Morph.*, 1892, Vol. 7, pp. 69–94.

Note on the Structure of the Mammalian Taste-Bulb. *Anat. Anzeiger*, 1893, Vol. 8, pp. 366–367.

The Development of the Organs of Taste. *Reference Hand-book of the Medical Sciences*, 1893, Vol. 9, pp. 657–659, figures, 600–607.

JOHN N. VAN DER VRIES :—

A.B., Hope College, 1896; Principal of School, East Saugatuck, Mich., 1896–97; Scholar in Mathematics, Clark University, 1897–98; Fellow, 1898–99.

FRANK L. O. WADSWORTH :—

E.M., Ohio State University, 1888; M.E., *ibid.*, 1889; B.S., *ibid.*, 1889; Assistant in Physics, *ibid.*, 1888–89; Fellow in Physics, Clark University, 1889–90; Fellow and Assistant, 1890–92; Special Assistant and Delegate from the Smithsonian Institution to the Bureau Internationale des Poids et Mesures, Paris, 1892; Senior Assistant in Charge, Astrophysical Observatory, Smithsonian Institution, 1892–94; Assistant Professor in Physics, University of Chicago, 1894–96; Assistant Professor of Astrophysics, Yerkes Observatory, 1896–97; Associate Professor of Astrophysics, *ibid.*, 1897–98; Special Engineering and Expert Work, Pittsburg and Washington, 1898–99; Director of the Allegheny Observatory, May, 1899–; Assistant Editor, *Astrophysical Journal*; Associate Editor, *Harper's Scientific Memoirs*; Member Astronomical and Astrophysical Society of America.

Author of :—

Some New Forms of Dynamos. *Electrical World*, Sept. 13, 1890, Vol. 16, pp. 183–184.

On the Relation between Rise of Temperature and Current in Electric Conductors. *Ibid.*, Feb. 27, 1892, and March 12, 1892, Vol. 19, pp. 145–146, 180–181.

Application of Interference Methods to Base Line Measurement. Philosophical Society, Washington, Nov., 1892.

Report of the Smithsonian Astrophysical Observatory. *Smithsonian Ann. Rep.*, Appendix V., 1893, pp. 60–63.

Electric Controls and Governors for Astronomical Instruments. *Astronomy and Astrophysics*, April, 1894, Vol. 13, pp. 266–271.

A Simple Method of determining the Eccentricity of a Graduated Circle with One Vernier. *Am. Jour. of Sci.*, May, 1894, 3d ser., Vol. 47, pp. 373–376.

The Manufacture of Very Accurate Straight Edges. *Jour. of the Franklin Institute*, July, 1894, Vol. 90, pp. 128. Reprinted in *American Machinist*, Aug. 2, 1894.

An Improved Form of Littrow Spectroscope. *Philosophical Magazine*, July, 1894, 5th ser., Vol. 38, pp. 137–142.

A New Design for Large Spectroscope Slits. *Am. Jour. of Sci.*, July, 1894, 3d ser., Vol. 48, pp. 19–20.

Some New Double Motion Mechanisms. *Astronomy and Astrophysics*, Aug., 1894, Vol. 13, pp. 627–628. Reprinted in *Zeits. f. Instrumentenkunde*, Jan., 1895, Vol. 15, pp. 23–25.

Fixed Arm Spectroscopes. *Philosophical Magazine*, Oct., 1894, 5th ser., Vol. 38, pp. 337–351. Reprinted in *Astronomy and Astrophysics* as No. 9 of the series, The Modern Spectroscope, Dec., 1894, Vol. 13, pp. 836–840.

Ein neuer Spektroskopspalt mit Doppelbewegung. *Zeits. f. Instrumentenkunde*, Oct., 1894, Vol. 14, pp. 354–356.

A Simple Method of mounting an Equatorial Axis on Ball Bearings. *Astronomy and Astrophysics*, Nov., 1894, Vol. 13, pp. 723–728.

A New Method of magnetizing and astatizing Galvanometer Needles. *Philosophical Magazine*, Nov., 1894, 5th ser., Vol. 38, pp. 483–488.

An Improved Form of Interrupter for Large Induction Coils. *Am. Jour. of Sci.*, Dec., 1894, 3d ser., Vol. 48, pp. 495–501.

Description of a Very Sensitive Form of Thomson Galvanometer and Some Methods of Galvanometer Construction. *Philosophical Magazine*, Dec., 1894, 5th ser., Vol. 38, pp. 553–558.

General Considerations respecting the Design of Astronomical Spectroscopes. Forming No. 10 of the series, The Modern Spectroscope. *Astrophysical Journal*, Jan., 1895, Vol. 1, pp. 52–79.

Bemerkungen über Versilberungsflüssigkeiten und Versilberung. *Zeits. f. Instrumentenkunde*, Jan., 1895, Vol. 15, pp. 23–27. Reprinted in the *Astrophysical Journal*, March, 1895, Vol. 1, pp. 252–260.

The Design of Electric Motors for Constant Speed. *Astrophysical Journal*, Feb., 1895, Vol. 1, pp. 169–177.

Some New Designs of Combined Grating and Prismatic Spectroscopes of the Fixed Arm Type and a New Form of Objective Prism. Forming No. 11 of the series, The Modern Spectroscope. *Ibid.*, March, 1895, Vol. 1, pp. 232–247.

Einfacher Unterbrecher für grosse Induktionsapparate. *Zeits. f. Instrumentenkunde*, July, 1895, Vol. 15, pp. 248–250.

A New Multiple Transmission Prism of Great Resolving Power. No. 13 of the series, The Modern Spectroscope. *Astrophysical Journal*, Nov., 1895, Vol. 2, pp. 264–272.

Fixed Arm Concave Grating Spectroscopes. No. 14, The Modern Spectroscope. *Ibid.*, Dec., 1895, Vol. 2, pp. 370–382.

A Very Simple and Accurate Cathetometer. *Am. Jour. of Sci.*, Jan., 1896, Vol. 1, pp. 41–49. Reprinted in *Philosophical Magazine*, Feb., 1896, Vol. 41, 132–153.

The Use and Mounting of the Concave Grating as an Analyzing or Direct Comparison Spectroscope. No. 15, The Modern Spectroscope. *Astrophysical Journal*, Jan., 1896, Vol. 3, pp. 47–62.

A Simple Optical Device for completely isolating or cutting out any Desired Portion of the Diffraction Spectrum and Some Further Notes on Astronomical Spectroscopes. No. 16, The Modern Spectroscope. *Ibid.*, March, 1896, Vol. 3, pp. 149–162.

A Note on Mr. Burch's Method of Drawing Hyperbolas and on a New Hyperbolagraph. *Philosophical Magazine*, April, 1896, Vol. 41, pp. 372–375.

Review of Boy's Work on the Newtonian Constant of Gravitation. *Astrophysical Journal*, April, 1896, Vol. 3, pp. 308–311.

The Conditions of Maximum Efficiency in the Use of the Spectrograph. No. 18, The Modern Spectroscope. *Ibid.*, May, 1896, Vol. 3, pp. 321–347.

Review of Langley's Report on the Smithsonian Astrophysical Observatory for 1895. *Ibid.*, May, 1896, Vol. 3, pp. 398–401.

The Objective Spectroscope. No. 19, The Modern Spectroscope. *Ibid.*, June, 1896, Vol. 4, pp. 54–76.

Review of Professor Stoney's paper on the Equipment of the Astrophysical Observatory of the Future. *Ibid.*, Oct., 1896, Vol. 4, pp. 239–242.

A Note on the Preparation of Phosphorescent Barium Sulphide. *Ibid.*, Nov., 1896, Vol. 4, pp. 308–309.

A Note on a Combined Equatorial Telescope and Polar Heliostat. *Ibid.*, Nov., 1896, Vol. 4, p. 310.

On a New Form of Mounting for Reflecting Telescopes, devised by the late Arthur Cowper Ranyard. *Ibid.*, Feb., 1897, Vol. 5, pp. 132–142.

A Note on a New Form of Fluid Prism. *Ibid.*, Feb., 1897, Vol. 5, p. 149.

On the Resolving Power of Telescopes and Spectroscopes for Lines of Finite Width. *Memorie della Società degli Spettroscopisti Italiani*, Jan., 1897, Vol. 26, pp. 8–22. *Philosophical Magazine*, May, 1897, Vol. 43, pp. 317–343.

Thermal Measurements with the Bolometer by the Zero Method. *Astrophysical Journal*, April, 1897, Vol. 5, pp. 268–276.

The Application of the Interferometer to the Measurement of Small Angular Deflections of a Suspended System. *Physical Review*, May–June, 1897, Vol. 4, pp. 480–497.

Tables of the Practical Resolving Power of Spectroscopes. *Astrophysical Journal*, June, 1897, Vol. 6, pp. 27–36.

Ueber das Auflösungsvermögen von Fernrohren und Spectroskopen für Linien von endlicher Breite. *Ann. der Physik u. Chemie*, June, 1897, Vol. 61, pp. 604–630.

On the Conditions which determine the Limiting Time of Exposure of Photographic Plates in Astronomical Photography. *Astronomische Nachrichten*, Vol. 144, pp. 97–110.

The Effect of the General Illumination of the Sky on the Brightness of the Field at the Focus of a Telescope. *Monthly Notices of Royal Astronomical Soc.*, June, 1897, Vol. 57, pp. 586–589.

A Note on Spider Lines. *Ibid.*, pp. 589–591.

On the Conditions which determine the Ultimate Optical Efficiency of Methods for observing Small Rotations, and on a Simple Method of doubling the Accuracy of the Mirror and Scale Method. *Philosophical Magazine*, July, 1897, Vol. 44, pp. 83–97.

On the Conditions of Maximum Efficiency in Astrophotographic Work. Part I. General Theory of Telescopic Images of Different Forms of Radiating Sources. *Astrophysical Journal*, Aug., 1897, Vol. 6, pp. 119–125.

A Comparison of the Photographic and of the Hand and Eye Methods of delineating the Surface Markings of Celestial Objects. *Popular Astronomy*, Aug., 1897, Vol. 5, pp. 200–209.

Astronomical Photography. *Knowledge*, Aug. and Sept., 1897, Vol. 20, pp. 193–195, 216–221.

A Note on the Effect of Heat on Phosphorescence. *Astrophysical Journal*, Aug., 1897, Vol. 6, pp. 153–155.

Adam Hilger. *Ibid.*, pp. 139–141.

Review of Dr. Braun's Die Gravitations Constante die Masse und mittlere Dichte der Erde. *Ibid.*, pp. 157–159.

Sur le Pouvoir Séparateur des Lunettes et de Spectroscopes pour les Raies de Largeur Finie. *Jour. de Physique*, Aug., 1897, Vol. 6, pp. 409.

A Determination of the Specific Resistance and Temperature Coefficient of Oil in Thin Films and the Application of these Results to the Measurement of the Thickness of Oil Films in Journal Bearings. *Physical Review*, Aug., 1897, Vol. 5, pp. 75–97.

On the Photography of Planetary Surfaces. *Observatory*, Sept., Oct., Nov., 1897, Vol. 20, pp. 333–341, 365–370, 401–410.

On the Conditions required for attaining Maximum Accuracy in the Determination of Specific Heat by the Method of Mixtures. *Am. Jour. of Sci.*, Sept., 1897, Vol. 4, pp. 265–282.

On the Effect of the Size of an Objective on the Visibility of Linear Markings on the Planets. *Astronomical Journal*, Oct. 6, 1897, Vol. 18, pp. 41–45.

On the Reduction of Observations. *Observatory*, Oct. 1897, Vol. 20, pp. 380–383.

Note on the General Theory of Telescopic Images. *Astrophysical Journal*, Dec., 1897, Vol. 6, p. 422.

On the Theory of Lubrication and the Determination of the Thickness of the Film of Oil in Journal Bearings. *Jour. of Franklin Institute*, Dec., 1897, Jan., 1898, Vols. 144–145.

On the Conditions of Maximum Efficiency in Astrophotographic Work. Part II. Effect of Atmospheric Aberration on the Intensity of Telescopic Images. *Astrophysical Journal*, Jan., 1898, Vol. 7, pp. 70–76.

A Note on the Discovery of an Error in the Papers of Struve and Lord Rayleigh dealing with the Application of the Principles of the Wave Theory to the Determination of the Intensity of the Images of Fine Lines and Extended Areas at the Focus of a Telescope. *Astrophysical Journal*, Jan., 1898, Vol. 7, pp. 77–85.

A Note on an Error in the Expression for the Intensity of Illumination at the Focal Plane of a Telescope due to an Infinitely Extended Luminous Area. *Astronomical Journal*, Jan., 1898, Vol. 18, pp. 124–126.

A Note on a New Form of Mirror for Reflecting Telescopes. *Popular Astronomy*, Feb., 1898, Vol. 5, pp. 516–524.

On the "Worthlessness" of Methods of Geometrical Optics in dealing with the Problems relating to the Definitive and the Delineating and Resolving Power of Telescopes. *Ibid.*, pp. 525–532.

A Note on the Figuring and Use of Eccentric and Unsymmetrical Forms of Parabolic Mirrors. *Astrophysical Journal*, Feb., 1898, Vol. 7, pp. 146–149.

A Note on the Result concerning Diffraction Phenomena recently criticised by Mr. Newall. *Monthly Notices of Royal Astronomical Soc.*, March, 1898, Vol. 58, pp. 286–291.

Notes on the Use of the Grating in Stellar Spectroscopic Work. *Astrophysical Journal*, March, 1898, Vol. 7, pp. 198–206.

CHARLES WALKER:—

B.C.E., University of Tennessee, 1885; M.A., *ibid.*, 1886; Assistant Professor of Chemistry and Physics, *ibid.*, 1886–89; Assistant in Chemistry, U. S. Naval Academy, Annapolis, 1889–90; Fellow in Chemistry, Clark University, 1890–93; Professor of Chemistry and Physics, Wisconsin State Normal School, 1893–94; Professor of Natural Science, Carson-Newman College, Mossy Creek, Tenn., 1896–.

Author of:—

Oxidation of Meta-Brom Toluene and Nitrotoluene Sulphamide. (With Dr. W. A. Noyes.) *Am. Chem. Jour.*, June, 1886, Vol. 8, pp. 185–190.

Oxidation of Para-xylene Sulphamide. (With Dr. W. A. Noyes.) *Ibid.*, April, 1887, Vol. 9, pp. 93–99.

The Condensation-Products of Acetacetic-ether Hydrazide and Oxalciticether Hydrazide. *Ibid.*, Dec., 1892, Vol. 14, pp. 576–586.

The Condensation-Products of Aromatic Hydrazydes of Acetacetic-ether. Indol and Pyrazol Derivatives. *Ibid.*, June, 1894, Vol. 16, pp. 430-443.

On the Action of Potassium Hydroxide on Orthomethoxyanilphenaminobenzoic Acid. *Ibid.*, 1897, Vol. 19, pp. 579-580.

ARTHUR J. WARNER:—

A.B., Marietta College O., 1889; A.M., *Ibid.*, 1897; Scholar in Physics, Clark University, 1889-90; Engaged in Electrical Work, Johns Hopkins University, 1890-92; Certificate in Electrical Engineering, *Ibid.*, 1893; With the Cherokee Mining Co., Chute, Ga., 1896-.

SHO WATASE:—

B.S., Sapporo, Japan, 1884; Student of Zoölogy, University of Tokio, 1884-86; Fellow in Biology, Johns Hopkins University, 1886-89; Bruce Fellow, *Ibid.*, 1889-90; Ph.D., Johns Hopkins University, 1890; Lecturer and Assistant in Morphology, Clark University, 1890-92; Reader in Cellular Biology, University of Chicago, 1892-93; Instructor in Anatomy and Physiology of the Cell, *Ibid.*, 1893-95; Assistant Professor in Cellular Biology, *Ibid.*, 1895-99; Professor of Cellular Biology, Imperial University, Tokio, Japan, 1899-.

Author of:—

Caryokinesis and the Cleavage of the Ovum. *J. H. U. Circulars*, April, 1890, Vol. 9, pp. 55-56.

On the Morphology of the Compound Eyes of Arthropods. *Quar. Jour. of Micr. Sci.*, June, 1890, N. S., Vol. 31, pp. 143-158, 1 pl.

On Caryokinesis. *Woods Holl Biological Lectures*, 1890. Ginn & Co., Boston, 1891, pp. 168-187.

Studies on Cephalopods. I. Cleavage of the Ovum. *Journal of Morphology*, Jan., 1891, Vol. 4, pp. 247-302, 4 pls.

The Origin of the Sertoli's Cell. *American Naturalist*, May, 1892, Vol. 26, pp. 443-444.

On the Significance of Spermatogenesis. *Ibid.*, July, 1899, Vol. 33, pp. 624-626.

On the Phenomena of Sex Differentiation. *Jour. of Morph.*, July, 1892, Vol. 6, pp. 481-493.

Homology of the Centrosome. *Ibid.*, May, 1893, Vol. 8, pp. 433-444.

On the Nature of Cell Organization. *Woods Holl Biological Lectures*, 1893. Ginn & Co., Boston, 1894, pp. 83-103.

Origin of the Centrosome. *Ibid.*, 1894. Ginn & Co., Boston, 1895, pp. 273-287.

On the Physical Basis of Animal Phosphorescence. *Ibid.*, 1895. Ginn & Co., Boston, 1896, pp. 101-118.

Microsomes and their Relation to the Centrosome. *Science*, Feb. 5, 1897, N. S., Vol. 5, pp. 230-231.

Protoplasmic Contractibility and Phosphorescence. *Ibid.*, 1898. (In press.)

OLIVER F. WATTS:—

A.B., Bowdoin College, 1889; A.M., *Ibid.*, 1892; Scholar in Chemistry, Clark University, 1889-90; Instructor in Physics, Chemistry, and Mathematics, Franklin Academy, Malone, N. Y., 1892-93; Instructor in Physics, High School, Waltham, Mass., 1893-.

ARTHUR GORDON WEBSTER:—

A.B., Harvard University, 1885; Instructor in Mathematics, *Ibid.*, 1885-86; Parker Fellow, *Ibid.*, 1886-89; Student, Universities of Berlin, Paris, and Stockholm, 1886-90; Ph.D., University of Berlin, 1890; Docent in Physics, Clark University, 1890-92; Assistant Professor of Physics, 1892-; Resident Fellow, American Academy of Arts and Sciences; Fellow, American Association for the Advancement of Science; Member, American Mathematical Society, American Physical Society.

Author of:—

Versuche über eine Methode zur Bestimmung des Verhältnisses der elektromagnetischen zur elektrostatischen Einheit der Elektricität. (Inaugural-dissertation.) Berlin, 1890.

A National Physical Laboratory. *Pedagogical Seminary*, June, 1893, Vol. 2, pp. 90–101.

Unipolar Induction and Currents without Difference of Potential. *Electrical World*, April 14–21, 1894, Vol. 23, pp. 491–492, 523–524.

On a Means of producing a Constant Angular Velocity. *Am. Jour. of Sci.*, May, 1897, Vol. 3, pp. 379–382.

A Rapid Break for Large Currents. *Ibid.*, pp. 383–386.

A New Instrument for measuring the Intensity of Sound. (With B. F. Sharpe.) *Report British A. A. S.*, Toronto, 1897, p. 554. Also *Proc. A. A. A. S.*, Boston, 1898, p. 135.

The Theory of Electricity and Magnetism, being Lectures on Mathematical Physics. Macmillan & Co., London, 1897. 563 pp.

An Experimental Determination of the Period of Electrical Oscillations. (Elihu Thomson Prize, Paris, 1896.) *Physical Review*, May–June, 1898, Vol. 6, pp. 297–314.

Note on Stokes's Theorem in Curvilinear Coördinates. *Bull. Am. Math. Soc.*, June, 1898, 2d ser., Vol. 4, pp. 438–441.

A New Chronograph and a Means of Rating Tuning-forks. *Proc. A. A. A. S.*, Boston, 1898, p. 135.

A Geometrical Method for Investigating Diffraction by a Circular Aperture. *Ibid.*, p. 136.

Report on the State of the Mathematical Theory of Electricity and Magnetism. *Ibid.*, pp. 103–112. Also *Science*, Dec. 9, 1898, Vol. 8, pp. 809–819.

Two Lowell Institute Lectures on Electricity and Magnetism, Light, and the Ether, 1897.

Six Lectures for the Colloquium of the American Mathematical Society, 1898.

JULIUS B. WEEMS:—

B.S., Maryland Agricultural College, 1888; Instructor in Chemistry and Mathematics, *ibid.*, 1888–89; Student, Johns Hopkins University, 1889–91; Chemist at Phosphate Mines, Florida, 1891–92; Fellow in Chemistry, Clark University, 1892–94; Ph.D., Clark University, 1894; On Special Research at New York Experimental Station, Geneva, N. Y., Oct., 1894–March, 1896; Professor of Agricultural Chemistry, Iowa State College of Agriculture and Mechanic Arts, and Chemist, Iowa Experiment Station, Ames, Ia., March, 1896–; Chemist, Iowa Geological Survey, Jan., 1899–; Member: German Chemical Society, American Chemical Society, Society of Chemical Industry of London, Society for Promotion of Agricultural Science, American Academy of Political and Social Science; Fellow, Iowa Academy of Science.

Author of:—

On Electrosyntheses by the Direct Union of Anions of Weak Organic Acids. *Am. Chem. Jour.*, Dec., 1894, Vol. 16, pp. 569–588.

The Chemical Composition of Squirrel-tail Grass. *Iowa Experiment Station Bull.*, No. 30, pp. 320–331.

Studies on Milk Preservatives. *Ibid.*, No. 33, pp. 499–504.

Soil Moisture. *Ibid.*, No. 33, pp. 606–615.

The Adulteration of Food. *Rep. of State Dairy Com. of Iowa*, 1896, pp. 312–315.

Soil Moisture. *Iowa Experiment Station Bull.*, No. 36, pp. 823–848.

Milk Preservatives. *Ill. State Dairymen's Ass'n*, 1898, pp. 103–110.

Chemistry and some of its Relations to Agriculture. *Rep. of the Iowa State Agric. Soc.*, 1898, pp. 42–48.

GERALD M. WEST:—

A.B., Columbia College, 1886; A.M., *ibid.*, 1889; Ph.D., Columbia College, 1890; Fellow in Anthropology, Clark University, 1890–91; Assistant in Anthropology, 1891–92; First Assistant in Anthropology, Bureau of Ethnology, World's Columbian Exposition, 1892–93; Docent in Ethnology, University of Chicago, 1893–94; Curator of Physical Anthropology, Field Columbian Museum, Chicago, 1894.

Author of:—

The Status of the Negro in Virginia during the Colonial Period. (Thesis for the Doctorate.) New York, 1890. 76 pp.

The Growth of the Breadth of the Face. *Science*, July 3, 1891, Vol. 18, pp. 10–11.

Eye-Tests on School Children. *Am. Jour. of Psy.*, Aug., 1892, Vol. 4, pp. 595–596.

The Growth of the Body, Head, and Face. *Science*, Jan. 6, 1893, Vol. 21, pp. 2–4.

The Anthropometry of American School Children. *Mem. Internat. Congress of Anthropology*, 1893 (Chicago, 1894), pp. 50–58.

Anthropometrische Untersuchungen über die Schulkinder in Worcester, Mass., Amerika. *Arch. f. Anthropologie, Braunschweig*, 1893, Vol. 22, pp. 13–48.

The Growth of the Human Body. *Educational Review*, Oct., 1896, Vol. 12, pp. 284–289.

Observations on the Relation of Physical Development to Intellectual Ability, made on the School Children of Toronto, Canada. *Science*, Aug. 7, 1896, N. S., Vol. 4, pp. 156–159.

A. HARRY WHEELER:—

S.B., Worcester Polytechnic Institute, 1894; Instructor in Mathematics, English High School, Worcester, 1894–Dec., 1896; and 1899–; Scholar in Mathematics, Clark University Dec., 1896–June, 1899.

WILLIAM MORTON WHEELER:—

Graduate, German and English Academy, Milwaukee, Wis., 1880; Graduate German-American Normal College, Milwaukee, Wis., 1883; Ward's Natural Science Establishment, Rochester, N. Y., 1883–85; Teacher of German and Assistant in Biology, Milwaukee Public High School, 1885–88; Curator, Milwaukee Public Museum, 1887–90; Fellow and Assistant in Morphology, Clark University, 1890–92; Ph.D., Clark University, 1892; Student at the University of Würzburg and University of Liége; Occupant of the Smithsonian Table at the Zoölogical Station, Naples, 1893–94; Instructor in Embryology, University of Chicago, 1892–95; Assistant Professor of Embryology, *ibid.*, 1895–99; Professor of Zoölogy, University of Texas, 1899.

Author of:—

Spiders of the Sub-family Lyssomanæ. (With G. W. and E. G. Peckham.) *Trans. Wis. Acad. Science, Arts and Letters*, Vol. 7, 1888, pp. 222–256, Pls. xi. and xii.

On Two New Species of Cecidomyid Flies producing Galls on Antennaria plantaginifolia. *Proc. Wis. Nat. Hist. Soc.*, April, 1889, pp. 209–216.

Two Cases of Insect Mimicry. *Ibid.*, pp. 217–221.

Ueber drüsenartige Gebilde im ersten Abdominal-segment der Hemipterenembryonen. *Zool. Anzeiger*, 1889, 12 Jahrg., pp. 500–504, 2 fig.

Homologues in Embryo Hemiptera of the Appendages to the First Abdominal Segment of other Insects. *American Naturalist*, 1889, pp. 644–645.

The Embryology of Blatta germanica and Doryphora decem-lineata. *Jour. of Morph.*, Sept., 1889, Vol. 3, pp. 291–386, 7 pl.

On the Appendages of the First Abdominal Segment of Embryo Insects. *Wis. Acad. Science, Arts and Letters*, Sept. 30, 1890, Vol. 8, pp. 87–140, Pls. I–III.

Ueber ein eigenthümliches Organ im Locustidenembryo. *Zool. Anzeiger*, 13 Jahrg., 1890.

Note on the Oviposition and Embryonic Development of Xiphidium ensiferum Scud. *Insect Life*, 1890, Vol. 2, pp. 222–223.

Descriptions of Some New North American Dolichopodidæ. *Psyche*, 1890, Vol. 5, pp. 337–343, 355–362, 373–379.

The Supposed Bot-fly Parasite of the Box-Turtle. *Ibid.*, 1890, Vol. 5, p. 403.

Hydrocyanic Acid secreted by Polydesmus virginiensis Drury. *Ibid.*, 1890, Vol. 5, p. 442.

The Embryology of a Common Fly. *Ibid.*, 1891, Vol. 6, pp. 97–99.

The Germ-band of Insects. *Ibid.*, 1891, Vol. 6, pp. 112–115.

Neuroblasts in the Arthropod Embryo. *Jour. of Morph.*, Jan., 1891, Vol. 4, pp. 337–343, 1 fig.

Concerning the "Blood-tissue" of the Insecta. *Ibid.*, 1892, Vol. 6, pp. 216–220, 233–236, 253–258, Pl. vii.

A Contribution to Insect Embryology. (Inaugural Dissertation.) *Jour. of Morph.*, April, 1893, Vol. 8, pp. 1–160, 6 pls.

The Primitive Number of Malpighian Vessels in Insecta. *Psyche*, 1893, Vol. 6, pp. 457–460, 485–486, 497–498, 509–510, 539–541, 545–547, 561–564, 2 figs.

Syncoelidium pellucidum, a New Marine Triclad. *Jour. of Morph.*, April, 1894, Vol. 9, pp. 167–194, 1 pl.

Planocera inquilina, a Polyclad inhabiting the Branchial Chamber of Sycotypus canaliculatus Gill. *Ibid.*, April, 1894, Vol. 9, pp. 195–201, 3 figs.

Protandric Hermaphroditism in Myzostoma. *Zool. Anzeiger*, 17 Jahrg., 1894.

The Behavior of the Centrosomes in the Fertilized Egg of Myzostoma glabrum Leuckart. *Jour. of Morph.*, Jan., 1895, Vol. 10, pp. 305–311.

The Problems, Methods, and Scope of Developmental Mechanics. (Translated from the German of Wilhelm Roux.) *Biological Lectures*, Marine Biological Laboratory, Woods Holl, 1894, pp. 149–190.

The Sexual Phases of Myzostoma. *Mitth. a. d. Zool. Station zu Neapel*, 1896, Vol. 12, pp. 227–302. Pls. x.–xii.

The Genus Ochthera. *Entomological News*, April, 1896, Vol. 7, pp. 121–123, 1 fig.

Two Dolichopodid Genera New to America. *Ibid.*, May, 1896, Vol. 7, pp. 152–156.

A New Genus and Species of Dolichopodidæ. *Ibid.*, June, 1896, Vol. 7, pp. 185–189, 1 fig.

A New Empid with Remarkable Middle Tarsi. *Ibid.*, June, 1896, Vol. 7, pp. 189–192, 3 figs.

An Antenniform Extra Appendage in Dilophus tibialis Loew. *Arch. f. Entwick. Mech. d. Organismen*, 1896, Vol. 3, pp. 261–268, Pl. xvi.

The Maturation, Fecundation, and Early Cleavage of Myzostoma glabrum Leuckart. *Arch. de Biologie*, 1897, Vol. 15, pp. 1–77, Pls. i.–iii.

A Genus of Maritime Dolichopodidæ New to America. *Proc. Cal. Acad. Sci., Zoöl.*, July, 1897, 3d ser., Vol. 1, pp. 145–152, Pl. iv.

A New Genus of Dolichopodidæ from Florida. *Zoölogical Bulletin*, Feb., 1898, Vol. 1, pp. 217–220, 1 fig.

A New Peripatus from Mexico. *Jour. of Morph.*, Oct., 1898, Vol. 15, pp. 1–8, 1 pl.

George Baur's Life and Writings. *American Naturalist*, Jan., 1899, Vol. 33, pp. 15–30.

Anemotropism and Other Tropisms in Insects. *Arch. f. Entwick. Mech. d. Organismen*, 1899, Vol. 8, pp. 373–381.

New Species of Dolichopodidæ from the United States. *Proc. Cal. Acad. Sci., Zoöl.*, 3d ser., Sept., 1899, Vol. 2, pp. 1–77, Pls. i.–iv.

The Development of the Urinogenital Organs of the Lamprey. *Zool. Jahrbücher, Abth. f. Morph.*, 1899, Bd. 13, pp. 1–88, Pls. i.–vii.

The Life-History of Dicyema. *Zool. Anzeig.*, April, 1899, Vol. 22, pp. 169–176.

J. Beard on the Sexual Phases of Myzostoma. *Ibid.*, July, 1899, Vol. 22, pp. 281–288.

Caspar Friedrich Wolff and the Theoria Generationis. *Biological Lectures*, Marine Biological Laboratory, Woods Holl, 1899.

GUY MONTROSE WHIPPLE:—

A.B., Brown University, 1897; Scholar and Assistant in Psychology, Clark University, 1897–98; Assistant in Psychology, Cornell University, 1898–.

Author of:—

The Influence of Forced Respiration on Psychical and Physical Activity. *Am.*

Jour. of Psy., July, 1898, Vol. 9, pp. 560–571.

On Nearly Simultaneous Clicks and Flashes. *Ibid.*, Jan., 1899, Vol. 10, pp. 280–286.

HENRY S. WHITE:—

A.B., Wesleyan University, 1882; Assistant in Astronomy and Physics, *ibid.*, 1882–83; Instructor in Mathematics, Hackettstown, N. J., 1883–84; Tutor in Mathematics, Wesleyan University, 1884–87; Ph.D., University of Göttingen, 1891; Assistant in Mathematics, Clark University, 1890–92; Associate Professor of Mathematics, Northwestern University, 1892–94; Noyes Professor of Pure Mathematics, *ibid.*, 1894–; Member American Mathematical Society.

Author of:—

Ueber zwei covariante Formen aus der Theorie der Abel'schen Integrale auf vollständigen, singularitätenfreien Schnittcurven zweier Flächen. *Math. Annalen*, 1890, Vol. 36, pp. 597–601.

Abel'sche Integrale auf singularitätenfreien, einfach überdeckten, vollständigen Schnittcurven eines beliebig ausgedehnten Raumes. *Nova Acta Leop.-Carol. Akad.*, 1891, Vol. 57, pp. 41–128.

On generating Systems of Ternary and Quaternary Linear Transformations. *Am. Jour. of Math.*, July, 1892, Vol. 14, pp. 274–282.

A Symbolic Demonstration of Hilbert's Method for deriving Invariants and Covariants of Given Ternary Forms. *Ibid.*, pp. 283–290.

Review of Klein's Evanston Lectures. *Bull. N. Y. Math. Soc.*, Feb. 1894, Vol. 3, pp. 119–122.

Reduction of the Resultant of a Binary Quadric and n-ic by Virtue of its Semi-combinant Property. *Ibid.*, Oct., 1894, Vol. 1, pp. 11–15.

Semi-combinants as Concomitants of Affiliants. *Am. Jour. of Math.*, July, 1895, Vol. 17, pp. 235–265.

Kronecker's Linear Relation among Minors of a Symmetric Determinant. *Bull. Am. Math. Soc.*, Feb., 1896, Vol. 2, pp. 136–138.

Numerically Regular Reticulations upon Surfaces of Deficiency higher than 1. *Ibid.*, Dec., 1896, Vol. 3, pp. 116–121.

The Cubic Resolvent of a Binary Quartic Derived by Invariant Definition and Process. *Ibid.*, April, 1897, Vol. 3, pp. 250–253.

Collineations in a Plane with Invariant Quadric or Cubic Curves. *Ibid.*, Oct., 1897, Vol. 4, pp. 17–23.

Inflexional Lines, Triplets, and Triangles associated with the Plane Cubic Curve. *Ibid.*, March, 1898, Vol. 4, pp. 258–260.

The Construction of Special Regular Reticulations on a Closed Surface. *Ibid.*, May, 1898, Vol. 4, pp. 376–382.

Elliott's Algebra of Quantics. Review. *Ibid.*, July, 1898, Vol. 4, pp. 545–549.

The Cambridge Colloquium. *Ibid.*, Oct., 1898, Vol. 5, pp. 57–62.

Report on the Theory of Projective Invariants; the Chief Contributions of a Decade. *Ibid.*, Jan., 1899, Vol. 5, pp. 161–175.

CHARLES O. WHITMAN:—

A.B., Bowdoin College, 1868; Principal Westford Academy and Master in the English High School, Boston, 1869–75; Ph.D., University of Leipzig, 1878; Fellow, Johns Hopkins University, 1878–79; Professor of Zoölogy, Imperial University of Japan, 1879–81; Naples Zoölogical Station, 1881–82; Director, Allis Lake Laboratory, 1886–89; Director, Marine Biological Laboratory, Woods Holl, Mass., 1888–; Professor of Animal Morphology, Clark University, 1889–92; Head Professor of Zoölogy, University of Chicago, 1892–; Editor of: *Journal of Morphology*, 1887–; *Biological Lectures* from the Marine Biological Laboratory, Woods Holl, Mass., 1890–; *American Naturalist*, Department of Microscopy, 1883–86; *Zoölogical Bulletin*, 1897–99 (continued in *Biological Bulletin*, 1899–).

Author of: —

The Embryology of Clepsine. *Quar. Jour. Micr. Sci.*, 1878, Vol. 18, pp. 215–315.

Ueber die Embryologie von Clepsine. *Zool. Anzeiger*, 1878, Vol. 1, pp. 5–6.

Changes Preliminary to Cleavage. *Proc. A. A. A. S.*, 1878, Vol. 27, pp. 263–270.

Do Flying Fish Fly? *American Naturalist*, Sept., 1880, Vol. 14, pp. 641–653.

Zoölogy in the University of Tokio, Yokohama, 1881, pp. 1–44.

Methods of Microscopical Research in the Zoölogical Station of Naples. *American Naturalist*, Sept., 1882, Vol. 16, pp. 697–706.

A New Species of Branchiobdella. *Zool. Anzeiger*, Sept. 10, 1882, Vol. 5, pp. 1–2.

The Advantages of Study at the Naples Zoölogical Station. *Science*, July 27, 1883, Vol. 2, pp. 93–97.

A Rare Form of the Blastoderm of the Chick, and its Bearing on the Question of the Formation of the Vertebrate Embryo. *Quar. Jour. Micr. Sci.*, 1883, Vol. 23, pp. 375–397.

A Contribution to the Embryology, Life-History, and Classification of the Dicyemids. *Mitth. aus d. Zool. Station zu Neapel*, Jan. 23, 1883, Vol. 4, pp. 1–89, 5 pls.

On the Development of some Pelagic Fish Eggs. (With Alexander Agassiz.) *Proc. Am. Acad. Arts and Sciences*, 1884, N. S., Vol. 12, pp. 23–75.

The External Morphology of the Leech. (With Alexander Agassiz.) *Ibid.*, 1884, N. S., Vol. 12, pp. 76–87.

The Connective Substance in the Hirudinea. *American Naturalist*, Oct., 1884, Vol. 18, pp. 1070–1071.

The Segmental Sense-Organs of the Leech. *Ibid.*, Nov., 1884, Vol. 18, pp. 1104–1109.

The Pelagic Stages of Young Fishes. (With Alexander Agassiz.) *Mem. Mus. Comp. Zoölogy*, 1885, Vol. 14, pp. 1–56.

Methods in Microscopical Anatomy and Embryology. Boston, 1885. 255 pp.

The Germ-Layers of Clepsine. *Zool. Anzeiger*, 1886, Vol. 1, pp. 1–6.

The Leeches of Japan. *Quar. Jour. Micr. Sci.*, April, 1886, Vol. 26, pp. 317–416. 5 pls.

Biological Instruction in Universities. *American Naturalist*, June, 1887, Vol. 21, pp. 507–519.

A Contribution to the History of the Germ-Layers in Clepsine. *Jour. of Morph.*, Sept., 1887, Vol. 1, pp. 105–182, 3 pls.

The Kinetic Phenomena of the Egg during Maturation and Fecundation. *Ibid.*, Dec., 1887, Vol. 1, pp. 227–252.

The Seat of Formative and Regenerative Energy. *Ibid.*, July, 1888, Vol. 2, pp. 27–49.

Address at the opening of the Marine Biological Laboratory, July 17, 1888. *First Annual Report for the Year 1888*, pp. 24–31.

The Development of Osseous Fishes. (With Alexander Agassiz.) II. The Pre-embryonic Stages of Development. Part I. The History of the Egg from Fertilization to Cleavage. *Mem. Mus. Comp. Zoölogy*, 1889, Vol. 14, pp. 1–40.

Some New Facts about the Hirudinea. *Jour. of Morph.*, April, 1889, Vol. 2, pp. 586–599.

Specialization and Organization, Companion Principles of all Progress. The Most Important need of American Biology. *Woods Holl Biological Lectures*, 1890. Ginn & Co., Boston, 1891, pp. 1–26.

The Naturalist's Occupation. *Ibid.*, 1890. Ginn & Co., Boston, 1891, pp. 27–52.

Spermatophores as a Means of Hypodermic Impregnation. *Jour. of Morph.*, Jan., 1891, Vol. 4, pp. 361–406, 1 pl.

Description of Clepsine Plana. *Ibid.*, pp. 407–418, 1 pl.

Metamerism of Clepsine. *Leuckart's Festschrift*, 1892, pp. 385–395.

The Marine Biological Laboratory, Friday Chapel Address. *University News*, Chicago, Dec. 17, 1892.

General Physiology and its Relations to Morphology. *Fifth Annual Report Marine Biological Laboratory*, 1892. Reprinted in *American Naturalist*, Sept., 1893, Vol. 27, pp. 802–807.

A Marine Biological Observatory. *Pop. Sci. Mo.*, Feb., 1893, Vol. 42, pp. 459–471.

A Marine Observatory the Prime Need of American Biology. *Atlantic Monthly*, June, 1893, Vol. 71, pp. 808–815.

A Sketch of the Structure and Development of the Eye of Clepsine. *Spengel's Zool. Jahrbücher*, 1893, Vol. 6, pp. 616–625.

The Inadequacy of the Cell-Theory of Development. *Jour. of Morph.*, August, 1893, Vol. 8, pp. 639–658; also *Woods Holl Biological Lectures*, 1893. Ginn & Co., Boston, 1894, pp. 105–124.

The Work and the Aims of the Marine Biological Laboratory. *Woods Holl Biological Lectures*, 1893. Ginn & Co., Boston, 1894, pp. 235–242.

Evolution and Epigenesis. *Ibid.*, 1894. Ginn & Co., 1895, pp. 205–224.

Bonnet's Theory of Evolution. *Ibid.*, 1894. Ginn & Co., 1895, pp. 225–240.

The Palingenesia and the Germ Doctrine of Bonnet. *Ibid.*, 1894. Ginn & Co., 1895, pp. 241–272.

The Egg of Amia and its Cleavage. (With A. C. Eycleshymer.) *Jour. of Morph.*, Feb., 1897, Vol. 12, pp. 309–354. 2 pls.

Some of the Functions and Features of a Biological Station. Presidential Address to the Society of American Naturalists, Ithaca meeting, 1897. *Woods Holl Biological Lectures*, 1896–97. Ginn & Co., Boston, 1898, pp. 231–242; also in *Science*, Jan. 14, 1898, Vol. 7, pp. 37–44.

The Centrosome Problem and an Experimental Test. *Science*, Feb. 5, 1897, N. S., Vol. 5, p. 67.

Lamarck and "A Perfecting Tendency." *Ibid.*, Jan. 21, 1898, Vol. 7, p. 99.

Apathy's Grief and Consolation. *Zool. Anzeiger*, May 1, 1899, Vol. 22, pp. 196–197.

Myths in Animal Psychology. *Monist*, July, 1899, Vol. 9, pp. 524–537.

Animal Behavior. *Woods Holl Biological Lectures*, 1898, pp. 285–338.

FRANK B. WILLIAMS:—

C.E., Missouri State University, 1890; M.S., *ibid.*, 1893; Teaching Fellow in Mathematics, *ibid.*, 1892–95; United States Assistant Engineer, Tennessee River Improvement, 1896–97; **Scholar in Mathematics, Clark University, 1897–98; Fellow, 1898–99.**

Author of:—

Note on the Finite Continuous Groups of the Plane. *Proc. Am. Acad. of Arts and Sci.*, Nov., 1899, Vol. 35, pp. 97–107.

J. FRANCIS WILLIAMS:—

C.E., Rensselaer Polytechnic Institute, 1883; B.S., *ibid.*, 1884; Ph.D., University of Göttingen, 1886; University of Berlin, 1887; Director, Technical Museum of Pratt Institute, Brooklyn, N. Y., 1887–89; **Docent in Mineralogy, Clark University, 1889–90**; Assistant Professor of Geology, Cornell University, 1890–91. Died Nov. 9, 1891.

Author of:—

Tests of Rutland and Washington County Slates. *Van Nostrand's Eng. Mag.*, 1884, No. 188.

Ueber den Monte Amiata in Toscana und seine Gesteine. Stuttgart, 1887.

Igneous Rocks of Arkansas. *Annual Report of the Geological Survey*, Arkansas, 1890, Vol. 2. 457 pp. Illustrated.

ALBERT P. WILLS:—

B.E.E., Tufts College (with Honors in Electricity), 1894; **Scholar in Physics, Clark University, 1894–95; Fellow, 1895–Jan., 1897; Ph.D., Clark University, 1897**; Professor of Physical Sciences, Colorado State Normal School, Jan., 1897–June, 1898; Student in Physics, Universities of Göttingen and Berlin, 1898–99; Associate in Applied

Mathematics and Physics, Bryn Mawr College, 1899–.

Author of: —

On the Susceptibility of Diamagnetic and weakly Magnetic Substances. *Philosophical Magazine*, May, 1898. 5th ser., Vol. 45, pp. 432–447; also *Physical Review*, April, 1898, Vol. 6, pp. 223–238.

Molekulare Susceptibilität paramagnetischer Salze. (With O. Liebknecht.) *Verhandl. der deuts. physik. Gesellschaft*, Sitz. vom 30 Juni, 1899 (to be published later *in extenso*).

Zur thermometrischen und kryogenen Verwendung des Kohlensäureschnees. (With H. du Bois.) *Verhandl. der deuts. physik. Gesellschaft.* Sitz. vom 30 Juni, 1899. (To be published later *in extenso*.)

On the Magnetic Shielding Effect of Trilamellar Spherical and Cylindrical Shells. *Physical Review*, Oct., 1899. Vol. 9, pp. 193–213.

MINOSUKE YAMAGUCHI: —

LL.B., Tokio Law School, 1892; Student in Philosophy, De Pauw University, 1894–97; A.B., Lombard University, 1897; **Scholar in Psychology, Clark University, 1897–98**; Graduate Student, Yale University, 1898–99.

ALBERT H. YODER: —

Teacher in Public Schools, Dakota, 1883–87; Graduate, State Normal School, Madison, So. Dak., 1888; Superintendent of Schools, *ibid.*, 1888–91; A.B., University of Indiana, 1893; **Scholar in Pedagogy, Clark University, 1893–94**; Principal, San Francisco Normal School, 1894–95; Scholar in Psychology, University of Chicago, 1895–96; Specialist in Pediatrics, Northwestern University Medical School, 1896; President of the Faculty and Professor of Philosophy and Pedagogy, Vincennes University, 1896–; Editor of the Bulletin of the Preparatory Teachers' Department, Vincennes University, Nov. 1896–.

Author of: —

The Study of the Boyhood of Great Men. *Pedagogical Seminary*, Oct., 1894, Vol. 3, pp. 134–166.

A Syllabus for the Study of Pubescence. *Child Study Monthly*, Feb., 1896, Vol. 1, pp. 280–283.

Investigations in Pubescence. *Trans. Ill. Soc. for Child-Study*, 1897, Vol. 2, No. 2, pp. 61–64.

Pubescence. *Northwestern Monthly*, May, 1896, Vol. 6, pp. 597–600.

LEWIS EDWIN YORK: —

Tutor in Mathematics, Mt. Union College, 1891–93; B.S., Mt. Union College, 1894; Superintendent of Public Schools, Newton Falls, O., 1894–96; Graduate, King's School of Oratory, 1896; President Duquesne College, 1896–97; Ph.D. (*pro merito*), Duquesne College, 1897; **Scholar in Pedagogy, Clark University, 1897–98**; Superintendent Public Schools, Kingsville, O., 1898–.

Author of: —

America's Need — Men. *Pleasures*, Oct., 1893.

Thoughts on Oratory. *Dynamo*, Jan., 1896.

J. W. A. YOUNG: —

A.B., Bucknell University, 1887; A.M., *ibid.*, 1890; Instructor in Mathematics, Bucknell Academy, 1887–88; University of Berlin, 1888–89; **Fellow in Mathematics, Clark University, 1889–92; Ph.D., Clark University, 1892**; Associate in Mathematics, University of Chicago, 1892–94; Instructor in Mathematics, *ibid.*, 1894–97; Assistant Professor of Mathematical Pedagogy, *ibid.*, 1897–; Investigating Methods of Teaching Mathematics in Prussia, 1897–98; Member American Mathematical Society.

Author of: —

On the Determination of Groups whose Order is a Power of a Prime. *Am. Jour. of Math.*, April, 1893, Vol. 15, pp. 124–178.

Bachmann's Theory of Numbers. *Bull. N. Y. Math. Soc.*, June, 1894, Vol. 3, pp. 216-222.

Theory of Numbers and of Equations. *Bull. Am. Math. Soc.*, 1895, 2d ser., Vol. 2, pp. 97-105.

Zur mathematischen Lehrbücherfrage: Eine schulstatistische Untersuchung. *Hoffmann's Ztsch. f. math. u. naturwiss. Unterricht*, Sept., 1898, Vol. 29, pp. 410-414.

The Elements of the Differential and Integral Calculus. (With C. E. Linebarger.) D. Appleton & Co., New York. (In press.)

www.ingramcontent.com/pod-product-compliance
Lightning Source LLC
Chambersburg PA
CBHW022125020426
42334CB00015B/770
9783741151439